MODERN HUMANITIES RESEARCH ASSOCIATION

TUDOR & STUART TRANSLATIONS

VOLUME 9

General Editors
ANDREW HADFIELD
NEIL RHODES

ENGLISH RENAISSANCE TRANSLATION THEORY

ENGLISH RENAISSANCE TRANSLATION THEORY

Edited by

Neil Rhodes
with
Gordon Kendal and Louise Wilson

MODERN HUMANITIES RESEARCH ASSOCIATION
2013

Published by
The Modern Humanities Research Association,
1 Carlton House Terrace
London SW1Y 5AF

First published 2013

ISBN (hardback) 978–1–907322–05–1
ISBN (paperback) 978–1–78188–041–8

Copies may be ordered from www.tudor.mhra.org.uk

MHRA TUDOR AND STUART TRANSLATIONS

For details of published and forthcoming volumes please visit our website:

www.tudor.mhra.org.uk

TABLE OF CONTENTS

PART TWO: LITERARY TRANSLATION

PART THREE: TRANSLATION IN THE ACADEMY

GENERAL EDITORS' FOREWORD

The aim of the *MHRA Tudor & Stuart Translations* is to create a representative library of works translated into English during the early modern period for the use of scholars, students, and the wider public. The series will include both substantial single works and selections of texts from major authors, with the emphasis being on the works that were most familiar to early modern readers. The texts themselves will be newly edited with substantial introductions, notes, and glossaries, and will be published both in print and online.

The series aims to restore to view a major part of English Renaissance literature which has become relatively inaccessible and to present these texts as literary works in their own right. For that reason it will follow the same principle of modernisation adopted by other scholarly editions of canonical literature from the period. The series will have a similar scope to that of the original *Tudor Translations* published early in the last century, and while the great majority of the works presented will be from the sixteenth century, like the original series it will not be rigidly bound by the end-date of 1603. There will, however, be a very different range of texts with new and substantial scholarly apparatus.

The *MHRA Tudor & Stuart Translations* will extend our understanding of the English Renaissance through its representation of the process of cultural transmission from the classical to the early modern world and the process of cultural exchange within the early modern world.

Andrew Hadfield
Neil Rhodes

PREFACE

This edition is designed to be used both as a stand-alone volume and in conjunction with EEBO. In accordance with the policy for the series as a whole, the texts presented here follow modern conventions for spelling and punctuation. I have also transliterated Greek characters, since this may help readers with no knowledge of the language to recognise the stem of the words. For readers who wish to consult the original-format texts on EEBO, STC numbers are identified in the Textual Notes and EEBO image numbers are given for references to texts cited in the commentary, except in the case of some major works where I have cited good modern editions. I have also given USTC numbers in the commentary for texts published outside the domains of EEBO when it seems helpful to do so. The texts themselves are based on EEBO facsimiles, but original copies have been consulted where those are imperfect or unreliable. In the case of manuscript sources, texts are based on the originals, except in the case of Queen Elizabeth where good facsimiles are available.

In preparing this edition I have been responsible for the selection and editing of the texts, with the exception of Gavin Douglas and Laurence Humphrey, as well for as for the introduction, commentary, glossary and bibliography. Gordon Kendal has been responsible for editing Douglas and for editing and translating Humphrey. I am grateful to Dr Kendal for help with some of the Latin sources, and in particular for his explanation (and emendation) of the passage from Brunfels in the letter by Richard Eden (**31**.). Louise Wilson has been responsible for the collation of the printed texts and for the preparation of the textual notes, with the exception of the manuscript sources, which were consulted by me. Although I have had sole responsibility for the preparation of the texts and for all textual decisions, including the modernisation policy, I have frequently relied on the advice and good judgement of Dr Wilson in making these decisions. I would also like to thank Stephen Halliwell once again for his advice on the Greek, and in particular for his erudite comments on Ascham's misquotation of Sophocles (**51**.).

I have been fortunate in having had both institutional and external support to enable me to complete this edition. The

MHRA granted me a part-time Research Associate post for eleven months between October 2010 and August 2011 to help with preparing the first volumes in the present series for publication, and also with the collation work for my own edition. Louise Wilson was appointed to this position. I am grateful to the MHRA for this assistance and also to the British Academy, which awarded me a Small Research Grant from 2010–12 for visits to the British Library and to libraries in Oxford and Cambridge. The School of English at St Andrews granted me two semesters' leave from February 2011, when most of the work for the edition was undertaken, and the AHRC awarded me a four month Research Fellowship in 2012 to complete the commentary and write the introduction. I am grateful, as ever, for the support of my colleagues, especially to Alex Davis, Lorna Hutson, Andy Murphy and the late Barbara Murray, as well as to the AHRC, in helping me to finish this project.

In the final stages I was exceptionally fortunate in being able to draw upon the combined learning of Anne Coldiron, Fred Schurink and Andrew Taylor, each of whom read large portions of the edition. I have silently incorporated a great many of their suggestions, which will have made an enormous improvement to the work. I am also grateful to David Swensen for research assistance in the final stages. It is a pleasure, too, to be able to thank José María Pérez Fernández for his peerless hospitality at the University of Granada, where I have had the opportunity to present some of my work on translation and on the 'common' in the Faculty of Translation and the Department of English. A final word of thanks goes to my co-General Editor and travelling companion on the visits to Granada, Andrew Hadfield, for many lively conversations on translation matters and the development of this series, as well as for his help in negotiating the restaurants and tapas bars of that fine city. He also read the final text and I am extremely grateful for his comments and advice.

Neil Rhodes

ABBREVIATIONS

CWE	*Collected Works of Erasmus*
CWM	*Collected Works of St Thomas More*
EEBO	*Early English Books Online*
KJB	*King James Bible* (the 'Authorised Version')
OED	*Oxford English Dictionary*
OHLTE 1	*The Oxford History of Literary Translation in English: Volume 1, To 1550*, ed. by Roger Ellis (Oxford: Oxford University Press, 2008)
OHLTE 2	*The Oxford History of Literary Translation in English: Volume 2, 1550–1660*, ed. by Gordon Braden, Robert Cummings, and Stuart Gillespie (Oxford: Oxford University Press, 2011)
STC	*Short-Title Catalogue*
USTC	*Universal Short-Title Catalogue*

INTRODUCTION

The aim of this volume is to provide a companion to the editions in the MHRA *Tudor and Stuart Translations* series by assembling the most significant discussions of the principles underlying English translation practice from Caxton through to the 1620s. It also aims to extend and complement the extremely valuable collections of English Renaissance literary criticism edited by Brian Vickers and Gavin Alexander, neither of which includes much material that is explicitly concerned with translation.[1] The project does, of course, presuppose that translation in this period can be viewed as a distinct category of composition in the first place, which is at least open to debate. It is possible, as Warren Boutcher has argued, to see translations as '"original" texts by those who happened to be translating',[2] and translation as part of a continuum that includes imitation, paraphrase, and commonplacing, as well as what we might consider to be original composition. Although Roger Ascham treated *translatio linguarum* and *imitatio* discretely in his pedagogical work, *The Schoolmaster* (1570), the most comprehensive account of the theory and practice of translation to be written by an Englishman during the sixteenth century, Laurence Humphrey's *Interpretatio linguarum* [The translation of languages] (1559), takes *interpretatio* to mean 'imitation' as well as 'translation' in its modern and more literal sense.[3] In a culture in which literary excellence is as likely to be defined by successful assimilation as by originality, almost all texts have to be understood as a dialogue with their sources.[4] The key source text for Renaissance translation theory itself is Cicero's *De Optimo genere oratorum* ['On the best kind of

[1] See *English Renaissance Literary Criticism*, ed. by Brian Vickers (Oxford: Clarendon Press, 1999); *Sidney's 'The Defence of Poesy' and Selected Renaissance Literary Criticism*, ed. by Gavin Alexander (London: Penguin, 2004).

[2] Warren Boutcher, 'The Renaissance' in *The Oxford Guide to Literature in English Translation*, ed. by Peter France (Oxford: Oxford University Press, 2000), pp. 45–55 (p. 46).

[3] I am grateful to Gordon Kendal and Fred Schurink for this point.

[4] The Renaissance understanding of 'invention' as the finding of appropiate material in authorities, as well as achieving uniqueness and independence of expression and thought, is central here.

orator'], which established the principle of translating sense for sense rather than word for word, and once this has been accepted, the border-line between translation and other forms of derivative composition starts to dissolve.

Nonetheless, it is indisputable that throughout the period the terms 'translation' and 'translated' are used on title-pages and in prefaces to define a literary work which the author has converted from one language into another. The prefaces frequently describe the difficulties the writer has faced in executing his or her task successfully, the particular challenges posed by the language of the source text, and the strategy adopted to produce a version in English that captures the life and spirit of the original. These prefaces supply most of the material gathered in the present volume. Some writers such as John Harington explicitly contrast the roles of translator and author (or what Harington calls the 'maker').[5] In the spate of anthologies and printed commonplace books that appear at the end of the century to celebrate the emergence of an English national literature, translations and translators are usually identified as such.[6] And this is to speak only of secular literature: there is certainly no doubt that in the case of the English Bible translation existed as a distinct and violently contentious activity in the minds of its opponents and defenders alike.

If 'translation' is a debatable category, then 'Renaissance' is perhaps even more so. But while I use the term 'early modern' in this edition where it seems appropriate, in the case of translation it is a good deal easier to justify the term 'Renaissance' than it is to explain in what sense it is 'modern'. It is worth reiterating here F. O. Matthiessen's well-known observation that 'A study of Elizabethan translation is a study of the means by which the Renaissance came to England'.[7] It now has the evidential support of the Warwick *Renaissance Cultural Crossroads* database, which allows us to chart the remarkable growth in printed English translations in the course of the sixteenth century, most significantly in the 1570s, the decade leading up to the publication of

[5] See **41**. 44–6.

[6] See for example Robert Allott, *Englands Parnassus: or the choycest Flowers of our Moderne Poets* (London, 1600), STC 378.

[7] F. O. Matthiessen, *Translation: An Elizabethan Art* (Cambridge, MA: Harvard University Press, 1931), p. 1.

the first major work of Elizabethan poetry, *The Shepheardes Calender* (1579).[8] The modern translator, Edith Grossman, has observed that:

> the broadening of horizons that comes with translation does not affect only readers, speakers, and writers of a language, but the very nature of language itself. The more a language embraces infusions and transfusions of new elements and foreign turns of phrase the larger, more forceful, and more flexible it becomes as an expressive medium.[9]

Grossman is making a general point, but what she says is precisely illustrated by developments in England in the second half of the sixteenth century and defines what we mean by a 'renaissance'. Other resources provide material sustenance to the idea of the Renaissance. English scholars have long had access to the STC (and ESTC), which has had the unfortunate side-effect of reinforcing a sense of the independence both of English book production and the Anglophone community itself. With the appearance of the St Andrews *Universal Short Title Catalogue* we can begin to move to a much better understanding of Britain's part in the broader European processes of cultural transmission from the classical to the early modern world, and of cultural exchange within the early modern world.[10] Translation is central to these processes, as it is more locally to the English literary renaissance.

If it is relatively easy to defend the terms 'translation' and 'Renaissance' in the title of this volume, the same cannot be said of 'theory'. The first monograph on the subject, by Flora Ross Amos, concluded that no coherent set of principles could be elicited from a study of English Renaissance translation, while more recently Massimiliano Morini has reminded us that with the exception of Laurence Humphrey, whose book was written

---

[8] See Brenda Hosington, dir., *Renaissance Cultural Crossroads* <http://www.hrionline.ac.uk/rcc/> [accessed 8 March 2012]. The greatest leap in the number of titles published is from 370 in 1560–1569 to 571 in 1570–1579. In the last two decades of the century (615 in the 1580s and 611 in the 1590s) the numbers level off.

[9] Edith Grossman, *Why Translation Matters* (New Haven: Yale University Press, 2010), pp. 22–3.

[10] See Andrew Pettegree, dir., *Universal Short-Title Catalogue* <http://www.ustc.ac.uk/> [accessed 8 March 2012].

in Latin and published abroad, there is no work that could be described as an English theoretical treatise on translation.[11] There is nothing, for example, that is comparable with Leonardo Bruni's *De Interpretatione recta* ['On the correct way to translate', *c.* 1425], one of the foundational texts of humanism, or with Etienne Dolet's reworking of Bruni's ideas in his *La Maniere de bien traduire d'une langue en aultre* ['The best way of translating from one language to another', *c.* 1540]. But there is nonetheless a considerable body of dialogue about the nature of translation, and its dangers and difficulties, produced in English during the period. In the case of Bible translation that dialogue is intensely polemic and often focused on very specific issues of verbal change; in the case of secular literature, translators almost invariably introduce their work with some consideration either of the competing claims of letter and spirit, or of the resources of English itself, or of the status of translation more generally; and all translators, whether religious or secular, argue for the benefits of their work (spiritual, cultural, social, or economic) as a process of 'making common', where 'common' is to be taken as something shared rather than something low or coarse. To describe this as 'theory' is probably to claim too much, but it is a convenient shorthand. It may also be justified if we try to understand these texts in relation to modern translation theory as it has developed from the 1970s, with the emergence of 'translation studies', to the historical and anthropological turn post-2000. This has entailed a move away from specifically linguistic concerns to broader questions of transnationalism and cultural transposition.[12] It is my hope that the present volume will help to open up some of these issues to further debate, whether or not they may properly be described as 'theoretical'.

---

[11] See Flora Ross Amos, *Early Theories of Translation* (New York: Columbia University Studies in English and Comparative Literature, 1920), p. 99 (Amos is referring specifically to secular translation); Massimiliano Morini, *Tudor Translation in Theory and Practice* (Ashgate: Aldershot, 2006), p. 17.

[12] This might be illustrated by a comparison between L. G. Kelly's account of 'modulated transposition' in *The True Interpreter: A History of Translation Theory and Practice in the West* (Oxford: Basil Blackwell, 1979), pp. 159–62, and Peter Burke's account of 'cultural translation' in *Cultural Translation in Early Modern Europe*, ed. by Peter Burke and R. Po-chia Hsia (Cambridge: Cambridge University Press, 2007), pp. 7–10.

And we must finally ask whether there is anything distinctively 'English' about this material: why not just 'Renaissance Translation Theory', which could then include Erasmus, whose work on translation was certainly influential in England. The first answer to this is that every language has its own idiom, as English translators frequently observe, and this means that translators specifically address the case of their own vernacular, even if the problems they discuss are common to other vernaculars. (This was a subject in which Erasmus had very little interest.) The point can be extended into academic contexts, where the educational experience of schoolboys consisted primarily of understanding the particular relationship between Latin, and sometimes Greek, and their own vernacular. This was an experience in which translation was again central and which left its mark on those who became writers themselves. The second answer is that for historical reasons, as we shall see, the issue of Bible translation is both more prominent and more vexed in England than it is elsewhere.[13] Since there is also an intimate relationship between the role of grammar in theological interpretation and its function in secular literary theory, as Brian Cummings has eloquently shown,[14] there are significant points of connection between the religious and the secular in English Renaissance translation theory.

These considerations have determined the organization of the present edition. The first section, 'Translating the Word of God', covers religious works in general, though it is focused principally on issues of Bible translation. It has three main components: Tyndale's making of the first English Bible and the debate with More; the first Catholic English Bible and the debate between Gregory Martin and William Fulke; and the evolution of the King James version of 1611. The section also presents paraphrase as a version of translation. The second section is simply called

[13] Including in Scotland where there was no equivalent to the polemical exchanges between Tyndale and More and Fulke and Martin. Nor was there a Bible in Scots. The first English-language Bible printed in Scotland is Edinburgh, 1579, STC 2125.

[14] See Brian Cummings, *The Literary Culture of the Reformation: Grammar and Grace* (Oxford: Oxford University Press, 2002), especially pp. 20–26. In the present volume the one writer to deal explicitly with both religious and secular translation is Laurence Humphrey.

'Literary Translation' and covers all secular translation in English aimed at the general reader. The terms 'literary' and 'literature' here are taken in their earliest and broadest sense. The section includes discussion not just of fictional works, but also of history, philosophy, medicine, and more general compilations of knowledge. The final section, 'Translation in the Academy', contains accounts by teachers, or by others writing for the educational market, of the pedagogical uses of different types of translation practice. In the remainder of this introduction I have deliberately left the challenge to the translator posed by poetry until the end of the two sections on translating the word of God and on literary translation. In the case of poetry, whether religious or secular, it is not simply the challenge of greater verbal density that has to be addressed, but also the question as to whether metre itself can be translated.

2.

It is difficult to think of a more dangerous literary activity, or one in which the stakes could be higher, than translating the Bible into English in the 1520s. William Tyndale's translation of the New Testament, printed at Worms and smuggled into England from January 1526, lit the fuse for the English Reformation. Tyndale himself, still in exile, was garotted and burned at the stake ten years later. Martin Luther, on the other hand, who had translated the New Testament into German in 1522, providing Tyndale with a contemporary vernacular model for his own work, survived to die of natural causes in 1546. The reason why English Bible translation was uniquely dangerous, and significant, is to do with timing. As Miles Coverdale points out in the first Bible licensed for publication in England (1535), other countries in Europe already had the Scriptures available to them in their own languages (**6**. 20–22): among the non-Latinate peoples, English speakers constituted the only major language group not to have direct access to the word of God. Officially, the Catholic Church had no objection in principle to Bible translation, and this is the position that Thomas More states in the *Dialogue Concerning Heresies* (1529) and Gregory Martin restates in his preface to the first Catholic English Bible (1582). In *Heresies* More argued that a good thing should not be denied to the many because a few draw evil from it (**3**. 199–203), but three years later he had shifted his ground, and in the *Confutation of Tyndale's Answer* (1532) he declared emphatically that there should be no translation into English 'until men better amend' (**5**. 247–48). More's reasons are clear: the vernacular Bible has become a Trojan horse for heresy. In England, then, timing meant that Bible translation and Reformation were more completely synonymous than they were elsewhere in Europe.[15]

This does not mean that there were no English Bibles before Tyndale. Tyndale himself points out that there were Old English versions of the Scriptures, as does William Fulke in his debate with Martin over the Catholic English Bible (**1**. 119–23, **12**. 200–28). The problem was that the principal English Bible before Tyndale was the Wycliffite Bible of the 1380s, which was irrevocably tainted with heresy; so much so, in fact, that it led to Archbishop Thomas Arundel's *Constitution against Gospellers* (1409), formulated at a conference in Oxford, which placed such tight restrictions on Bible translation that they effectively shut it down altogether. Arundel decreed that:

> no man hereafter by his owne authoritie, translate any text of the Scripture into English, or any other tongue, by way of a booke, libell [booklet], or treatise, and if [that] no man read anye suche book libell or treatise, nowe lately set foorth inthe time of John Wickliffe, or sithence, or hereafter to be set forth, in part or in whole, privily, or apertly [privately or publicly]: upon paine of greater excommunication, untill the said translation be allowed by the Ordinary of the place [ecclesiastical authority], or (if the case so require) by the Councell provinciall: He that shall do contrary to this shal likewise be punished as a favorer of error & heresie.[16]

Tyndale had tried to get his plan for an English Bible approved by the Bishop of London, Cuthbert Tunstall, presenting him with a translation from Isocrates to establish his credentials, and when the proposal was rejected he decided that he would have to do the work abroad. Tyndale and More, and later in the century

[15] See Ian Green, *Print and Protestantism in Early Modern England* (Oxford: Oxford University Press, 2000).

[16] John Foxe, *Actes and Monuments* (London, 1583), STC 11225, sig. FFFf.ii^r, image 560.

Gregory Martin and William Fulke, argue over whether Arundel did or did not amount to a ban on Bible translation, but perhaps the most succinct verdict on the Oxford Constitutions was offered by Miles Smith in the preface to the King James Bible, where he calls them 'an unprofitable gift' (**15d**. 262).

After completing his New Testament Tyndale published *The Obedience of a Christian Man* (1528), a work that aimed to dissociate reform from rebellion by emphasising the duties of subjects to rulers. Its preface, though, is concerned with Bible translation and it is here that Tyndale makes his unequivocal declaration 'that the Scripture ought to be in the mother tongue' (**1**. 3–4). The principle that everyone should have access to the word of God in their own language, unmediated by the Church, is fundamental to Protestantism, but the centrality of Scripture in reformed Christianity places an enormous burden of responsibility on the translator. If the individual is alone before God with a Bible in their hands, he or she needs to know that the text that holds the key to their salvation is an authentic representation of His word.[17] But how is that to be achieved in a modern vernacular and with more than one intervening translation? And what do those translations intervene between? What, in fact, is the pure source? These questions are at the heart of sixteenth-century Bible translation through to 1611 and the different answers to them have important implications for translation theory in general.

The original texts of the Old Testament were first written down in Hebrew. They were translated into Greek in the third century BC in Egypt. According to tradition, Ptolemy II Philadelphus commissioned 72 translators to work in separate cells for 72 days, during which they all produced an identical version of the Bible.[18] This version is known as the Septuagint, and the story of its inception is clearly meant to establish it as inspired and therefore completely authentic. The original language of the New

[17] See James Simpson, *Burning to Read: English Fundamentalism and its Reformation Opponents* (Cambridge, MA: Harvard University Press, 2007), pp. 68–105.

[18] See Philo of Alexandria, *On the Life of Moses* 2. 6–7 in *Philo*, trans. by F. H. Colson and G. H. Whitaker, 10 vols (London: Heinemann, 1950), 6: 273–95 (465–71). The origin of the story is the 'Letter of Aristeas', written *c*. 130 BC.

Testament was also Greek, since this was the language of the communities to which the Apostles and St Paul preached.[19] But when Latin superseded Greek as the common language of the eastern Mediterranean, the Bible texts began to be translated into Latin in a process that was inevitably vulnerable to the charge of degradation, either on account of scribal corruption or simply through their distance from the source. These early Latin Bible texts are known as the *Vetus Latina*. In time it was recognised that there had to be a single, authoritative Latin text of the Bible and this was undertaken by St Jerome on the authority of Pope Damasus between 382 and 406. Dismissing the story of the Septuagint translation as a fabrication of the 'first lying author',[20] and along with it the belief that the Septuagint version was inspired, Jerome went back to the original Hebrew for this new Latin version of the Old Testament; for the New Testament he sought out the best texts of the original Greek. What Jerome produced was the *Biblia Sacra Vulgata*, better known as the Vulgate – the standard Bible throughout the Middle Ages, the basis of all Church commentary, and finally decreed by the Catholic Church to be the authentic text at the Council of Trent in 1546.[21]

Two features of the Vulgate immediately bring into focus a fundamental paradox in translation theory, and one that has particular resonance in the sixteenth-century debates on Bible translation. This is that while the aim of translation is to make texts common, the desire for authenticity drives the good translator back to the pure source. Jerome returned to what he called

---

[19] There are some differences in the language of the Septuagint and the New Testament, though both were written in *koinē* or 'common' Greek, which superseded the four classical Greek dialects.

[20] Jerome, 'Preface to the Pentateuch' in *Western Translation Theory*, ed. by Douglas Robinson (Manchester: St Jerome, 2002), p. 30.

[21] '[The council] decides and declares that the old well known Latin Vulgate edition which has been tested in the church by long use over so many centuries should be kept as the authentic text in public readings, debates, sermons and explanations; and no one is to dare or presume on any pretext to reject it', session 4, 8 April 1546; see *Decrees of the Ecumenical Councils*, ed. by Norman P. Tanner (London: Sheen & Ward, 1990), 2: 664.

[22] Jerome, 'Preface to the Four Gospels' in *The Principal Works of St Jerome*, trans by W. H. Fremantle, *Nicene & Post-Nicene Fathers*, ed. by Philip Schaff and Henry Wace (Edinburgh: T. and T. Clark, 1996), 6: 488; *Epistles* 106. 2. 3 to Sunnias and Fretela (cited by Miles Smith, preface to the KJB (**15d**. 404)).

the 'fountain-head' of the Hebrew and Greek,[22] but what he created from these was common or 'vulgar' Latin. Although the most famous English Bible, the King James or Authorised Version, achieved an elevated style, it is important to remember that the story of Bible translation is for the most part one of vulgarisation, punctuated by attempts to return to the pure source. The early Bible texts were written in languages that were commonly understood at the time, from Hebrew (and then Aramaic), to Greek, to Latin. The problem with the Vulgate Latin was its longevity. By the time of the Reformation Jerome's text had been around for over a thousand years, and what was once a vernacular was now only understood by an educated minority. The fact that a text referred to as 'vulgar' was now only intelligible to an elite was a paradox pointed out by Erasmus in the preface to his revised Latin translation of the New Testament.[23]

The case of the Vulgate also highlights another aspect of translation theory that is specific to the task of transmitting the word of God: this is the conflict between the inspired and philological views of translation.[24] The first view, illustrated by the Septuagint legend, holds that the translator is simply God's medium or instrument, which gives the written text an absolute guarantee of purity and authenticity. The second view, which is that of Jerome, is that the translator can never presume wholly to comprehend the essence of the word of God, but must try to reconstruct the best possible text of His utterance by philological method. This view presents Bible translation as an entirely human activity within the domain of language skills. The logic of these positions is that in the inspired view there should only ever be one text, whereas in the philological view there may be

[23] See 'Foreword' to the *Novum Instrumentum* [New Testament], 3rd edn (1522) in Erasmus, *The Praise of Folly and Other Writings*, ed. and trans. by Robert M. Adams (New York: W. W. Norton, 1989), pp. 134–35. Erasmus called his preface the *Paraclesis*. On the complex relationship between pure source and common language in Erasmus's approach to the New Testament see Paul Botley, *Latin Translation in the Renaissance: The Theory and Practice of Leonardo Bruni, Giannozzo Manetti and Desiderius Erasmus* (Cambridge: Cambridge University Press, 2004), pp. 115–63.

[24] See W. Schwarz, *Principles and Problems of Biblical Translation: Some Reformation Controversies and their Background* (Cambridge: Cambridge University Press, 1955), pp. 15–16.

many, since it concedes that the translator's work is one of approximation. It was the fear of multiple texts and the consequent possibility of schism that led Augustine, Jerome's contemporary, to challenge his new Latin translation and reaffirm the status of the Septuagint as an inspired text.[25] This conflict is replayed in the sixteenth century where the philological view is represented by Erasmus and the inspirational view (with some qualifications) by Luther, but this does not reflect the division that had opened up between Catholics and Protestants in quite the way one might expect. Luther is in some respects closer to Augustine, yet it is Protestantism that produces multiple Bible texts, as Gregory Martin was quick to point out. On the other hand, as part of its response to Protestantism, the Catholic Church decided to give the Vulgate the unique authority of an inspired text, despite its having been constructed by Jerome on philological principles. Singleness and multiplicity, purity and commonness, are key points of contention in sixteenth-century debates about Bible translation, and these debates are conducted along sectarian lines, but it is not easy to attribute a coherent set of principles about translation to one side or the other.

Tyndale himself illustrates the point. If one difference between the fourth and sixteenth centuries is the Reformation, another is humanism, in which philological method and the principle of returning to the sources were combined in a pan-European rediscovery of classical literature. What worked for secular literature could also work for Holy Scripture, and here the central figure is Erasmus, who is in turn a model for Tyndale. Tyndale's theology may have been much closer to Luther's, but as a scholar and a linguist he was Erasmian.[26] As Tyndale's master and More's friend, Erasmus is the third point of a triangular relationship, and Tyndale delighted in using the evidence of his translation work to counter More's increasingly violent opposition to an English Bible (**4**. 44–56). Erasmus's own project was the *Novum Instrumentum*, not a vernacular Bible, but a better Latin

[25] For a Protestant view of the dissension between Augustine and Jerome, see Fulke **10**. 123–77 below; also Schwarz, pp. 37–44.

[26] On Tyndale's translation of Erasmus's *Enchiridion*, see David Daniell, *William Tyndale: A Biography* (New Haven: Yale University Press, 1994), pp. 64–74; on the Erasmian view that God exists in language, see Cummings, *Literary Culture of the Reformation*, p. 199.

version of the New Testament. In order to achieve this he went back to the pure source of the Greek, examining the existing manuscripts to produce an authoritative text on which the new translation could be based: 'we Latins have but a few small streams, a few muddy pools, the Greeks possess crystal-clear springs and rivers that run with gold', he had written as early as 1501.[27] It was a long-running project, eventually appearing in 1516 to become the first printed Greek text of the New Testament, with his new translation and (in 1522) Jerome's Vulgate in parallel.[28] The rationale for the new text was supported by the 'Annotations', which were the most controversial part of the whole exercise. It was the Greek text of Erasmus's revised edition of 1522 that Tyndale used as a source for the first printed English translation of the New Testament, represented by the Cologne fragment of 1525 and the complete version printed at Worms the following year. But as a scholar Tyndale outdid his master in one important respect: he had managed to learn Hebrew. So for the Old Testament too he was able to return to the original source, using one of the editions of the Hebrew text published at Venice (1517) or Alcala (1522).[29] Tyndale's aim was a common, vernacular Bible, accessible to all classes of people and central to family life (**1**. 36), but to produce this he followed the humanist principle of drawing upon the 'clearest springs' available.

One crucial question that Tyndale had to address if his Bible was to find acceptance was the adequacy of a vernacular as unrefined as English for the transmission of the mysteries of the divine word. Since writers were still debating, forty years later, whether English was capable of producing great literature, given the relative poverty of its vocabulary, this was clearly a point of

---

[27] Erasmus, *Correspondence*, ed. and trans. R. A. B. Mynors and D. F. S. Thomson, *CWE* 2 (Toronto: University of Toronto Press, 1974-), p. 25.

[28] Erasmus explicitly advocates translation of the Bible into the vernaculars in the *Paraclesis*; see *The Praise of Folly and Other Writings*, trans. by Adams, p. 121. It is possible that Erasmus's statement persuaded Tyndale to undertake his translation. The *Paraclesis* was itself translated into English by William Roye as *An Exhortation to the Diligent Studye of Scripture* (Antwerp: Hans Luft, 1529).

[29] See *An Answer unto Sir Thomas More's Dialogue*, ed. by Anne M. O'Donnell and Jared Wicks (Washington, DC: Catholic University Press of America, 2000), p. xxi. This was the Masoretic text with pointings, the authoritative Hebrew text of the Jewish Bible.

substance. Tyndale's answer is that English is in fact a better vehicle for rendering the Greek and Hebrew originals than Latin because of its greater affinity with those languages.[30] To the opponents of English translation he retorts: 'They will say it cannot be translated into our tongue, it is so rude. It is not so rude as they are false liars. For the Greek tongue agreeth more with the English than the Latin. And the properties of the Hebrew tongue agreeth a thousand times more with the English than with the Latin' (**1**. 107–10). What he means by this is that the languages correspond more closely in terms of word order, so the English translator does not have to 'seek a compass' in the way that the Latin translator does: in Latin there will be periphrasis, whereas English will be more direct. Since word order itself might be regarded as part of the mystery of Holy Scripture, this is a good point to make, though Tyndale qualified it as the work of revising his translations progressed.[31] One way in which it might be illustrated is in the hospitality of the languages towards the related forms of gnomic utterance (Hebrew), aphorism (Greek), and proverbial saying (English). This is exploited by Tyndale to create some of the most characteristic and memorable verbal structures in the English Bible, preserved over centuries through the King James version. As Gerald Hammond has pointed out, this is what Tyndale himself called the 'sore [sharp] and strong' style when describing the letters of St Paul.[32]

Thomas More was not one of those who regarded English as 'rude' and inadequate (**3**. 304), and he left a considerable body of his own writing in the vernacular, unlike Erasmus, who never bothered to learn the language, despite his Anglophilia. So where were the lines of opposition drawn in the fierce polemics between More and Tyndale over Bible translation? At the heart of the dispute is the transparency or otherwise of Holy Scripture. For Tyndale, God's word can be read literally and the sense is open to common understanding. In arguing that it is not, the Church

[30] On the affinity between English and Greek see **20**. 7–14.

[31] Cummings, *Literary Culture of the Reformation* (2002), p. 200.

[32] See 'The Sore and Strong Prose of the English Bible' in *English Renaissance Prose: History, Language, and Politics*, ed. by Neil Rhodes (Tempe, AZ: MRTS, 1997), pp. 19–34. On Tyndale's use of proverbs see Daniell, *William Tyndale* (1994), pp. 17, 24, 129–30, 135.

indulges in 'juggling' (a favourite word) and 'sophistry'; it aims to awe unlearned people by emphasising the complexity of Scripture, 'and so delude them with descanting upon it with allegories', as he writes in the preface to the Pentateuch (**2**. 49). However, though the meaning of Scripture may be transparent, not everybody is able to perceive this, and in order to understand it, the law of God must already be written on your heart (**4**. 131–33). At this point Protestant theology seems to transfer the principle of inspiration from translator to reader: the good translator needs the human resources of scholarship and linguistic expertise, but the good reader needs inspiration to see the sense and grasp the truth. More's position is very different and is essentially hierarchical.[33] The mysteries of Holy Scripture are complex and open to different interpretations, so the danger of vernacular translations is that they encourage the ignorant to be 'busy' and to start debating matters which they can't possibly understand. This is why Moses had to ascend a hill to receive the tablets while the people waited below (**3**. 256–67). What this means is that the only safe authority for the interpretation of Scripture is the accumulated learning and wisdom of the Church, and for More collective tradition (including oral tradition) is the key to right understanding. To translate correctly you need to observe 'the common custom and usage of speech' (**5**. 126). Interestingly, the debate about translation seems to produce on the one hand a position which is both demotic and exclusive, and on the other a position which is elitist yet inclusive.

The other main area of contention shows succinctly how theological difference may be condensed into issues of translation. Violent conflict could be generated over the translation of single words, since in some cases entire doctrinal structures rested upon them. These are what More called 'words of weight' in the *Dialogue Concerning Heresies*, and he does so in exactly the kind of riddling way that would seem to confirm Tyndale's accusation of 'juggling': 'as weighty be they as any lightly can be, but I mean that every one of them is more than thrice three in number' (**3**. 38). The terms he identifies as crucial are Tyndale's preference

[33] The difference is summed up in the distinction between *sola scriptura* ['by scripture alone'], the doctrine that the Bible contains everything that is necessary for salvation, and what the Protestants referred to as the 'unwritten verities' of Catholic Church tradition.

for 'elders' over 'priests', 'congregation' over 'Church', and 'love' over 'charity' (**3**. 46–50, **5**. 1–10). Although More focuses on the issue of (mis-) translation, the real grounds of his objection are not difficult to see. The first two strike at Church hierarchy and the institution of the Church itself, while the last weakens any association of love with good works. Tyndale would argue that the Vulgate (itself a translation) is an integral part of the institution of the Church, which is why it is essential to go back to the original Greek and Hebrew. He also needles More by reminding him that his close friend Erasmus had translated Greek *ekklēsia* as *congregatio* in the *Novum Instrumentum*.[34] For Tyndale, 'congregation' is a levelling term, but for More it is a secularising one: detached from its institutional sense 'congregation' could refer to any kind of assembly, he claims. In his *Answer to More* Tyndale argues that *ekklēsia* can be translated as 'congregation' rather than 'Church' because the context ('circumstance') will indicate whether the word is to be understood in an ecclesiastical sense (**4**. 20–22). In the *Confutation of Tyndale's Answer* More then seizes upon the word 'circumstance' and shifts it from the general sense of 'context' to its more specific dialectical and rhetorical sense of the defining attributes of a thing under particular conditions; these are 'accidents' rather than the essential features of the thing itself. So 'circumstance' in this sense, More argues, allows the translator complete liberty of definition, and he claims sarcastically that 'he may translate the world into a football if he join herewith certain circumstances' (**5**. 84–86). By fixing on the rhetorical meaning of the term, More cleverly finds a way of throwing back Tyndale's charges of 'juggling' and 'poetry' on himself; by appealing to 'circumstance' for meaning rather than the consensual authority of tradition, Tyndale gives the translator the license of fiction, 'a great long tale' in which he may 'make any word understood as it like himself'. Though Tyndale claims to give the literal sense of the Scriptures, More's point is that he is really using translation as a cloak for redefinition, and then as an instrument for the deinstitutionalisation of religion.

Within four years of More's *Confutation* both he and Tyndale had been executed for their beliefs, and Tyndale's Bible transla-

[34] On the argument between Tyndale and More over the translation of key terms see Cummings, *Literary Culture of the Reformation*, pp. 192–96.

tions were not republished in England in their original form. But his work was continued by Miles Coverdale, and before Tyndale's death in 1536 a vernacular Bible had for the first time been printed in England. Coverdale was on his own admission no great linguist, but he was a far more irenic figure than either Tyndale or More and he was content to see his contributions simply as part of a wider whole. Although he makes his theological position clear when he refers to 'the darkness of men's traditions' in the prologue to the English Bible of 1535, he is adamant that diversity of translation need not be the cause of sectarianism and division. Just as different peoples may speak different languages yet be unified through faith 'and be one in love, even so may diverse translations understand one another' (**6**. 60). After the violence and hatred of the More-Tyndale polemics, the benign serenity of this is extraordinary. Its vision is almost that of Donne, a century later, imagining the state beyond death and observing that '*Gods* hand is in every *translation*; and his hand shall binde up all our scattered leaves againe, for that *Librarie* where every *booke* shall lie open to one another'.[35] It is echoed in Hilary Mantel's highly partisan *Wolf Hall*, where the principal sponsor of English Bible translation during the 1530s, Thomas Cromwell, 'wonders again if the dead need translators; perhaps in a moment, in a simple twist of unbecoming, they know everything they need to know'.[36] Then, there will be complete understanding, but even here on earth Coverdale believes that, though there will be failings in the translation, 'love shall construe all to the best' (**6**. 85). Amid the convulsions of the Reformation his was a forlorn and, in a quite specific sense, unworldly hope.

Yet though both translation theory and the act of translation itself are pivotal to the English Reformation, many of the problems confronting the translator remain the same in all historical and confessional conditions. The most crucial of these is whether to translate word for word or sense for sense. Jerome addressed this issue in his letter to Pammachius, deciding that while with secular literature it was allowable – indeed preferable

[35] John Donne, *Devotions upon Emergent Occasions*, ed. by Anthony Raspa (New York: Oxford University Press, 1987), p. 86 ('Meditation 17').

[36] Hilary Mantel, *Wolf Hall* (London: Fourth Estate, 2009), p. 152. (Mantel's novel is acidly anti-More, but Tyndale is spared her scrutiny.)

– to translate sense for sense, this would be presumptuous in the case of the divine word: 'I myself not only admit but freely proclaim that in translating from the Greek (except in the case of the holy scriptures where even the order of the words is a mystery) I render sense for sense and not word for word.' But while acknowledging that word order is part of the divine mystery, Jerome also concedes that when the Apostles and Evangelists quote from the Old Testament they 'have sought to give the meaning rather than the words, and [. . .] have not greatly cared to preserve forms or constructions'.[37] Jerome's position on this central question is ambivalent, because he did not himself follow the word-for-word principle in his own Bible translation, and his subsequent point about the Apostles conveying only the meaning when citing the Old Testament may be intended to justify that procedure.[38]

All translation theory ultimately refers to this key point, whether or not the matter being translated refers to Holy Scripture. Thomas Norton, for example, explaining his method in his translation of Calvin (1561; preface 1562) is concerned about the fullness and density of his author's style, which packs so much into a small space that it is difficult for the translator to avoid circumlocution in conveying the meaning. But he decides that even though a more direct style might reflect the 'natural manner' of English, it would sacrifice faithfulness to the original, which is essential in 'matters of religion'. This means that the translator must respect not just the 'grammatical construction', but even 'the very building and order' of the original, so he is determined 'to follow the words so near as the phrase of the English tongue would suffer me' (**8**. 36–37).[39] Norton's reference to 'building' represents writing as craft and suggests that literal translation is a brick-by-brick procedure. This is scarcely achievable in practice, but Norton had recently written *Gorboduc* with Thomas Sackville, the first blank verse tragedy in English, and in the quotations from Virgil in Calvin Norton also uses blank verse, following Surrey's example in the two books of the *Aeneid*

[37] *Principal Works of St Jerome*, ed. by Schaff and Wace, VI, 113, 117.

[38] See Schwarz, pp. 34–35.

[39] The term 'phrase' can refer specifically to word order, as in Elyot's use of the Greek *phrasis* (**20**. 9–10), though Quintilian understands it more broadly as *elocutio*; see *Institutio oratoria*, VIII.i.1.

published in 1557. Here is somebody who is very much alive to the possibility of finding new forms of correspondence between the very different languages of Latin and English.

At the other end of the spectrum from word for word translation is paraphrase. In the sixteenth century this usually refers to a form of Biblical commentary that offers an expanded version of the original text in order to elucidate it. In addition to his Latin translation of the New Testament Erasmus had written a series of paraphrases on it, beginning in 1517, and in the 1540s Henry VIII's last queen, Katherine Parr, set up a team to translate the whole of Erasmus's work into English.[40] Its leader was Nicolas Udall, later the author of *Ralph Roister Doister*, which has a similarly seminal role in comedy as *Gorboduc* does in tragedy. Udall's definition of paraphrase, though, presents it in terms that are exactly the opposite of Norton's account of the literal method: it is 'a plain setting forth of a text or sentence more at large, with such circumstance of more or other works as may make the sentence open, clear, plain, and familiar' (**7b**. 1–3). Paraphrase, in fact, is not quite translation, as Francis Marbury indicates in the preface to a work by Robert Rollock when he says that 'a good translator is neither a paraphrast nor a periphrast, which is committed by needless changing or adding words' (**14**. 21–23: it is 'needless' change, of course, that distinguishes periphrasis from paraphrase). But while from the translator's perspective the paraphrast may seem to enjoy great freedom, from the author's perspective the role is frustratingly restrictive. Erasmus himself complained that in paraphrase 'the writers pen is kept shut within the enclosure of an exceeding strait grate'.[41] The difference depends upon how writers define their relationship with the source text. It is telling that Erasmus (in Udall's translation) uses the terms 'strait' when it is the essential function of paraphrase to 'open up' the source text, and 'grate', not 'gate', which suggests the bars of the prison cell.

Although the translators' description of both their task and their method move between the two poles of freedom and confinement, their aims are fairly consistent: the terms Udall uses

[40] Under Edward VI the English *Paraphrases* were required to be made available in every church at the expense of the parish.

[41] *Paraphrase on the Gospel of Matthew*, trans. by Nicholas Udall (London: 1548), STC 2854.5, sig. Cii^{r}, image 18.

to define paraphrase and those that Tyndale uses to describe his Bible translation are remarkably similar and identify their goal as democratic enlightenment. The contrast between light and darkness is fundamental to the self-image of Protestant Bible translation (**1**. 9–23). The text most frequently cited in support of this is Matthew 5.15: 'Neither do men light a candle, and put it under a bushel, but on a candlestick; and it giveth light to all that are in the house'.[42] It is echoed directly, if rather clumsily, in Marbury's likening of the author to the light and the translator to the candlestick (**14**. 4–13, cf. **7a**. 52), which makes the translator's role passive. Although Miles Smith uses the metaphor in the preface to the KJB (**15d**. 163), he also figures translation more aptly as the opening of a window. Translation is both enlightening and, because the sun shines on all alike, inclusive. There is some irony in the fact that Erasmus's work was so frequently coopted by Protestants in support of these ideals, both by Parr and Udall in the case of the *Paraphrases* and by Tyndale in the case of the *Novum Instrumentum* and the ferocious debate with More. This is not simply because Erasmus was More's 'dearling', as Tyndale put it. In his preface to the 1516 *Novum Instrumentum*, known as the *Paraclesis*, Erasmus imagined the ploughman chanting a holy text as he toiled in the fields and women 'of the lowest rank' reading the Epistles of St Paul,[43] but the Bible texts that he published were in Greek and Latin. There is no record in his voluminous output of any work written in one of the modern European vernaculars.

Erasmus's work did, however, provide a Greek New Testament that Protestant translators could claim was a purer source text than the Vulgate at the same time as it exposed the inadequacy of the latter by setting a new Latin translation alongside it. The Protestant challenge to the Catholic Church on translation, then, was twofold: first, that it was keeping people in darkness by denying them texts of the divine word in their own language; and second, that its own preferred Latin translation was corrupt and thus lacked authority. And if, as the Church claimed, there was no ban on vernacular Bible translation, then it is not surprising that Tyndale posed the question,

[42] See also Mark 4.21 and Luke 8.16. The converse is Mark 4.33–34 (see **3**. 228–31). (Bible quotations are from the KJB unless otherwise specified.)
[43] Erasmus, *The Praise of Folly and Other Writings*, p. 121.

'how happeneth that ye defenders translate not one yourselves?' (**4**. 92–93). English Catholics were slow to respond to Tyndale's challenge, and between 1531, the year of Tyndale's *Answer to More*, and 1582, when the first Catholic English Bible was printed at Rheims, at least five independent Protestant versions of the Bible had been published in English: Coverdale was followed by 'Matthew's Bible' (by John Rogers); the Great Bible of 1539, which was appointed to be read in churches; the Geneva Bible of 1560, produced by Protestant exiles under Mary and containing Calvinist marginal commentary that the later Church of England found contentious; and the Bishops' Bible of 1568, an unsuccessful attempt at displacing the Geneva version.[44]

So when Gregory Martin, an exiled Jesuit based at the English College of Douai-Rheims, began work on a Catholic English Bible in the late 1570s, he did so with the awareness both of a considerable body of philological scholarship that cast doubt on the reliability of the Vulgate text, and also of half a century of Protestant Bible translation. The Catholic project was essentially to reassert the adequacy and authority of the traditional Latin text, which it did by emphasising both the integrity of the Vulgate as the authentic expression of the divine word and the integrity of Church tradition. In the face of diversity and schism the Catholic voice would speak for one text and one Church. Although Protestant translators align themselves with humanist scholarship and argue that they have returned to the well-springs of truth in the original Hebrew and Greek texts, they have nonetheless produced many *different* translations, despite their claims for the purity of their sources. The main thrust of Martin's *Discovery of the Manifold Corruptions of the Scriptures* (1582), which he wrote when he was working on his translation of the Bible, is that heresy works through disintegration: Protestantism is mocked for its continual internal dissension, and philological method in Bible scholarship is presented as a scene of pedantic squabbling (**9**. 225–39) and as a means of picking and choosing readings from source texts that best suit the translators' theology (**9**. 267–79). Martin also cleverly sets the Hebrew and Greek sources of the Protestant Bibles at odds with each other by pointing out that because they only allow the Hebrew to be

[44] We could also include in this list Richard Taverner's Bible of 1539 and Laurence Tomson's version of Beza's Latin New Testament of 1576.

authentic for the Old Testament, and the Greek for the New, they have to falsify the New Testament Greek at those points where Christ or the Apostles quote the Old Testament in order to make their Septuagint Greek agree with the Hebrew (**9**. 123–71). In contrast with all this, the premise of the Catholic Bible is the reduction of multiplicity to unity in the single text of the Vulgate and the single language of Church Latin in a process of recovery that aims to transcend the post-Babel confusion of tongues.

As a result, Martin must not only use the Vulgate as the source text, but he must also produce an extremely literal translation. It is furthermore a reluctant translation, despite his assertion in the preface that the Church has never 'wholly condemned all vulgar versions of the Scriptures' (**11**. 42), since translation represents multiplicity, which in turn leads to heresy. So where Tyndale argues that the affinity English has with Greek and Hebrew means that his vernacular Bible actually sounds like English, for Martin it is a virtue of his own translation that it still sounds like Latin. Its Latinate quality, which involves the coining of terms such as 'exaninate' and 'repropitiate' (examples quoted by Fulke: **10**. 389–90) is a way of preserving the solemnity of the Vulgate and maintaining a distance from the common people and from common speech. Although the Church had indeed sanctioned Bible translation in earlier times, Martin argues, these translations were not to be found in the hands of taverners, or, for that matter, women, but were kept in colleges and monasteries and the private homes of a few especially devout men (**11**. 128–54). In a gesture towards Erasmus's *Paraclesis*, which deliberately undoes its purpose, Martin claims that the ploughman could certainly have chanted the Psalms as he worked, but without understanding them, since he would not have had access to the translations. One problem with this uncompromisingly elitist stance is that it does not address the point that the Vulgate itself was originally 'vulgar'.[45] Nonetheless, Martin's defence of his

[45] This point had been debated in the 'Great Controversy' of the 1560s, the most important Protestant-Catholic debate on English Bible translation and related doctrinal issues between Tyndale and More and Martin and Fulke; see John Rastell, *A Treatise intitled, Beware of M. Jewel* (Antwerp, 1566), STC 20729, sigs I6^{r}–K2^{r}, images 75–78. The Jesuit Rastell's work is an attack on John Jewel's defence of the English Church, *Apologia pro Ecclesia Anglicana*, published in both Latin (1562) and English (1564).

translation method also enables him to make an interesting charge against the Protestant translations, which is that by neglecting 'the majesty [. . .] of that venerable style of Christ's spirit', they end up treating the word of God as though it were secular literature, gratuitously beautifying the language (**11**. 180–94). This has the surprising effect of reversing the positions in the Tyndale-More exchanges, where Tyndale had sneered at More's 'poetry'. And yet it has a certain logic to it: Tyndale was ideologically anti-literary, but More had also defined his agenda as a secularising one. Fifty years on, it seems that mainstream English Protestantism had become more willing to allow that its appeal to the 'common' could extend the category of 'literature' to embrace the works of both God and man.

Martin's opponent was William Fulke, who had become the official voice of English Protestantism, engaging in print with numerous Catholic controversialist works and orally in public disputations with Catholic prisoners, including Edmund Campion. In his *Defence of Translations* he argues that the philological method is the path to salvation and that the truth of Holy Scripture must come from 'the first fountains and springs rather than out of any streams that are derived from them' (**10**. 120–22). While that image derives ultimately from Jerome, Fulke also argues that even Augustine, Jerome's opponent on the subject of Bible translation, agreed on the necessity of returning to these sources, despite having only Latin, and that as his mother tongue (**10**. 313–18). On the tricky subject of Old Testament Greek quoted in the New, he retorts that Christ and the Apostles never quote from the Septuagint in a way that disagrees 'in sense and substance of matter [. . .] from the truth of the Hebrew text' (**10**. 187–91). This certainly moves away from the principle of literal translation in the case of Scripture, and that position is reinforced a little later when he argues, crucially, that the translator working 'for the ignorant people's instruction may sometimes depart from the etymology or common signification or precise turning of word for word' (**10**. 251–53).[46] In its abandonment of the literal principle in order to further common

[46] In a reprise of the Tyndale-More polemics, but with the roles reversed, Fulke also points out that Martin is not consistent in translating key words such as Church and priest (**10**. 272–75).

understanding, this gets close to the core of the differences in Protestant and Catholic approaches to English Bible translation.

That difference is extended in Fulke's massive attack on the Rheims New Testament of 1582, which he reprints in parallel with the text of the Bishops' Bible and challenges section by section. What Fulke offers is a defence of the common and an appeal for true vulgarisation in defiance of the false authority, as he sees it, of the Vulgate. He points out that the original language of the New Testament was not vulgar Latin but common Greek, adding that what was once vulgar is now ecclesiastical (**12**. 42; 100). The fact that some parts of the Bible are difficult to understand doesn't mean that they should not be translated, but that people should be given interpretative aids (**12**. 60). Confronting the Catholic Church itself, he moves into full polemical stride: papists are like the Pharisees, an elite sect who withhold knowledge from the common people and leave them in darkness (**12**. 126–33). Rome is the 'Babylonian harlot' who flouts the law of nature itself, Fulke implies, 'in restraining that which God hath left to be most free and general' (**12**. 253–55). Holy Scripture should be common knowledge, indifferent to distinctions of rank; and where Martin deplored the idea of the divine word being tossed to and fro in taverns, Fulke suggests that entertainers should be engaged instead to read from an English Bible at feasts so that 'the servants, prentices, slaves, and drudges of the house may be made equal with angels' (**12**. 335–37). And as for rank, so for gender: Fulke cites the Greek Church Father, Chrysostom, to show that the Bible should be available to 'boys and girls' and to 'holy persons of both sexes' (**12**. 329, 376). It is a vital inclusion, not least because it reinforces the real meaning of the term 'the mother tongue'.

Fulke's egalitarian rhetoric is difficult to resist – spreading the word of God throughout society is surely an unqualified good – so it is important to remember that there are two sides to this argument in relation to translation theory. Multiple translations necessarily have the effect of destabilising the reader's sense of the authority of the text, and where the source author is God Himself, getting it right is a matter of life or death, salvation or damnation. Popularisation can lead to degradation or, worse, perversion of the divine word. So we should not be surprised by the tone of the debates about Bible translation from Tyndale and More to Martin and Fulke. The fury that drives them is a measure of what is at stake, and the anxiety that underlies it comes from an awareness of how easily the 'honey' or 'manna' of God's word can become poison. This is what made Thomas More change his position on Bible translation between *Heresies* and the *Confutation*. Despite Fulke's assertion that 'none but spiders can suck poison out of wholesome flowers, which poison yet is not in the good flowers but in the evil nature of the spider' (**12**. 264–66), most translators in the early modern period, and not just those engaged in the perilous work of Bible translation, felt that spiders were everywhere.[47] They are the enemies of translation, figured in the type of the arch-critic, Zoilus, who had notoriously found fault even with Homer.[48] As Thomas James puts it, in a rather elaborate metaphor intended to justify the coarse-spun material of his translation of the Italian Protestant Antonio Brucioli: 'finest threads be not ever the best, for then spiders would undo weavers and spinners . . . sucking sour out of sweet and drawing forth poison from honey' (**13**. 36–40). These 'Zoiluses', he complains, 'do shoot the venom of their tongues against painful [careful] translators of books' (**13**. 64–65). Zoilus, and his scornful companion, Momus (also cited by James) hover balefully behind the prefaces to a great many translations of the period, divine and secular.

They are certainly present at the opening of Miles Smith's address to the King James or Authorised Version of the Bible, where Smith, who was both a translator and one of the two final reviewers of the KJB, defends the work against 'calumniation' and 'cavil' and presents James himself in an improbably heroic role ('his royal heart was not daunted or discouraged', **15d**. 52–53) as the authoriser of the project, persevering in the face of fierce obloquy. In fact, the origins and progress of the KJB were rather less embattled than Smith suggests. James had proposed a new translation of the Bible in 1602 at his last meeting of the General Assembly of the Church of Scotland before ascending the English throne; then, at the Hampton Court conference of January 1604, which had been convened to sort out

[47] And some poets: John Donne writes in 'Twickenham Garden' of the 'spider love, which transubstantiates all, / And can convert manna to gall', *The Poems of John Donne*, ed. by Robin Robbins (Pearson: Harlow, 2008), I, 254–55.

[48] On Zoilus and Momus, see Heidi Brayman Hackel, *Reading Material in Early Modern England: Print, Gender and Literacy* (Cambridge: Cambridge University Press, 2005), pp. 9–10, 122–23.

various demands from the Puritan wing of the Church, he was receptive to what seems to have been an opportunistic suggestion from John Rainolds, the Puritans' principal spokesman, for a new English Bible.[49] Rainolds's intention may have been to get the Geneva Bible accepted as the official Bible of the Church of England, but since James deplored its polemical Calvinist marginal comments (especially the one that seemed to allow disobedience to kings), this was never likely to work. Instead, he used the occasion to instigate a new translation fashioned more to his liking. This is why the account of what happened at Hampton Court, written by the anti-Puritan William Barlow, ends with James 'smiling' (**15a**.).

James appointed Richard Bancroft, Bishop of London and soon to be translated to Canterbury, to set up a team of translators. There were 47 in all, divided into six 'companies' with two each based at Westminster, Oxford, and Cambridge (see **15b**. note 4), and Bancroft also issued a set of rules (**15c**.). Despite the formidable resources of scholarship assembled, this was not expected to be a wholly new translation, but a revision of the Bishops' Bible of 1568 with readings to be selected from Protestant Bibles from Tyndale to Geneva. After all the intense debate over the translation of key terms, from Tyndale and More onwards, it was decided that the 'old ecclesiastical words' (eg. 'church' rather than 'congregation') should be used.[50] In another rejection of Puritan views, marginal notes were to be restricted to the explanation of Hebrew and Greek terms. The rest of the instructions are concerned to establish the translation as essentially a collaborative enterprise, with every individual's work checked over by other members of the company, with the complete text agreed by conference and then sent on for further review. The procedures for the KJB were later reported to the Synod of Dort in 1618, where the policy for the marginalia was elaborated and a preference expresssed for the Septuagint over

[49] The Scottish proposal of 1602 is recounted in Spottiswoode's *History of the Church of Scotland* (1655); see David Norton, *The King James Bible: A Short History from Tyndale to Today* (Cambridge: Cambridge University Press, 2011), pp. 82–83. Norton is the best guide to the evolution of the KJB.

[50] The Anglican revision of radical Protestantism in the context of Bible translation is rehearsed in David Edgar's play, *Written on the Heart*, performed by the RSC in 2011, where the ghost of Tyndale confronts Lancelot Andrewes, who represents the KJB translators.

the Vulgate for certain books (**15e**). The difference between Hampton Court and Dort was that the first conference was organised by a conservative Protestant establishment to negotiate with the Puritans, while the second was organised by a Calvinist establishment to resist the new conservative movement of Arminianism. The KJB was intended to be a monument to the Church of England's middle way. In this respect it follows the vision of translation as a 'common work of building' described by Nicholas Udall and reflected in the collaboration between the Puritan and conservative wings of the Church cleverly enforced by James.

After paying tributes to the King's efforts in setting up the new translation, Smith's preface presents the Bible as a panacea, and the ultimate source text by the ultimate author (**15d**. 60–100), in relation to which all tongues are barbarous (**15d**. 107–18). He then recounts the genealogy of Bible translation, pointing out that vernacular translations had enabled people to read Scripture in their mother tongue even before Christianity was general throughout the Roman Empire, so this is not just a recent fashion devised by Thomas Cromwell. It is at this point that he cites Catholic opposition to the vernacular Bible, dismissing the highly circumscribed permission for Bible translation granted by Rome as 'an unprofitable gift' (262). The insistence that translation should be profitable, that it should contribute to the 'common profit', which is an older term for 'common weal' and 'common wealth',[51] is constantly reiterated in the prefaces to secular translations, as we shall see. It underlines the Protestant commitment to the ideal of vernacular Bible translation as a socially inclusive distribution of spiritual benefit summed up in the maxim quoted by Thomas James, '*Bonum quo communius, eo melius*, Good, the commoner it is, the better it is' (**13**. 91–92). But what is also striking here is Smith's citation of secular literature to make the point, for the phrase comes from Sophocles' tragedy, *Ajax*. Nor is this an isolated instance: he cites Aristotle's *Metaphysics* (295–97) to argue for the importance of precursors and to pay tribute to earlier English Bible translators, and Sophocles again

[51] On the terminology of the 'common weal', see David Rollison, *A Commonwealth of the People: Popular Politics and England's Long Social Revolution, 1066–1649* (Cambridge: Cambridge University Press, 2010), pp. 13–21.

when he quotes the line from *Electra*, 'matters of such weight and consequence are to be speeded with maturity' (428–29), to explain why this translation was not finished in 72 days, as the Septuagint was supposed to have been. The allusions to Greek tragedy in Smith's preface to the KJB are part of a Protestant tradition of philhellenism, illustrated most powerfully in the figure of Sir John Cheke, first Regius Professor of Greek at Cambridge, who had read through the whole of Sophocles twice in his lectures of the 1540s and who had also worked on a translation of the New Testament into pure 'Anglo-Saxon' English.[52] They reinforce the point that English Protestantism has moved away from its radical, anti-literary origins onto a more humane centre ground.

For Catholics Greek continued to be a minefield. Gregory Martin had accused Protestant translators of treating Holy Scripture like secular literature, but he also, rather rashly, decided to quote Demosthenes in order to discredit what he saw as the worst mistranslations, such as 'carcass' for 'soul' and 'grave' for 'hell', and asked, tauntingly: 'what are those? words or wonders?'[53] There may be good theological grounds for rejecting those translations, but citing a Greek orator does nothing to demonstrate that. Instead, it draws attention to the purely rhetorical effect of the words themselves. The terms 'carcass' and 'grave' are too ordinary to be 'wonders', and that ordinariness is, of course, part of the point; but Fulke was quick to spot that 'wonders' was an entirely apt description of some of Martin's more exotic Latinisms, as we saw above.[54]

The crucial issue of lexical choice in Bible translation is addressed by Smith at the end of the preface, where his discussion ultimately focuses on the concept of freedom. Explaining why the

[52] See Paul Strope Needham, 'Sir John Cheke at Cambridge and at Court', Unpublished PhD diss., Harvard University, 1971, p. 145; John Cheke, *The Gospel according to Saint Matthew*, ed. James Goodwin (Cambridge: J. and J. J. Deighton, 1843). On Protestant philhellenism see Victor Skretkowicz, *European Erotic Romance: Philhellene Protestantism, Renaissance Translation and English Literary Politics* (Manchester: Manchester University Press, 2010), especially pp. 24–26.

[53] Quoted by Fulke; see **10**. 392–93 below.

[54] On the vocabulary of the Douai-Rheims Bible, see David Norton, *A History of the Bible as Literature: Volume 1, From Antiquity to 1700* (Cambridge: Cambridge University Press, 1993), pp. 122–35.

KJB translators have not always translated the same words in the same way, he argues that 'the wise had rather have their judgements at liberty in differences of readings, than to be captivated to one', and suggests that being over-precise in this respect is likely only to encourage the atheist. 'For is the kingdom of God become words or syllables?', he asks; 'why should we be in bondage to them if we may be free' (491–92). This is a striking declaration for a scholar to make, since it seems to equate philological exactitude with tyranny and to associate 'freedom' in translation – that is to say, flexibility in choice of words – with social and political freedom. Smith then reinforces the association by suggesting that to choose some words and reject others might lay the translators open to the charge of 'unequal dealing toward a great number of good English words'.[55] This remarkable extension of the translators' responsibility into the political domain is nonetheless consistent with the aim of social inclusiveness that drives English Protestant Bible translation from the start. Here its effect is twofold: first, it invites the reader to conclude that the kingdom of God has indeed become words and syllables, since its rhetorical strategy depends upon the personification of the words at the translators' disposal; second, its almost playful suggestion that every decent English word should be given a chance of immortality in the new English Bible draws the Anglican Church away from the dark side of Calvinism at the same time as it affirms the fullness and sufficiency of the English vocabulary itself.

This affirmation points us towards the purely secular considerations of literary translation, which is one of the objections that Catholics made against the Protestant translators' approach to their task. But there is one book of the Bible that is especially able to act as a bridge between divine and secular translation theory and which even Protestants worried might be subject to inappropriate popularisation. This is the Psalms, which because they take

---

[55] There is a similar theme in Thomas Smith's *De Republica Anglorum*; see Cathy Shrank, *Writing the Nation in Reformation England, 1530–1580* (Oxford: Oxford University Press, 2004), p. 228.

[56] Hebrew poetry was based on parallelism rather than metre or rhyme, but there was little understanding of this before Robert Lowth's *Praelectiones Academicae de Sacra Poesi Hebraeorum* ['On the Sacred Poetry of the Hebrews'] (1754).

the form of poetry provide a specific set of questions and challenges for translators.[56] There is a wide range of English Psalm translation and a number of poets from Wyatt onwards attempted versions of the Psalms alongside their secular literary work. But because these were sung poems there was always the suspicion that they might degenerate into pop songs. This is the other way of looking at Erasmus's singing ploughman; it is satirically referenced in *1 Henry IV* where Falstaff says 'would I were a weaver – I could sing psalms, or anything' (2.5.119–20), and in the Clown's account in *The Winter's Tale* of a Puritan who 'sings psalms to hornpipes' (4.3.40–41).[57] So Catholics such as Gregory Martin who felt that popular versions of the Psalms were an officially sanctioned degradation of the Scriptures had a point. It was Elizabeth's first Archbishop of Canterbury, Matthew Parker, not a weaver, who published an English Psalter in 'rhyme', which in this case meant the ballad metre.[58]

English Psalm translation was practised by those of the highest rank, though it was experienced by those of the lowest. King James himself worked on Psalm translation, and it was probably the knowledge of this that held back George Wither from publishing his own versions until after the King's death. Wither's reflections on his method, published in *A Preparation to the Psalter* (1619) are interesting and innovative. He begins by arguing that verse has all 'the gravity' that becomes Holy Scripture because every word and syllable has to be considered in terms of quantity and number (**16**. 19–22) and 'weighed' accordingly, since 'gravity' implies weight as well as sober majesty. Wither's point is to identify his procedure with the forms of classical verse and dispel any associations with vulgar English rhyme, and when he goes on to explain that he has used different metres for different Psalms 'with an intent to suit the matter of each Psalm, so near as I could, to such numbers as might most

---

[57] *The Norton Shakespeare based on the Oxford Edition*, ed. by Stephen Greenblatt (New York: W. W. Norton, 1997), pp.1181, 2919; see also Tessa Watt, *Cheap Print and Popular Piety, 1550–1640* (Cambridge: Cambridge University Press, 1991), pp. 39–73.

[58] For his justification of this project, see Matthew Parker, *The Whole Psalter* (London, 1567), STC 2729, sigs B1^{v}-B2^{r}, image 6. But it was the Sternhold and Hopkins Psalter (1562) which was the most overwhelmingly popular version in English metre; see Hannibal Hamlin, *Psalm Culture and Early Modern English Literature* (Cambridge: Cambridge University Press, 2004), pp. 19–50.

aptly express it' (126–27), he may well be thinking of the metrical variety found in collections of odes, especially those of Horace, with his debts to the Greek lyricists. His preference for 'variety of metre' chimes with the preference for 'variety of senses' in the vocabulary of the KJB (**15d**. 441), and both celebrate a new sense of the abundant literary and poetic resources of English. Ultimately, though, what aligns Wither's method with the principles of the KJB translation is the attempt to balance grammar and simplicity – an aim that transcends the generic differences of poetry and prose. He wants to maintain that poetry has 'a power above the reach of common language' (42), and that the translation must express that, but also in order for the expressions of the original Hebrew or Greek to 'have the same power', they must be converted as far as possible 'into such plain and easy words as are becoming the language which they are reduced into' (165–67). With that as his goal, but still confining himself 'wholly to the text', he claims that he has 'carried an indifferent regard both to the sense and the words' (194–95).[59]

King James's arrangements for the translation process of the new Bible, with their expectations of bonding between the puritan and conservative wings of the Church, was his most skilful application of the political vision outlined in his first speech to parliament of March 1604. Here James proclaimed the union of the two kingdoms, 'which is the other inward Peace annexed to my Person', arguing that the integrity of the realm depended upon the assimilation of oppositional religious groups, both Catholic and puritan.[60] Negotiating between the two extremes of loose, vernacular coarseness and the kind of scrupulous *ad verbum* fidelity to source that takes no account of the idiom of the target language, Wither's translation theory is in its own terms equally characteristic of the English preference for the middle way.

---

[59] On 'indifference' see **15d**. 507 and note.

[60] King James VI and I, *Selected Writings*, ed. by Neil Rhodes, Jennifer Richards and Joseph Marshall (Aldershot: Ashgate, 2003), pp. 293–306 (p. 295).

3.

Coverdale correctly observed that the Reformation was driven by translation and printing (**6**. 64–65), but this was a union that predated Protestant efforts to make common the word of God. The very first book to be printed in English (though not in England) was a translation: Caxton's *Recuyell of the Histories of Troy*, which he produced at Bruges in 1473–4. This is a chivalric and essentially secular work, despite Caxton's claim in the preface that the matter should all be conformable to Christian doctrine, and one that was certainly not designed for the mass market. With its careful detailing of provenance it has the feel of a manuscript, a luxury item translated not just from French into English, but from one court culture to another. But despite the high status intent, the new technology soon forces Caxton to confront the logic of what we can now call 'publication'. In a later preface to his Virgil translation, *Eneydos*, he rehearses the dilemma of the writer who has to convert the diversity of speech into the uniformity demanded by print. English, he realises, is fundamentally unstable, having changed over his lifetime, but also varying from shire to shire; so how does a translator find a common form of the language? The problem, in fact, lies in the very notion of the 'common', with its double sense of something shared and something of low status. In a revealing observation, Caxton says that anyone of 'reputation in his country will utter his communication and matters in such manners and terms that few men shall understand them' (**18**. 55–57). This use of the term 'communication' shakes off its medieval origins in medieval 'commun' and Latin 'communis' and is also at odds with our modern understanding of the term, which implies inclusivity rather than exclusivity. Caxton is happy to state in the preface to *Eneydos* that his audience consists of the noble and the learned, not the common people (73–75), but the print medium still requires him to find a common language for his translations. He ends up by explaining, as English translators so often do, that he has sought a *via media*, negotiating between the 'over-rude' (too coarse) and the 'curious' (ornate). At the very inception of English print translation, then, there is a conflict between the desire to preserve rank and status and the principle of accessibility implicit in the new technology itself.

The Protestant legitimisation of making common, and thus of the whole translation process in England, tends to obscure the fact that anxieties about rank and status are endemic in discussions about translation all the way through the early modern period. These may have a straightforwardly social dimension, as they do with Caxton (and it is worth remembering here that some of the earliest English print translations were by aristocrats like Woodville and Tiptoft, who were working in an elite cultural framework),[61] but in the course of the sixteenth century these anxieties also cover textual degradation, the unwelcome popularisation of professional 'secrets', the vulgarisation or simplification of learning ('dumbing down') and the lowly role of the translator himself – or herself – in relation to the original invention of the author.

All these construct translation as a vertical process of transmission; but there is a horizontal axis too, which is evident in Caxton's comments on dialectal diversity.[62] The best illustration of this is provided by Gavin Douglas's *Eneados* (1513), the most significant translation of a work of secular literature into any form of English in the first half of the sixteenth century. Douglas was a Scottish nobleman who would certainly not have suffered from status anxiety, but he still feels obliged to make the conventional apology for the inadequacy of his rendering of the original. What he does not apologise for is the inadequacy of 'our language' (**19**. 13), a mixture of Scots and 'southern' which retains the vigorous or 'busteous' qualities of his native tongue but is willing to be receptive to English, just as Latin was to Greek. Nor does Douglas feel any inhibitions about following in the footsteps of his English predecessor. In fact, he is extremely rude about Caxton's Virgil, pointing out that he wasn't even translating from Latin, and observing sarcastically that when he got to a bit that he didn't understand he claimed that it was

[61] Caxton published *The Dictes and Sayengs of the Philosophres* and Christine de Pizan's *Moral Proverbes*, translated by Anthony Woodville, Earl Rivers (1477–79) and a translation of Cicero's *De Amicitia* by John Tiptoft, Earl of Worcester (1481).

[62] The distinction between vertical and horizontal approaches to translation was formulated by Gianfranco Folena in 1973; see *Volgarizzare e tradurre* (Torino: Einaudi, 1993), pp. 12–13, though Susan Bassnett-McGuire points out that Roger Bacon had a similar idea in the thirteenth century; see *Translation Studies*, 3rd edn (London: Routledge, 2002), p. 57.

'feignit' – as if the whole of the *Aeneid* wasn't fiction in the first place (100–1). Douglas's scornful account of Caxton's remoteness from the original texts leads him to do some detailed explanation of his own practice, and also to a particularly striking image for the predicament of the translator:

> Wha is attachit until a stake, we see,
> May gae nae further, but wrele about that tree (156–57).

The image of the translator being tied to a stake has associations for us that it would not have done for Douglas, whose work is pre-Reformation, but it vividly captures the situation of the writer who can only wander a certain distance from his source text, like a tethered goat, and who is forced to circle around the original in the search for adequate verbal equivalents in his own tongue. Douglas's frustration at not being able to 'transcend' the source is echoed in complaints that secondary tasks in the form of translation or paraphrase are more difficult than original authorship, because the translator has less freedom. In the modern era, liberation from this mired and compromised state is what Benjamin was to offer in his concept of translation as a reflection of 'the suprahistorical kinship of languages' and a reaching towards 'the very nucleus of pure language'.[63]

Both Douglas's account of the characteristics of his own vernacular and his image of the translator's lack of freedom may be situated on the horizontal plane of translation theory, but the opening prologue to *Eneados* also shows how easily these issues can be constructed on the more familiar vertical line of high and low textual status. After all, Douglas is at pains to stress that Virgil represents the summit of poetic achievement in the prestige language of Latin, which is why he is so dismissive of Caxton's translation, working as he does through the intermediary and lower status language of French.[64] But the established binary of elite Latin and lowly vernacular was about to be complicated by

[63] Walter Benjamin, 'The Task of the Translator', in *Illuminations*, ed. by Hannah Arendt (London: Pimlico, 1999), pp. 74, 80.

[64] Though we should also remember that in a different configuration of language economies French is high status through its role in the law and in diplomacy, as well as at court. On the complex issue of French and English language status in the late fifteenth century, see Ardis Butterfield, *The Familiar Enemy: Chaucer, Language, and Nation in the Hundred Years War* (Oxford: Oxford University Press, 2009), pp. 308–49.

a third element. When Douglas was translating Virgil in 1513 the teaching of Greek had scarcely begun in either Scotland or England, but in the next few years posts in Greek were established at Cambridge and Oxford and by the 1540s the subject was thriving at both universities. The pioneer of translation from Greek into English was Sir Thomas Elyot, who probably learned the language from the Oxford medic Thomas Linacre, and it is in his translation of Isocrates' *To Nicocles* as *The Doctrinal of Princes* (1533) that Elyot makes the claim that 'the form of speaking used of the Greeks called in Greek, and also in Latin, *phrasis*, much near approacheth to that which at this day we use than the order of the Latin tongue' (**20**. 9–11).[65] This echoes Tyndale's similar claims for the affinity between Greek and English, but in a secular context, and its implications for the perceived hierarchy of classical and vernacular languages are interesting. If English and Greek are closer than English and Latin (and similar claims were made for the affinity between Greek and other vernaculars), then Greek must surely be of lower rank than Latin. Yet it was the older of the two tongues, from which Latin itself borrowed, and in the Renaissance many Greek texts were first translated into Latin before reaching any of the modern vernaculars, suggesting that it was it, not Greek, which had the subsidiary role. So Greek was a disruptive force in the early sixteenth century, leaving the status of Latin uncertain, and for that reason, as far as religion was concerned, it was a radical force, as we have already seen.

Elyot himself, however, was certainly no radical and his Hellenic interests drew him into the circle of Sir Thomas More, not that of the reformers. The fact that he managed also to get on good terms with Cromwell says a great deal about the precarious nature of political alignments in the 1530s, but something too about the ambivalent status of Greek. For More and his circle Greek was the language of dialogue, of civilised philosophical debate constructed as play; for Tyndale it was the language

[65] On the affinity between Greek and English, see J. B. Trapp, 'The Conformity of Greek and the Vernacular: The History of a Renaissance Theory of Language', in *Classical Influences on European Culture, AD 500–1500* (Cambridge: Cambridge University Press. 1971), pp. 239–44.

[66] R. R. Bolgar, *The Classical Heritage and Its Beneficiaries* (Cambridge: Cambridge University Press, 1954), p. 313 (citing Richard Croke, the first Reader in Greek at Cambridge).

of the pure source, the word of God as it was faithfully recorded in the gospels. But Greek also represented a third and quite different sphere of knowledge, for it was seen as the language of medicine and science, of economics and public administration.[66] Elyot made one English translation of a Lucianic work, which reflects his associations with More, but otherwise his publications had entirely pragmatic ends in view and their watchword is common profit (**21**. 2–7).[67] It is this aspect of Greek that inspires Elyot's career as a writer and translator. In contrast with both More and Tyndale, but also in contrast with the courtly reference points that guided Caxton, Elyot redefined the role of translator as that of public servant.

In this he may well have been influenced by Linacre, and it is no coincidence that the leading light among early English Greek scholars was a medic. Galen remained the principal medical authority for much of the sixteenth century, and Galen, like his predecessor Hippocrates, was a Greek. Medical treatises from antiquity were published in Latin translation during the Renaissance, but to make these secret stores of professional knowledge available to the general public in the vernacular was a completely different matter. In doing just that, though he was only translating from the French, the physician Thomas Phaer defended himself in terms that echo modern conflicts between public benefit and the vested interests of healthcare professionals. For Phaer there is a moral imperative 'to declare that to the use of many which ought not to be secret for lucre of a few, and to communicate the fruit of my labours to them that will gently and thankfully receive them' (**22**. 18–21). Thomas Gale, who produced an English translation of Galen from Latin (1566), puts forward a similar argument, though less eloquently, adding that he doesn't intend that weavers should become surgeons and thinks that everyone should stick to his own profession (**34**. 56–62). Both Phaer and Gale cite the parable of the talents in defence of their support for communication over secrecy, and Phaer writes movingly about the duty imposed upon us by God to use the gifts he has given us for the general good. The underlying principle of

[67] The Lucian translation was *A dialogue betwene Lucian and Diogenes* (London, [1532?]), i.e. the pseudo-Lucianic *Cynicus*. The Latin translations of Lucian by Erasmus and More (Paris, 1506) were very influential and often reprinted.

communication – the dissemination of knowledge 'to the end that we should in common help one another' (**22**. 58–59) – reconfigures translation as a work of Christian charity. In doing so it links the Protestant desire to make common the word of God, which drives Bible translation, to the secular purposes of common profit.

It would be misleading, however, to imply that translators in sixteenth-century England usually go to Greek sources for material likely to be of social benefit to the nation. Medicine is a specific case, and though there are translations of Plutarch's *Moralia* and Xenophon's *Oeconomicus*, the key text in the field of moral philosophy is Cicero's *De Officiis* [On duties], which appeared in a highly successful translation by Nicholas Grimald in 1556. Grimald starts by saying that he has discovered 'profits and commodities' by joining experience of the world with deep reading, and that 'the most profitable part of philosophy' is that concerning manners, which is what Cicero covers in *De Officiis* under the general rubric of social duties. What this kind of book teaches us, he suggests, is 'the open use of living' (**27**. 4–12). This nicely chosen phrase shows how broadly we should understand the terms 'profit' and 'commodity' in the context of early modern translation. These words appear over and over again in translators' prefaces, as writers try to establish the usefulness of their works, but they are not limited to the narrow economic sense that they have today. Grimald goes on to argue that his translation will do for England what has already been done in other countries, and that since this nation is more 'given to civility and humanity than others', it will become 'peerless' when guided by Cicero's precepts (46–50). Following in Grimald's footsteps, John Dolman translated another of Cicero's works of moral philosophy, the *Tusculan Questions* (1561). Unlike Grimald, Dolman is worried that he will be accused of 'the unprofitable disclosing of the mysteries of Lady Philosophy' (**28**. 82), though it is unclear who would stand to gain from Cicero's work remaining secret. His anxiety may have something to do with his target audience, which he describes as 'a mean [i.e. middling] sort of men' (85). Seventy years earlier, though gradually acquiring commissions from merchants like himself, Caxton had discussed audience in terms of the three estates; with Dolman we are already seeing the emergence of what would become the great English middle class. How far down the social order the precepts of 'civility and humanity' might be expected to reach would have been debatable, but as Dolman realises, the mission of the vernacularisation of the classics was precisely to extend that reach.

If the term 'translation theory' is to mean anything, it has to be concerned with how you translate as well as why and for whom. This was a burning issue, quite literally, in the case of Bible translation, and Douglas had commented on the methodology of verse translation in the opening prologue to *Eneados*, but Grimald is the first English writer to offer a set of principles for the translation of secular prose. This is appropriate, since Cicero was the pre-eminent model for style in the sixteenth century, based on his prestige as an orator rather than a philosopher. A translation, Grimald says, should follow the rules for an oration: 'that it be short and without idle words, that it be plain and without dark sense, that it be probable and without any swerving from the truth'. He then amplifies this advice:

> For if it be not as brief as the very author's text requireth, whatso is added to his perfect style shall appear superfluous and to serve rather to the making of some paraphrase or commentary. Thereto, if it be uttered with ink-horn terms, and not with usual words, or if it be phrased with wrested or far-fetched forms of speech, not fine, but harsh, not easy, but hard, not natural, but violent, it shall seem to be. (175–81)

The stylistic virtues the translator should aim for, then, are conciseness, perspicuity, and fluency, the last being implied by the term 'natural': the original should be so perfectly converted into the natural idiom of the target language that it should not seem like a translation. What Grimald's prescription reinforces is the essential link between communication as making common and communication as effective speech – between goal and method.

The association of the orator and the translator derives from Cicero's *De Optimo genere oratorum*, which was a much cited authority in Renaissance discussions of translation, though its authorship is now disputed. Supposedly a preface to Cicero's own Latin translations of Demosthenes and Aeschines, it became a model for humanist translations of the classics in the Renaissance. It plays a central role in what is certainly the most comprehensive account of the theory and practice of translation written by an Englishman in the sixteenth century, Laurence Humphrey's *Interpretatio linguarum* (1559). Although Humphrey's book is particularly concerned with the translation of Greek into Latin, which is what Cicero himself had done,[68] and is itself written in Latin, it outlines a general set of principles for translation, which certainly include translation into the vernacular. Indeed, Humphrey lists the achievements of English translators towards the end of his work. But he begins by pointing out that the very terms 'translation' and 'translator' have a range of meanings, and the fact that he prefers *interpretatio* (in Greek *hermēneia*) to *translatio* alerts the reader to the principle that translation is always concerned with the elucidation of meaning.[69] This has obvious resonance for Bible translation. But throughout the work he uses a variety of alternative terms for the translation process to give a more nuanced sense of what the translator is doing in different contexts and to indicate the range of the semantic field of *interpretatio* (see headnote below). He then outlines three different kinds of translation: the over-literal, which he associates with pedagogical spoon-feeding; the too-free, when the translator loses sight of his original and writes as though he were an independent author; and the middle way, which is obviously the best. The four qualities we should expect in a good translation are that it should be comprehensive, appropriate, attractive, and aptly suited (**29**. 145–46), where the second term (*propria*) indicates that every language has its own idiom or defining character which the translator must attempt to reproduce. Like Grimald, Humphrey thinks that the translator's watchword should be perspicuity, which should run through everything we are saying, like blood (304–5). This might seem a slightly odd metaphor to use for the principle of clarity, but its purpose is to suggest that by finding the right form of words to elucidate the meaning of the original, the good translator will produce a living imitation of his source text.

---

[68] His example of translation from Hebrew is from Obadiah (see Humphrey (1559), p. 590).

[69] Tyndale claims that 'faythfully I have interpreted' the New Testament in the epilogue to the Worms printing of 1526 and that he 'nether was holpe with englysshe of eny that had interpreted the same, or soche lyke thinge in the scripture before tyme', *The New Testament translated by William Tyndale*, ed. by W. R. Cooper (London: British Library, 2000), p. 544.

Humphrey then explains what the requirements of a good translator are, and it is here that we see the links both between the translator and the orator and also, most crucially, between translating the word of God and translating secular literature. The qualities we should look for in a translator, he says, are natural gifts, learning, fidelity, and diligence (325–27). Humphrey uses the last of these to make an explicit parallel between oratory and translation by substituting diligence for delivery in the well-known story of Demosthenes' response to the question as to which was the most important element in oratory (484).[70] But it is fidelity (*fides*) that is the key term here. Humphrey echoes Quintilian in requiring the faithful translator, like the orator, to be a good man (441), and the wider implications of this become clearer in the section on imitation that follows. Imitation is, of course, a writing practice closely related to that of translation, but it also operates as a principle for translation itself and Humphrey offers translators three models for their work: Christ in sacred writings, Cicero in secular prose, and Virgil in poetry. Humphrey casts the model in the role of inspirational leader, as Theseus was for Hercules (522–23), so imitation is given a heroic rather than a servile colour. What this means in terms of translation practice is that we have to incorporate ourselves (the bodily metaphor reappears) into the expressive character of the original, 'putting on the living image and likeness of his language as far as possible' (535–36). Cicero's complete success in translating Greek into Latin means that 'the whole of Cicero is a pattern of how to express oneself, a live example' (616–17). But the ultimate model for imitation, the pattern of all that we should seek to become, is of course Jesus Christ. In the context of translation we have to understand that Christ is, as it were, translating himself – that which God has already expressed in Hebrew – and it is this that makes *fides* the touchstone of Humphrey's work. Faithfulness to the original ('faithful and sure interpretation', as Grimald put it, **27**. 184) is the principle that connects secular translation to the greater and

[70] Demosthenes answered that the first was 'pronunciation' [delivery]'; the second, 'pronunciation'; and the third, 'pronunciation'. This was widely cited in the Renaissance; see for example Thomas Wilson, *The Arte of Rhetorique* (London, 1553), STC 25799, sig. Gg1^{r}, image 126. ('Action' is often given for 'pronunciation'.)

more comprehensively demanding task of translating the work of God.[71]

Humphrey's book was published not in London, but in Basel, where he had gone to escape the re-institution of Catholic doctrine in England under Mary. In that respect his work is part of the mid-century translation activity stimulated by the Protestant experience of exile. This produced the Geneva Bible, Hoby's *Courtier* and Wilson's Demosthenes, the last two works coming from the circle which had gathered around Sir John Cheke at Padua. Towards the end of *Interpretatio linguarum*, after his roll-call of fine English translators in which Cheke's achievements are praised, Humphrey makes the comparativist point that it is good to have 'a taste of foreign ways' (933–34), citing the example of Wilson.[72] Protestantism had been the driver of Bible translation (and vice versa: the two are so closely linked), but the flowering of secular English translation and translation theory in the mid-Tudor period is partly attributable to the cultural dislocation of Protestants under Mary.

Cheke's role here is central. He had been appointed as the first Regius Professor of Greek at Cambridge, where he developed the subject so successfully that he could claim to have attracted audiences of over two hundred for his lectures.[73] But his commitment to Greek studies went hand in hand with a deep respect for his native tongue and Thomas Wilson recalls how he would spontaneously translate from one language to the other in these lectures, a practice that he seems to have repeated in the Greek reading group at Padua (**36**. 1–27, 114–20). It was Cheke's encouragement of the written exercise of double translation at St John's College that Ascham publicised in *The Schoolmaster* (**51**. 203–73) and which another of Cheke's pupils, William Cecil, recommended to the young John Harington.[74] Cecil also acted as a patron of translation, employing both Richard Eden (**31**.) and Arthur Golding (**32**.), who lived for a time at Cecil's house on the

[71] The different approaches to faithfulness in Scriptural and secular translation, observed by Jerome, are illustrated by Horace warning of the dangers of the *fidus interpres* in *Art of Poetry*, ll. 134–35.

[72] In some respects a rather unfortunate example, since Wilson was tortured after being arrested in Rome in 1558.

[73] Needham, 'Sir John Cheke at Cambridge and at Court', p. 145.

[74] See John Harington, *Nugae Antiquae* (London: Vernor and Hood, 1804), p. 131 (letter of 1578).

Strand. In exile at Padua, Wilson says, Cheke 'would English his matters out of the Latin or Greek upon the sudden, by looking of the book only, without reading or construing anything at all' (**36**. 114–16); and it was here that Wilson conceived his translation of Demosthenes. Here too Thomas Hoby, another St John's alumnus, completed his *Courtier*. It is ironic that Humphrey should have said that the importance of translation lay in teaching (**29**. 717), for though he became President of Magdalen College, Oxford, he is not on record as having been inspirational as a tutor and lecturer. It is difficult to estimate the influence of his treatise, which was not reprinted, but there is absolutely no doubt of the cultural impact of Cheke's teaching.[75] Though his own translations remained unpublished, the work of his pupils was hugely influential, and these pupils included the future Edward VI. Through Ascham his legacy is even reflected in Queen Elizabeth, who continued to meet with her former tutor after ascending the throne and who was herself a considerable translator (**23**., **43**.).

Cheke is also central because he draws together the three fields of translation activity represented in the present volume: translating sacred texts, literary translation, and pedagogy. His own translation work included the gospels of Matthew and part of Mark in English and Latin versions of Sophocles and Demosthenes, now lost.[76] Our record of his ideas about translation comes mainly from Wilson's reminiscences and the brief letter that Hoby published with his translation of Castiglione. His legacy, however, is extensive and his influence had a reach far outside the academy. For William Cecil translation was a first step towards empire building, which was why he employed Richard Eden to work on Peter Martyr.[77] For Thomas Hoby it was part of a process of catching up, which England would have to do if it was to compete with other countries in what we would now call the knowledge economy:

---

[75] The question as to whether a scholar could have more impact through teaching or publication is raised by Udall at **7a**. 77–89 below.

[76] See *John Bale's Catalogue of Tudor Authors: An Annotated Translation of Records from the Scriptorum illustrium maioris Brytanniae catalogus (1557–1559)*, ed. by J. Christopher Warner (Tempe, AZ: MRTS, 2010), pp. 149–50.

[77] See Andrew Hadfield, *Literature, Travel, and Colonial Writing in the English Renaissance, 1545–1625* (Oxford: Oxford University Press, 1998), pp. 71–91.

> In this point (I know not by what destiny) Englishmen are much inferior to well most other nations [. . .] [and] if they will mark well the truth, they shall see at this day where the sciences are most turned into the vulgar tongue, there are best learned men, and comparing it with the contrary they shall also find the effects contrary. (**30**. 102–3, 116–19)

This does not mean that translation is a threat to academics, he claims, somewhat provocatively: 'the translation of Latin or Greek authors doth not only not hinder learning, but it furthereth it; yea, it is learning itself, and a great stay to youth' (138–40). For Thomas Wilson, translating Demosthenes was a way of engaging with the political and military threat posed by Spain.[78] The last instance is a useful reminder that alongside the rhetoric of democratisation, much translation activity in the sixteenth century was occasional and directed towards pragmatic ends.[79]

The belief that translation is vital to England's cultural development, which Hoby uses to counter charges of dumbing down, is closely linked to an awareness of Italy's superiority. William Thomas, who published books on Italian language and history, is another writer who warns that England is backward in terms of 'civil knowledge' because it doesn't have the sciences in its own language (**25**. 13–21); Morley complains that Italians and the French are much more prompt at translating works from Latin than the English (**26**. 32–35), and Grimald and Painter (**35**. 80) make similar points. Later, both Daniel's correspondent, 'N. W.', and John Florio quote Giordano Bruno to the effect that from 'translations all sciences had their offspring' (**40**. 23; **47**. 206). All agree that Italy is the leader of the field. It was also in Italy that Greek was first introduced to the West, so there is a certain symmetry in Cheke's efforts to keep the flame of Greek studies alive among the English community in Padua in the 1550s, however unwelcome his residence there may have been.

---

[78] See Alastair J. L. Blanshard and Tracey A. Sowerby, 'Thomas Wilson's Demosthenes and the Politics of Tudor Translation', *International Journal of the Classical Tradition*, 12 (2005), 46–80.

[79] See Fred Schurink, 'Introduction', in *Tudor Translation*, ed. by Schurink (Basingstoke: Palgrave Macmillan, 2011), pp. 1–17.

While he was strongly committed to his own vernacular as well as to Greek,[80] Cheke would have been rather less enthusiastic about his countrymen developing 'a taste of foreign ways', as Humphrey put it. Alongside complaints that England is not producing enough translation, there are frequent admissions in the mid-century that English is a relatively impoverished language and might not have the resources to do the work effectively, but there is much less agreement about how the process of enrichment should work.[81] Cheke's gospel translation leaves no doubt as to where he stands on the matter of imported foreign vocabulary, since it is scrupulously confined to words of pure Anglo-Saxon origin, preferring 'ofspring of adders' to Tyndale's 'generation of vipers', and for translation itself, 'trutorn'.[82] In the letter to Hoby he makes an explicit statement of his position, which has often been quoted:

> I am of this opinion that our own tongue should be written clean and pure, unmixed and unmangled with borrowing of other tongues; wherein, if we take not heed, by time, ever borrowing and never paying, she shall be fain to keep her house as bankupt' (**30**. 253–57).

But Hoby's own translation is far from being 'pure' in the way that Cheke's Matthew is, and Hoby's borrowing is natural, not strained, and 'seemeth to grow out of the matter and not to be sought for', as Cheke himself acknowledges. In fact, Cheke's use of the financial metaphor in the debate about 'ink-horn terms',[83] reveals a fundamental inconsistency in his position as an advocate for translation. Translators constantly reiterate that

[80] In addition to his translation of Matthew, Cheke headed a campaign for the reform of Greek pronunciation with his close ally, Thomas Smith. This was linked to an agenda for English: 'in the case of Greek there was no dispute about the writing; in the case of English, the other way round', Thomas Smith, *De recta et emendata linguae Anglicae scriptione, Dialogus* in *Literary and Linguistic Works*, vol. 3, ed. by Bror Danielsson (Stockholm: Almquist and Wiskell, 1983), p. 39.

[81] The classic account of the sixteenth-century debate on English vernacular enrichment is R. F. Jones, *The Triumph of the English Language* (Stanford: Stanford University Press, 1953); on borrowing and neologising see pp. 94–141.

[82] Cheke, *Matthew*, pp. 46, 73.

[83] The expression starts to be used from the mid-sixteenth century for what Caxton would have called 'curious' terms, but it is perhaps more significant to see what this is contrasted with: Cheke's 'pure' is Caxton's 'rude'.

what they do is for the public good, that it enriches the commonwealth. In broad economic terms they are free-traders. Cheke, however, is a protectionist, and in more specifically financial terms what seems to worry him is the fiscal deficit. The most forceful challenge to this kind of thinking comes from George Pettie in his preface to Guazzo. Pettie argues that if English has 'cracked its credit', this must have happened very recently, since it has been borrowing words from other languages for centuries, and he points out rather neatly that even the words 'plain' and 'common' come from Latin. Whether a word is old or new, native or foreign, should have no effect upon its innate value. For Pettie, borrowing is investment for growth: 'Why should not we do as much for the posterity as we have received of the antiquity?' (**38**. 81–82), he asks. Cheke's contribution to the translation culture of mid-sixteenth century England was very considerable, but as far as the economic and financial argument is concerned it was Pettie who turned out to be right.

The financial metaphor, which is encountered most frequently in the ideas of verbal coinage and of language as a treasury or thesaurus, is one of a range of images for translation.[84] In addition to economics, these tend to work in the figurative fields either of the body (clothing, digestion) or of international relations (immigration, conquest).[85] But none of these provides much of a context for understanding what Cheke's real concerns are here. His antipathy towards foreign imports has less to do with national bankruptcy – whatever that might mean in terms of language – than with a strong attachment to the ideal of linguistic purity, which is how his letter to Hoby begins. The ideal of the pure source was shared by both humanism and Protestantism, as we have seen in relation to Bible translation, and it is also evident in Cheke's concern with the correct pronunciation of Greek. It is an ideal that is fraught with anxieties about the translation

---

[84] A humanist precedent for the representation of language as coinage can be found in Valla's preface to his Latin translation of Thucydides, where he derives it from Quintilian's *nummus*: see Nancy S. Struever, *Theory as Practice: Ethical Enquiry in the Renaissance* (Chicago: University of Chicago Press, 1992), p. 129.

[85] On metaphors for translation, see A. E. B. Coldiron, 'Commonplaces and Metaphors', in *OHLTE* (2), pp. 109–17; Morini, pp. 35–61; Theo Hermans, 'Images of Translation: Metaphor and Imagery in the Renaissance Discourse on Translation', in *The Manipulation of Literature*, ed. by Hermans (London: Croom Helm, 1985), pp. 103–35.

process, which can so easily be construed as one of degradation and contamination. This has its own Biblical source in Genesis 26.15, where the Philistines are reported to have filled the Israelites' wells with earth. Humphrey alludes to it when he argues that Christ's role as translator was to open 'those very wells which the Pharisees and rabbis (offspring of the Philistines) had blocked with the foul stagnancies of their verbal obscurities' (549–52).[86] But the merely human translator, acutely conscious that his or her work can only be an approximation of the original, is more likely to worry that all they will ever be able to offer the reader is dirty water. Florio asks hopefully in the preface to his translation of Montaigne: 'Can the well-springs be so sweet and deep, and will the well-drawn water be so sour and smell?' (**47**. 212–13). But a great deal hangs on that term 'well-drawn'. In the end it was left to Chapman to provide an adequate answer to this problem when he took up the challenge of translating Homer, the purest spring of all in secular literature. 'All tongues have enriched themselves from their original' by borrowing, he argues in the preface to *Achilles' Shield*, 'and therefore for current wits to cry from standing brains, like a brood of frogs from a ditch, to have the ceaseless, flowing river of our tongue tuned into their frog pool [. . .] would soon bring the plague of barbarism amongst us' (**44b**. 107–11). Chapman's contrast of the standing pool and the flowing river is perfectly judged because it answers the purists in their own language. Where Cheke imagines a nation writing clean, pure English by living off its own wealth, and mixing metaphors to do so, Chapman sees only a stagnant pond.

Outside the field of metaphor, however, fear of degradation reflects real issues about the relationship between source text and translation.[87] Many texts were translated from intermediary languages rather than directly from the original. Greek texts often found their way into the modern vernaculars through Latin translation, but some also arrived in English via French, the best-known example being North's Plutarch, based on Amyot.

---

[86] On well-springs of pure and muddy water as Biblical source, see Hester Lees-Jefferies, *England's Helicon: Fountains in Early Modern Literature and Culture* (Oxford: Oxford University Press, 2007), pp. 103–21; and in a secular context, Neil Rhodes, *Shakespeare and the Origins of English* (Oxford: Oxford University Press, 2004), pp. 124–26.

[87] We should also bear in mind that degradation is distinct from contamination and produces a different kind of anxiety.

This might also happen at the lower end of the market, as in the case of romance where French was frequently a staging post between Spanish and English. Attitudes to French varied: it did not quite have the prestige that Bembo had claimed for Italian in his *Prose della volgar lingua* (1525), but some writers, like John Healey, the translator of Theophrastus, thought that Greek could be translated into French a good deal more happily than into Latin (**49**. 18–22), though he brushes aside wilder claims that French was actually a more venerable language than Greek. In cases where the source text itself was French, writers were suitably respectful, with Richard Carew commenting admiringly on 'the Venus of the French' (**48**. 33). But Chapman reacted violently to suggestions that his English Homer might have relied on the French of Hugues Salel, which he dismisses as 'poor and unpleasing' (**44c**. 153–64), while earlier he had scoffed at Arthur Hall's translation of Homer and branded it as 'born lame and defective' because it had been delivered by the 'French midwife' (**44b**. 52–53). Chapman also defended himself against the 'envious windfucker' who claimed that he had just used Latin paraphrases of Homer (**44c**. 225–30) and he goes to some lengths to establish his credentials as a Hellenist. In fact, Chapman's source text was the parallel Greek-Latin edition of Spondanus, which had an extensive commentary, and his translation could not have been completed without Latin aids. In this respect he was no different from a great many translators, including the prolific Philemon Holland, who worked from multiple translations alongside an original-language edition.[88] The practice is again validated by Bible translation, where hybridity of material is held to be a guarantee of the purity of the end product.[89]

This last point is one of the fundamental paradoxes of Renaissance translation theory. The idea that translation represents a process of serial degradation as it moves telephonically from one language to another is easy to understand; but it is complicated by the model of Bible translation, which is always the translation of a translation and which therefore invites the translator to recover the purity of the original through synthesis.

[88] See Gordon Braden in *OHLTE* (2), p. 97.

[89] In addition to multiple source texts the KJB translators also compared modern foreign-language translations of the Bible; see Gerald Hammond, 'The Authority of the Translated Word of God', *Translation and Literature*, 2 (1993), 17–36.

Considerations of source text or 'copy' text also reopen the issue of vertical and horizontal lines of translation. Chapman's angry defence of his scholarship posits a vertical line of transmission and a linguistic hierarchy, but the process of collation in much actual and entirely conscientious translation practice operates on a horizontal plane looking back to the concerns of a purist such as Cheke; these considerations remind us that there is difference between degradation (dumbing down) and contamination (crossing over), and that the first may be positively constructed as collaborative progress just as the second may be seen as enrichment.

There is no doubt, however, that the vertical model for translation is the dominant one in the minds of most commentators on the translation process, and this has implications for the status of the translator himself, or herself (the question of gender is certainly relevant here). Though Erasmus claimed that paraphrase was more difficult than original writing, and Douglas implied as much when he said that the translator was tied to a stake, there was general agreement that the translator's role was secondary. This could be qualified: Sir John Harington said that he 'would wish to be called rather one of the not worst translators than one of the meaner makers' (**41**. 45–46). The unidentified 'N. W.', writing from Oxford to Samuel Daniel about his translation of Paolo Giovio, went further: translation has the same relation to original authorship as disposition does to invention in rhetoric, he argues, where 'disposition' means dissemination and 'blazing [. . .] inventions abroad in this famous island' (**40**. 17–18). But the most elaborate disquisition on the subject of the translator's secondary status came from John Florio in the preface to his Montaigne. Here he describes his previous literary labour (his Italian-English dictionary) as his 'last birth', designating this 'masculine' on account of its being primary and independent and therefore of high status. The analogy he draws is with the mythical loosing of Bacchus from Jupiter's thigh. His translation of Montaigne, on the other hand, is a 'defective edition' and therefore a female birth, 'since all translations are reputed females, delivered at second hand' and Florio's role as a translator is comparable with Vulcan's in hatching Minerva from Jupiter's brain (**47**. 13–21). It is difficult to imagine what Florio's dedicatees would have made of this, since they were not only female but mothers themselves; nor would they have been much enlightened by Florio's sudden switching of his own part in the business to that of 'fondling foster-father', presumably to escape the suggestion that he might be transgender. In fact, the unintended consequence of Florio's rather confused imaging of translation as a 'female birth' is the hint that it might be primary after all.

But Florio's mythological metaphors do point us to the very real issue of gender and translation. There certainly were women translators in the sixteenth century, though they do not feature strongly in the present volume, partly because much of their work was unpublished and it was in the context of print publication that theorising about the nature of translation tended to take place.[90] Moreover, some of this work is of considerable importance: the only surviving translation of Greek tragedy into English, for example, is Jane Lumley's version of Sophocles' *Iphigeneia at Aulis*, which she made as a New Year's gift for her father.[91] This was a private, family affair, as was the young Princess Elizabeth's translation of Marguerite de Navarre, which she presented to her stepmother Katherine Parr on a similar occasion, but some work by women did make it into print. The most significant translation by a woman in this period is undoubtedly Anne Bacon's *Apology of the Church of England*, which was the official defence of the newly established Anglican Church and distributed to every parish in the country. The Latin original had been written by Bishop John Jewel in 1562 and a translation commissioned by the Archbishop of Canterbury, Matthew Parker. When this proved to be inadequate, Anne, one of the remarkable Cooke sisters and mother of Francis Bacon, offered her own version instead. C. S. Lewis – hardly a proto-feminist – judged that 'if quality without bulk were enough, Lady

[90] There are excellent accounts by Patricia Demers, *Women's Writing in English: Early Modern England* (Toronto: University of Toronto Press, 2005), pp. 64–98, and Chris Laoutaris, 'Translation/Historical Writing' in *The History of British Women's Writing, 1500–1610*, ed. by Caroline Bicks and Jennifer Summit (London: Palgrave Macmillan, 2010), pp. 296–327. See also *Women and Translation in Early Modern England and France*, ed. by Marie-Alice Belle, in *Renaissance and Reformation/Renaissance et Réforme*, 36 (2013).

[91] This is also the first play extant by an English woman; see *Three Tragedies by Renaissance Women Writers*, ed. by Diane Purkiss (London: Penguin, 1998). Jane (née Fitzalan) was the daughter of the Earl of Arundel, who had taken considerable care with her education. Her translations of Isocrates into Latin also survive in manuscript.

Bacon might be put forward as the best of all sixteenth-century translators'.[92]

For Queen Elizabeth herself language skills were an essential tool in the daily business of government, but also a mark of scholarly accomplishment and cultural finesse. The only one of her six languages that would have been of little practical use to her was classical Greek, yet she continued to read Greek with Ascham after becoming queen. In her childhood translation of Marguerite, she wrote that 'the wit of man or woman [shall] wax dull and unapt to do or understand anything perfectly unless it be always occupied upon some manner of study' (**23**. 9–12), and she managed to live by this maxim, producing her translation of part of Horace's *De Arte poetica* at the age of sixty-five.

Florio's underlying point, which is that the secondary status of translation makes it an appropriately feminine activity, might charitably be construed as a version of the modesty topos, disclaiming undue credit for his own labours. But then Florio was not a woman, and recent scholarship has done much to establish both the significance of early modern women's writing in general and the more specific contribution of translation within that. Danielle Clarke, for example, has made the valuable suggestion that Florio's designation of translation as female may imply that 'the cultural function of both translation and women is to reproduce and transmit cultural and economic capital'.[93] More negatively, since it did not presume to the status of original invention, translation could be seen as a suitably passive skill, like embroidery, in which an educated woman could exercise her mind without appearing forward or outspoken.

But some women, of course, were both outspoken and also translators, like Mildred Cecil, Anne Bacon's sister and wife of

---

[92] C. S. Lewis, *English Literature in the Sixteenth Century, Excluding Drama* (Oxford: Clarendon Press, 1954), p 307. See also Mary Ellen Lamb, 'The Cooke Sisters: Attitudes Towards Learned Women in the Renaissance', in *Silent But for the Word: Tudor Women as Patrons, Translators, and Writers of Religious Works*, ed. by Margaret Patterson Hannay (Kent, OH: The Kent State University Press, 1985), pp. 107–25; Patricia Demers, '"Nether bitterly nor brablingly": Lady Anne Cooke Bacon's Translation of Bishop Jewel's *Apologia Ecclesiae Anglicanae*', in *English Women, Religion, and Textual Production, 1500–1625*, ed. by Micheline White (Farnham: Ashgate, 2011), pp. 205–17.

[93] Danielle Clarke, 'Translations', in *The Cambridge Companion to Early Modern Women's Writing*, ed. by Laura Lunger Knoppers (Cambridge: Cambridge University Press, 2009), pp. 167–80 (p. 172).

Sir William Cecil, who was considered by the Spanish ambassador to be rather too clever and an undue influence on her husband.[94] Mildred was another Greek scholar and one of the few women to comment on their own translation practice. In a letter to Lady Somerset, which she sent with a translation of a sermon of St Basil, she writes:

> I have somewhat superstitiously observed the nature of the Greek phrase, not omitting the congruity of English speech, but rather the use, that the treaty of so good an author should not in too much serving the English tongue lese his own efficacy and value (**24**. 26–27).[95]

Since she was not intending to publish her own work, there was no need for her to observe the principle of making common, and she wants the translation still to sound like Greek: this is an elite taste shared between friends – almost, perhaps, the female equivalent of Thomas More's Hellenophile circle. The most outspoken woman translator writing in the sixteenth century, however, was working at the opposite end of the cultural spectrum. The Spanish ambassador would at least have approved of the fact that Mildred Cecil was translating a work of piety, even if it did have a Protestant agenda, but he would have been shocked by a woman translating and publishing one of his own country's romances, which is what Margaret Tyler did, and not from intermediary French. Tyler herself remarks on the fact that she might have been expected to confine herself to a work of divinity, but argues that if men think it's perfectly fitting to dedicate romances to women, and therefore (presumably) to read them, then why should they not also translate them (**37**. 84–93).

Since the great majority of translators' prefaces take the form of apology, their tone tends to be defensive, but the effect of Tyler's doubly subordinate role as a female translator has the

[94] Conyers Read, *Mr. Secretary Cecil and Queen Elizabeth* (London: Jonathan Cape, 1955), pp. 35, 336.

[95] See also Jane Stevenson, *Women Latin Poets: Language, Gender, and Authority, from Antiquity to the Eighteenth Century* (Oxford: Oxford University Press, 2005), pp. 263–66. On the ways in which women rewrite their own position and agency as translators see Brenda M. Hosington, 'Tudor Englishwomen's Translations of Continental Protestant Texts: The Interplay of Ideology and Historical Context', in *Tudor Translation*, ed. by Fred Schurink (London: Palgrave Macmillan, 2011), pp. 121–42.

effect of making her preface all the more forceful and challenging. She is untroubled by some of the anxieties that beset her male counterparts, arguing, like William Painter for example, that chivalric romance is morally inspiring, but adding (*pace* Painter) that it really doesn't matter whether it is truthful or not.[96] And rather than nervously anticipating criticism from the learned, Tyler offers her work confidently to the court of public opinion, declaring that she doesn't 'fear the speech of the people if I be found backward' (32). She seems, in fact, to have been inspired by the example of her own material, which she claims will instil 'courage' in the young with its stories of military prowess. Her own role here is like that of a drummer in battle, who contributes by inciting others to fight while being just as exposed to death or injury. This is a highly intelligent rewriting of the female translator's position with regard to both agency and vulnerability in a context which is supplied by the subject matter of the source text itself. It also adds substance to Tyler's point that women have always been co-opted by men as necessary partners in the production of chivalric romance.

Tyler uses her military matter to comment perceptively on translation and gender, but not to define the relationship between the translator and her source text as a power struggle. Male translators, however, do sometimes see their work as an act of conquest and subjugation. One of the least apologetic of all sixteenth-century English translators is Thomas Drant, who is confident that he can improve on his source text, which is Horace's satires (*Sermones*). Some of his metaphors of improvement are drawn from craft-work, as he describes the way he has both blunted and sharpened the cutting edge of Horace's wit, 'helping him to ebb and helping him to rise' (**33**. 31). But the image is given an unexpected twist when he suddenly reconfigures the text as one of the spoils of conquest. Referencing Deuteronomy 9.1, and God's promise to the children of Israel that they shall possess nations mightier than themselves, Drant declares that 'I have done as the people of God were commanded to do with their captive women that were handsome and beautiful: I have shaved

[96] Painter slides between the terms 'history' and 'novelle' for his material. On the difference between chivalric romance and the *novella* see Lorna Hutson, *The Usurer's Daughter: Male Friendship and Fictions of Women in Sixteenth-Century England* (London: Routledge, 1994), pp. 91–98.

off his hair and pared off his nails' (45–47). Given the date at which Drant was writing (1566), it is astonishing that he can feel able to represent his urbane Roman precursor as both female and barbarian, and English as a superior, civilising force. Christian zeal will have helped (Drant was Archdeacon of Lewes), but gendering the source text itself as female is still in striking contrast to the ways in which both Tyler and Florio represent the translation process.

Drant's figuring of translation as an act of conquest and civilisation, however, is not unique, and by the start of the new century, when confidence in the power of English had grown, it might have seemed more plausible. In 1601 Philemon Holland, the most voluminous of English Renaissance translators, wrote in his preface to Pliny that critics of translation were rejecting the opportunity 'to triumph now over the Romans in subduing their literature under the dent of the English pen, in requital of the conquest sometime over this island' (**46**. 73–75). Fifty years earlier, William Thomas had thought that the English were good at fighting, but backward in translation (**25**. 10–21); now translation can be seen as an extension of war by other means. This retains a vertical model for the translation process, but with a complete role-reversal between source text and target language. Behind it lies the medieval theory of the translation imperii, in which history is represented as a succession of transfers of power from one great empire to another.[97] In the case of England, Holland is being somewhat premature.

Thomas Fuller called Holland the 'translator general in his age', though not very flatteringly,[98] and his vast labours in the conversion of Greek and Latin prose into English may have given him a satisfied sense of empire building. But neither his claim to be paying back the Romans, nor Drant's more exotic reference to cleaning up wild female captives, are really representative of English thinking about translation in the period (though both are frequently cited). Elsewhere in the preface to Holland's Pliny,

[97] On the relationship between *translatio imperii* and *translatio studii* in the early Renaissance, see Karlheinz Stierle, '*Translatio Studii* and Renaissance: From Vertical to Horizontal Translation', in *The Translatability of Cultures: Figurations of the Space Between*, ed. by Sanford Budick and Wolfgang Iser (Stanford, CA: Stanford University Press, 1996), pp. 55–67.

[98] Thomas Fuller, *The History of the Worthies of England*, ed. by P. A. Nuttall (London: Thomas Tegg, 1840), III, 287.

and also in the preface to his Livy published the year before, there is a recognition that the relationship between translation and source text is essentially receptive. Dedicating his Livy to Elizabeth, Holland praises her benign policy towards aliens, which allows him to represent Livy as an immigrant applying for citizenship. He 'arrived long since and conversed as a mere stranger in this your famous island' – that is to say, he has long been available in England in Latin – but now 'humbly craveth Your Majesty's favour to be ranged with other free denizens of that kind' (**45**. 26–30). The metaphor combines the political and linguistic senses of 'naturalisation' and echoes Hoby's *Courtier*, where the courtier is presented as an Italian who has 'strayed about this realm' but is now 'become an Englishman' (**29**. 9, 18); though here Hoby's hospitable intentions are restrained by Cheke's wary advice that he should try to use the 'old denizened words' in his translation (**29**. 265). It's one thing to give a home to immigrants, but we shouldn't let them corrupt our language. Cheke's guarded welcome to Hoby's stranger seems of a piece with his financial concerns, but his urging of caution was not much heeded in Elizabethan England. Cheke himself had, after all, been an English stranger in Italy and after Elizabeth's accession there was a reciprocal welcome for European Protestants in London like Florio's father. These immigrants, some of whom became foreign language teachers, are the human embodiment of translation. They represent the actual link between textual migration and the migration of people in early modern Europe, which is captured in the metaphors of immigration and naturalisation in translators' prefaces.[99] They also demonstrate another way in which Protestantism is a driver of translation practice in the sixteenth century.

So receptivity rather than conquest is the underlying principle of translation in this period and we should think in terms of exchange rather than follow the more familiar paradigm of post-colonialist theory. The point is illustrated by a key term in Holland's preface to Pliny. In a passage that argues a forceful

[99] On the 'migration' of texts see Andrew Pettegree, 'Translation and the Migration of Texts', in *Borders and Travellers in Early Modern Europe*, ed. by Thomas Betteridge (Ashgate: Aldershot, 2007), pp. 113–25; on the immigrants themselves, see Pettegree, *Foreign Protestant Communities in Sixteenth-Century London* (Oxford: Clarendon Press, 1986).

case for making Pliny common, Holland says that the translation should not be 'appropriate to the learned only, but accommodate to the rude peasant of the country' (**46**. 45–46). On the face of it this is simply a point about stylistic level: the translation should be expressed in a way that is intelligible to the common people. But the concept of 'accommodation' is also the point at which the vertical and horizontal planes of translation intersect. Accommodation is the key principle of cultural translation, which extends the principle of sense for sense at the verbal level to that of cultural equivalence.[100] Richard Carew demonstrates this in his translation of Henri Estienne when he says that he has changed 'entre Paris et Lyon' to 'betwixt York and London' and 'chien de St Roche' to 'Toby's dog' (**48**. 46–48). Closely related to the concept of accommodation is 'domestication', and together these terms underline the hospitable ethos of translation represented in the sense of its offering a home to strangers.[101] This is present even in Drant's image of the captive women, since in Deuteronomy the point of the hairstyling and nail-paring is to make the women fit to enter the homes of their captors as wives. But the best example of translation as both accommodation and domestication is the actual and metaphorical one of John Florio, the Anglo-Italian who had married Samuel Daniel's sister and who lodged at the home of Lucy, Countess of Bedford while translating Montaigne. In the prefatory poem to the published text Daniel writes that Florio has enabled Montaigne's 'happy settling in our land' and that he has '[p]laced him in the best lodging of our speech /And made him now as free as if born here' (418, 422–23). This observation on the naturalisation of Montaigne as a 'free' English citizen prompts Daniel to reflect on the greater freedom of the international community of letters where 'th'intertraffic of the mind' is not impeded by national boundaries. But it also reflects upon Florio's own family history,

[100] See Burke and Po-chia Hsia, eds, *Cultural Translation in Early Modern Europe*, especially pp. 7–10, where accommodation is understood as adaptation.

[101] There are other ways of representing domestication: Lawrence Venuti sees it as an inherent part of the invisibility of the translator which enforces the 'multiple hierarchies and exclusions' of the hegemonic body of Anglo-American linguistic dominance; see *The Translator's Invisibility* (London: Routledge, 1995), p. 17; on translation and welcome, see Paul Ricoeur, 'Being a Stranger', trans. Alison Scott-Baumann, in *Theory, Culture & Society*, 27 (2010), 37–48.

so it is appropriate that Daniel should return to the domestic sphere at the end of his poem. Echoing the earlier metaphor of 'the best lodging of our speech' with the reminder that since 'a guest in gratefulness, / For the great good the house yields him within' does not complain about the accommodation, so, '[w]hilst England English speaks', we should not complain about the inadequacy of English for the purposes of translation (448–50).

At the turn of the seventeenth century, then, a democratisating programme of translation goes hand in hand with a confidence in the ability of English to accommodate the best of classical and European literature, and this has come about through an extraordinary degree of linguistic receptivity. From Homer to Montaigne, or (we might say) from the most ancient and bardic to the most modern and sophisticated of writers, English-speaking readers now had a wealth of foreign literature available to them in their own language. The test of this new confidence is in poetry. Poetry is the highest form of literary expression, but the complexity of its verbal effects also poses the greatest challenge for translators: Morley had to explain that he wasn't able to do anything with Petrarch's rhymes, for example (**26**. 61). At the summit of the hierarchy of poetic genre is epic, and the outstanding exponents of the form are Virgil in Latin and Homer in Greek, so how English translators approach these writers is central to an understanding of their strategies for assimilating and reproducing in English the greatest achievements of classical literature. The term from modern translation theory that seems most useful in this context is 'dynamic equivalence', which echoes what Queen Elizabeth called 'the force and form of speech' (**43**. 38) in her translation of Horace and responds to some of the specific issues involved in the translation of metre. The verse epics of Homer and Virgil, like all classical poetry, were written in quantitative metre, which was based on quite different principles from the accentual-syllabic metres of native English 'rhyme', as it was referred to in the sixteenth century, usually with contempt. In quantitative metre feet are measured in terms of long and short syllables, which correspond to the numerically ordered harmonies of music; this kind of verse is altogether superior to the crude beats of accentual-syllabic metre with its rhymed line endings. The question for English translators of classical poetry, then, was whether a metre could be found that could act as the dymamic equivalent of this more elevated form of poetic expression.

Douglas's Virgil stuck to a native verse form. Surrey, who had read Douglas's poem in manuscript, attempted something new, adapting Italian *versi sciolti* for the blank verse form that was to become the staple of English verse drama and epic. But Surrey's experiment was not immediately understood, which was why Roger Ascham referred to his metre as 'lame', and other writers argued that in order to reproduce the height of Virgil's style translators would have to reconstruct a version of the classical hexameter in English.[102] This was what Richard Stanyhurst tried to do in his 1582 translation of the *Aeneid*, arguing that the only way to get rid of all the low-grade 'rhyming' poets who were being published was for the learned to devote themselves to 'the true making of verses in such wise as the Greeks and Latins' (**39**. 122–27). This inevitably requires some adjustment: Stanyhurst explains that English translators don't need to follow the quantities of Latin words when assigning quantities to syllables in English, any more than the Romans needed to be tied to the Greek, which was the source of their own metres (135–39). This seems reasonable, but it pushes Stanyhurst towards a position that effectively undermines the case for using quantitative metres in the first place. Since those metres ultimately refer to the harmonious order of the divine creation, they represent a universal template for prosody comparable with the pre-Babel condition of language when there was no need for translation at all. But to justify his method of assigning quantities to words in English Stanyhurst argues that every language has its own law; that aesthetic considerations should determine quantity; that 'nothing may be done or spoken against nature, and that art is also bound to shape itself by all imitation to nature' (180–88). This is tantamount to saying that poets should respond to and shape the natural properties of their language rather than conform to an externally imposed pattern, which is what Daniel was to argue in his *Defence of Ryme* (1603). As if to acknowledge the contradiction, Stanyhurst balances his approximations of

[102] Roger Ascham, *The Scholemaster* (London, 1570), STC 832, fo. 61^{v}, image 68. Puns on 'feet' are common in Elizabethan writing about metre. On Elizabethan experiments with hexameter, see Derek Attridge, *Well-weighed Syllables: Elizabethan Verse in Classical Metres* (London: Cambridge University Press, 1974).

classical hexameter with a conscientiously 'natural' and rustic English vocabulary. But the combination was not well received. Puttenham deplored the coarseness of the language, while the metre prompted this outburst from Thomas Nashe: 'Master *Stannyhurst* (though otherwise learned) trod a foule lumbring boystrous wallowing measure, in his translation of Virgil'.[103] Stanyhurst's Virgil is certainly odd, but it is perhaps more readable today than the iterative jog-trot of some Elizabethan fourteeners. In the broader terms of translation theory the point is that metre, while not being a meta-language, is a system of organising language that is so intrusive that it must itself be translated. Hence the need for 'dynamic equivalence'. English would establish blank verse as the dynamic equivalent of the classical hexameter, but in 1582 the matter was not yet settled.

By the time Chapman started publishing his translations of Homer in 1598, defenders of classical metre had mostly fallen silent, though the issue was to have a final airing in the debate between Campion and Daniel in 1602–03.[104] But Chapman's vigorous defence of native English verse forms as adequate vehicles for rendering classical epic meant that he preferred rhyme over blank verse, so his English Homer first appeared in rhymed fourteeners (now rather old-fashioned) and, in the case of *Achilles' Shield*, decasyllabic rhyming couplets. In this he was driven partly by his animosity towards Julius Caesar Scaliger, who had elevated Virgil over Homer in his influential *Poetices* (1581), where he had also asserted the claims of art over nature.[105] This was anathema to Chapman and pushed him to construct Homer in terms similar to those in which Romanticism would later construct Shakespeare. Writing in the preface to *Achilles' Shield* he says that Homer's verse is the expression of

[103] George Puttenham, *The Art of English Poesy*, ed. by Frank Whigham and Wayne A. Rebhorn (Ithaca: Cornell University Press, 2007), Book 3, Chapter 23; *The Works of Thomas Nashe*, ed. by R. B. McKerrow, rev. by F. P. Wilson (Oxford: Blackwell, 1958), I, 299.

[104] See Neil Rhodes, 'Framing and Tuning in Renaissance English Verse', in *Renaissance Transformations: The Making of English Writing and its World* (1480–1650), ed. by Margaret and Thomas Healy (Edinburgh: Edinburgh University Press, 2009), pp. 32–47.

[105] On Scaliger's elevation of Virgil above Homer, see *Poetices libri septem* (Lyons, 1561), Book 5,'De Imitatione et Iudicio'; on Scaliger, art, and nature, see Fernand Hallyn, 'Cosmography and Poetics', in *The Cambridge History of Literary Criticism*, vol. 3., p. 444.

'an absolute and full soul; Virgil's out of a courtly, laborious, and altogether imitatory spirit' (**44b**. 9–11). This is remarkably similar to the eighteenth-century comparisons of Shakespeare and Jonson in which Jonson is always negatively represented as a writer of secondary status because less 'original'. It is one of the main objects of Chapman's prefaces to the various editions of his Homer translations to emphasise the inspired and bardic quality of his subject and to claim this as something that English, being 'more conformable, fluent and expressive' than other languages (32), is uniquely able to convey. Homer is the true original and only English is capable of capturing that originality, he argues: '[he] hath appeared like an angel from a cloud or the world out of chaos, when no language can make comparison of him with ours if he be worthily converted' (48–51).

In the preface to *The Iliads* (1611) he explains how this is to be achieved, and he does so by taking a position that is diametrically opposed to that of the advocates for classical metres in English. Music in poetry derives from rhyme, he argues, and the profusion of monosyllables in English (generally thought to be a deficiency) make for better rhymes and therefore better music; accentual-syllabic metre is also a virtue, so that all told, he notes in the margin, 'Our English language [is] above all others for rhythmical poesy' (**44c**. n. 43). Having established that English has the resources to give an adequate rendering of the Greek original, the final question is how the translation itself can be executed without loss. Chapman does this by representing translation in its ideal form as a transmigration of souls. Dismissing literal prose translation, he says that in these 'th'other's full soul cannot make / The ample transmigration to be shown / In nature-loving poesy' (35–37). Chapman's implicit claim is that his translation has a status comparable with the source because he has been able to convey 'the absolute and full soul' of Homer, as he put it earlier. This is probably the boldest claim for the original status of translation to be made during the English Renaissance.

While the general tenor of Chapman's prefaces to Homer might be seen as proto-Romantic, there is another aspect to them that presents his work in a very different light. Most translators' prefaces are essentially defensive, as we have seen: they anticipate the carping criticisms of the hordes of Zoiluses and Momuses who are waiting to find fault with the translators' honest labour.[106] Some, like Drant and Tyler, go against the grain by appearing confident or insouciant. Chapman, however, is nakedly aggressive. In the prefaces to both *Achilles' Shield* and *The Iliads* there is an extraordinary level of vituperation directed against 'Detraction' and 'Envy', and throughout the prefaces he defends his work by suggesting that a just appreciation of it depends upon the capacities of the reader. It is the reader, not the translator, who is on trial. In the preface to *Achilles' Shield* the reader is in fact addressed as the 'Understander', with the observation that 'You are not everybody' (58), and to this discriminating audience Chapman confides that 'my desire and strange disposition in all things I write is to set down uncommon and most profitable coherents for the time' (74–76). Chapman's Homer represents a high-water mark of confidence in the capacities of English for translation, but in its presumption of a readership sufficiently discerning to share the values of the author it is less proto-Romantic than proto-Augustan. In becoming so, it moves away from the spirit of making common which was the guiding principle of translation in the sixteenth century.

4.

Translating the word of God and the translation of secular literature both aim to develop common understanding. Translation for the reading public has the goal of enriching the nation and the individual by providing access to knowledge, both spiritual and secular, that would otherwise be closed to the unlearned. Translation in the academy, however, has a different aim, which is less to further understanding than to aid composition; or, rather, understanding is principally a means to the ultimate goal of achieving eloquence in Latin.[107] But academic writers also

[106] The Zoiluses (or Zoili or Zoilists) are rarely identified, but we can assume that they are essentially an academic breed. Since it was Cambridge that produced most of the translators in the sixteenth century we may tentatively associate them with a more conservative Oxford. (The most notable exception at Oxford is Laurence Humphrey.)

[107] Mastery of Latin was, of course, a prerequisite for studying any work of learning that had not been translated. But translation as an exercise was specifically directed toward composition and expression.

recognise that translation exercises help to develop expressive competence in English, which some see as part of their mission as teachers. John Brinsley writes in *Ludus Literarius* that one of the functions of translation is 'to help to proceed as well in our English tongue as in the Latin [. . .] to attain variety and copy of English words to express their minds easily [. . .] and so in time to come to propriety, choice and purity, as well in our English as in the Latin' (**54**. 107–12). Though Brinsley was writing in 1612, we can take his educational ideas and practice to be representative of the common regime in the Elizabethan grammar schools.[108]

We might expect that earlier in the sixteenth century there would have been little confidence in the eloquence of the vernacular among schoolmasters, and even less interest in promoting it. We might also expect there to have been an absolute prohibition on the use of printed English translations of classical authors in the classroom. After all, the evil of 'cribbing', with the help of translations from Bohn's library of the classics, was to become a familiar theme of the Victorian school story. But none of this seems to have been true even in the early sixteenth century,[109] and throughout the early modern period pedagogical attitudes towards translation were rather less purist and censorious than they became in later centuries. This is strikingly illustrated by John Palsgrave's English translation of the neo-Latin comedy, *Acolastus* (1540), dedicated to Henry VIII, which makes various observations on the shortcomings of schoolmasters. Palsgrave is impatient with those who show off their erudition by explaining one Latin word with another, as well as with more rustic teachers whose spoken English is too poor to make them suitable as tutors in noble families. To remedy this

[108] See Peter Mack, *Elizabethan Rhetoric: Theory and Practice* (Cambridge: Cambridge University Press, 2002), pp. 11–14, 18–19. On the curriculum, see also Quentin Skinner, *Reason and Rhetoric in the Philosophy of Hobbes* (Cambridge: Cambridge University Press, 1996), pp. 19–40.

[109] On the adequacy of English, see for example *Terens in Englysh* (Paris, *c*. 1520), STC 23894, sig. Ai^{v}, image 2. Mack cites William Kempe, *The Education of Children in Learning* (London, 1588) on the use of translation in the classroom at p. 14; Colin Burrow, however, gives a more skeptical view in 'Shakespeare and Humanistic Culture', in *Shakespeare and the Classics*, ed. by Charles Martindale and A. B. Taylor (Cambridge: Cambridge University Press, 2004), pp. 9–27.

he has produced an English *ekphrasis* on the Latin play, which he claims has not been attempted before anywhere else in Europe (**50**. 90–93), though the play (written by a Dutchman) had in fact been popular as an educational text in several other countries. The title-page is explicit about the classroom use of translation, presenting *Acolastus* as 'translated into our English tongue after such manner as children are taught in the grammar school' (3–4), and it offers a bilingual text with marginal notes that key each Latin expression (*phrasis*) to its English equivalent. Palsgrave's work represents translation in the academy as a two-way process: it is both a vehicle for learning Latin and a means of improving English. When claiming originality for his exercise he is quick to point out that this is not because other vernaculars are so eloquent that they are not in need of improvement, and he cites the work of leading European humanists who have drawn attention to the discrepancy between the poor state of their own vernaculars and the best Latin models (98–123). It is not entirely clear from Palsgrave's examples whether he is referring to barbarism in other modern languages or in the standard of Latinity in these countries, but he evidently thinks there is a relationship between the two. Latin will be taught more effectively through the medium of translation and the vernacular will be improved by its acquaintance with pure Latinity.

It is no coincidence that we should begin to consider translation in the academy with reference to drama. The term Palsgrave uses for his work, *ekphrasis*, is a rhetorical term for an extended and vivid piece of description, but it also has the sense of 'speaking picture'. It is an illustration of language as living speech. Its model is Terence and it was Terence who supplied the conversational Latin of the *Vulgaria* – bilingual textbooks used for the elementary teaching of grammar – and also Nicholas Udall's *Floures for Latine spekynge* (1534), which paired familiar English and Latin phrases. The use of drama in the classroom reminds us that translation is an oral as well as a written exercise in the early modern period and that eloquence in both Latin and English is an ideal for speech as well as for writing. The reason that Terence was used so widely was that he represented an easy style of Latin that was also regarded as particularly 'pure'. As Maurice Kyffin puts it in his translation of *Andria* (1588), the first complete translation of one of Terence's comedies to be printed in England,[110] he has undertaken to 'make common' his work (**53**. 29) not because the play offers good entertainment, but because 'the Latin is pure and eloquent, much commended by Tully himself' (75–76). This purity is crucial to Terence's status as a model author for Latin language learning, but it is a quality also allied to familiarity, so that in his translation Kyffin says that he has used 'the most known, usual, and familiar phrases in common speech to express the author's meaning' (84–85). It is revealing that he also boasts of having at one point rejected the translation of a learned scholar in favour of his own interpretation, citing the authority of Erasmus's proverb collection, the *Adagia*. The combination of purity and familiarity is an Erasmian ideal, and one that led him to proverbs in the first place, but it is also a Protestant ideal. Pure and common Terence represents for education and Latinity the combination of values that Tyndale and subsequent Bible translators aspired to in their English renderings of the word of God.

Roger Ascham also appears to endorse the virtues of common speech in his book *Toxophilus*, where he cites the maxim from Aristotle's *Topica* that we should aim 'to speake as the common people do, to thinke as wise men do'.[111] But there he was addressing the yeomen archers of England, and he had a rather different audience in mind for his pedagogical work, *The Schoolmaster* (1570), which is pitched more at the elite private tutor than the common grammar schools. In Ascham's own case, as tutor to Princess Elizabeth, 'elite' meant royalty. Palsgrave had a similar experience as tutor to Henry VIII's younger sister, Mary, but unlike Palsgrave, Ascham did not really see the improvement of the vernacular as part of the schoolmaster's job. This does not mean that he was uninterested in translation, but that he was interested in it only as an exercise to develop fluency in Latin and Greek. The use of printed translations as grammatical helps is certainly not part of his scheme. Ascham is often credited with the formulation of 'double translation', and, through his use of this method in teaching Princess Elizabeth, with the future queen's remarkable facility in languages. But Ascham was following the practice of his mentor, John Cheke, at Cambridge, and both men would have read the letter on double translation

[110] *Terens in Englysh* is also a version of *Andria*, but is not complete.

[111] Roger Ascham, *Toxophilus* (London, 1545), STC 837, sig. Ai^{r}, image 5.

by the younger Pliny, which Ascham quotes in *The Schoolmaster* (**51**. 211–17).[112] What Ascham recommends is that the tutor should himself translate an obscure passage from Cicero into plain English and give it to his pupil to translate back into Latin. The result can then be compared with the Ciceronian original (28–44). The second exercise is for the tutor to compose a letter, or the kind of narrative that Aphthonius recommends at the start of the *Progymnasmata*, which the pupil will then translate into Latin unaided. The exercise of double translation itself involves the retranslation of passages into English, or vice versa, as Ascham explains in his account of John Whitney, the boy he was tutoring at the home of Sir Anthony Denny alongside Princess Elizabeth: 'I read unto him Tully, *De amicitia*, which he did every day twice translate, out of Latin into English and out of English into Latin again'. This was combined with a version of the first exercise: 'I did translate it myself into plain English and gave it him to turn into Latin' (101–4, 109–10). The closest that Ascham gets to saying that his method will help to improve expression in English is when he claims that it is superior to grammar school exercises because it doesn't just deliver 'single commodity' (158; i.e. only one kind of benefit). But his real purpose is to argue that only double translation will fully embed Latinity so that it becomes, as it were, second nature.

Ascham also distinguishes *translatio linguarum* from the related exercises of *paraphrasis, metaphrasis* and *imitatio*. He is unenthusiastic about the first two, pointing out that even though Quintilian had recommended them, Cicero had been against them (163–81), and they are certainly not suitable for younger scholars. The charge against paraphrase is that it involves a reformulation rather than a mere translation of the original text, and since the best authors will have already chosen the best form of words, paraphrase will inevitably mean a change for the worse (275–301), unless the source text itself is in barbarous Latin. The same is true of metaphrase, which requires the further shift of verse into prose or prose into verse. Imitation is different, of course, because it acknowledges the superiority of the original and tries to assimilate it into a wholly distinct composition rather

[112] Ascham's method is discussed in William E. Miller, 'Double Translation in English Humanistic Education' in *Studies in the Renaissance*, 10 (1963), 163–74.

than convert it into another (and weaker) version of the same thing.[113]

Ascham is quite consciously offering an elite model of teaching practice, in which double translation is central, and he is rather dismissive of the ordinary grammar schools. At one point he recalls the common school of his own childhood in the North, where learning 'was tied only to [the pupils'] tongue and lips, and never ascended up to the brain and head' (55–57). It is this kind of school, however, that John Brinsley is concerned with in *Ludus Literarius*. This work is constructed as a dialogue between two schoolmasters, Spoudeus and Philoponus, with Philoponus representing the views of the author, and when Brinsley reaches the subject of translation he cites Ascham directly, pointing out that teachers don't have the time to organise a double translation regime in the grammar schools (**54**. 20–23). What he proposes instead is that pupils should be taught Latin with the aid of 'grammatical translations', and this represents another key distinction between translation in the academy and literary translation for the general reading public. From Cicero and Horace onwards there was general agreement that it was better to translate sense for sense than word for word, except (in the Christian era) in the case of Holy Scripture. But this is no help to children who are trying to understand the grammar of the original text, and the translations that Brinsley made and published are scrupulously literal, designed as far as possible to show pupils the exact correspondence between the Latin and English syntax of every sentence. Through Philoponus he itemises twenty-one benefits of this kind of translation (56–174), explaining that where the literal sense of a phrase seems convoluted or clumsy he has placed it in the margin with an explanatory note, and substituted a more natural expression substituted in the text. Responding to Spoudeus's worry that using translations is a form of cheating, and encourages idleness, Philoponus says that this can be avoided if they are not presented as interlinear or parallel text (261–79). On the broader question of their educational value, Philoponus presents the use of grammatical translation as part of a two-stage process of 'analysis and genesis' (169–74); when making their own translations, pupils do them

[113] For the long section on *imitatio* which is not included in the present volume, see Vickers, ed., *English Renaissance Literary Criticism*, pp. 140–61.

'first plainly, then artificially' (312–13). What this means is that grammatical understanding leads on to rhetorical composition, and in the latter the guiding principles should be always to take into account the context of the passage and then aim for propriety and liveliness (328–32). This is the kind of education that Shakespeare is likely to have had at his country grammar school in Stratford-upon-Avon.

Sixteenth-century translators constantly emphasise the 'commodity' of their work, meaning that it has social and cultural benefit, but the school text-book presents translation as commodity in the more modern sense of the term. Abraham Fleming, who combined studying at Cambridge with work in a variety of roles in London print shops, says that he has been urged by a friend to publish his translation of Virgil's *Eclogues* in order to help 'young beginners in grammatical exercises' (**52**. 36–37). His familiarity with print technology enables him to present the work as offering every possible convenience for the budding scholar, including an alphabetical glossary of proper names and a 'handgrip' of notes (101), though he complains that the printer has ignored his annotations from other authors in order to cut costs. Nonetheless, Fleming makes economy his own selling point. Since he claims that the translation includes some of the features of a commentary and a dictionary, it offers 'a mitigation of expense, or (that I may speak more familiarly) a saving of money' (118–20). And when the translation was reissued with the *Georgics* in 1589, he suggests an even greater saving: the translation would be able to take the place of the schoolmaster himself.[114]

The most elaborate use of print technology for translation in the academy is represented by the work of Joseph Webbe, who breaks all of Brinsley's rules about avoiding interlinear and parallel glossing in printed translations with his complex system of connected boxes keying Latin to English phrases. Webbe's system for his translation of Cicero and other school authors was intended to support a highly individual teaching method for which he obtained a patent from parliament. Since he had himself grown up speaking Latin, his project was to resuscitate it as a living language, making it available for familiar and colloquial

[114] See Andrew Wallace, *Virgil's Schoolboys: the Poetics of Pedagogy in Renaissance England* (Oxford: Oxford University Press, 2010), p. 162.

use and not simply as the medium for learned discourse in print. This agenda is illustrated by the prefatory matter to his translation of Cicero's *Familiar Epistles* (1620), where he has an imaginary conversation with Cicero himself. Being 'ever of an affable disposition', Cicero invites Webbe to give his friend (the dedicatee of the translation) a volume of his letters. When Webbe asks 'In what language?', and Cicero replies, 'English', Webbe blushes at the thought of the greatest orator of all time seeing his supreme eloquence reduced to such a homely idiom. But Cicero reassures him, saying that the more 'ordinary' the discourse, the more likely it is to win universal acceptance, and he should not assume that everybody who wants to read his letters will be able to understand the original Latin (**55**. 39–58).

It would be fair to say that in all the previous defences of translation written during the early modern period, nobody had ever thought that they might get the author of the source text itself to legitimise its translation into an entirely unknown language. This bold move is part of Webbe's plan to make Latin contemporary: Cicero's endorsement of the familiar helps to endorse lowly English, but it also helps the reader to see Latin itself as a familiar language. So at the heart of Webbe's pedagogy is a determination that pupils should learn to speak Latin in its own idiom, a goal that can only be achieved by use and not by following the prescriptions of grammar. His *Appeal to Truth*, which is heavily indebted to the ideas of the Flemish scholar Cominius, represents the most outspoken attack on grammar, and on teachers who put precept before practice, in early modern England. Although it may seem reasonable to suppose that 'those which in speech proceed by art, rules, and reason ought to speak better than those that follow the people' (**56**. 56–58), this is not in fact the case. Rather, 'we begin not by art but by nature and proceed by use, custom, authority, and exercise, governed by the ear' (85–86). As far as translation is concerned, where middling scholars and would-be poets go wrong is in ignoring 'the judgement of the ear' (222). Leaving aside the question as to whether Webbe's method is likely to have been successful, his work is a striking illustration of how much discussion of the uses of translation in the academy in this period focuses on the spoken dimension of both language learning and composition. It is striking, too, that in the case of Webbe's own translations, the typography of the printed page is used not to erode the oral, as Walter Ong famously argued with regard to Ramus, but to reinforce it.[115]

Webbe also provides us with a last word on the subject of dumbing down. When he attacks 'Leonardus Aretinus and his followers' Webbe is in fact, whether consciously or not, attacking the entire programme of humanism. As well as being the author of the first important Renaissance treatise on translation, Leonardo Aretino Bruni was also the originator of the term *studia humanitatis*,[116] so Webbe's rejection of humanist philology gives us the sense of an ending. Ascham's methods may have worked for Elizabeth, but the ideals they represented were scarcely within reach of any but a tiny minority of pupils. Webbe had his own, equally idealistic agenda for Latin as a living language, but in his desire to sweep away grammar he also looks forward to a point in the future when, for the student as well as for the general reader, the translation would gradually start to replace the source.

[115] See Walter J. Ong, *Ramus, Method, and the Decay of Dialogue* (Cambridge, MA: Harvard University Press, 1958).

[116] See Paul Oskar Kristeller, *Renaissance Concepts of Man* (New York: Harper & Row, 1972), p. 7.

FURTHER READING

Alexander, Gavin, ed., *Sidney's 'The Defence of Poesy' and Selected Renaissance Literary Criticism* (London: Penguin, 2004)

Amos, Flora Ross, *Early Theories of Translation* (New York: Columbia University Studies in English and Comparative Literature, 1920)

Bassnett-McGuire, Susan, *Translation Studies*, 4th edn (London: Routledge, 2013)

Belle, Marie-Alice, ed., *Women and Translation in Early Modern England and France*, in *Renaissance and Reformation/Renaissance et Réforme*, 36 (2013)

Botley, Paul, *Latin Translation in the Renaissance: The Theory and Practice of Leonardo Bruni, Giannozzo Manetti and Desiderius Erasmus* (Cambridge: Cambridge University Press, 2004)

Boutcher, Warren, 'The Renaissance' in *The Oxford Guide to Literature in English Translation*, ed. by Peter France (Oxford: Oxford University Press, 2000)

Braden, Gordon, Robert Cummings, and Stuart Gillespie, eds, *The Oxford History of Literary Translation in English: Volume 2, 1550–1660* (Oxford: Oxford University Press, 2011)

Burke, Peter and R. Po-chia Hsia, eds, *Cultural Translation in Early Modern Europe* (Cambridge: Cambridge University Press, 2007)

Clarke, Danielle, 'Translations' in *The Cambridge Companion to Early Modern Women's Writing*, ed. by Laura Lunger Knoppers (Cambridge: Cambridge University Press, 2009), pp. 167–80

Cummings, Brian, *The Literary Culture of the Reformation: Grammar and Grace* (Oxford: Oxford University Press, 2002)

Daniell, David, *William Tyndale: A Biography* (New Haven: Yale University Press, 1994)

Ellis, Roger, ed., *The Oxford History of Literary Translation in English: Volume 1, To 1550* (Oxford: Oxford University Press, 2008)

Gillespie, Stuart, *English Translation and Classical Reception: Towards a New Literary History* (Oxford: Wiley-Blackwell, 2011)

Grossman, Edith, *Why Translation Matters* (New Haven: Yale University Press, 2010)

Hammond, Gerald, *The Making of the English Bible* (Manchester: Carcanet, 1982)

Hannay, Margaret Patterson, ed., *Silent But for the Word: Tudor Women as Patrons, Translators, and Writers of Religious Works* (Kent, OH: The Kent State University Press, 1985)

Hermans, Theo, 'Images of Translation: Metaphor and Imagery in the Renaissance Discourse on Translation', in *The Manipulation of Literature*, ed. by Hermans (London: Croom Helm, 1985), pp. 103–35

Höfele, Andreas and Werner von Koppenfels, eds, *Renaissance Go-Betweens: Cultural Exchange in Early Modern Europe* (New York: Walter de Gruyter, 2005)

Kelly, L. G., *The True Interpreter: A History of Translation Theory and Practice in the West* (Oxford: Basil Blackwell, 1979)

Lathrop, Henry Burrowes, *Translations from the Classics into English from Caxton to Chapman* (Madison, WI: University of Wisconsin Press, 1933)

Lindeman, Yehudi, 'Translation and the Renaissance: A Context and a Map', *Canadian Review of Comparative Literature*, 8 (1981), 204–16

Matthiessen, F. O., *Translation: An Elizabethan Art* (Cambridge, MA: Harvard University Press, 1931)

Miller, William E., 'Double Translation in English Humanistic Education', *Studies in the Renaissance*, 10 (1963), 163–74

Morini, Massimiliano, *Tudor Translation in Theory and Practice* (Aldershot: Ashgate, 2006)

Norton, David, *A History of the Bible as Literature: Volume 1, From Antiquity to 1700* (Cambridge: Cambridge University Press, 1993)

—, *The King James Bible: A Short History from Tyndale to Today* (Cambridge: Cambridge University Press, 2011)

Norton, Glyn P., *The Ideology and Language of Translation in Renaissance France and their Humanist Antecedents* (Geneva: Droz, 1984)

Pettegree, Andrew, 'Translation and the Migration of Texts', in *Borders and Travellers in Early Modern Europe*, ed. by Thomas Betteridge (Ashgate: Aldershot, 2007), pp. 113–25

Rener, Frederick M., *Interpretatio: Language and Translation from Cicero to Tytler* (Amsterdam: Rodopi, 1989)

Rhodes, Neil, 'Status Anxiety and English Renaissance Translation' in *Renaissance Paratexts*, ed. by Helen Smith and Louise Wilson (Cambridge: Cambridge University Press, 2011), pp. 107–20

Robinson, Douglas, ed., *Western Translation Theory from Herodotus to Nietzsche*, 2nd edn (Manchester: St Jerome, 2002)

Schurink, Fred, ed., *Tudor Translation* (Basingstoke: Palgrave Macmillan, 2011)

Schwarz, W., *Principles and Problems of Biblical Translation: Some Reformation Controversies and their Background* (Cambridge: Cambridge University Press, 1955)

Simpson, James, *Burning to Read: English Fundamentalism and its Reformation Opponents* (Cambridge, MA: Harvard University Press, 2007)

Steiner, George, *After Babel: Aspects of Language and Translation*, 3rd edn (Oxford: Oxford University Press, 1998)

Venuti, Lawrence, *The Translator's Invisibility* (London: Routledge, 1995)

Vickers, Brian, ed., *English Renaissance Literary Criticism* (Oxford: Clarendon Press, 1999)

Weissbort, Daniel and Astradur Eysteinsson, eds., *Translation - Theory and Practice: A Historical Reader* (Oxford: Oxford University Press, 2006)

PART ONE
TRANSLATING THE WORD OF GOD

1. William Tyndale, *The Obedience of a Christian Man* (1528)

[William Tyndale (1494?–1536) was born in Gloucestershire and educated at Magdalen Hall, Oxford (later incorporated into Hertford College). He is the translator of the first printed English Bibles: a New Testament printed at Cologne in 1525, most of which is lost; a complete New Testament printed at Worms in 1526; and the first five books of the Old Testament (the Pentateuch) printed at Antwerp by Martin de Keyser in 1530. A revised New Testament appeared from the same press at Antwerp in 1534 and much of this and the Pentateuch was assimilated in revised form into the King James Bible of 1611 (the 'Authorised Version'). Tyndale's bible translations were smuggled into England from March 1526 where they were denounced as heretical and burned; Tyndale himself met the same fate at Vilvorde near Antwerp in 1536.

The Obedience of a Christian Man was printed by de Keyser at Antwerp in 1528. It is a social and political treatise concerned with the duties of a Christian within the family and the kingdom, which are referred ultimately to the individual's duty towards God. Its emphasis on the subject's necessary obedience towards the monarch enabled it to find favour with Thomas Cromwell and his circle, and with Henry VIII himself, despite its dangerous advocacy of a vernacular bible. The argument that the Scriptures should be available in English is central to the opening preface to the reader.

William Tyndale, *The Obedience of a Christian Man*, ed. by David Daniell (London: Penguin, 2000); Stephen Greenblatt, *Renaissance Self-Fashioning: from More to Shakespeare* (Chicago: University of Chicago Press, 1980); David Daniell, *William Tyndale: A Biography* (New Haven: Yale University Press, 1994); James Simpson, *Burning to Read: English Fundamentalism and its Reformation Opponents* (Cambridge, MA: Harvard University Press, 2007); Brian Cummings, *The Literary Culture of the Reformation: Grammar and Grace* (Oxford: Oxford University Press, 2009)]

William Tyndale, otherwise called William Hychins,[1] unto the reader.

That thou mayest perceive how that the Scripture ought to be in the mother tongue and that the reasons which our spirits make for the contrary are but sophistry and false wiles to fear thee from the light, that thou mightest follow them blindfold and be their captive, to honour their ceremonies and to offer to their belly.

First God gave the children of Israel a law by the hand of Moses in their mother tongue, and all the prophets wrote in their mother tongue, and all the Psalms were in the mother tongue. And there was Christ but figured and described in ceremonies, in riddles, in parables, and in dark prophecies. What is the cause that we may not have the Old Testament with the New also, which is the light of the Old, and wherein is openly declared before the eyes that there was darkly prophesied? I can imagine no cause verily except it be that we should not see the work of Antichrist and juggling° of hypocrites. What should be the cause that we which walk in the broad day should not see as well as they that walked in the night, or that we should not see as well at noon as they did in the twilight? Came Christ to make the world more blind? By this means Christ is the darkness of the world and not the light, as he sayeth himself (John 8).

Moreover, Moses sayeth (Deuteronomy 6), 'Hear, Israel, let these words which I command thee this day stick fast in thine heart, and whet them on thy children and talk of them as thou sittest in thine house and as thou walkest by the way, and when thou liest down and when thou risest up, and bind them for a token to thine hand, and let them be a remembrance between thine eyes, and write them on the posts and gates of thine house.' This was commanded generally unto all men. How cometh it that God's word pertaineth less unto us than unto them? Yea, how cometh it that our Moseses forbid us and command us the contrary, and threat us if we do, and will not that we once speak of God's word? How can we whet God's word (that is, put it in practice, use, and exercise) upon our children and household, when we are violently kept from it and know it not? How can we (as Peter commandeth) give a reason of our hope when we wot° not what it is that God hath promised or what to hope? Moses

[1]The Tyndales of Gloucestershire also took the name of Hychins or Hutchins.

also commandeth in the said chapter: 'If the son ask what the testimonies, laws, and observances of the Lord mean, that the father teach him. If our children ask what our ceremonies (which are more than the Jews' were) mean, no father can tell his son.'[2] And in the eleventh chapter he repeateth all again for fear of forgetting.

They will say, haply, the Scripture requireth a pure mind and a quiet mind. And therefore the layman, because he is altogether cumbered with worldly business, cannot understand them. If that be the cause, then it is a plain case that our prelates understand not the Scriptures themselves. For no layman is so tangled with worldly business as they are. The great things of the world are ministered by them, neither do the laypeople any great thing but at their assignment.

If the Scripture were in the mother tongue, they will say, then would the laypeople understand it every man after his own ways. Wherefore serveth the curate but to teach them the right way? Wherefore were the holy days made but that the people should come and learn? Are ye not abominable schoolmasters in that ye take so great wages, if ye will not teach? If ye would teach, how could ye do it so well and with so great profit, as when the laypeople have the Scripture before them in their mother tongue? For then should they see by the order of the text whether thou jugglest° or not. And then would they believe it, because it is the Scripture of God, though thy living be never so abominable. Where now, because your living and your preaching are so contrary, and because they grope out in every sermon your open and manifest lies, and smell your insatiable covetousness, they believe you not when you preach truth. But alas, the curates themselves, for the most part, wot no more what the New or Old Testament meaneth than do the Turks. Neither know they of any more than that they read at Mass, matins, and evensong, which yet they understand not. Neither care they but even to mumble[3]

[2] **Marg.** No, nor Sir John his ghostly children. ['Sir John' is a contemptuous name for an ignorant priest; cf. Spenser's gloss to 'May' in *The Shepheardes Calender*, 'Our sir Iohn) a Popishe priest. A saying fit for the grosenesse of a shepheard, but spoken to taunte vnlearned Priestes', *The Shorter Poems*, ed. by Richard A. McCabe (London: Penguin, 1999), p. 86.]

[3] mumble] to chew feebly, turning the food over in the mouth, and hence to speak indistinctly. 'Mumbling' became a theme of Protestant attacks on Church Latin as meaningless noise. Thomas Key in Udall's edition of Erasmus's

up so much every day, as the pie° and popinjay° speak they wot not what, to fill their bellies withal. If they will not let the layman have the word of God in his mother tongue, yet let the priests have it, which for a great part of them do understand no Latin at all, but sing and say and patter° all day, with the lips only, that which the heart understandeth not.

Christ commandeth to search the Scriptures (John 5). Though that miracles bear record unto his doctrine, yet desired he no faith to be given either unto his doctrine or unto his miracles, without record of the Scripture. When Paul preached (Acts 17), the other searched the Scriptures daily, whether they were as he alleged° them. Why shall not I likewise see whether it be the Scripture that thou allegest? Yea, why shall I not see the Scripture and the circumstances and what goeth before and after, that I may know whether thine interpretation be the right sense, or whether thou jugglest and drawest the Scripture violently unto thy carnal and fleshly purpose? Or whether thou be about to teach me or to deceive me?

Christ sayeth that there shall come false prophets in his name and say that they themselves are Christ; that is, they shall so preach Christ that men must believe in them, in their holiness and things of their imagination, without God's word. Yea, and that against-Christ or Antichrist that shall come is nothing but such false prophets that shall juggle with the Scripture and beguile the people with false interpretations, as all the false prophets, scribes, and Pharisees did in the Old Testament. How shall I know whether ye are that against-Christ or false prophets or no, seeing ye will not let me see how ye allege the Scriptures? [. . .]

The sermons which thou readest in the Acts of the Apostles and all that the Apostles preached were no doubt preached in the mother tongue. Why then might they not be written in the mother tongue? As if one of us preach a good sermon, why may it not be written? St Jerome also translated the Bible into his mother

---

Paraphrases (see **7**. below) lists 'mumbling up of psalmes not understand' among other popish 'trumpery', STC 2854.5, sig. a1^{v}, image 131, and Calvin in Norton's translation (see **8**. below) also deplores 'mumbling not understanded', *Institution* (1561), STC 4415, sig. M1^{v}, image 438. See also Carla Mazzio, *The Inarticulate Renaissance: Language trouble in an age of eloquence* (Philadelphia: University of Pennsylvania Press, 2008), pp. 33–35.

tongue.[4] Why may not we also? They will say it cannot be translated into our tongue, it is so rude. It is not so rude as they are false liars. For the Greek tongue agreeth more with the English than with the Latin.[5] And the properties of the Hebrew tongue agreeth a thousand times more with the English than with the Latin. The manner of speaking is both one, so that in a thousand places thou needest not but to translate it into the English word for word, when thou must seek a compass[6] in the Latin, and yet shalt have much work to translate it well-favouredly, so that it have the same grace and sweetness, sense, and pure understanding with it in the Latin as it hath in the Hebrew. A thousand parts better may it be translated into the English than into the Latin. Yea, and except my memory fail me and that I have forgotten what I read when I was a child, thou shalt find in the English chronicle how that King Æthelstan caused the Holy Scripture to be translated into the tongue that then was in England and how the prelates exhorted him thereunto.[7] [. . .]

Man's wisdom is plain idolatry, neither is there any other idolatry than to imagine of God after man's wisdom. God is not man's imagination, but that only which he sayeth of himself. God is nothing but his law and his promises; that is to say, that which he biddeth thee do and that which he biddeth thee believe and hope. God is but his word, as Christ sayeth (John 8): 'I am that I say unto you; that is to say, that which I preach am I. My words are spirit and life.' God is that only which he testifieth of himself, and to imagine any other thing of God than that is damnable idolatry. Therefore, sayeth the 118th Psalm, 'Happy are they

---

[4] St Jerome (*c.* 347–420) was commissioned by Pope Damasus to revise the *Vetus Latina*, the Bible of the Latin-speaking Christians, in 380–01. The result was the Vulgate, which became the standard Latin text of the Bible up to the time of the Reformation and continued to be so for Catholics.

[5] Sir Thomas Elyot also claimed an affinity between Greek and English in the preface to his translation of Isocrates (see **20**. below).

[6] seek a compass] find a more roundabout means of expression (periphrasis).

[7] Æthelstan is usually regarded as the first king of a united England. The *Anglo-Saxon Chronicle* records his defeat of the Scots at Brunanburh, but not his institution of a vernacular Bible. There are, however, several Old English Bible translations: notably, the first fifty Psalms by Alfred, King of Wessex (*c.* 900), part of the Pentateuch by Ælfric, Abbot of Eynsham, and the Wessex Gospels (both *c.* 990). The earliest English versions of any part of the New Testament are probably by Aldred, provost of St Cuthbert's, Chester-le-Street, Northumbria (950–70).

which search the testimonies of the Lord'; that is to say, that which God testifieth and witnesseth unto us. But how shall I that do when ye will not let me have his testimonies or witnesses in a tongue which I understand? Will ye resist God? Will ye forbid him to give his spirit unto the lay as well as unto you? Hath he not made the English tongue? Why forbid ye him to speak in the English tongue, then, as well as in the Latin?

Finally, that this threatening and forbidding the laypeople to read the Scripture is not for love of your souls, which they care for as the fox doth for the geese, is evident and clearer than the sun, inasmuch as they permit and suffer you to read[8] Robin Hood, and Bevis of Hampton, Hercules, Hector, and Troilus, with a thousand histories and fables of love and wantonness and of ribaldry as filthy as heart can think, to corrupt the minds of you withal, clean contrary to the doctrine of Christ and of his Apostles. For Paul (Ephesians 5) sayeth: 'See that fornication and all uncleanness or covetousness be not once named among you, as it becometh saints; neither filthiness, neither foolish talking, nor jesting, which are not comely. For this ye know that no whoremonger, other unclean person, or covetous person, which is the worshipper of images, hath any inheritance in the kingdom of Christ and of God.' And after, sayeth he, 'through such things cometh the wrath of God upon the children of unbelief.' Now seeing they permit you freely to read those things which corrupt your minds and rob you of the kingdom of God and Christ and bring the wrath of God upon you, how is this forbidden for love of your souls?

A thousand reasons more might be made, as thou mayest see in *Paraclesis Erasmi* and in his preface to the paraphrases of Matthew,[9] unto which they should be compelled to hold their

[8] **Marg**. Read what thou wilt: yea, and say what thou wilt save the truth. [Both Tyndale and More are contemptuous of the fabulous heroes of English ballad and romance and classical legend (see **3**. 277 below).]

[9] Desiderius Erasmus (1466–1536), born in Rotterdam, was the leading Northern European humanist and an inspirational figure for Tyndale. The *Paraclesis* is the preface to his Greek New Testament with revised Latin translation, the *Novum Instrumentum* (1516), where he argues that the Scriptures should be available to the unlearned in their own language. (Tyndale's New Testament was based on Erasmus's Greek text.) Erasmus made a similar case for the vernacular in the preface to the *Paraphrase on Matthew* (1522); see *Collected Works of Erasmus* 45, trans. and ed. by Dean Simpson (Toronto: University of Toronto Press, 2008), 17–18.

peace or to give shameful answers. But I hope that these are sufficient unto them that thirst the truth. God for his mercy and truth shall well open them more; yea, and other secrets of his godly wisdom, if they be diligent to cry unto him, which grace grant God. Amen.

2. William Tyndale, *The First Book of Moses called Genesis* (1530)

[The book described on its title-page as *The First Book of Moses called Genesis* is in fact Tyndale's version of the Pentateuch, translated from the original Hebrew (see Introduction, pp. 11–12). It is the first translation from Hebrew into English and all subsequent English versions of the early books of the Old Testament are indebted to it. Tyndale went on to translate Jonah (1531) and Joshua to 2 Chronicles, which John Rogers used for the 'Matthew Bible' of 1537. Each book of Tyndale's Pentateuch has a prologue, but it is the opening address to the reader that describes his initial attempts to gain support for a Bible in English.

See *Tyndale's Old Testament*, ed. by David Daniell (New Haven: Yale University Press, 1992); Werner Schwarz, *Principles and Problems of Biblical Translation: Some Reformation Controversies and their Background* (Cambridge: Cambridge University Press, 1955); A. C. Partridge, *English Biblical Translation* (London: Andre Deutsch, 1973); Gerald Hammond, *The Making of the English Bible* (Manchester: Carcanet, 1982); David Norton, *A History of the Bible as Literature: Volume 1, From Antiquity to 1700* (Cambridge: Cambridge University Press, 1993); Gerald Hammond, 'The Sore and Strong Prose of the English Bible' in *English Renaissance Prose: History, Language, and Politics*, ed. by Neil Rhodes (Tempe, AZ: MRTS, 1997), pp. 19–34; David Daniell, *The Bible in English: Its History and Influence* (New Haven: Yale University Press, 2003); David Norton, *The King James Bible: A Short History from Tyndale to Today* (Cambridge: Cambridge University Press, 2011); and headnote **1**.]

W. T. to the Reader.

When I had translated the New Testament, I added an epistle unto the latter end, in which I desired them that were learned to amend [it] if aught were found amiss. But our malicious and wily hypocrites which are so stubborn and hard-hearted in their wicked abominations that it is not possible for them to amend anything at all (as we see by daily experience when their both livings and doings are rebuked with the truth) say, some of them that it is unpossible to translate the Scripture into English, some that it is not lawful for the laypeople to have it in their mother tongue, some that it would make them all heretics, as it would no doubt from many things which they of long time have falsely taught, and that is the whole cause wherefore they forbid it, though they other cloaks° pretend. And some, or rather everyone, say that it would make them rise against the King, whom they themselves (unto their damnation) never yet obeyed, and lest the temporal rulers should see their falsehood, if the Scripture came to light, causeth them so to lie.

And as for my translation, in which they affirm unto the laypeople (as I have heard say) to be I wot° not how many thousand heresies, so that it cannot be mended or corrected,[1] they have yet taken so great pain to examine it, and to compare it unto that they would fain have it and to their own imaginations and juggling terms, and to have somewhat to rail at, and under that cloak to blaspheme the truth that they might with as little labour, as I suppose, have translated the most part of the Bible. For they which in times past were wont to look on no more Scripture than they found in their Duns[2] or such like devilish doctrine, have yet now so narrowly looked on my translation that there is not so much as one 'I' therein if it lack a title over his head,[3] but they have noted it, and number it unto the ignorant people for a heresy. Finally, in this they be all agreed to drive you from the knowledge of the Scripture, and that ye shall not have

---

[1] Cuthbert Tunstall (1474–1559), Bishop of London, preached a sermon on 26 October 1526 at St Paul's alleging two thousand errors in the translation and ordering copies to be burned.

[2] Duns Scotus (*c.*1265–1308), scholastic theologian who challenged Aquinas by emphasising the primacy of will over intellect, thus reducing the human capacity to make rational moral choices. Taken in the Reformation to be representative of the pedantic definitions and distinctions of scholasticism, he is the origin of the term 'dunce'.

[3] i.e. the more obtuse adherents of scholasticism who have scrutinised Tyndale's translation complain if they find the simplest word without a heading.

the text thereof in the mother tongue, and to keep the world still in darkness to the intent they might sit in the consciences of the people through vain superstition and false doctrine, to satisfy their filthy lusts, their proud ambition and unsatiable covetousness, and to exalt their own honour above king and emperor, yea, and above God himself.

A thousand books had they liefer° to be put forth against their abominable doings and doctrine than that the Scripture should come to light. For as long as they may keep that down, they will so darken the right way with the mist of their sophistry, and so tangle them that either rebuke or despise their abominations with arguments of philosophy and with worldly similitudes and apparent reasons of natural wisdom, and with wresting the Scripture unto their own purpose, clean contrary unto the process, order, and meaning of the text, and so delude them in descanting° upon it with allegories, and amaze them [by] expounding it in many senses before the unlearned laypeople, when it hath but one simple literal sense whose light the owls cannot abide, that though thou feel in thine heart and art sure how that all is false that they say, yet could'st thou not solve their subtle riddles.

Which thing only moved me to translate the New Testament, because I had perceived by experience how that it was impossible to establish the laypeople in any truth, except the Scripture were plainly laid before their eyes in their mother tongue, that they might see the process, order, and meaning of the text. For else whatsoever truth is taught them, these enemies of all truth quench it again, partly with the smoke of their bottomless pit whereof thou readest (Apocalypse 9), that is, with apparent reasons of sophistry and traditions of their own making, founded without ground of Scripture, and partly in juggling with the text, expounding it in such a sense as is impossible to gather of the text, if thou see the process, order, and meaning thereof.

And even in the Bishop of London's house I intended to have done it. For when I was so turmoiled in the country where I was that I could no longer there dwell (the process whereof were too long here to rehearse) I this wise thought in myself, this I suffer because the priests of the country be unlearned, as God it knoweth there are a full ignorant sort which have seen no more Latin than that they read in their porteouses° and missals which yet many of them can scarcely read, except it be Albertus's *De secretis mulierum*[4] in which yet, though they be never so sorely learned, they pore day and night and make notes therein and all to teach the midwives, as they say, and Lyndwood,[5] a book of constitutions to gather tithes, mortuaries,° offerings, customs, and other pillage, which they call not theirs, but God's part and the duty of Holy Church, to discharge their consciences withal. For they are bound that they shall not diminish, but increase all thing unto the utmost of their powers, and therefore (because they are thus unlearned, thought I) when they come together to the alehouse, which is their preaching place, they affirm that my sayings are heresy. And besides that, they add two of their own heads° which I never spake, as the manner is to prolong the tale to short the time withal, and accuse me secretly to the Chancellor and other Bishop's officers. And indeed when I came before the chancellor, he threatened me grievously, and reviled me and rated me as though I had been a dog, and laid to my charge whereof there could be none accuser brought forth (as their manner is not to bring forth the accuser), and yet all the priests of the country were that same day there. As I this thought, the Bishop of London came to my remembrance, whom Erasmus (whose tongue maketh of little gnats great elephants, and lifteth up above the stars whosoever giveth him a little exhibition°) praiseth exceedingly, among other in his annotations on the New Testament, for his great learning.[6] Then thought I, if I might come to this man's service, I were happy. And so I got me to London, and through the acquaintance of my master came to Sir Harry Gilford, the King's Grace's Controller, and brought him

[4] Albertus Magnus (1193/1206–1280), *On the Secrets of Women.*

[5] William Lyndwood (*c.*1375–1446), whose book on ecclesiastical law, the *Provinciale*, went through many editions before the Reformation. Tyndale's point is that the priests are so ignorant that they will only attempt to read a book in Latin if there is a sexual or financial interest.

[6] Tunstall had been part of the circle of Greek scholars at Oxford (which included Thomas More) where Erasmus stayed on his first visit to England in 1499, and he had helped him with his work for the Greek New Testament. There is no reference to Tunstall in Erasmus's *Annotations*, but in a letter to Pieter Gillis (7 May 1515) he calls Tunstall and More 'two of the best scholars in the whole of England [. . .] both great friends of mine', Letter 332 in *The Correspondence of Erasmus*, trans. by R. A. B. Mynors and D. F. S. Thomson (Toronto: University of Toronto Press, 1976), *CWE* 3: 85.

an oration of Isocrates[7] which I had translated out of Greek into English, and desired him to speak unto my Lord of London for me, which he also did as he showed me, and willed me to write an epistle to my Lord and to go to him myself which I also did, and delivered my epistle to a servant of his own, one William Hebblethwaite, a man of mine old acquaintance. But God which knoweth what is within hypocrites saw that I was beguiled, and that that counsel was not the next way unto my purpose, and therefore he got me no favour in my Lord's sight.

Whereupon my Lord answered me, his house was full, he had more than he could well find, and advised me to seek in London, where he said I could not lack a service. And so in London I abode almost a year, and marked the course of the world, and heard our praters, I would say our preachers, how they boasted themselves and their high authority; and beheld the pomp of our prelates, and how busy they were (as they yet are) to set peace and unity in the world, though it be not possible for them that walk in darkness to continue long in peace, for they cannot but either stumble or dash themselves at one thing or another that shall clean unquiet all together;[8] and saw things whereof I defer to speak at this time, and understood at the last not only that there was no room in my Lord of London's palace to translate the New Testament, but also that there was no place to do it in all England, as experience doth now openly declare.

Under what manner therefore should I now submit this book to be corrected and amended of them which can suffer nothing to be well? Or what protestation should I make in such a matter unto our prelates, those stubborn Nimrods,[9] which so mightily fight against God and resist his Holy Spirit, enforcing with all craft and subtlety to quench the light of the everlasting testament, promises, and appointment made between God and us; and heaping the fierce wrath of God upon all princes and rulers,

---

[7] Isocrates] Greek rhetorician and educationalist (436–338 BC) who also wrote on political questions. It is not known which oration Tyndale translated, but a case has been made for *Demonicus* (Lathrop 1967) and *Panegyricus* (Daniell 1994). However, the theme of the duties of subjects in *Nicocles, or the Cyprians* is reflected in Tyndale's *Obedience* and would have made a prudent choice (see also **20**. below).

[8] unquiet all together] bring everything into a state of unquietness.

[9] Nimrod was supposed to have been responsible for building the Tower of Babel, so he figures as the original enemy of translation (see Genesis 11.1–9).

mocking them with false, feigned names of hypocrisy, and serving their lusts at all points, and dispensing with them even of the very laws of God, of which Christ himself testifieth (Matthew 5) that not so much as one tittle thereof may perish or be broken. And of which the Prophet sayeth (Psalm 118): ‘Thou hast commanded thy laws to be kept *meod*’, that is in Hebrew, exceedingly, with all diligence, might, and power, and have made them so mad with their juggling charms and crafty persuasions that they think it full satisfaction[10] for all their wicked living to torment such as tell them truth, and to burn the word of their soul’s health and slay whosoever believe thereon.

Notwithstanding yet I submit this book and all other that I have either made or translated, or shall in time to come (if it be God’s will that I shall further labour in his harvest), unto all them that submit themselves unto the word of God to be corrected of them, yea, and moreover to be disallowed and also burnt, if it seem worthy when they have examined it with the Hebrew, so that they first put forth of their own translating another that is more correct.

3. Thomas More, *A Dialogue Concerning Heresies* (1529)

[Sir Thomas More (1478–1535) was born in London and educated at Oxford where he studied under the Greek scholars Thomas Linacre and William Grocyn. He then trained as a lawyer and was called to the Bar in 1502. He was a long-standing friend of Erasmus, whom he met in London in 1499; he and Erasmus collaborated on Latin translations of Lucian, and Erasmus’s *Moriae Encomium* [Praise of Folly] (1511) puns on his name. More’s own most famous work is *Utopia* (1516). His early humanist activities were superseded by theological disputation when he was employed by Henry VIII to reply to Luther in the *Responsio ad Lutherum* (1523). In 1528 he was engaged by Tunstall to search for heresy in recent publications, and this led to the polemical exchanges with Tyndale. He was created Lord Chancellor in 1529, but after refusing to acknowledge Henry as Supreme Head of the Church of England as established by the Act of Supremacy in 1534, he was imprisoned in the Tower, then tried and executed for treason.

[10] satisfaction] In the theological sense of atonement for sin.

The *Dialogue Concerning Heresies* (to use the title given in the *Workes* (1557)) was written shortly before More became Lord Chancellor. Despite the subject of the work, More's humanism survives in the civilised and hospitable elements of the dialogue form. More's interlocutor ('The Messenger') is a young scholar who has been influenced by heretical, Lutheran opinions at university (probably Cambridge). The work is in four books, and at the beginning of the fourth book, which specifically addresses the issue of Bible translation, the scholar has just returned from visiting his friends at the university.

See *A Dialogue Concerning Heresies*, ed. by Thomas M. C. Lawler, Germain Marc'hadour and Richard C. Marius, *CWM* 6, (New Haven: Yale University Press, 1981); Rainer Pineas, *Thomas More and Tudor Polemics* (Bloomington: Indiana University Press, 1968); Stephen Greenblatt, *Renaissance Self-Fashioning: From More to Shakespeare* (Chicago: University of Chicago Press, 1980); David Daniell, *William Tyndale: A Biography* (New Haven: Yale University Press, 1994); Simpson, *Burning to Read*.]

Book 3, Chapter 8

The author showeth why the New Testament of Tyndale's translation was burned, and showeth for a sample certain words evil and of evil purpose changed.

But now, I pray you, let me know your mind concerning the burning of the New Testament in English, which Tyndale lately translated, and, as men say, right well, which maketh men much marvel of the burning.

It is, quoth I, to me great marvel that any good Christian man, having any drop of wit in his head, would anything marvel or complain of the burning of that book if he know the matter, which whoso calleth the New Testament calleth it by a wrong name, except they will call it Tyndale's testament or Luther's testament.[1]

[1] Martin Luther (1483–1546), instigator of the Reformation with the circulation of his ninety-five theses through Germany and beyond in 1517. He published his German translation of the New Testament in 1522 and Tyndale used this in addition to Erasmus's Greek and Latin texts and the Vulgate. Luther's influence is also evident in the format of the Cologne fragment and its prologue, but there is no evidence that Luther and Tyndale ever met.

For so had Tyndale, after Luther's counsel, corrupted and changed it from the good and wholesome doctrine of Christ to the devilish heresies of their own that it was clean a contrary thing.

That were marvel, quoth your friend, that it should be so clean contrary, for to some that read it, it seemed very like.

It is, quoth I, nevertheless contrary and yet the more perilous, for like as to a true silver groat,° as false copper groat is nevertheless contrary, though it be quicksilvered over, but so much the more false in how much it is counterfeited the more like to the truth, so was the translation so much the more contrary in how much it was craftily devised like, and so much the more perilous in how much it was to folk unlearned more hard to be discerned.

Why, quoth your friend, what faults were there in it?

To tell you all that, quoth I, were in a manner to rehearse you all the whole book wherein there were found, and noted wrong, and falsely translated above a thousand texts by tale.°[2]

I would, quoth he, fain hear some one. He that should, quoth I, study for that should study where to find water in the sea. But I will show you for ensample two or three such as every one of the three is more than thrice three in one.

That were, quoth he, very strange, except you mean more in weight, for one can be but one in number.

Surely, quoth I, as weighty be they as any lightly can be, but I mean that every one of them is more than thrice three in number.

That were, quoth he, somewhat like a riddle.

This riddle, quoth I, will soon be read, for he hath mistranslated three words of great weight and every one of them is, as I suppose, more than thrice three times repeated and rehearsed in the book.

Ah, that may well be, quoth he, but that was not well done. But, I pray you, what words be they?

The one is, quoth I, this word 'priests'; the other, 'the Church'; The third, 'charity'. For 'priests', wheresoever he speaketh of the priests of Christ's Church, he never calleth them 'priests', but always 'seniors'; the Church he calleth always the 'congregation'; and charity he calleth always 'love'. Now do these names in our English tongue neither express the things that be meant by them, and also there appeareth, the circumstances well considered, that

[2] See **2**. n. 1 above.

he had a mischievous mind in the change. For first, as for priests and priesthead, though that of old they used commonly to choose well elderly men to be priests, and therefore in the Greek tongue priests were called *presbiteri*, as we might say, 'elder men', yet neither were all priests chosen old, as appeareth by St Paul writing to Timothy, *nemo iuventutem tuam contemnat*, 'let no man condemn thy youth', nor every elder man is not a priest. And in our English tongue this word 'senior' signifieth nothing at all, but is a French word used in English more than half in mockage, when one will call another 'my Lord' in scorn. And if he mean to take the Latin word *senior*, that word in the Latin tongue never signified a priest, but only an elder man. By which name of elder men, if he would call the priests Englishly, then should he rather signify their age than their office, and yet the name doth in English plainly signify the aldermen[3] of the cities and nothing the priests of the Church. And thus may we perceive that rather than he would call a priest by the name of a priest, he would seek a new word he neither wist nor cared what.

Now where he calleth the Church always the 'congregation', what reason had he therein?[4] For every man well seeth that though the Church indeed be a congregation, yet is not every congregation the Church, but a congregation of Christian people, which congregation of Christian people hath been in England always called and known by the name of the Church, which name what good cause or colour could he find to turn into the name of 'congregation', which word is common to a company of Christian men or a company of Turks?

Like wisdom was there in the change of this word 'charity' into 'love'. For though charity be always love, yet is not, ye wot well, love always charity.[5]

---

[3] aldermen] The word goes back to Old English and refers to those who exercise authority under the king: 'senior' is its first gloss in the OED.

[4] Erasmus had provided an answer to this question in his note to Romans 16.5 in the *Novum Instrumentum*, where he says that *ecclesia* may be taken to mean the building itself rather than a meeting of Christians, which is conveyed by *congregatio* (see *CWM* 6: 2, 681).

[5] The Vulgate translates Greek *agapē* as *charitas*, e.g. at the key place of 1 Corinthians 13.

Book 3, chapter 14

The author answereth the doubt moved before in the eleventh chapter concerning the constitution provincial,[6] *and that the clergy is therein far from the fault that is imputed to them in that point, showing also that the clergy hath not forbidden the Bible to be made and read in English.*

But now to the matter we were in hand with. Ye said ye would make answer for the law whereby the clergy of this realm hath forbidden all the people to have any Scripture translated into our tongue which is, as I said, in my mind an evil-made law.

Marry, quoth I, that is soon answered. Lay the charge to them that made it.

Marry, quoth he, so I do, for who made that construction but they.

Surely, quoth I, nobody else, nor they neither.

No, quoth he, what every man knoweth it.

Verily, quoth I, many men talk of it, but no man knoweth it, for there is nonsuch indeed. There is of truth a constitution that speaketh of such matter, but nothing of such fashion. For ye shall understand that the great arch-heretic, Wycliffe,[7] whereas the Holy Bible was long before his days by virtuous and well-learned men translated into the English tongue, and by good and godly people with devotion and soberness well and reverently read, took upon him of a malicious purpose to translate it of new. In which translation he purposely corrupted that holy text, maliciously planting therein such words as might in the readers' ears serve to the proof of such heresies as he went about to sow, which

[6] This is the *Constitution against Gospellers* (1409), also known as the 'Constitutions of Arundel', which resulted from a synod convened at Oxford in 1407 by Thomas Arundel, Archbishop of Canterbury, to combat Lollardy. For the constitution on English Bible translation see Introduction, pp. 7–8. The punishment for heresy of burning dates from this period.

[7] John Wycliffe (d. 1384) was the most prominent English opponent of papal authority and official Church teaching before the Reformation. His belief in the centrality of Scripture, and the Gospels in particular, as a model for Christian life inspired the first complete English translation of the Bible. The translation was first attributed to him by the chronicler Henry Knighton, writing before 1394, but it is unlikely that Wycliffe himself had a direct hand in it. Supporters of Wycliffe were referrred to as Lollards from as early as 1382. Arundel's Constitutions were a response to this new threat to Church authority.

he not only set forth with his own translation of the Bible, but also with certain prologues and glosses which he made thereupon. And these things he so handled (which was no great mastery), with reasons probable and likely to laypeople and unlearned, that he corrupted in his time many folk in the realm, and by other ill books which he made in Latin, being after borne into Bohemia and there taught by John Huss[8] and others, he was the occasion of the utter subversion of that whole realm, both in faith and good living, with the loss also of many a thousand lives. And as he began again the old heresies of those ancient heretics whom and whose errors the Church of Christ had condemned and subdued many divers ages afore, so doth Luther again begin to set up his. For all that he hath in effect he hath of him, saving that, lest he should seem to say nothing of his own, he added some things of himself of such manner sort as there was never heretic before his days neither so wicked that he would for sin, nor so foolish that he durst for shame, write, say, or, I trow, think the like.

I long, quoth he, to hear some of them, for the man is taken for wiser than to mean so madly, as men bear him in hand.[9]

Well, quoth I, that shall we see soon when we come thereto. But for our present purpose, after that it was perceived what harm the people took by the translation, prologues, and glosses of Wycliffe, and also of some other[s] that after him helped to set forth his sect, then for that cause and forasmuch as it is dangerous to translate the text of Scripture out of one tongue into another, as holy St Jerome testifieth,[10] forasmuch as in translation it is hard alway to keep the same sentence° whole – it was, I say, for these causes, at a council held at Oxford, provided upon great pain that no man should from thenceforth translate into the English tongue or any other language, of his own authority, by way of book, libel, or treatise, nor no man openly or secretly any such book, libel,° or treatise read, newly made in the time of the said John Wycliffe or since, or that should be made any time

[8] Jan Hus (1369?-1415), follower of Wycliffe in Bohemia and the principal conduit of Wycliffe's ideas to the sixteenth-century English reformers. Hus's burning in 1415 precipitated two decades of war in Bohemia and Saxony.

[9] bear him in hand] accuse him.

[10] 'The labour is one of love, but at the same time both perilous and presumptuous', Jerome to Pope Damasus, in 'Preface to The Four Gospels', in *Principal Works of St Jerome*, ed. by Schaff and Wace (1996), VI, 487.

after, till the same translation were by the diocesan° or, if need should require, by a provincial council approved. And this is a law that so many so long have spoken of, and so few have in all this while wrought to seek whether they say truth or no. For I trow that in this law ye see nothing unreasonable, for it neither forbiddeth the translations to be read that were already well done of old before Wycliffe's days, nor damneth his because it was new, but because it was nought,° nor prohibiteth new to be made, but provideth that they shall not be read, if they be mismade, till they be by good examination amended, except they be such translations as Wycliffe made, and Tyndale, that the malicious mind of the translator had in suchwise handled it as it were labour lost to go about to mend them.

Book 3, chapter 16

The messenger rehearseth some causes which he hath heard said by some of the clergy wherefore the Scripture should not be suffered in English, and the author showeth his mind that it were convenient to have the Bible in English. And therewith endeth the third book.

Sir, quoth your friend, yet for all this I can see no cause why the clergy should keep the Bible out of laymen's hands that can° no more but their mother tongue.

I had weened,° quoth I, that I had proved you plainly that they keep it not from them. For I have showed you that they keep none from them but such translation as be either not yet approved for good, or such as be already reproved for nought, as Wycliffe's was, and Tyndale's. For as for other old ones that were before Wycliffe's days remain lawful, and be in some folk's hands had and read.

Ye say well, quoth he, but yet, as women say, somewhat it was alway that the cat winked when her eye was out.[11] Surely so it is

[11] the cat winked when her eye was out] Proverbial: see Bartlett Jere Whiting, *Proverbs, Sentences, and Proverbial Phrases from English Writings mainly before 1500* (Cambridge, MA: Harvard University Press, 1968), C92. 'Wink' means to close one or both eyes, not as in the modern sense. Cf. *Jacke Jugeler* (1565): 'Sumwhat it was sayeth the proverbe olde / That the Catte winked when here iye was out / That is to saye no tale can be tolde / But that sum Englyshe may be piked therof out', STC 14837a, sig. Eii^{v}, image 20.

for nought that the English Bible is in so few men's hands when so many would so fain have it.

That is very truth, quoth I, for I think that though the favourers of a sect of heretics be so fervent in the setting forth of their sect that they let° not to lay their money together and make a purse among them for the printing of an evil-made or evil-translated book, which though it hap to be forbidden and burned, yet some be sold ere they be spied, and each of them lose but their part, yet I think there will no printer lightly be so hot to put any Bible in print at his own charge, whereof the loss should lie wholly in his own neck and then hang upon a doubtful trial whether the first copy of his translation was made before Wycliffe's days or since. For if it were made since, it must be approved before the printing. And surely how it hath happed that in all this while God hath either not suffered or not provided that any good, virtuous man hath had the mind in faithful wise to translate it, and thereupon either the clergy, or at the least wise some one Bishop to approve it, this can I nothing tell. But howsoever it be, I have heard and hear so much spoken in the matter, and so much doubt made therein, that peradventure it would let° and withdraw any one Bishop from the admitting thereof without the assent of the remanant.° And whereas many things be laid against it, yet is there in my mind not one thing that more putteth good men of the clergy in doubt to suffer it than this: that they see sometime much of the worse sort more fervent in calling for it than them whom we find far better, which maketh them to fear lest such men desire it for no good, and lest if it were had in every man's hand there would great peril arise, and that seditious people should do more harm therewith than honest folk should take fruit thereby. Which fear I promise you nothing feareth me, but that whosoever would of their malice or folly take harm of that thing that is of itself ordained to do all men good, I would never for the avoiding of their harm take from others the profit which they might take and nothing deserve to lose. For else if the abuse of a good thing should cause the taking away thereof from other that would use it well, Christ should himself never have been born, nor brought his faith into the world, nor God should never have made it neither if he should for the loss of those that would be damned wretches, have kept away the occasion of reward from them that would with help of his grace endeavour them to deserve it.

I am sure, quoth your friend, ye doubt not but that I am full and wholly of your mind in this matter that the Bible should be in our English tongue, but yet that the clergy is of the contrary and would not have it so that appeareth well in that they suffer it not to be so. And over that, I hear in every place almost where I find any learned man of them, their minds all set thereon to keep the Scripture from us. And they seek out for that part every rotten reason that they can find, and set them forth solemnly to the show, though five of those reasons be not worth a fig. For they begin as far as our first father, Adam, and show us that his wife and he fell out of Paradise with desire of knowledge and cunning.° Now if this would serve, it must from the knowledge and study of Scripture drive every man – priest and other – lest it drive all out of Paradise. Then say they that God taught His disciples many things apart, because the people should not hear it, and therefore they would the people should not now be suffered to read all.[12] Yet they say further that it is hard to translate the Scripture out of one tongue into another, and specially, they say, into ours, which they call a tongue vulgar and barbarous. But of all things specially they say that Scripture is the food of the soul and that the common people be as infants that must be fed but with milk and pap,° and if we have any stronger meat it must be chammed° afore by the nurse and so put into the baby's mouth. But methinks, though they make us all infants, they shall find many a shrewd brain among us that can perceive chalk from cheese well enough, if they would once take us our meat in our own hand. We be not so evil-toothed but that within a while they shall see us cham it ourself as well as they, for let them call us young babies and° they will, yet by God they shall for all that well find in some of us that an old knave is no child.[13]

Surely, quoth I, such things as ye speak is the thing that, as I somewhat said before, putteth good folk in fear to suffer the Scripture in our English tongue, not for the reading and receiving but for the busy chamming thereof, and for much meddling with such parts thereof as least will agree with their capacities. For undoubtedly, as ye spake of our mother Eve, inordinate appetite of knowledge is a means to drive any man out of Paradise, and

[12] See Mark 4.33–4.

[13] an old knave is no child] Proverbial: see Whiting (1968), K81. A variation is 'an old knave is no fool', which Lear's fool plays with at *King Lear* II.4.73–82.

inordinate is the appetite when men unlearned, though they read it in their language, will be busy to ensearch° and dispute the great mysteries of Scripture, which, though they hear, they be not able to perceive. This thing is plainly forbidden us that be not appointed nor instructed thereto. And therefore holy St Gregory Nazianzanus,[14] that great solemn doctor, sore toucheth and reproveth all such bold, busy meddlers in the Scripture, and showeth that it is in Exodus, by Moses ascending up upon the hill where he spake with God, and the people tarrying beneath, signified that the people be forbidden to presume to meddle with the high mysteries of Holy Scripture, but ought to be content to tarry beneath and meddle no higher than is meet for them; but receiving from the height of the hill by Moses that that is delivered them, that is, to wit, the laws and precepts that they must keep and the points they must believe, look well thereupon and often, and meddle well therewith: not to dispute it, but to fulfil it. [. . .][15]

And thus in these matters, if the common people might be bold to cham it, as ye say, and to dispute it, then should ye have the more blind the more bold, the more ignorant the more busy, the less wit the more inquisitive, the more fool the more talkative of great doubts and high questions of Holy Scripture and of God's great and secret mysteries, and this not soberly of any good affection, but presumptuously and unreverently at meat and at meal. And there, when the wine were in and the wit out, would they take upon them with foolish words and blasphemy to handle Holy Scripture in more homely manner than a song of Robin Hood. And some would, as I said, solemnly take upon them like as they were ordinary readers[16] to interpret the text at their pleasure, and therewith fall themself and draw down others with them into seditious sects and heresies, whereby the Scripture of God should lose his honour and reverence, and be by such unreverent and unfitting demeanour among much people quite and clean abused unto the contrary of that holy purpose that God

---

[14] St Gregory Nazianzanus] Gregory of Nazianzus (c.325–389), Greek Father of the Church and Bishop of Constantinople. He had studied rhetoric at Athens and was noted for his eloquence.

[15] See Exodus 24.15–18.

[16] ordinary readers] *Not* the 'general public', but persons appointed at the Inns of Court to deliver authoritative explanations of legal statutes. More himself held this office at Lincoln's Inn (as did his descendant, John Donne, though in an honorary capacity).

ordained it for. [. . .] And therefore, as I say, forsooth, I can in no wise agree with you that it were meet for men unlearned to be busy with the chamming of Holy Scripture, but to have it chammed unto them. For that is the preacher's part, and theirs that after long study are admitted to read and expound it, and to this intent weigh all the words, as far as I perceive, of all holy doctors that anything have written in this matter.

But never meant they, as I suppose, the forbidding of the Bible to be read in any vulgar tongue. Nor I never yet heard any reason laid why it were not convenient to have the Bible translated into the English tongue, but all those reasons, seemed they never so gay and glorious at the first sight, yet when they were well examined, they might in effect, for ought that I can see, as well be laid against the holy writers that wrote the Scripture in the Hebrew tongue, and against the blessed Evangelists that wrote the Scripture in Greek, and against all those in like wise that translated it out of every of those tongues into Latin, as to their charge that would well and faithfully translate it out of Latin into our English tongue. For as for that our tongue is called barbarous is but a fantasy, for so is, as every learned man knoweth, every strange language to other. And if they would call it barren of words, there is no doubt but it is plenteous enough to express our minds in anything whereof one man hath used to speak with another.

Now as touching the difficulty which a translator findeth in expressing well and lively the sentence° of his author, which is hard alway to do surely, but that he shall sometime minish° either of the sentence or of the grace that it beareth in the former tongue, that point hath lain in their light that have translated the Scripture already either out of Greek into Latin, or out of Hebrew into any of them both, as by many translations which we read already to them that be learned appeareth.

Now as touching the harm that may grow by such blind bayards[17] as will, when they read the Bible in English, be more busy than will become them. They that touch that point harp upon the right string and touch truly the great harm that were likely to grow to some folk, howbeit not by the occasion yet of the English translation, but by the occasion of their own lewdness

[17] blind bayards] bay horses, proverbially a type of recklessness, especially (as here) in one who is blind to the light of knowledge.

and folly, which yet were not in my mind a sufficient cause to exclude the translation and to put other folk from the benefit thereof, but rather to make provision against such abuse and let a good thing go forth. No wise man were there that would put all weapons away because manquellers° misuse them, nor this letted not, as I said, the Scripture to be first written in a vulgar tongue. For the Scripture, as I said before, was not written but in a vulgar tongue such as the whole people understood, nor in no secret ciphers, but such common letters as almost every man could read. For neither was the Hebrew, nor the Greek tongue, nor the Latin neither, any other speech than such as all the people spake. And therefore if we should lay that it were evil done to translate the Scripture into our tongue, because it is vulgar and common to every Englishman, then had it been as evil done to translate it into Greek or into Latin, or to write the New Testament first in Greek or the Old Testament in Hebrew, because both those tongues were as very vulgar as ours. And yet should there, by this reason also, not only the Scripture be kept out of our tongue, but, over that, should the reading thereof be forbidden both all such laypeople and all such priests too as can no more than their grammar, and very scantly that. All which company, though they can understand the words, be yet as far from the perceiving of the sentence in hard and doubtful texts as were our women, if the Scripture were translated to our own language.

Howbeit, of truth, seldom hath it been seen that any sect of heretics hath begun of such learned folk as nothing could else[18] but the language wherein they read the Scripture, but there hath alway commonly these sects sprung of the pride of such folk as had, with the knowledge of the tongue, some high persuasion in themself of their own learning beside. To whose authority some other folk have soon after – part of malice, part of simpleness, and much part of pleasure and delight in newfangledness – fallen in and increased the fashion. But the head hath ever commonly been either some proud, learned man, or at the least, beside the language, some proud smatterer° in learning. So that if we should, for fear of heretics that might hap to grow thereby, keep the Scripture out of any tongue, or out of unlearned mens' hands, we should for like fear be fain to keep it out of all tongues, and out of learned mens' hands too, and wot° not whom we might

[18] nothing could else] knew nothing else.

trust therewith. Wherefore there is, as me thinketh, no remedy but if any good thing shall go forward, somewhat must needs be adventured, and some folk will not fail to be nought. Against which things provision must be made that as much good may grow and as little harm come as can be devised, and not to keep the whole commodity from any whole people because of harm that by their own folly and fault may come to some part. As though a lewd surgeon would cut off the leg by the knee to keep the toe from the gout or cut off a man's head by the shoulders to keep him from the toothache [. . .]

Now if it so be that it would haply be thought not a thing meetly to be adventured to set all on a flush° at once, and dash rashly out Holy Scripture in every lewd° fellow's teeth, yet thinketh me there might such a moderation be taken therein as neither good virtuous layfolk should lack it, nor rude and brash brains abuse it. For it might be with diligence well and truly translated by some good Catholic and well-learned man, or by divers dividing the labour among them and after conferring their several parts together each with other. And after that might the work be allowed and approved by the ordinaries,° and by their authorities so put unto print as all the copies should come whole unto the Bishop's hand, which he may after his discretion and wisdom deliver to such as he perceiveth honest, sad,° and virtuous, with a good monition° and fatherly counsel, to use it reverently with humble heart and lowly mind, rather seeking therein occasion of devotion than of dispicion,° and providing as much as may be that the book be after the decease of the party brought again and reverently restored unto the ordinary. So that, as near as may be devised, no man have it but of the ordinary's hand, and by him thought and reputed for such as shall be likely to use it to God's honour and merit of his own soul. Among whom, if any be proved after to have abused it, then the use thereof to be forbidden him either forever or till he be waxen wiser.

4. William Tyndale, *An Answer to More's Dialogue* (1531)

[Tyndale's *Answer* to More's *Dialogue* begins by addressing More's claim that he has deliberately mistranslated certain key words, and then goes through the four books answering what appear to be the most plausible charges against him. Much of the *Answer* is also cast as dialogue. The passages here deal with the translation of *ecclesia* and whether or not the Church has proscribed Bible translation.

See William Tyndale, *An Answer unto Sir Thomas Mores Dialogue*, ed. by Anne M. O'Donnell and Jared Wicks (Washington, DC: Catholic University Press of America, 2000)]

Why Tyndale used this word 'congregation' rather than 'church' in the translation of the New Testament.

Wherefore inasmuch as the clergy, as the nature of those hard and indurate adamant stones[1] is to draw all to them, had appropriated unto themselves the term that of right is common unto all the whole congregation of them that believe in Christ, and with their false and subtle wiles had beguiled and mocked the people and brought them into the ignorance of the word, making them understand by this word 'church' nothing but the shaven flock of them that shore° the whole world, therefore in the translation of the New Testament, where I found this word *ecclesia* I interpreted it by this word 'congregation'. Even therefore did I it and not of any mischievous mind or purpose to establish heresy, as Master More untruly reporteth of me in his *Dialogue*, where he raileth on the translation of the New Testament.

And when Master More sayeth that this word 'church' is known well enough, I report me unto the consciences of all the land whether he say truth or otherwise, or whether the laypeople understand by 'church' the whole multitude of them that profess Christ or the juggling sprites only. And when he sayeth that 'congregation' is a more general term, if it were, it hurteth not, for the circumstance doth ever tell what congregation is meant. Nevertheless, yet sayeth he not the truth, for wheresoever he sayeth a congregation, there may I say a church also, as the church of the devil, the church of Satan, the church of wretches, the church of wicked men, the church of liars, and a church of Turks thereto.

For Master More must grant (if he will have *ecclesia* translated throughout all the New Testament by this word 'church') that

[1] adamant stones] very hard stones, but with magnetic properties.

'church' is as common as *ecclesia*. Now is *ecclesia* a Greek word and was in use before the time of the Apostles,[2] and taken for a congregation among the heathen where was no congregation of God or of Christ. And also Lucas[3] himself useth *ecclesia* for a church or congregation of heathen people thrice in one chapter, even in the 19th of the Acts, where Demetrius the goldsmith or silversmith had gathered a company against Paul for preaching against images.

Howbeit Master More hath so long used his figures of poetry that, I suppose, when he erreth most, he now by reason of a long custom believeth himself that he sayeth most true. Or else, as wise people when they dance naked in nets believe that no man seeth them,[4] even so Master More thinketh that his errors be so subtly couched that no man can espy them [. . .]

But how happeth it that Master More hath not contended in like wise against his dearling Erasmus all this long while. Doth not he change this word *ecclesia* into 'congregation', and that not seldom in the New Testament?[5] Peradventure he oweth him a favour because he made *Moria* in his house,[6] which book, if [it] were in English then should every man see how that he then was far otherwise minded than he now writeth. But verily I think that as Judas betrayed not Christ for any love that he had unto the

[2] See More, *The Confutation of Tyndale's Answer*, ed. by L. A. Schuster et al., 3 vols (New Haven: Yale University Press, 1973), *CWM* 8:3, 1523; Cummings, *Literary Culture of the Reformation*, p. 193.

[3] Lucas] i.e. Luke, assumed also to be the author of Acts.

[4] Or else [. . .] seeth them] i.e. like those who behave as though their faults are concealed when they are in fact exposed for all to see. Proverbial (see M. P. Tilley, *A Dictionary of the Proverbs in England in the Sixteenth and Seventeenth Centuries* (Ann Arbor: University of Michigan Press, 1950), N.130), but also rich in metaphor. Cf. Tyndale, *The Obedience of a Christian Man*, ed. by David Daniell (Harmondsworth: Penguin, 2000), p. 103, and Fulke, *Defence of Translations*, STC 11430.5, p. 160, image 130: 'Nowe you have gotten a fine nette to daunce naked in, that no ignorant blinde bussard can see you. The maskes of your nette be the ambiguous and abusiue significations of this worde priest'.

[5] Erasmus uses the term *congregatio* for Greek *ekklēsia* at Acts 5.11 and in eight other places, but generally prefers Latin *ecclesia*. See also **3**. 71–72 above and **5**. 178–80 below.

[6] Erasmus planned *Moriae Encomium* [Praise of Folly] when travelling from Italy to England in 1509 and claimed to have written it in a few days while staying at More's house in Bucklersbury, London.

high priests, scribes and pharisees, but only to come by that wherefore he thirsted, even so Master More (as there are tokens evident) wrote not these books for any affection that he bare unto the spirituality, or unto the opinions which he so barely defendeth, but to obtain only that which he was an hungered for.

Chapter 14

MORE:[7] Wycliffe was the occasion of the utter subversion of the realm of Bohemia, both in faith and good living, and of the loss of many a thousand lives.[8]

TYNDALE: The rule[s] of their faith are Christ's promises, and the rule of their living, God's law. And as for loss of lives, it is truth that the Pope slew, I think, a hundred thousand of them because of their faith, and that they would no longer serve him; as he slew in England many a thousand, and slew the true king[9] and set up a false, unto the effusion of all the noble blood and murdering up of the commonalty,[10] because he should be his defender.

MORE: The constitution of the Bishops is not that the Scripture shall not be in English, but that no man may translate it by his own authority, or read it, until they had approved it.[11]

TYNDALE: If no translation shall be had until they give licence or till they approve it, it shall never be had. And so it is all one in effect to say 'there shall be none at all in English', and to say, 'till we admit it', seeing they be so malicious that they will none admit, but feign all the cavillations they can to prove it were not expedient. So that if it be not had spite of their hearts, it shall never be had. And thereto they have done their best to have had it enacted by parliament that it should not be in English.[12]

---

[7] Speakers are identified in the margin in *1531*.

[8] See **3**. 112–18 above.

[9] true king] Tyndale claims that Richard II was the rightful king, who was murdered for his support for the Wycliffites, and Henry IV crowned because he resisted them.

[10] commonalty] the common people, i.e. (at this time) all who are neither nobility nor clergy.

[11] See **3**. 137–45 above.

[12] enacted by parliament [. . .] be in English] Tyndale's translations of the New Testament and Pentateuch were banned on 22 June 1530 because 'corruptly translated'; see Stanford E. Lehmberg, *The Reformation Parliament: 1529–1536* (Cambridge: Cambridge University Press, 1970), pp. 120–23.

Chapter 16

The messenger asketh him, 'If there be an old, lawful translation before Wycliffe's, how happeneth it that it is in so few men's hands, seeing so many desire it?' He answereth, 'The printer dare not print it, and then hang on a doubtful trial, whether it were translated since or before; for if it were translated since, it must be first approved.'[13]

What may not Master More say, by authority of his poetry?[14] There is a lawful translation that no man knoweth', which is as much as no lawful translation. Why might not the bishops show which were that lawful translation, and let it be printed? Nay, if that might have been obtained of them with large money, it had been printed, ye may be sure, long ere this. But, sir, answer me hereunto: how happeneth that ye defenders translate not one yourselves, to cease the murmur of the people, and put to your own glozes,° to prevent heretics? Ye would no doubt have done it long since, if ye could have made your glozes agree with the text in every place. And what can you say to this, how that, besides they have done their best to disannul all translating by parliament, they have disputed before the King's grace that it is perilous and not meet, and so concluded that it shall not be, under a pretence of deferring it of certain years, where Master More was their special orator, to feign lies for their purpose.

MORE: Nothing discourageth the clergy so much as that they of the worst sort most calleth after it. [15]

TYNDALE: It might well be Pharisees full of holiness long not after it, but publicans that hunger after mercy might sore desire it. Howbeit, it is in very deed a suspect thing, and a great sign of a heretic to require it.

Then he juggleth° with allegories. Sir, Moses delivered them all that he had received of God, and that in the mother tongue, in which all that had the heart thereto studied, and not the priests only, as thou mayest see in the Scripture (Deuteronomy 31. 9–13). And the Apostles kept nothing behind, as Paul testified (Acts 20) how he had showed them all the counsel of God, and had kept

[13] See **3**. 182–86 above.

[14] poetry] Rhetorical trickery involving the figurative rather than the literal sense; the charge is amplified by the references to 'glozes' and to More as 'orator'.

[15] See **3**. 197–98 above.

nought back. Should the laypeople less hearken unto the expositions of the prelates in doubtful places, if the text were in their hands when they preached?

MORE: The Jews give great reverence unto the Bible, and we sit on it.

TYNDALE: The Pope putteth it under his feet and treadeth on it, in token that he is lord over it, that it should serve him, and he not it.

MORE: God hath ordained the ordinaries° for chief physicians.

TYNDALE: They be lawyers ordained of the Pope and can° no more skill of the Scripture than they that never saw it; yea, and have professed a contrary doctrine. They be right hangmen to murder whosoever desireth, for the doctrine that God hath given to be the ordinary of our faith and living.

And when he maketh so great difficulty and hardness in Paul's epistles, I say it is impossible to understand either Peter or Paul, or aught at all in the Scripture, for him that denyeth the justifying of faith in Christ's blood. And again, it is impossible to understand in the Scripture more than a Turk for whosoever hath not the law of God written in his heart to fulfil it; of which point, and of true faith too, I fear me that you are void and empty, with all your spirituality, whose defender ye have taken upon you to be, for to mock out the truth for lucre and vantage.°[16]

5. Thomas More, *The Confutation of Tyndale's Answer* (1532)

[More's *Confutation* of Tyndale's *Answer* runs to nearly two thousand pages, quoting Tyndale and rebutting him paragraph by paragraph and sometimes sentence by sentence. The humanist tenor of the *Dialogue of Heresies* has been replaced by a sustained polemic supported by a vast amount of theological scholarship. The passages here return to the question of mistranslation and respond to Tyndale's attacks on the 'poetry' of More's humanist writings and his collaboration with Erasmus.

See More, *The Confutation of Tyndale's Answer*, ed. by L. A. Schuster et al., *CWM* 8, 3 vols (New Haven: Yale University Press, 1973).]

---

[16] Cf. Tyndale's translation of Matthew 25.27: 'Then at my commynge shulde I have receaved my money with vauntage'.

Book 2, chapter 1

So was it now that among other tokens of Tyndale's evil intent in his translation I showed as for ensample that he changed commonly this word 'Church' into this word 'congregation', and this word 'priest' into this word 'senior', and 'charity' into 'love', and 'grace' into 'favour', 'confession' into 'knowledge', and 'penance' into 'repentance', with many words more, which he changeth and useth daily, as in turning 'idols' into 'images', and 'anointing' into 'smearing', 'consecrating' into 'charming', 'sacraments' into 'ceremonies', and 'the ceremonies' into 'witchcraft', and yet many more.

Now showed I there the causes why Tyndale did evil in translating the Scripture into our tongue with such manner [of] changes, and showed also the things that might well make every man perceive that he meant therein the setting forth of some heresies, as appeareth in my said dialogue. Which things, if I should here again rehearse and repeat, and in like wise all other things against which Tyndale doth object, it were too long a work, and as much as to plant and set into this book mine whole dialogue again. Wherefore in all such things I must needs remit° the reader unto the dialogue [it]self.

Now cometh Tyndale, and for answer thereof, and to disprove all that I lay against him in the translating of divers of these words, showeth that the Latin text and the Greek may be his excuse and defence, forasmuch as the words in the Latin text and the Greek do, as he sayeth, signify such things as he hath expressed in his English translation, by those English words that I find the fault in. [. . .]

But yet to the intent ye may the better perceive how wisely the man defendeth the matter, in such wise as he showeth both lack of learning, and more lack of wit, and most lack of grace, he doth at the last confess himself that he made the changes for the setting forth of his heresies, which was the point that I laid to his charge as the very thing for which his translation was very well worthy to be burned.

Book 2, chapter 2

In the second chapter, Tyndale sayeth that he changed this word 'Church' into this word 'congregation' in the New Testament, where he found this word *ecclesia* in Latin, because that the clergy had, he sayeth, brought the people into the ignorance of the true signification of this word 'Church', making them understand thereby nothing but the clergy.

First, this is undoubtedly false, whatsoever Tyndale say. For albeit that men call the clergy by the name of the Church, as the part ordained of God to be the more spiritual part thereof, yet is there no man I suppose so rude but that he knoweth and so heareth the clergy preach also themself that of the Church of Christ is every Christian man, and that the whole Church is the whole Christian people, and therefore they call it the Catholic Church that is universal, by which word never man was, I ween,° so mad to mean only the priests, how boldly soever Tyndale against his own conscience report himself to every other man's. I would also, because he reporteth him so much to other men's conscience, fain wit of Tyndale by his own conscience where he had ever heard any priest either preach or write, or so much as say the word that only the clergy is the Church, and none of the Church but they. I suppose themself have not given themself the name. The word is English, and they teach not every man his mother tongue, as men teach children their ABC. But the good people have of old time, though they know themself also for part of the Church, yet because the Church signified a holy name of a Christian company gathered together in God, have therefore, of humility on their own part and reverence toward them, used to call the clergy by that name, accounting them for the more godly part of that whole godly company. [. . .]

But now that thing that good folk have of good mind begun, and many hundred years continued, Tyndale as one of another sort would utterly have changed, and rather than laymen should have any such reverent mind to priests as to call them the Church, he would take it from them both, and, putting away from both that holy name of Church, would call them both by the name of congregation, a word without any signification of Christendom any more than of Jews or Turks.

TYNDALE: To this answereth Tyndale and sayeth: 'If this word "congregation" were a more general term than this word

"Church", it hurteth not, for the circumstance[1] doth ever declare what thing is meant thereby.'[2]

MORE: If the setting of the circumstance make all well enough, he needeth not much to care what word he changeth nor how. For he may set such circumstances of his own device that he may make men perceive what he meaneth. For so he may translate the world into a football if he join therewith certain circumstances, and say this round, rolling football that men walk upon and ships sail upon, in the people whereof there is no rest nor stability, and so forth, a great long tale with such circumstances, he might, as I say, make any word understood as it like himself, whatsoever the word before signified of itself. But surely the word 'congregation' with the circumstances in the text would not have served when he translated it first to make the English reader to take it for the Church, no more than 'idols' for 'images', or 'images' for 'idols', as he translateth in like wise, or 'repenting' for 'doing penance',[3] which he changeth too. But marry he hath added unto his translation such circumstances since that the order of priesthood is right nought, but that every man, woman, and child is as very a priest as a priest indeed, and that every man and woman may consecrate the body of Christ and say Mass as well as any priest, and hear confession and assoil° as well as may a priest, and that there is no difference between other folk and priests, but all one congregation and company without any difference save an appointment to preach, and also that the common, known people of all Christian realms – clergy, lay-people, and all – be not the Church, nor be no part of the Church

---

[1] circumstance] Here, 'context'. But More then uses the term in the more specific sense of 'accidents', a set of variable attributes that define a thing (or person, or action) in particular conditions. As a lawyer he may also be thinking of Quintilian's discussion of 'circumstance' in *Institutio oratoria* V.10.104–10; see also Greenblatt , *Renaissance Self-Fashioning*, pp. 102–03.

[2] See Tyndale, *Answer*, STC 24437, sig. A7^{r}, image 7.

[3] 'repenting' for 'doing penance'] Another crucial term: the Protestant translation of 'do penance' (*poenitentiam agite* in the Vulgate) as 'repent' effectively abolished the sacrament of penance with its requirement to perform good deeds; see 'Of penance' in Tyndale, *Obedience*, ed. by Daniell, p. 115. Tyndale argues for the translations 'repent' and 'repentance' in the prologue to the revised New Testament (1534), STC 2826, sigs *viii^{v}–**i^{v}, images 9–10, but Erasmus had laid the philological grounds for this in his correction of the Vulgate translation in the *Novum Instrumentum*. See Simpson, *Burning to Read*, pp. 72–76.

because they use sacraments and ceremonies and divine service in churches, but that the Church is a secret congregation of unknown, chosen heretics, scattered abroad in corners and studying to destroy the Church. [. . .]

TYNDALE: 'For wheresoever', sayeth he, 'that I may say a "congregation", there I may say a "Church" also, as the Church of the Devil, the Church of Satan, the Church of wretches, the Church of wicked men, the Church of liars, and a Church of Turks thereto.'[4]

MORE: This is lustily said of Tyndale and like a man. But it pleaseth him not to consider that I said that this word 'congregation' is indifferent unto Turks and Christian men, and unto all other companies and a company of Christian men, so that it as well signifieth a company of Turks as of Christian men, and that this word 'Church' doth signify a company of Christian people and is not indifferent to a company of Turks and of Christian men. And I said, and yet I say, that this is true of the usual signification of these words themself in the English tongue, by the common custom of us English people that either now do use these words in our language, or that have used [them] before our days. And I say that this common custom and usage of speech is the only thing by which we know the right and proper signification of any word, insomuch that if a word were taken out of Latin, French, or Spanish, and were for lack of understanding of the tongue from whence it came used for another thing in English than it was in the former tongue, then signifieth it in England none other thing than as we use it and understand thereby whatsoever it signify anywhere else. Then say I now that in England this word 'congregation' did never signify the number of Christian people as Christian people, with a connotation or consideration of their faith or Christendom, no more than this word 'assembly', which hath been taken out of the French, and now is by custom become English, as 'congregation' is out of the Latin. [. . .]

In the end of this chapter Tyndale telleth me that I have been so long used in my figures of poetry that when I err most, I do now, as he supposeth, by reason of a long custom, believe myself that that I say most true, or else as wise people, when they dance naked in a net, believe that no man see them.[5] Even so, he sayeth,

---

[4] See Tyndale, *Answer*, sig. A7^{v}, image 7.

[5] See **4**. 40–42 above.

that I think mine errors so subtly couched that no man can spy them. As for mine errors, how subtly they be couched I cannot tell, nor what other men shall spy I cannot say. But surely, if I could spy any in my writing myself, I would not fail both to confess it to God and the world and forsake it. Now if I be by custom of poetry so blinded that I cannot see mine errors, but ween that my lies were true, yet if I find any that can show them me, I shall soon amend the fault. But I have one good likelihood that I do not err or lie after such fashion as Tyndale telleth me, in that if it so were, Tyndale then that pryeth thereupon so narrowly, and with such eagle's eyes as he hath, were very likely to spy it, namely sith I go so bare, dancing naked in a net. And I am sure if he spied any such thing in me, he would of his charity be so good to me as to tell me. But surely he hath spied none yet. For all that he hath hitherto pored out° and called mine errors be but his own and turn upon his own top every one.[6] And as for my poetry, verily I can° little else, and yet not that neither. But it had been good for Tyndale's soul, and a thousand souls beside, that he had meddled but with poetry instead of Holy Scripture all the days of his life. For of poetry, though there should have come little good, yet could there never have come such a heap of harm to Christian people as he hath of his blind malice brought into this realm by his untrue translating, and more untrue construing of the Holy Scripture of God, most maliciously making the blessed word of God to serve him for an instrument to drive men to the devil.

And yet if poetry be, as Tyndale calleth it, nothing but feigning and lying, then is he cunning enough, and can, I assure you, make as much poetry upon any part of Scripture as any poet can in England upon any part of Virgil. And he useth in his writing much plain poetry, wherewith he danceth naked not all in a net, but for the more part so stark naked without any net at all that there is not the breadth of a silken thread to cover his poetry, of which points of his plain, open poetry I have showed you some already, and shall anon show you many more.

Then he asketh me why I have not contended with Erasmus, whom he calleth my dearling, of all this long while for translating of this word *ecclesia* into this word *congregatio*.[7] And then he

[6] turn upon his own top] rebound upon his own head.

[7] See Tyndale, *Answer*, image 8. On Erasmus's translation of *ekklēsia* see **4**. 44–47 above.

cometh forth with his feat° proper taunt that I favour him of likelihood for making of his book of *Moria* in my house. There had he hit me low, save for lack of a little salt. I have not contended with Erasmus my dearling, because I found no such malicious intent with Erasmus my dearling as I find with Tyndale. For had I found with Erasmus my dearling the shrewd intent and purpose that I find in Tyndale, Erasmus my dearling should be no more my dearling. But I find in Erasmus my dearling that he detesteth and abhorreth the errors and heresies that Tyndale plainly teacheth and abideth by, and therefore Erasmus my dearling shall be my dear dearling still. And surely if Tyndale had either never taught them, or yet had the grace to revoke them, then should Tyndale be my dear dearling too. But while he holdeth such heresies still, I cannot take for my dearling him that the devil taketh for his dearling.

Now for his translation of *ecclesia* by *congregatio*, his deed is nothing like Tyndale's. For the Latin tongue had no Latin before used for 'the Church' but the Greek word *ecclesia*, therefore Erasmus in his new translation gave it a Latin word. But we had in English a proper English word therefore, and therefore was no such cause for Tyndale to change it into a worse. Erasmus also meant none heresy therein, as appeareth by his writing against heretics,[8] but Tyndale intended nothing else thereby, as appeareth by the heresies that himself teacheth and abideth by. And therefore was there in this matter no cause for me to contend with Erasmus as there was to contend with Tyndale, with whom I contend for putting in 'congregation' instead of 'Church', except that Tyndale peradventure meaneth that I should have been angry with Erasmus because that instead of 'congregation' in his Latin translation he had not put in our English word 'Church'.

As touching *Moria*, in which Erasmus under the name and person of 'Moria', which word in Greek signifieth 'folly', doth merely touch and reprove such faults and follies as he found in any kind of people, perusing every state and condition, spiritual

[8] After much prompting by the Church hierarchy, Erasmus reluctantly agreed to write two 'diatribes' against Luther on the freedom of the will in 1524 and 1526–27; see A *Discussion of Free Will* and *Hyperaspistes* in *CWE* vols 76 and 77. More strongly encouraged him to fight against heresy in a letter of 18 December 1526; see *St Thomas More: Selected Letters*, ed. by Elizabeth Frances Rogers (New Haven, CT: Yale University Press, 1961), pp. 161–65.

and temporal, leaving almost none untouched, by which book Tyndale sayeth that if it were in English, every man should then well see that I was then far otherwise minded that I now write. If this be true, then the more cause have I to thank God of amendment. But surely this is untrue. For, God be thanked, I never had that mind in my life to have holy saints' images or their holy relics out of reverence. Nor if there were any such thing in *Moria*, that thing could not yet make any man see that I were myself of that mind, the book being made by another man, though he were my dearling never so dear. Howbeit that book of *Moria* doth indeed but jest upon the abuses of such things after the manner of the disour's° part in a play, and yet not so far neither by a great deal as the messenger doth in my dialogue, which I have yet suffered to stand still in my dialogue,[9] and that rather yet by the counsel of other men than of myself.

For albeit that it be lawful to any man to mislike the misuse of every good thing, and that in my dialogue there [be] not only those evil things rehearsed, but answered also and soiled,° and the goodness of the thing itself well used is plainly confirmed and proved. Yet hath Tyndale by erroneous books in setting forth Luther's pestilent heresies so envenomed the hearts of lewdly disposed persons that men cannot almost now speak of such things in so much as a play, but that evil hearers wax a great deal the worse.

And therefore in these days in which Tyndale hath (God amend him) with the infection of his contagious heresies so sore poisoned malicious and newfangled folk that the King's Highness, and not without the counsel and advice not of his nobles only, with his other counsellors attending upon His Grace's person, but also of the right virtuous and special, well-learned men of either university and other parts of the realm specially called thereto, hath, after diligent and long consideration had therein, been fain for the while to prohibit the Scripture of God to be suffered in English tongue among the people's hands, lest evil folk by false drawing of every good thing they read into the colour and maintenance of their own fond fantasies, and turning all honey into poison, might both deadly do hurt

---

[9] More's point is that the figure of the Messenger in *Heresies* is potentially more subversive than Erasmus's Folly. He evidently still sees *Heresies* as a humanist work like Erasmus's.

unto themself, and spread also that infection further abroad. I say therefore, in these days in which men by their own default misconstrue and take harm of the very Scripture of God, until men better amend, if any man would now translate *Moria* into English, or some works either that I have myself written ere this,[10] albeit there be none harm therein, folk yet being (as they be) given to take harm of that that is good, I would not only my dearling's books, but mine own also, help to burn them both with mine own hands rather than folk should (though through their own fault) take any harm of them, seeing that I see them likely in these days so to do.

6. Miles Coverdale, *Biblia: The Bible Faithfully Translated into English* (1535)

[Miles Coverdale (1488–1569) was an Augustinian friar based in Cambridge who came under the influence of the religious reformers, especially Robert Barnes, during the 1520s. In exile on the continent from 1528, where he assisted Tyndale with the Pentateuch, he was responsible for the first complete printed English Bible in 1535, when he returned to England. He went on to produce the 'Great Bible' of 1539, which was based on a revision of the Matthew Bible of 1537, not his own earlier text. He was exiled twice more: in the 1540s, and in the 1550s under Mary, though he had been made Bishop of Exeter in the intervening period under Edward VI. During his last period of exile he was a contributor to the Geneva Bible (1560), returning to England for the last time in 1559.

Coverdale's Bible of 1535 was printed at Antwerp by de Keyser and dedicated to Henry VIII, who was by now supportive of Bible translation. It was reissued by John Nicolson at Southwark shortly afterwards. Coverdale was not a skilled linguist and he stated that his sources were Latin and German translations, not the original Hebrew and Greek texts, though his principal source was in fact the proscribed English translation by Tyndale. His Latin sources were the Vulgate, Erasmus's *Novum Instrumentum* (1516) and Sanctes Pagninus's very literal translation of 1528; his

[10] *Moriae Encomium* was translated into English by Sir Thomas Chaloner in 1549 and *Utopia* by Ralph Robinson in 1551.

German sources were Luther (1522, 1534) and the Zurich Bible of 1524–29.

The Coverdale Bible, 1535, introd. by S. L. Greenslade (Folkestone: Dawsons, 1975); Brooke Foss Westcott, *A General View of the History of the English Bible*, rev. by W. A. Wright (London: Macmillan, 1905); Norton, *Bible as Literature*; Simpson, *Burning to Read*; David Lawton in *OHLTE* (1) pp. 226–29.]

A Prologue. Miles Coverdale unto the Christian Reader.

Considering how excellent knowledge and learning an interpreter of Scripture ought to have in the tongues, and pondering also mine own insufficiency therein and how weak I am to perform the office of a translator, I was the more loath to meddle with this work. Notwithstanding, when I considered how great pity it was that we should want it so long, and called to my remembrance the adversity of them which were not only of ripe knowledge, but would also with all their hearts have performed that they began, if they had not had impediment – considering, I say, that by reason of their adversity it could not so soon have been brought to an end, as our most prosperous nation would fain have had it – these and other reasonable causes considered, I was the more bold to take it in hand. And to help me herein I have had sundry translations, not only in Latin, but also of the Dutch[1] interpreters, whom because of their singular gifts and special diligence in the Bible, I have been the more glad to follow for the most part, according as I was required. But to say the truth before God, it was neither my labour nor desire to have this work put in my hand. Nevertheless, it grieved me that other nations should be more plenteously provided for with the Scripture in their mother tongue than we;[2] therefore, when I was instantly required, though I could not do so well as I would, I thought it yet my duty to do my best, and that with a good will.

[1] Dutch] German, i.e. 'high Dutch'.

[2] European printed vernacular bibles before 1500 included German (1466); Italian (1471); Dutch (1477); Catalan (1478); French (1479); parts were also translated into Spanish and Portugese.

Whereas some men think now that many translations make division in the faith and in the people of God, that is not so. For it was never better with the congregation of God than when every Church almost had the Bible of a sundry translation. Among the Greeks, had not Origen a special translation? Had not Vulgarius one peculiar, and likewise Chrysostom? Besides the Seventy Interpreters,[3] is there not the translation of Aquila, of Theodotion, of Symmachus, and of sundry other? Again, among the Latin men thou findest that every one almost used a special and sundry translation; for insomuch as every bishop had the knowledge of the tongues, he gave his diligence to have the Bible of his own translation. The doctors, as Irenaeus, Cyprianus, Tertullian, St Jerome, St Augustine, Hilarius, and St Ambrose upon diverse places of the Scripture read not the text all alike.

Therefore ought it not to be taken as evil that such men as have understanding now in our time exercise themselves in the tongues and give their diligence to translate out of one language into another. Yea, we ought rather to give God high thanks therefore, which through his spirit stirreth up men's minds so to exercise themselves therein. Would God it had never been left off after the time of St Augustine, then should we never have come into such blindness and ignorance, into such errors and delusions. For as soon as the Bible was cast aside and no more put in exercise, then began every one of his own head to write whatsoever came into his brain and that seemed to be good in his own eyes, and so grew the darkness of men's traditions. And this same is the cause that we have had so many writers which seldom made mention of the Scripture of the Bible, and though they sometimes alleged° it, yet was it done so far out of season and so wide from the purpose that a man may well perceive how that they never saw the original.

Seeing then that this diligent exercise of translating doth so much good and edifieth in other languages, why should it do evil in ours? Doubtless like as all nations in the diversity of speeches may know one God in the unity of faith, and be one in love, even

[3] Seventy Interpreters] Responsible for the Septuagint, the Greek translation of the Old Testament from the Hebrew made in Egypt in the 3rd and 2nd centuries BC. This was the source of the first Latin translation, the *Vetus Latina*, made in the 2nd century AD.

so may diverse translations understand one another, and that in the head, articles and ground of our most blessed faith, though they use sundry words. Wherefore methinks we have great occasion to give thanks unto God that he hath opened unto his Church the gift of interpretation° and of printing, and that there are now at this time so many which with such diligence and faithfulness interpret the Scripture to the honour of God and edifying of his people, whereas (like as when many are shooting together) every one doth his best to be nighest the mark. And though they cannot all attain thereto, yet shooteth one nigher than another and hitteth it better than another – yea, one can do it better than another. Who is now then so unreasonable, so despiteful, or envious, as to abhor him that doth all his diligence to hit the prick° and to shoot nighest it, though he miss and come not nighest the mark. Ought not such one rather to be commended and to be helped forward that he may exercise himself the more therein?

For the which cause, according as I was desired, I took the more upon me to set forth this special translation, not as a checker,° not as a reprover or despiser of other men's translations (for among many as yet I have found none without occasion of great thanksgiving unto God), but lowly and faithfully have I followed mine interpreters, and that under correction. And though° I have failed anywhere, as there is no man but he misseth in something, love shall construe all to the best without any perverse judgement.

7. Nicholas Udall, *The Paraphrase of Erasmus upon the New Testament* (1548)

[Nicholas Udall (1504–66) was educated at Corpus Christi College, Oxford, a recent foundation which promoted the study of Greek. He was implicated in the distribution of Lutheran works there in 1527–8. His first publication was a manual for conversational Latin, *Floures for Latine Spekynge* (1534), based on Terence and many times reprinted, but his best known work is the seminal English comedy *Ralph Roister Doister*, not published until 1566. In 1534 he was also appointed Headmaster of Eton. His first translation of Erasmus was the *Apophthegms* (1542), and in 1543 he was appointed by the Queen, Katherine

Parr, to lead a team to translate all of Erasmus's Latin *Paraphrases* into English.

Erasmus's *Paraphrases on the New Testament*, beginning with Romans in 1517, proceeded alongside his revisions of the text of the New Testament [the *Novum Instrumentum*] and presented his 'philosophy of Christ' to the wider public. The popularising aspects of the *Paraphrases* appealed to Protestants, but the translation project initiated by Katherine Parr had to wait until after the death of Henry VIII for publication. The English *Paraphrases* included contributions from Princess Mary and from Katherine herself; also from Coverdale, Leonard Cox, Thomas Key, and John Olde. Udall was responsible for editing the first volume and for the translations of the paraphrases of Luke and possibly also Matthew and Acts. The royal Injunctions of 1547 required every church in England to keep a copy of the translations.

See E. J. Devereux, 'The Publication of the English Paraphrases of Erasmus', *Bulletin of the John Rylands University Library of Manchester*, 51 (1969), 348–67; Albert Rabil, 'Erasmus' Paraphrases of the New Testament', in *Essays on the Works of Erasmus*, ed. by Richard L. De Molen (New Haven, CT: Yale University Press, 1978), pp. 145–61; Stephen Alford, *Kingship and Politics in the Reign of Edward VI* (Cambridge: Cambridge University Press, 2002); Hilmor M. Pabel and Mark Vessey, eds, *Holy Scripture Speaks: The Production and Reception of Erasmus's Paraphrases on the New Testament* (Toronto: University of Toronto Press, 2002); Janel Mueller, ed., *Katherine Parr: Complete Works and Correspondence* (Chicago: Chicago University Press, 2011).]

a) [Epistle to King Edward VI]

Now as touching the translators of such books as this, although I have at this present the less to say, because I myself have in a small portion of this work filled one room of some other man that might have been able to do it better than I have done, yet can I not but wish that among so many Your Majesty's most ample and bounteous exhibitions,° and so many other godly acts to be done as are daily brought and offered to the gracious direction of Your Highness, of your most dear uncle, being governor of your royal person during this time of your minority, and under

Your Majesty our Protector,[1] and of the other your most honourable counsellors, this thing also might be preferred to your considerations, how necessary a thing it were that some able, worthy, and meet persons, for doing such public benefit to the commonweal as translating of good works and writing of chronicles, might by some good provision and means have some condign sustentation° in the same. For what realm almost (England excepted) hath not all the good authors that ever wrote translated into the mother tongue, whereby the people are made prudent and expert men in the tract of all affairs, either touching any discipline or else any civil matters? And in Germany, what good work of divinity is there which they have not in their own language to the unestimable edifying of the people in the due knowledge of God?

For what hath been or is in any commonweal the foundation of spreading abroad the knowledge of God's word but only the setting forth of the Bible with other good and godly treatises for the declaration of the same? What thing hath the whelps of the Romish Antichrist so fiercely always barked against as at the translating of Scripture and other books concerning matters of religion into the vulgar tongue for the use of the people? What any one thing is there against the which there hath in all Christian realms, as long as it might prevail, been either sorer decrees, laws, or inhibitions ordained, or more terrible execution of all kinds of torments and deaths invented, devised, and put in use than against the setters forth of books concerning religion? What one thing hath papistry in all countries more eagerly conspired, more subtly compassed, or more earnestly practised to oppress than the coming forth of Scripture and other divine works in the vulgar tongue, whereof the rude multitude might gather knowledge? Against what thing hath there in these last years until Christ, like fire being hidden under wood, would needs mount up and appear abroad maugre° the head of the Romish Pharoah and all his tyranny; against what thing, I say, hath there been either more sorer thunderbolts shot – of depraving, of accursing, of slandering, of defacing, of condemning, and of burning – than against books of Scripture matters translated or written in the

[1] Edward Seymour (1506–52), Duke of Somerset, was Lord Protector of England during Edward's minority between Henry's death in 1547 and his indictment in October 1549.

mother language and against the authors of the same? Until the Bible and other good treatises for the explanation of the same were in Christian regions turned and set forth in the vulgar languages, what kind of idolatry, superstition, popery, error, ignorance, or counterfeit religion did not reign? As long as the candlelight of the Gospel was kept hidden under the bushel, what king, what prince, what country, what people did not the blind popish guides lead, as one that is blindfold may be led, till both fell in the pit?[2] But when and wheresoever it hath pleased God by his special mercy, grace, and providence to show open the light of the Gospel and true doctrine, there hath at once all popish trumpery even of itself vanished away, as a mist is dispersed with the heat of the sun, as smoke is consumed in the air, as dust is blown and scattered abroad with a puff of wind, as the night giveth place to the bright day, and as darkness vanisheth at the clear light of the sun. Contrariwise, where the word of God cannot yet get any entry to take place, nor the books of Holy Scripture obtain to be published to the people, what eye doth not see and what Christian heart doth not lament and bleed to consider in what blindness, superstition, error, unquietness of conscience, and trouble of mind, the silly° people do live?

It is therefore no small benefit that such persons do to a common weal, which are willingly travailers in this kind of writing. For as for new books of trifling vanities and profane arguments we need none, there are daily so many written; but to have such works made common to the public use of the unlearned multitude, as are the principal best, and have been written by noble clerks° of undoubted learning, knowledge, and godliness, therein consisteth such a public benefit as (if I should not now be suspected and deemed to hunt for myself) is in mine estimation worthy public thanks and regard. For (as Erasmus in his third book of apophthegms, as well by a sapient answer of Socrates, as also by two other pretty stories, the one of Leonicenus and the other of William Warham, late Archbishop of Canterbury, doth declare[3]) much more good and a much

[2] See Matthew 5.15, a favourite authority for the benefits of translating the word of God (cf. **14**. 8–11 below), as is the proverb 'If the blind lead the blind they will both fall into the ditch', the subject of a famous contemporary painting by Pieter Bruegel the Elder.

[3] See Erasmus, *Apophthegms*, trans. by Nicolas Udall (1542): 'Socrates beeyyng demaunded for what cause he would not beare some publique office in

greater benefit to a commonweal doth such a one as translateth or composeth any fruitful book or treatise, which by going abroad throughout a whole realm may profit all pastors, curates, students, and all people universally, than any man is able to do by preaching, teaching, or giving instructions to one company alone, or in one place or country and no more, though he should never so rightly, never so diligently, or never so cunningly do the same. Now, besides that such a translator travaileth not to his own private commodity,° but to the behoof and public use of his country; besides that the thing is such as must so throroughly occupy and possess the doer, and must have him so attent° to apply that same exercise only that he may not during that season take in hand any other trade of business whereby to purchase his living; besides that the thing cannot be done without bestowing of long time, great watching, much pains, diligent study, no small charges as well of meat, drink, and books, as also of other necessaries, the labour self[4] is of itself a more painful° and a more tedious thing than for a man to write or prosecute any argument of his own invention. A man hath his own invention ready at his own pleasure without lets° or stops to make such discourse as his argument requireth, but a translator must of force in manner at every other word stay and suspend both his cogitation and his pen to look upon his author, so that he might in equal time make thrice so much as he can be able to translate. But whether of both a man shall apply himself to do, he can in the meanwhile do nothing else; he cannot during the season bestow himself on any other occupation for his living, and his necessities and also charges in the meantime nevertheless do grow as well as other men's. Whereof it cometh to pass that a number of such as would be right willing and diligent to do good in the common weal with this kind of service, yet through default of necessary maintenance, cannot; and certain that hath both living and vacant time enough, for as much as they see the pains of travail so great, the hire nothing at all, and the captiousness of some maligners

governing the comenweale sens that he could singlare good skyll howe to administer the same: answered, that persone to dooe muche better seruice in a cytee whiche dyd make a great noumbre of menne apte & mete to bee rewlers in a comenweale, then hym that could well governe the same in his own person only', STC 10443, fol. 4^{v}, image 25. The stories of Leonicenus, an Italian physician who was the first translator of Galen into Latin, and Warham follow.

[4] the labour self] that same labour.

against the truth so ready to deprave° the diligent labour of studious writers, are for the most part of them better contented (according to the accustomed proverb) to play for naught than to work for naught. And by this means lie almost all good books hidden from the people and all disciplines unknown.

b) To the gentle Christian reader.

For a paraphrase is a plain setting forth of a text or sentence more at large, with such circumstance of more and other words as may make the sentence° open, clear, plain, and familiar, which otherwise should perchance seem bare, unfruitful, hard, strange, rough, obscure, and dark to be understood of any that were either unlearned or but meanly entered.°[1] And what is this but a kind of exposition, yea, and that of the most pithy and effectual sort? [. . .]

And where the said Erasmus, far otherwise than a great number of the scholastical sort and other unlettered expositors of these last blind seasons, hath written these his paraphrases in as ornate a style as he hath the most part of his other volumes, is not (as some barbarous blunderers have for safeguard and defence of their own poor honesties alleged) a thing unseeming for books of Holy Scripture matters. For divinity, like as it loveth no cloaking, but loveth to be simple and plain, so doth it not refuse eloquence if the same come without injury or violation of the truth. For who writeth more ornately than the Greek divines: Basil, Gregory Nazianzanus, Theophilactus, Chrysostom? Or who in Latin more elegantly than Lactantius, Jerome, and divers others? Albeit in this English paraphrase the translators have of purpose

[1] paraphrase] The first citation in OED. Erasmus wrote in the preface to the Paraphrase on the Gospel of Matthew, also translated by Udall: ‘the writers penne is kept shut within the enclosure of an excedyng streyght grate, because it is debarred from that libertie, which all other sortes of commentaries doe suffer and receive (for a paraphrase also is reputed as a kynde of commentarie)’. Erasmus also says that whereas in writing a commentary the author is at liberty to admit that he does not understand a particular place in the text, ‘one that maketh a paraphrase hath not the lyke liberie or power’, STC 2854.5, sig. Cii^{r}, image 18. Francis Marbury distinguishes translation from paraphrase at **14**. 21 below, and see also Ascham at **50**. below.

studied rather to write a plain style than to use their elegancy of speech, partly because there cannot in all points be expressed in the English tongue the grace that is in the Latin, much less (of myself I speak) the pleasantness that is in the style of Erasmus, a man of most excellent learning and exquisite eloquence in this kind (though indeed not altogether a Ciceronian, but yet feat,° pleasant, sweet, elegant, and sensible), and partly because there was a special regard to be had to the rude and unlettered people, who perchance through default of attaining to the high style should also thereby have been defrauded of the profit and fruit of understanding the sense, which thing that they might do was the only purpose why it was first translated, and now by the King's most excellent Majesty willed to be read. For as for the learned, [they] are able enough to help themselves without any translations at all.

Neither are these translations to be depraved,° because some reader would perhaps otherwise have turned some things than he shall here read it. For no two interpreters there be that in translating out of any one tongue into another would agree in all points of style or inditing,° as (best for this purpose) it may appear by the ancient Fathers of the Church, whose allegations of places of Holy Scripture most commonly vary in words and agree not but in sense. And the same interpreter that would have translated some part hereof better than it now is would in some other points perchance have done it worse. Therefore every man gently° take and interpret another's labours and bear with his infirmity, if not in consideration of his study and travail, yet at least wise for respect of his good zeal and godly intent to further knowledge. If it come to the hands of such as can and will, without disdain or arrogancy, take his pen and emend anything that his good and uncorrupt judgement shall see meet to be corrected, I suppose that besides the reward of God and the public thanks of his country, he shall also privately deserve and receive immortal thanks of the translators, whose desire is to have it well. Neither do I suppose any to be of such mind that he would disdain or be grieved to see his thing bettered, as in this great work some things are indeed here and there otherwise penned than the first translators wrote it. For this is a common work of building, to the which are hired many sundry men of occupation; and in case some man be making a door, a window, or a frame, though another of the same occupation put his hand to the bettering or perfecting of it, yet is not the so doing any displeasure, nor cause of grutch° to the other, but rather a beautifying of his doing and a cause of rendering thanks to the party that of good will and zeal, without presumption, did put his helping hand to a good purpose. And semblably,° in this common work of the Gospels' vineyard (forasmuch as every labourer hath his eye directed to the only mark of setting forth the glory of God and His most holy word), no man meaneth any rebuke or derogation to his fellow when he emendeth something that was to be reformed or altered, but rather seemeth to crave the like help of the other again in his own doings, because it is evident that any man can further see, and can be a more indifferent judge in another man's doings than he can be in his own. Giving therefore first laud, praise, and thanks to God for all his gifts, and then to our most excellent king, Edward VI, for so gracious accepting, favouring, and maintaining honest and godly studies, let every man employ his good talents that God hath given him to the public use of serving and profiting his country, and to the common edifying each of other in Jesus Christ Our Lord.

8. Thomas Norton, *The Institution of Christian Religion by Calvin* (1562)

[Thomas Norton (1530/2–84) was educated at Michaelhouse, Cambridge and the Inner Temple. By 1550 he had become tutor to the children of Edward Seymour, Duke of Somerset (after he had lost the position of Protector) and in *c.* 1556 he married Margaret Cranmer, daughter of the martyred Archbishop. His early translation work included the preparation of the index for the *Paraphrases* of Erasmus (see **7**. above). As an original writer he is best known for *Gorboduc*, co-authored with Thomas Sackville, the first English blank verse tragedy. As a parliamentarian and lawyer he was active in the persecution of Catholics: he petitioned Elizabeth for the execution of Thomas Howard, fourth Duke of Norfolk and Mary, Queen of Scots, and was involved in the trial of Edmund Campion, organising the disputations in which William Fulke took part (see **10**. below, headnote).

Jean Calvin (1509–64), French Protestant reformer, was the most important Protestant theologian of the sixteenth century after Luther and a key influence on the early Protestant Church in England. His *Christianae religionis institutio*, first published at Basel in 1536 and completely revised towards the end of his life, was his seminal work. He produced his own translation of the work into French and supervised further translations as the Latin text of his work was revised and expanded. Based in Geneva from 1541, he preached some two thousand sermons there (also in French) and provided shelter for English and Scottish exiles during the reign of Mary. His theology is principally associated with the doctrines of predestination and justification by faith alone, but he also emphasised the centrality of Scripture for our knowledge of God.

John Dawes, a schoolmaster and translator of Heinrich Bullinger's sermons, had originally been commissioned to translate the *Institutes* (as they are generally known). However, his work was rejected, and the printer, Edward Whitchurch (Norton's stepfather), asked Norton to undertake it instead. The source text for the translation is *Institutio Christianae religionis* (Geneva: Robert Estienne, 1559), the fifth and final edition of Calvin's work. The preface to the reader did not appear until the second edition.

See Francis Higman, 'Calvin's Works in Translation', in *Calvinism in Europe, 1540–1620*, ed. by Andrew Pettegree, Alistair Duke and Gillian Lewis (Cambridge: Cambridge University Press, 1994), pp. 82–99; John Craig, 'Forming a Protestant Consciousness? Erasmus's *Paraphrases* in English Parishes, 1547–1666' in *Holy Scripture Speaks: The Production and Reception of Erasmus's Paraphrases on the New Testament*, ed. by Hilmor M. Pabel and Mark Vessey (Toronto: University of Toronto Press, 2002), pp. 313–58; Marie Axton in *ODNB*]

The translator to the readers.

At the first edition of this book I considered how the author thereof had of long time purposely laboured to write the same most exactly, and to pack great plenty of matter in small room of words; yea, and those so circumspectly and precisely ordered to avoid the cavillations of such as, for enmity to the truth therein conceived, would gladly seek and abuse all advantages which might be found by any oversight in penning of it, that the sentences were thereby become so full as nothing might well be added without idle superfluity, and again so nighly pared[1] that nothing could be minished° without taking away some necessary substance of matter therein expressed. This manner of writing, beside the peculiar terms of arts and figures,[2] and the difficulty of the matters themselves being throughout interlaced with the schoolmen's controversies,[3] made a great hardness in the author's own book in that tongue wherein otherwise he is both plentiful and easy, insomuch that it sufficeth not to read him once unless you can be content to read in vain.

This consideration encumbered me with great doubtfulness for the whole order and frame of my translation. If I should follow the words, I saw that of necessity the hardness in the translation must needs be greater than was in the tongue wherein it was originally written. If I should leave the course of words, and grant myself liberty after the natural manner of mine own tongue to say that in English which I conceived to be his meaning in Latin, I plainly perceived how hardly I might escape error; and on the other side, in this matter of faith and religion how perilous it was to err. For I durst not presume to warrant myself to have his meaning without his words, for they that wot° what it is to translate well and faithfully, specially in matters of religion, do know that not the only grammatical construction of words sufficeth, but the very building and order, to observe all advantages of vehemence or grace by placing or accent[4] of words, maketh much to the true setting forth of a writer's mind. In the end, I rested upon this determination, to follow the words so near as the phrase of the English tongue would suffer me. Which purpose I so performed that if the English book were printed in such paper and letter as the Latin is, it should not exceed the Latin in quantity. Whereby, beside all other commodities° that a faithful translation of so good a work may bring, this one benefit is moreover provided for such as are desirous to attain some knowledge of the Latin tongue (which is at this time to be wished in many of those men for whose profession this book most fitly

[1] nighly pared] closely reduced.

[2] arts and figures] technical vocabulary and expressions.

[3] Norton refers to Calvin's engagement with scholastic theology. This was concerned with the logical analysis of definitions and distinctions, which was the cause of much academic controversy.

[4] accent] emphasis; predates the first citation as a noun in the OED.

serveth) that they shall not find any more English than shall suffice to construe the Latin withal, except in such few places where the great difference in the phrases of the languages enforced me: so that, comparing the one with the other, they shall both profit in good matter and furnish themselves with understanding of that speech wherein the greatest treasures of knowledge are disclosed.

In the doing hereof, I did not only trust mine own wit or ability, but examined my whole doing from sentence to sentence throughout the whole book, with conference and overlooking of such learned men as my translation being allowed by their judgement,[5] I did both satisfy mine own conscience that I had done truly, and their approving of it might be a good warrant to the reader that nothing should herein be delivered him but sound, unmingled,° and uncorrupted doctrine, even in such sort as the author himself had first framed it. Beside all this, I privately required many and generally all men with whom I ever had any talk of this matter, that if they found anything either not truly translated or not plainly Englished, they would inform me thereof, promising either to satisfy them or to amend it. Since which time I have not been advertised by any man of anything which they would require to be altered. Neither had I myself, by reason of my profession being otherwise occupied, any leisure to peruse it. And that is the cause why at this time you have no change at all in the work, but altogether as it was before.

Indeed, I perceived many men, well-minded and studious of this book, to require a table° for their ease and furtherance. Their honest desire I have fulfilled and have added hereunto a plentiful table, which I have translated out of the Latin, wherein the principal matters discoursed in this book are named by their due titles in order of alphabet, and under every title is set forth a brief sum of the whole doctrine taught in this book concerning the matter belonging to that title or commonplace.[6] And therewith is added the book, chapter, and section or division of the chapter, where

[5] The translation was checked sentence by sentence by David Whitehed.

[6] commonplace] Topic or subject heading. Although usually associated with humanist rhetoric and the classical literary tradition, Protestant commonplace collections such as Pietro Martire (Peter Martyr) Vermigli's *Loci communes* (1576; English translation 1583) were published in sixteenth-century England. Norton's first published translation, *An Epistle unto the Duke of Somerset* (1550) was taken from a work by Vermigli.

the same doctrine is more largely expressed and proved. And for the readier finding thereof, I have caused the number of chapters to be set upon every leaf in the book and quoted the sections also by their due numbers with the usual figures of algorism.° Moreover, whereas in the last edition the evil manner of my scribbling hand, the interlining of my copy, and some other causes well known among workmen of that faculty, made very many faults to pass the printer, I have in this impression caused the book to be composed by the printed copy and corrected by the written; whereby it must needs be that this is much more truly done than the other was, as I myself do know above three hundred faults amended. Thus, on the printer's behalf and mine, your ease and commodity, good readers, is provided for; now resteth your own diligence for your own profit in studying it.

To spend many words in commending the work itself were needless. Yet thus much I think I may both not untruly and not vainly say, that though many great learned men have written books of commonplaces of our religion, as Melanchthon, Sarcerius,[7] and others, whose works are very good and profitable to the Church of God, yet by the consenting judgement of those that understand the same, there is none to be compared to this work of Calvin, both for his substantial sufficiency of doctrine, the sound declaration of truth in articles of our religion, the large and learned confirmation of the same, and the most deep and strong confutation of all old and new heresies, so that (the Holy Scriptures excepted) this is one of the most profitable books for all students of Christian divinity. Wherein, good readers, as I am glad for the glory of God, and for your benefit, that you may have this profit of my travail, so I beseech you let me have this use of your gentleness° that my doings may be construed to such good end as I have meant them, and that if anything mislike you by reason of hardness, or any other cause that may seem to be my default, you will not forthwith condemn the work, but read it oftener; in which doing you shall find (as many have confessed to me they have found by experience) that those things which at

[7] Philipp Melanchthon (1497–1560) was an important German reformer and Christian humanist, a correspondent of both Luther and Calvin. He was the author of an influential commonplace collection, *Loci communes* (1521) and a widely used Greek grammar; Erasmus Sarcerius (1511–89), German Lutheran, whose own *Loci communes* were translated by Richard Taverner for Cromwell in 1538.

the first reading shall displease you for hardness shall be found so easy as so hard matter would suffer, and for the most part more easy than some other phrase which should with greater looseness and smoother sliding away deceive your understanding. I confess indeed it is not finely and pleasantly written, nor carrieth with it such delightful grace of speech as some great wise men have bestowed upon some foolisher things, yet it containeth sound truth set forth with faithful plainness, without wrong done to the author's meaning; and so if you accept and use it, you shall not fail to have great profit thereby, and I shall think my labour very well employed.

9. Gregory Martin, *A Discovery of the Manifold Corruptions of the Scriptures* (1582)

[Gregory Martin (1542?–1582) was a Scholar and subsequently Fellow and Lecturer in Greek at St John's College, Oxford, where he formed a life-long friendship with Edmund Campion. A committed Catholic, he resigned his Fellowship in 1568 for religious reasons and became tutor to the son of Thomas Howard, Duke of Norfolk. After the Duke's arrest in 1569 he fled to the recently founded English College at Douai where he was joined by Campion. Ordained a priest in 1573, Martin later spent eighteenth months teaching English seminarians in Rome before returning to the college in 1578, when it transferred to Rheims. In this year he published *A Treatise of Schism*, which addressed the problems facing Catholics in England, and began work on an English translation of the Bible, which he completed by 1580.

A Discoverie of the Manifold Corruptions of the Holy Scriptures by the Heretickes of our Daies was the product of Martin's work on the Catholic English Bible. In it he aims to expose the various ways in which Protestants have used translation to misrepresent and pervert the meaning of Holy Scripture. He reported to Campion that the work was nearly complete in 1579. The translation of the New Testament itself was published in 1582 at Rheims, while for financial reasons the Old Testament did not appear until 1609–10.

See Westcott, *History of the English Bible*; Greenslade, *Cambridge History of the Bible, Vol. 3*; Norton, *History of the Bible as Literature*; Douglas Robinson, ed., *Western Translation*

Theory from Herodotus to Nietzsche (Manchester: St Jerome, 1997); Alexandra Walsham, 'Unclasping the Book? Post-Reformation English Catholicism and the Vernacular Bible', *Journal of British Studies*, 42 (2003), 141–66; Andrew Taylor in *OHLTE* (2), 121–40; Thomas M. McCoog in *ODNB*.]

The Preface containing Five Sundry Abuses or Corruptions of Holy Scriptures, common to all heretics and agreeing specially to these of our time; with many other necessary advertisements to the reader.[1]

As it hath been always the fashion of heretics to pretend° Scriptures for show of their cause, so hath it been also their custom and property to abuse the said Scriptures many ways in favour of their errors.

1. One way is to deny whole books thereof, or parts of books, when they are evidently against them. So did (for example) Ebion all St Paul's Epistles, Manicheus the Acts of the Apostles, Alogiani St John's Gospel, Marcion many pieces of St Luke's Gospel, and so did both these and other heretics in other books, denying and allowing what they list, as is evident by St Irenaeus, St Epiphanius, St Augustine, and all antiquity.

2. Another way is to call into question at the least and make some doubt of the authority of certain books of Holy Scriptures, thereby to diminish their credit. So did Manicheus affirm of the whole New Testament that it was not written by the Apostles; and peculiarly of St Matthew's Gospel that it was some other man's under his name, and therefore not of such credit but that it might in some part be refuted. So did Marcion[2] and the Arians

[1] The debate between Martin and Fulke (nos **9–12**) relies upon voluminous citation of authorities from both parties and it is beyond the scope of the present edition to gloss all of these. I have identified what seem to me to be the most significant citations. I have also used the footnotes to expand and translate those references given by Martin or Fulke either in the body of text or the margin, identifying the former as either GM or WF. Biblical citations and translations of brief phrases of Latin and Greek are given in the text [Ed.].

[2] Marcion of Sinope, near Pontus (*c*. 85–160), proposed a NT canon consisting of only eleven books: a version of Luke and the epistles of St Paul.

deny the Epistle to the Hebrews to be St Paul's, and Alogiani the Apocalypse to be St John's the Evangelist.[3]

3. Another way is to expound the Scriptures after their own private conceit° and fantasy,° not according to the approved sense of the holy ancient Fathers and Catholic Church. So did Theodorus Mopsuestites[4] affirm of all the books of the Prophets and of the Psalms that they spoke not evidently of Christ, but that the ancient Fathers did voluntarily draw those sayings unto Christ which were spoken of other matters. So did all heretics that would seem to ground their heresies upon Scriptures and to avouch them by Scriptures expounded according to their own sense and imagination.

4. Another way is to alter the very original text of the Holy Scripture by adding, taking away, or changing it here and there for their purpose. So did the Arians in sundry places, and the Nestorians in the first Epistle of St John, and especially Marcion, who was therefore called *Mus Ponticus*, the mouse of Pontus, because he had gnawen (as it were) certain places with his corruptions, whereof some are said to remain in the Greek text until this day.[5]

5. Another way is to make false translations of the Scriptures for the maintenance of error and heresy. So did the Arians (as St Jerome noteth in Isaiah 26) read and translate Proverb 8, *Dominus creavit me in initio viarum suarum*, that is, 'The Lord created me in the beginning of his ways', so to make Christ, the wisdom of God, a mere creature. St Augustine also[6] noteth it as the interpretation of some Pelagian (Genesis 3): *Fecerunt sibi vestimenta* for *perizomata* or *campestria*, that is, 'They made

---

[3] See Epiphanius, *Panarion* (a compilation of some eighty early heresies), 2.69; Eusebius, *Ecclesiastical History* 4.27; Epiphanius and Augustine on the heresies of the Alogiani [GM].

[4] Act. Synod 5 [GM].

[5] **Marg**. Tertullian, *Against Marcion*, 51.1; 51.5. [Tertullian (*c*. 160–*c*. 220) was the earliest major Christian theologian writing in Latin. His treatise against Marcion was one of a series of polemics against heresy. Martin wants to establish the point that his source text, the Vulgate, is more accurate than the Greek original.]

[6] Augustine, *Against Julian*, 5.2 [GM].

themselves garments', whereas the word of the Scripture is 'breeches' or 'aprons', proper and peculiar to cover the secret parts.[7] Again the selfsame heretics did read falsely Romans 5: *Regnavit mors ab Adam usque ad Moysen etiam in eos qui peccaverunt in similitudinem praevaricationis Adamae;*[8] that is, 'Death reigned from Adam to Moses, even on them that sinned after the similitude of the prevarication of Adam', to maintain their heresy against original sin that none were infected therewith, or subject to death and damnation, but by sinning actually, as Adam did. Thus did the old heretics.

6. What these of our days? Is it credible that being so well warned by the condemnation and detestation of them, they also would be as mad and impious as those? Heretics, gentle reader, be always like heretics, and howsoever they differ in opinions or names, yet in this point they agree, to abuse the Scriptures for their purpose by all means possible. I will but touch four points of the five before mentioned, because my purpose is to stay upon the last only and to decipher their corrupt translations. But if I would stand upon the other also, were it not easy to show the manner of their proceeding against the Scriptures to have been thus: to deny some whole books and parts of books; to call other some into question; to expound the rest at their pleasure; to pick quarrels to the very original and canonical text; to fester and infect the whole body of the Bible with cankered translations? [. . .]

16. The fourth point is of picking quarrels to the very original text, for alter and change it I hope they shall not be able in this watchful world of most vigilant Catholics. But what they would do if all Bibles were only in their hands and at their commandment, guess by this: that Beza,[9] against the evidence of all copies both Greek and Latin (in his *Annotations upon the New Testament* set forth in the year 1556) thinketh *pōrōsis* [turning

[7] secret parts] the genitalia; predates the first citation in the OED (1577).

[8] **Marg.** Augustine, Epistle 89 and *On the Earning and Remission of Sins*, 1.ii.

[9] Beza] Théodore de Bèze (1519–1605), French Protestant and follower of Calvin who settled in Geneva. He published a Latin translation of the NT with annotations in 1556. In 1565 he brought out a Greek NT with his own translation and the Vulgate in parallel columns, modelled on Erasmus's *Novum Instrumentum*, with expanded annotations. It was the annotations that were especially controversial.

into stone] is more than should be in the text (Matthew 10); and *to ekeuomenon* [the pouring out] (Luke 21); and *proskunein autois* [to prostrate themselves] (Acts 7). The first, against Peter's supremacy; the second, against the real presence of Christ's blood in the B[lessed] Sacrament; the third, against the making of whatsoever images, whether they be adored or no. Thus you see how the mouse of Geneva (as I told you before of Marcion, the mouse of Pontus) nibbleth and gnaweth about it, though he cannot bite it off altogether.

17. He doth the like in sundry places, which you may see in his *Annotations*, Acts 7. 16, where he is saucy° against all copies, Greek and Latin, to pronounce corruption, 'corruption', avouching and endeavouring to prove that it must be so, and that with these words, to what purpose should the Holy Ghost, or Luke, add this (Acts 8. 20)? But because those places concern no controversy, I say no more but that he biteth at the text, and would change it according to his imagination if he might; which is too proud an enterprise for Beza, and small reverence of the Holy Scriptures so to call the very text into controversy, that whatsoever pleaseth not him crept out of the margent into the text, which is his common and almost his only conjecture.

18. He biteth sore at the word *anatōlē* [sunrise] (Luke 1.78), and will not translate that, but the Hebrew word of the Old Testament; but at *ōdinas* (Acts 2.24) much more; and at *hebdomēkonta pente* [seventy-five] (Acts 7.14) exceedingly. But yet after he hath said all that he could against it, he concludeth that 'he durst not, and that he had a conscience, upon conjecture to change anything'. And therefore all this is gnawing only.[10] But in the third of Luke he maketh no conscience at all to leave out these words (verse 36), *qui fuit Cainan* [who was from Cainan], not only in his own translation, but in the vulgar Latin which is joined therewith, saying in his *Annotations*, *non dubitavimus expungere*, that is, 'we doubted not to put it out'. And why? 'By the authority of Moses' (Genesis 11), whereby he signifieth that it is not in the Hebrew where this posterity of Shem is reckoned. And so to maintain the Hebrew verity, as they call it, in the Old

[10] **Marg.** Beza reconcileth the Greek text of the New Testament with the Hebrew text of the Old by putting out of the Greek text so much as pleaseth him.

Testament, he careth not what become of the Greek in the New Testament, which yet at other times, against the vulgar Latin text, they call the Greek verity, and the pure fountain, and that text whereby all translations must be tried.

19. But if he have no other way to reconcile both Testaments but by striking out in the Greek of the New all that agreeth not with the Hebrew of the Old Testament, then let him alter and change so many words of our Saviour himself, of the Evangelists, and of the Apostles, as are cited out of the Old Testament and are not in Hebrew, which places they know are very many, and when need is, they shall be gathered to their hands. Let him strike out (Matthew 13.14–15; Acts 28.26–27) the words of our Saviour and St Paul cited out of Isaiah (Isaiah 6.9–10), because they are far otherwise in the Hebrew. Strike out of the Epistle to the Galatians these words, 'upon a tree' (Galatians 3.13), because in the Hebrew it is only thus: 'cursed is he that is hanged' (Deuteronomy 11), in fine.[11] Yea, strike out of David's Psalms that which concerneth our redemption upon the cross much nearer, 'they have pierced my hands and my feet' (Psalm 21), because in Hebrew there is no such thing. Let them control the Apostle for saying, *dedit*, 'he gave gifts' (Ephesians 4), because it is both in the Hebrew and Greek, *accepisti*, 'thou tookest gifts' (Psalm 67); and for *corpus aptasti* [you have prepared a body] (Hebrews 10), let them put *aures perforasti* [you have opened my ears], because it is so in the Hebrew (Psalm 40). To be short, if all must be reformed according to the Hebrew, why doth he not in St Stephen's sermon cut off the number of five souls from seventy-five, because it is not in the Hebrew?

20. Must such difficulties and diversities be resolved by chopping and changing, hacking and hewing the sacred text of Holy Scripture? See into what perplexities wilful heresy and arrogancy hath driven them: to discredit the vulgar Latin translation of the Bible, and the Fathers' expositions according to the same (for that is the original cause of this), and besides that, they may have always this evasion, 'It is not so in the Hebrew, it is otherwise in the Greek', and so seem jolly fellows and great clerks unto the ignorant people. What do they? They admit only the Hebrew in

[11] in fine] in the end; in short.

the Old Testament, and the Greek in the New, to be the true and authentical text of the Scripture. Whereupon this followeth, that they reject, and must needs reject, the Greek of the Old Testament (called the Septuagint) as false, because it differeth from the Hebrew.[12] Which being rejected, thereupon it followeth again, that wheresoever those places so disagreeing from the Hebrew are cited by Christ or the Evangelists and Apostles, there also they must be rejected, because they disagree from the Hebrew; and so yet again it followeth that the Greek text of the New Testament is not true, because it is not according to the Hebrew verity, and consequently the words of our Saviour and writings of his Apostles must be reformed (to say the least), because they speak according to the Septuagint and not according to the Hebrew.[13]

21. All which must needs follow, if this be a good consequence: 'I find it not in Moses, nor in the Hebrew, therefore I struck it out', as Beza doth and sayeth concerning the foresaid words, *qui fuit Cainan*. This consequence, therefore, let us see how they will justify, and withal let them tell us whether they will discredit the New Testament because of the Septuagint, or credit the Septuagint because of the New Testament; or how they can credit one and discredit the other, where both agree and consent together; or whether they will discredit both for credit of the Hebrew; or rather, whether there be not some other way to reconcile both Hebrew and Greek, better than Beza's impudent presumption, which if they will not maintain, let them flatly confess that he did wickedly, and not (as they do) defend every word and deed of their masters, be it never so heinous, or salve it at the least.

22. Alas! How far are these men from the modesty of the ancient Fathers, and from the humble spirit of obedient Catholics, who seek all other means to resolve difficulties rather than to do violence to the sacred Scripture, and when they find no way, they

[12] **Marg**. Their perplexity in defending both the Hebrew text of the Old Testament and Greek text of the New.

[13] Quotations from the OT in the Vulgate NT were given in the Greek of the Septuagint. Martin's point is that since the Protestant Bibles always prefer the Hebrew text to the Septuagint translation, they have to alter the very words of Christ in order to apply this choice consistently.

leave it to God. St Augustine, concerning the difference of the Hebrew and the Greek, sayeth often to this effect, that it pleased the Holy Ghost to utter by the one that which he would not utter by the other.[14] And St Ambrose thus: 'We have found many things not idly added of the seventy Greek interpreters.'[15] St Jerome, though an earnest patron of the Hebrew (not without cause, being at that time perhaps the Hebrew verity indeed) yet giveth many reasons for the differences of the Septuagint; and concerning the foresaid places of St Luke, he doth give a reason thereof, both for the Seventy, and for the Evangelist that followed them, neither doubting of the truth thereof, nor controlling them 'by the authority of Moses' (as Beza speaketh), that is, by the Hebrew.[16] Others say concerning Cainan, that Moses might leave him out in the genealogy of Shem by the instinct of the same spirit that St Matthew left out three kings in the genealogy of our Saviour (Matthew 1), where if a man would control the Evangelist by the Hebrew of the Old Testament that is read in the books of the Kings, he should be as wise and as honest a man as Beza. Lastly, Venerable Bede thinketh it sufficient in this very difficulty of Cainan to marvel at it reverently rather than to search it dangerously.[17] And thus far of picking quarrels to the original text, and their good will to alter and change it as they list, if they might be suffered.

23. Which also may be proved by all their false translations (being the principal point I mean to speak of) most evidently. For as now they translate falsely to their purpose, because they cannot alter the text, so would they, if it were possible, have the text agreeable to their translation. For example, he that translateth 'ordinances', when it is in the original Greek text 'justifications' and 'traditions',[18] he would rather that it were 'ordinances' also in the Greek; but because he cannot bring that about, he

---

[14] **Marg**. Augustine, *The City of God*, 18. 43; *On Christian Doctrine*, 2. 15 [GM].
[15] **Marg**. Ambrose, *On the Six Days of Creation*, 3. 5 [GM].
[16] **Marg**. Jerome, preface to the Paralipomena [the Greek name for the books of Chronicles, retained in the Vulgate]; commentary on Isaiah 28 [GM].
[17] **Marg**. Bede, preface to Acts [GM].
[18] At Colossians 2.8 Tyndale has 'the tradicions of men & ordinaunces after the worlde and not after Christ' (New Testament, revised 1534), STC 2826, fol. ccxci^{v}, image 312; but it is not clear what Martin is referring to here. Cf. ll. 286–96 below.

doth at the least what he can, to make the ignorant believe it is so, by so translating it.

24. And this of all other is the most fine and subtle treachery against the Scriptures, to deceive the ignorant readers withal (which St Paul calleth 'the secret things of dishonesty and adulterating of the word of God' (2 Corinthians 4), as it were mingling water with wine, like false vintners), when they give them for God's word, and under the name of God's word, their own words, and not God's, forged and framed, altered and changed, according to differences of times, and variety of new opinions, and diversity of humours and spirits, diversely and differently, one heretic not only correcting his fellow every day, but one eagerly refuting and refelling° another. Bucer[19] and the Osiandrians and Sacramentaries against Luther, for false translations; Luther against Münster, Beza against Castalio,[20] Castalio against Beza, Calvin against Servetus, Illyricus both against Calvin and Beza. The Puritans control° the grosser Calvinists of our country; yea, the later translations of the selfsame heretics control the former exceedingly, not only of oversights but of wilful falsifications, as it is notorious in the later editions of Luther and Beza, and in our English Bibles set forth in diverse years, from Tyndale, their first translator, until this day; yea, which is more, the English translators of Beza's New Testament control him and his translation, which they protest to follow, being afraid sometimes and ashamed to express in English his false translations in the Latin.[21]

25. But in this catalogue of dissentions, falsifiers, and disagreeing translators, I will not greatly rip up° old faults neither abroad nor at home. I leave Luther's false translations into the German

[19] Martin Bucer (1491–1559), German reformer who hoped to unite Protestants and Catholics and who also attempted to mediate between Luther and Zwingli. He was exiled to England in 1549 where he enjoyed the patronage of Archbishop Thomas Cranmer and helped to influence the second edition of the Book of Common Prayer (1552).

[20] Sebastian Castalio, or Châteillon (1515–63), French preacher and theologian, who produced the freest and most literary Latin translation of the Bible in the early modern period (1551) with Cicero as his model.

[21] An English translation of Beza's New Testament was published by Laurence Tomson in 1576; it was incorporated into the Geneva text of 1587.

tongue to the credit of Staphylus and Emserus,[22] and other German writers of his own time, that saw them and read them and reckoned the number of them in the New Testament only about 1400 heretical corruptions.[23] I leave Calvin's and Beza's French corruptions to so many worthy men as have noted them in their French books against the said heretics;[24] Tyndale's and his companions corruptions in their first English Bible to our learned countrymen of that age, and namely to the right reverend father and confessor Bishop Tunstall, who in a sermon openly protested that he had found in the New Testament only, no less than two thousand. If we know it not, or will not believe it, strangers in their Latin writings testify it to the world.[25]

26. But I omit these as unknown to our country, or to this age, and will deal principally with the English translations of our time, which are in every man's hands within our country. [. . .]

48. In the New Testament, we ask them, will you be tried by the ancient Latin translation, which is the text of the Fathers and the whole Church? 'No, but we appeal to the Greek'. What Greek, say we, for there be sundry copies, and the best of them (as Beza confesseth) agree with the said ancient Latin, for example in St Peter's words: 'Labour that by good works you may make sure your vocation and election' (2 Peter 1). Doth this Greek copy please you? 'No', say they, 'we appeal to that Greek copy which hath not those words, "by good works", for otherwise we should grant the merit and efficacy of good works towards salvation; and generally to tell you at once by what Greek we will be tried, we like best the vulgar Greek text of the New Testament, which is most common and in every man's hands.

49. Well, say we, if you will needs have it so, take your pleasure in choosing your text, and if you will stand to it, grant us that Peter was chief among the Apostles, because your own Greek text sayeth, 'the first, Peter' (Matthew 10). 'No', sayeth Beza, 'we will

---

[22] **Marg.** Staphylus, *Apology*, part 2; Esmerus, preface to the *Annotations* on Luther's New Testament.

[23] **Marg.** William Lindanus, *Dubitantius*, pp. 84–5.

[24] **Marg.** Vigor and the rest.

[25] **Marg.** Lindanus, *Dubitantius*, p. 98. On Tunstall see **2**. n. 1 above.

grant you no such thing, for these words were added to the Greek text by one that favoured Peter's primacy'. Is it so? Then you will not stand to this Greek text neither. 'Not in this place', sayeth Beza.

50. Let us see another place. You must grant us, say we, by this Greek text, that Christ's very blood which was shed for us is really in the chalice, because St Luke sayeth so in the Greek text. 'No', sayeth Beza, 'those Greek words came out of the margent into the text, and therefore I translate not according to them, but according to that which I think the truer Greek text, although I find it in no copies in the world'. And this his doing[26] is maintained and justified by our English Protestants in their writings of late.

51. Well yet, say we, there are places in the same Greek text as plain for us as these now cited, where you cannot say it came out of the margent, or it was added falsely to the text: as 'stand and hold fast the traditions' etc. (2 Thessalonians 2). By this text we require that you grant us traditions delivered by word of mouth, as well as the written word, that is, the Scriptures. 'No', say they, 'we know the Greek word signifieth "tradition" as plainly as possible, but here and in the like places we rather translate it "ordinances", "instructions", and what else soever'. Nay sirs, say we, you cannot so answer the matter, for in other places you translate it duly and truly, 'tradition', and why more in one place than in another? They are ashamed to tell why, but they must tell, and shame both themselves and the devil, if ever they think it good to answer this treatise, as also why they changed 'congregation', which was always in their first translation, into 'Church' in their later translations, and did not change likewise 'ordinances' into 'traditions', 'elders' into 'priests'.

52. The cause is that the name of 'Church' was at first odious unto them because of the Catholic Church which stood against them, but afterward this name grew more in favour with them because of their English Church, so at length called and termed. But their hatred of priests and traditions continueth still, as it first

[26] **Marg**. See chapter 1, number 37; chapter 17, number 11. [The reference is to Beza's Latin New Testament (1556).]

began, and therefore their translation also remaineth as before, suppressing the names both of the one and of the other.

10. William Fulke, *A Defence of the Translations of the Holy Scriptures* (1583)

[William Fulke (1536/7–1589) was a graduate of St John's College, Cambridge and wrote two early scientific books attacking astrology and meteorology before returning to St John's as a Fellow in 1564. As part of a radical Puritan faction he was involved in confrontation and controversy from early in his career and this helped to prime him for his assault on Martin and the Catholic English Bible in the 1580s. With the patronage of the Earl of Leicester he became Master of Pembroke College, Cambridge, in 1578, serving as Vice-Chancellor of the university from 1581–82, and he succeeded Bishop John Jewel as the principal defender of the theology of the Church of England against Catholic attacks. With official encouragement he published rebuttals of some twenty-one Catholic controversial works, but his most important writing is undoubtedly that of the debate with Martin on the theory of Bible translation.

A Defence of the Translations of the Holy Scriptures might be seen as an extension into print of the public disputations Fulke had held with Catholic prisoners. The most famous of these was with Martin's friend Edmund Campion in the Tower before his execution in 1581. Fulke responds to Martin's *Discovery* paragraph by paragraph and in doing so reprints his text in its entirety.

See William Fulke, *A Defence of the Sincere and True Translations of the Holy Scriptures into the English Tongue*, ed. by C. H. Hartshorne (Cambridge: Cambridge University Press, 1843); Richard Bauckham in *ODNB*; and headnote **9**.]

MARTIN: The Preface containing five sundry abuses or corruptions of Holy Scriptures, common to all heretics, and agreeing specially to these of our time, with many other necessary advertisements to the reader.

As it hath been always the fashion of heretics to pretend Scriptures for show of their cause, so hath it been also their custom and property to abuse the said Scriptures many ways in favour of their errors.[1]

FULKE: Whether these five abuses have been common to all heretics, and whether it hath been the fashion of all heretics to pretend Scriptures for show of their cause, though I will spare now to enquire of, as a thing wherein learned men at the first sight may espy the great skill that Martin pretendeth to have in discerning of heretics and heresies, yet will I show (by the grace of God) that none of these five abuses are committed by us or our catholic[2] translations, and that the popish heretics are, in some sort or other, guilty of them all.

1.[3] First, we deny no one book of the canonical Scripture that hath been so received of the Catholic Church for the space of 300 years and more, as it hath been often proved out of Eusebius, St Jerome, and other ancient authorities, but the papists, in advancing apocryphal books to be of equal credit with the canonical Scriptures, do in effect deny them all. Besides that, to add unto the word of God is as great a fault as to take away from it, the one being forbidden under as heavy a curse as the other. Those blasphemies of Pighius and Eccius, the one calling the Holy Scripture a nose of wax and a dumb judge, the other terming the Gospel written to be a black gospel and an inky divinity, and that of Hosius, acknowledging none other express word of God, but only this one word, *ama*, or *dilige*, 'love thou' — what other thing do they import, but a shameless denial of all books of the Holy Scripture indeed, howsoever in word they will seem to admit them?[4] [. . .]

4.[5] The original text of the Holy Scripture we alter not, either by adding, taking away, or changing of any letter or syllable for any

[1] Subsequent passages from Martin in Fulke's work are not reproduced here but cited by line references to the text of this edition.
[2] catholic] orthodox, belonging to the true faith, as distinct from 'Roman Catholic'.
[3] See **9**. 9–15 above. Fulke reprints Martin's work section by section but it seemed proper to preserve its independence in this edition [Ed.].
[4] Pighius, *Assertion of Church Hierarchy* (1538), 3.3. fol. 80; Eck, *Apologia for Catholic Principles* (1542), fol. 74; Hosius, *On the Express Word of God*, 1.628 [WF].
[5] See **9**. 35–42 above.

private purpose, which were not only a thing most wicked and sacrilegious, but also vain and impossible. For seeing not only so many ancient copies of the original text are extant in divers places of the world,[6] which we cannot, if we would, corrupt, and that the same are multiplied by printing into so many thousand examples, we should be rather mad than foolish if we did but once attempt such a matter for maintenance of any of our opinions. As also it is incredible that Marcion, the mouse of Pontus, could corrupt all the Greek copies in the world (as Lindanus, of whom you borrowed that conceit, imagineth) in those places in which he is charged by Tertullian. For Marcion's heresy was not so generally received by the Greek Church that all men would yield unto him; neither was Tertullian so sound of judgement in the Latin Church that whatsoever he judged to be a corruption in Marcion must of necessity be so taken. But if adding and detracting from the Scripture be proper notes of heretics, who can purge Stephen Gardiner and Gregory Martin?[7] The one for adding unto a verse of the Psalm this pronoun *se*, 'himself', to prove the carnal presence, citing it thus, *Escam se dedit timentibus eum*, 'He gave himself to be meat to them that fear him', whereas the words of the Prophet, according to the Hebrew, Greek, and Latin, are no more but *Escam dedit*, 'He hath given meat' etc. The other, in his fond book of schism, citing this text out of 1 Corinthians 10, as many papists do against the certainty of faith, *Qui stat, videat ne cadat*, 'He that standeth, let him take heed he fall not', whereas not only the truth of the Greek, but even the vulgar Latin translation hath *Qui se existimat stare*, 'He that thinketh or supposeth that he standeth, let him take heed that he fall not'. But of such additions and detractions used by the Romish rats, far worse than the mice of Pontus, we shall have more occasion to speak hereafter.

---

[6] The number of manuscripts of the Greek New Testament available to scholars at the time of the Reformation was actually quite small; many more are now known.

[7] Stephen Gardiner (1495/8–1555), Catholic Bishop of Winchester, imprisoned during Edward VI's reign, who became Lord Chancellor under Mary. See *A Detection of the Devil's Sophistrie* (1546), fol. 69 b., on Psalm 111.4–5; Martin, *Treatise of Schism* [WF].

5.[8] As touching false and heretical translations, which is the chief argument of this book, I doubt not but, by the grace of God, to clear our English translators from any wilful corruptions for the maintenance of any error or heresy, such as were those of the Arians and Pelagians,[9] which Gregory Martin, as though he uttered some great piece of skill, doth so diligently express. I shall have occasion also to show that the papists themselves of our times, maintaining their corrupt vulgar translation against the truth of the original texts of Greek and Hebrew, are most guilty of such corruption and falsification, whereof although they be not the first authors, yet by obstinate defending of such errors, they may prove worse than they which did first commit them. For the authors of that vulgar translation might be deceived, either for lack of exact knowledge of the tongues, or by some corrupt and untrue copies which they followed, or else perhaps that which they had rightly translated, by fault of the writers and negligence of the times might be perverted. But these men frowardly° justifying all errors of that translation, howsoever they have been brought in, do give plain testimony that they are not led with any conscience of God's truth, but wilfully carried with purpose of maintaining their own errors, lest, if they did acknowledge the error of the Romish church in that one point, they should not be able to defend any one iota of their heresy, whose chief colour is the credit and authority of that particular and false Church, rather than any reason or argument out of the Holy Scriptures or testimony of the most ancient Christian and catholic Church. [. . .]

18.[10] But you say that Beza, to maintain the Hebrew verity of the Old Testament, careth not what become of the Greek in the New Testament. You should have made your antitheton° more full (wherein it seemeth you pleased yourself not a little) if you had said that Beza, to maintain the Hebrew verity of the Old Testament, careth not what becometh of the Greek corruption in the New Testament, and so you should have spoken both more eloquently and more truly. But at other times, you say, against

[8] See **9**. 43–60 above.
[9] those of the Arians and Pelagians] The Arians denied the Trinity by defining Christ as an inferior being to God. The Pelagians denied original sin.
[10] See **9**. 118–22 above.

the vulgar Latin text, they call the Greek text the Greek verity, and the pure fountain, and that whereby all translations must be tried. We say indeed that by the Greek text of the New Testament all translations of the New Testament must be tried, but we mean not by every corruption that is in any Greek copy of the New Testament, and much less that the Hebrew text of the Old Testament should be reformed after the Greek of the New where it is uncorrupted, and least of all where any copy is guilty of a manifest error as in this place now in question. [. . .]

20.[11] Who alloweth or who can abide chopping and changing, or hacking and hewing, the sacred text of Holy Scriptures? As for the perplexities, whereunto you feign that wilful heresy and arrogancy hath driven us, is of your weaving; for (God be praised!) we can well enough with good conscience and sound knowledge, that may abide the judgement of all the learned in the world, defend both the Hebrew text of the Old Testament and the Greek text of the New, not of purpose to discredit the vulgar Latin translation and the expositions of the Fathers, but to fetch the truth, upon which the hope of our salvation is grounded, out of the first fountains and springs rather than out of any streams that are derived from them; and this we do agreeable to the ancient Fathers' judgements. For who knows not what fruitful pains St Jerome took in translating the Scripture out of the original tongue? Neither would he be dissuaded by St Augustine, who although he misliked that enterprise at the first, yet afterward he highly commended the necessity of the Greek and Hebrew tongues for Latin men, to find out the certain truth of the text in the infinite variety of the Latin interpretations; for thus he writeth: *contra ignota signa propria magnum remedium est linguarum cognitio. Et Latinae*, etc.:

> Against unknown proper signs the knowledge of tongues is a great remedy. And truly, men of the Latin tongue, whom we have now taken in hand to instruct, have need also of two other tongues unto the knowledge of the divine Scriptures, namely the Hebrew and the Greek, that recourse may be had unto the former copies if the infinite variety of the Latin interpreters shall bring any doubt, although we find oftentimes in the

[11] See **9**. 147–71 above.

books Hebrew words not interpreted, as *Amen, Alleluia, Racha, Osanna*,etc.

and a little after, *sed non propter haec pauca*, etc. :

But not for these few words, which to mark and inquire of it is a very easy thing, but for the diversities, as it is said, of the interpreters, the knowledge of those tongues is necessary. For they that have interpreted the Scriptures out of the Hebrew tongue into the Greek tongue may be numbered, but the Latin interpreters by no means can be numbered. For in the first times of the faith, as a Greek book came into every man's hand, and he seemed to have some skill in both the tongues, he was bold to interpret it. Which thing truly hath more helped the understanding than hindered, if the readers be not negligent, for the looking upon many books hath oftentimes made manifest sundry obscure or dark sentences.[12]

This is St Augustine's sound judgement of the knowledge of tongues and diversity of interpretations for the better understanding of the Scriptures. But let us see what be the absurdities that you gather of our defending the original texts of both the tongues. First, we must needs reject the Greek of the Old Testament, called Septuagint, as false, because it differeth from the Hebrew. Where it is not only different in words, but also contrary in sense, why should we not? But if it retain the sense and substance, although it express not the same words, we need not reject it. St Jerome, who was required by Paula and Eustochium to expound the Prophets not only according to the truth of the Hebrew, but also after the translation of the Septuagint, whereof he divers times complaineth, upon the 1st of Nahum sayeth expressly that it was against his conscience always to follow the same: *Ignoscite prolixitati*, etc.:

Pardon me that I am so long, for I cannot, following both the story and the tropology[13] or doctrine of manners, comprehend both briefly; most of all, seeing that I am so greatly tormented or troubled with the variety of the translation, and against my

[12] Augustine, *On Christian Doctrine*, II. 11, 12 [WF].

[13] tropology] Here, a secondary sense of the Scripture relating to morals; in other contexts it can refer to figurative discourse.

> conscience sometimes I am compelled to frame a consequence of the vulgar edition[14]

– which was the Septuagint. This was St Jerome's opinion of the Septuagint translation.

But upon rejection of that translation, say you, it followeth that wheresoever those places so disagreeing from the Hebrew are cited by Christ, or the Evangelists and Apostles, there also they must be rejected because they disagree from the Hebrew; and so the Greek text of the New Testament is not true, and consequently the words of our Saviour and writings of his Apostles, speaking according to the Septuagint, must at least be reformed. It is an old saying, and a true, that one inconvenience being granted, many do follow, and so you may heap up a hundred after this manner. But for answer I say that neither our Saviour, nor his Apostles, citing any place out of the Old Testament, do bring anything disagreeing in sense and substance of matter (the purpose for which they allege it considered) from the truth of the Hebrew text. Therefore there is no need that the Seventy[15] in those places should be rejected – although our Saviour Christ, speaking in the Syrian tongue,[16] is not to be thought ever to have cited the text of the Seventy, which is in Greek, and his Apostles and Evangelists, using that text, regard the substance of the sentence and not the form of words. For many times they cite not the very words of the Greek Seventy neither; and St Jerome, [in] *In Catalogo scriptorum Ecclesiasticorum* [Towards a Catalogue of Ecclesiastical Writings], which is set as a preface to St Matthew's Gospel, telleth you expressly that in the Hebrew example of St Matthew, which he had, wheresoever the evangelist St Matthew, either in his own person or in the person of Our Lord and Saviour, useth the testimonies of the Old Testament, he followeth not the authority of the seventy translators, but the Hebrew, of which these are two places: 'out of Egypt have I called my son',

---

[14] the vulgar edition] Jerome, commentary on Nahum 1. Although Fulke understands 'vulgar edition' to refer to the Septuagint, Jerome may be referring to the old Latin Bible, the *Vetus Latina*.

[15] the Seventy] i.e. the seventy translators of the Septuagint.

[16] The Syrian tongue] Aramaic, which includes Syriac was the common language of the Jewish people and is therefore thought to be the language of Jesus Christ.

and 'he shall be called a Nazarite'.[17] See you not what a perilous perplexity we are in by defending both the Hebrew text of the Old Testament and the Greek of the New, when neither are contrary to the other?

21.[18] No whit of that doth follow by striking out *qui fuit Cainan*, because it is not found in Moses; and therefore we have nothing to do to justify your vain consequence, grounded upon an absurdity of your own devising. But we must tell you whether we will discredit the New Testament because of the Septuagint? No, not for a thousand millions of Septuagints, nor for all the world will we credit the Septuagint against the truth of the Old Testament. But whatsoever is cited out of the Seventy in the New is not contrary to the Hebrew in the Old; and therefore the way of reconciliation is easily found without discrediting both, or either of both, in those places. And in this place, which is a mere corruption, borrowed out of the corruption of the Septuagint, or a Judaical addition (Genesis 11), I think there is no better way of reconciling than to strike it clean out, as Beza hath done; which generation neither is in the Hebrew verity nor in your own vulgar Latin translation (either Genesis 11 or 1 Paralipomena[19] 1). Beside that, it maketh a foul error in the computation of time, adding no less than 230 years between Arpachshad and Shelah, more than the Hebrew verity or the vulgar Latin agreeing therewith doth number, and therefore he was more presumptuous that out of the corrupt and false text of the Septuagint added the same unto the genealogy in St Luke than Beza, which by the authority of Moses removed the same. If you will still persist to defend the authority of the Septuagint against the Hebrew verity, which like an atheist you deride, at leastwise defend your own vulgar Latin translation of the Old Testament, and deliver yourself out of that perplexity in which you would place us between the Hebrew of the Old and the Greek of the New Testament, seeing no less doubts entangleth you between the Latin of the New and the Latin of the Old, differing altogether alike as the Greek and the Hebrew do. [. . .]

---

[17] See Matthew 2.23 and Jerome, 'Letter to Pammachius', *Principal Works of St Jerome*, ed. by Schaff and Wace, vol. VI, p. 115; cf. **3**. 135 above.

[18] See **9**. 172–87 above.

[19] Paralipomena] Chronicles

23.[20] You shall never be able to prove by any translation of ours, though perhaps in some we may err, that we have any purpose either to falsify the truth or to change the text, though it were possible for us. In translating we have dealt with a good conscience, albeit not always peradventure we have attained to the full truth, which in translating out of one tongue into another is a very hard point thoroughly to observe. Your example of 'ordinances' translated for that which in the Greek is 'justifications' and 'traditions', when you show where and by whom it is so translated, you shall receive an answer. In the meantime, I say, a translator that hath regard to interpret for the ignorant people's instruction may sometimes depart from the etymology or common signification or precise turning of word for word, and that for diverse causes. You yourselves translate not *ecclesia* always 'the Church', but sometimes 'the assembly'; nor *seniores*, 'elders', but 'seniors' or 'ancients'. Neither would you translate *presbyter* always 'a priest' if you translated the Old Testament. In the story of Susannah you would not call them priests that laid wait for her honesty and life, yet in your vulgar Latin they are called priests. So are they called *presbuteroi* in Greek in the New Testament, which you turn sometimes 'priests', sometimes 'ancients', and sometimes 'seniors'.[21]

24.[22] By false translations wilfully and of purpose to falsify the truth of God's word is as gross and as abominable treachery as to corrupt the very text, although I think St Paul, speaking of the covertures or cloaks of dishonesty, and adultering of the word of God (2 Corinthians 4), meaneth a further cunning than false translations. That those whom you call heretics find fault with one another's translations, they do none otherwise than you popish heretics. Do not you, Gregory Martin, in the 7th chapter and 33rd section of this book, find fault with all the Catholics, as you term them, that translate *sheol, sepulchrum*, 'a sepulchre', and not always 'hell'? If Bucer or Zwingli do justly observe any

[20] See **9**. 215–24 above.

[21] e.g. Martin's annotation to 1 Peter 5.1: 'because we follow the vulgar Latin translation, we say *Seniors* or *Senior*: whereas otherwise we might and should say according to the Greek, *The Priests* [. . .] so translateth Erasmus, and Beza himself', New Testament, STC 2898, p. 665, image 354. This is a particular complaint of More's against Tyndale's translation, see **3**. 46–70 above.

[22] See **9**. 225–48 above.

error in Luther, or Luther in Münster, or Beza in Castalio the Anabaptist, or Calvin in Servetus the horrible heretic, yea, and if froward and schismatical Illyricus can discover any error committed by Calvin and Beza, the truth loseth nothing when the errors of men are found out by what means soever. That you speak of the Puritans controlling the grosser Calvinists of our country, I know not what you mean, neither do I think you can justify your words for translation of the Scriptures. Where you say the later translations of the selfsame heretics control the former exceedingly, not only of oversights, but of wilful falsifications, it is a wilful and impudent slander; yet you blush not to say it is notorious. How, I pray you? You answer: in the later editions of Luther and Beza, and in our English Bibles set forth in diverse years, from Tyndale, their first translator. That Luther, Beza, and the later translators of the English Bibles have corrected some small faults that have escaped in their former editions, it may be granted. But do Luther and Beza therefore accuse themselves, or the later English translators the former, of wilful falsifications? I think those brute beasts, to whom Ambrose ascribeth the art of making syllogisms,[23] if they could speak, would not conclude thus brutishly. Certain it is that Balaam's ass did reason substantially. But much more, you say, the English translators of Beza's New Testament do control him and his translation, being sometimes afraid and ashamed to express his false translations. If it be so, they are more modest than you, which seem to be afraid or ashamed of nothing so much as lest you might seem to fail in unshamefastness.° But to the purpose: if they think Beza, as all men may err, hath somewhat trodden awry, is it a fault to avoid his step, or a proud controlling or accusing him of falsification? Nevertheless, whereinsoever Luther, Beza, or the English translators have reformed any of their former oversights, the matter is not so great that it can make a heresy. Yea, if you were of St Augustine's judgement, you would acknowledge that the multitude and diversity of translations is for the benefit of them that be ignorant in the tongues, yea, and of them also that be learned in them oftentimes, that of diverse men's translations they may judge which is the aptest. [. . .][24]

---

[23] Ambrose, On the Six Days of Creation, 6.4 [WF].

[24] Augustine, *On Christian Doctrine*, II.11 [WF].

35. In the margent: 'You will not charge us with forsaking the old approved Latin text, though it be an ill sign and to our evident confusion.' St Augustine, though a mere Latin man, whom you yourself do after confess to have understood but one tongue well, and that was even his mother tongue, learned (as he confesseth) of his nurses, is not so addicted to the Latin translation but that he would have men to seek to the Hebrew and Greek fountains,[25] which you like a blasphemous hypocrite deny to be the true and authentical Scriptures indeed, allowing only the vulgar Latin translation, as though neither the Churches of Greece, Syria, Armenia, Ethiopia, nor any other in the world which have not the vulgar Latin, had not the true and authentical Scriptures. And though your vulgar Latin hath for many years been of great authority in the Latin Church, from the time when the knowledge of the Hebrew and Greek tongues have decayed, yet it is utterly false that you say that it hath been of great authority with all the Fathers of the Latin Church; whereas there is not one that lived within 400 years after Christ that knew it, but almost every one followed a several translation. And St Augustine, in the place before cited, telleth you that there were innumerable translations out of the Greek into the Latin. Again, that your vulgar Latin is full of many errors and corruptions I have showed by the confession of Isidorus Clarius and Lindanus, two of your own profession; of which the one took pains by the Hebrew and Greek to correct it, the other showed means how it should be corrected.[26] And where you say that Luther and his followers forsook it for none other cause in the world but that it is against them, it is utterly untrue. For beside that they have made clear demonstration of many palpable errors therein, which they that have any forehead° amongst you cannot deny, they

[25] Augustine accepted that Latin translations of the Bible should be emended on the authority of the Septuagint and that the Greek New Testament should have precedence over the Latin where the variety of Latin translations is confusing; see *De Doctrina Christiana*, II.53–56, ed. and trans. by R. P. H. Green (Oxford: Clarendon Press, 1995), pp. 81–83.

[26] Isidore Clarius (1495–1555) produced a new edition of the Vulgate and played a major role in the Council of Trent where the Vulgate was declared sacred and canonical in the first decree of April 1546. Although his text was accepted, his commentary was condemned. William Lindanus (1525–88) wrote *On the Best Way of Interpreting the Scriptures* (1558) and Fulke later attributes to him the view that the Vulgate translator was an incompetent Latinist.

have and do daily convince you of horrible heresies, even out of your own corrupt, vulgar translation. Finally, whosoever shall read what Calvin and Kemnitius have written against the Council of Trent for authorising that translation,[27] shall plainly see that they had something else to allege against it, which nothing at all concerneth their opinions that be contrary to the popish heresy [. . .]

22. If this English word 'priest'[28] by custom of speech did signify no more than the Greek word *presbuteros*, we would no less use it in our translations than 'Bishops' and 'deacons', which offices, though they be shamefully abused by the papists, yet the abuse of the words maketh no confusion between the ministers of the Law and of the Gospel as this word 'priest' doth, by which the Jewish sacrificers are rather understood than the preachers of the Gospel and ministers of the sacraments. But whereas the etymology of this English word 'priest' cometh from *presbyter*, you charge us with great folly and malice that for *sacerdos* we translate 'priest' and for *presbyter*, 'elder'.[29] To this I answer, we are not lords of the common speech of men, for if we were we would teach them to use their terms more properly, but seeing we cannot change the use of speech, we follow Aristotle's council, which is to speak and use words as the common people useth, but to understand and conceive of things according to the nature and true property of them;[30] although for my part I like well of the French translation, which for *hiereis* or *sacerdotes* always translateth *sacrificateurs*, sacrificers, and for *presbyteri*, where they signify the ministers of the word and sacraments, *prêtres*, 'priests'. But this diversity being only of words and not of matter

[27] The Council of Trent was convened in order to arrive at a definitive statement of Catholic doctrines in response to the new Protestant theology and met from 1545 to 1563. Calvin responded to the decrees on the Vulgate in session four of Trent in his Antidote to the Council of Trent, November 1547.

[28] See Martin, *Discovery*, STC 17503, sigs Ci^{v}–Cii^{r}, images 60–61.

[29] See also Thomas More, **3**. 53–68 above.

[30] Aristotle's council [. . .] property of them] Aristotle, *Topica*, II, 21. A popular maxim, cf. Tilley, W 530; quoted by Roger Ascham: 'He that wyll wryte well in any tongue, muste folowe thys councel of Aristotle, to speake as the common people do, to thinke as wise men do', *Toxophilus* (1545), STC 837, sig. a1^{r}, image 5; and by Francis Bacon, 'loquendum ut vulgus, sentiendum ut sapientes', *The Advancement of Learning*, ed. by Michael Kiernan (Oxford: Oxford University Press, 2000), p. 117.

or meaning, reasonable men will take an answer, fools and quarrellers will never acknowledge any satisfaction [. . .]

Chapter 21

MARTIN. We may say unto you as Demosthenes said unto Aeschines *ti tauta; rhēmata ē thaumata*, what are these? words or wonders?' Certainly they are wonders, and very wonderful In Catholic men's ears, and whether it be sincere and not heretical dealing I appeal to the wise and indifferent reader of any sort.[31]

FULKE. For all the terms quarrelled at in this section we have answered before, except perhaps for the term of 'love' which is used instead of 'charity', expressing what charity is in deed and not, as it is commonly taken of the common people, as an attack on charity when they call alms 'charity'. No man that could abide the people to be instructed would cavil at the explication of the word 'charity' by 'love', when in the English tongue the word 'charity' is either not understood or taken for another thing than the Latin word *charitas* doth signify. As for the wonders of words that Demosthenes spake of, I know not where more properly they shall be found than in your affected novelties of terms, such as neither English nor Christian ears ever heard in the English tongue: 'scandal', 'prepuce', 'neophyte', 'depositum', 'gratis', 'parasceve', 'paraclete', 'exaninate', 'repropritiate', and a hundred such like inkhorn° terms. Yea, I would gladly know why, among so many Greekish and Latin-like terms, *gazophylacium* is not 'a gazophilace', but 'a treasury'; *encaenia* 'the dedication' and not 'the encaenes', as well as 'pasce', 'Pentecost', 'azymes', 'parasceve': belike the Church must have treasure, and the feast of dedication must not be hid in a new-found term. Why should *adventus* be sometime 'the coming' and sometimes 'the advent', except it were for the sound of the time of advent, before the feast of the nativity of Christ?

[31] See Martin, *Discovery*, STC 17503, p. 306, image 171. The reference is to Demosthenes, *Oration against Aeschines*. Jerome cites the same speech in the 'Letter to Pammachius', quoting Cicero's prologue to his own translation of Demosthenes (now lost), where he says that he has approached the task not just as a translator, but as an orator (see Schaff and Wace, p. 114). Cf. also Laurence Humphrey **28**. 607–39 below.

Why should Latin words be translated in Greekish terms, as *scissuras* into 'schisms', *aemulatores* 'zelators' and suchlike (Romans 11; Acts 10)? These and such other be wonders of words, that wise men can give no good reason why they should be used.

11. Gregory Martin, *The New Testament Translated Faithfully into English* (1582)

[Martin's *New Testament* was presumably undertaken at the request of William Allen, founder of the English College at Douai. The source text is the Vulgate, so this is a translation of a translation, and it is also extremely literal. However, Martin's Greek language skills enabled him to compare the Vulgate with its Greek originals and this is reflected in the notes and commentary. He was assisted by Allen himself, John Bristow, William Rainolds (brother of the King James Bible translator, John Rainolds), and Thomas Worthington. Bristow was probably the author of the notes, which were designed not merely to explain difficult places but also 'specially for the discoverie of the corruptions of divers late translations, and for clearing the controversies in religion, of these daies' (tp.). The NT notes and the earlier polemical treatise form a single project, but Martin did not live to see his Catholic English Bible in print.]

The Preface to the Reader treating of these three points: of the translation of Holy Scriptures into the vulgar tongues, and namely into English; of the causes why this New Testament is translated according to the ancient vulgar Latin text; and of the manner of translating the same.

The Holy Bible long since translated by us into English, and the Old Testament lying by us for lack of good means to publish the whole in such sort as a work of so great charge and importance requireth, we have yet through God's goodness at length fully finished for thee, most Christian reader, all the New Testament, which is the principal, most profitable, and comfortable piece of Holy Writ, and as well for all other institution of life and doctrine, as specially for deciding the doubts of these days, more proper and pregnant° than the other part not yet printed.

Which translation we do not for all that publish upon erroneous opinion[1] 1) of necessity that the Holy Scriptures should always be in our mother tongue, or 2) that they ought, or were, ordained by God, to be read indifferently[2] of all, or 3) could be easily understood of everyone that readeth or heareth them in a known language, or 4) that they were not often through man's malice or infirmity pernicious and much hurtful to many; or 5) that we generally and absolutely deemed it more convenient in itself, and more agreeable to God's word and honour or edification of the faithful, to have them turned into vulgar tongues than to be kept and studied only in the ecclesiastical learned languages. Not for these nor any such like causes do we translate this sacred book, but upon special consideration of the present time, state, and condition of our country, unto which divers things are either necessary or profitable and medicinable now, that otherwise in the peace of the Church were neither much requisite nor perchance wholly tolerable.

1. In this matter, to mark only the wisdom and moderation of Holy Church and the governors thereof on the one side, and the indiscreet zeal of the popular, and their factious leaders, on the other, is a high point of prudence. These latter, partly of simplicity, partly of curiosity, and specially of pride and disobedience, have made claim in this case for the common people, with plausible pretences many, but good reasons none at all. The other, to whom Christ hath given charge of our souls, the dispensing of God's mysteries and treasures (among which Holy Scripture is no small store) and the feeding his family in season with food fit for every sort (Matthew 24.45; 1 Corinthians 4.1), have neither of old nor of late ever wholly condemned all vulgar versions of Scripture, nor have at any time generally forbidden the faithful to read the same; yet they have not by public authority prescribed, commanded, or authentically ever recommended any such interpretation to be indifferently used of all men.

The Armenians say they have the Psalter and some other pieces translated by St Chrysostom into their language, when he was banished among them; and George the Patriarch in writing his

[1] **Marg**. Translation of Scriptures into the vulgar tongues not absolutely necessary or profitable, but according to the time.

[2] indifferently] indiscriminately, but with the more specific meaning that the Scriptures cannot be converted into different languages without essential loss.

life signifieth no less. The Slavonians affirm they have the Scriptures in their vulgar tongue, turned by St Jerome, and some would gather so much by his own words in his epistle to Sophronius, but the place indeed proveth it not.[3] Ulfilas surely gave the Scriptures to the Goths in their own tongue, and that before he was an Arian. It is almost three hundred years since James, Archbishop of Genoa, is said to have translated the Bible into Italian. More than two hundred years ago, in the days of Charles V, the French king, was it put forth faithfully in French,[4] the sooner to shake out of the deceived people's hands the false, heretical translations of a sect called Waldenses. In our own country, notwithstanding the Latin tongue was ever (to use Venerable Bede's words[5]) common to all the provinces of the same for meditation or study of Scriptures, and no vulgar translation commonly used or occupied of the multitude, yet they were extant in English even before the troubles that Wycliffe and his followers raised in our Church, as appeareth as well by the testimony of Malmesbury recording that Venerable Bede translated divers parts into the vulgar tongue of his time,[6] and by some pieces yet remaining, as by a provincial constitution of Thomas Arundel, Archbishop of Canterbury, in a council held at Oxford, where strait° provision was made that no heretical version set forth by Wycliffe or his adherents should be suffered, nor any other in or after his time be published or permitted to be read, being not approved and allowed by the Diocesan° before,[7] alleging° St Jerome for the difficulty and danger of interpreting the Holy Scripture out of one tongue into another, though by learned and Catholic men.[8] So also it is there insinuated that neither the translations set forth before that heretic's time, nor other afterward being approved by the lawful ordinaries,° were

[3] Jerome, letter 134, to Augustine. [GM]. [Jerome was born in Dalmatia in modern Croatia and his mother tongue would have been 'Slavonian' (Serbo-Croat). Sophronius was his own middle name, not that of a correspondent.]

[4] This probably refers to the *Bible historiale* completed in 1297 (not in the reign of Charles V) by Guyart des Moulins, which remained the principal French Bible for two centuries. It combines portions of the Vulgate with historical commentary.

[5] Bede, *The Ecclesiastical History of the English People* (731), 1.1 [GM].

[6] See William of Malmesbury, preface to *Deeds of the Kings of the English* (1125), which was modelled on Bede.

[7] **Marg**. See Lyndwood, *Provinciale*, Book 5, 'On Magistrates'.

[8] On the Constitutions of Arundel and Jerome see **3**. ns 6 and 10 above.

ever in our country wholly forbidden, though they were not (to say the truth) in quiet and better times, much less when the people were prone to alteration, heresy, or novelty, either hastily admitted or ordinarily read of the vulgar, but used only, or specially, of some devout, religious, and contemplative persons, in reverence, secrecy, and silence, for their spiritual comfort.

Now since Luther's revolt also, divers learned Catholics, for the more speedy abolishing of a number of false and impious translations put forth by sundry sects, and for the better preservation or reclaim of many good souls endangered thereby, have published the Bible in the several languages of almost all the principal provinces of the Latin Church;[9] no other books in the world being so pernicious as heretical translations of the Scriptures, poisoning the people under colour of divine authority, and not many other remedies being more sovereign against the same, if it be used in order, discretion, and humility, than the true, faithful, and sincere interpretation opposed thereunto.

2. Which causeth the Holy Church not to forbid utterly any Catholic translation, though she allow not the publishing or reading of any absolutely and without exception or limitation, knowing by her divine and most sincere wisdom how, where, when, and to whom these her Master's and Spouse's gifts are to be bestowed to the most good of the faithful; and therefore neither generally permitteth that which must needs do hurt to the unworthy, nor absolutely condemneth that which may do much good to the worthy. Whereupon, the order which many a wise man wished for before was taken by the Deputies of the late, famous Council of Trent[10] in this behalf and confirmed by supreme authority that the Holy Scriptures, though truly and catholicly translated into vulgar tongues, yet may not be indifferently read of all men, nor of any other than such as have express licence thereunto of their lawful ordinaries, with good testimony from their curates or confessors that they be humble, discreet, and devout persons and like to take much good and no harm

---

[9] The first Catholic vernacular Bibles published in response to Protestant translations were the German Bibles of Johann Dietenberger (1534) and John Eck (1537). Flemish (Vinck) and French (de Leuze and Larben) Bibles were printed at Louvain in 1548 and 1550, and a Polish Bible (Leopolita) at Cracow in 1561.

[10] **Marg.** Index of Prohibited Books, regulation 4 [GM]. [The first Index was published in 1557 and reissued in 1559. The Council of Trent authorised a less draconian version, published in 1564 and known as the Tridentine Index.]

thereby. Which prescript, though in these days of ours it cannot be so precisely observed as in other times and places, where there is more due respect of the Church's authority, rule, and discipline, yet we trust all wise and godly persons will use the matter in the meanwhile with such moderation, meekness, and subjection of heart as the handling of so sacred a book, the sincere senses of God's truth therein, and the holy canons, counsels, reason, and religion do require.

Wherein, though for due preservation of this divine work from abuse and profanation, and for the better bridling of the intolerable insolency of proud, curious, and contentious wits, the governors of the Church, guided by God's spirit as ever before, so also upon more experience of the malady of this time than before have taken more exact order both for the readers and translators in these later ages than of old. Yet we must not imagine that in the primitive Church[11] either everyone that understood the learned tongues wherein the Scriptures were written, or other languages into which they were translated, might without reprehension read, reason, dispute, turn, and toss the Scriptures; or that our forefathers suffered every schoolmaster, scholar, or grammarian that had a little Greek or Latin straight to take in hand the Holy Testament; or that the translated Bibles into the vulgar tongues were in the hands of every husbandman, artificer, prentice, boys, girls, mistress, maid, man; that they were sung, played, alleged° of every tinker, taverner, rhymer, minstrel; that they were for table talk, for ale-benches, for boats and barges, and for every profane person and company. No, in those better times men were neither so ill, nor so curious of themselves so to abuse the blessed book of Christ; neither was there any such easy means before printing was invented to disperse the copies into the hands of every man as now there is.

They were then in libraries, monasteries, colleges, churches, in Bishops', priests', and some other devout principal laymen's houses and hands,[12] who used them with fear and reverence and specially such parts as pertained to good life and manners; not meddling but in pulpit and schools (and that moderately too) with the hard and high mysteries and places of greater difficulty.

[11] **Marg.** The Holy Scriptures never read of all persons indifferently at their pleasure.

[12] **Marg.** Where and in whose hands the Scriptures were in the primitive Church.

The poor ploughman could then in labouring the ground sing the hymns and Psalms either in known or unknown languages, as they heard them in the Holy Church, though they could neither read nor know the sense, meaning, and mysteries of the same. [. . .]

4. [. . .] But the case now is more lamentable,[13] for the Protestants and such as St Paul calleth *ambulantes in astutia*, 'walking in deceitfulness' (2 Corinthians 4.2), have so abused the people and many others in the world, not unwise, that by their false translations they have instead of God's law and testament, and for Christ's written will and word, given them their own wicked writing and fantasies,° most shamefully in all their versions, Latin, English, and other tongues, corrupting both the letter and sense by false translation, adding, detracting, altering, transposing, pointing, and all other guileful means; specially where it serveth for the advantage of their private opinions, for which they are bold also, partly to disauthorise quite, partly to make doubtful, divers whole books allowed for canonical Scripture by the universal Church of God this thousand years and upward; to alter all the authentical and ecclesiastical words used since our Christianity into new, profane novelties of speeches agreeable to their doctrine; to change the titles of works, to put out the names of the authors,[14] to charge the very Evangelist with following untrue translation, to add whole sentences proper to their sect into their Psalms in metre, even into the very Creed in rhyme[15] – all which the poor, deceived people say and sing as though they were God's own word, being indeed through such sacrilegious treachery made the Devil's word.[16]

---

[13] **Marg.** The Scriptures have been falsely and heretically translated into the vulgar tongues, and sundry other ways sacrilegiously abused, and so given to the people to read.

[14] **Marg.** Beza, Annotations on Luke 1.78.

[15] **Marg.** See the tenth article of their creed in metre. [Archbishop Matthew Parker had published a version of the Psalms in English 'rhythme' in *The Whole Psalter* (1567), citing Ambrose and Bede in his support, STC 2729, sig. B1^{v}, image 6. Luther had produced a rhyming version of the Creed.]

[16] **Marg.** All this their dealing is noted (as occasion serveth) in the annotations upon this Testament, and more at large in a book lately made purposely of that matter, called *A Discovery* etc. [ie. **9**. above].

To say nothing of their intolerable liberty and licence to change the accustomed callings° of God, angel, men, places, and things used by the Apostles and all antiquity, in Greek, Latin, and all other languages of Christian nations, into new names, sometimes falsely and always ridiculously, and for ostentation taken of the Hebrews to frame and fine° the phrases of Holy Scriptures after the form of profane writers, sticking not for the same to supply, add, alter, or diminish as freely as if they translated Livy, Virgil, or Terence;[17] having no religious respect to keep either the majesty or sincere simplicity of that venerable style of Christ's spirit, as St Augustine speaketh, which kind the Holy Ghost did choose of infinite wisdom to have the divine mysteries rather uttered in, than any other more delicate,° much less in that meretricious[18] manner of writing that sundry of these new translators do use. [. . .]

This we profess only, that we have done our endeavour with prayer, much fear and trembling, lest we should dangerously err in so sacred, high, and divine a work; that we have done it with all faith, diligence, and sincerity; that we have used no partiality for the disadvantage of our adversaries, nor no more license than is sufferable in translating of Holy Scriptures, continually keeping ourselves as near as is possible to our text and to the very words and phrases which by long use are made venerable, though to some more profane or delicate ears they may seem more hard or barbarous,[19] as the whole style of Scripture doth lightly to such at the beginning acknowledging with St Jerome that in other writings it is enough to give in translation sense for sense, but that in Scriptures, lest we miss the sense we must keep the very words.[20] We must, sayeth St Augustine, speak according to a set rule, lest license of words breed some wicked opinion concerning the things contained under the words.[21] Whereof our holy forefathers and ancient Doctors had such a religious care that they would not change the very barbarisms and incongruities of

[17] Martin (following Jerome) defends his own practice by arguing that the word of God must be translated literally, not freely or sense for sense in the way that classical literature might be translated.

[18] meretricious] Predates the first citation in OED (Francis Bacon, *New Atlantis*, 1626) where the term refers to the embraces of a prostitute.

[19] **Marg**. Augustine, *Confessions*, Book 3, chapter 5.

[20] **Marg**. See Jerome, 'Letter to Pammachius'.

[21] **Marg**. Augustine, *On the City of God*, Book 10, chapter 5.

speech which by long use had prevailed in the old readings or recitings of Scriptures [. . .]

In this our translation, because we wish it to be most sincere, as becometh a Catholic translation, and have endeavoured so to make it, we are very precise and religious in following our copy, the old vulgar approved Latin,[22] not only in sense, which we hope we always do, but sometime in the very words also and phrases, which may seem to the vulgar reader and to common English ears not yet acquainted therewith, rudeness or ignorance; but to the discreet reader that deeply weigheth and considereth importance of sacred words and speeches, and how easily the voluntary translator may miss the true sense of the Holy Ghost, we doubt not but our consideration and doing therein shall seem reasonable and necessary. Yea, and that all sorts of Catholic readers will in short time think that familiar which at the first may seem strange, and will esteem it more when they shall be taught to understand it,[23] than if it were the common known English.

12. William Fulke, *The New Testament, with a Confutation of Manifest Impiety* (1589)

[Fulke's *New Testament* aimed to provide a comprehensive refutation of Martin's work, including its all-important annotations. The text of the Rheims NT is presented in parallel with that of the Bishops' Bible of 1568. In order to complete this massive project Fulke worked with two assistants for nine months in 1587–88 while lodging at the London home of his publisher, Christopher Barker. The topicality of the work is underlined by the fact that its completion coincided with the defeat of the Great Armada, Philip of Spain's attempt to return England to the Catholic faith.]

---

[22] The Vulgate had only been 'approved', i.e. decreed to be authoritative, at the Council of Trent in 1546.

[23] **Marg.** See the last Table at the end of the book [STC 2884, sigs Eeeeeii^{r}-Eeeeeii^{v}, images 425–26, 'The Explication of Certain Wordes in this Translation, not familiar to the vulgar reader'. Some words from Rheims were adopted in the KJB, such as 'communicate' in the sense of 'distribute'; see Norton, *King James Bible* (2011), pp. 29–32.]

The Confutation of this Preface

1.[1] If the whole Bible had been translated by you, and that long since, into the English tongue, it is [a] marvel that it hath lain so long by you for lack of good means to publish it.[2] You have published books of as great charge and much less importance within these twenty-eight years, but such, indeed, by which you had more hope to win unto your credit and cause than you have by the Holy Bible, though you perverted it with never so partial translation and poisoned it with never so heretical and blasphemous annotations, as you have done your edition of the New Testament. You were wont to boast of the zeal of Popes, cardinals, and other great prelates of the Romish sect for the conversion of our nation unto their obedience. Were they also so strait-laced that none of them can find in their purses to bear the charges of printing a work so necessary, or at leastwise profitable, as you hold the translation of the Scriptures to be for the maintenance of the Catholic religion? Or do you not rather, as the Family of Love[3] used to do for their works, craftily beg of your favourers in England larger exhibition° upon colour of printing your translation of the Bible? When it is not hard to gather that you were purposed indeed to set it forth, and would use such means as you may in those parts, the forbearing of the money, though your printer took it upon interest, might be paid for in the sale of one impression, although it so might happen that a number of them were confiscated, or miscarried in the ways, as chanced to some of these your books. But whoso seeth what unnecessary charge you have put yourselves unto in printing this your translation in so large a volume may easily perceive you set

[1] See **11**. 6–14 above. As in his reply to Martin's *Discovery*, Fulke reprints his preface to the New Testament paragraph by paragraph.

[2] lack [. . .] to publish it] Martin attributed the non-appearance of the Catholic English Bible, completed in 1580, to the poor state of the finances of the English College at Douai-Rheims, but the failure to publish may also have been due to perceived scholarly weakness; see Hammond, *Making of the English Bible*, pp. 156–57.

[3] Family of Love] A dissenting religious community founded by 'H. N.' (Hendrik Niclaes) and related to the Anabaptists. The English Familists were the subject of a satirical play, *The Family of Love* (1608) formerly attributed to Thomas Middleton. Fulke claims that they used the pretext of publication costs as a fund-raising strategy and suggests that the exiled Catholics are doing the same.

it not forth for poor men's profit, and that by so excessive price, of so small a part of the whole Bible, you mean to discourage your friends from waiting for all the rest.[4] What advantage you have in this part for deciding the doubts of these days, we shall examine in the several places where you pretend to take it.

2. You are afraid to give over your old impudent proposition that ignorance of the Scriptures is the mother of popish devotion.[5] And therefore you hold it an erroneous opinion that 'the Holy Scriptures should be always in our mother tongue, or that they ought, or were ordained by God, to be read indifferently° of all'. Whereas it is certain that the Holy Scripture of the Old Testament was by God's ordinance first written in the mother tongue of the Jews, and the New Testament in the Greek tongue, which was the mother tongue to a great part of the world and that language which was most generally understood among the Gentiles, unto whom the Gospel was preached (John 5.39).[6] Our Saviour Christ commandeth not only a reading, as you yourselves confess, but also a deep search of the Scriptures unto all the Jews indifferently. St Paul commendeth the education of Timothy in knowledge of the Scriptures from his infancy (2 Timothy 3.15). Which authorities prove that the Holy Scriptures were ordained by God to be read and known indifferently of all, and therefore ought to be translated into the mother tongues of all nations that all may read and know them. Another erroneous opinion you account it to think that 'the Scriptures can be easily understood of everyone that readeth or heareth them in a known language', which if it were admitted, yet it followeth not that the Scriptures ought not to be in a known language, because they cannot be easily understood of everyone that readeth or heareth

[4] The Rheims NT was handsomely printed and expensive, in contrast to the cheap and popular Geneva Bible of 1560.

[5] See **11**. 15–30 above.

[6] Fulke is referring to the *koinē*, which was the common dialect of Greece spoken throughout the Eastern Mediterranean after Alexander, superseding the regional dialects of classical Greek such as Attic and Ionic. This is the language of the Septuagint, the New Testament and some of the early Church Fathers. Its Latin name *communis* indicates its status as the common language of the communities to which the Apostles preached. It was itself superseded by Latin, but Fulke's point is that this is the original 'vulgar' language of the early Church, not the Latin of the Vulgate.

them, but rather that everyone that readeth or heareth them ought more diligently to study and exercise himself in them, more often hear and read them, and more fervently pray to God for aid of his Spirit that he may understand them. And yet it is certain that albeit some places of the Scripture are not easy to be understood of all men, yet there are many parts of them, and so many as are able to instruct us unto salvation, so plain and easy as they may be understood of everyone that readeth or heareth them. And of this judgement is St Augustine, answering this objection of the obscurity of the Scriptures: *magnificem igitur et salubriter*, etc.:

> Therefore hath the Holy Ghost magnifically and wholesomely so tempered the Holy Scriptures that by plain and open places he might provide against famine; by dark places, he might wipe away loathsomeness. For nothing almost is gathered out of those obscurities which is not found most plainly uttered in some other place.[7]

And in the chapter immediately before, he showeth that by reason of the diversity of languages, the same sound of words not serving all nations, the Scriptures were translated into divers tongues that they might be generally known: *ex quo factum est*, etc.:

> whereof it is come to pass that even the Holy Scriptures, by which so great diseases of men's wits are helped, being proceeded from one tongue, which might conveniently spread over all the world through divers languages of the interpreters, being dispersed far and wide might become known of the nations to their salvation.

By both of which places it is evident that St Augustine deemed it more convenient in itself, and more agreeable to God's word, honour, and edification of the faithful, to have the Scriptures turned into vulgar tongues than to be kept and studied in any learned language whatsoever. Now why you should account any one tongue more than another to be ecclesiastical, you are able to give no sound reason, seeing God hath called His Church of all tongues and nations and sanctified them all to the preaching of the Gospel and the praise of his name. As for the Latin tongue,

[7] Augustine, *On Christian Doctrine* 2.6 [WF].

which you would most willingly have to be counted an ecclesiastical tongue, was for many hundred years after Christ the common vulgar and popular tongue in most part of the West Churches, of those nations that were subject to the Roman Empire. And why it is now ecclesiastical that then was vulgar, I know no cause but that Antichrist, whose tongue it is, blasphemously challenging to be the head of the Church, hath chosen and authorised it to be ecclesiastical in contumely of all other languages, which the Holy Ghost, descending upon the Apostles in cloven tongues hath consecrated to the preaching of Christ Jesus and to the magnifying and setting forth of the great praises of God (Acts 2).[8] That through man's malice or infirmity the Scriptures are often made pernicious and hurtful to many, it is no greater reason to keep them from the knowledge of most men than it were to deprive all men from meat and drink because many do abuse them to the destruction of both their bodies and souls. As for the special consideration that procured this edition, when you do express it, we may better judge of it. In the meantime, we can conceive none other but that which is the practice of many heretics: when you could not altogether suppress the knowledge of the Holy Scriptures whereby your errors are discovered, you thought it the next way for your purpose, by your partial translation, as much as you could, to obscure them, and by your heretical annotations to pervert them, that the one should make them unprofitable, the other also hurtful.

3.[9] The wisdom of the popish synagogue and the governors thereof is the wisdom of the old serpent, and of the children of this world, which are oftentimes wiser in their kind than the children of light, with whom it is a high point of prudence to provide for themselves by what unjust means soever. So have the popish clergy always endeavoured by depriving the common people of the reading of the Holy Scriptures, and following their predecessors, the Jewish lawyers,[10] have taken away the key of

---

[8] i.e. the Church's granting to Latin a unique ecclesiastical status is at odds with the gift of tongues from the Holy Ghost at Pentecost, which enabled the Apostles to preach the word of God to everyone in their own language.

[9] See **11**. 31–46 above.

[10] Jewish lawyers] The 'scribes and Pharisees' that Christ attacks at Luke 11.37–54 as an elite group which has taken away the key of knowledge from the people.

knowledge, of the same policy that they did, lest their wickedness being commonly discovered by the light, they should lose that estimation which through blind ignorance they have commonly obtained (Luke 11. 25, Deuteronomy 4.6, John 5.39, 2 Peter 1.19, 2 Timothy 3.15, Acts 17.11). And they which have made claim for the common people in this case, whom of your charity you call the popular, and their seditious leaders, of godly zeal and true simplicity, not of curiosity, pride, and disobedience, have both made it and justified it with better reasons than all the proud papists in the world are able to avoid. For what greater reasons can be alleged than the authority of God in the Old Testament, and of Christ our Saviour and his Apostles in the New, and the practice of the primitive Church, and the consent of the most ancient and approved Fathers of the same, which have been brought to prove that the Holy Scriptures ought to be known of all Christians?[11] But the governors of the popish, anti-Christian Church, arrogating to themselves the name and dignity of the dispensing of God's mysteries and treasures (among which, the Holy Scripture – as you confess – is no small store), by maintaining that ignorance is the mother of devotion, declare that they would willingly, if they could, abolish all knowledge of the Holy Scriptures from the common people's hearts. And whereas you say that 'of old, they have not ever condemned all vulgar versions of Scripture, nor generally forbidden the faithful to read them', let the registers of Bishops be searched, where it will appear that many have been accused and condemned as heretics for having, reading, or hearing the Holy Scriptures in the English tongue, without any exception taking against the truth of the translation. And that the governors of the popish Church 'have not by public authority prescribed, commanded, or authentically ever recommended any interpretation of Scriptures into the vulgar tongue to be indifferently used of all men', they have declared sufficiently thereby that they were not the ministers of God and Christ, nor successors of his Apostles, nor of the ancient Fathers of the primitive Church, all which, as is noted before, have by public and lawful authority always prescribed, commanded, and authentically recommended, as the Holy Bible and the writings

[11] For the long list of references to the OT, NT, and the Church Fathers providing authority for the dissemination of Scripture in the vernacular see Fulke, *New Testament*, STC 2888, sig. A2^{r}, image 6.

of the Fathers are most plentiful witnesses, the Holy Scriptures of God to be known, read, and understood of all sorts of Christians indifferently, and without exception of any, which of necessity implieth the translation of the same into all vulgar languages, without which it is not possible for all sorts of Christians to read them, know them, and understand them.

4.[12] Seeing the Armenians were converted to the faith long before St Chrysostom came amongst them, it is not to be doubted but they had the whole Scriptures in their vulgar tongue long before his time.[13] And their confession lately set forth doth plainly argue that they have the whole Bible in their own language at this day. To justify that the Slavonians say of St Jerome's translation into their tongue, his own words are these: *translationem diligentissimem emendatam olim mea lingua hominibus dederim*, 'I say not this that I would bite my predecessors, or think that anything is to he detracted from them, whose translation being most diligently corrected, I have given long ago to the men of my language'. Now the Slavonians were the men of Jerome's language or mother tongue, as he testifieth himself of the place of his nativity in *In Catalogo*, for whose use he might translate the vulgar Latin Bible, which was according to the Septuagint's, after he had most diligently corrected it. But if this place prove it not sufficiently, at leastwise he sayeth plainly that the Scripture was translated into the tongues of many nations.[14] Beside these, the Syrians, Arabians, and Ethiopians had of ancient time the Holy Scriptures in their several languages, as it is manifest by those parts of them which are at this day brought from them into this part of the world. The Spaniards have the Old Testament translated of ancient time into their mother tongue.[15] Walafridus testifieth that the Dutch tongue is the same which was the language of the Goths and Getes, into which, since the days of Ulfilas, by whom they were first convened, some wise men of that nation have translated the Holy Scripture.[16] In our

[12] See **11**. 47–85 above.

[13] The Armenians were converted in 300, but the Bible was not translated until a century later, during the period of Chrysostom's exile.

[14] Jerome, letter to Pope Damasus: 'Preface to the Gospels' [WF].

[15] Manuscripts of Old Testament readings by medieval Spanish Jews exist, which they took with them after their expulsion from Spain in 1492.

[16] Walafridus Strabo, *On Ecclesiastical Matters*, 7 [WF].

own country, not only the Saxon translations of divers parts of the Holy Scripture yet remaining – some in print, some in libraries – but even the testimony of Bede, whom you quote and cite most impudently for the contrary, doth prove that vulgar translations of the Holy Scriptures in his time were commonly used and occupied of the faithful multitude. His words are these: *Hac in praesenti iuxta numerum librorum quibus lex divina scripta est, quinque gentium linguis, unam eandemque, summa veritatis et verae sublimitatis scientiam scrutatur et confitetur. Anglorum videlicet, Britonum, Scottorum, Pictorum et Latinorum, quae meditatione scripturarum caeteris omnibus est facta communis*:

> This island (sayeth Bede), at this present, according to the number of the books in which the law of God is written, doth search out and confess one and the self-same knowledge of the highest truth and of the true height in five tongues; namely, of the Angles, of the Britons, of the Scots, of the Picts, and of the Latins, which in meditation of the Scripture is made common to all the rest.[17]

He meaneth that learned men of all the four nations studied the Scriptures by help of the Latin tongue and such commentaries and treatises of the elder Fathers as were written therein. But he sayeth expressly that the knowledge of the highest truth, which is not to be found but in the Holy Scriptures, and according thereunto was both searched out and confessed in the mother tongue of the other four nations, by which he meaneth the Christians unlearned in the Latin tongue. A manifest testimony whereof are many parts of Scripture in the Saxon language yet remaining to be seen and read.[18]

That the Scriptures were extant in English both before and after Wycliffe's time and not of his translation, beside your conjecture out of Lyndwood, it is manifestly proved by so many ancient written copies of the English Bible, differing in translation, yet to be showed, of which Wycliffe's translation could be but one. Notwithstanding that the Pharisaical clergy condemned

---

[17] Bede, *Ecclesiastical History*, 1.15.

[18] See **1**. n. 7 above. There was a a revival of interest in Anglo-Saxon during the sixteenth century as Protestants tried to recover evidence of an early English-speaking Church independent of Rome. One result of this is the great collection of manuscripts made by Archbishop Matthew Parker held by Corpus Christi College, Cambridge.

the reading of them for heresy, let the acts of public writings remaining in the registers testify. And of what devilish policy they kept the laws of God in secrecy and silence, which he commanded to be uttered in all places and times, to the edifying of all sorts of Christians, howsoever you seek to smooth it, God's children do plainly espy it.

5.[19] How pernicious heretical translations of the Scriptures are which poison the people under colour of divine authority. If we had not learned sufficiently by the corruptions of old heretics, this translation of yours doth give plentiful testimony, which being helped forward with heretical annotations, as it were with stings to make way for the poison to enter, hath no small force to deceive the simple. But the best is, we are assured that they shall not prevail finally, but in them whom the Lord acknowledgeth not for his. In the meantime, not only the remedy of true and sincere translation out of the fountain and original text is to be opposed, but also the fraud of the adversary, as occasion serveth, to be discovered and laid open.

6.[20] The popish Church, arrogating to herself divine wisdom in restraining that which God hath left to be most free and general, declares that she is the Babylonical harlot, the spouse of Antichrist, who exalteth himself above all divine authority and controlleth the wisdom of God in everything that is contrary to his devilish presumption: as in the use of images, of the cup in the Lord's Supper, of marriage in the Church ministers, of meats in times made by him more religious, and such other.[21] The true Church of God teacheth the true use of the Scriptures, even out of the Scriptures themselves, and discourageth not men from reading of them, as it were from a dangerous discourse whereby they are like to take harm, knowing that none but spiders can

[19] See **ll**. 86–96 above.

[20] See **ll**. 97–121 above.

[21] The representation of the Pope as the Antichrist and the Roman Church as the Whore of Babylon derives from Protestant readings of Revelation. On the rise of the English apocalyptic tradition through Bale and then Foxe, see Katharine R. Firth, *The Apocalyptic Tradition in Reformation Britain* (Oxford: Oxford University Press, 1979), pp. 32–110. Its most memorable expression in the service of the Church of England is in Spenser, *The Faerie Queene*, Book One, published in 1590, the year after Fulke's *New Testament*.

suck poison out of wholesome flowers, which poison yet is not in the good flowers but in the evil nature of the spider.[22] The Holy Scriptures, learned even from a man's infancy, are able to make him wise unto salvation, and being well studied of the man of God are able to make him perfect and ready unto all good works, and to execute every part of his office (2 Timothy 3.15).

7.[23] That the governors of the popish Church have taken straiter° order for readers and translators of the Scriptures than the Fathers of the primitive Church of Christ did, it is not to preserve the word of God from profanation or to bridle the proud curiosity of the contentious, as it is pretended, but to suppress the light of truth, which displayeth their gross and palpable abuses both in doctrine and conversation.

But where you say that the Holy Scriptures were never read of all persons indifferently, it is a most impudent assertion, set down without any show of proof and contrary to most manifest arguments of antiquity. We acknowledge the Fathers of the ancient Church were careful to keep the holy treasure of God's word from abuses, but that they did not by prohibiting or restraining the reading of it, but by diligent teaching and exhorting of men to the right use of it. Therefore, where you say 'we must not imagine that in the primitive Church everyone which understood the Scriptures in the learned tongues wherein they were written, or in other languages into which they were translated, might without reprehension, read, reason, dispute, turn, and toss the Scriptures', it is utterly false, for with reverence of God's mysteries, and to the end they were given, every man might not only without reprehension, but with good liking and commendation of the godly Fathers read, reason, dispute, and search, which is to turn and toss the books of the Scriptures. It is recorded generally of all the faithful in Berea that they daily searched the Scriptures even to examine the doctrine of the Apostles by them (Acts 17. 11). Irenaeus sayeth that 'all the Scriptures both of the Prophets and of the Gospels may be alike heard of all men'.[24] Chrysostom exhorteth all men indifferently to read the Scriptures and 'to call their neighbours to the

[22] Cf. James 13.45–61.

[23] See **11**. 122–44 above.

[24] **Marg**. Irenaeus, *Against Heresies*, 2.35.

hearing of them'. Also, he taketh away the vain excuses of them which alleged that they were worldly men, had wife, children, and household to look unto, and prayeth that they would not deceive themselves, saying that 'they which are entangled with such cares have more need to seek remedy by reading of the Holy Scriptures'.[25] And he sayeth, 'the reading of the Scripture is more necessary for laymen than for the monks'. And he sayeth, 'the people ought as soon as they come at home from the church to turn over the holy books and to call their wives and children together to the conference of those things which are said'. Again, 'it is no excuse', sayeth he, 'to say, "I have not read what Paul sayeth", but a fault'.[26] Further, where you say we must not imagine that our forefathers suffered every schoolmaster, scholar, or grammarian that had a little Greek or Latin straight to take in hand the Holy Testament, St Augustine is plainly against you, for he sayeth that 'they which turned the Scriptures out of the Hebrew tongue into the Greek tongue may be numbered, but the Latin interpreters cannot be numbered. For in those first times of the faith, as the Greek book came into any man's hands which seemed to himself to have some skill in both the tongues, he was bold to translate it'.[27] That the translated Bibles were in the hands and godly use of all sorts of men, women, children, how base soever their degree and calling was, is partly showed already; and more particularly, St Jerome sayeth that in the country of Bethlehem, the husbandman, the ploughman, the shepherd, the reaper, the vine-dresser did sing the Psalms of David and made none other noise.[28] Chrysostom sayeth the knowledge of the Scripture is most necessary for children, *pueris*, 'boys and girls', because you so term them and exhorteth their parents to cause them from their tender years to be exercised in the reading of the Holy Scriptures. That the Scriptures may be read at the table, he showeth, and that players, rhymers,° and jesters, instead of their lewd practices, should be commanded in recompense of their entertainment to read the Holy Scriptures, whereby the servants, prentices,

[25] Chrysostom, *On Genesis*, Homily 7; Homily 21 [WF].

[26] Chrysostom, *Commentary on Matthew*, Homily 2; Homily 5; *Epistle on Hebrews*, Homily 17 [WF].

[27] Augustine, *On Christian Doctrine*, 2.11 [WF].

[28] Jerome, on behalf of Paula and Eustochium, letter to Marcella [WF].

slaves, and drudges of the house may be made equal with angels.[29] St Augustine also exhorteth the people to read the Scripture at the table and meats.[30] As for boats and barges, which serve for men's travel, seeing God commanded his laws to be spoken of in journeys, and Christ himself preached out of boats or barges, there is no cause why his Holy Scriptures may not be read in them also. Neither did the ancient Fathers account any true Christian, or company of Christians, to be a profane person or company, but rather, of a company of profane persons by diligent reading of the Scriptures to be made a holy Church of God.[31] And although there was not so easy means, before printing was invented, to disperse the copies of the Bible into every man's hand, yet by the continual labour of the stationers, notaries, or book-writers, which in those times supplied the want of printers, there was a sufficient number of copies for every man that would buy them, or else Chrysostom should in vain have exhorted all the laymen of his time to buy them Bibles or at least the New Testament: *Audite obsecro seculares omnes*, etc., 'Hear, I pray you, all ye laymen. Provide you Bibles which are the medicines of the soul, if you will nothing else; at leastwise get the New Testament, the Apostle, the Acts, the Gospels, continual and diligent teachers.'[32] It is a frivolous pretence, therefore, of the scarcity of copies, for whatsoever will be commonly sold and well paid for, by diligence of workmen will soon be made plentiful.[33]

8.[34] They were in all men's hands that were desirous to read them, and were to be bought of common stationers or book-sellers, as it appeareth by the saying of Chrysostom cited in the section next before, not only in libraries, monasteries etc., and some devout principal laymen's houses and hands. And as devout laymen did use them well then, so do such men use them well now, learning out of them such things as be necessary and

[29] Chrysostom, *Epistle on Ephesians*, Homily 20; *On Genesis*, Homily 10; *Commentary on Matthew*, Homily 49 [WF].

[30] Augustine, *De Temp*. 56 [WF]

[31] Chrysostom, *Commentary on Matthew*, Homily 49 [WF].

[32] Chrysostom, *Epistle on Colossians*, Homily 9 [WF].

[33] Fulke is exaggerating: manuscript books were available before printing and were certainly 'well paid for', but their cost meant that they were not 'commonly sold'.

[34] See **11**. 145–55 above.

profitable for them to know, and leaving higher mysteries and hard places to the discussing of the learned. That the husbandmen of whom St Jerome speaketh sang the Psalms in an unknown tongue, which they could neither read nor know the sense, meaning, or mysteries of them, it is boldly affirmed and unpossible to be proved. Such singing of Psalms with the lips, not understood with the heart, no godly wise man would have allowed, much less commended, as he doth, calling them their songs of love, the shepherds' whistles, the instruments of tillage.[35] And as those holy persons of both sexes, to whom St Jerome commendeth the reading and meditation of the Scripture, used them to the glory of God and the building up of their souls in faith and godliness, so, God be thanked, at these days many thousands of faithful Christians with like zeal, reverence, humility, and all other virtues requisite, do read the Holy Scriptures in their mother tongue, and by daily reading do greatly profit in piety and charity, as well virgins as married folk, parents and children, princes and subjects, pastors and people.

13. Thomas James, *A Commentary upon the Canticle of Canticles by Brucioli* (1598)

[Thomas James (1572/3–1629) was educated at Winchester College and New College, Oxford, where he was elected to a Fellowship. He was appointed as the first Librarian of the Bodleian Library in 1602 and corresponded on library matters with the founder, Thomas Bodley himself until the latter's death in 1613, proposing the deposit arrangement with the Stationers' Company in London. The translation of Brucioli was his first publication, and another translation, *The Moral Philosophy of the Stoicks* by Guillaume du Vair, appeared in the same year, but

[35] See Jerome, on behalf of Paula and Eustochium, 'Letter to Marcella' (Letter 46.12): 'in the cottage of Christ all is simple and rustic: and except for the chanting of psalms there is complete silence. Wherever one turns the laborer at his plough sings alleluia, the toiling mower cheers himself with psalms, and the vine-dresser while he prunes his vine sings one of the lays of David. These are the songs of the country; these, in popular phrase, its love ditties: these the shepherd whistles; these the tiller uses to aid his toil', *Principal Works of St Jerome*, ed. by Schaff and Wace, VI, 65. On the voicing of words not understood see **1**. n. 3 above.

the rest of his large output consisted mainly of anti-Catholic polemic. The source text is *Commento di Antonio Brucioli in tutti i sacrosanti libri del Vecchio & Nuovo Testamento dalla hebraica verita, e fonte Greco, per esso tradotti in lingua Toscana* (Venice: Francesco Brucioli e fratelli, 1542–47). *La Cantica* is treated in the second book (1546).

Antonio Brucioli (1495–1566) was an Italian humanist from Florence whose translation of the Bible (1532) became the version preferred by Italian Protestants until Giovanni Diodati's translation of 1603 (annotated edition, 1607). His biblical commentaries (1542–46) were suspected of Lutheranism and he was brought before the Venetian Inquisition in 1555; after he failed to retract he was summoned again in 1558 and imprisoned. His secular work includes Italian translations of Aristotle's *Rhetoric* (1545) and Pliny's *Natural History* (1548).

See Andrew Taylor in *OHLTE*, pp. 55–63; R. Julian Roberts in *ODNB*.]

The translator to the courteous and Christian reader.

A Christian I presume thou art that readest this book;[1] courteous I call thee, because I hope to find thee so; it is as much as I desire, and surely no less doth mine author deserve. His name is Brucioli, by birth an Italian, his country (as I guess) Florence, and therefore a stranger;° if a stranger, entreat him as a stranger, that is, gently and kindly, and know that it is thy duty, if it be not thy courtesy so to do, for there is a duty which belongeth unto strangers, commanded in the Law and commended in the Gospel.[2] As a stranger by birth, so good must be done unto him in general, but as he is not a stranger from the faith, so we are bound to show him special favour, for so the apostle St Paul willeth us for to do: 'Do good', sayeth he, 'unto all men, but especially or chiefly to those which are of the household of faith.'[3] Of this household was Brucioli, and not of that other household

[1] this book] The 'Canticle of Canticles' is one of the three books of Solomon, widely known as the 'Song of Songs' or 'Song of Solomon'.

[2] For the Law see Deuteronomy 10.19: 'Love ye therefore the stranger, for ye were strangers in the land of Egypt'; cf. Exodus 22.21; Leviticus 19.34; and for the Gospel, Romans 12.13.

[3] Galatians 6.10.

of good works, where none but merit-mongers[4] and superarrogant or supererogating papists dwell. Read his commentary and thou wilt confess as much. There is often mention of faith, of justification by faith only, of faith and justification by imputation:° still, faith comes in, as if our actions were as insipid and unpleasant without faith as the old sacrifices were unsavoury without salt. The Law requireth salt in all sacrifices, Brucioli requireth faith in every action: he maketh it the subject of his discourse, brings it in in every chapter, in every page, yea, almost in every line, as if it were the centre whereunto all the lines of his commentary must of force have been drawn.

Embrace his book, therefore, in thine hands, and entertain his doctrine into thine heart. Scorn him not because he is not attired after the fine Italian fashion, for this were to accept of him for his good apparel and not for his good parts, which St James noted for a fault in the Jews.[5] Brucioli is now in England and not in Italy, and therefore must be content with such apparel as our country affords. He hath the best that could be gotten for him, for indeed it is all that could be gotten: either he must have this or none, and better this than none, for I hope it is good and strong, though it be not very costly and fine. The finest threads be not ever the best, for then spiders would undo weavers and spinners and be set awork more than they be, and yet I cannot say but they work too fast many times; but, alas, it is in sucking sour out of sweet and drawing forth poison from honey. These creatures I do not like: the lion naturally hateth the mouse, the sheep a wolf, and naturally I do abhor these men from my very heart; and therefore if any spider come upon my book, it shall be lawful for any man either to sweep, or else to blow him away, for he is but a light person of himself and easily blown away that spendeth his time in this sort, how heavy soever he prove to others.[6] They say there be no spiders in Ireland, their houses are built of such a wood as breedeth none. O that England were as Ireland in this respect, and that all our houses were built of this

[4] merit-mongers] those who believe in earned entitlement to reward from God (James's coinage).

[5] James 2.2.

[6] On spiders cf. Fulke **12**. 264–66; see also Alexandra Walsham, 'The Spider and the Bee: the Perils of Printing for Refutation in Tudor England', in *Tudor Books and Readers: Materiality and the Construction of Meaning*, ed. by John N. King (Cambridge: Cambridge University Press, 2010), pp. 163–90.

kind of timber, then would the house of God go better forward than it doth and we should be fitter men to be temples of the Holy Ghost than we are. But now the world is as full of these wicked creatures as ever Egypt swarmed with frogs. There was no house, no place in Egypt but there were frogs to be found: there is no place, no house almost in England where there are not some of these venomous spiders to be found. A man shall find them everywhere in city and fields, in beds and at board, in court and country. If a young man write, they say his head is too green; if an old man, they say his best is past; if a man of middle age, they say at that time his body is more fit for action than contemplation; so that neither old, nor young, nor middle-aged writers can please them, and no marvel for I think they cannot please themselves.

But chiefly these spider-catching Zoiluses[7] do shoot the venom of their tongues against painful° translators of books, which seek other men's profits and not their own, reaping not the fruit of that which they have sown, and like candles spending themselves to give others light. 'But what!', sayeth Master Momus[8] with his crew of carping knights, 'these men mar all with their translations. It was never well with us (that is, that are learned) since so many books were translated into English. Their labour were better spared than employed – they corrupt books, misinterpret writers, are enemies unto the commonwealth, and enemies to all good learning.' If this be all they have to say, they say in word somewhat, in effect nothing: for either they take that for a fault which is not so indeed, or else they know not how to distinguish the abuse from the thing, and so speak against they know not what.

Translators have their faults and abuses as well as other men, as when they translate foolish and unprofitable, or wicked and ungodly books, or else mistranslate and misinterpret books, and then the abuse proceedeth either of malice or of ignorance: if of

[7] Zoiluses] Zoilus was a Cynic philosopher of the 4th century BC who was notorious for the severity of his attacks on Homer. He became the type of the carping critic and is frequently cited by sixteenth-century translators in anticipation of pedantic objections to their work.

[8] Momus] A satirical figure from classical literature, used by Lucian to mock the Stoics. He is a familiar figure in Elizabethan satire (e.g. Thomas Lodge, *A Fig for Momus*, 1595) and has a similar role to that of Zoilus in translators' prefaces.

malice, their reproof is just; if of ignorance, blame them not unless it be affected, for the best that is may miss in a strange° language, when no man knoweth all in his own tongue. And thus far reacheth their complaint against the abuse of translations, which may in no wise be excused. As for the harm that cometh by making learning too common, men of common judgement may by vulgar examples easily refute them. The sun and moon, fire and water, are profitable and yet common. The philosopher sayeth, *Bonum quo communius, eo melius*, 'good, the commoner it is, the better it is.'[9] If it be true in philosophy, it is true in divinity, and therefore St Paul wisheth that all men were learned as he was and that all men could speak with divers tongues as he did, etc.[10] I would that these men which think they have St Paul's learning had St Paul's zeal (so it were according to knowledge) to seek other men's good and not their own. For now merchants do not monopolise the goods of a city more than these do appropriate unto themselves the learning of whole universities, and when they have it, what do they with it but keep it unto themselves? Because I would not be of this odious sect of men, most courteous and Christian reader, I have at vacant° times translated according to that measure of knowledge which God hath given me, both this book and some others, as *The History of the Jesuits* and *Moral Philosophy of the Stoics*, which with permission of my superiors I mean shortly to publish, if God will and health permit me so to do.

14. Francis Marbury, in *A Treatise of God's Effectual Calling by Robert Rollock* (1603)

[Francis Marbury (1555–1611), educated at Christ's College, Cambridge, was a Puritan preacher and author of a moral interlude, 'The Contract of Marriage between Wit and Wisdom'. He was also the father of the pioneer American settler, Anne Hutchinson. The text reproduced here is from Marbury's address

[9] A much quoted maxim, especially by those defending the popularization of professional knowledge: e.g. John Hester, *The Pearle of Practise* [on medicine and surgery] (1594), STC 13253, *ii^{v}, image 3, who also alludes to Momus, and John Florio, **46**. 218–19. The source may be Aristotle, *Nicomachean Ethics* 1.2.8 discussing private and public benefit.

[10] I Corinthians 14.5.

to the reader prefatory to Henry Holland's translation of a Latin work by Robert Rollock.

Robert Rollock (1555–99), minister in the Church of Scotland, was taught Hebrew by James Melville at the University of St Andrews and in 1583 became master of the new college at Edinburgh. His application of Ramist dialectic to the scriptures made him a popular author of biblical commentary. Rollock's translator, Henry Holland, was the son of the prolific translator Philemon Holland and also a printer and bookseller. Holland's source text is *Tractatus de vocatione efficaci* (Edinburgh, 1597).

See *The Diary of Mr. James Melvill, 1556–1601* (Edinburgh: Bannatyne Club, 1829); T. N. S. Lennam, 'Francis Merbury, 1555–1611', *Studies in Philology*, 65 (1968), 207–22.]

To the Reader.

Although the greater part both of authors and translators of books may be taxed of officiousness, and not a few of ungodliness, yet are there some whose merits in this kind do outweigh the demerits of the other. These are either those worthy lights themselves, or else those second candlesticks to translate the light into, which God specially in these latter years hath bestowed as gifts (to use St Paul's word) upon his Church, to the edification of it. It is true indeed in one sense that both the one and the other are but candlesticks, for the light is God's; but otherwise comparatively the author is the light and the translator is, as it were, another candlestick to translate the light into,[1] and that for those which through ignorance of the tongue could not attain to the light when it shone out of the author's own lamp. Now although there seem no great gifts to be required in a translator, yet the truth is that if he be not of good discretion to choose the fittest works; of good speech to express the author's sentence° with fittest words; and of so great apprehension and former store° that by that which he seeth in the author he hath attained to more than peradventure the author himself saw or minded, his defectiveness will bring him in danger of showing what gifts are required in a translator. For a good translator is neither a

[1] Cf. Matthew 5.15; Mark 4.21; Luke 8.16 and **15d**. 161–63 below.

paraphrast nor a periphrast,[2] which is committed by needless changing or adding words. He so behaveth himself that the comparing of the original will commend his fidelity, and that they which know of no original would take the translator for the author himself. He must naturalise[3] his translation for the reader without injuring the gift of the author in the native work. But these seem critic rules[4] to the irregular, which offend against their authors to please themselves. For as there are many translations of unworthy works, so are there many transportations of worthy works, which like plants ill taken up rejoice not to grow in the soil into which they are translated.

And yet nevertheless it cannot without injury be denied that this age hath afforded many excellent translations of excellent and learned authors to the benefit of our people, amongst whom Master Rollock, the reverend author of this work, deserveth an eminent place, as also this work itself is very acceptable, together with the translator's godly labour in this and other things commodious to the Church of Christ. This inclined me the rather to commend it to thee in these few lines, not as taking upon me anything, but as a poor man where he is better known is sometimes engaged for a rich. This labour is become ours not only because it is thus well Englished, but also because the author is a Scottishman, which is now to the wise-hearted a synonymy of an Englishman.[5] And it shall be to the praise of both the nations to receive both mutual and common benefits without that emulation which was betwixt Israel and Judah.

---

[2] neither a paraphrast nor a periphrast] The distinction is between someone who rewords or gives a free rendering of a passage in order to make it clearer and someone who expresses him/herself in a roundabout way. On paraphrase see **7b**. n. 1 above; 'periphrast' is borrowed from Greek *periphrastēs* and is the first recorded use of the word in English.

[3] naturalise] The senses of granting citizenship, making something native or common, and introducing a foreign word into the language are usages which all date from the second half of the sixteenth century (see Introduction, pp. 53–55). But 'naturalise' may be understood here in the modern sense of 'respect the idiom of the target language'.

[4] i.e. unnecessarily prescriptive and precise.

[5] Following the Union of Crowns of England and Scotland in 1603.

15. The King James Bible

a) William Barlow, *The Sum and Substance of the Conference at Hampton Court* (1604)

[William Barlow (*c*. 1565–1613), educated at St John's College, Cambridge; Dean of Chester at the time of the Hampton Court conference and subsequently Bishop of Lincoln. An opponent of the Calvinist doctrine of predestination and a supporter of the Divine Right of Kings, he was employed by James to preach against the Scottish Presbyterian, Andrew Melville. He was a KJB translator, leading the second Westminster company.

The Hampton Court conference was convened in January 1604 in order to consider demands from the Puritans to be exempted from certain ceremonial Church practices. These demands were made in the millenary Petition presented to James in April 1603, immediately after he succeeded Elizabeth. The Puritans won few concessions and the real 'substance' of the conference turned out to be the unscheduled suggestion from their representative, John Rainolds, for a new translation of the Bible. Barlow's own position was unsympathetic to Puritanism, but his report is generally thought to be the most reliable available record.

See (for the section as a whole) *The Bible: Authorized King James Version*, ed. by Robert Carroll and Stephen Prickett (Oxford: Oxford University Press, 2008); Westcott, *History of the English Bible*; Alfred W. Pollard, *Records of the English Bible: the Documents Relating to the Translation and Publication of the Bible in English, 1525–1611* (London: Oxford University Press, 1911); Greenslade, *Cambridge History of the Bible, Vol. 3*; Ward Allen, ed., *Translating for King James: Notes Made by a Translator of King James's Bible* (London: Allen Lane, 1970); Partridge, *English Biblical Translation*; Hammond, *The Making of the English Bible*; Norton, *History of the Bible as Literature: Vol. 1*; Erroll F. Rhodes and Líana Lupas, eds., *The Translators to the Reader: the Original Preface of the King James Version of 1611 Revisited* (New York: American Bible Society, 1997); Daniell, *Bible in English*; Gordon Campbell, *Bible: The Story of the King James Version* (Oxford: Oxford University Press, 2010); Norton, *The King James Bible*.]

After that, [Dr Rainolds[1]] moved His Majesty that there might be a new translation of the Bible, because those that were allowed in the reigns of Henry VIII and Edward VI were corrupt and not answerable to the truth of the original. For example, first, Galatians 4.25, the Greek word *susoikei* is not well translated, as now it is, 'bordereth', neither expressing the force of the word, nor the Apostle's sense, nor the situation of the place. Secondly, Psalm 105.28, 'they were not obedient'; the original being, 'they were not disobedient'. Thirdly, Psalm 106, verse 30, 'Then stood up Phineas and prayed'; the Hebrew hath 'executed judgement'.

To which motion there was at the present no gainsaying, the objections being trivial and old, and already in print, often answered. Only my Lord of London[2] well added that if every man's humour should be followed, there would be no end of translating. Whereupon his Highness wished that some especial pains should be taken in that behalf for one uniform translation (professing that he could never yet see a Bible well translated in English, but the worst of all His Majesty thought the Geneva[3] to be), and this to be done by the best learned in both the universities; after them to be reviewed by the Bishops and the chief learned of the Church; from them to be presented to the Privy Council; and lastly to be ratified by his royal authority. And so this whole Church to be bound unto it, and none other. Marry withal, he gave this caveat (upon a word cast out by my Lord of London) that no marginal notes should be added, having found in them which are annexed to the Geneva translation (which he saw in a Bible given him by an English lady) some notes very partial, untrue, seditious, and savouring too much of dangerous and traitorous conceits. As, for example, Exodus 1.19, where the

[1] Rainolds] John Rainolds (1549–1607), President of Corpus Christi College, Oxford, was a Calvinist with scholarly expertise in both Hebrew and Greek. He was the principal spokesman for the Puritans, but also had a significant role in the KJB as a member of the Oxford company (under John Harding) which translated the Prophets.

[2] i.e. Richard Bancroft; see headnote to **15b**.

[3] Geneva] The Geneva Bible was translated by English Calvinists in exile during the reign of Mary (1553–58). A cheap and extremely popular bible, many editions contain extensive commentary. The 1576 revision by Laurence Tomson was based on the 1565 edition of Beza's Latin translation (1556), strongly attacked by Gregory Martin (*Discovery*, STC 17503, bii[r] ff. image 10 ff.). The first Scottish printing was by Alexander Arbuthnot, Edinburgh, 1579, from which the quotations below are taken.

marginal note alloweth disobedience to kings, and 2 Chronicles 15.16, the note taxeth Asa for deposing his mother only, and not killing her.[4] And so concludeth this point, as all the rest, with a grave and judicious advice. First, that errors in matters of faith might be rectified and amended. Secondly, that matters indifferent[5] might rather be interrupted and a gloss added, alleging from Bartolus' *De regno*[6] that, as better a king with some weakness than still a change, so rather a Church with some faults than an innovation. 'And surely', sayeth His Majesty, 'if these be the greatest matters you be grieved with, I need not have been troubled with such importunities and complaints as have been made unto me. Some other more private course might have been taken for your satisfaction', and withal, looking upon the lords, he shook his head, smiling.

b) Letter from King James to Richard Bancroft, Bishop of London (1604)

[Richard Bancroft (1544–1610) was a Scholar of Christ's College, Cambridge, who developed a reputation as a conformist preacher and opponent of Puritanism during the 1580s. He was engaged in combatting the anti-episcopal satire of the Marprelate pamphlets in 1588–89 and was responsible for the detection of the printing press near Manchester. Appointed Bishop of London in 1597, he was a staunch defender of Church hierarchy at the Hampton Court conference. At the time of James's letter on the setting up of the new Bible translation he was about to succeed Archbishop Whitgift, who had died earlier in the year, as Archbishop of Canterbury.]

---

[4] At Exodus 1.19 the King of Egypt commands the Jewish midwives to kill all newborn males, but they disobey the order. The note reads: 'Their disobedience herein was lawful, but their dissembling evil'. At 2 Chronicles 15.16 the note on 'mother' reads: 'Or grandmother: and herein he shewed that he lacked zeale: for she ought to have dyed both by the covenant and by the Lawe of God, but he gave place to foolish pitie, & wolde also seme after a sorte to satisfie the Law', STC 2125, pp. 26, 207, images 36, 224.

[5] i.e. things which are neither good nor bad in themselves; here, things without theological implications.

[6] Bartolus] Bartolus da Sassoferrato (1313–57), Italian professor and author of many legal works, including *De Regno et regali potestate*, on the extent of a king's power.

After my hearty commendations unto Your Lordship[1] I have received letters from His most excellent Majesty, the tenor whereof followeth:

Right trusty and well beloved, we greet you well. Whereas we have appointed certain learned men, to the number of four-and-fifty,[2] for the translating of the Bible, and that in this number divers of them have either no ecclesiastical preferment at all, or else so very small as the same is far unmeet for men of their deserts and yet we of ourself in any convenient time cannot well remedy it. Therefore we do hereby require you that presently you write in our name, as well to the Archbishop of York as to the rest of the Bishops of the province of Canterbury, signifying unto them that we do will, and straitly° charge every one of them, as also the other Bishops of the province of York, as they tender our good favour towards them, that (all excuses set apart) when any prebend° or parsonage, being rated in our book of taxations, the prebend to twenty pound at the least and the parsonage to the like sum and upwards, shall next upon any occasion happen to be void, and to be either of their patronage and gift, or the like parsonage so void to be of the patronage or gift of any person whosoever, they do make stay thereof, and admit none unto it, until certifying us of the avoidance of it, and of the name of the patron (if it be not of their own gift) we may commend for the same some such of the said learned men as we shall think fit to be preferred to it: not doubting of the Bishops' readiness to satisfy us herein, or that any of the laity, when we shall in time move them to so good and religious an act, will be unwilling to give us the like due contentment and satisfaction: we ourself having taken the same order for such prebends and benefices as shall fall void in our gift.[3] What we write to you of others, you must apply it to yourself, as also not forget to move the said Archbishop and all the Bishops, with their Deans and chapters of both provinces, as touching the other point to be imparted

[1] Your Lordship] The addressee is probably John Jegon, Bishop of Norwich.

[2] four-and-fifty] there are only 47 known translators of the KJB.

[3] James had not provided any funding for the translation, hence this elaborate instruction to the Bishops to produce some remuneration for those involved in what would be a lengthy and demanding task. (They were not very responsive.) The issue of funding for translation had been raised in a rather different by Nicholas Udall; see **7a**. 89–120.

otherwise by you unto them. Furthermore, we require you to move all our Bishops to inform themselves of all such learned men within their several dioceses, as having especial skill in the Hebrew and Greek tongues, have taken pains in their private studies of the Scriptures for the clearing of any obscurities either in the Hebrew or in the Greek, or touching any difficulties or mistakings in the former English translation, which we have now commanded to be thoroughly viewed and amended, and thereupon to write unto them, earnestly charging them and signifying our pleasure therein, that they send such their observations either to Mr Lively, our Hebrew reader in Cambridge, or to Dr Harding, our Hebrew reader in Oxford, or to Dr Andrews, Dean of Westminster, to be imparted to the rest of their several companies,[4] that so our said intended translation may have the help and furtherance of all our principal learned men within this our kingdom.

Given under our signet at our Palace of Westminster, the two and twentieth of July, in the second year of our reign of England, France and Ireland, and of Scotland, the seven and thirtieth.

Your Lordship may see how careful his Majesty is for the providing of livings for these learned men. I doubt not therefore but your lordship will have that due regard of his Majesty's request herein, as it is fit and meet, and that you will take such order both with your chancellor, register, and such your Lordship's officers, who shall have intelligence of the premises, as also with the Dean and chapter of your cathedral church, whom his Majesty likewise requireth to be put in mind of his pleasure herein, not forgetting the latter part of his Majesty's letter touching the informing of yourself of the fittest linguists within your diocese for to perform, and speedily to return that which his Majesty is so careful to have faithfully performed. I

[4] The KJB translators were divided into six companies based at Westminster, Oxford, and Cambridge. The first Westminster company (led by Lancelot Andrewes) was responsible for Genesis to II Kings; Cambridge (Edward Lively, then either Robert Spalding or Andrew Byng) for I Chronicles to the Song of Solomon; and Oxford (John Harding) for the Prophets. The second Cambridge company (led by John Duport) was responsible for the Apocrypha; Oxford (Thomas Ravis) for the Gospels, Acts, and Revelation; and Westminster (William Barlow) for the Epistles. For notes on all the translators see Campbell, *Bible: The Story of the King James Version* (Oxford: Oxford University Press, 2010), pp. 276–94, and Norton, *The King James Bible*, pp. 54–62.

could wish your Lordship would for my discharge return me in some few lines the time of the receipt of these letters, that I may discharge that duty which his Majesty by these his letters hath laid upon me; and so I bid your Lordship right heartily farewell.

From Fulham this 31st of July, 1604.
Your Lordship's loving friend and brother,
Ric. London.

c) Richard Bancroft, *Rules to be Observed in Translating the Bible* (1604)

1. The ordinary° Bible read in the Church, commonly called the 'Bishops' Bible',[1] to be followed, and as little altered as the truth of the original will permit.

2. The names of the Prophets and the holy writers, with the other names in the text, to be retained as near as may be, accordingly as they are vulgarly used.

3. The old ecclesiastical words to be kept, as the word 'Church' not to be translated 'congregation' etc.[2]

4. When any word hath divers significations, that to be kept which hath been most commonly used by most of the ancient Fathers, being agreeable to the propriety of the place and the analogy of faith.[3]

5. The division of the chapters to be altered either not at all, or as little as may be, if necessity so require.

---

[1] The Bishops' Bible] Translated under the authority of Matthew Parker, Archbishop of Canterbury, and published in 1568. Expensively produced, and the official Bible during Elizabeth's reign, but not as popular as Geneva.

[2] See **3**. 46–82 and **4**. 1–37 above.

[3] analogy of faith] The Protestant hermeneutic principle which holds that, since the Bible is a harmonious whole with no internal contradictions, any interpretation of a difficult passage must be checked for consistency with a similar passage where the sense is clearer; often stated as 'Scripture must explain Scripture'.

6. No marginal notes at all to be affixed, but only for the explanation of the Hebrew or Greek words, which cannot without some circumlocution so briefly and fitly be expressed in the text.[4]

7. Such quotations of places to be marginally set down as shall serve for the fit reference of one Scripture to another.

8. Every particular man of each company to take the same chapter, or chapters, and having translated or amended them severally by himself where he thinketh good, all to meet together, confer what they have done, and agree for their parts what shall stand.

9. As any one company hath dispatched any one book in this manner, they shall send it to the rest, to be considered of seriously and judiciously, for His Majesty is very careful in this point.

10. If any company, upon the review of their book shall doubt or differ upon any place, to send them word thereof, note the place and withal send their reasons, to which if they consent not, the difference to be compounded at the General Meeting, which is to be of the chief persons of each company, at the end of the work.

11. When any place of special obscurity is doubted of, letters to be directed by authority to send to any learned man in the land for his judgement on such a place.

12. Letters to be sent from every Bishop to the rest of his clergy, admonishing° them of this translation in hand, and to move and charge as many as being skilful in the tongues; and having taken pains in that kind, to send his particular observations to the company, either at Westminster, Cambridge, or Oxford.

13. The Directors in each company to be the Deans of Westminster and Chester for that place, and the King's Professors in the Hebrew or Greek in either university.

[4] This is intended to be in direct contrast to the Geneva Bible; see **15a**. 23–31.

14. These translations to be used when they agree better with the text than the Bishops' Bible: Tyndale's; Matthew's; Coverdale's; Whitchurch's; Geneva.[5]

15. Besides the said Directors before mentioned, three or four of the most ancient and grave divines in either of the universities, not employed in the translating, to be assigned by the Vice-Chancellor, upon conference with the rest of the heads, to be overseers of the translations, as well Hebrew as Greek, for the better observation of the fourth rule above specified.[6]

d) Miles Smith, *The Translators to the Reader* [Preface to the King James Bible], 1611

[Miles Smith (d. 1624) was born in Hereford and retained an association with the cathedral throughout his life. He studied at Corpus Christi and Brasenose Colleges, Oxford, from *c.* 1568, eventually becoming a Doctor of Divinity in 1594. By the time Bancroft was assembling the team of scholars for the new translation of the Bible, Smith had won a reputation as an outstanding classicist and expert in oriental languages (Chaldaic, Syriac, and Arabic). He was involved in the KJB from start to finish, as a member of the revision committee and as one of the two final reviewers (with the Bishop of Winchester, Thomas Bilson). His own work was on the prophetic books of the Old Testament. He was appointed Bishop of Gloucester in 1612, but subsequently became involved in a bitter dispute with the Dean, William Laud, whose Arminian theology he opposed.

David Norton has noted that the KJB preface 'has been a casualty of its length, and is rarely reprinted' (*King James Bible* (2011), p. 117). The text below is reduced to about half the length of the original.

See John Tiller in *ODNB*; and headnote to **15.a**.]

---

[5] Matthew's; Whitchurch's] John Rogers (martyred under Mary) used the pseudonym 'Thomas Matthew' and combined Tyndale and Coverdale (1537). Edward Whitchurch and Richard Grafton were the printers of the Great Bible (1539)

[6] Rule 15 appears only in the Egerton manuscript.

The best things have been calumniated[1]

Zeal to promote the common good, whether it be by devising anything ourselves, or revising that which hath been laboured by others, deserveth certainly much respect and esteem, but yet findeth but cold entertainment in the world. It is welcomed with suspicion instead of love, and with emulation instead of thanks; and if there be any hole left for cavil to enter (and cavil, if it do not find a hole, will make one) it is sure to be misconstrued, and in danger to be condemned. This will easily be granted by as many as know story,° or have any experience. For was there ever anything projected, that savoured any way of newness or renewing, but the same endured many a storm of gainsaying, or opposition? A man would think that civility, wholesome laws, learning, and eloquence, synods, and Church maintenance (that we speak of no more things of this kind) should be as safe as a sanctuary, and out of shot, as they say, that no man would lift up the heel,[2] no, nor dog move his tongue against the motioners° of them. For by the first, we are distinguished from brute beasts led with sensuality; by the second, we are bridled and restrained from outrageous behaviour, and from doing of injuries, whether by fraud or by violence; by the third, we are enabled to inform and reform others, by the light and feeling that we have attained unto ourselves; briefly, by the fourth, being brought together to a parley face to face, we sooner compose our differences than by writings, which are endless; and lastly, that the Church be sufficiently provided for is so agreeable to good reason and conscience, that those mothers are held to be less cruel that kill their children as soon as they are born, than those nursing fathers and mothers (wheresoever they be) that withdraw from them who hang upon their breasts (and upon whose breasts again themselves do hang to receive the spiritual and sincere milk of the word) livelihood and support fit for their estates. Thus it is apparent that these things which we speak of are of most necessary use, and therefore that none either without absurdity can speak against them, or without note of wickedness can spurn against them. [. . .]

[1] Section headings have been taken from the marginalia of *1611*.
[2] Cf. Psalm 41.9.

His Majesty's constancy, notwithstanding calumniation, for the survey of the English translations

This, and more to this purpose, His Majesty that now reigneth (and long, and long may he reign, and his offspring forever, himself and children, and children's children always[3]) knew full well, according to the singular wisdom given unto him by God, and the rare learning and experience that he hath attained unto; namely, that whosoever attempteth anything for the public (specially if it pertain to religion, and to the opening and clearing of the word of God) the same setteth himself upon a stage to be glouted° upon by every evil eye,[4] yea, he casteth himself headlong upon pikes, to be gored by every sharp tongue. For he that meddleth with men's religion in any part, meddleth with their custom, nay, with their freehold; and though they find no content in that which they have, yet they cannot abide to hear of altering. Notwithstanding, his royal heart was not daunted or discouraged for this or that colour, but stood resolute, 'as a statue immovable, and an anvil not easy to be beaten into plates', as one sayeth.[5] He knew who had chosen him to be a soldier, or rather a captain, and being assured that the course which he intended made much for the glory of God, and the building up of his Church, he would not suffer it to be broken off for whatsoever speeches or practices. [. . .]

The praise of the Holy Scriptures

The Scriptures then being acknowledged to be so full and so perfect, how can we excuse ourselves of negligence if we do not study them; of curiosity, if we be not content with them? Men talk much of *eiresionē*,[6] how many sweet and goodly things it had hanging on it; of the philosopher's stone,[7] that it turneth copper

---

[3] Cf. Ezekiel 37.25.

[4] Smith may be echoing James's own use of this image for the exposure of the monarch to public gaze in *Basilikon Doron* (Edinburgh, 1603), STC 14349, sig. I4^{r}, image 73.

[5] **Marg**. Suidas [supposed author of a Greek lexicon in the tenth century].

[6] **Marg**. An olive bow wrapped about with wool, whereupon did hang figs and bread, and honey in a pot, and oil [cf. Plutarch, *Theseus*, 22.5].

[7] philosopher's stone] The illusory substance that alchemists believed could turn base metals into gold.

into gold; of cornucopia, that it had all things necessary for food in it; of panaces the herb, that it was good for all diseases; of catholicon[8] the drug, that it is instead of all purges; of Vulcan's armour,[9] that it was an armour of proof against all thrusts and all blows, etc. Well, that which they falsely or vainly attributed to these things for bodily good, we may justly and with full measure ascribe unto the Scripture for spiritual. It is not only an armour, but also a whole armoury of weapons, both offensive and defensive, whereby we may save ourselves and put the enemy to flight. It is not a herb, but a tree, or rather a whole paradise of trees of life, which bring forth fruit every month, and the fruit thereof is for meat, and the leaves for medicine. It is not a pot of manna, or a cruse° of oil, which were for memory only, or for a meal's meat or two, but, as it were, a shower of heavenly bread sufficient for a whole host, be it never so great, and, as it were, a whole cellar full of oil vessels, whereby all our necessities may be provided for and our debts discharged. In a word, it is a panary° of wholesome food against finewed° traditions; a physician's shop (St Basil calleth it) of preservatives against poisoned heresies;[10] a pandect° of profitable laws against rebellious spirits; a treasury of most costly jewels against beggarly rudiments; finally, a fountain of most pure water springing up unto everlasting life. And what marvel? The original thereof being from heaven, not from earth; the author being God, not man; the inditer,° the Holy Spirit, not the wit of the Apostles or Prophets; the pen-men, such as were sanctified from the womb and endued with a principal portion of God's spirit; the matter – verity, piety, purity, uprightness; the form – God's word, God's testimony, God's oracles, the word of truth, the word of salvation, etc.; the effects – light of understanding, stableness of persuasion, repentance from dead works, newness of life, holiness, peace, joy in the Holy Ghost; lastly, the end and reward of the study thereof, fellowship with the Saints, participation of the heavenly nature, fruition of an inheritance immortal, undefiled, and that never shall fade away: happy is the man that delighteth in the Scripture, and thrice happy that meditateth in it day and night.

[8] panaces [. . .] catholicon] both terms mean a panacea or universal remedy, the latter usually containing rhubarb (first citation in the OED).

[9] Vulcan's armour] The armour made by Hephaestus (Vulcan) for Achilles in *Iliad* 18.

[10] **Marg**. Basil, *Exegetic Homilies*, Psalm 1.

Translation necessary

But how shall men meditate in that which they cannot understand? How shall they understand that which is kept close in an unknown tongue? As it is written, 'Except I know the power of the voice, I shall be to him that speaketh a barbarian, and he that speaketh shall be a barbarian to me' (1 Corinthians 14.11). The Apostle excepteth no tongue: not Hebrew the ancientest, not Greek the most copious, not Latin the finest. Nature taught a natural man to confess that all of us in those tongues which we do not understand are plainly deaf; we may turn the deaf ear unto them. The Scythian counted the Athenian, whom he did not understand, barbarous;[11] so the Roman did the Syrian, and the Jew (even St Jerome himself calleth the Hebrew tongue barbarous, belike because it was strange to so many),[12] so the Emperor of Constantinople[13] calleth the Latin tongue barbarous, though Pope Nicolas do storm at it;[14] so the Jews long before Christ called all other nations *Lognazim*, which is little better than barbarous. Therefore, as one complaineth that always in the Senate of Rome there was one or other that called for an interpreter,[15] so, lest the Church be driven to the like exigent,° it is necessary to have translations in a readiness. Translation it is that openeth the window, to let in the light; that breaketh the shell, that we may eat the kernel; that putteth aside the curtain, that we may look into the most holy place; that removeth the cover of the well, that we may come by the water, even as Jacob rolled away the stone from the mouth of the well, by which means the flocks of Laban were watered (Genesis 29.10). Indeed, without translation into the vulgar tongue, the unlearned are but like children at Jacob's well, which was deep (John 4.11), without a bucket or something to draw with, or as that person mentioned by Isaiah, to whom when a sealed book was delivered with this motion, 'Read this, I pray thee', he was

---

[11] **Marg.** Clement of Alexandria, *Stromata*, Book 1 [chapter 16, referring to the Scythian, Anarcharsis]. A relativist point: the Greek word *barbaros* referred to all non-Hellenes in mimicry of their unintelligible speech. Scythians were widely taken to be a type of the barbarian.

[12] **Marg.** Jerome, Letter to Damasus [Epistle 20.4].

[13] **Marg.** Michael, son of Theophilus [the Byzantine Emperor, Michael III].

[14] **Marg.** Petrus Crabbe, ed. *Conciliorum omnium* (1538), Book 2.

[15] **Marg.** Cicero, *De Finibus* [On the Ends of Good and Evil], 5. [29].

fain to make this answer, 'I cannot, for it is sealed' (Isaiah 29.11).

The translation of the Old Testament out of the Hebrew into the Greek

While God would be known only in Jacob, and have his name great in Israel, and in none other place, while the dew lay on Gideon's fleece only, and all the earth besides was dry; then for one and the same people, which spake all of them the language of Canaan, that is, Hebrew, one and the same original in Hebrew was sufficient.[16] But, when the fulness of time drew near, that the sun of righteousness, the Son of God, should come into the world, whom God ordained to be a reconciliation through faith in his blood, not of the Jew only, but also of the Greek, yea, of all them that were scattered abroad; then lo, it pleased the Lord to stir up the spirit of a Greek Prince (Greek for descent and language) even of Ptolemy Philadelph, King of Egypt, to procure the translating of the Book of God out of Hebrew into Greek.[17] This is the translation of the Seventy Interpreters, commonly so called, which prepared the way for our Saviour among the Gentiles by written preaching, as St John Baptist did among the Jews by vocal. For the Grecians, being desirous of learning, were not wont to suffer books of worth to lie moulding in kings' libraries, but had many of their servants, ready scribes, to copy them out, and so they were dispersed and made common. Again, the Greek tongue was well known and made familiar to most inhabitants in Asia, by reason of the conquest that there the Grecians had made, as also by the colonies, which thither they had sent.[18] For the same causes also it was well understood in many places of Europe, yea, and of Africa too. Therefore the word of God, being set forth in Greek, becometh hereby like a candle set upon a candlestick, which giveth light to all that are in the house,[19]

[16] **Marg**. Augustine, *Against Faustus*, Book 12, chapter 32.

[17] The legendary story of the Septuagint is preserved in the *Letter to Aristeas*, probably from the second century BC. See **6**. note 3 above.

[18] Smith refers to the common or *koinē* Greek widely spoken in the eastern Mediterranean and Asia Minor after the conquests of Alexandria. See also **12**. n. 6 above.

[19] Cf. Matthew 5.15; Mark 4.21; Luke 8.16.

or like a proclamation sounded forth in the marketplace, which most men presently take knowledge of; and therefore that language was fittest to contain the Scriptures, both for the first preachers of the Gospel to appeal unto for witness, and for the learners also of those times to make search and trial by. It is certain that that translation was not so sound and so perfect, but that it needed in many places correction; and who had been so sufficient for this work as the Apostles or Apostolic men? Yet it seemed good to the Holy Ghost, and to them, to take that which they found (the same being for the greatest part true and sufficient), rather than making a new, in that new world and green age of the Church, to expose themselves to many exceptions and cavillations, as though they made a translation to serve their own turn, and therefore bearing witness to themselves, their witness not to be regarded. This may be supposed to be some cause why the translation of the Seventy was allowed to pass for current. [. . .]

Translation out of Hebrew and Greek into Latin

There were also within a few hundred years after Christ translations many into the Latin tongue, for this tongue also was very fit to convey the Law and the Gospel by, because in those times very many countries of the West, yea of the South, East, and North, spake or understood Latin, being made provinces to the Romans. But now the Latin translations were too many to be all good, for they were infinite (*Latini interpretes nullo modo numerari possunt*, sayeth St Augustine).[20] Again, they were not out of the Hebrew fountain (we speak of the Latin translations of the Old Testament), but out of the Greek stream, therefore the Greek being not altogether clear, the Latin derived from it must needs be muddy. This moved St Jerome, a most learned father, and the best linguist, without controversy, of his age or of any that went before him, to undertake the translating of the Old Testament out of the very fountains themselves, which he performed with that evidence of great learning, judgement, industry, and faithfulness, that he hath forever bound the Church unto him in a debt of special remembrance and thankfulness.

[20] **Marg**. Augustine, *Of Christian Doctrine*, Book 2, chapter 11 ['the Latin translators can in no way be numbered'].

The translating of the Scripture into the vulgar tongues

Now though the Church were thus furnished with Greek and Latin translations, even before the faith of Christ was generally embraced in the Empire (for the learned know that even in St Jerome's time, the Consul of Rome and his wife were both ethnics,° and about the same time the greatest part of the Senate also),[21] yet for all that the godly learned were not content to have the Scriptures in the language which themselves understood, Greek and Latin (as the good lepers were not content to fare well themselves, but acquainted their neighbours with the store that God had sent, that they also might provide for themselves (2 Kings 7.9)), but also for the behoof and edifying of the unlearned which hungered and thirsted after righteousness, and had souls to be saved as well as they, they provided translations into the vulgar for their countrymen, insomuch that most nations under heaven did shortly after their conversion hear Christ speaking unto them in their mother tongue, not by the voice of their minister only, but also by the written word translated. If any doubt hereof, he may be satisfied by examples enough, if enough will serve the turn. First St Jerome sayeth, *Multarum gentium linguis Scriptura ante translata docet falsa esse quae addita sunt* etc., i.e., 'The Scripture being translated before in the languages of many nations doth show that those things that were added (by Lucian or Hesychius) are false.'[22] So St Jerome in that place. The same Jerome elsewhere affirmeth that he, the time was, had set forth the translation of the Seventy *suae linguae hominibus*, *i.e.*, for his countrymen of Dalmatia.[23] [. . .] In like manner Ulfilas is reported by Paulus Diaconus and Isidore (and before them by Sozomen) to have translated the Scriptures into the Gothic tongue;[24] John, Bishop of Seville by Vasseus, to have turned them into Arabic, about the year of Our Lord 717;[25] Bede by Cistertiensis, to have turned

[21] **Marg**. Jerome, Epistle 23; Ammianus Marcellinus; Zosimus.

[22] **Marg**. Jerome, Preface to the Gospels (Vulgate) [cf. **12**. note 14 above].

[23] **Marg**. Jerome, Preface to the Psalms (Vulgate).

[24] **Marg**. Paulus Diaconus, *Historia miscella*, 12; Isidore, *History of the Goths*; Sozomen, *Historia ecclesia*, 6.37.

[25] **Marg**. Johannes Vaseus, *Rerum Hispaniae memorabilium annales* [Annals of Spain].

a great part of them into Saxon;[26] Efnard by Trithemius, to have abridged the French Psalter, as Bede had done the Hebrew, about the year 800; King Alfred by the said Cistertiensis, to have turned the Psalter into Saxon;[27] Methodius by Aventinus (printed at Ingolstadt) to have turned the Scriptures into Slavonian;[28] Valdo, Bishop of Frising, by Beatus Rhenanus, to have caused about that time the Gospels to be translated into Dutch rhyme, yet extant in the library of Corbinian;[29] Valdus by divers to have turned them himself or to have gotten them turned into French about the year 1160; Charles the Fifth of that name, surnamed 'the Wise', to have caused them to be turned into French about 200 years after Valdus his time, of which translation there be many copies yet extant, as witnesseth Beroaldus.[30] Much about that time, even in our King Richard the Second's days, John Trevisa translated them into English, and many English Bibles in written hand are yet to be seen, with divers translated, as it is very probable, in that age.[31] [. . .] So that to have the Scriptures in the mother tongue is not a quaint conceit lately taken up, either by the Lord Cromwell in England, or by the Lord Radevile in Polonie, or by the Lord Ungnadius in the Emperor's dominion,[32] but hath been thought upon, and put in practice of old, even from the first times of the conversion of any nation; no doubt because it was esteemed most profitable to cause faith to grow in men's hearts the sooner

[26] Venerable Bede (672/3–*c.* 735), of Jarrow and Wearmouth in Northumbria, is the author of *Historia ecclesiastica gentis Anglorum*, an account of the conversions of the Anglo-Saxons to Christianity, but left no Bible translations. The source of the story is William of Malmesbury, *Gesta regum Anglorum* [The History of the English Kings].

[27] **Marg**. Polydore Vergil, *Historia Anglorum* [English History], 5. [See also **1**. n. 7.]

[28] **Marg**. Johannes Aventinus, *Annales Boiorum*, 4.

[29] **Marg**. About the year 900; see Beatus Rhenanus, *Rerum Germanicarum*.

[30] **Marg**. Matthaeus Beroaldus, *Chronicum Scripturae sacrae*, 4.8.

[31] Trevisa] John of Trevisa (1326–1412) translated Higden's *Polychronicon* from the Latin. Caxton's preface to the 1482 edition, STC 13438, sig. a3^{v}, image 3, mentions Trevisa as a Bible translator, but there is no record of his work.

[32] Thomas Cromwell (*c.* 1485–1540) sponsored the publication of the Bible in English from Coverdale (1535) to the Great Bible (1539), which he ordered to be distributed to every parish in the country. Mikolaj Radziwill funded a Protestant Polish translation and Baron Ungnad von Sonnegg a translation into Serbo-Croat (both 1563).

and to make them to be able to say with the words of the Psalm, 'As we have heard, so we have seen' (Psalm 48. 8).

The unwillingness of our adversaries that the Scriptures should be divulged in the mother tongue

Now the Church of Rome would seem at the length to bear a motherly affection towards her children, and to allow them the Scriptures in their mother tongue: but indeed it is a gift, not deserving to be called a gift, an unprofitable gift:[33] they must first get a licence in writing before they may use them, and to get that, they must approve themselves to their confessor, that is, to be such as are, if not frozen in the dregs, yet soured with the leaven of their superstition. Howbeit, it seemed too much to Clement the Eighth that there should be any licence granted to have them in the vulgar tongue, and therefore he overruleth and frustrateth the grant of Pius the Fourth.[34] So much are they afraid of the light of the Scripture (*lucifugae scripturarum*, as Tertullian speaketh)[35] that they will not trust the people with it, no, not as it is set forth by their own sworn men – no, not with the licence of their own Bishops and inquisitors. Yea, so unwilling they are to communicate the Scriptures to the people's understanding in any sort, that they are not ashamed to confess that we forced them to translate it into English against their wills.[36] This seemeth to argue a bad cause, or a bad conscience, or both. Sure we are, that it is not he that hath good gold that is afraid to bring it to the touchstone, but he that hath the counterfeit; neither is it the true man that shunneth the light, but the malefactor, lest his deeds should be reproved (John 3.20); neither is it the plain-dealing merchant that is unwilling to have the weights or the

[33] **Marg**. Sophocles, *Ajax*, 655 ['the gifts of enemies are no gifts and bring no profit'; also included in Erasmus, *Adagia*, 1.3.35].

[34] **Marg**. See the observation (set forth by Clement VIII's authority) upon the fourth rule of Pius IV's making in the Index of Prohibited Books. [The Index of Clement VIII (1596) retracted even the highly circumscribed permission for Catholics to read vernacular translations of the Bible; see also **11**. n. 9. The Latin Bible published under Clement, known as the Clementine Vulgate (1592), was standard until 1979].

[35] **Marg**. Tertullian, On the Resurrection of the Dead, 47. 17.

[36] See Martin, *New Testament*, STC 2884, sig. B2^{r}, image 6.

meteyard° brought in place, but he that useth deceit. But we will let them alone for this fault, and return to translation. [. . .]

A satisfaction to our brethren

[. . .] We are so far off from condemning any of their labours that travailed before us in this kind, either in this land or beyond sea, either in King Henry's time or King Edward's (if there were any translation or correction of a translation in his time[37]), or Queen Elizabeth's of ever-renowned memory, that we acknowledge them to have been raised up of God for the building and furnishing of his Church, and that they deserve to be had of us and of posterity in everlasting remembrance. The judgement of Aristotle is worthy and well-known: 'If Timotheus had not been, we had not had much sweet music; but if Phrynis (Timotheus his master) had not been, we had not had Timotheus.'[38] Therefore blessed be they, and most honoured be their name, that break the ice, and giveth onset upon that which helpeth forward to the saving of souls. Now what can be more available thereto than to deliver God's book unto God's people in a tongue which they understand, since of a hidden treasure, and of a fountain that is sealed, there is no profit? [. . .] Therefore let no man's eye be evil, because His Majesty's is good; neither let any be grieved that we have a Prince that seeketh the increase of the spiritual wealth of Israel (let Sanballats and Tobiahs do so, which therefore do bear their just reproof)[39], but let us rather bless God from the ground of our heart, for working this religious care in him, to have the translations of the Bible maturely considered of and examined. For by this means it cometh to pass, that whatsoever is sound already (and all is sound for substance, in one or other of our editions, and the worst of ours far better than their authentic vulgar)[40] the same will shine as gold more brightly, being rubbed and polished; also, if anything be halting, or superfluous, or not so agreeable

[37] No new English bible translations were published during the reigns of Edward VI (1547–53) or Mary (1553–58), but Edward's reign saw the publication of *The Book of Common Prayer* (1549; revised 1552).
[38] **Marg**. Aristotle, *Metaphysics* 2.1.[4].
[39] See Nehemiah 4.1–3.
[40] authentic vulgar] This may refer either to Martin's translation or to the Vulgate itself.

to the original, the same may be corrected, and the truth set in place. And what can the King command to be done that will bring him more true honour than this? And wherein could they that have been set awork approve their duty to the King, yea, their obedience to God and love to his saints, more than by yielding their service, and all that is within them, for the furnishing of the work? But besides all this, they were the principal motives of it, and therefore ought least to quarrel it; for the very historical truth is that upon the importunate petitions of the Puritans at His Majesty's coming to this crown, the conference at Hampton Court having been appointed for hearing their complaints, when by force of reason they were put from all other grounds, they had recourse at the last to this shift, that they could not with good conscience subscribe to the Communion book, since it maintained the Bible as it was there translated, which was, as they said, a most corrupted translation.[41] And although this was judged to be but a very poor and empty shift,° yet even hereupon did His Majesty begin to bethink himself of the good that might ensue by a new translation, and presently after gave order for this translation which is now presented unto thee. Thus much to satisfy our scrupulous brethren.

An answer to the imputations of our adversaries[42]

Now to the latter we answer that we do not deny, nay, we affirm and avow, that the very meanest translation of the Bible in English set forth by men of our profession (for we have seen none of theirs of the whole Bible as yet)[43] containeth the word of God, nay, is the word of God. As the King's speech which he uttered in Parliament, being translated into French, Dutch, Italian, and Latin, is still the King's speech, though it be not interpreted by every translator with the like grace, nor peradventure so fitly for phrase, nor so expressly for sense, everywhere. [. . .]

[41] corrupted translation] i.e. that of the Bishops' Bible (1568); see **15a** above.

[42] adversaries] i.e. the translators of the Catholic English Bible; see **9** and **11** above.

[43] The Catholic English Old Testament was published at Douai in 1610–11, too late to have any impact on the KJB.

Yet before we end, we must answer a third cavil and objection of theirs against us for altering and amending our translations so oft, wherein truly they deal hardly and strangely with us. For to whomever was it imputed for a fault (by such as were wise) to go over that which he had done, and to amend it where he saw cause? St Augustine was not afraid to exhort St Jerome to a *palinodia* or recantation;[44] the same St Augustine was not ashamed to retractate, we might say revoke, many things that had passed him, and doth even glory that he seeth his infirmities.[45] If we will be sons of the Truth, we must consider what it speaketh, and trample upon our own credit, yea, and upon other men's too, if either be any way a hindrance to it. This to the cause. Then to the persons, we say that of all men they ought to be most silent in this case. For what varieties have they, and what alterations have they made, not only of their service books, portesses,° and breviaries, but also of their Latin translation?[46] [. . .]

The difference that appeareth between our translations, and our often correcting of them, is the thing that we are specially charged with; let us see therefore whether they themselves be without fault this way (if it be to be counted a fault, to correct) and whether they be fit men to throw stones at us. *O tandem maior parcas insane minori*, 'They that are less sound themselves ought not to object infirmities to others.'[47] If we should tell them that Valla, Stapulensis, Erasmus, and Vives found fault with their vulgar translation, and consequently wished the same to be mended, or a new one to be made, they would answer peradventure that we produced their enemies for witnesses against them, albeit they were in no other sort enemies than as St Paul was to the Galatians for telling them the truth (Galatians 4.16), and it were to be wished that they had dared to tell it them plainlier and oftener.[48] But

---

[44] Augustine, Epistle 40.7. See *The Confessions and Letters of St Augustin*, in *Nicene & Post-Nicene Fathers*, vol. 1, ed. by Philip Schaff (Edinburgh: T. and T. Clark, 1996), p. 274.

[45] **Marg**. Augustine, *Retractions*; cf. Epistle 28.4: *video etiam interdum vitia mea* [sometimes I see my own faults].

[46] The Vulgate itself had been revised and the revision approved at the Council of Trent; see **10**. n. 27 above.

[47] **Marg**. Horace, [*Satires* 2.3.326; Smith paraphrases the sense].

[48] Lorenzo Valla (1407–57), Italian humanist whose *Collatio Novi Testamenti* (1442) pioneered a critical comparison of the Vulgate with the Greek New Testament and was a model for Erasmus's method in the *Novum Instrumentum*. (Erasmus edited the first printed edition of 1505.) Faber Stapulensis (Jacques

what will they say to this, that Pope Leo the Tenth allowed Erasmus' translation of the New Testament, so much different from the vulgar, by his Apostolic Letter and Bull; that the same Leo exhorted Pagnine to translate the whole Bible and bear whatsoever charges was necessary for the work?[49] Surely, as the Apostle reasoneth to the Hebrews, that if the former Law and Testament had been sufficient, there had been no need of the latter (Hebrews 7.11; 8.7), so we may say, that if the old vulgar had been at all points allowable, to small purpose had labour and charges been undergone, about framing of a new. [. . .]

The purpose of the translators, with their number, furniture, care etc.

But it is high time to leave them, and to show in brief what we proposed to ourselves, and what course we held in this our perusal and survey of the Bible. Truly, good Christian reader, we never thought from the beginning that we should need to make a new translation, nor yet to make of a bad one a good one (for then the imputation of Sixtus had been true in some sort, that our people had been fed with gall of dragons instead of wine, with whey instead of milk)[50], but to make a good one better, or out of many good ones, one principal good one, not justly to be excepted against; that hath been our endeavour, that our mark. To that purpose there were many chosen that were greater in other men's eyes than in their own, and that sought the truth rather than their own praise. [. . .] If you ask what they had before them, truly it was the Hebrew text of the Old Testament, the Greek of the New. These are the two golden pipes, or rather

Lefèvre d'Etaples, 1460?-1536), author of the first complete translation of the Bible into French (1530). Juan Luis Vives (1492?-1540), Spanish Erasmian humanist and tutor to Mary Tudor who advocated the use of the vernacular in education.

[49] **Marg.** Sixtus Senens [Sanctes Pagninus (1470–1536)]. Leo X had authorized Erasmus's new Latin translation of the New Testament, *Novum Instrumentum* (1516), with the Vulgate and original Greek in parallel, and had lent manuscripts to help with the task. He had also authorized Pagninus's very literal Latin translation (1528), which was the first Latin translation of the Old Testament undertaken directly from the Hebrew since the Vulgate.

[50] Sixtus Quintus, *Biblia Sacra Vulgatae* (1590), preface. The Sistine Vulgate was closely related to the Clementine Vulgate; see note 34 above.

conduits, where-through the olive branches empty themselves into the gold. St Augustine calleth them precedent, or original tongues, St Jerome, fountains.[51] The same St Jerome affirmeth,[52] and Gratian hath not spared to put it into his decree, that 'as the credit of the old books' (he meaneth of the Old Testament) 'is to be tried by the Hebrew volumes, so of the New by the Greek tongue' (he meaneth by the original Greek). If truth be to be tried by these tongues, then whence should a translation be made, but out of them? These tongues, therefore, the Scriptures we say in those tongues, we set before us to translate, being the tongues wherein God was pleased to speak to his Church by his Prophets and Apostles. Neither did we run over the work with that posting haste that the Septuagint did, if that be true which is reported of them, that they finished it in seventy-two days;[53] neither were we barred or hindered from going over it again, having once done it, like St Jerome, if that be true which himself reporteth, that he could no sooner write anything, but presently it was caught from him, and published, and he could not have leave to mend it;[54] neither, to be short, were we the first that fell in hand with translating the Scripture into English, and consequently destitute of former helps, as it is written of Origen, that he was the first in a manner, that put his hand to write commentaries upon the Scriptures, and therefore no marvel, if he overshot himself many times.[55] None of these things: the work hath not been huddled up in seventy-two days, but hath cost the workmen, as light as it seemeth, the pains of twice seven times seventy-two days and more: matters of such weight and consequence are to be speeded with maturity,[56] for in a business of moment a man feareth not the blame of convenient slackness. Neither did we think much to consult the translators or commentators – Chaldee, Hebrew,

---

[51] **Marg.** Augustine, *On Christian Doctrine*, 3.3.[7]; Jerome, Epistle to Sunnias and Fretela [106.2].

[52] **Marg.** Jerome, Epistle to Lucinius [71.5]; Gratian, *Decretum*, Distinctio 9. [This was an authoritative collection of canon law composed in the twelfth century. Here Gratian quotes Jerome.]

[53] **Marg.** Josephus, *Jewish Antiquities*, 12 [107].

[54] **Marg.** Jerome, Letter to Pammachius against Jovinian [Epistles 48.2].

[55] Origen's commentaries were written between 222 and 230; see Eusebius, *Ecclesiastical History*, 6.23.

[56] **Marg.** Sophocles, *Electra* [320, 'A man often hesitates when he is engaged in a great task'].

Syrian, Greek, or Latin – no, nor the Spanish, French, Italian, or Dutch; neither did we disdain to revise that which we had done, and to bring back to the anvil that which we had hammered, but having and using as great helps as were needful, and fearing no reproach for slowness, nor coveting praise for expedition, we have at length, through the good hand of the Lord upon us, brought the work to that pass that you see.

Reasons moving us to set diversity of senses in the margin, where there is great probability for each

Some peradventure would have no variety of senses to be set in the margin, lest the authority of the Scriptures for deciding of controversies by that show of uncertainty should somewhat be shaken. But we hold their judgement not to be sound in this point. For though 'whatsoever things are necessary are manifest', as St Chrysostom sayeth,[57] and as St Augustine, 'In those things that are plainly set down in the Scriptures, all such matters are found that concern faith, hope, and charity.'[58] Yet for all that, it cannot be dissembled, that partly to exercise and whet our wits, partly to wean the curious from loathing of them for their everywhere plainness, partly also to stir up our devotion to crave the assistance of God's spirit by prayer, and lastly, that we might be forward to seek aid of our brethren by conference, and never scorn those that be not in all respects so complete as they should be, being to seek in many things ourselves, it hath pleased God in his divine providence here and there to scatter words and sentences of that difficulty and doubtfulness, not in doctrinal points that concern salvation (for in such it hath been vouched that the Scriptures are plain) but in matters of less moment. [. . .] Therefore, as St Augustine sayeth, that variety of translations is profitable for the finding out of the sense of the Scriptures,[59] so diversity of signification and sense in the margin, where the text is not so clear, must needs do good, yea, is necessary, as we are

[57] **Marg**. Chrysostom, *On Thessalonians*, 2.3 [Homily 14].

[58] **Marg**. Augustine, *On Christian Doctrine*, 2.9.

[59] **Marg**. Augustine, *On Christian Doctrine*, 2.14.21 [Augustine is cited to support 'diversity of signification' in the margin, but this is not the same as the interpretative commentary of the Geneva Bible marginalia which James had forbidden.]

persuaded. We know that Sixtus Quintus expressly forbiddeth that any variety of readings of their vulgar edition should be put in the margin[60] (which though it be not altogether the same thing to that we have in hand, yet it looketh that way), but we think he hath not all of his own side his favourers for this conceit. They that are wise had rather have their judgements at liberty in differences of readings, than to be captivated to one, when it may be the other. [. . .]

Reasons inducing us not to stand curiously upon an identity of phrasing

Another thing we think good to admonish° thee of, gentle reader, that we have not tied ourselves to a uniformity of phrasing or to an identity of words, as some peradventure would wish that we had done, because they observe that some learned men, somewhere, have been as exact as they could that way. Truly, that we might not vary from the sense of that which we had translated before, if the word signified the same thing in both places (for there be some words that be not of the same sense everywhere), we were especially careful, and made a conscience,[61] according to our duty. But that we should express the same notion in the same particular word, as for example, if we translate the Hebrew or Greek word once by 'purpose', never to call it 'intent'; if one where 'journeying', never 'travelling'; if one where 'think', never 'suppose'; if one where 'pain', never 'ache'; if one where 'joy', never 'gladness', etc. Thus to mince the matter we thought to savour more of curiosity° than wisdom, and that rather it would breed scorn in the atheist than bring profit to the godly reader. For is the kingdom of God become words or syllables?[62] Why should we be in bondage to them if we may be free, use one precisely when we may use another no less fit as commodiously? [. . .] We might also be charged (by scoffers) with some unequal dealing towards a great number of good English words. For as it

[60] **Marg**. Sixtus Quintus, *Biblia Sacra Vulgatae* (1590), preface 5.

[61] i.e. made it a matter of conscience.

[62] words or syllables] This may echo Jerome: '[Christ] made it his care to formulate dogmas rather than to hunt for words and syllables', *Principal Works of St Jerome*, ed. by Schaff and Wace, VI, 115.

is written of a certain great philosopher, that he should say that those logs were happy that were made images to be worshipped, for their fellows, as good as they, lay for blocks behind the fire; so if we should say, as it were, unto certain words, 'Stand up higher, have a place in the Bible always', and to others of like quality, 'Get ye hence, be banished forever', we might be taxed peradventure with St James his words, namely, 'to be partial in ourselves and judges of evil thoughts'.[63] Add hereunto that niceness in words[64] was always counted the next step to trifling, and so was to be curious about names too;[65] also that we cannot follow a better pattern for elocution than God himself. Therefore He, using divers words in his Holy Writ, and indifferently[66] for one thing in nature, we, if we will not be superstitious, may use the same liberty in our English versions out of Hebrew and Greek for that copy or store that he hath given us. Lastly, we have on the one side avoided the scrupulosity of the Puritans, who leave the old ecclesiastical words and betake them to other, as when they put 'washing' for 'baptism'[67] and 'congregation' instead of 'Church'; as also on the other side we have shunned the obscurity of the papists, in their 'azymes', 'tunic', 'rational', 'holocausts', 'prepuce', 'pasche', and a number of such like, whereof their late translation is full,[68] and that of purpose to darken the sense, that since they must needs translate the Bible, yet by the language thereof it may be kept from being understood. But we desire that the Scripture may speak like itself, as in the language of Canaan,[69] that it may be understood even of the very vulgar.

---

[63] James 2.4.

[64] niceness in words] Being over-precise or pedantic in choice of vocabulary.

[65] **Marg.** Eusebius, *Praeparatio Evangelica*, 12.8., following Plato, [*Statesman*, 261].

[66] indifferently] i.e. the sense can be conveyed in a variety of ways without compromising the meaning of the divine author. 'Indifference' in this sense of verbal latitude is known as adiaphorism.

[67] As does Sir John Cheke in his purist English translation of Matthew and part of Mark, which attempted only to use vocabulary of Anglo-Saxon origin and was not published until the nineteenth century. See Cheke, *The Gospel according to Saint Matthew*, ed. by James Goodwin (Cambridge, 1843), p. 80.

[68] See the preface to the Old Testament in Gregory Martin, *The Holy Bible* (Douai, 1609–10), STC 2207, sig. †5^{r}, image 5. Following James's instruction on the 'old ecclesiastical words' (see **15b** above) the KJB translators had tried to steer a middle way between Geneva and Rheims.

[69] i.e. as in the original Hebrew of the Old Testament.

e) Samuel Ward, Report to the Synod of Dort (1618)

[Samuel Ward (1572–1643) was a Scholar of Christ's College, Cambridge, who was appointed Master of Sidney Sussex College, Cambridge, in 1610 and Lady Margaret's Professor of Divinity in the university in 1623. Sidney Sussex was a recent foundation with a Puritan reputation and Ward himself was a firm Calvinist. He was responsible for translating the Apocrypha for the KJB as a member of the second Cambridge company. His letter is dated 20 November [1618].

The Synod of Dort was a meeting of representatives from the eight reformed Churches organised by the Dutch Reformed Church and held at Dordrecht in 1618–19. Its purpose was to debate the challenge to Calvinist doctrine from Arminianism, which was condemned as heresy. The Synod also initiated an official translation of the Bible into Dutch and Ward's report of the procedures for the KJB is relevant to this. Ward was one of five British delegates chosen by King James to attend the Synod.

The Latin text of the original was unpublished and is held at Exeter College, Oxford; see *The British Delegation and the Synod of Dort (1618–1619)*, ed. by Anthony Milton (Woodbridge: The Boydell Press, 2005).]

The theologians of Great Britain offered a written explanation of the design and plan in accordance with which the business of the very accurate English version was instituted by the most serene King James, of what plan was observed in distributing the work, and what rules were laid down for the translators; with the intent that any points which might be judged useful to us might be taken from it. A copy of this document is subjoined.

Method which the English theologians followed in the version of the Bible. The theologians of Great Britain, unwilling to give a sudden and unconsidered answer to so important a question, considered it their duty to hold an early consultation, and since honourable mention has been made of the very accurate English translation lately set forth, with great care and at great expense by the most serene King James, to notify to this numerously attended synod the design and plan with which this sacred business was furnished by his most serene Majesty.

Firstly, in the distribution of the work he willed this plan to be observed: the whole text of the Bible was distributed into six sections, and to the translation of each section there were nominated seven or eight men of distinction, skilled in languages.

Two sections were assigned to certain London theologians; the remaining four sections were equally divided among the theologians of the two universities.

After each section had finished its task, twelve delegates, chosen from them all, met together and reviewed and revised the whole work.[1]

Lastly, the Very Reverend the Bishop of Winchester, Bilson,[2] together with Dr Smith, now Bishop of Gloucester, a distinguished man, who had been deeply occupied in the whole work from the beginning, after all things had been maturely weighed and examined, put the finishing touch to this version.

The rules laid down for the translators were of this kind:

In the first place, caution was given that an entirely new version was not to be furnished, but an old version, long received by the Church, to be purged from all blemishes and faults; to this end there was to be no departure from the ancient translation unless the truth of the original text or emphasis demanded.

Secondly, no notes were to be placed in the margin, but only parallel passages to be noted.

Thirdly, where a Hebrew or Greek word admits two meanings of a suitable kind, the one was to be expressed in the text, the other in the margin. The same to be done where a different reading was found in good copies.

Fourthly, the more difficult Hebraisms and Graecisms were consigned to the margin.

Fifthly, in the translation of Tobit and Judith, when any great discrepancy is found between the Greek text and the old vulgate Latin, they followed the Greek text by preference.

---

[1] The 'Committee of Revisers' included John Bois, who left extensive notes (see *Translating for King James*, ed. by Ward Allen (London: Allen Lane, 1970)), Andrew Downes, John Harmer and (possibly) William Hutchison.

[2] Thomas Bilson (1546/7–1616) had been a Fellow of New College, Oxford, and Headmaster of its sister institution, Winchester College, before becoming Bishop of Winchester. His work on church government stands alongside that of Hooker and he was a candidate for the Archbishopric of Canterbury in 1604 and again in 1611, when George Abbot was appointed.

Sixthly, that words which it was anywhere necessary to insert into the text to complete the meaning were to be distinguished by another type, small roman.

Seventhly, that new arguments should be prefixed to every book, and new headings to every chapter.

Lastly, that a very perfect genealogy and map of the Holy Land should be joined to the work.

16. George Wither, *The Psalms*

[George Wither (1588–1667) studied at Magdalen College, Oxford, and the Inns of Court, and worked in a variety of literary genres throughout a long career. As a satirist he was the author of the highly successful *Abuses Stript and Whipt* (1613); he was a writer of pastoral, forming part of a circle with William Browne, Christopher Brooke, John Davies of Hereford, and Michael Drayton, sometimes known as the Jacobean Spenserians; and he published *A Collection of Emblems* in 1635. A pirated edition of his *Works* appeared in 1620. During the Civil Wars he fought on the Parliamentarian side, was associated with the radical Levellers, and was initially close to Cromwell during the Protectorate. After the Restoration, then in his seventies, he was charged with seditious libel and imprisoned for a time in the Tower of London.

A Preparation for the Psalter represents Wither's preliminary thoughts on a replacement for the extremely popular, long-standing metrical versions of the Psalms by Sternhold and Hopkins. This was a project which had been encouraged by King James and the *Preparation* was published in a grand folio edition dedicated to Prince Charles. Wither worked on his psalm translations during the early 1620s, at the same time that James himself was attempting his own versions, and he published related material in *Exercises upon the First Psalme* (1620) and *The Hymns and Songs of the Church* (1623). The complete *Psalmes of David* was not published until 1632, and then only in Amsterdam, dedicated to Princess Elizabeth.

Rivkah Zim, *English Metrical Psalms: Poetry as Praise and Prayer* (Cambridge: Cambridge University Press, 1987); Norton, *History of the Bible as Literature: Vol. 1*; Ian Green, *Print and Protestantism in Early Modern England* (Oxford: Oxford

University Press, 2000), pp. 503–52; Hannibal Hamlin, *Psalm Culture and Early Modern English Literature* (Cambridge: Cambridge University Press, 2004); Donald Mackenzie in *OHLTE* (2), pp. 141–54; Michelle O'Callaghan in *ODNB*.]

a) *A Preparation to the Psalter* (1619)

Chapter 2

To oppose this my proceeding I do expect an army of imputations,° and that many objections shall be brought against me to make frustrate my pains, for I have discovered a whole troupe of them ready to try the strength of my apologies. And these are framed by three sorts of men.[1] The first are such as absolutely except against the whole work. The second dislike only some particulars, or the manner of doing it. And the third take exceptions against me for undertaking it. The former of these three may also be divided into two companies. The one of them disallows all translations of Holy Scriptures into metre. The second allow metre but are obstinate against all new translations. To silence the first I could produce many reverend men, and of authority in the Church, that have mentioned the translation of some parts of the Holy Scripture into verse with approbation and respect; but because they would seem to give reasons for their dislike I choose rather to confute their reasons.

First, whereas they say that verse cannot retain that gravity which becometh the authority of Holy Scriptures, it is false; for how can that speech be denied to have in it gravity wherein every word and syllable must be considered in quantity and number?°[2] Or who can be so ignorant to think so, but such as are altogether

[1] **Marg**. The three sorts of men that except against the author's undertaking.

[2] **Marg**. Their first objection answered, who disallow all translations of the Holy Scriptures into verse. [Wither's point properly refers to verse in classical, i.e. quantitative, metre in which syllables are designated long or short rather than stressed or unstressed as in native English verse. The term 'verse' did not have the modern associations of being a lighter or less serious form of poetry, but referred to poetry that observed the rules of classical metre. However, by the time Wither was writing it was generally accepted that accentual-syllabic verse had its own 'numbers'.]

strangers unto the Muses? For in every language verse hath more elegances than prose can have. And I am of opinion (not without warrant of good authority)[3] that it was partly by reason of the extraordinary majesty and pleasingness which is in numbers that the Holy Ghost chose in them, rather than otherwise, to set down these mysteries as the most fitting language to express sacred things, which shall hereafter appear more at large.[4]

Again, they have supposed it impossible for the translator so to keep himself to the original (in a matter where every letter and syllable is of such moment), but that either for the measure or the rhyme he shall be sometime forced to let go much of the true meaning of the words. But this is also a mistake. For I am certain that if there be anyone who can in prose deliver entirely the truest and most proper sense of these poems, it may be as well expressed in verse. Yea, I believe, and dare maintain, that they may be much better and more naturally done into numbers than into prose.

For if they have at all times (as those who understand them know) a power above the reach of common language, then questionless in expressing things of their own quality they have much more efficacy, and that which is at first written in measured words[5] can never be so well and fitly opened as by the key of poesy.[6] The reason is, there are so many phrases peculiar to that kind of writing, so many metaphors unusual in prose, so many hyperboles, and a multitude of such liberties and conceits as are only proper to itself, that they can never be retained in prose but either the translator will mar the simplicity becoming that speech, or quite darken the majesty of his original, especially if he be one of those many who are not respective° to the quality of numbers.[7]

---

[3] **Marg**. Augustine, *On Sacred Music*, Book 6.

[4] **Marg**. See chapter 9.

[5] measured words] Words in metre, but also with the sense of 'carefully weighed or calculated' (the first citation in the OED for this sense is Wither, *The Dark Lantern* (1653); see Wing 3152, p. 7, image 9); there is a similar double sense in 'gravity' as both 'solemnity' and 'weight' in the metrical sense.

[6] **Marg**. That which was at first written in verse can never be so gracefully turned into prose as into numbers.

[7] i.e. the translator must be responsive to the greater imaginative and rhetorical range in poetry and also have a good ear.

And what is it else which maketh the blockish multitude to lay on poesy that unjust and shameful imputation of lying, but their ignorance of those deep allegories and becoming liberties which it challengeth?[8] Or else their not understanding of the beauty and use which they have in their own places, because they often find them improperly thrust into a language uncapable of such elegancies? [. . .]

Nothing comes to perfection but by degrees. They [our forefathers] laboured according to their talent; we must do according to ours; and those that come after ought, as far as God shall enable them, to amend what we shall happen to oversee. For every generation should as much as in them lieth make plain the work of God to such as shall come after. But now this age is most especially bound thereunto above all that are past. For during many generations before us, such a general ignorance was spread over all Christendom that both the sacred Scriptures, and that holy tongue wherein they were first delivered, was so rarely understood that much corruption crept in, and very few were able to search the fountain from whence the words of life sprang. But considering that former rarity, the knowledge thereof is now common; and, we may say, that God hath in a manner miraculously sent down the gift of tongues again into the Church as he did in the time of the Apostles, and it is almost a wonder to see how frequent the understanding of languages is now become. Which doubtless is vouchsafed that we might make use thereof to his glory, which we can no way better set forth than in making such a plain and easy delivery of his word in our own tongues as shall be most significant and suitable to the majesty thereof. [. . .]

And therefore I turn to those that are only so curious° as to meddle with the manner of handling of this subject[9] [. . .] Some of those would have it a paraphrase, and think that the sense is rather to be followed than the words, because by taking that liberty, as Buchanan, Hessus, Beza, and others in the Latins have

---

[8] **Marg.** The cause why poesy hath been slandered with lying. [The charge that poets lie goes back to Plato's *Republic* and is answered by Sidney in the *Apology for Poetry* (1595), but it is a charge that applies to fictional literature in general and not just to metrical verse. In a scriptural context the negative view of 'poetry' is repeated by Tyndale; see **4**. 14 above.]

[9] **Marg.** Of such things as may be objected against the liberty which may be used in a translation.

done, it would seem, as they think, more graceful in the translation.[10] True it is that the pains would be much less, and peradventure the verse would be more pleasing also to some readers. But I find no such want of ornament in our Prophet's expressions as that I need to borrow them elsewhere, nor is often his way of delivery so difficult as that it must require many circumstances to illustrate his meaning.[11] Or though in my own conceit° his phrases might not appear so plain and powerful as the addition of some other words would make them, yet (reserving° only the proprieties of our language) I have chosen rather to confine myself wholly to the text. Yea, in the smallest things I have taken no liberty but what I find warrantable both by much and good authority, lest I should seem to distrust the force of God's own words and teach his Holy Spirit how to speak.

Some other again there be that would tie me to keep every Hebraism unaltered; some will take dislike because I have not followed that one translation which they affect. Some would have them all in one kind of verse. And some again are displeased because every Psalm is not composed in the same measure whereinto we have it already turned in our common Psalms books.[12] And beside these, so many objections I have heard as makes me think I have adventured upon the only task which is subject to every man's censure: yea, as Jerome said when he was to interpret° one of these Psalms, *aggredior opus difficilimum*, 'I undertake a most difficult task'.[13] And if it were possible so to shape these Psalms as they might be pleasing to each particular man's fancy, I should bring to light the most strange and shapeless chimera that ever was formed by imagination, for there is scarce a cobbler but will undertake to tell you something that is to be

---

[10] George Buchanan (1506–82), Scots Protestant humanist and tutor to James VI and 1, and Eobanus Hessus (1488–1540) both published metrical Latin paraphrases of the Psalms. Beza (Théodore de Bèze) wrote Psalm paraphrases in both Latin and his native French, collaborating with Clément Marot on a vernacular psalter which was completed in 1562. For Buchanan see George Buchanan, *Poetic Paraphrase of the Psalms of David (Psalmorum Davidis paraphrases poetica)*, ed. and trans. by Roger P. H. Green (Paris: Libraire Droz, 2011).

[11] **Marg**. God's word needs no circumstances to give it ornament. [On 'circumstances', see **5**. n. 1 above.]

[12] On the variety of English versions of the Psalms before Wither, see Zim, *English Metrical Psalms*.

[13] **Marg**. Jerome, Letter to Cyprian [Epistle 40, paragraph 2].

done in this business. But it is the judicious and godly man whom I seek to satisfy; as for the rest, neither are they nor their objections worth thinking on, much less a reply.

And yet because charity commands me to be regardless of none, and seeing my aim is to instruct and benefit all men what I may, I would gladly give everyone what satisfaction I might.[14] And forasmuch as it appears somewhat questionable why I should make use of so many kinds of verse in my translation, I protest that I have not done it out of any special affectation of variety, but with an intent to suit the matter of each Psalm, so near as I could, to such numbers as might most aptly express it. For sometime the Prophet describes the person, sometime the condition; now he prays, anon he prophesies. In one Psalm he blesseth, in another he pronounceth judgement. In this he reckoneth up God's benefits; in that he singeth his praises and returneth thanks for them. Here again he setteth down things present, there he relateth things past; in some he laments his sins, in others triumphs over the enemies of the Church – yea, so often varies his subject as it were absurd to imagine that so many sundry passions and such different inventions may be expressed so naturally in one or some few kinds of verse as in many. Yea, the method or manner of speech which the Prophet may use (even in subjects of one nature) will many times require alteration in the numbers, as those who are any whit acquainted with poesy shall easily find. But, howsoever, I have not followed the advice of my own brains in what I have done. For if those that were learned in the Hebrew have not been deceived, there is variety of numbers also in the original. Moreover, because there be some who, not out of self-conceit but through weakness, may take offence, because I have not according to the example of a few modern interpreters altogether used the Hebrew phrase, I have a desire also to satisfy them.[15] Which I should quickly do if they could but understand how decent and proper it were to use the most known dialect[16] of that language which we undertake to deliver

[14] **Marg**. The reason why I have used variety of measures.

[15] Josephus, *Antiquities of the Jews*, Book 7, chapter 10; Jerome, Epistle 155 and preface to *The Chronicle*; Eusebius, preface to Job; Rabbi David Kimchi on Psalm 4.

[16] dialect] 'idiom' or 'manner of speech' rather than a regional variation of a language.

our minds in; for that is ever best translated, and with most ease understood, which we express in words and phrases suitable to our own tongue.[17] And they who think, out of a reverend respect of the Hebrew, to preserve always in their versions her own natural speech, instead of the right which they imagine to give that sacred tongue, do much injure it, because the same phrases which have an extraordinary emphasis in their own language, being verbatim reduced into another, are many times of no force; as would appear if we should, word for word, translate some of those proverbs which are usual in other countries.[18] And certain I am that if ancient authority could not be found to make good my assertion, yet reason makes it manifest. And therefore my opinion is that every translator of the Holy Scriptures ought so to convert those Hebraisms or Graecisms as (if it were possible) they might have the same power, and that into such plain and easy words as are becoming the language which they are reduced° into, rather than by mingling them improperly to overthrow the majesties or confound the properties of both.

Let them either make such English as is intelligible and of force, or else leave the Hebrew words wholly unaltered, as the Apostles and sometime the Fathers have done.[19] For if they undertake to be interpreters, it is fit they should naturalise those phrases they borrow before they insert them among ours, except they be such as have so extraordinary a force that they seem to import more to the reader's mind than other words are able to do, or such as appear doubtful to the interpreter; for some of both sorts I think there be.[20] And they are not only to be interpreted according to our abilities, but religiously to be preserved also, unaltered by the translators; and the reason of this St Jerome gives, whose words are these: *propter vernaculum linguae uniuscuiusque idioma, non posse apud alios sonare ut apud suos*

[17] for that [. . .] own tongue] The argument that the best translations accommodate themselves to the natural idiom of the target language is discernible in earlier discussions of secular verse (see Stanyhurst, **38**. 182–88 below), but rarely stated with such clarity.

[18] **Marg**. See Jerome, 'Letter to Pammachius'.

[19] **Marg**. Maranatha, Raca. & suchlike [both terms of anathema or curse. [Augustine had specified these words as examples of the untranslatable; see *On Christian Doctrine* 2.34; trans. by Green (1995), p. 73.]

[20] **Marg**. Such are *Selah*, *Allelujah* &c.[*Selah* is used frequently in the Psalms and indicates a pause].

dicta sunt, et multo melius esse non interpretata ponere, quam vim eorum interpretatione tenuare.[21]

For my own part, I protest, so careful hath my proceeding been in this to keep a decent mean that I have neither neglected to make use of the Hebrew phrase, where it might appear anything more powerful than ours or be easy and suitable to the language; nor confined myself unto it, where without violating the text I might make it more perspicuous by the English dialect. And because I know that whosoever follows the sense over-securely, without great heed to the words, may sometime make a sense of his own, and seeing he who addicts himself wholly to the words, without much care of the sense, may oftentimes make nonsense, therefore I have evermore carried an indifferent° regard both to the sense and the words, which middle way every man ought to keep; or else, according to the saying of the poet: *Incidit in Scyllam cupient vitare Charybdim*, 'He doth on Scylla run, that would Charybdis shun.'[22]

Moreover, that no man may be justly offended, nor my own conscience troubled for anything purposely committed in my metrical translation, I have as near as I was able kept myself to the very words of the Psalms, and have been fearful to take unto me the liberty of coining new words or of expressing myself in phrases borrowed from a heathen poet, as some endeavouring this work have done.[23] For I know it is unseemly, and to mix them with the sacred word of God must needs be more distasteful to the ear of a good and zealous Christian than a garment of linsey-woolsey[24] is to a Jew. And I remember Athanasius hath a caveat for it: 'take heed', sayeth he, 'that out of affectation of eloquence you seek not to trim the Psalms (and prayers of the Prophets) with new-coined phrases of the time, lest you adulterate the sense or put one matter for another. But according to that simplicity wherein they are written, recite and sing them, so the

[21] **Marg**. Jerome to Marcella, Epistle 63, paragraph 2 ['because of the native idiom of any tongue, some things cannot be said, so it is much better not to translate them than to give a weak translation'. The reference should be to Epistle 26.2; Epistle 63 is to Theophilus].

[22] Proverbial (and recorded in Erasmus, *Adagia* 1.5.4).

[23] **Marg**. New words, or foreign phrases are as much as may be avoided in the translations of holy Scriptures.

[24] linsey-woolsey] A textile combining linen and wool which religious law forbids Jews to wear.

Holy Ghost who hath spoken them will acknowledge his own words and further your desires'.[25] To this purpose are his words, and yet I do not think it is to be understood, as some would have it, that Athanasius intended they should be repeated by all men and at all times in the original tongue. For he himself did not so, nor do I think that he meant to bind men unto such translations as should word for word interpret the Scriptures, without regard of what beseemed the language into which it was turned, for he also made use of another kind of version. And that the Scriptures are sometime better translated when they are interpreted according to their sense than word for word is the opinion of St Jerome, Epistle 71, *Ad Pammachium, de optime genere interpretandi.* [. . .][26]

Chapter 3

I have endeavoured a translation of the Psalms into verses of several kinds, keeping (so near as I could do) even the very words of our English translation, because I would give the less cause of offence to the captious reader.[27] And where I am compelled to use synonyms, I have been so careful to get words of the same power that I have no more differed from that version than two prose translations agreeing in the same sense may differ one from another, saving in such things as by the consent both of Protestant and papist interpreters° may be indifferently taken, either this way or that, without prejudice to the matter; nor have I done so much but where some necessity in the number or the propriety of our tongue did seem to require it. And to my knowledge I have neither for conceit in the measure, nor for other end, left out or put in any one word by which the sense may be either made more, or less, or mistaken. Yea, if the words in the prose were of that nature (or so placed) as they might seem to bear a double interpretation, I have laboured so to turn them into verse that I have not confined them to any one sense, but preserved the

[25] Athanasius (Archbishop of Alexandria), Letter to Marcellinus, 'On the Interpretation of the Psalms'. For a modern translation, see *The Life of Antony and the Letter to Marcellinus*, trans. by Robert C. Gregg (New York: Paulist Press, 1980). This is the earliest work on psalm-reading and held in high esteem.

[26] 'On the best way of translating'. The reference should be to Epistle 57.

[27] **Marg**. The order of proceeding used by this author in his employment about the Psalms.

liberty of a twofold understanding. For those that do not so, geld the Scriptures and many times run on with a sense far from the meaning of the Holy Ghost, which I have ever been so fearful of that, when I might have tied sentences together with much more elegancy, I have chosen for the reason afore-specified rather to use such simple expressions as you shall find. And since I first entered into this subject, I still kept with me so much consideration as to remember that such holy things were neither to be handled rashly nor used as exercises of vain wit. Yea, I know that the beauty of these poems consisteth not in those ornaments of speech which make plausible° other writings. But, as St Paul sayeth of his Gospel, 'it is in demonstration of the spirit and of power' (1 Corinthians 2.4). And I hope, therefore, that those who are judicious, though they have had their ears seasoned with the music of other poesy, will consider that it is necessary and decent these odes should be expressed in a phrase rather answerable to their gravity than in that which is every way suitable to the language of other poems.[28] And I think also that somewhat the more plainness is to be used, because it is a subject wherein applause is not so much to be sought for, as this that the meanest capacities be fitted as well as the best pleased.

b) *The Psalms of David Translated into Lyric Verse* (1632)

A Preface to the Reader.

This translation long since finished in blurred° papers (and often called for) I lately made legible to others, and it had my leave to seek a public pass into the world, which if it merit to obtain, be the fault theirs who shall oppose it. I waited long to see a more exact performance, but none appearing, answerable to the dignity of our English muses, I have sent forth my essay to provoke others to discover their endeavours on this subject, that, choice being had, the best might receive the best approbation.

I have had more care to suit the capacity of the vulgar than to observe those criticisms which arride° the learned, yet I hope with

[28] odes [. . .] other poems] Cf. Ephesians 5.19. The term 'ode' (Greek ōdē = 'song') also points towards the metrical variety of Horace's *Odes* and the Greek tradition he imitates.

so much discretion that the best judgements shall have no cause to despise it. For though the language be plain, it is significant, and such a dialect[1] as is likely to continue unchanged, when fantastical expressions will grow as unfashionable as our clothes. It is also briefer by above a fourth part[2] than the translations which I have yet seen in any language of Europe, and preserves likewise the words of the prose, the fullness of the sense, and the relish of the Scripture phrase as well as any of them. Which, considering how much other vulgar tongues have ignorantly been preferred before our[s] (how difficultly the Hebrewisms are contracted, how much the often translation from one matter and from one person to another interrupts brief knitting of things together, and how much the frequent rhymes and other things considerable in lyric translations interrupt such briefness) is a great honour to our language; especially seeing my brevity hath made no Psalm obscurer, but rather so easy to be understood that some readers have confessed it hath been instead of a comment unto them in sundry hard places.[3]

If you expect such elegant-seeming paraphrases as are composed by those who, selecting easy and passionate Psalms, have trimmed them up with rhetorical illustrations (suitable to their fancies and the changeable garb of affected language), I shall deceive your expectation, for I have purposely avoided those descants and confined myself to the grave and simple language of the text. And I was thereby the better kept from wandering after mine own sense as in their circumlocutions they have done. Beside, their versions are fitted rather to be read than sung, which giveth a greater liberty to the translator. For though it be most graceful in a reading-poem when the period° is cast sometime into one part of the line or stanza and sometime into another, yet in a lyric composition, where the same staff° is often reiterated to one tune, the periods and words of the same quantity must be always observed in the same places. For if there be not always a decent pause in the matter when the tune is ended, or if in the singing the natural quantity of the word be adulterated, or, if we be not careful that a full

[1] dialect] See **16a**. 150.

[2] a fourth part] a quarter.

[3] i.e. the transparency of the expression makes the translation its own commentary. This presents translation as interpretation.

point[4] fall not where the tune is in the height of a continuing strain,[5] it will sound very absurdly to a judicious ear, as may appear by offering to sing some of those composures° which are plausible° in reading.

[4] full point] full stop, i.e. at the end of a sentence. The musical structure must be tied to the grammatical structure: sound must work in harmony with sense.
[5] in the height [. . .] strain] in the middle of a melodic line.

PART TWO
LITERARY TRANSLATION

17. William Caxton, *The Recuyell of the Histories of Troy* (1473–74)

[William Caxton (*c.* 1422–1491) was born in Kent and became a mercer and merchant adventurer who turned to translation and printing quite late in his career. Based for thirty years in Bruges, he became governor of the English Nation there in 1463. As a diplomat mixing with the aristocracy he would have been aware of the trade in luxury manuscripts between the Burgundian court and England and realised that this could be commercially exploited by a printing press. This was set up first at Bruges in 1472 and then from 1475–76 at Westminster, where the German Wynkyn de Worde acted as his foreman. The first book printed in England was *The Canterbury Tales*, published in late 1476 or early 1477, and over a hundred more publications followed. These included his own translations of Aesop, Christine de Pizan, the *Golden Legend*, and the *Aeneid*, all from French sources. A manuscript survives of Caxton's translation of Ovid's *Metamorphoses* from the *Ovide moralisée*, but there is no evidence that it was ever printed.

The *Histories of Troy* was Caxton's first translation into English, dedicated to Margaret, Duchess of Burgundy, who may also have commissioned it. Begun in 1468/69, it was interrupted by political events in England, in which Caxton had a diplomatic role, and completed at Cologne in 1471. It was at Cologne that he first acquired a printing press and learned the trade. Caxton returned to Bruges in December 1472 and the book was printed there at some point over the next two years. The work acknowledges the tradition that the heroes of ancient Greece were the ancestors of the Dukes of Burgundy. The source text is Raoul Lefèvre's *Recueil des histories de Troies* (1464).

See N. F. Blake, *Caxton and his World* (London: Andre Deutsch, 1969); Miguel Márquez, 'Aspects of Vocabulary Building in Caxton's *Recuyell of the Historyes of Troy*', *English Studies*, 72 (1991), 328–49; Lotte Hellinga, *Caxton and Early Printing in England* (London: British Library, 2010); A. E. B. Coldiron, 'William Caxton', in *OHLTE* (1), pp. 160–69.]

Here beginneth the volume entitled and named *The Recuyell*° *of the Histories of Troy* composed and drawn out of diverse books of Latin into French by the right venerable person and worshipful man, Raoul le Fèvre, priest and chaplain unto the right noble, glorious, and mighty prince in his time Philip, Duke of Bourgogne,[1] of Brabant etc. in the year of the incarnation of Our Lord God a thousand, four-hundred, sixty-and-four, and translated and drawn out of French into English by William Caxton, mercer of the city of London, at the commandment of the right high, mighty, and virtuous princess, his redoubted lady, Margaret,[2] by the grace of God Duchess of Bourgogne, of Lautrec, of Brabant etc. Which said translation and work was begun in Bruges in the county of Flanders the first day of March, the year of the incarnation of Our said Lord God a thousand, four-hundred, sixty-and-eight, and ended and finished in the holy city of Cologne, the nineteenth day of September, the year of Our said Lord God, a thousand, four-hundred, sixty-and-eleven etc.

Prologue to Book 1

When I remember that every man is bounden by the commandment and counsel of the wise man to eschew sloth and idleness, which is mother and nourisher of vices, and ought to put myself unto virtuous occupation and business, then I, having no great charge of occupation, following the said counsel took a French book, and read therein many strange and marvellous histories, wherein I had great pleasure and delight, as well for the novelty of the same as for the fair language of French, which was in prose so well and compendiously set and written, which methought I understood the sentence° and substance of every matter. And for so much as this book was new and late made and drawn into French, and never had seen it in our English tongue, I thought in myself it should be a good business to translate it into our English, to the end that it might be had as well in the royalme of England as in other lands, and also for to pass therewith the time, and thus concluded in myself to begin this said work, and forthwith took pen and ink and began boldly to run forth as blind

[1] Bourgogne] Burgundy.

[2] Margaret] Sister of Edward IV, she married Philip, Duke of Burgundy, in 1468.

[3] blind Bayard] See **3**. 309 above.

Bayard[3] in this present work, which is named *The Recuyell of the Trojan Histories*. And afterward when I remembered myself of my simpleness and unperfectness that I had in both languages, that is to wit in French and in English, for in France was I never, and was born and learned mine English in Kent, in the Weald, where I doubt nor is spoken as broad and rude English as in any place of England, and have continued by the space of thirty years, for the most part in the countries of Brabant, Flanders, Holland, and Zealand; and thus when all these things came tofore° me, after that I had made and written five or six quires[4] I fell in despair of this work, and purposed no more to have continued therein, and those quires laid apart, and in two year after laboured no more in this work, and was fully in will to have left it, till on a time it fortuned that the right high, excellent, and right virtuous princess, my right redoubted lady, my lady Margaret, by the grace of God sister unto the King of England and of France, my sovereign lord[5] [. . .] sent for me to speak with her good grace of diverse matters, among the which I let her Highness have knowledge of the foresaid beginning of this work, which anon commanded me to show the said five or six quires to her said grace. And when she had seen them, anon she found a default in my English,[6] which she commanded me to amend, and moreover commanded me straitly° to continue and make an end of the residue then not translated, whose dreadful commandment I durst in no wise disobey, because I am a servant unto her said grace and receive of her yearly fee and other many good and great benefits, and also hope many more to receive of her Highness, but forthwith went and laboured in the said translation after my simple and poor cunning,° also nigh as I can following mine author, meekly beseeching the bounteous highness of my said lady that of her benevolence list° to accept and take in gree° this simple and rude work here following. And if there be anything written or said to her pleasure, I shall think my labour well employed, and whereas there is default that she aret° it to the simpleness of my cunning, which is full small in this behalf, and

[4] quires] Four sheets of paper folded to form eight leaves.

[5] A long list of her further titles is omitted.

[6] default in my English] Margaret may have judged Caxton's English to have fallen short of the high style apropriate to courtly culture (Hellinga, *William Caxton and Early Printing*, p. 108).

require and pray all them that shall read this said work to correct it and to hold me excused of the rude and simple translation.

Epilogue to Book 2

Thus endeth the second book of *The Recuyell of the Histories of Troy*, which books were late translated into French out of Latin by the labour of the venerable person Raoul le Fèvre, priest, as afore is said, and by me, indign° and unworthy, translated into this rude English by the commandment of my said redoubted lady, Duchess of Bourgogne. And forasmuch as I suppose the said two books be not had tofore this time in our English language, therefore I had the better will to accomplish this said work, which work was begun in Bruges and continued in Ghent and finished in Cologne, in the time of the troublous world,[7] and of the great divisions being and reigning, as well in the royalmes of England and France as in all other places universally through the world, that is to wit the year of Our Lord a thousand, four-hundred, seventy-one. And as for the third book, which treateth of the general and last destruction of Troy, it needeth not to translate it into English, forasmuch as that worshipful and religious man, Dan John Lydgate,[8] monk of Bury, did translate it but late, after whose work I fear to take upon me, that am not worthy to bear his penner° and ink-horn after him to meddle me in that work. But yet forasmuch as I am bound to contemplate my said lady's good grace, and also that his work is in rhyme,[9] and as far as I know it is not had in prose in our tongue, and also peradventure he translated after some other author than this is, and yet forasmuch as diverse men be of diverse desires, some to read in rhyme and metre and some in

---

[7] troublous world] In 1470 Caxton was involved in diplomatic negotiations between England and the Hanseatic merchants, but these were interrupted by the Earl of Warwick's rebellion and the deposition of Edward IV, who fled to the Low Countries. Edward regained his throne in 1471 after the dispute was settled.

[8] Lydgate] (*c.* 1370–1449/50?) was prior of Hatfield Regis near Bury St Edmunds and a poet who acknowledged Chaucer as his master. His *Troy Book* was based on the *Historia destructionis Troiae* of Guido delle Colonne (1287) and was completed in 1420. It was first printed in 1513 by Richard Pynson on the order of Henry VIII as *The Hystorye, sege and dystruccyon of Troye* (STC 5579).

[9] rhyme] A general term for verse in native English metre.

prose, and also because that I have now good leisure, being in Cologne, and have none other thing to do at this time, in eschewing of idleness, mother of all vices, I have delibered° in myself for the contemplation of my said redoubted lady to take this labour in hand, by the sufferance and help of Almighty God, whom I meekly supply° to give me grace to accomplish it to the pleasure of her that is causer thereof, and that she receive it in gree of me, her faithful, true, and most humble servant, etc.

Epilogue to Book 3

Thus end I this book, which I have translated after mine author as nigh as God hath given me cunning, to whom be given the laud and praising. And forasmuch as in the writing of the same my pen is worn, mine hand weary and not steadfast, mine eyen dimmed with overmuch looking on the white paper, and my courage° not so prone and ready to labour as it hath been, and that age creepeth on me daily and feebleth all the body, and also because I have promised to divers gentlemen and to my friends to address to them as hastily as I might this said book, therefore I have practised and learned at my great charge and dispense° to ordain° this said book in print, after the manner and form as ye may here see, and is not written with pen and ink as other books be, to the end that every man may have them at once. For all the books of this story named *The Recuyell of the Histories of Troy* thus imprinted as ye here see, were begun in one day and also finished in one day, which book I have presented to my said redoubted lady as afore is said, and she hath well accepted it and largely rewarded me, wherefore I beseech Almighty God to reward her everlasting bliss after this life, praying her said grace and all them that shall read this book not to disdain the simple and rude work, neither to reply against the saying of the matters touched in this book, though it accord not unto the translation of other which have written it. For diverse men have made diverse books which in all points accord not, as Dictys, Dares,[10]

[10] Dictys, Dares] Dictys Cretensis and Dares Phrygius supposedly recorded first-hand accounts of the Trojan War. The works attributed to them (*Ephemeris belli Troiani* and *Historia de excidio Troiae*), which actually date from late antiquity, were popularised in the medieval period by Guido delle Colonne.

and Homer. For Dictes and Homer, as Greeks, say and write favourably for the Greeks, and give to them more worship than to the Trojans, and Dares writeth otherwise than they do, and also as for the proper names, it is no wonder that they accord not, for some one name in these days have diverse equivocations after the countries that they dwell in, but all accord in conclusion the general destruction of that noble city of Troy and the death of so many noble princes, as kings, dukes, earls, barons, knights, and common people, and the ruin irreparable of that city that never since was re-edified, which may be ensample to all men during the world how dreadful and jeopardous it is to begin a war, and what harms, losses, and death followeth. Therefore the Apostle sayeth, 'All that is written is written to our doctrine',[11] which doctrine for the common weal I beseech God may be taken in such place and time as shall be most needful in increasing of peace, love, and charity, which grant us He that suffered for the same to be crucified on the rood-tree. And say we all Amen for charity.

18. William Caxton, *Eneydos* [The Aeneid] (1490)

[The translation of the *Aeneid* was dedicated to Arthur, Prince of Wales (before he could read). Caxton's work is at some distance from Virgil's original, as Douglas contemptuously points out in the Prologue to his own translation (see **19**. 59–121), leaving out large parts of the poem and giving particular prominence to the story of Dido and Aeneas. The source text is Guillaume le Roy's French version (1483) of an Italian paraphrase, together with Boccaccio's *De Casibus illustrium virorum*. See also *Caxton's Eneydos*, ed. by W. T. Culley and F. J. Furnivall (London: EETS, 1890); *Caxton's Own Prose*, ed. by N. F. Blake (London: André Deutsch, 1973).]

[11] Romans 15.4. The KJB translation, 'For whatsoever things were written aforetime were written for our learning, that we through patience and comfort of the scriptures might have hope' better emphasizes the moral resources of history, which is Caxton's point here.

After divers works made, translated, and achieved, having no work in hand, I sitting in my study[1] where as lay many divers pamphlets and books, [it] happened that to my hand came a little book in French, which late was translated out of Latin by some noble clerk° of France, which book is named Eneydos, made in Latin by that noble poet and great clerk, Virgil. Which book I saw over and read therein how after the general destruction of the great Troy, Aeneas departed bearing his old father Anchises upon his shoulders, his little son Iulus[2] on his hand, his wife with much other people following, and how he shipped and departed, with all the history of his adventures that he had ere he came to the achievement of his conquest of Italy, as all along shall be showed in this present book. In which book I had great pleasure by cause of the fair and honest terms and words in French, which I never saw tofore° like, ne none so pleasant ne so well-ordered. Which book as meseemed should be much requisite to noble men to see, as well for the eloquence as the histories, how well that many hundred years past was the said book of Eneydos with other works made and learned daily in schools, specially in Italy and other places, which history the said Virgil made in metre. And when I had advised me in this said book, I delibered° and concluded to translate it into English, and forthwith took a pen and ink and wrote a leaf or twain, which I oversaw again to correct it. And when I saw the fair and strange terms therein, I doubted that it should not please some gentlemen which late blamed me, saying that in my translations I had over-curious° terms which could not be understood of common people, and desired me to use old and homely terms in my translations.

And fain would I satisfy every man, and so to do took an old book and read therein, and certainly the English was so rude and broad that I could not well understand it. And also My Lord Abbot of Westminster[3] did show to me late certain evidences written in Old English for to reduce° it into our English now used. And certainly it was written in such wise that it was more like to Dutch than English.[4] I could not reduce ne bring it to be

[1] my study] Possibly Caxton's bookshop (Blake).

[2] Iulus] Alternative name for Ascanius, Aeneas's son.

[3] Abbot of Westminster] John Estney, abbot from 1474 to 1498.

[4] Dutch] German. Early modern 'Dutch' covered both German ('High Dutch') and Dutch/Flemish ('Low Dutch').

understood. And certainly our language now used varieth far from that which was used and spoken when I was born, for we Englishmen be born under the domination of the moon, which is never steadfast, but ever wavering, waxing one season and waneth and decreaseth another season, and that common English that is spoken in one shire varieth from another.[5] Insomuch that in my days happened that certain merchants were in a ship in Thames for to have sailed over the sea into Zeeland, and for lack of wind they tarried at Foreland and went to land for to refresh them. And one of them, named Sheffield, a mercer, came into a house and asked for meat, and specially he asked after eggs, and the goodwife answered that she could speak no French. And the merchant was angry, for he also could speak no French, but would have had eggs, and she understood him not. And then at last another said that he would have eyren; then the goodwife said that she understood him well.[6]

Lo, what should a man in these days now write, eggs or eyren? Certainly it is hard to please every man, by cause of diversity and change of language, for in these days every man that is in any reputation in his country will utter his communication and matters in such manners and terms that few men shall understand them.

And some honest and great clerks have been with me and desired me to write the most curious terms that I could find, and thus between plain rude and curious I stand abashed.° But in my judgment the common terms that be daily used are lighter° to be understood than the old and ancient English. And forasmuch as this present book is not for a rude, uplandish° man to labour therein ne read it, but only for a clerk and a noble gentleman that feeleth and understandeth in feats of arms in love and in noble chivalry, therefore in a mean between both I have reduced and translated this said book into our English, not over-rude ne curious, but in such terms as shall be understood by God's grace according to my copy. And if any man will entermete° in reading of it and findeth such terms that he cannot understand, let him

[5] On the 'Renaissance discovery of dialect' and the emergence of 'common English' see Paula Blank, *Broken English: Dialects of English and the Politics of Language in Renaissance Writings* (London: Routledge, 1996), pp. 7–32; see also **20**. n. 1 below.

[6] The distinction is between northern (eggs) and southern (eyren) forms of English.

go read and learn Virgil or the epistles of Ovid, and there he shall see and understand lightly all, if he have a good reader and informer, for this book is not for every rude and uncunning man to see, but for clerks and very gentlemen that understand gentleness and science.[7]

Then I pray all them that shall read in this little treatise to hold me for excused for the translating of it, for I knowledge myself ignorant of cunning to emprise° on me so high and noble a work. But I pray Master John Skelton,[8] late created Poet Laureate in the University of Oxford, to oversee and correct this said book and to address and expone where as shall be found fault to them that shall require it, for him I know for sufficient to expone° and English every difficulty that is therein. For he hath late translated the epistles of Tully[9] and the book of Diodorus Siculus,[10] and divers other works out of Latin into English, not in rude and old language, but in polished and ornate terms craftily, as he that hath read Virgil, Ovid, Tully, and all the other noble poets and orators to me unknown. And also he has read the nine Muses and understood their musical sciences,[11] and to whom of them each science is appropred°. I suppose he has drunk of Helicon's well.[12] Then I pray him and such other to correct, add, or minish° where he or they shall find fault, for I have but followed my copy in French as nigh as me is possible, and if any word be said therein well, I am glad, and if otherwise I submit my said book to their correction. Which book I present unto the high-born, my to-coming° natural and sovereign lord Arthur[13] by the grace of God

---

[7] gentleness and science] noble and chivalrous behaviour; learning. Caxton identifies his audience as the first two of the three 'estates' or social ranks.

[8] Skelton] John Skelton (*c.* 1460–1529) claimed to have received this honour from the university senate (see 'Against Garnesche'). He left Oxford to become tutor to Prince Henry (later Henry VIII).

[9] Tully] Cicero

[10] Skelton translated Poggio Bracciolini's *Bibliotheca Historica of Diodorus Siculus* in 1488. Rhetorically elaborate and with many neologisms, the translation was a strained attempt to show off the expressive capabilities of English.

[11] musical sciences] i.e. the various arts and branches of knowledge governed by the Muses.

[12] Helicon's well] Mount Helicon was the site of the two springs sacred to the Muses, Aganippe, and Hippocrene (the latter associated with poetic inspiration).

[13] Arthur] The eldest son of Henry VII and only three years old at the time of Caxton's dedication.

Prince of Wales, Duke of Cornwall, and Earl of Chester, first-begotten son and heir unto our most dread, natural, and sovereign lord and most Christian king, Henry the VII, by the grace of God King of England and of France and Lord of Ireland, beseeching his noble grace to receive it in thank of me his most humble subject and servant. And I shall pray unto Almighty God for his prosperous increasing in virtue, wisdom, and humanity, that he may be equal with the most renowned of all his noble progenitors.

And so to live in this present life, that after this transitory life he and we all may come to everlasting life in heaven. Amen.

19. Gavin Douglas, *Eneados* [The Aeneid] (1513)[1]

Edited by Gordon Kendal

[Gavin Douglas (*c.* 1476–1522) was born into a noble Scottish family and was a member of the regency council after James IV was killed at Flodden in 1513, the year he completed his translation of the *Aeneid.* His principal earlier work was the dream-allegory, *The Palace of Honour* (1501) and he is also the author of a moral allegory, *King Heart*. The humanist scholars John Major and Polydore Vergil were among his acquaintance. He was appointed Bishop of Dunkeld in 1515 and died in London, probably of the plague, while on a diplomatic mission to secure help from Henry VIII in the Scottish troubles.

Douglas set out to translate the *Aeneid* in 1511, encouraged by his kinsman, Henry, Lord Sinclair. The poem is written in Middle Scots, though with elements of 'southern', as Douglas concedes in the prologue, to produce what Gordon Kendal describes as 'a complex blend of proto-Scots and proto-English' (p. xviii). He uses decasyllabic rhyming couplets and includes all Virgil's twelve books, plus a thirteenth book written by Maphaeus Vegius in 1428. *Eneados* was not printed until 1553, but Surrey read the poem in manuscript in the 1540s and it influenced his own translation of *Aeneid* 2 and 4 (printed 1557), which represent

[1] The text and annotations are taken from Gavin Douglas, *The Aeneid (1513)*, ed. by Gordon Kendal, 2 vols (London: MHRA, 2011) with some additional glosses and notes by Neil Rhodes.

the first examples of blank verse in English. Douglas's translation was highly praised by C. S. Lewis in *English Literature in the Sixteenth Century* (1954). The source text is the edition printed at Paris in 1500/01 with the commentary by Jodocus Badius Ascensius and there is evidence of Douglas's use of Ascensius in his translation.

Note: in Scots, 'a' often corresponds to English short 'o' or long 'a-e' (strang/strong, mak/make), 'ai' to long 'o' (wrait/wrote), 'au' to long 'o' (saul/soul), 'ei' to short 'e' or long 'y' (deid/dead, heich/high), guttural 'ch' (thoct/thought), and 'k' to 'tch' (sic/such).

See also Priscilla Bawcutt, *Gavin Douglas: A Critical Study* (Edinburgh: Edinburgh University Press, 1976); Robert Cummings, '"To the Cart the Fift Quheill": Gavin Douglas's Humanist Supplement to the *Eneados*', *Translation and Literature*, 4 (1995), 131–56; Gordon Kendal, *Translation as Creative Retelling: Constituents, Patterning and Shift in Gavin Douglas' Eneados* (Saarbrucken: Lambert Academic Publishing, 2010).]

Far greater difference betwixt my blunt endite *writing*
And thy sharp sugurat sang Virgilian,
Sae wisely wrocht with never a word in vain.
My wavering wit, my cunning (feeble at all),[1]
My mind misty, there may nocht miss a fall:
Strae for this ignorant blabbering imperfite *(worth only straw)*
Beside thy polished terms redimite! *beautiful*
And naetheless, with support and correction,
For natural love and friendful affection
Whilk I bear to thy works and endite
(Although, God wit, I knaw therein full lite), *little*
And that thy facund sentence micht be sung *eloquent, meaning*
In our language as weel as Latin tongue –
'As weel'! na, na: impossible were, perdee!
Yet with your leave, Virgil, to follow thee,
I wald into my rural, vulgar gross
Write some savouring of thy *Eneados*.
But sair I dreid for to distain thee quite

[1] at all] i.e. 'altogether'.

Through my corruptit cadence imperfite –
'Distain thee'! na, forsooth, that may I nocht:
Weel may I shaw my borrel, busteous thocht, *rough, vigorous*
But thy work shall endure in laud and glory,
But spot or fault, condign eterne memory.
Though I offend, unharmit is thy fame,
Thine is the thank, and mine shall be the shame [. . .]
First I protest, beaux sirs (by your leave),
Be weel advisit, my work ere ye repreif,
Consider it warely, read ofter than aince: *carefully*
Weel at ae blenk slee poetry nocht tane is. *glance, clever*
And yet, forsooth, I set my busy pain
As that I should, to mak it braid and plain,
Keeping nae southern, but our ain language,
And speaks as I learnit when I was page. *child*
Nor yet sae clean all southern I refuse,
But some word I pronounce as neighbour does,
Like as in Latin been Greek terms some.
Sae me behovit whilom (or then[2] be dumb)
Some bastard Latin, French, or English use –
Where scant were Scots I had nae other choice;
Nocht for our tongue is in the selfin scant, *because, in itself*
But for that I the fouth of language want – *fullness*
Whereas the colour of his property, *where, quality*
To keep the sentence, thereto constrainit me;
Or then to mak my sang short sometime,
Mair compendious, or to likely my rhyme.[3]
Therefore good friends, for a jimp or a bourd, *quirk, joke*
I pray you note me nocht at every word. *criticise*
The worthy clerk hecht Laurence of the Vale,[4] *called*
Amang Latins a great patron (sans fail),
Grants, when twelve years he had been diligent
To study Virgil, scant knew he what he meant;
Then thou or I, my friend, when we best ween *think*
To have Virgil read, understand, and seen –

[2] or then] S. 'or than'; possibly 'rather than', but cf. 44 below.

[3] to likely my rhyme] *OED* (B.3) quotes this for the sense of 'adorn, embellish', but the sense of 'fit, resemble' seems better.

[4] Lorenzo Valla (1407–1457), Italian humanist rhetorician and author of *Elegantiae linguae Latinae*; a major influence on Erasmus.

The richt sentence perchance is far to seek.
The ilk work twelve years first was in making eik,
And nocht correct when the poet gan decease.
Thus for small faults, my wise friend, hauld thy peace.
Adhering to my protestation,
Though William Caxton,[5] of English nation,
In prose has prent a book of English gross,
Cleping it *Virgil in Eneados*,
Whilk that he says of French he did translate,
It has naething ado therewith, God wit,
Nor nae mair like than the devil and Saint Augustine.[6]
Have he nae thank therefore – but lost his pain –
Sae shamefully that story did pervert.
I read his work with harms at my heart
That sic a book, but sentence or ingine, *skill*
Should be entitlit after the poet divine.
His ornate golden verses, mair than gilt,
I spittit for despite to see sae spilt *disfigured*
With sic a wicht, whilk truly (by mine intent) *by such a man*
Knew never three words of all that Virgil meant.
Sae far he chops,[7] I am constrainit to flyte.[8]
The three first books he has owerhippit quite, *skipped*
Saving a little touching Polydorus
And the tempest sent furth by Aeolus:
And that full simply on his ain guise –
Virgil them wrait all on another wise –
For Caxton puts in his book out of tune
The storm furth sent by Aeolus and Neptune;
But wha that reads Virgil soothfastly *truthfully*
Shall find Neptune save Aeneas' navy.
Me list nocht shaw how the story of Dido
By this Caxton is hail pervertit so,

[5] Caxton] *Eneydos*, ed. by W. T. Culley and F. J. Furnivall (London: EETS, 1890). See **18**. above.

[6] Augustine] Bishop and saint (354–430), who was personally important for Douglas. His controversial exchanges with Jerome on Bible translation are frequently cited by both Catholics and Protestants in the sixteenth century.

[7] chops] S. 'chowps'. Coldwell suggests 'mumbles', but it is more likely to be (with 'far') 'assaults haphazardly', skewing the entire plot.

[8] flyte] chide, quarrel; also with a more specific sense in sixteenth-century Scots of an abusive contest in verse, as in 'The Flyting of Dunbar and Kennedy'.

That (beside where he feigns to follow Bocace)[9]
He runs sae far frae Virgil in mony place,
On sae prolix and tedious fashion,
Sae that the fourth book of *Eneadon*,
Touching the love and deith of Dido queen,
The twapart of his volume doth contain, *two-thirds*
That in the text of Virgil (traist me)
The twelfth part scarce contains, as ye may see.
The fifth book, of the feasts funeral,
The lusty games, and plays palestral: *athletics*
That is owerhippit quite and left behind;
Naething thereof ye shall in Caxton find.
The sixth book eik, he grants that wants hail,
And (for thereof he understood nocht the tale)
He calls it 'feignit', and nocht for to believe.
Sae is all Virgil perchance! for, by his leave,
Juno nor Venus gods[10] never were;
Mercury, Neptune, Mars, nor Jupiter;
Of Fortune eik, nor her necessity,
Sic things nocht authentic are, wit we;
Nor yet admits[11] that quaint philosophy[12]
Haulds sauls hops frae body to body;
And mony things whilk Virgil did rehearse,
Though I them write furth following his verse.
Nor Caxton shrinks nocht siclike things to tell,
As nocht were fable but the passage to hell;
But traist weel, wha that ilk sixth book knew,
Virgil therein a heich philosopher him shew,
And, under the clouds of dark poetry,
Hid lies there mony notable history.

[9] Bocace] Giovanni Boccaccio (1313–75), author of books on history and mythology, including *De genealogia deorum gentilium* [On the genealogy of the pagan gods], as well as his *Decameron*. Caxton refers to Boccaccio's 'fall of noblys' (*De casibus virorum illustrium*, translated by Lydgate as *The Fall of Princes*) in *Eneados* Book 6.

[10] gods] S. 'goddes'; C. 'goddessis'.

[11] admits] The subject might be 'we' or 'Virgil' or even 'authenticity'; the sense is 'accept as true'.

[12] quaint philosophy] a reference to Pythagoras's theory of the transmigration of souls.

For sae (the poets') be their crafty cures:[13] *skilful concerns*
In similitudes, and under quaint figures,
The soothfast matter to hide and to constrain.
All is not false, traist weel, in case they feign. *in the event*
Their art is sae to mak their works fair,
As in the end of Virgil I shall declare [. . .]

Wherefore, ye gentle readers, I beseek,
Traist on nae wise that this my work be sic,
Whilk did my best, as my wit micht attain,
Virgil's verses to follow, and naething feign.
Ye worthy nobles, read my works forthy, *therefore*
And cast this other book on side far by,
Whilk, under colour of some French strang wicht, *foreign*
Sae Frenchly[14] lees, uneath twa words gaes richt. *scarcely*
I nald ye traist I said this for despite, *would not*
For me list with nae English books flyte,
Nor with nae bogle nor brownie[15] to debate, *fight*
Neither auld ghaists nor spirits deid of late;
Nor nae man will I lakin or despise, *disparage*
My works till authorise by sic wise.
But touching Virgil's honour and reverence,
Whaever contrare, I maun stand at defence. *must*
And but my book be fundin worth sic three,
When it is read, do warp it in the sea, *throw*
Thraw it in the fire or rend it, every crumb.
Touching that part, lo! here is all and some.
Syne I defend and forbids every wicht *forbid*
That can nocht spell their paternoster richt
For till correct, or yet amend Virgil,
Or the translator blame in his vulgar style.
I knaw what pain is to follow him foot-het. *hot-foot*
Albeit thou think my sang intricate, *complicated in meaning*
Traist weel, to follow a fixed sentence or matter,

[13] Alternative punctuation is possible: taking 'be' as 'by' would mean substituting 'to-hide' and 'to-constrain' in l. 118.

[14] Frenchly] S. 'frenschlie' can mean 'frankly'; perhaps a pun.

[15] bogle nor brownie] The first is a bad, night-time goblin and the second a more benevolent spirit.

Is mair practic, difficult, and mair straiter *practically challenging*
(Though thine ingine be elevate and heich)
Than for to write always at liberty.
If I had nocht been to ae bounds constrainit,
Of my bad wit perchance I could have feignit
In rhyme a ragment twice as curious, *discourse, ingenious*
But nocht by twenty part sae sententious. *full of meaning*
Wha is attachit until a stake, we see,
May gae nae further, but wrele about that tree. *writhe*
Richt sae am I to Virgil's text ybound:
I may nocht flee, less than a fault be found; *unless*
For, though I wald transcend and gae beside,
His work remains, my shame I can nocht hide.
And thus I am constrainit, as near I may,
To hauld his verse and gae nae other way,
Less some history, subtle word, or the rhyme
Causes me mak digression sometime.
Sae though in my translation eloquence scant is,
Nae lusty cast of oratory Virgil wants;
(My studious brain, to comprehend his sentence,
Let me never taste his flood of eloquence).
And thus, forsooth, because I was not free,
My work is mair obscure and gross, perdee;
Whereof, God wit, Virgil has nae wyte: *blame*
Though mine be blunt, his text is maist perfite [. . .]

Though venerable Chaucer – principal poet but peer,
Heavenly trumpet, horologe, and regular, *clock, regulator*
In eloquence balmy, conduit and dial, *sundial*
Milky fountain, clear strand, and rose royal,
Of fresh endite, through Albion island braid –
In his *Legend of Notable Ladies* said
That he could follow word by word Virgil,[16]
Wiser than I micht fail in lacker style. *worse*
Sometime the text maun have an exposition,
Sometime the colour will cause a little addition,
And sometime of ae word I maun mak three:

[16] 345] On Dido, see *The Legend of Good Women*, ll. 1002–03; but Chaucer means only that he could (if he wished) tell the story in full.

In witness of this term *oppetere*.[17]
Eik (weel I wit) certain expositors seir *various*
Maks on ae text sentence diverse to hear,
As them appears, according their intent;
And for their part shaw reasons evident.
All this is ganing – I will weel it sae be – *fitting*
But ae sentence to follow may suffice me.
Sometime I follow the text as near I may,
Sometime I am constrainit another way.
Beside Latin our language is imperfite:
Whilk in some part is the cause and the wyte,
Why that of Virgil's verse the ornate beauty
Until our tongue may nocht observit be; *in*
For there been Latin words mony ane
That in our leed ganing translation has nane, *language*
Less than we minish their sentence and gravity,
And yet scant weel exponit. Wha trows nocht me,
Let them intepret *animal* and *homo*,
With mony hundred other terms more,
Whilk in our language, soothly (as I ween),
Few men can tell me clearly what they mean.
Betwixt *genus*, *sexus*, and *species*
Diversity to seek in our leed I cease.
For *obiectum* and *subiectum* alsa
He were expert, could find me terms twa
Whilk are as rife amang clerks in school
As ever fowls plungit in lake or pool.
Logicians knaws herein mine intent,
Under whase bounds lurks mony strange went. *path*
Whereof the process, as now, we maun let be. *discourse*
But yet, touching our tongue's penurity
(I mean, unto compare of fair Latin,
That knawn is maist perfect language fine):
I micht also, percase, come lither speed *sluggish*
For *arbor* or *lignum*[18] until our leed

---

[17] *oppetere*] *Aeneid* 1.96. In the marginal notes to the manuscript of the poem held by Trinity College, Cambridge, Douglas writes: '*Oppetere* is as meikle to say as *ore terram petere*, like as Servius expones the samen term, whilk to translate in our tongue is *with mouth to seek, or bite, the earth*. And lo! That is a hail sentence for ane of Virgil's words'.

[18] *arbor* or *lignum*] tree or wood.

To find different proper terms twain,
And thereto put circumlocution nane.
Richt sae, by about-speech oftentimes,
And soothable[19] words, we compile our rhymes. *true*
God wit, in Virgil are terms mony a hunder
For to expone made me a fellon blunder. *great trouble*
To follow allenarly Virgil's words, I ween, *only*
There should few understand me, what they mean:
The beauty of his ornate eloquence
May nocht all time be keepit with the sentence.
Saint Gregory[20] eik forbids us to translate
Word after word, but sentence follow algate; *always*
'Wha haulds', quod he, 'of words the properties,
Full oft the verity of the sentence flees'.
And to the samen purpose we may apply
Horace[21] in his *Art of Poetry*:
'Press nocht,' says he, 'thou traist interpreter,
Word after word to translate thy matter'.
Lo! he repreifs, and haulds misseeming,[22] *unbecoming*
Aye word by word to reduce onything [. . .] *translate*

Else have I said there may be nae compare *already*
Betwixt his verses and my style vulgar:
Although he stand in Latin maist perfite,
Yet stood he never weel in our tongue endite,
Less than it be by me now at this time.
If I have failit, bauldly repreif my rhyme,
But first, I pray you, graip the matter clean; *probe*
Reproach me nocht till the work be owerseen.

---

[19] soothable] S. 'seuthable'; C. 'semabill'.

[20] Gregory] Gregory the Great (*c.* 540–604), pope and theologian; see e.g. *Epistle* 10: 'Dum enim non sunt qui sensum de sensu exprimunt, sed transferre verborum semper proprietatem volunt, omnem dictorum sensum confundunt.' (For while nobody renders meaning through meaning, but wants all the time to be translating the particular character of the words, they muddle the whole sense of what is being expressed.)

[21] Horace] 65–8 BC; see ll. 133–34: 'nec verbo verbum curabis reddere fidus interpres' (a faithful translator does not laboriously translate word for word). On the complex nature of the historical debate, see Rita Copeland, *Rhetoric, Hermeneutics, and Translation in the Middle Ages* (Cambridge: Cambridge University Press, 1991), especially chs 1 and 2.

[22] misseeming] First citation in the OED.

Be nocht ower studious to spy a mote in my ee,
That in your ain a ferry-boat[23] can nocht see,
And do to me as ye wald be done to.
Now hark, sirs, there is nae mair ado,
Wha list attend, give audience and draw near.
Methocht Virgil begouth on this manner: *began*
'I the ilk umwhile that in the small ait reed *formerly, oat(en)*
Tonit my sang, syne frae the woods gaed,
And fields about taucht to be obeisant
(Though he were greedy) to the busy husband,
A thankful work made for the pleuchman's art;
But now the horrible, stern deeds of Mart . . .' [24]

20. Thomas Elyot, *The Doctrinal of Princes by Isocrates* (1533)

[Sir Thomas Elyot (*c.* 1490–1546) was a humanist and diplomat whose best known work is *The Governor* (1531). It is unclear whether he attended Oxford University, but he seems to have studied law at the Middle Temple and medicine under Thomas Linacre, who taught him Greek. He became part of Sir Thomas More's circle and produced an English version of the pseudo-Lucianic *Cynicus*, which More had translated from Greek into Latin. He was made ambassador to the Emperor Charles V in the year *The Governor* was published, dedicated to Henry VIII, but the embassy was unsuccessful and he fell out of favour. His later works include *The Castle of Health* (1534?) and the first Anglo-Latin dictionary (1538).

The Doctrinal of Princes is a version of one of the Cyprian orations of Isocrates, *Ad Nicoclem* [To Nicocles], which delivers pithy advice on conduct for rulers. The fact that Isocrates was sympathetic to monarchy (unusually for an early fourth-century Athenian) gave his writings some currency in Tudor England, identifying him with the 'mirror for princes' genre. Elyot's work is generally agreed to be the first extant translation directly from

[23] ferry-boat] In Matthew 7.3 'beam' is 'trabs', which can be anything made of wood, including a ship; D.'s word seems more likely to be a clergy joke than serious exegesis.

[24] 279–84] These render lines usually considered spurious but mentioned in Suetonius's *Life*; they link the *Aeneid* with Virgil's earlier *Eclogues* (*Bucolics*) and *Georgics*.

Greek into English. However, we do not know his source text, and there had been at least four different Latin translations of the oration printed before 1533 (Venice, 1480; Bologna, 1505; 's-Hertogenbosch, 1516; Paris, 1529).

See also Henry Burrowes Lathrop, *Translations from the Classics into English from Caxton to Chapman* (Madison, WI: University of Wisconsin Press, 1933); Stanford E. Lehmberg, *Sir Thomas Elyot, Tudor Humanist* (Austin: University of Texas Press, 1960); Greg Walker, *Writing Under Tyranny: English Literature and the Henrician Reformation* (Oxford: Oxford University Press, 2005); Cathy Shrank, 'Sir Thomas Elyot and the Bonds of Community' in *The Oxford Handbook of Tudor Literature*, ed. by Mike Pincombe and Cathy Shrank (Oxford: Oxford University Press, 2009), pp. 154–69.]

Sir Thomas Elyot, Knight, to the reader.

This little book, which in mine opinion is to be compared in counsel and short sentence with any book, Holy Scripture excepted, I have translated out of Greek, not presuming to contend with them which have done the same in Latin, but to the intent only that I would assay if our English tongue might receive the quick and proper sentences pronounced by the Greeks. And in this experience I have found (if I be not much deceived) that the form of speaking used of the Greeks called in Greek, and also in Latin, *phrasis*,[1] much near approacheth to that which at this day we use than the order of the Latin tongue: I mean in the sentences and not in the words, which I doubt not shall be affirmed by them who, sufficiently instructed in all the said three tongues, shall with a good judgement read this work.[2] And where

[1] *phrasis*] In his *Dictionary* Elyot defined 'phrasis' as 'The proper fourme, or maner of speache, which in one countrye is oftentimes diverse: as Southerne, Northerne, Devenysshe, Kentysshe [. . .]', STC 7659, sig. Rv^{r}, image 107 (this predates the first use of the term dialect in English). Here, however, the term seems to refer to syntax or word order.

[2] Philologists in other countries in the early modern period, including Budé in France, made the claim that their own vernaculars were closer to Greek than to Latin; see John Considine, *Dictionaries in Early Modern Europe: Lexicography and the Making of Heritage* (Cambridge: Cambridge University Press, 2008), pp. 61–63, 204–06.

I have put at the beginning these words, vessel, plate, or for that which is in Greek, brass or gold wrought, it is perceived of every wise man for what intent I did it. Finally, the chief cause of this my little exercise was to the intent that they which do not understand Greek nor Latin should not lack the commodity[3] and pleasure which may be taken in reading thereof. Wherefore, if I shall perceive you to take this mine enterprise thankfully, I shall that little portion of life which remaineth (God sending me quietness of mind) bestow in preparing for you such books in the reading whereof ye shall find both honest pastime and also profitable counsel and learning.

21. Thomas Elyot, *The Knowledge which Maketh a Wise Man* (1533)

[The book is part of Elyot's wider agenda for the dissemination of knowledge. It is related to the translation of Isocrates in its exploration of the role of the counsellor to monarchy, but it also reflects Elyot's other Greek interests as it takes the form of a series of dialogues between Plato and Aristippus. The preface uses the familiar complaint against detractors who draw poison from 'sweet milk' to contrast royal generosity and support for literary endeavours.]

The Proem of Sir Thomas Elyot, Knight.

God, unto whom all men's hearts be opened and the will of man speaketh, is my witness that to the desire of knowledge, whereunto I have hitherto been ever of my nature disposed, I have joined a constant intent to profit thereby my natural country, whereunto, according to the sentence° of Tully,[1] we be most specially bounden. Wherefore after I had applied the more part of my life in perusing diligently every ancient work that I might

---

[3] commodity] The term combines the senses of commercial value and social benefit. It is frequently reiterated in sixteenth-century English writing about the usefulness of translation.

[1] Tully] Cicero.

come by, either Greek or Latin, containing any part of philosophy necessary to the institution of man's life in virtue, I have endeavoured myself to set forth such part of my study as I thought might be profitable to them which should happen to read or hear it. But divers men, rather scorning the benefit than receiving it thankfully, do show themselves offended (as they say) with my strange terms. Other, finding in my books the thing dispraised which they do commend in using it, like a galled horse abiding no plasters° be alway gnapping° and kicking at such examples and sentences as they do feel sharp, or do bite them, accounting to be in me no little presumption that I will in noting other men's vices correct *Magnificat*,[2] since other much wiser men, and better learned than I, do forbear to write anything. And which is worse than all this, some will maliciously divine or conject that I write to the intent to rebuke some particular person, coveting to bring my works and afterward me into the indignation of some man in authority.

Thus unthankfully is my benefit received, my good will consumed, and all my labours devoured. Such is of some men the nature serpentine that, lapping sweet milk, they convert it forthwith into poison to destroy him of whose liberality they late had received it. How incomparably be these men unlike to the most excellent prince, our most dear sovereign lord, whose most royal person I heartily beseech God to preserve in long life and honour.[3] His Highness benignly receiving my book, which I named *The Governor*,[4] in the reading thereof soon perceived that I intended to augment our English tongue, whereby men should as well express more abundantly the thing that they conceived in their hearts (wherefore language was ordained), having words apt for the purpose, as also interpret out of Greek, Latin, or any other tongue into English as sufficiently as out of any one of the said tongues into another. His Grace also perceived that throughout the book there was no term new made by me of a Latin or

[2] correct *Magnificat*] See n. on **41**. 59 below.

[3] i.e. Henry VIII. On the relationship between Elyot's literary work and the monarchy see Greg Walker, *Writing Under Tyranny: English Literature and the Henrician Reformation* (Oxford: Oxford University Press, 2005), pp. 123–275.

[4] Elyot's best-known work (1531), reprinted seven times to 1580, sets out a programme of education for the English ruling classes in political and moral philosophy. Its translations from Greek sources include Xenophon, Plato, Lucian, and Plutarch.

French word but it is there declared so plainly by one mean or other to a diligent reader that no sentence is thereby made dark or hard to be understood. Ne the sharp and quick sentences,° or the round° and plain examples set out in the verses of Claudian the poet[5] in the second book, or in the chapters of 'Affability', 'Benevolence', 'Beneficence', and of the diversity of flatterers, and in divers other places, in any part offended His Highness.

22. Thomas Phaer, *The Regiment of Life* [Jehan Goeurot] (*c.* 1544)

[Thomas Phaer (1510–1560) was a lawyer and physician practising in Wales, whose *Book of Children* is regarded as a foundational work of paediatrics. He is best-known as the co-author of the first complete translation of the *Aeneid* into English (if the language of Douglas's poem is disqualified), which went through eight editions between 1558 and 1620. The work was completed by Thomas Twyne after Phaer's death. Written in rhyming fourteeners, Phaer's translation was highly praised in the Elizabethan period (this was one of the few points on which Gabriel Harvey and Thomas Nashe agreed), and he was described by Puttenham as one of the best poets of Mary's reign in *The Arte of English Poesie*.

Phaer's translation from the French of Goeurot was printed with his own *Treatise of the Pestilence*, probably in 1543, and again with *The Book of Children* in 1544. The text reproduced here is described as 'The preface to the booke of chyldren', but it is followed by *The Regiment of Life*, to which it refers. All three works were printed together in 1546.

See also Paula Blank, 'Languages of Early Modern Literature in Britain' in *The Cambridge History of Early Modern English Literature*, ed. by David Loewenstein and Janel Mueller (Cambridge: Cambridge University Press, 2002), pp. 141–69; Philip Schwyzer in *ODNB*.]

[5] Claudian] Roman poet writing under the Emperor Honorius *c.* 395–404. The verses cited in *The Governor* ('Though that thy power stretcheth both far and large', STC 7636, fol. 98, image 105) were politically risky.

The Preface to *The Book of Children*.

Although (as I doubt not) every good man will interpret this work to none other end but to be for the comfort of them that are diseased, and will esteem no less of me by whom they profit than they will be glad to receive the benefits, yet forasmuch as it is impossible to avoid the teeth of malicious envy, I thought it not unnecessary to prevent the furies of some which are ever gnawing and biting upon them that further any godly sciences. To those I protest that in all my studies I never intended, nor yet do intend, to satisfy the minds of any such pick-faults (which will do nothing but detract and judge other, snuffing at all that offendeth the noses of their momish[1] affections, howsoever laudable it be other ways), but my purpose is here to do them good that have most need, that is to say children, and to show the remedies that God hath created for the use of man to distribute in English, to them that are unlearned, part of the treasure that is in other languages; to provoke them that are of better learning to utter their knowledge in suchlike attempts; finally, to declare that to the use of many which ought not to be secret for lucre of a few, and to communicate the fruit of my labours to them that will gently and thankfully receive them, which if any be so proud or supercilious that they immediately will despise, I shall friendly desire them, with the words of Horace: *quod si meliora novisti, candidus imparti, si non, his utere mecum.*[2] If they know better, let us have part; if they do not, why repine they at me? Why condemn they the thing that they cannot amend? Or if they can, why dissimule° they their cunning? How long would they have the people ignorant? Why grutch° they physic to come forth in English? Would they have no man to know but only they? Or what make they themselves – merchants of our lives and deaths? – that we should buy our health only of them, at their prices? No good physician is of that mind. For if Galen,[3]

---

[1] momish] carping. Derived from Momus (see **13**. 68 above). First citation in the OED which wrongly glosses the word as 'foolish'.

[2] *Quod* [. . .] *mecum*] A misquotation of Horace, *Epistles* 1.6.67–68: '*si quid novisti rectius istis* [. . .]' (If you know better ones [i.e. precepts], then be frank and pass them on; if not, make use of these with me).

[3] Galen] The most important medical authority from antiquity up to the early seventeenth century. His work was translated into Latin by Leonicenus (see **7**. 80 above) and into English by Thomas Gale, who also cites Avicenna, Pliny, and Celsus (see **33**. below).

the prince of this art, being a Grecian wrote in Greek; King Avicenna of Araby in the speech of his Arabians; if Pliny, Celsus, Serenus, and other of the Latins wrote to the people in the Latin tongue; Marsilius Ficinus (whom all men assent to be singularly learned) disdained not to write in the language of Italy; generally, if the intent of all that ever set forth any noble study have been to be read of as many as would, what reason is it that we should hugger-mugger[4] here among a few the thing that was made to be common to all?

Christ sayeth, 'no man lighteth a candle to cover it with a bushel, but setteth it to serve every man's need',[5] and these go about not only to cover it when it is lighted, but to quench it afore it be kindled (if they might by malice), which as it is a detestable thing in any godly science, so methinketh in this so necessary an art it is exceeding damnable and devilish to debar the fruition of so many inestimable benefits which our heavenly father hath prepared for our comfort and innumerable uses, wherewith he hath armed our impotent nature against the assaults of so many sicknesses; whereby his infinite mercy and abundant goodness is in nothing else more apparently confessed by the which benefits, as it were with most sensible arguments spoken out of heaven, he constraineth us to think upon our own weakness and to knowledge that in all flesh is nothing but misery, sickness, sorrows, sin, affliction and death – no, not so much strength as by our own power to relieve one member of our bodies diseased. As for the knowledge of medicines, comfort of herbs, maintenance of health, prosperity, and life, they be his benefits, and proceed of him to the end that we should in common help one another, and so live together in his laws and commandments. In the which doing we shall declare ourselves to have worthily employed them, and, as fruitful servants, be liberally rewarded; otherwise, undoubtedly the talent that we have hidden shall be digged up and distributed to them that shall be more diligent[6] – a terrible confusion afore so high a justice, and at such a court where no wager of law shall be taken, no proctor° limited to defend the cause, none exception allowed to reprove the witness, no counsel

[4] hugger-mugger] secretly hoard; cf. the parable of the talents below.
[5] Matthew 5.15; Luke 11.33. Phaer cites the texts commonly used to support vernacular translation of the Bible.
[6] See Matthew 25.14–30 and Luke 19.12–28 (the parable of the talents).

admitted to qualify the glosses.[7] The very bare text shall be there alleged: *cur non posuisti talentum in fenus*. Why hast thou not bestowed my talent to the vantage?°

23. Elizabeth Tudor (Princess Elizabeth), 'The Glass of the Sinful Soul' [Marguerite of Navarre] (1544)

[Elizabeth (1533–1603) was educated by Protestant tutors in the 1540s, appointed by Henry VIII but supervised by her stepmother, Katherine Parr. She became an impressive linguist, with competence in Latin, Greek, French, Italian, and Spanish. Her first Latin tutor was William Grindal, succeded by Roger Ascham in 1548, who also taught her Greek and who claimed in *The Schoolmaster* that she continued to read Greek daily after she ascended the throne. Her Latin was of an order that enabled her not only to deal with routine government and diplomatic business, but also to make extempore speeches on her visits to Oxford and Cambridge. Unlike her successor, James I, Elizabeth did not put her literary work into print.

Elizabeth made her translation 'The Mirror of the Sinful Soul' as a gift for Queen Katherine for the New Year of 1545 when she was eleven years old. Her French tutor is likely to have been the Huguenot Jean Bellemain and a further translation from French, made in 1545, is from the first chapter of the Calvin's *Institutes* (French language edition, 1541). The source text for the translation from Marguerite de Navarre is *Le Miroir de l'âme pécheresse* published by Antoine Augereau (Paris, 1533), USTC 9396, a poem which Elizabeth here renders in prose. Elizabeth's work was published in 1548 by John Bale as *A Godly Meditacyon of the Christen Sowle*.

See also Anne Lake Prescott, 'The Pearl of the Valois and Elizabeth I: Marguerite de Navarre's *Miroir* and Tudor England' in *Silent But for the Word: Tudor Women Writers as Patrons, Translators, and Writers of Religious Works*, ed. by Margaret Patterson Hannay (Kent, OH: The Kent State University Press, 1985); Elizabeth I, *Translations, 1544–1589*, ed. by Janel Mueller and Joshua Scodel (Chicago: University of Chicago Press, 2009).]

[7] qualify the glosses] show the negative interpretations of our actions in a better light. This predates the first citation of 'gloss' in the OED.

To our most noble and virtuous Queen Katherine,[1] Elizabeth, her humble daughter, wisheth perpetual felicity and everlasting joy.

Not only knowing the affectuous° will and fervent zeal the which Your Highness hath towards all godly learning, as also my duty towards you, most gracious and sovereign princess; but knowing also that pusillanimity and idleness are most repugnant unto a reasonable creature and that, as the philosopher[2] sayeth, even as an instrument of iron or of other metal waxeth soon rusty unless it be continually occupied, even so shall the wit of a man or woman wax dull and unapt to do or understand anything perfectly unless it be always occupied upon some manner of study. Which things considered hath moved so small a portion as God hath lent me to prove° what I could do.[3] And therefore have I (as for assay° or beginning, following the right notable saying of the proverb aforesaid) translated this little book out of French rhyme into English prose, joining the sentences together as well as the capacity of my simple wit and small learning could extend themselves. The which book is entitled or named *The Mirror or Glass of the Sinful Soul*, wherein is contained how she (beholding and contempling° what she is) doth perceive how of herself and of her own strength she can do nothing that good is or prevaileth for her salvation, unless it be through the grace of God, whose mother, daughter, sister, and wife by the Scriptures she proveth herself to be. Trusting also that through His incomprehensible love, grace, and mercy she, being called from sin to repentance, doth faithfully hope to be saved.

And although I know that, as for my part which I have wrought in it, as well spiritual as manual, there is nothing done as it should be, nor else worthy to come in your grace's hands, but rather all unperfect and uncorrect; yet do I trust also that, howbeit it is like a work which is but new begun and shapen, that the file of your excellent wit and godly learning in the reading of

---

[1] Katherine Parr (1512–1548), Henry VIII's last queen, who had strong Protestant sympathies.

[2] the philosopher] Aristotle; but cf. also Ovid, *Tristia* 5.12.21: 'My wit, injured by long rusting, is dull, much inferior to what it was before', quoted in Nanus Mirabellius's popular commonplace book *Polyanthea*, which was a major source for Elizabeth's own *Sententiae* (Mueller and Scodel).

[3] On talent as a loan from God see **22**. 60–64 above and many Renaissance poems (Shakespeare, Sonnet 4; Milton, Sonnet 16).

it, if so it vouchsafe your highness to do, shall rub out, polish, and mend (or else cause to mend) the words or, rather, the order of my writing, the which I know in many places to be rude and nothing done as it should be. But I hope that, after to have been in your grace's hands, there shall be nothing in it worthy of reprehension, and that in the meanwhile no other, but your highness only, shall read it or see it, lest my faults be known of many. Then shall they be better excused, as my confidence is in your grace's accustomed benevolence, than if I should bestow a whole year in writing or inventing ways for to excuse them. Praying God Almighty, the maker and creator of all things, to grant unto Your Highness the same New Year's Day[4] a lucky and a prosperous year, with prosperous issue and continuance of many years in good health and continual joy, and all to His honour, praise, and glory. From Ashridge[5] the last day of the year of Our Lord God, 1544.

24. Mildred Cecil, 'An Homily or Sermon of St Basil' (*c.* 1548)

[Mildred Cecil (1526–89) was the eldest daughter of Sir Anthony and Lady Anne Cooke and one of five remarkable and highly educated sisters. Walter Haddon described a visit to their home as like 'living among the Tusculans' and Roger Ascham specifically praised Mildred's knowledge of Greek, ranking her second only to Lady Jane Grey for her scholarly accomplishments. Her sister Anne, who became the mother of Francis Bacon, translated sermons by Bernardo Ochino and also published a translation of Bishop Jewel's *Apologia Ecclesiae Anglicanae*; Elizabeth translated a work on the doctrine of transubstantiation, *A Way of Reconciliation*, and married another translator, Sir Thomas Hoby; Katherine married Sir Henry Killigrew, and the last sister, Margaret, died young. Mildred herself was the wife of Sir William Cecil and was thought by the Spanish ambassador, Guzman de Silva, to be exceptionally clever and to hold a great influence over him.

[4] The translation as New Year's gift was an English tradition. Some of Erasmus's translations (eg. Lucian's *Toxaris* to Richard Foxe in 1506) were presented in this way.

[5] Ashridge] a manor in Buckinghamshire belonging to the crown.

Mildred Cecil had a particular interest in the early Greek fathers of the Church such as Chrysostom, Gregory Nazianzanus and Cyril, as well as Basil. This was an interest shared by a number of Protestant scholars, including Sir John Cheke, whose only published translations were Latin versions of Chrysostom. De Silva saw Mildred as highly committed to the reformed Church, describing her as 'a much more furious heretic than [Cecil] is' (Read, p. 336). Her translation of a sermon of St Basil was sent as a gift to Lady Somerset, wife of the Lord Protector (*c.* 1548). Mildred Cecil's enthusiasm for Basil is recorded in the epitaph written by her husband.

See Marjorie K. McIntosh, 'Sir Anthony Cooke: Tudor Humanist, Educator and Religious Reformer', *Proceedings of the American Philosophical Society*, 119:3 (1975), 233–50; Conyers Read, *Mr. Secretary Cecil and Queen Elizabeth* (London: Jonathan Cape, 1955); Mary Ellen Lamb 'The Cooke Sisters: Attitudes Towards Learned Women in the Renaissance' in *Silent But for the Word: Tudor Women as Patrons, Translators, and Writers of Religious Works*, ed. by Margaret Patterson Hannay (Kent, OH: The Kent State University Press, 1985), pp. 107–25; Jane Stevenson, *Women Latin Poets: Language, Gender, and Authority, from Antiquity to the Eighteenth Century* (Oxford: Oxford University Press, 2005); Elaine Treharne, '*Tristis Amor*: An Unpublished Verse Love Letter from Elizabeth Dacre Howard to Sir Anthony Cooke', *Renaissance Studies*, forthcoming]

An Homily or Sermon of Basil the Great,[1] Archbishop of Caesaria, upon the saying of Moses in the fifteenth chapter of Deuteronomy, 'Take heed to thyself' etc.

To the very noble and virtuous Duchess of Somerset,[2] her right good lady and mistress

[1] The only work by Basil to be published in English during the early modern period was *An Exhortation* [. . .] *to the studie of humaine lernynge* (1557), which justified the reading of pagan poets by Christians and explained how the good could be separated from the bad. This is an important humanistic document, translated into Latin by Leonardo Bruni; the English translation is by William Barker, who also translated Xenophon.

[2] Duchess of Somerset] Anne Seymour (*c.* 1510–1587), wife of the Lord Protector.

Like as poor debtors, most honourable and my very good lady, desiring to pay that their poverty keepeth back, and seeking honestly to may that they would, use for the continuance of their creditors' favour either to pay some small part to prolong the remanent° or to intercede by friends to diminish the debt, so I your humble servant and debtor, knowing in heart my earnest zeal to serve your vertuous contentation,° and seeing indeed the weakness of my thin power to ensure the same, thought meeet with these few leaves thus by me translated to move your goodness either to take them as some small part of my service I owe or instead of some mean° friend to entreat for my debt. Albeit my labour herein be indeed neither worthy to serve ne the one ne the other, yet I trust the author whose commendation my words can smally enlarge will claim such favour that my labour coming in his company be thought as welcome for his sake as my good will meant to send it for his own, whereof the one I hope through your grace's gentle acceptance, the other I doubt not through the author's worthy deserving. I have somewhat superstitiously° observed the nature of the Greek phrase,[3] not omitting the congruity of English speech, but rather the use, that the treaty° of so good an author should not in too much serving the English tongue lese° his own efficacy and value, thinking it less fault that the author should speak Greekish English and save his own sense than English Greek and confound it with a doubtful, in this showing the property of the tone,[4] in the other the verity of the matter. The lord God preserve your grace with his favour to the performation° of his honour and all our comforts.

Your Grace's in service
Mildred Cecil

25. William Thomas, 'The Book of the Sphere' (*c.* 1551)

[William Thomas (d. 1554) was of Welsh descent, though nothing further is known about his parentage and education. He travelled in Italy in the 1540s, publishing *The Historie of Italie* (1549),

[3] phrase] idiom, expression; or, as in Elyot **20**. 10, word order.
[4] tone] This would seem to mean 'characteristic style' rather than to refer to a quality of sound, but the first citation in the *OED* for that sense is 1641.

which was heavily indebted to Machiavelli, and the first English-Italian primer, *Principal Rules of the Italian Grammer* (1550). He also published a narrative of his travels in Italian (1552). Employed by the Privy Council under Edward VI, he became involved with Wyatt's rebellion on Mary's accession and was tried and executed for treason.

The preface to the translation of Sacrobosco is an early defence of English as a modern vernacular entirely adequate for the furthering of knowledge in the arts and sciences. In pressing his case Thomas echoes continental writers such as Du Bellay in France, whose *La Deffence et Illustration de la Langue Françoyse* (1549) was a seminal apology for the mother tongue, and also those writers in Italy who were engaged in promoting *la lingua volgare*. There are many early printed texts of Johannes de Sacrobosco's *De Sphaera*, originally written in the thirteenth century. Thomas's source text may have been the edition published in Venice (1545), USTC 854137.

See also Andrew Hadfield, *Literature, Travel, and Colonial Writing in the English Renaissance, 1545–1625* (Oxford: Oxford University Press, 1998); Cathy Shrank, *Writing the Nation in Reformation England, 1530–1580* (Oxford: Oxford University Press, 2004); Jonathan Woolfson, 'Thomas Hoby, William Thomas, and Mid-Tudor Travel to Italy' in *The Oxford Handbook of Tudor Literature*, ed. by Mike Pincombe and Cathy Shrank (Oxford: Oxford University Press, 2009).]

Unto the high and mighty prince, Harry, Duke of Suffolk,[1] William Thomas wisheth all health and honour, with long life.

The toward° beginning of virtue that by the proof of your tender years, my lord, do already appear in you – appear, I say, at the fair blossom of the spring, before the full harvest summit hath moved me to address this my little work unto you: to the intent it should not only be a means to guide the same unto the

[1] Suffolk] Henry Brandon, 2nd Duke of Suffolk (1535–1551). Thomas's dedication must have been written before July 1551 when Henry and his brother Charles both died of the sweating sickness. Like Henry Hastings, the dedicatee of Hoby's *Courtier*, Brandon was tutored by John Cheke and Roger Ascham alongside Prince Edward.

foundation of necessary knowledge, but also that under your grace's name our nation should find the lack that unto this hour hath been the enemy of all our glory. For notwithstanding that in deeds of arms our predecessors have prevailed against infinity of strangers,° triumphing now in France, now in Spain, now in Flanders, in Scotland, Ireland, and elsewhere, yet because that in civil knowledge they have not had the grounded sciences that unto many estrange° nations through the benefit of their own tongues have been common, therefore also have they not had that glorious representation of sapience° that should cause the strangers to apply° their happy success in things, not unto fortune's mutability, but unto their own politic and prudent government – a thing undoubtedly not a little to be lamented amongst us. But lief° as the physician, until he have found the cause of the person's infirmity, cannot well minister unto him any effectual medicine, so neither is it possible to provide a remedy unto this default until the original occasion thereof be tried out. Wherefore, seeing that our nation is no less prompt of capacity and quick of memory than other nations be, I would now see what should be the cause that amongst so many thousands of us as have studied the Latin tongue, it is almost hard to find any good author in our own mother tongue.

Surely, if I take not my mark amiss, the fault hereof consisteth in the bringing up of our youth. For the child hath no sooner learned his ABC but straightways his master putteth the Latin grammar in his hand and so proceedeth in teaching him the Latin tongue ere ever he can speak good English. And what teacheth he him, trow you? – Ovid; Virgil; Tully; Aristotle, and such other as the master himself doth sometime scarcely well understand. Wherein the child consumeth the flower of his learning youth, and if he arrive out at the writing of a pistle in Latin, then it be cause enough, though well he cannot write half a pistle in English, for then may he proceed unto *dialectica* and consequently *ad autem orationem*, to see whether he can surmount Cicero in the Latin eloquence. But the master seeth not here the inconvenience of this disorder because he thinketh the speaking and writing of Latin sufficient for a learned man, and considereth not that they who at these days write in the Latin tongue travail to carry water from their own wells unto the sea. Whereas the study of Latin should be to draw the worthy things of the same unto their own tongues, because is it possible to build well without foundation or reap wheat where hath been sown no corn? Can the scholar write without matter whereof, or think we with the only study of the Latin tongue to attain the well understanding of Virgil, Aristotle, or any other such? No, surely, no, that is not the right way.

26. Henry Parker (Lord Morley), *The Triumphs of Petrarch* (*c.* 1555)

[Henry Parker, 10th Baron Morley (1480/81–1556) grew up in the household of Lady Margaret Beaufort. A conservative in religion, he was – extraordinarily – on good terms with both Thomas Cromwell and Mary Tudor, presenting copies of Machiavelli (including *Il Principe*) to Cromwell and devotional works to Mary. Most of his writing remained in manuscript and the translation of Petrarch was not published until the end of his life, when he wrote the preface to the young Lord Maltravers.

Petrarch (1304–1374) is one of the three Italian writers (with Dante and Boccaccio) credited with having raised the Italian vernacular to classic status. English translations date back to Chaucer, but he was particularly influential on the development of the sonnet form in England during the sixteenth century through the *Canzoniere*. The *Trionfi* are written in terza rima (interlocking tercets rhyming ABA, BCB), which explains why Morley had so much difficulty with the rhyme, and are also addressed to the Laura of the *Canzoniere*. The translation probably dates from the late 1520s and was presented to Henry VIII, as were a number of Morley's other translations from Latin and Italian. These include some of Plutarch's *Lives*, from late fifteenth-century Latin versions, and the first forty-six lives of Boccaccio's *De claris mulieribus* [On famous women].

See also D. D. Carnicelli, ed., *Lord Morley's Tryumphes of Fraunces Petrarcke* (Cambridge, MA: Harvard University Press, 1971); Marie Axton and James P. Carley, eds, *Triumphs of English: Henry Parker, Lord Morley: Translator to the Tudor Court* (London: British Library, 2000)].

Unto the most toward young gentle Lord Maltravers,[1] son and heir apparent to the worthy and noble Earl of Arundel.

The fables of Aesop, most toward° young Lord, are not only had in commendation among the philosophers, as with Plato, Aristotle, and diverse other of the most excellent of them, but also the divines, when in their preachings there cometh to their purpose any matter to rehearse to the rude people, they allege the allegory sense of them to the much edification of the hearers. I say, therefore, that among other his witty fables (not to you, noble gentleman, unknown)[2] he telleth how that the cock scraping on the dunghill found a precious stone, and when he saw it, disdaining, he spurned it from him, saying 'What have I to do with thee? Thou canst not serve me to no kind of use', and so despising it, left it whereas it lay on the dunghill still. Even so, there be a number of that sort that percase° when they shall either hear read, or themself read, this excellent *Triumphs* of this famous clerk, Petrarch, shall little set by them and peradventure cast it from them, desiring rather to have a tale printed of Robin Hood or some other dunghill matter than of this, which I dare affirm, yea, and the Italians do the same, that the divine works set apart, there was never in any vulgar speech or language so notable a work so clerkly done as this his work. And albeit that he setteth forth these six wonderful-made *Triumphs* all to the laud of his lady, Laura, by whom he made so many a sweet sonnet that never yet no poet nor gentleman could amend nor make the like, yet who that doth understand them shall see in them comprehended all moral virtue, all philosophy, all storial° matters and, briefly, many divine sentences [and] theological secrets declared. But, alas, who is he that will so read them that he will mark them, or what printer will not say that he may win more gain in printing of a merry jest than suchlike excellent works? Surely, my good lord, very few or none, which I do lament at my heart, considering that as well in French as in the Italian (in the which both tongues I have some little knowledge), there is no excellent work in the Latin but that straightways they set it forth in the vulgar, most commonly to their kings and noble princes of

[1] Maltravers] Henry Fitzalan, Lord Maltravers (1538–1566), son of Henry, 12th Earl of Arundel.

[2] Aesop's *Fables* were studied at the start of the school curriculum as part of elementary Latin language learning.

their region and countries. As one of late days that was Groom of the Chamber with that renowned and valiant prince of high memory, Francis, the French king, whose name I have forgotten,[3] that did translate these *Triumphs* to that said king, which he took so thankfully that he gave to him for his pains a hundred crowns to him and to his heirs of inheritance to enjoy to that value in land forever, and took such pleasure in it that, wheresoever he went among his precious jewels, that book was always carried with him for his pastime to look upon, and as much esteemed by him as the richest diamond he had.

Which said book, when I saw the copy of it, I thought in my mind how I, being an Englishman, might do as well as the Frenchman, did translate this said work into our maternal tongue, and after much debating with myself did, as your lordship doth see, translate the said book to that most worthy king, our late sovereign lord of perpetual memory, King Henry the Eighth, who as he was a prince above all other most excellent, so took he the work very thankfully, marvelling much how I could do it and thinking verily I had not done it without help of some other, better knowing the Italian tongue than I. But when he knew the very truth, that I had translated the work myself, he was more pleased therewith than he was before, and so what His Highness did with it is to me unknown, one thing is, that I did it in such haste that doubtless in many places (if it were again in my hands) I think I could well amend it, albeit that I profess I have not erred much from the letter but in the rhyme, which is not possible for me to follow in the translation, nor touch the least point of the elegancy that this elegant poet hath set forth in his own maternal tongue.

But as it is, if in the translation there be anything to be amended, or any will deprave° it, I shall pray you, most noble young lord, the very mirror of all the young noble gentlemen of this realm in virtue, in learning, and in all other feats appertaining to such a lord as you be, to defend it against those that will more by envy than by knowledge deprave it; and then I do not fear but those that know and can speak the Italian will bear with the simple translation and commend the work, as it is so much commendable that it cannot be too dear bought.

[3] Morley is referring to Simon Bougouyn, valet de chamber to Francis 1 (1494–1547), who translated the *Trionfi* into French *c.* 1525. (An earlier French translation had been done by Georges de la Forge (Paris, 1514), USTC 26291).

27. Nicholas Grimald, *Cicero's Three Books of Duties* (1556)

[Nicholas Grimald (1519/20–1562) studied first at Cambridge and then at Oxford, where he became a Fellow of Merton College. A friend of John Bale and a protégé of the Protestant Bishop of London, Nicholas Ridley, he seems to have changed his religion under Mary in order to escape possible execution. His writings include Latin dramas on Christian themes, forty poems in the first edition of Tottel's *Songes and Sonnetes* (1557), which contain examples of blank verse and the heroic couplet, and various translations mentioned by John Bale in his catalogue of famous British writers (including Hesiod, Xenophon, and Plato), which have not survived.

Cicero (106–43 BC), Roman orator and moral philosopher, was regarded as a model for prose style in the sixteenth century and had a significant place in the school curriculum. As a rhetorician he was studied in Latin and it is the moral philosophy that is translated into English. Much the most popular text was *De Officiis* [On duties], which had a major influence on humanist political and social thought and was recommended by Elyot in *The Governor*. The first and rather poor translation was by Richard Whittington (1534), but Grimald's, published by Tottel, was extremely successful and went through eight editions by the end of the century. A Latin text was added to the translation in the second edition of 1558, but almost nothing of Cicero had been printed in England in Latin before the second half of the century and Grimald would have worked from an imported continental edition, probably that in *Opera Ciceronis* (Paris: Robert Estienne, 1555), USTC 151874.

See also Gerald O'Gorman, ed., *Marcus Tullius Ciceroes Thre Bokes of Duties* (Washington: Folger Shakespeare Library, 1990); Howard Jones, *Master Tully: Cicero in Tudor England* (Nieuwkoop: de Graaf, 1998); Robert Cummings 'Classical Moralists and Philosophers' in *OHLTE* (2), pp. 371–89; Michael G. Brennan in *ODNB*.]

To the Right Reverend Father in God and his singular good Lord, Thomas, Bishop of Ely,[1] one of the King and Queen's Majesties' most honourable Privy Council.

Having recourse of late, right reverend father, to the old studies that I once applied in the university, and getting some fruit of quiet life to the perusing and recording of those things wherewith in time past I felt myself greatly both delighted and furthered, I gave my mind chiefly to such kind of learning as would serve best both to the order of my study and also to the governance of my life; so that, comparing my experience and reading together, I might make my private diligence in studying do service to the open use of living. In following of which intent, what by increase of judgement for years, what by travelling abroad in the world, I found ever more and more so new profits and commodities° that whereas, methought, I had seen but the shadow of things, now I begin more to see, as it were, the whole body thereof. And most of all, this proof I have, in the greatest and most profitable part of philosophy, which is concerning manners, and namely in the books that of duties be written by Marcus Tullius Cicero, a matter containing the whole trade,° how to live among men discreetly and honestly,[2] and so rightly pointing out the pathway to all virtue, as none can be righter, only Scripture excepted. Insomuch that when I had well considered all together, I said with myself concerning this as did a certain learned man, not long ago, by Homer. This is the fifth time I have read over this author, and as oft as I read him, so oft somewhat I find that I marked not before and that hath need to be deeply pondered, so that I fancied at the first he was easy, but now, methinks, he requires a very heedful and a musing reader.

---

[1] Thomas Thirlby (*c.* 1500–1570) held diplomatic posts in addition to his bishopric under both Edward and Mary. He was deprived of Ely under Elizabeth for his Catholic sympathies, but he was a prudently chosen dedicatee for Grimald in 1556. The subject matter of Cicero's work responds to Thirlby's secular offices.

[2] honestly] Adapted from Ciceronian *honestas*, this is a key term in Tudor humanist discourse on social duty, covering a range of meanings from 'self-restraint' to 'simplicity', though Thomas Cooper also glosses it as 'of good reputation' and 'comely' in his *Thesaurus* (1565), STC 5686, sig. LLL4[r], image 346. See Jennifer Richards, *Rhetoric and Courtliness in Early Modern Literature* (Cambridge; Cambridge University Press, 2003), esp. pp. 26–28, 69, 92 (on Grimald).

Wherefore, not without marvellous great pleasure, espying that either in private life, to attain quietness and contentation;° or in office-bearing, to win fame and honour; or in every estate, both to avoid disorder and enormity, and also to keep a right rule and commendable behaviour, this book plainly is the mirror of wisdom, the fortress of justice, the master of manliness, the school of temperance, the jewel of comeliness, I wished many more to be partners of such sweetness as I had partly felt myself. And to declare that I meant no less than I wished, I laid to my helping hand, endeavouring by translation to do likewise for my countrymen as Italians, Frenchmen, Spaniards, Dutchmen, and other foreigns have liberally done for theirs. So, chiefly for our unlatined people, I have made this Latin writer English, and have now brought into light that from them so long was hidden, and have caused an ancient writing to become, in a manner, new again, and a book used but of few to wax common to a great many. So that our men, understanding what a treasure is among them for the fashioning of their life, and being by nature most of all other nations given to civility and humanity[3] when they shall be aided and directed by these perfect precepts, may in all points of good demeanour become people peerless.

Yet judge I all this labour little-worth, and smally or nothing able to prevail, without your honourable lordship were patron hereof, to whom I do dedicate both my good heart and my work also (I call it mine, as Plautus and Terence called the comedies theirs which they made out of Greek),[4] not as to teach your lordship ought that you have not already, but by your authority to get it the more estimation with other. For as Tully's treatise, being so full of learning, asketh a learned man's judgement, which whoso refuse, they show themselves to be unwise, even so such a noble counsellor of England seemeth most meet to receive so noble a senator of Rome into a strange region. Doubtless, among so many honourable deeds of your lordship's it shall not be the least honourable if ye do Marcus Tullius this honour to

[3] humanity] Another key term, adapted from Latin *humanitas*. Although principally referring to humane letters, as in modern 'arts and humanities', it was starting to acquire the sense of compassion towards others in sixteenth-century England. 'Civility' and 'humanity' are coupled elsewhere in the period, e.g. in Udall's translation of Erasmus's *Paraphrases*, STC 2854.5, fol. vii, image 7.

[4] Plautus and Terence worked in the tradition of Greek New Comedy introduced by Menander.

welcome him hither, and to be the very cause that so famous a Roman may become familiar with our Englishmen. So shall a worthy peer be worthily entreated as very courtesy requireth, so your lordship's judgement must needs be well-liked, which is wont to allow lovely knowledge and goodness, so will the common people more highly esteem the thing as it is expedient for them to do, and the sooner also will they follow these wholesome lessons, which is full necessary in a well-ordered state. To be short: your lordship, for a chosen patron; my translation, for a welcome work; and Tully shall be taken for such a Tully as he is. And like as Marcus Cicero, with the authority of a father, commended these books to his young Cicero, so when our English youth shall behold them once authorised by so reverend a father in God, no doubt they will be the rather in love with them, and will count it pleasant painstaking here to enrich themselves with informations of virtue, ensamples out of stories, moral doctrine, politic prudence, antiquity, variety of marvellous matters so cunningly and oratorically treated and endited,° as he was able to declare and express who was the first and the chief that ever clad Lady Philosophy in Roman attire.

N. G. to the Reader.

[. . .] Tullius, in his grave years, after he had heard a number of learned men, after he had read the most approved authors, after he had endited so many volumes and his style was waxen ripe, his wit sage, his learning full, his judgement perfect, enterprised to draw this draught, and made it of such excellence as we may well wonder at in viewing, and yet not attain in following. Tullius, having done many glorious acts, in a state of government most triumphant, learned the most part of these lessons by experience. Tullius, out of the Greek authors, of whom also some had been governors of flourishing empires, translated a great deal.[5] Tullius to Marcus, his well-beloved son, abiding even at Athens among

[5] Cicero's translations from Greek include Xenophon's *Oeconomicus* (on household government), which is closely related to *De Officiis*. He addressed some of the issues concerned with translating Greek moral philosophy into Latin in *De Finibus bonorum et malorum* [On the ends of good and evil] 1.1–4 and some of the general principles of translation in *De Optimo genere oratorum* [On the best kind of orator].

the best philosophers, was not afraid to send this parcel of philosophy. No doubt as welcome it was to the learned Athenians as the Greeks' doings were to the Romans, or as nowadays the French and Italians' well-framed writings be to those Englishmen that understand them; yea, and so much the more welcome as it was a rare thing then to see that kind of knowledge expressed in pure Latin. But in Rome, in Italy, in Europe, in all quarters where Latin speech had place, O, so it was embraced at all times, of all men, in every degree, order, and estate. Rulers have here found much witty policy appertaining to the governance of realms. Householders and parents have picked out of these books virtuous instructions for their children and their servants. Doctors and divines have here met with moral sentence and ensamples very excellent. Civil lawyers have espied, touching justice and equity, both rules appointed and cases discussed. Schoolmen have taken here-hence problems and questions to debate at large, and have fetched from hence philosophical conclusions with reasons and arguments to prove and to disprove. Orators have been well-furnished hereby with sundry graces and ornaments of speech, and in the like manner of matter have marked how to bestow their style. Rhetoricians, who for their exercise do use declamations, have taken out of this commonplaces, like large fields where men may walk at liberty. Schoolmasters never wist of finer phrases for to make their scholars acquainted with the very vein of the Latin language. At few words, all men that of wisdom be studious, may get somewhat herein to sharp the wit, to store the intelligence, to feed the mind, to quicken the spirit, to augment the reason, to direct the appetite, to frame the tongue, to fashion the manners: moreover to rule, to obey, to dispute, to determine, to teach, to persuade, and to every needful purpose in a man's life.

Unless the self thing witness as much as I say, let me not be credited, but in case both the book speak for itself, and to my testimonial I am able to adjoin princely peers, well-beknown and well-approved, then shall both the worthiness of the work and also the weight of the authority win credit and assent. Tully's *Duties*, when Caesar Augustus had read over, still standing on his feet, as he again delivered them to his nephew, of whom he had them: 'Eloquent', quoth he, 'was this man'.[6] Eloquent he was

[6] Plutarch, *Life of Cicero*, 49.3.

indeed, and one that loved well his country. Tully's *Duties* had Severus, the noble emperor, in so great price and reputation, that of all the Romans' books, to read them he thought him best apaid.° Tully's *Duties* have I known good clerks and well-learned men bear about in their bosoms, laying it full near their hearts that they would have lodged in their heads, and entirely loving Tully's heavenly company which way soever they went. Tully's *Duties* did Erasmus the Rotterdammer so greatly commend that in making mention of them he could not choose but break forth into these words: 'What? Writeth an ethnic° all this to ethnics? A profane man to the profane? Yet in his precepts of conversation, O Lord, what an equity, what a holiness, what sincerity, what verity? How well doth all together accord with nature? How is all framed even by good reason? What a conscience requireth he of such as govern that state? How plainly sets he before our eyes the marvellous and the amiable beautifulness of virtue? How much, how religiously, yea, how like a divine doth he teach of helping and relieving other men; of getting and maintaining of love and friendship; of the contempt of those vanities for which the common sort of Christian folk will either do or suffer they care not what?'[7] Finally, he deemeth them full worthy and full meet both for schoolmasters in their schools to read unto the youth, and also for old men again and again to use and to peruse.

These riches and treasures of wit and wisdom, as Cicero transported out of Greece into Italy, so have I fetched from thence and conveyed them into England, and have caused also Marcus Tullius (more than he could do when he was alive) to speak English. Marvellous is the matter, flowing the eloquence, rich the store of stuff, and full artificial° the enditing; but how I in our manner of speech have expressed the same, the more the book be perused, the better it may chance to appear. None other translation in our tongue have I seen but one, which is of all men of any learning so well liked that they repute it and count it as none.[8] Yet if ye list to compare this somewhat with that nothing, peradventure this somewhat will seem somewhat the more.

---

[7] Erasmus to Voecht (Jacobus Tutor), September 1519, in the preface to a new edition of *De Officiis*; see *CWE* 7, trans. R. A. B. Mynors (1987), pp. 71–73 (p. 72). Erasmus was referring to the edition printed by Martens (Louvain, 1519).

[8] Richard Whittington, *The thre bookes of Tullyes offices* (London: Wynkyn de Worde, 1534), STC 5278.

Howbeit look, what rule the rhetorician gives in precept to be observed of an orator in telling of his tale – that it be short and without idle words, that it be plain and without dark sense, that it be probable° and without any swerving from the truth – the same rule should be used in examining and judging of [this] translation.[9] For if it be not as brief as the very author's text requireth, whatso is added to his perfect style shall appear superfluous and to serve rather to the making of some paraphrase or commentary. Thereto, if it be uttered with ink-horn terms,[10] and not with usual words, or if it be phrased with wrested° or far-fetched forms of speech, not fine, but harsh, not easy, but hard, not natural, but violent, it shall seem to be. Then also, in case it yield not the meaning of the author, but either following fancy or misled by error forsakes the true pattern, it cannot be approved for a faithful and sure interpretation which ought to be taken for the greatest praise of all. These points, as I have studied to perform, so where I have not always attained unto them, I shall desire you, gentle reader, gently to consider both the excellence of the author, who is a perfect orator, and also the greatness of the matter, which is profound philosophy.

Nevertheless, such as be exquisite° in both the languages already may (and that with some profit and pleasure) try what I have done and what they can do, all under one, if, laying my translation apart, they will set the Latin before them and so assay° their own vein. Either they shall like themselves the better when they confer it with my poor workmanship, or else perchance con° me the more thank for attempting, following, and accomplishing of this enterprise. Be it so, one hath neither the Latin nor the English eloquence, yet by the benefit of nature, sith a man may do much, namely if he thereto adjoin use and exercise, here is for him occasion both to whet his wit and also to file his tongue. For although an Englishman hath his mother

[9] Grimald follows Cicero in adapting the rules of oratory to translation. See Humphrey **29**. 607–38. The term 'probable' has a particular application in rhetoric, where the speaker's ability to convey credible truths is essential; a 'probable' translation is one that carries conviction on account of its faithfulness to the original.

[10] ink-horn terms] affected neologisms, usually Latinate. Though a derogatory expression, it was acknowledged for much of the sixteenth century that English vocabulary was deficient in its resources for translation, especially in the case of technical terms. See also Pettie, **38**. 58.

tongue and can talk apace, as he learned of his dame, yet it is one thing to tittle-tattle, I wot° not how, or to chatter like a jay, and another to bestow his words wisely, orderly, pleasantly, and pithily. Such as have English meetly° well and but a smattering or small taste in the Latin, which number is great among the scholars of this realm, may hereby fall into such acquaintance and familiarity with this most excellent Latin man that neither shall his device seem hard, nor his art obscure, nor his style strange. I dare well say, if this work hap into a good student's hand, he will not think it enough to run it over once, as we fare with trifles and toys, but advisedly and with good leisure three or four or five times, he will read it, and read it, and read it again. First by the principal points, by the definitions and the divisions, to see what is treated, how far-forth, in what order, and with what variety; then, to mark the precepts, reasons, conclusions, and commonplaces; after, unto the said places to refer all the stories, with the verses poetical; finally, as well in the English as the Latin, to weigh well properties of words, fashions of phrases, and the ornaments of both. Moreover, many clerks I have known ere this, which could conceive and understand full well, whose tongue nevertheless in utterance and use of speech was in a manner maimed; yea, and some that could also speak Latin readily and well-favouredly, who to have done as much in our language and to have handled the same matter, would have been half blank.[11] What need more words? I desire my travail none otherwise to be taken in worth than the diligent peruser shall in effect find fruit thereof.

28. John Dolman, *Tusculan Questions* [Cicero] (1561)

[John Dolman was born in Newbury, Berkshire, son of the clothier Thomas Dolman, who was manager to John Wincombe, fictionalised by Thomas Deloney in *Jack of Newbury*. He is mentioned in Laurence Humphrey's *Life of Bishop Jewel* as one of Jewel's pupils at Corpus Christi College, Oxford, where he graduated BA in 1557. He was admitted to the Inner Temple in 1560, when he was working on his translation of Cicero, and he

[11] On Latin language learning as the cause of inadequacy in English see William Thomas, **25**. 30–53 above.

followed this with a contribution to the 1563 edition of the *Mirror for Magistrates* on the tragedy of Lord Hastings.

Cicero wrote the *Tusculan Questions* (also known as the *Tusculan Disputations*) at his country villa at Tusculum where he retired after the death of his daughter. Composed in five books, it addresses the fear of death, how to cope with the sufferings and misfortunes of life, and the moderation of the passions. Dolman acknowledges Grimald's work as his precedent in making Cicero's moral philosophy available in the vernacular, but it was less successful and was not reprinted.

See also Louis B. Wright, 'Translations for the Elizabethan Middle Class', *The Library*, 13 (1932), 312–31; Lily B. Campbell, 'John Dolman', *ELH*, 4 (1937), 192–200.]

To the Right Reverend Father in God, John, Bishop of Sarum.[1]

Right Honourable, when as partly by the counsel of them as might command me, and partly by mine own consent, I left the university and began to apply myself to the study of the common laws of the realm, I felt myself chiefly hindered therein with the intermeddling° of those studies, the which, not without great delight, I had aforetime used. The which, because I was loath to continue, to the defrauding of the expectation of those with whom to trifle it had been impiety, I minded to take my farewell of some such part of philosophy as both might be most profitable to the quiet leading of my life, to whatsoever trade I should give myself, and also should be so pleasant that it might even cloy me with delight. Which my desire to satisfy, when I sought many books, yet found I none more meet than this, which whiles I read I must needs confess that I was never more delighted with any work, except it were the sacred volume of the Holy Scriptures. Wherefore, when I had perused it over and found such profit and pleasure therein as it were not possible to find the like in any ethnic° writer, I wished all men the like delight as the reading of it brought unto me. And because I could not misdoubt but the learned had already tried into the intent that the unlearned also

[1] Bishop of Sarum] John Jewel (1522–71), Bishop of Salisbury and the principal spokesman for the newly established Anglican church in *An Apologie, or aunswer in defence of the Church of England* (1562).

might have some fruition thereof, and that our country might at length flow with the works of philosophy, I endeavoured myself, although not eloquently, yet plainly, to translate the same into our English tongue.

And considering that there was none more meet to have the protection of so grave and learned a work than your honour; remembering also that the first attempt of the same part of philosophy, translated by Master Grimald, passed forth under the protection of one of that honourable vocation to the which also it hath pleased God after sundry troubles to call you, I thought it my duty in respect of many benefits by your lordship on me bestowed, to dedicate unto you this my simple travail, thinking that nothing could be unwelcome to your honour that savoured [of] Tully, whom I am not ignorant how much you were wont to esteem. Wherefore I hope that, like as your lordship was wont to be delighted with the Roman Tully, even so this English Tully (although not adorned with like eloquence by the translator, yet varying nothing in sense) you will not disdain.

The Preface to the Reader

If thankfulness for so simple desert may cause thee to requite him with any part of the like gentleness, who took upon him this travail, such as it is, only for thy commodity,° gentle reader, then stay a while from the reading of Tully and harken favourably to this little communication that I crave at thy hands. I mind only to excuse myself briefly unto thee, and so to dismiss thee. The matters which I think colourably° may and will be objected unto me are these: first, the lack of years and eloquence to attempt so weighty a book as the very sages of the university have let lie still, even from the time that it was first written unto this day; then, the profaning[2] of the secrets of philosophy, which are esteemed only of the learned and neglected of the multitude, and therefore unmeet to be made common for every man.

[2] profaning] Degrading something that is held to be exclusive by making it accessible to ordinary people. This predates the first citation in the OED (Sir Thomas Browne, 1643). The revealing of professional 'secrets' was a complaint made especially against vernacular medical books; see Thomas Gale **34**. below.

First, as for mine own unableness for years, I answer by Plato and this mine author, that I know nothing but that which my soul, now settled in my body, recounteth as things learned before.[3] And the soul shall never have the body more apt to whatsoever thing it listeth to dispose him than in his youth, which is in manner the greenness of the same. Since, therefore, the body, which hath no knowledge but by reason of the soul, is in youth most apt and able to execute the inventions of the same, what cause is there why the wit, being one of the principal parts of the soul, should not chiefly in this nimbleness of the body utter her force and virtue?

Then, as for lack of eloquence, first this, I think, they will all grant: that it is not possible for any man to express the writings of Tully in English so eloquently as he hath uttered the same in Latin. Then, for mine own translation, forasmuch as it must of necessity be either more simple than the style of Tully, or else more foolish and full of crooked° terms (for Tully's mean° none can attain), I had rather to be partner of the favour due to simplicity and plainness than with foolish and far-fetched words to make my translation seem more dark to the unlearned and more foolish to the wise. By which my plainness, without counterfeit eloquence, if I have gotten no other commodity, yet thus much I am sure of, that I have thereby escaped the just reproof that they deserve which think to cloak their ignorance with inkhorn terms. For unless it were in such things as the logicians term 'names of art',[4] for the which we have no proper English words, I have used none but the plain and accustomed terms.

Now as touching the second objection, which containeth the unprofitable disclosing of the mysteries of Lady Philosophy, as Master Grimald termeth her, I think that sufficiently satisfied if they consider that, besides the rascal multitude and the learned

[3] soul [. . .] learned before] Socrates's theory of anamnesis is introduced in Plato, *Meno* 86b and developed in *Phaedo*. Dolman's college, Corpus Christi, was the leader in the development of Greek studies at Oxford in the early sixteenth century. (There were, however, no English translations of Plato in the period.)

[4] names of art] More usually, 'terms of art'. Dolman echoes Grimald on 'inkhorn terms' (**27**. 178), but his reference to logicians also looks back to medieval scholasticism and the verbal pedantry expressed in 'new terms of art' criticised by Bacon in *The Advancement of Learning* (1605), STC 1164, sig. E3^{r}, image 19.

sages, there is a mean sort of men,[5] which although they be not learned, yet, by the quickness of their wits, can conceive all such points of art as nature could give. To those I say there is nothing in this book too dark, especially inasmuch as the reading of one book will open another. And thus, in my opinion, I am discharged of unprofitable revealing of the secrets of philosophy, inasmuch as both, I hope, it shall do much good to this sort of men aforementioned, and also, I am sure, it can be nothing hurtful to the learned, but shall much more inflame all liberal wits with the desire of knowledge when they shall see so worthy matters contained in one little book of that which we term philosophy or learning.

Besides these there are yet other faults, as the misprinting of many words and the ill printing of some Greek words in Latin letters, and of the verses also, otherwise than they should be read. But the blame thereof I utterly refuse [. . .] I beseech thee, gentle reader, to place each man's fault by himself that I may be forced to father no other man's faults than mine own; which, as I know to be more than I would they were, so I shall desire thee to weigh them with gentleness, knowing that if such as have greater knowledge to set forth things more exactly should hear my plainness not overmuch discommended, they then should be much more provoked with hope of the marvellous fame that their doings should deserve, if they listed to employ some pains in attempting the like. Of the which as I know there is a great number (in both the universities inespecially), so I would wish that either they, ceasing any longer to envy knowledge to our English tongue, would stain[6] the same with better, or else that they would not disdain to afford their favourable words to such as express their good will in the same, although not so well as it might be, yet as their eloquence will permit them. And thus much to the learned reader whom I make the judge of my work, though I permit the reading of it to all other.

[5] mean sort] An early reference to the 'middling sort' or what would become the middle classes (significant, in view of Dolman's background and connection with Deloney); see Keith Wrightson, 'Estates, Degrees, and Sorts: Changing Perceptions of Society in Tudor and Stuart England' in *Language, History and Class*, ed. by P. J. Corfield (Oxford: Blackwell, 1991), pp. 30–52.

[6] stain] Used figuratively to mean 'eclipse' or 'put in the shade' and therefore to 'replace'.

But now, thou unlearned reader, forasmuch as whatsoever I did, I did it for the desire I had to profit thee, it shall be thy part, of the worst to think the best. For had it not been for thy commodity, I could well enough have suppressed mine ignorance with silence, and so, by concealing that little which I know, although not blazed° my simple skill, yet well have avoided the necessity of excuse in such things as I deserve reprehension. But so much I tendered thy profit that I had rather to say somewhat (although not so perfectly as some other might), than for lack of my little labour to let so worthy a book lie unknown unto thee. Thus, whiles I study to profit thee, I am fain to submit my doings to the judgement of every curious carper. Wherefore, inasmuch as I have brought thee (who towards these things was no otherwise than blind) by my travail to the sight hereof and caused thee to be rid from blindness (which is so loathsome a thing that it is almost grown into a proverb that a blind man would be glad to see his nighest fellow hanged, because then he should see), then truly, though I crave no praise at thy hands (because it is a token of ignorance to be praised of the ignorant), yet I may be bold to desire so much of thee as Apelles commanded the foolish shoemaker to perform; who, whenas he beheld the picture of a man drawn by Apelles, so lively that the senses of man would have doubted whether it were a picture or a living creature, not contented with the sight of it, which was more meet for a prince to behold than him, began to find fault with his show. Apelles, knowing that he was a shoemaker, took it in good part and with the pencil amended the fault; but the shoemaker, by likelihood somewhat proud that he was able to find fault with Apelles' works, came again the second day and began to dispraise the proportion of his face. Wherewithal, Apelles, being much moved, stepped forth and said, 'No further than thy shoe, souter',° showing thereby that no man ought to talk further than his skill will bear him.[7] Megabizes esteemed Alexander as a prince, whiles he stood in his school and said nothing, but when he began to talk of things which he knew not, he said unto him that even his little children would laugh him to scorn.

Wherefore, shortly to make an end and to send thee to Tully, do thou neither praise nor dispraise further than thy cunning will

[7] The story is told in Pliny, *Natural History*, 35, which is also the source of the reference to Megabizes.

bear thee, for they are both alike faults, but rightly weigh and remember the words of Tully, to whom I now send thee to enjoy such pleasure as at the first, whiles I myself read him, I friendly wished unto thee.

29. Laurence Humphrey, *Interpretatio linguarum* [The translation of languages][8] (1559)

Translated by Gordon Kendal[9]

[Laurence Humphrey (1527?-1590) was among other things a Protestant theologian and a president of Magdalen College, Oxford. His work on translation, concerned primarily but not exclusively with translation from Greek and Hebrew into Latin, has a practical orientation. He aims to advise and encourage translators and expositors of all kinds, and to raise the status of their craft. For him *interpretatio* has a wider connotation than the modern 'translation' and – to indicate various aspects of linguistic mediation – he alternates it with a number of other words (e.g. *convertere*, *explicare*, *exponere*, *exprimere*, *imitare*, *reddere*, *tradere*, *traducere*, *transferre*, *transfundere*, *vertere*), each having its own semantic versatility. The sense he intends by a particular word on a particular occasion is best determined by context. Interpreters (learned, fluent, fastidious in their command of language, concerned to enhance humanity by undoing the curse of Babel) are the modern equivalent of the classical orator, key figures in the renascent culture of Humphrey's time. But he grounds their importance theologically too, and for him St Paul is as significant as Cicero: like God in Christ, the *interpres* is a mediator of truth, a salvific teacher. So their character no less than their technical skill is important. Translating for Humphrey is essentially a communal endeavour, with translators helping one another as well as their readers. His handling of the whole subject is cumulative and recapitulatory

[8] The full title is: *Interpretatio linguarum: seu de ratione convertendi & explicandi autores tam sacros quam prophanos, Libri tres* [The translation of languages: or the method of rendering and expounding both sacred and secular authors, three books].

[9] The translation has also been annotated by Gordon Kendal with some additional notes by Neil Rhodes.

rather than strictly linear, and he frequently takes up earlier topics and expands them, sometimes with changes in terminology that can cause confusion. A particularly valuable feature of the work, impossible to reproduce in this selection, is his detailed analyses of actual examples of translation.

See also Glyn P. Norton, *The Ideology and Language of Translation in Renaissance France and their Humanist Antecedents* (Geneva: Droz, 1984); Frederick M. Rener, *Interpretatio: Language and Translation from Cicero to Tytler* (Amsterdam: Rodopi, 1989); J. W. Binns, *Intellectual Culture in Elizabethan and Jacobean England: The Latin Writings of the Age* (Leeds: Francis Cairns, 1990).]

[*1. The importance of translation*]

Anyone who knows how to speak can testify that language has many sorts of value. It brings distinction and benefit to a state, provided you put it to use. But if you merely know it, without ever exercising it openly, then – while indeed you have in your possession a treasure – it is shut away and useless, like a sword that you grasp but keep in its sheath. A sword gets its value in being used, and in the same way language shows its gleaming edge when brought out, but grows dull when hidden away. What is more, if when you speak you use a strange language, a language that others do not know, that is no different from remaining silent. People will marvel in astonishment and not understand you. You may acquire a reputation for being wise but you will do them no good, and many will just think (as St Paul remarks) that you are a barbarian, indeed mad.[1] Speech of this sort simply passes into the air, not into the ear. It is babbling and gabbling rather than proper speaking.

It is God who enables us to express ourselves through language; hence doing this intelligibly, in ways suited and familiar to people's hearing and perception, will bring benefit not just privately to the proprietor of the material, but also in general

[1] I Corinthians 14.11 and 23. The whole chapter is a key passage for Humphrey's understanding of the importance of translation. The 'tongues' mentioned there are usually taken by scholars now to refer to the psychological phenomenon of *glossolalia*, rather than to foreign languages.

to everyone who hears him. And when an accurate translation is provided something more than just useful is going on, something wonderfully godlike, whether through the live voice in public assemblies, or through pen and writings for the sake of posterity. This is how – by practising the good office of translation – we can incite some people to virtue and urge them into the fellowship of the Christian religion, and call others back out of vice and superstition; and (in brief) be of mutual help and benefit to one another on any matter whatever. Thus all the weird uttering and confusion that Babel engendered has been annulled by this ability we have to translate. The situation is that nothing need be private – language, speech, words – but everything may be regarded (in line with Pythagoras' precept) as a common possession among friends.[2] We acknowledge God the Holy Spirit to be the author of this remarkable gift, and the Apostle, having spoken of the different kinds of tongues that have come from God, proceeds right away to the matter of translating them: making it clear that languages are of little significance unless they express themselves plainly; and that their chief benefit individually and collectively is to explain clearly and teach whatever is spoken or written in them. These matters are discussed extensively in the twelfth and fourteenth chapters of [I] Corinthians as vital for a Christian congregation, so that anything that concerns the consolation, encouragement, and mutual upbuilding of all may not be some unintelligible noise like the unclear sound of flutes, but be proclaimed loud and clear in the church, like trumpets with a clear message.[3]

This is translation [*interpretatio*], called by the Greeks *hermēneia*. 'Translator' is an ambiguous word and can be understood in various ways. For present purposes I take it to mean someone who brings clarity to some particular form of language or idiom generally less well known, translating [*interpretatione*] it into words that are better known and more familiar; or who turns something [*convertit*] from a foreign language into one that is more common and widely used. I am not presuming to say in

[2] common possession among friends] This echoes the first of Erasmus's *Adagia*: *Amicorum communia omnia* ('Between friends all is common'); see also Kathy Eden, *Friends Hold All Things in Common* (New Haven, CT: Yale University Press, 2001).

[3] I Corinthians 14.6–8.

what this art of translation consists, but it is possible to give some guidance as to approach and method.[4] It is astonishing that so far nobody has done this – especially in the present age, when all the fine arts have begun to blossom and when so many men of distinction and excellence have emerged in every kind of discipline, and more especially indeed since every day there are pupils at school, professors in universities, theologians in pulpits, working away at something that is so plainly relevant and widely beneficial, and that matters to so many of us. [1–4]

[2. *The qualities of a good translation*]

Broadly speaking, there are three kinds of translation. (It is possible to imagine a variety of different ways of translating, just like ways of speaking, but I want at present to distinguish them briefly in this way.) The first kind is rather crude and lacking in refinement, since there is no distancing in it from the actual words. We might say it is overscrupulous or unduly restrained. To this category belong those who have rendered word for word Homer, Euripides, Sophocles, Aristophanes, and other poets. I believe their idea is (like nurses forcing into infants' mouths morsels of food already chewed and broken up, prattling childishly to the little prattlers) to give a sort of helping hand to beginners, people ignorant of Greek and having no teacher with whom to discuss things, and to bring them to some slender understanding of the poets. At one time this may well have been all right, in the bad old days, when nobody could venture to teach or learn languages without being suspected of heresy. But frankly, in this golden age of learning, it is bound to seem as though – in cutting everything up into little bits and allocating individual words in such a way that nothing is left for the pupils to ponder and investigate carefully for themselves – they are looking to their own idleness rather than to any benefit to the students. It is not a bad plan, at the outset of training, to show clearly and in detail to people learning the basics of prose what each word in itself means, and then to move them on gradually step by step to something more advanced. But when someone is teaching them to crawl when they ought to be soaring up into the heights of poetry,

[4] On Humphrey's method see Norton, *The Ideology and Language of Translation*, pp. 11–14.

if the teacher is seizing upon things that are relatively trivial and neglecting more important matters, it is as if he wants them to be back in their cradles whimpering while he softly and delicately feeds and nurtures them on this 'pap', humouring their idleness and sloth and plainly encouraging them to be lazy. Imagine teaching an adult, who is already able to jump and run, how to move along slowly step by step with infants, progressing gradually: it is like that when someone is in effect teaching people grown to maturity in the reading of the Greeks to become children again, and summoning them back to their cradles when they might be undertaking tasks weightier and more grown-up. Things learned quickly, with no mental challenge, are quickly lost. They stick longer if acquired with toil. Indeed, so long as learners are glued to the individual words, they are not even learning. The meaning is lost or obscured, so that a skilled translator is needed to deal with these supposedly 'clear' translations they claim to be providing for raw beginners. [14–16]

The next method, favoured by some translators nowadays, has the opposite fault. It is freer and looser and allows itself too much licence. While the former method keeps strictly within limits, this one with quite shameless audacity leaps across boundaries, luxuriating in synonyms, playing with unnecessary tropes, wantonly sporting with metaphors, brazenly making up words, tossing aside the natural ones and piling up exotic ones, striving for fancy embellishments where there is no occasion for them; veritably (as the saying goes) 'putting perfume on lentils'. It offers sumptuous and garish expressions, and puts on a gaudy show, when the meaning requires restraint and simplicity. It is ponderous in light matters, tragic in comic, raging hot in cool, frigid in passionate. In brief, it follows completely its own inclination and bent, and pays no attention to the author chosen for consideration – as if there were no difference between a 'writer' and a 'translator'. But a writer [*scriptor*] is free to say whatever he wants, in whatever order, and with whatever words he likes (so long as they are of acceptable quality). A translator, however, has a firm objective in front of him, with limits beyond which he cannot stray if he wishes to render the author's meaning faithfully and discharge his duty satisfactorily. The former pursues his own ideas; the latter ideas found in someone else. The former has freedom; the latter is under compulsion not to present us with what he has thought up for himself, but must rather establish what the author has conceived, and settle for taking from the language into which he is translating words that – in representing how the author expresses himself and decks out his language – say the same thing in the same shape and fashion. [22–24]

It remains to discuss the third method, the 'middle way'. This has features in common with both of the preceding. It is straightforward but learned, elegant but faithful. It is neither puffed up beyond measure nor so low as to be mean. It is restrained, balanced, moderate, in love with neither squalor nor profusion but with neatness of arrangement. [30]

The essential qualities of the translation we are aiming at are these: it should be comprehensive [*plena*], naturally appropriate [*propria*], attractive [*pura*], and aptly suited [*apta*]. In my view these are its constituent parts.

I call a translation 'comprehensive' when it gives the sense in full, so that every part of the meaning has its parallel, and it corresponds fully throughout to what the author has in mind, with nothing left out and nothing added. For almost everyone – through inattention or taking his eyes from the target – lets some words escape and others flow to excess; while there are those who just wander all over the place and fail to 'hit the nail on the head', as the old saying goes. For this perfect agreement three things need to be carefully considered in every text: first, the subject matter and meaning; next the way the words are structured and applied; finally the rhythm (that is, as Cicero says, the way in which the words are shaped and linked together). The Greeks called subject matter *pathēmata tēs psychēs*,[5] truly that which minds have thought and devised. Dialecticians call it *inventio*. We need to examine extremely carefully what the author's points are, identifying how the argument proceeds, whether the assertions are established and grounded in terms of 'natures' or 'causes and effects' or in other ways. The 'structure' [*forma*] of the words – in Greek *schēmatismos* – refers to the complexion and, so to speak, the 'attire' of what is being said and meant: whether affirmative or negative, direct or interrogative in form, categorical or hypothetical; then whether they are straightforward [Greek *haplē*] or imitative [Greek *mimētikē*] (that is, whether it is a continuous, unbroken narrative or one that has dialogues punctuating it and splitting it up). Finally, we should be sensitive to its 'rhythm'

---

[5] 'states or impressions of the mind'.

[*numeros*] – the Greek rhetoricians call it *rhythmon* – and whatever relates to its composition [Greek *synthēkē*] and arrangement, to the way the meaning is set out. If these various aspects are scrutinised, you will not lose any of the meaning and ideas, any of the style and construction, that the author meant to observe. Contrariwise, if they get only fleeting attention you will go utterly astray. Good writers never produce anything bad or superfluous: hence nothing should be cut away or removed. [31–33]

We have next to discuss 'natural appropriateness', the ingrained way of speaking evident in every language.[6] For the Romans it is 'Latinity', for Greeks 'Hellenism', for Athenians 'Atticism', for Jews 'Hebraism': whereby everything is designated accurately, fittingly, and faithfully, in its own proper terms. For Aristotle in Greek the way is 'not to surround things with general notions but to call them by their own names'.[7] The first of our race to do this was Adam when in Paradise he gave things names of their own.[8] All praise to a translator who uses literal language,[9] in the fashion of country folk and rustics who express themselves rather crudely but clearly, and call a spade a spade: simple folk, innocent of the obfuscations of rhetoricians who play around with words to amplify or condense things, and in other ways darken and obscure their topic or envelop it in circumlocutions; making a hill into a mountain, a mule into a lion, a flea into an elephant, a midget into a Hercules. So we need to keep our eyes open for things that are similar, like superstition and religion, audacity and courage, and vices which deceptively resemble a type of virtue. For we should not express rough things smoothly, or bitter things sweetly, nor hide bad things under a fine name, or draw a respectable curtain over wickedness. Our language should stay literal: in this way we shall not depart from

[6] Humphrey is concerned here with respecting as far as possible the way in which the source language 'maps' reality by using words that stick closely and naturally to the facts. Etymology, analogy, and sound were important tools in determining this. For the ancient discussion about 'nature' and 'convention' see Plato's *Cratylus*. Cicero was by no means a strict 'analogist': see *Orator* 155–62; also Horace, *Art of Poetry* 70–72. The different question of respecting an author's style is dealt with under 'aptness' below.

[7] *Rhetoric* III.5.3.

[8] Genesis 2.19–20.

[9] literal language] Humphrey has the Greek *kyriolegein*.

our original, but render each word naturally (though not to the point of absurdity). [41–42]

It is useful for the translator to have a good grasp of etymology, with a knowledge of the languages from which words are derived. For words often have the same rationale. If you are wanting to translate *boēthein* [help], you will find nothing more suitable or natural than *succurrere* [run to assist] because the key elements in each word are the same: *boēthein*[10] means to run up to the voice of someone who is calling out or in difficulty (like *boēdromein*). [43–44]

[Still on this question of 'appropriateness': while Cicero is of course outstanding in the way he uses Latin and absorbs Greek ideas naturally into his own language, there is a danger of following him in the wrong way, especially when we are dealing with sacred texts which particularly demand literalness in translation.] Longolius[11] was a man of noble spirit who strove always for the best, but he lacked something of that healthy outlook which the Italians have, and was well-nigh swept away into this pernicious profanity, eager to impose on us a Ciceronian Gospel and to subject God's Holy Word to the heathen eloquence of Cicero. But it is rather for every device of rhetoric and all Cicero's richness to be subject to God's Word, to assist it rather than correct it, to serve it rather than lord over it, to follow in its due place rather than to take the lead. It should, in brief, be shedding light on it, not spreading darkness over it or impairing its sacred perfection with the triflings of human eloquence. For in what way is that any different from using a Lesbian rule,[12] if the mistress to whom all the arts should minister and serve is bent and turned to their own will? I am not denying that the divine Word can be expressed and spoken in a Ciceronian way (indeed I am greatly in favour of that and I shall try to indicate this later), but it has to be in such a way 'Ciceronian' (by which I mean fine and

---

[10] *boēthein*] Greek *boē* is 'shout', *thein* (and *dromein*) is 'run'.

[11] Christophorus Longolius (1488–1522), friend of Pope Leo X and Italian humanists.

[12] Lesbian rule] Originally a mason's tool made of (malleable) lead to fit around curves, then figuratively any governance or principle that is over-accommodating; mentioned by Aristotle in *Ethics* V.10. It also appears in Erasmus, *Adagia* 1.5.93 where it is explained as doing things the wrong way round, as when theory is accommodated to fact, not fact to theory, and when law is suited to conduct and not conduct to law.

graceful and elegant) that it is still 'Christian'. Christ must still be Christ, the Gospel still the Gospel, and faith and baptism and all the things we have learned and absorbed through reading and hearing them proclaimed in schools and pulpits: everything must be secure and preserve its true glory. When Cicero was unable to translate something appropriately into Latin from his Greek sources, he left it in Greek – e.g. 'philosophy', 'rhetoric', 'geometry', and many other examples scattered throughout his books – though he sometimes employs circumlocution, as when he speaks of 'study of wisdom' or 'art of speaking'.[13] [51–52]

The third essential quality is 'attractiveness', in Greek *katharotēs*. The translation should be clear and graceful, because using the right words will not be any good if they are unpleasing and ugly (though the beauty must not displace or damage the meaning). If this attractiveness does not come of its own accord we need to seek for it. For it is a truly wonderful and godlike thing not only to give to people who understand Latin an accurate and proper sense of what men of conspicuous learning have written, but much more to translate it with faultless grace and purity, so that their meaning may be not only understood but read with keen pleasure. Certainly, to my mind, nobody who cannot transmit another's thoughts and ideas with elegance and beauty is worthy of the great name of translator. [57–58]

[The fourth essential quality is 'aptness'.] A right and proper translation maintains the highest degree of suitability of expression throughout, for the essence of translating is to be just right, and anything ill-fitting is a major offence; and whoever produces something unseemly, something inappropriate to the subject and persons concerned, is an incompetent bungler. If we do not wish – like poor stage actors– to show ourselves up badly, telling our tale clumsily, we need to weigh carefully the nature of what is being discussed, and by whom. Not all subject matters are the same, nor is there only one way of expressing them. Hence Aristotle gives good advice: 'conform[14] with the subject matter'[15] – express it appropriately, because grand matters should not be treated bombastically, matters in the middle range should not be overdone, and plain matters should not be expressed meanly and

[13] 'study of wisdom' or 'art of speaking'] Greek *philosophia* and *rhētorikē technē*.
[14] conform] Literally in Greek 'be analogous'.
[15] *Rhetoric* III.7.1–2.

meagrely. Rather, those three categories of the rhetoricians – grand, intermediate, plain – should each be established and expressed in its own place. For the same shoe does not fit every foot, nor every garment Hercules. So too not every style of speech fits every subject, but serious matters need expressing with dignity, matters in the middle range with moderation, and the lowliest matters in a low and plain sort of style. Then we need to give consideration to who the persons are. Writers differ considerably, for poets need one kind of language, orators another, historians another; and within these categories one is grander, richer, fuller than another; another is more polished, neater, more elegant; another is rougher, meaner, drier. Indeed, the same writer does not always stay the same or speak in the same way on all occasions. Virgil creeps on the ground in his *Bucolics*, speaking about trees and lowly tamarisk shrubs. In the *Georgics* he is a good deal more refined and flowery. And in the *Aeneid*, 'he who once tuned his song on a slender reed and then, leaving the woods, did good work for the farmer by compelling the fields nearby to obey the labourer, however greedy, now sings of the terrible arms of Mars and of the Man':[16] making war indeed sound warlike. [81–83]

We should watch out lest, in our efforts on behalf of the original language, we set insufficient store by the one that we are using. We need to be at pains all the time to make use of words that are customary and proper within the language into which we are translating. Otherwise you will turn out many a strange and dark and clumsy absurdity, because – while indeed there is some kinship and similarity among all languages – there is clear and manifest difference too. [99–100]

By way of companion to these [four] essential qualities I now add 'clarity' [*perspicuitas*], something that supremely assists understanding and is indispensable in practice. Rather like blood, it should run through every part of what we are saying. For what is the point of language if it is so indistinct that nobody can understand it, so obscure as to be incomprehensible? Aristotle calls this quality *saphēneia* and he declares it to be of crucial importance, saying that language should not even be spoken, and is not performing its function, if it does not signify

[16] Four lines of verse (found in Suetonius) which were often placed at the beginning of the *Aeneid*.

clearly and plainly.[17] A translator will express himself lucidly and distinctly if he calls to mind and keeps fixed in his memory what I have already said about natural appropriateness, about attractiveness, and about aptness. For naturalness and clarity are inseparable companions, and there is nothing more lucid than attractiveness, while in contrast nothing is more obscure than uncouth language. If something fits well it is clear, while if it is translated unsuitably and awkwardly it presents more of an obstacle, hindering the reader's progress and getting in the way of his understanding. [114–15]

[*3. The requirements for a good translator*]

It remains for me to deal as briefly as I can with the actual formation of the translator. There are accordingly four major requirements in the making and establishing of a translator: the right natural gifts [*natura*], fine learning [*doctrina*], religious fidelity [*fides*], and outstanding application to the work [*diligentia*]. [115–16]

We ought, then, to begin with 'natural talent', it being first in rank as well as in time. The pagans thought of this as a kind of prodigious power, or a god. I believe it to be a kindling and breathing of the Holy Spirit, imparted and bestowed so that a man has the enthusiasm to undertake tasks and the resolution to complete them. It is a sort of exceptional gift from God. [116–17]

Training can help this natural excellence but it cannot create it. It can polish it but not instil it, reshape and improve it but not bestow it as a gift or endowment. Erasmus, a translator of felicitous dexterity if ever there was one, while he may have many equals – perhaps even betters – in expressive power and strength and dignity of language, as well as in renown for Ciceronian diction, nevertheless (such is the ease of his style, his gentle and even flow) he appears – in virtue of a certain impressive natural power, a sharpness of wit, a precision of judgement, in short because of this whole natural capacity of which I am speaking – second to none. [119]

[Next is 'learning'.] For we do not want a translator lacking in culture and learning, a mere labourer who has none of the equipment of knowledge, only the empty noise and clatter of words.

[17] *Rhetoric* III.2.1.

Frequently the path he is entering will not be uniformly level or smooth. It will be sown with thickets and thorns. There will be many an obstacle, and delays and difficulties will occur. These are things with which a knowledgeable and learned craftsman will deal easily. [125–26]

True, solid, genuine learning is split into two parts, of which one is called 'knowledge' [*cognitio*, Greek *gnōsis*] and the other 'diction' [*oratio*, Greek *logos*]. This distinction I have taken from St Paul, for at the beginning of the [first] Epistle to the Corinthians, after mingling compliments with greetings and gratitude, he commends them because they amply abound in those very riches and resources of the mind, namely in speech [*sermo*][18] and in knowledge [*scientia*]. 'Knowledge' means knowledge of things, while 'diction' means knowing about words and how to express oneself.

It is necessary in the first place to make a great effort to become knowledgeable about divine as well as human matters, so that the translator may be equipped theoretically and practically to deal with all sorts of important subjects. This cultural expertise underlies and supports language: it is a knowledge of humanity and the liberal arts that sheds light on things. We quite rightly blame a translator who is deficient in words, inarticulate, a mere infant in expressing himself – because he lacks the wherewithal for laying bare matters that are hidden away and essentially recondite, and for opening them up so that people can hear and read them. In the same way there is no escaping censure for anyone who aspires to execute the lofty and challenging duty of translation but who – owing to his ignorance of what is most relevant – does so naked and unarmed. [127–28]

However, the translator's special concern is with articulating subject matter, so his main task is to refine and cultivate his language. This area covers specifically the 'logical' in diction – whatever has a bearing on the arrangement and fabric and structure of speech. There is, too, the matter of different languages,[19] but I am going to deal briefly first with the arts of Grammar, Rhetoric, and Dialectic. These arts are primary and basic, of course, but for the translator they are invaluable beyond all the

[18] The biblical text (I Corinthians 1.5) has *verbum* and *scientia*.

[19] He argues at length (134–70) for the study of Greek and Hebrew as well as Latin.

rest. Once Grammar has been grasped and understood it seems the lowest of the low – and to be sure it is, since that is precisely where the foundation lies – but if you try to do without Grammar as the base when laying out and building up any of the other matters, you will never reach the summit, and the whole apparatus, however splendid and brilliant, will sink and crash to the ground. [130]

Rhetoric these days is in a bad way, not indeed through any intrinsic defect of its own but just because of human fashions. We need to revive it and restore it to its proper dignity. It teaches us about the figurative qualities of words and languages, it indicates how discourses are divided up and arranged, it shows how meanings can be embellished or adapted, it sets out rules for making language ornate and attractive and more expansive, and it outlines the ways in which speech is conceived and structured. All of this is essential if authors are even to be understood or explained, never mind translated, so that you grasp accurately what they mean, and convey with due precision and skill the inherent import of each. [131–32]

Dialectic (according to Plato) raises men's eyes from the dirt they are stuck in and turns demagogues into teachers.[20] Paul requires this in a bishop: that they learn *orthotomein*,[21] to 'divide (or discern) rightly' God's word. This is the genuine study of language – not something that lays snares for people and deludes them with its sophistical 'probabilities' – and its influence is not confined (as many imagine) to the schools, to sheltered nooks and thinking-shops where people quibble and argue. At root it is not a mere love of bandying words. Rather, it explains propositions and passages in the sacred books, it divides genera into species, distinguishes true from false, discriminates ambiguities; and finally – what is crucial and has a particular bearing on our present project – it brings a clarity of understanding which enables the translator to see what the writer means, to understand how he makes his point, and to bring a clear perception and judgement to the way his exposition, argument, and conclusion are ordered. For unless these things are attended to (as was also shown earlier) the translator will lose track of what is meant,

[20] e.g. *Republic* VII.533.c.

[21] *orthotomein*] Greek literally 'to cut straight'; cf. II Timothy 2.15 and Hebrews 4.12.

or of the arrangement of words and the sequenced connection of the statements; and in consequence will be saying something different or laying the argument out differently. [132–33]

Next we need to discuss 'fidelity'[22] and religion. For when we are dealing with secular authors we need to show fidelity, and with sacred authors devotion and faith. Translating faithfully means translating in the way one ought to do, and also with the right frame of mind. Both are essential. If we are faithful we shall not distort the sense but give it in full and without adulteration; not patching on to it anything of our own, and not cutting away from it anything of the author's. A translator will show fidelity in not putting down casually and carelessly, with a sort of heedless abandon, whatever happens to come to his pen: rather, he will work as accurately and as discerningly as he can, following the rules I laid down earlier when I was discussing translation itself. As I have said, that is the way to work faithfully and in the way one ought. Now the translator's frame of mind needs to be considered too, and there are three things a faithful translator should avoid. I take the trusty [*fidum*] and faithful [*fidelem*] translator to be a 'good' man:[23] someone who will not follow his own inclination, who will not seek for praise, and who will not seek his own benefit. For [first] personal inclination blinds and does not want to see the truth, and (to be sure) it is not the least of the plagues that afflict students – and a poison in religion – when what ought to be carried out with right and careful judgement is corrupted through giving way to personal or party feelings. [170–1]

We ought [secondly] to reckon this itchy hankering after idle praise as a pestilence and an abomination wherever it occurs. What a blessing it would surely be if we could get harmony and agreement among translators! Let me be perfectly frank and honest: this restlessness, this anxiety that possesses some folk to meddle [Greek: *polypragmosynē*] and to toss dust in others' eyes,[24] is an abhorrence. At the slightest provocation they desert the well-trodden highway, discontented with others' translations,

[22] With *fides* Humphrey draws on a range of meanings, from personal reliability and integrity to deep loyalty and deference to the text's author (especially – but not exclusively – when that is God).

[23] Compare Quintilian on the orator, *Institutio oratoria* I.9.

[24] The Latin expression is *oculos cornicum configunt* (pierce crows in their eyes).

and make up new translations of their own, more concerned to produce things that are novel and different than things that are better. They hunt out non-existing 'defects'[25] and they make a great song and dance over trifles; and if they come upon some word incorrectly translated then the whole book is re-worked and sent back to the press for publication. This gives them a reputation for being acute and clear-sighted, while everyone else appears dim and blind. [172]

Apart from personal inclination and glory, there is a third distortion of aim: the pursuit of profit and gain.[26] Things are in a bad way when something which should have been done out of a love of letters is undertaken out of a love of money. Even in money-making trades, with paid employees, this is considered a vice. Among those who cultivate the Muses and aim at distinction in the liberal arts, it is truly the depth of baseness. Far be the goddess-queen of this world, love of gain and covetousness, from the virgin Muses! One must fear, however, that people employed and paid to translate, hiring themselves out, will go about their business fraudulently, and will be less than trustworthy in discharging their affairs. This I in part deduce to be the case, because when their translations are compared with the original we notice various inversions, corruptions, omissions, superfluities; sometimes several lines at a time have been removed – all with the idea of fooling the reader and jeopardising the printer, or whoever else is paying them. I refrain from names, but I have seen it done, and heard of it. [174–75]

Last of all comes 'diligence', hand-maiden and servant of all the rest. What Demosthenes says of delivery,[27] I say of diligence: I reckon it to be first, second, third. It is what secures, facilitates, guards, and preserves everything necessary; and without it you will never accomplish anything remarkable or important. For what is the point of the other qualities, however illustrious or distinguished, if diligence is not there as an incentive, a sort of

[25] In Latin *in scirpo nodum quaerentes* (looking for a knot in a bulrush).

[26] This contrasts sharply with Udall's complaint that there is no adequate financial support for translation (see **7a**. 89–120 above).

[27] Cicero, *Orator* XVII.56. The anecdote was frequently quoted in the Renaissance: see for example Thomas Wilson, *The Arte of Rhetorique* (1553), STC 25799, sig. Gg1^{r}, image 126; Francis Bacon, 'Of Boldness' in *Essayes* (1625), STC 1148, pp. 62–63, image 37. Here it underlines Humphrey's analogy between oratory and translation.

spur? Being diligent, careful, zealous is vital to a good nature. A field may be good but if it is not tilled it becomes barren: in the same way a fertile and prolific talent will go bad and (as we might say) run wild unless it is refreshed and maintained by constant care. And how is the translator to acquire his breadth of learning, all the knowledge he needs, and that taste and fullness and grace in the way he expresses himself, if this diligence (Greek: *philoponia*) is lacking? [180–81]

Some hate this diligence and, instead of publishing their work properly they dash ahead with it and toss it forth, bragging they will translate in one month what others can barely do in six. But on publication it is apparent how deficient, crude, and full of errors they are. People like this need therefore repeatedly to be warned against precipitancy in writing or publishing. Horace rightly advises keeping things under cover till the ninth year.[28] This seems ridiculous if we look at it superficially, but on closer and fuller investigation it is truly a golden rule. For if things are to endure they need the application of time and care. Second thoughts are wiser and craftsmen do better in their later work. What you did not see yesterday you will notice more clearly tomorrow. Each day learns from the preceding one, and you grow wise where formerly you were foolish. [186–87]

[*4. Imitation and practice*]

[The way to excel in translating is through imitation and practice.][29] Cicero defines imitation as what drives us with systematic application to seek to resemble others in the way we express ourselves.[30] For whatever the sphere in which someone is less able, that person should there copy another who is more able, and take his example from him. We are made in such a way that by ourselves we can accomplish little. But with assistance and (so to speak) under others' auspices we can do and dare a great deal.

[28] *Art of Poetry* 388.

[29] In summary: 'Christ in Christianity, Cicero in Latin prose, Virgil in hexameter verse' (697–8). On imitation see Roger Ascham (**51**. below); George W. Pigman III, 'Versions of Imitation in the Renaissance', *Renaissance Quarterly*, 33 (1980), 1–32; Thomas M. Greene, *The Light in Troy: Imitation and Discovery in Renaissance Poetry* (New Haven, CT: Yale University Press, 1982).

[30] *Ad Herennium* I.2.3; Humphrey reads 'velimus' (want) rather than 'valeamus' (be able).

'One man is no man' and having someone else to partner what ability one has makes one stronger and firmer. Hercules had his Theseus. But if beside us we have not just a partner but a leader we will fight more stoutly and follow the commander's battle-standards with more spirit.

The same sort of thing is true of imitation in writing and in speaking. It means taking one's model from someone else, following it, heeding it, submitting to it. An ape exhibits the gestures, the signs, the mannerisms, the habitual actions of human beings: our imitating will be the more serious about reproducing the entire likeness of someone else, following him through the tracks and traces he has left, familiarising ourselves with his whole way of writing (incorporating ourselves in it, so to speak), making a full surrender of ourselves to his principles: in short, putting on the living image and likeness of his language as far as possible, taking his example as a kind of template for our own writing. [215–16]

[In the sacred writings, what better model than God himself in Christ?] For whom else can we take as teacher, whom more learned or holier than God, the sole and utterly reliable interpreter of his own will? It was he who gave the Law, and it was he also who set it forth with fresh clarity. The Father delivered it, and he sent his Son to explain it. The Saviour himself made this quite clear (in Matthew) in not only translating into the Greek language the laws on murder, adultery, divorce, swearing oaths and perjury, vengeance, love and hatred (laws issued and established for the Jews in their own language) and leaving them for us in translated form: but – being an expositor [*enarrator*] as well as a translator [*interpres*] – in also opening up through his teaching those very wells which the Pharisees and rabbis (offspring of the Philistines)[31] had blocked with the foul stagnancies of their verbal obscurities. So I firmly believe that in Christ Jesus, the author of the New Testament, there is a kind of pattern not only for living aright but also for expressing things aright, an altogether definitive likeness of God. If we are really serious in giving care and application to conforming to that pattern we shall be following the best of leaders, we shall never go astray, and we shall discharge the duty and vocation of the finest of

[31] See the story in Genesis 26.15.

translators. For God's mysteries should only ever be set forth in the language that God uses. [217–18]

[In prose writing Cicero is clearly a superlative model, both for his style and for the way he absorbs and re-expresses Greek ideas. But there are dangers for the translator in regard to prose, and limitations in regard to verse.] It is a big question nowadays just how Cicero is to be imitated. We need to be careful here, and the more so, the easier it is to go wrong. It is a fine thing to imitate the best, but to imitate them improperly is a bad thing. Some there are who claim to be imitating Cicero and who shelter under his name and authority: people whom, if what they actually did were as good as their intentions, I should be commending to students for imitation no less than Cicero. But in this matter of scholarship, considering what seems to me an extremely important topic – the nature of imitation in sacred and secular writings – it is not what people may say that deserves attention: rather, we need to consider how they do it and what reasons have influenced them. And the authority of men ought to count for less than the weight of the reasons they adduce. So if someone claims to be a Ciceronian while wandering all over the place, adding things or cutting them out at will, turning everything upside down, changing (mutilating, rather) the whole design, and often leaving out entire sentences: then to my mind his way of translating is neither right nor Ciceronian, even if he insert various words or phrases lifted (wrenched out, rather) from Cicero, words which may be fine enough in themselves but which are forced and far-fetched, and fail to express the pith and sense of what the Greek words say. I think we need to turn our backs on this free and easy method, and look for a different approach. Neither in what he has said, nor by his actual example, does this broad and winding way of proceeding have Cicero's approval – these people will never maintain that. He left no prototype of translation, whole and complete, for us to imitate; or, if he did, it has not survived. All he did was insert ideas here and there throughout his writings, as the context required, with an eye to basic meaning rather than to individual words. A 'translator' [*interpres*] would not have done that, but Cicero – so sparing in his explicit translations – wanted to remain freer, as well he might. [242–44]

Note how he writes in the first book of *De Officiis*, explaining the whole matter quite clearly and showing us plainly what his habitual practice was in translating [*convertendo*]. 'Therefore', he says, 'I particularly follow[32] the Stoics, at least on the present occasion and for the present enquiry, not in the way that translators [*interpretes*] do but (in my usual fashion) by using my own judgement and free will to draw out from the original sources as much as, and in whatever way, I think right.'[33] Notice he says 'in my usual fashion', so he is not just telling us what he has done in *De Officiis* but is stating his practice when translating [*transferendo*] on other occasions. And indeed he says the very same thing about those two famous, and contrary, speeches which he is said to have rendered into Latin (and he is quoted by Jerome): 'I translated [*converti*] the finest, and contrary, speeches of the two greatest Athenian orators, Aeschines and Demosthenes, not as a translator but as an orator'; and so on.[34] From this it is clear that Cicero declined and refused the title of 'translator', nor has anything been published (at the present time at least) which could give translators a model by which they could comprehensively regulate and fashion themselves. That the whole of Cicero is a pattern of how to express oneself, a live example, is now a byword. But that any one single part of it can be taken as a model for accurate and definitive translating, with nothing lacking: that is something that no-one will easily demonstrate. Without question, he copied many things from many people, as I acknowledge now and as I shall show more clearly later. Demosthenes – easily the greatest of orators – gave us Cicero as an orator, Aristotle made him a dialectician, Plato turned him into a philosopher (though with Aristotle's help in other areas): in sum, he has no excellence which he did not derive from Greece. Still, this does not mean that he regularly and explicitly cites their ideas: no, his usual practice is rather to put them to use.[35] [245–46]

---

[32] follow] Humphrey follows the reading 'sequimur' rather than the future tense 'sequemur' found in other editions.

[33] *De Officiis* I.II.6.

[34] *De Optimo Genere Oratorum* [On the best way of speaking] V.14, quoted in Jerome *Epistle* 57.7. See ll. 755–56 below; also Fulke, **10**. 372–76 above.

[35] 'Cicero, for all his greatness, is a thoroughgoing Greek. You will now (I imagine), honest reader, [after Humphrey's detailed analysis of Cicero's policy] understand how he imitated the Greeks in the theory of speaking and in philosophy: not just overtly translating [*aperte convertendo*] from Greek to Latin, but also tacitly hinting [*occulte adumbrando*] at particular topics in various places and in various ways. The same approach to imitation exists in Scripture: sometimes overt and apparent, sometimes tacit and latent.' [Humphrey (1559), p. 328]

There is a question whether [Cicero] ought to be followed in poetry. Granted that many seem to think that way, here is my reasoned judgement. We should consider him as a supreme orator, but not as a poet. True, he set forth many things in Latin verse, including Aratus and others, but there are others, poets of repute and fame, matchless and outstanding in the field, who have left us fine specimens in this art. Terence (whom Cicero calls his intimate friend), supremely elegant, a comedy writer both dazzling and quick, reckoned by an ancient poet to be a 'thief', is in the opinion of all scholars a rival of the Greeks.[36] Ovid writes elegiacs superbly. He took over many things from the Greeks into his *Metamorphoses*, especially from Homer, and to me he seems in all his books to be the most felicitous of poets, pouring out his verses spontaneously, with an easy dexterity (as he himself says), and what he wrote with care and consideration evidently deserves immortal credit and to rank in fame and repute with the greatest poets. Horace is supreme in lyrical verse, thoroughly Pindaric and for that very reason exemplary.

But, as I go over them all in my mind and think about them, I find – when heroic verse is under discussion – none to compare with Virgil. Hence everyone calls him 'the Poet', uniquely memorable on account of his reputation and the pre-eminence of his writing. So it is principally of his translating[37] that I shall now speak. In the *Bucolics* experts judge that he is surpassed by Theocritus, in the *Georgics* that he surpasses Hesiod, and in the *Aeneid* that he equals Homer. Whether this be true, I scarcely know, but I do know that his concern was less to imitate than to seek to excel, and that he invested no less glory in beautifying his poems than in imitating what he found before him. Nor will anyone ever read Virgil properly, much less understand him, who does not set alongside him the *Idylls* of Theocritus, whose contrivances, characters, ideas he closely followed. For what Theocritus devised in his first Idyll, Virgil has in the fifth and tenth Eclogue; and just as Virgil's shepherds vie with one another in singing, so Thyrsis and Aipolos (the goatherd) do in

[36] His creative reworking of earlier poets, notably Menander, gave rise to accusations of plagiarism, e.g. from his rival Luscius Lanuvinus.

[37] Humphrey's 'de eius praecipue imitatione' *could* mean 'imitating Virgil' (which would be more consistent with his prevailing use of the term), but the context suggests strongly simply 'translation': his way of adapting and reproducing earlier material.

Theocritus. They commonly make use of the same characters (Menalcas, Daphnis) and evidently the same notions are largely borrowed. [379–81]

[More examples follow, from the *Eclogues* and *Georgics*.] As for Virgil being completely Homeric in the *Aeneid*: surely the very opening is derived from Homer – 'I sing of arms and the man' and 'Muse, tell me the causes'?[38] Achilles swears by a sceptre[39] and Virgil imitates this.[40] What a brilliant image that is of Fame![41] (It is also in Hesiod.)[42] Homer often has 'but when they had removed the desire of food and drink'; so does Virgil.[43] But why should I go on, since the whole concept of the story is from Homer? What else is the account of the Trojan War than Homer's *Iliad*? The sailing, wandering, exile: surely this is Homer's *Odyssey*? The speeches, assemblies, Sinon, the narrator, Dido's hospitality: surely clear evidence of borrowing from Homer to be found scattered everywhere?[44] It is also characteristic of Homer to place a spondee in the fifth foot: here Virgil has copied both Homer's idea and his way of expressing it.[45]

But enough of pointing things out! I have now run through almost everything to do with imitation and its various elements, showing what imitation is, and whom and how we ought to imitate, whether it be in translating [*vertendis*] sacred theology or pagan writers, and whether prose or verse is being used. Accordingly, to these I give prime place: Christ in Christianity, Cicero in Latin prose, Virgil in hexameter verse. I do not reject others but as principal examples to follow in imitation these are the main authors, in my opinion. [384–87]

The translator's sole and chief end is the glory of God, who is the ruler and author of all that we do. Every single one of our actions (so the sacred Scriptures teach) is to be directed to the praise of his glorious name, for Christ is the Alpha (from whom all things must proceed) and the Omega (in whom all things must

[38] *Odyssey* I.1; Humphrey here and in what follows sets out the original in full.

[39] *Iliad* I.234.

[40] *Aeneid* XII.206–10.

[41] *Aeneid* IV.174 f.; *Iliad* II.93.

[42] See *Works and Days* 760 f.

[43] e.g. *Aeneid* VIII.184.

[44] More examples follow of how Virgil absorbs his Greek models: *Aeneid* I.211–13; I.369–70; IV.10, I.605–06.

[45] *Aeneid* I.617–18.

conclude). This is the purpose, then, which anyone wishing to discharge his task rightly and to do the work of an honest and responsible translator should keep constantly before his eyes. Then the proximate end is to benefit our neighbours. For Paul says ([I] Corinthians, chapter 14),[46] 'Whoever speaks in tongues builds up himself, but whoever prophesies[47] builds up the church'; and later, 'But now, brethren, if I come to you speaking in tongues, what good shall I do you unless I speak either in a revelation or with understanding or in prophecy or teaching?' We may speak thus about our translator because he is not translating for his own benefit but in order to equip with understanding people in the church who need a translator if they are to know anything at all. So all translation should be directed and governed in such a way that they get maximum benefit from it. It will not be complicated or obscure or crabbed, but easy and clear and plain. It will not be misleading or pretentious or disjointed, but true and faithful and precise and perfectly proportioned. So let the more pertinent and immediate aim be this: that readers or hearers be taught. For 'glory of God' seems a rather remote and exotic end, and is common to every occupation, activity, and project; while 'benefit to others' is rather vague and wide-ranging. Here then is something closer and more specific: to teach. [401–2][48]

[Humphrey's third Book deals with 'exercises' (*prae-exercitamenta*) and offers in turn 'certain maxims and rules which have a bearing on this type of work', then 'a variety of practical suggestions and patterns' for putting them into practice, and finally 'a miscellany of actual examples' (412–13). Much of the Book develops points already made earlier. Wide reading, for example, is vital if we are to be able to establish precisely what each word means.]

Words have above all a peculiar identity or natural meaning of their own[49] and we should therefore not distort their particular character. This is especially important in the Holy Scriptures, as Jerome attests in saying, 'I not only admit, I freely avow, that –

[46] I Corinthians 14.4–6.

[47] prophesies] Literally 'tells forth'.

[48] This is again in marked contrast to Udall, who argues that the social benefit of publication is greater than anything that can be achieved by teaching; see **7a**. 77–89 above.

[49] Greek *kyriotēs* and *idiotēs*; Latin *idiotismus*.

apart from the Holy Scriptures, where the very order of the words is a mystery – I do not render word for word but meaning for meaning'.[50] [424]

It would be a huge task to list everything that we should look out for and imitate in our reading, but it is clear by now what steps and approaches we should take to establish this natural meaning [*proprietas*]: through etymology, contrarieties, differences, choice of synonyms, onomatopoeia [*imitatio*],[51] close comparison of context and circumstances, carefully weighing things up, sticking close to the literal meaning of the topics we are translating, keeping things simple rather than complex, and in other ways which need not be enlarged upon here. This is certainly the simplest way, the truest, the safest, and the best. But sometimes it happens that this natural and straightforward approach is not available to us. It will not work, so we need to try something different. Hence I shall relax the severity of our discipline a little, to give ourselves wider access to other ways of handling the problem, and a way out of our perplexities. Horace is right when he advises, 'Faithful translator, do not worry about rendering word for word';[52] and Cicero often gave this advice too, for it is not always the case that words need merely to be counted: they need rather to be weighed.[53] Sometimes you will be unable to translate absolutely word for word, sometimes you will be able to do it, but clumsily. Cicero in his Prologue to the two mutually contrary speeches of Demosthenes and Aeschines says this, in virtually these words: 'I have not rendered them like a translator but like an orator, keeping the original meanings and their structures but with idioms and words that suit our usage; in which I did not consider it necessary to render word for word, but I have retained the essential character and meaning of the words'.[54] [433–35]

---

[50] *Epistle* 57.5.

[51] Cf. *Ad Herennium* IV.31.42.

[52] *Art of Poetry* 133–34.

[53] *De Optimo Genere Oratorum* V.14. Cicero's prescription is recorded by Gabriel Harvey at the start of two pages of manuscript notes at the end of his copy of *Interpretatio linguarum* (Trinity College, Cambrige, shelfmark III.18.74), It was frequently cited in the Renaissance; see for example Erasmus, letter to Nicholas Ruistre, Bishop of Arras, 17 November 1503, *CWE* 2, trans. by R. A. B. Mynors and D. F. S. Thomson, p. 177.

[54] *De Optimo Genere Oratorum* V.14. Humphrey's punctuation is slightly different from (e.g.) Loeb's and he has 'tam figuris quam verbis' instead of

Sometimes boldness is required, as I have shown in the rules I gave earlier, since new things demand new names. Nobody should think it a crime to depart from old-established tastes, or a sin to leave the beaten track (as if we must never introduce anything new but only use what we find in Cicero). Sometimes we have to do this in theological and historical subjects, and indeed (as mentioned earlier) with Cicero's own leave and permission. There are some areas of knowledge which claim to be a sort of law unto themselves – military, medical, legal, naval – and apparently have their own vocabulary appropriated after a fashion to their own particular discipline. It seems to me that John Cheke, of blessed memory, understood this; that one-time teacher of King Edward, a knight of great distinction, outstanding and illustrious in all sorts of ways, and exceptionally well versed in Greek and Latin, who in the emperor Leo's book[55] *On Military Tactics* (which he translated from Greek and dedicated to the most mighty king Henry VIII) did not shrink from the barbarous words in common use in military science at that time, when Greek eloquence was on the wane and language was growing ever more uncouth. [503–4]

[Of the three main areas in which the would-be translator should practise – speaking impromptu, careful reflection, and writing – the last is of greatest importance: 'by far supreme in guiding and bringing our powers of expression to accomplishment'.] We need to write often and at length because, just as reflection is more effective than extemporary speaking, so diligence in writing has greater value than pondering and judging. (But see Cicero for his praises of the pen.)[56] And we should each of us refine our own mother tongue by constant writing. For it is no less the business of learned men to transfer into their own

'tamquam figuris, verbis'; this accounts for a small difference in the translation here. On the widespread citation of Cicero's parallel between oratory and translation in the Renaissance, see L. G. Kelly *The True Interpreter: A History of Translation Theory and Practice in the West* (Oxford: Blackwell, 1979), p. 183.

[55] Sir John Cheke was the first Regius Professor of Greek at Cambridge. Though his own translations were from Greek into Latin (with the exception of his unpublished English version of the Gospel of St Matthew), he played a vital role in the development of English translation, as work by Thomas Hoby (**30**. below) and Thomas Wilson (**36**. below) testifies. Cheke's translation of the *Taktika* of Emperor Leo VI (d. 912) appeared in print in 1554, though he had presented it in MS to Henry VIII ten years earlier.

[56] e.g. *De Oratore* I.33.150.

language things that come from elsewhere than it is for merchants to transport here foreign goods and merchandise which are unavailable at home. The latter enrich the country with goods, the former generously enrich and adorn the language, the spirit, the mind of their citizens, filling out their common speech, amplifying it, and educating their rough and unpolished minds by means of the illustrious writings of the wise and learned of other countries. Cicero in various places mentions this as his own practice, for instance in the first book of *De Officiis*: 'In this matter I believe I have been of considerable help to our people, so that not only those without knowledge of Greek literature but even the educated reckon they have gained much in proficiency of expression and in judgement.'[57] By this he affirms himself to have shed light in Roman literature not only on philosophy but also on the art of oratory, imparting to his fellow citizens a knowledge of things foreign which was not available to them as a native growth at home. If other individuals and nations were to do this they would certainly develop their own language, and would through their hard work bring considerable benefit to the more ignorant among them. Hence we ought surely to applaud – and copy – the hard work of the Germans, the French, the Italians, and the Spaniards, who have diligently set about translating [*convertant*] into their own language books that deal with our holy and pure religion, or moral teaching, or the subtleties of the natural world, or knowledge of mathematical perplexities. In doing this they themselves become more learned, their citizens wiser, and their language more refined and graceful. [514–516]

[5. *English translators of recent times*]

Our catalogue of distinguished writers tells us that many translators [*interpretes*] once flourished in England.[58] But since oblivion, that all-consuming enemy of eternity, has destroyed virtually all memory of them, my wish is to revive this noble work (which brings benefit to individuals privately and to communities publicly) amid so great and blessed a crop of talented and learned

[57] *De Officiis* I.I.1.

[58] Thomas Nashe also offers a roll-call of translators who have flourished in England in his Preface to Robert Greene's *Menaphon*; see *The Works of Thomas Nashe*, ed. by R. B. McKerrow, rev. F. P. Wilson (Oxford: Blackwell, 1958), III, pp. 316–17.

men. Some very distinguished men, struck by how important the matter is, have made an auspicious start in reawakening this long-buried work of translation [*transferendi*].

The distinguished knight Henry Howard Surrey (a veritable Cicero and Virgil in his own language) was renowned in this field, equally adept in prose and verse – the view also of his teacher, Hadrian Junius, a foreigner but extremely learned.[59] He is said to have translated [*convertisse*] a good part of Virgil's *Aeneid* into English verse and measures,[60] to the praise and admiration of all who have seen it. He has left a sample of his poetic art also in several of the *Psalms* of David, in Solomon's *Ecclesiastes*, and elsewhere, and would have produced more, and with better finish, if the sentence of death had not struck him down mid-course, in the flower of his age and learning.

In the present age that golden knight Thomas Wyatt of Kent worked away at the same task, composing in English measures and bringing glory to his native language: a man distinguished both by descent and by talent, and said to have translated the whole *Psalter* in language that is elegant and tasteful.[61] [517–18]

[Surrey] also translated Boccaccio's *Epistle to Pinus* (consoling him on his exile) and he is said to have spoken Italian and French beautifully.

That Lincoln man of noble rank, Edmund Sheffield, who died with great bravery in the peasants' rising at Norwich,[62] composed in the Italian fashion what they call 'sonnets', and poems.

Thomas Chaloner, of knightly rank and the most eloquent of men, is also said to have shown great zeal in producing a fine translation of Erasmus's *Praise of Folly* for Thomas More.[63]

---

[59] Hadrian Junius (de Jonghe, 1511–75) came to England in 1542 as physician to the Duke of Norfolk and tutor to his son.

[60] A translation of books II and IV appeared in 1557, which is the first example of blank verse in English. (Humphrey is unaware of Gavin Douglas's full translation (1513), printed at London in 1553.) *Certain Chapters of the Proverbs of Solomon*, to which Surrey contributed paraphrases of *Ecclesiastes* and some psalms, was published in 1549–50 (STC 2760); see Simpson, *Burning to Read*, pp. 156–76. John Bale attributed the Boccaccio translation (see below) to Surrey, but it is now lost.

[61] Wyatt's translation of the penitential psalms (STC 2726) was printed in 1549.

[62] the peasants' rising at Norwich] Kett's rebellion (1549). Sheffield (1521–49) was a protégé of Thomas Cromwell. Cheke paid tribute to him after his death, but his poetry does not survive.

[63] Printed in 1549.

But there are others too who have busied themselves with distinction in other fields. For it is evident that all who seek to clarify [*explicare*] difficult and obscure authors in their native language deserve well of their country: people like the nobleman Richard Cavendish of Suffolk, translator of Euclid's *Geometry* – a task undertaken by the expert in the subject Tapley (who died at Basle), even if it was not published.[64]

Richard[65] Eden, cosmographer and alchemist, also translated [*vertit*] Peter Martyr Anglerius' book about the newly discovered islands.[66] [519–20]

Who will not admire and think worthy of all honour the distinguished Earl of Hertford,[67] Duke of Somerset, uncle of King Edward VI and His Majesty's governor and Protector, Edward Seymour? A nobleman celebrated for piety, kindness, and loving dedication to literature, who – in order to assuage his sorrow while he was held in custody in the Tower of London – showed also how he esteemed and loved this work of translation and study by writing (while bearing as a prisoner his own cross) a book *On Bearing the Cross*, and by translating from French into English Calvin's *On Consolation in Adversity*: an example to others to dispel sloth and revive diligence, while at the same this sweet medicine consoled him and kept up his own courage and spirits.[68] [521]

The distinguished Sir Thomas Elyot, renowned for the glory and splendour of his birth and for the brilliance of his literary works and writings, wrote many fine and eloquent things and also translated several, certainly – with some elegance – *The Friendship of Titus and Gisippus*.[69]

---

[64] A number of translators of Euclid were active at this time, among them Robert Recorde (1510–58) and the more elusive Tapley. The first published English translation was by Sir Henry Billingsley (1570).

[65] Richard] Humphrey has 'John'.

[66] The Italian writer Pietro Martire d'Anghiera (Peter Martyr) produced a series of books ('decades') between 1511 and 1525 on explorations in the New World, collected in 1530 under the title *De Orbe Novo*; Eden's partial English translation appeared in 1555 as *Decades of the New World*. See also **31**. below.

[67] Hertford] Humphrey has 'Hereford'.

[68] Somerset's translation of a letter sent by Calvin to Somerset himself was printed as *An Epistle both of Godly Consolacion and also of Advertisement* (1550), STC 4407.

[69] *The Friendship of Titus and Gisippus*] See the story in Boccaccio's *Decameron* VIII.8, retold in Elyot's *The Governor*.

Whoever translated Marcus Aurelius, either from Spanish or from Italian, deserves praise in my opinion for its Isocratic sweetness, its Ciceronian fulness, the wonderful dignity of its sentiment in many places, and the comeliness of its words everywhere.[70]

But those who established the enterprise of translating the Holy Scriptures, either because the most gracious king Henry VIII commanded it or because they themselves wanted to, give a clear enough indication by their example of what they would like others to do for other books. Of them my incapacity does not permit me to judge but I have enough piety and affection to praise and commend them for blessing me and everyone else with so great and remarkable a benefit. This godly work has been carried further by Edward VI, son of a most renowned and mighty father, and a man destined by his age and devotion to be another Josiah[71] and by his love of peace and wisdom to be another Solomon. After consulting leading men and taking advice from bishops, he saw to it that they were issued in an amended and improved form, and he ordered them to be read in public and to be kept and proclaimed in every church. And so that they might be better understood by the ordinary people Queen Katherine Parr, that fine flower of womanhood, took care to ensure that they would be comprehensible by having appended to them the *Paraphrases* of Erasmus: they too are available in churches for the benefit of the ignorant and uneducated.[72] This task was entrusted to those who with great experience had worked long and diligently in this field, especially to those men of great learning and devotion, Thomas[73] Caius and N[icholas] Udall. The latter of these undertook work that brought glory to himself and was not without benefit to his fellows, gathering together the best of Terence and translating [*vertendis*] it

---

[70] Antonio de Guevara's *The Golden Boke of Marcus Aurelius* (original Spanish version printed at Seville, 1528) was translated from a French version by Lord Berners in 1535 and many times reprinted. Sir Thomas North's translation, *The Diall of Princes* [. . .] *with the Famous Booke of Marcus Aurelius*, also from the French, was printed in 1557 (STC 12427). Humphrey may be referring to either work.

[71] See II Kings 22 f.

[72] See headnote to **7.** above.

[73] Thomas] Humphrey has 'D. I.'. Caius was also known as Thomas Key, translator of the *Paraphrase of the Gospel of St Mark*; see **7.** above.

gracefully into the vernacular,[74] producing a version [*convertendis*] of Erasmus's *Apophthegms*,[75] and in other ways too.

Would that other leaders among the learned might strive their utmost to translate [*traducendis*] other authors! It would surely be for the country's good. What is there to prevent the whole of Cicero at least from being expressed in English for English people? Why should Livy's *History* and the works of Plato and Aristotle not be published in our language? Others have worked hard elsewhere at translating [*transferendis*] much of what these have written, to help their own folk. And if people have realised how useful the works are that Thomas Wilson – that finest and most learned of men – has published for English readers on reasoning and rhetoric,[76] what is the obstacle to translating into English at least those principles of ethics and politics, taught privately to individuals, that bring the grace and order of good laws and practices to the nation as a whole? Thereby here at home we might grow in judgement and philosophical understanding, like other countries. For although I consider the decrees and resolutions of our own realm to be wholesome and well suited and right for us, still it will not be altogether a waste of time to know about the arrangements, the statutes, the laws of other nations. Having a taste of foreign ways (whether of the people who command and bear sway or of those too who are subject to authority and obey) I believe to be an advantage. In that way our own ways can be sometimes strengthened, sometimes changed, corrected, adjusted.

And if these works are a joy to know and an aid to our understanding, how much greater attention should we give to religion and to the holy writings which deal with sacred matters, ensuring that they reach out and spread among ordinary folk! Knowing these not only brings wisdom but helps people to grow and develop in true, pure devotion. In this category I include not just the Bible but the writings of the Church Fathers, ecclesiastical histories, and the record of early Christianity. Whoever sets his mind to this I shall regard as a good citizen and as deserving of all praise and honour. Hence I cannot fail at this point to

[74] *Flowers for Latin Speaking selected and gathered out of Terence and the same translated into English*, first printed in 1534.

[75] A translation of Erasmus's third and fourth books was printed in 1542.

[76] *The Rule of Reason* (1551) and *The Art of Rhetorique* (1553).

commend warmly the hard work of that fine and genuinely good man Peter Morwen, who – I gather– took on the task of translating the *Jewish Wars* of Josephus so that English people could understand it:[77] a task of great advantage to all his fellow-citizens and of value to his own country. [522–5]

In the universities of Oxford and Cambridge there have been many outstanding in the craft of translating [*vertendo*] who with steady application might be adept and proficient. The famous Magdalen School[78] in Oxford was never without them, indeed before my time it was always well supplied and subsequently, when I was a pupil, it was celebrated because of that outstanding master of translation [*interpretandi*], a teacher of mine worthy of many honours, memorable for learning and piety and eventually – as Bishop of Hereford – most deservedly a light to his profession. I mean John Harley of blessed memory, who, far from disdaining his native language, devoted as much effort to learning it as to learning others, and was so fond and observant of the particular character of his own language, its distinguishing features and beauties, that he used asterisks and different marks to draw attention to them, and would thrust a little line through the fancier expressions as if he were slaying them. When people gathered to hear him he would use his finger to draw attention to points worth noting, and where words were tantamount to Latin or Greek he would single them out and repudiate them. Rightly so, too. For how can it be right to roam around exclusively in foreign languages, while not knowing how people speak at home?

His successor was a most zealous master, with great felicity in translation, someone deeply engaged in it for a long time,

[77] Morwen published a translation of the work known as the *Yosippon*, by Joseph Ben Gorion writing as the Greek historian Flavius Josephus, with the title *A Compendious and Most Merveilous History of the Latter Tymes of the Jewes Commune Weale* (1558). Extremely popular with Protestants, it went through twelve editions to 1615.

[78] Magdalen School] Thomas Wolsey (and possibly William Tyndale) was educated at Magdalen School and was briefly a master there. A succession of headmasters published important Latin textbooks: John Anwykyll, *Vulgaria quedam abs Terencio* and *Compendium totius grammaticae* (1483), based on Valla; Robert Whittington, *Vulgaria* (1520), with examples in colloquial English; and, as Humphrey notes, Thomas Cooper, who revised Elyot's *Dictionary* as the *Thesaurus linguae Romanae et Britannicae* (1565). The various versions of the *Vulgaria* were the basis for the practice described by Humphrey in section 6.

exceedingly experienced certainly in either of the languages,[79] and as distinguished for his enthusiasm in religion as for his proficiency in letters: Thomas Cooper, amply familiar through the bulk and value of his writings, seeing that he not only produced a comprehensive account of the history of antiquity – publishing *Chronicles of All the Nations*[80] – but also expanded Thomas Elyot's Latin-English dictionary with a fresh store of words. I hope now he will hammer away at the same work and produce something worthy of his great piety or learning, neglecting no period of time, no illustrious public deed, nothing that has ever been done, so that the history which he has begun may be carried forward, and a work still unfinished may be brought up to the present time and given its final revision and polish. [526–28]

[6. *A particular technique*]

A popular practice exists among youngsters at school of passages being read aloud, with the pupils saying back in their native language what they have been given [in Latin] by their teachers. It may seem rather frivolous – child's play – but it will lead on to more serious things at the next stage if learner and teacher alike do their work properly, and if phrases in the languages are impressed truly on the pupils' minds while they are soft and tender and (like wax) pliant and easily worked on by whoever is fashioning them. Later they become as hard as rock and you will not find it easy to impress anything on them. However, it is imperative to move on in stages from this elementary lesson, so that when they are familiarised and trained in this exercise they may tell stories, discuss general points, reproduce the authors' more striking ideas and illustrations, sometimes touching on them in passing, sometimes investigating more carefully and in detail the way words and ideas are linked together. The greatest effect comes through retelling entire books from beginning to end, hour by hour, in everyday speech, for the sake of improving understanding and proficiency: whether fasting or feasting, to expound Sallust, or Livy, or Cicero's *De Officiis*, or the lives of the emperors or popes, or Josephus or other historians; some-

[79] either of the languages] i.e. Latin and Greek.

[80] Published in 1549, carrying on the work of Thomas Lanquet, who died in 1545.

times also to translate a chapter of the Bible. Their minds will thus be banqueted and fed with a kind of wholesome fodder, and they will acquire quickness and ease in their capacity to explain things.

But these academic exercises can go wrong in two ways. There are some who match one word to another but, if you ask them to say what it means, they are silent. On the other hand, there are teachers who give an overall translation, lumping all the meaning together, but fail to explain what essentially each particular word signifies. Hence it is important here to realise first that individual words have to be dealt with methodically and (as they say) 'construed' or built up grammatically; and then – much more importantly – that expressions in the vernacular should be intelligible: that is, they should be set forth faithfully and in a fit and proper manner. In this way not only will the meaning of the words be clear, but the differences in the way the languages express themselves will not be disguised. [544–46]

[Humphrey gives several examples, including one (549–53) from his own experience. The ten-year-old Edward Stafford (son of the late Sir William), turned an English version (which Humphrey had written for him) of one of Cicero's letters into competent but immature Latin. Humphrey had told him to keep as close as he could to the distinctive character of English, so that later comparison with Cicero's Latin could highlight the differences.]

[7. *Concluding remarks*]

Dear reader, the task I undertook is finished. I have set out certain general rules as helpfully as I could for the young and very young to understand, but in such a way that this craft [of translation] may be directed and improved by wise judgement and by careful attention to circumstances. Next I suggested various useful ways of enriching one's language. Finally, I have supplied enough actual examples – perhaps too many by now – to give pleasure by the attractiveness of the material, and by their serviceableness to make people better, and better informed. May the Guide and Protector of every work direct to the glory of His Name what I have here done with my own hands, and may He in whom we must work and live and die make it effective in the upbuilding of Church and State. [622]

30. Thomas Hoby, *The Courtier of Count Baldessar Castilio* (1561)

[Sir Thomas Hoby (1530–66) matriculated at St John's College, Cambridge, in May 1545, but left in 1547 without taking a degree. This may have been too late for him to have had much direct contact with John Cheke, the inspirational college tutor and Regius Professor of Greek, who had been appointed tutor to Prince Edward in 1544. Hoby then spent a year studying with Martin Bucer at Strasbourg. A committed Protestant, he remained abroad during Mary's reign and wrote about his experience of European courtly circles in his travel journals (unpublished until 1902). This included a stay at Padua in the company of Cheke and Thomas Wilson in 1554–55. Returning to England in 1555, he was knighted and appointed ambassador to France in 1566, dying at Paris in the same year.

Castiglione's *Il Cortegiano* (Venice, 1528) was the most famous courtesy or conduct book of the sixteenth century. By the time Hoby's translation was published the book was famous throughout Europe, having been translated into Spanish (1534) and French (1537). In Germany a Latin translation (1561) was followed by one in the vernacular (1565), while in England a Latin translation (by Batholomew Clerke) was published after the English version in 1571. Hoby began by translating Book 3 as a separate commission for Elizabeth Parr, Marchioness of Northampton, on his arrival in Paris in 1552 and finished it three years later at Padua. Hoby attempted to have the book published in 1557, when he sought Cheke's approval, but it seems to have been still too politically sensitive for the Marian authorities. There were three editions under Elizabeth and John Wolfe published a tri-lingual text (Italian, French and Hoby's English) in 1588, which underlines the pan-European status of the work.

See F. O. Matthiessen, *Translation: An Elizabethan Art* (Cambridge, MA: Harvard University Press, 1931); L. G. Kelly, *The True Interpreter: A History of Translation Theory and Practice in the West* (Oxford: Basil Blackwell, 1979); Baldassare Castiglione, *The Book of the Courtier* [trans. by Thomas Hoby], ed. by Virginia Cox (London: Dent, 1994); Peter Burke, *The Fortunes of The Courtier* (Cambridge: Polity Press, 1995); Mary Partridge, 'Thomas Hoby's English Translation of Castiglione's *Book of the Courtier*', *The Historical Journal*, 50.4 (2007), 769–86;

Massimiliano Morini, *Tudor Translation in Theory and Practice* (Ashgate: Aldershot, 2006).]

To the Right Honourable, the Lord Henry Hastings, son and heir apparent to the noble Earl of Huntingdon.[1]

Themistocles, the noble Athenian, in his banishment entertained most honourably with the King of Persia, willed upon a time to tell his cause by a spokesman, compared it to a piece of tapestry that, being spread abroad, discloseth the beauty of the workmanship, but folded together, hideth it, and therefore demanded respite to learn the Persian tongue to tell his own cause.[2] Right so, honourable lord, this courtier hath long strayed about this realm, and the fruit of him either little or unperfectly received to the common benefit; for either men skilful in his tongue have delighted in him for their own private commodity,° or else he hath eftsoons° spoken in piecemeal[3] by an interpreter to such as desired to know his mind and to practise his principles: the which how unperfect a thing it is, Themistocles and experience teach. But now, though late indeed, yet for all that at length, besides his three principal languages[4] in the which he hath a long time haunted all the courts of Christendom, he is become an Englishman (which many a long time have wished, but few attempted and none achieved) and well-willing to dwell in the court of England and in plight° to tell his own cause. In whose commendation I shall not need to use any long process of words, for he can so well speak for himself and answer to the opinion

[1] Hastings] (1536?-1595) Henry became 3rd earl in 1561. The family were Protestants implicated in the attempt to enthrone Lady Jane Grey and when Hoby was making this translation they were trying to demonstrate their loyalty to the Marian regime. Hastings himself had been tutored by Cheke and Ascham alongside Prince Edward and had met Hoby in Brussels in 1555.

[2] Themistocles] The Athenian general who had defeated the Persians at Salamis in 480 BC and who later fled to Persia. See Plutarch, 'Life of Themistocles' in *Lives* 29.3. For North's version of the story see STC 20066, p. 139, image 82.

[3] piecemeal] Refers to the extraction of 'sundry examples and pithy sentences' (l. 69 below) for courtesy manuals and commonplace books. Lodovico Dolce's 1552 edition of Castiglione assisted the practice by presenting the text as a set of precepts.

[4] three principal languages] i.e. Italian, French, and Spanish; on the European reception of *The Courtier* see Burke, *The Fortunes of the Courtier*.

men have a long time conceived of him, that whatsoever I should write therein were but labour in waste, and rather a diminishing than a setting forth of his worthiness, and a great deal better it were to pass it over with silence than to use briefness. Only for the little acquaintance I have with him, and for the general profit [that] is in him, my desire is he should now at his first arrival, a new man in this kind of trade,° be well entertained and much honoured.

And forsomuch as none but a noble young gentleman, and trained up all his lifetime in court and of worthy qualities, is meet to receive and entertain so worthy a courtier, that like may fellowship and get estimation with his like, I do dedicate him unto your good lordship that through your means and under your patronage he may be common to a great many. And this do I not because I suppose you stand in need of any of his instructions, but partly because you may see him confirm with reason the courtly fashions, comely exercises, and noble virtues that unawares have from time to time crept into you, and already with practice and learning taken custom in you, and partly to get him the more authority and credit through so honourable a patron. For no doubt, if you be seen willingly to embrace him, other young and courtly gentlemen will not shun his company, and so both he shall get him the reputation now here in England which he hath had a good while since beyond the sea in Italy, Spain, and France, and I shall think my small travail well employed and sufficiently recompensed. The honour and entertainment that your noble ancestors showed Castilio the maker,[5] when he was in this realm to be installed Knight of the Order for the Duke his master, was not so much as presently both he and this his handiwork shall receive of you.

Generally ought this to be in estimation with all degrees of men, for to princes and great men it is a rule to rule themselves that rule others, and one of the books that a noble philosopher[6] exhorted a certain king to provide him, and diligently to search, for in them he should find written such matters that friends durst

[5] Castiglione visited England in 1506, just before the events recounted in *Il Cortegiano*, to receive the Order of the Garter from Henry VII on behalf of the Duke of Urbino. He had been hosted by Hastings' grandfather, the 1st Earl of Huntingdon.

[6] noble philosopher] Probably Isocrates, *To Nicocles*; see **20.** above.

not utter unto kings; to men grown in years, a pathway to the beholding and musing of the mind and to whatsoever else is meet for that age; to young gentlemen, an encouraging to garnish their mind with moral virtues and their body with comely exercises, and both the one and the other with honest qualities to attain unto their noble end; to ladies and gentlewomen, a mirror to deck and trim themselves with virtuous conditions, comely behaviours and honest entertainment toward all men; and to them all in general, a storehouse of most necessary implements for conversation, use, and training up of man's life with courtly demeanours.

Were it not that the ancientness of time, the degree of a consul and the eloquence of Latin style in these our days bear a great stroke,[7] I know not whether in the invention and disposition of the matter, as Castilio hath followed Cicero[8] and applied to his purpose sundry examples and pithy sentences out of him, so he may in feat° conveyance° and like trade of writing be compared to him, but well I wot° for renown among the Italians he is not inferior to him. Cicero, an excellent orator, in three books of an orator unto his brother fashioneth such a one as never was, nor yet is like to be: Castilio, an excellent courtier, in three books of a courtier unto his dear friend fashioneth such a one as is hard to find and perhaps unpossible. Cicero bringeth into dispute of an orator Crassus, Scevola, Antonius, Cotta, Sulpitius, Catullus, and Caesar his brother, the noblest and chiefest orators in those days: Castilio to reason of a courtier, the lord Octavian Fregoso, Sir Frideric his brother, the lord Julian de Medici, the lord Caesar Gonzaga, the lord Francescomaria della Rovere, Count Lewis of Canossa, the lord Gaspar Pallavicino, Bembo, Bibiena, and other most excellent courtiers,[9] and of the noblest families in these days in Italy, which all afterward became princes, cardinals,

[7] bear a great stroke] have a great influence.

[8] Castiglione consciously models his dialogue on Cicero's *De Oratore*; see Richards, *Rhetoric and Courtliness*, pp. 47–55. Invention and disposition are the first two parts of rhetoric, dealing with the finding and organising of topics and arguments.

[9] Principal speakers in the dialogue, gathered at the court of Urbino. The two prominent literary figures are Pietro Bembo (1470–1547), a master of Ciceronian Latin prose style and author of love poetry in the Petrarchan tradition, and Bernardo Bibbiena (1470–1520), author of the comic drama, *La Calandria*.

bishops, and great lords, and some yet in life. Both Cicero and Castilio profess they follow not any certain appointed order of precepts or rules as is used in the instruction of youth, but call to rehearsal matters debated in their times to and fro in the disputation of most eloquent men and excellent wits in every worthy quality, the one company in the old time assembled in Tusculum[10] and the other of late years in the new palace of Urbino.

Where many most excellent wits in this realm have made no less of this book than the great Alexander did of Homer, I cannot sufficiently wonder that they have not all this while from time to time done a common benefit to profit others as well as themselves. In this point (I know not by what destiny) Englishmen are much inferior to well most other nations. For where they set their delight and bend themselves with an honest strife of matching others to turn into their mother tongue not only the witty writings of other languages, but also of all the philosophers and all sciences, both Greek and Latin, our men ween° it sufficient to have a perfect knowledge to no other end but to profit themselves, and (as it were) after much pains in breaking up a gap, bestow no less to close it up again, that others may with like travail follow after. And where our learned men for the most part hold opinion to have the sciences[11] in the mother tongue hurteth memory and hindreth learning, in my opinion they do full ill consider from whence the Grecians first, and afterward the Latins, fetched their knowledge. And without wading° to any further reasons that might be alleged, if they will mark well the truth, they shall see at this day where the sciences are most turned into the vulgar tongue, there are best learned men, and comparing it with the contrary they shall also find the effects contrary.[12] In Italy (where most translation of authors is), not only for philosophy, logic, humanity, and all liberal sciences both in Greek and Latin (leaving apart Barbarus, Naugerius,

[10] Tusculum] A city near Rome where Cicero had a villa and wrote several books, including *Tusculan Questions*. It is the setting for *De Oratore*, so providing the parallel with Urbino.

[11] sciences] i.e. arts and sciences, or the various branches of knowledge.

[12] Hoby is referring in particular to the numerous Italian translations of Aristotle, which included both the *Poetics* and scientific works such as the *Physics*. There were considerably more translations of Aristotle into Italian during the sixteenth century than intro any other vernacular.

Sannazarus, Bembus, Lazarus, and the rest that of very late days flourished), Genua, Tomitanus, Robertellus, Manutius, Piccolhomineus are presently very singular and renowned throughout all Christendom; but also for the same in the vulgar tongue with little or no sight at all in the Latin, Aretino, Gelli (a tailor in Florence), the lady Victoria Colonna, the lady Dionora Sanseverina, the lady Beatrice Loffreda, Veronica Gambara, Virginea Salvi,[13] and other infinite men and women are most famous throughout Italy, whose divine works and excellent style both in rhyme and prose give a sufficient testimony, not only of their profound knowledge and noble wit, but also that knowledge may be obtained in studying only a man's own native tongue. So that to be skillful and exercised in authors translated is no less to be called learning than in the very same in the Latin or Greek tongue.

Therefore the translation of Latin or Greek authors doth not only not hinder learning, but it furthereth it; yea, it is learning itself, and a great stay to youth, and the noble end to the which they ought to apply their wits that with diligence and study have attained a perfect understanding, to open a gap for others to follow their steps, and a virtuous exercise for the unlatined to come by learning, and to fill their mind with the moral virtues and their body with civil conditions, that they may both talk freely in all company, live uprightly though there were no laws, and be in a readiness against all kind of worldly chances that happen, which is the profit that cometh of philosophy. And he said well that was asked the question how much the learned differed from the unlearned. So much, quoth he, as the well-broken and ready horses from the unbroken. Wherefore I wot not how our learned men in this case can avoid the saying of Isocrates to one that among sundry learned discourses at table spake never a word: if thou be unlearned, thou dost wisely, but

[13] Aretino [. . .] Salvi] Castiglione's list of unlatinate writers includes Pietro Aretino (1492–1556), author of comedies and erotica and notorious as a satirist (known as 'the scourge of princes'); Giambattista Gelli (1498–1563), author of popular philosophical dialogues (there is an English translation of *Circes* by Henry Iden (1557)); Vittoria Colonna (1490–1547) and Veronica Gambara (1485–1550), both patrons of the arts and significant lyric poets in their own right (Colonna was also the addressee of some of Michelangelo's best known sonnets).

if thou be learned, unwisely; as who should say, learning is ill bestowed where others have not profited by it.[14]

As I, therefore, have to my small skill bestowed some labour about this piece of work, even so could I wish with all my heart profound learned men in the Greek and Latin should make the like proof, and every man store the tongue according to his knowledge and delight above other men in some piece of learning, that we alone of the world may not be still counted barbarous in our tongue, as in time out of mind we have been in our manners. And so shall we perchance in time become as famous in England as the learned men of other nations have been and presently are, and though the hardness of this present matter be such, and mine unskilfulness to undertake this enterprise so great, that I might with good cause have despaired to bring to an end it that many excellent wits have attempted, yet could I not choose but yield to the continual requests and often persuasions of many young gentlemen, which have may chance an opinion that to be in me, that is not in deed, and unto whom in any reasonable matter I were skilful in, neither I could nor ought of duty to want in fulfilling their desire. Notwithstanding a great while I forbore and lingered° the time to see if any of a more perfect understanding in the tongue, and better practised in the matter of the book (of whom we want not a number in this realm) would take the matter in hand to do his country so great a benefit. And this imagination prevailed in me a long space after my duty done in translating the third book (that entreateth of a gentlewoman of the court) persuaded thereto, in that I was informed it was then in some forwardness by another, whose wit and style was greatly to be allowed, but since prevented by death he could not finish it.[15] But of late being instantly craved upon afresh, I whetted my style and settled myself to take in hand the other three books (that entreat of the perfection of a gentleman of the court) to fulfil their petition in what I am able, having time and leisure thereto, the which I have done, though not in effect yet in appearance, and that in a great deal shorter time than the hardness of the matter required. And where it shall not perhaps thoroughly please by reason my small understanding in the

[14] There is no record of this in Isocrates.

[15] Probably William Thomas, executed for treason in 1554. See Partridge, 'Hoby's English Translation' and **24**. above.

tongue, and less practice in the matters herein contained, is not of force to give it the brightness[16] and full perfection in this our tongue that it hath in the Italian, it shall suffice yet that I have showed myself obedient in the respect a man ought to have toward his betters. And no more can they avoid the blame to charge me withal than I to undertake it. Beside that, I have declared my good will and well-meaning no less than if my cunning° were greater and could extend much farther. But peradventure the rudeness of this shall be an encouraging of some other to give the onset[17] upon other matters with a better ripeness of style and much more aptness, and so shall this yet somewhat profit both ways.

But the estimation it must get by your honour is the principal cause that setteth it out and maketh it worn with the hands of heedful readers. For in case you cheerfully receive it, men will reckon it good; if you allow it, worthy to be practised; if you commend it, worthy to pass from hand to hand. Therefore among the other good opinions men generally hold of you, let it not be the least that they may hold also no less of this that you allow and commend. And so shall you show undeserved kindness, I, bounden duty, and all others good will to embrace and to welcome it out of Italy into England. And thus shall Castilio be esteemed such a one as he is indeed, and wax familiar with all men, that of late was known of very few and so mangled with variety of judgements that he was (in a manner) maimed and lost a good piece of his estimation. But in case judgements now feint,[18] or mine interpretation seem not pithy but rude,° not proper but cold, there is no more imperfection in this courtier than in Cyrus himself in the translation of Xenophon into the Italian or any other tongue,[19] the one as necessary and proper for a gentleman of the court as the other for a king. And I shall desire my labour may so be taken well in worth as I have endeavoured

[16] force [. . .] brightness] The two rhetorical figures of *energia* and *enargeia* which are essential in recapturing the life of the original.

[17] give the onset] make a start.

[18] feint] Possibly 'deceive', but the sense is unclear.

[19] There were two translations of Xenophon's *Cyropaideia* into Italian as the *Vita di Cyro* by Hoby's time, by Poggio Bracciolini (Florence, 1521) and Lodovico Domenichi (Venice, 1548); the first English translation was by William Barker (1552).

myself to follow the very meaning and words of the author without being misled by fancy, or leaving out any parcel° one or other, whereof I know not how some interpreters° of this book into other languages can excuse themselves, and the more they be conferred,° the more it will perchance appear. Wherefore receive you this as a token of my good will, and so receive it that the fruit, whatever it be, may be acknowledged at your hands. And you pass expectation of men in this as in all other things, which no doubt is very great of you; and I, to acknowledge this benefit, where my ability stretcheth to nothing else, shall at the least evermore wish unto your Lordship long life, that you may go forward, as you do, in these beginnings, which promise a lucky end, to the honour of yourself, comfort of your friends, and forwardness of the common weal[20] of your country.

1556.
Your lord's most bounden Thomas Hoby

A Letter of Sir J. Cheke's.
To his loving friend, Master Thomas Hoby

For your opinion of my good will unto you, as you writ, you cannot be deceived; for submitting your doings to my judgement, I thank you; for taking this pain of your translation, you worthily deserve great thanks of all sorts. I have taken some pain at your request, chiefly in your preface: not in the reading of it, for that was pleasant unto me both for the roundness° of your sayings and well-speakings of the same, but in changing certain words which might very well be let alone, but that I am very curious° in my friends' matters, not to determine, but to debate what is best. Wherein I seek not the bestness haply by truth, but by mine own fancy and show of goodness.

I am of this opinion that our own tongue should be written clean and pure, unmixed and unmangled with borrowing of other tongues; wherein, if we take not heed, by time, ever borrowing and never paying, she shall be fain to keep her house as

[20] common weal] On 'commonwealth', 'common weal' and related terms see David Rollison, *A Commonwealth of the People: Popular Politics and England's Long Social Revolution, 1066–1649* (Cambridge: Cambridge University Press, 2010), esp. pp. 13–21.

bankrupt.[21] For then doth our tongue naturally and praisably utter her meaning when she borroweth no counterfeitness of other tongues to attire herself withal, but useth plainly her own with such shift° as nature, craft, experience, and following of other excellent doth lead her unto; and if she want at any time (as being unperfect she must), yet let her borrow with such bashfulness that it may appear that if either the mould of our own tongue could serve us to fashion a word of our own, or if the old denizened° words could content and ease this need, we would not boldly venture of unknown words.[22] This I say not for reproof of you, who have scarcely and necessarily used, where occasion serveth, a strange word so as it seemeth to grow out of the matter and not to be sought for, but for mine own defence, who might be counted over-strait° a deemer of things if I gave not this account to you, my friend and wise, of my marring this your handiwork.

But I am called away – I pray you pardon my shortness: the rest of my sayings should be but praise and exhortation in this your doings, which at more leisure I should do better.

From my house in Wood Street, the 16th of July, 1557.
Yours assured,
John Cheke

[21] bankrupt] Financial metaphors (most obviously that of 'coinage') were common in sixteenth-century discussions of language, especially in the context of borrowing; see Morini, *Tudor Translation*, pp. 42–44. But Cheke's analogy makes little sense: no contract for repayment is involved in the borrowing of foreign words and no language would be impoverished if it failed to export some of its terms. See also Pettie **38**. 68–74 below.

[22] Cheke's preference for 'pure' English vocabulary is most evident in his translation of Matthew and part of Mark; see John Cheke, *The Gospel according to St Matthew*, ed. by James Goodwin (London, 1843). Cf. also Arthur Golding in the preface to his continuation of Sidney's translation of de Mornay, *The Trewnesse of the Christian Religion* (1587): 'great care hath bene taken, by forming and deryving of fit names and termes, out of the fountaynes of our owne tongue [. . .] rather than by usuring Latin termes, or by borrowing the wordes of any forreine language', STC 18149, sig. *4v, image 5 (I am grateful to Liza Blake for this reference).

31. Richard Eden, Letter to Sir William Cecil (1562)

[Richard Eden (*c.*1520–1576) attended Christ's College, Cambridge, from 1534 to 1537 and then Queen's College, where he was tutored by Sir Thomas Smith, friend of Cheke and teacher of William Cecil. In 1552 he became secretary to Cecil and in that capacity produced translations of historical and topographical works as part of England's first tentative plans to challenge Spain as an imperial power. The most important of these is *The Decades of the New Worlde or West India* (1555) from Pietro Martire d'Anghiera (Peter Martyr) and Gonzalo Oviedo. His translation of Martin Cortes's work on navigation as *The Arte of Navigation* (1561) was the first manual on this subject to become available in English. Eden also influenced Richard Hakluyt, who reprinted some of his work in his *Principal Navigations* (1589). Laurence Humphrey refers to him in *Interpretatio linguarum* as a cosmographer and alchemist and the translator of Pietro Martire (p. 520). There is no record of his translation of Pliny referred to in the letter below, but his comments on the translation process itself are significant.

See Edward Arber, ed., *The First Three English Books on America* (Birmingham, 1885); Andrew Hadfield, *Literature, Travel and Colonial Writing in the English Renaissance, 1545–1625* (Oxford: Oxford University Press, 1998).]

As touching the which matter, right honourable, as it was no part of my device, but such as the Master of Savoy[1] had then in hand, as I suppose, no less to pleasure himself and his friend than for £20 thereof to be allotted to me for an earnest penny to begin the book, as he sayeth, even so am I right sorry that for so small a matter, and not so favourable a suit as I would have wished, not only Your Honour hath taken such pains, but that also such contention is risen thereof between the Master of Savoy and Master Baptist[2] of the Privy Chamber, that by reason thereof the

[1] Master of Savoy] Thomas Thurland, governor of the Hospital of the Savoy, a poor house on the Strand. (Thurland was responsible for ruining the institution's finances.)

[2] Master Baptist] Giovanni Battista Castiglione, Queen Elizabeth's Italian tutor as a child and a relation of the author of *Il Cortegiano*. He was appointed a Groom of the Privy Chamber on her accession.

pardon being stayed by Your Honour, the young gentleman his kinsman (as he hath informed me) is in danger of his life [. . .] And whereas the Master of Savoy told me that Your Honour somewhat doubted that the book could be translated into the English tongue, I assure your honour that this I dare say without arrogancy, that to translate the variable history of Pliny[3] into our tongue, I would be ashamed to borrow so much of the Latin as he doth of the Greek, although the Latin tongue be accounted rich and the English indigent and barbarous, as it hath been in time past much more than it now is, before it was enriched and amplified by sundry books in manner of all arts translated out of Latin and other tongues into English. And it is not unknown unto Your Honour that the Latins receiving both the science of philosophy and physic of the Greeks do still for the most part in all their translations use the Greek names, insomuch that for the better understanding of them, one Otto Brunfelsius,[4] a learned man, hath written a large book entitled *Onomasticon medicinae*, where he hath these words: *res ipsas, atque atra vocabula, scite, apposite, designateque efferre, atque ad Polycleti regulam quod aiunt exprimere, res est non minus difficilis quam gloriosa. Quo, nullum studii genus, maiori constat molestia. Id quod in causa esse reor, quod hodie tam pauci in ea palaestra sese exerceant*[5] etc. Again, it is not unknown unto Your Honour that once all tongues were barbarous and needy, before the knowledge of things brought in plenty of words and names, whereby it may well appear that men in the first age of the world had a short language, consisting of few words, which ever after increased by the knowledge and invention of things.[6] Exercise also maketh

[3] history of Pliny] See headnote to **46**. below.

[4] Brunfelsius] Brunfels was a Carthusian monk turned Lutheran, who was chiefly interested in the medicinal use of plants. His *Onomaonomastikon medicinae* (Strasbourg, 1534) was a comprehensive dictionary of their Greek and Latin names.

[5] *Onomasticon* [. . .] *exerceant*] 'Medical Terminology [. . .] To convey – perceptively, judiciously, and with exactness of outline – actual facts and obscure words, and to express them in accordance with the 'rule of Polycletus' (as they say), is as difficult as it is glorious; hence there is no branch of study that involves more trouble. That, I imagine, is why nowadays so few people undertake the challenge.' (Polycletus was a Greek sculptor renowned for his accuracy.)

[6] On early modern views on the origin of language, see Richard Waswo, *Language and Meaning in the Renaissance* (Princeton, NJ: Princeton University Press, 1987), pp. 284–85.

such words familiar, which at the first were difficult to be understood. For children at the first, as sayeth Aristotle,[7] call all men fathers, but shortly after, by exercise, call them by their names. And I have learned by experience that the mariners use many English words, which were as unknown unto me as the Chaldean tongue before I was conversant with them. It may therefore suffice that the words and terms of arts and sciences be known to the professors thereof, as partly by experience and partly by help of the dictionaries describing them *per proprium genus et differentiam*,[8] as the logicians teach, and as Georgius Agricola[9] useth to do in the Germany tongue, which as well in that part of philosophy as in all other was barbarous and indigent before it was by long experience brought to perfection.

32. Arthur Golding, *The Histories of Trogus Pompeius* (1564)

[Arthur Golding (1535/36–1606) studied at Jesus College, Cambridge, and in the early 1560s was employed by Sir William Cecil, living for a time at Cecil's home on the Strand. Between 1562 and 1565 he published five translations from Latin, including Trogus Pompeius and (on the instruction of Cecil) the first English version of Caesar's *Gallic Wars*. Much the most famous of these translations, however, is that of Ovid's *Metamorphoses* into fourteeners, which was widely influential, leaving its mark on *A Midsummer Night's Dream* and *The Tempest*. In later life he published numerous translations of religious works from both Latin and French, including work by Calvin. Golding's extraordinary output and, in the case of Ovid, his influence, was not matched by much reflection on the business of translation itself.

---

[7] Aristotle] *Physics* 1.1.

[8] *per* [. . .] *differentiam*] i.e. the technique (from Aristotle) of defining an object or idea by placing it first under a more general category, then marking out its distinctiveness from others in the same category by some specific differentiating feature.

[9] Georgius Agricola] (1494–55), a geologist, best known for his book *De Re metallica* (Basel, 1530). Eden may be confusing him Rudolph Agricola (1444–1485), whose *De Inventione dialectica* (1479; printed Cologne, 1520) dealt with the role of *loci* and commonplaces in argumentation, but neither scholar published in German.

Trogus Pompeius (Gnaeus Pompeius Trogus) was a Roman historian of the first century BC whose work survives only in the epitome by the later historian, Justin. Golding revised his translation in 1570 when it was 'newly conferred with the Latin copy', but the first Latin edition of Trogus Pompeius to be published in England did not appear until 1572. Golding's source text is likely to have been one of the editions published at Paris between 1502 and 1519.]

See Raphael Lyne, *Ovid's Changing Worlds: English 'Metamorphoses' 1567–1632* (Oxford: Oxford University Press, 2001); Morini, *Tudor Translation*; John Considine in *ODNB*.]

To the Reader.

Trogus Pompeius wrote the histories of the whole world from the beginning of the monarchy of Assyria unto the reign of the emperor Augustus, the abridgement of whose works, gathered out by Justin (who partly by his own industry, but more by the decay and loss of his author, Trogus, obtained the name of a famous historiographer), I have translated out of Latin into English, though not so eloquently as a number could have done, yet (I trust) according to the true sense and meaning of the author. Wherein albeit I may seem to some to have taken in hand a vain and frivolous travail, namely to put forth that thing in rude English which is written in good and pure Latin, yet notwithstanding, as well for the avoiding of idleness, the mother and nourisher of all vice, as also for the zeal I bear to this my native country, desirous to gratify, yea, and to profit such as have not understanding in the Latin tongue if I could, I have not stopped my race° until such time as I had attained to the final scope° of my prepensed° purpose, following the ensample of divers wise and well-learned, both of old time and also of our age, of all sorts of nations, whose study and travail hath always been to bring into their mother tongue such works as they found either in the Greek (the head and well-spring of all philosophy, cunning and learning) or in any other language worthy to be known and had in memory. And in like manner as oftentimes beautiful and well-favoured persons, turned out of their gorgeous apparel and costly attire into simple raiment, do like° the beholders as well as they did in their gayest garments, even in like wise (I trust) it may so come to pass that this my rude translation, void of ornate terms and elegant inditing,° may (as it were) in his plain and homely English coat be as well accepted of the favourable reader as when it were richly clad in Roman vesture; considering that the value and estimation of the history is no more abased thereby than should the virtue of a precious stone by setting it in brass or iron, or by carrying it in a closure of leather.[1]

33. Thomas Drant, *A Medicinable Moral* [Horace's satires] (1566)

[Thomas Drant (*c.*1540–1578) studied at St John's College, Cambridge, where he became a Fellow, and later held various ecclesiastical appointments, most notably that of Archdeacon of Lewes. Although he was known principally as a preacher, his work on epigram and satire in English was innovative (his first publication included 'certain of the special articles of the epigram'). *A Medicinable Morall* was followed by a translation of Horace's *Epistles*, including the *Art of Poetry*, which was published together with the satires [*Sermones*] in 1567, and in 1568 by *Epigrams and Sentences Spiritual in Vers* from Gregory of Nazianus. Other works, including a translation of the first five books of the *Iliad*, are now lost.

A Medicinable Morall is the first complete English translation of Horace's satires, though some of Wyatt's poems are imitations of Horace and Lewis Evans, a schoolmaster, had produced versions of the first two satires the year before Drant. The title-page claims that the satires are 'Englished according to the prescription of St Jerome', that is to say, sense for sense rather than word for word, as Jerome prescribed in the case of Bible translation. Drant couples Horace with the *Lamentations* of Jeremiah, giving the book as a whole a moralising, Christian character, and includes an anti-Catholic satire of his own in place of 1.5 in Horace.

[1] The metaphor of new clothing is one of the commonest figurative representations of translation in the early modern period; on the range of metaphors for translation in the period, see A. E. B. Coldiron in *OHLTE* (2), pp. 109–17. On the jewel in the box cf. Aelian [trans. by Abraham Fleming] *A Registre of Hystories* (1576), STC 164, sig. ¶3v, image 8.

See Colin Burrow, 'Horace at Home and Abroad: Wyatt and Sixteenth-Century Horatianism' in *Horace Made New: Horatian Influences on British Writing from the Renaissance to the Twentieth Century* (Cambridge: Cambridge University Press, 1993); Neel Mukherjee, 'Thomas Drant's Rewriting of Horace', *Studies in English Literature 1500–1900*, 40 (2000), 1–20; Gordon Braden in *OHLTE*, pp. 89–100.]

To the Reader.

Horace was excellent good in his time, a much zealous controller of sin, but chiefly one that with sharp satires and cutting quips could well display and disease a glozer.[1] The holy prophet Jeremiah[2] did ruefully and wailingly lament the deep and massy° enormities of his times, and earnestly prognosticate and forspeak the sorry and sour consequents that came after, and sauce with tears the hard plagues that had gone before. Therefore, as it is meet for a man of God rather to weep than to jest, and not undecent for a profane writer to be jesting and merry spoken, I have brought to pass that the plaintive prophet Jeremiah should weep at sin and the pleasant poet Horace should laugh at sin. Not one kind of music delighteth all passions, nor one salve for all grievances. If a man would calendar° in mind the sequel° of times, and whom the world dubbeth as worthies and culleth as her whelps,[3] and how for shows and prattling of piety she proclaimeth fools holy, admireth fools, magnifieth fools (and how for not prating of piety, or not glozing, she misjudgeth the wise, discrediteth the wise, profaneth the wise), not a thousand Democriti could suffice to laugh at the one, nor a thousand Heracliti be enough to weep at the other.[4] Horace, because he

[1] display [. . .] glozer] expose and discomfort a sychophant.

[2] Jeremiah] The Old Testament prophet traditionally regarded as the author of the book of *Lamentations*, in which the destruction of Jerusalem is seen as an act of divine retribution for the sins of its people.

[3] culleth as her whelps] kill off her unwanted offspring.

[4] Democriti [. . .] Heracliti] Followers of Democritus or Heraclitus, both Greek philosophers. Democritus was known as the laughing philosopher, reported by Seneca never to have appeared in public without mocking human folly, and Heraclitus as the weeping philosopher. Lucian presented them as a complementary package in 'Philosophies for Sale' and they were frequently paired in the Renaissance, e,g. by Montaigne (*Essays* 1.50).

was not in any such time wherein pretenced forwardness° was a harvest to those that pretended it, and a despoiling winter blast to that religion wherefore it seemed to be pretended, he never saw that with the view of his eye which his pensive° translator cannot but overview with the languish of his soul.[5]

Nonetheless, such vices as were then fledge° and incident into that age he assaileth fiercely and rattleth up bitterly. His eloquence is sometimes too sharp, and therefore I have blunted it, and sometimes too dull, and therefore I have whetted it, helping him to ebb and helping him to rise. I began this work (a thing of small account) two years agone or more, and have dispatched it by piecemeal, or inchmeal, with small prejudice or none to my study or profession. In the first and second satire I have taken it a note beyond the text: afterward plodded on much more precisely. At the beginning he is lofty, but afterward wonderfully calmed. I dare not warrant the reader to understand him in all places, no more than he did me. Howbeit, I have made him more lightsome, well nigh by the tone half (a small accomplishment for one of my continuance) and if thou canst not now in all points perceive him (thou must bear with me), in sooth the default is thine own. This is a true assertion: whoso but knew the least part of Horace his satires as they were before may now understand them all in their new English livery.

First, I have done as the people of God were commanded to do with their captive women that were handsome and beautiful: I have shaved off his hair and pared off his nails,[6] that is, I have wiped away all his vanity and superfluity of matter. Further, I have for the most part drawn his private carping of this or that man to a general moral. I have Englished things not according to the vein of the Latin propriety, but of our own vulgar tongue. I have interfarced° (to remove his obscurity and sometimes to

[5] Horace [. . .] soul] The sense is obscure, but Drant seems to be making a distinction between the vices of Horace's day and the more hypocritical states of sinfulness prevalent in the Christian era. Horace would not have been able to see the latter and readers must bring their Christian understanding to bear on his *Sermones* retrospectively. (This is echoed in the reference to 'self-help' in the final sentence of the passage.)

[6] Deuteronomy 21.11–12. 'And seest among the captives a beautiful woman, and hast a desire unto her, that thou wouldest have her to thy wife; /Then thou shalt bring her home to thine house; and she shall shave her head, and pare her nails.'

better his matter) much of mine own devising. I have pieced his reason, eked° and mended his similitudes, mollified his hardness, prolonged his curtal° kind of speeches, changed and much altered his words, but not his sentence;° or at least, I dare say, not his purpose. For short, if thou canst credit me, do so. If not, ask counsel at his interpreters.° And if something shall seem to thee strangely or not reasonably done, thou shalt find, I am sure, that it came so to pass not upon negligence but judgement. Otherwise, if any will deceive himself in misjudging, he shall have much ado to make me angry. For whatso is spoken of me sinisterly° through the speaker's either evil will or small skill, my fashion is to be loath to hear it, but not wroth° to revenge it. The poet is thus: sometimes he wadeth very far in fetching out his matter, and sometimes he is brittle° and soon broken off from his matter, so that thou be deep-witted to begin with him and well-witted to take him with thee. Thou must, gentle reader, bring in thy self help to the understanding of him and will likewise to thine own amendment, or else it will but fall out with thee according to the tenor of this distich.[7]

34. Thomas Gale, *Certain Works of Galen's* (1566)

[Thomas Gale (*c.* 1507–1567) was a London surgeon and a spokesman for the Company of Barber Surgeons, who also served in the armies of both Henry VIII and Philip II of Spain. His experience as an army surgeon informs his treatise *Certain Works of Chirurgery* (1563), which deals extensively with the treatment of wounds. This important work opens with a dialogue on the theory of surgery.

Certain Works of Galen's claims to be the first English translation of the Greek physician who was still the principal medical authority in the sixteenth century. (The first translation, via French, actually appears in a compilation entitled *The Questyonary of Cyrurgyens* (1542)). Galen's *Methodus medendi* was a set text for the entry examination for the Barber Surgeons Company and Gale translates from the Latin texts of this work

[7] i.e. you will suffer in the same way that the objects of this satire do. (A 'distich' is two lines of verse, usually a rhyming couplet, but Drant uses the term here to refer to the two books of Horace's *Sermones*.)

and of Galen's works on the natural faculties and the humours. The Latin versions of Galen which Gale uses as his source texts were made by Thomas Linacre. A partial translation of *Methodus medendi* had also been made by John Caius, but it remained unpublished.

See Mary C. Erler, 'The First English Printing of Galen: The Formation of the Company of Barber-Surgeons', *HLQ*, 48 (1985), 159–71; Max Satchell in *ODNB*.]

To the Right Honourable Sir Henry Neville, Knight[1]

And forasmuch as your lordship beareth such a singular love unto the same art [i.e. surgery], I am therefore moved to dedicate these my simple travails unto your honour to be the patron and defender thereof, for I do perceive that now in our time no good enterprise can be gone about but false detraction and envy is like to overthrow the same, which hath moved me, forasmuch as you are a noble man, the rather to dedicate my travails unto your honour to be my aid and succour in the defending of this my small travail, which, I protest, I have not taken in hand neither for vainglory, neither yet for any worldly profit or gain. For since the first time that I began to set out any part of this art in our English tongue, I have both sustained great displeasure and also lost many profits of those which were in times past my special friends, and the greatest matter that they have to say against me is only that I go about to make everybody cunning in the art of medicine with setting forth of these my works in the English tongue. But if it shall please your good lordship to understand my bounden duty, first to Almighty God, of whom I have received the talent, and also my duty to my natural country, whom I ought to profit with my talent according to the saying of our saviour Jesus Christ, which sayeth: 'he that hideth his talent in the ground and useth it not to the profit of his neighbour, it shall be taken from him again'.[2] Wherefore, my good Lord, I think it my duty to set forth these things for the commodity of the commonwealth of my country. [. . .]

[1] Neville] A godson of Henry VIII and a groom of the privy chamber.

[2] See Matthew 25.14–30 and Luke 19.12–28; cf. also Thomas Phaer, **22**. 41–70 above.

Now, my singular good Lord, if they shall say it is not good because it is in the English tongue, then I must allege° unto them, the famous men which were the chief setters forth of the same art, as Hippocrates and Galen[3] amongst the Grecians, whatsoever they might understand by foreign languages, either else gather by reason or by experience or observation of time – all these, whatsoever they were, they did write them in Greek, which was their own language and tongue, to that end they might the better be understood and sooner be learned. Also in like manner the worthy Arabians, as that noble king Avicenna, Averroes, Albucasis, Mesue, and a great sort more of worthy men, which did collect and translate many noble works of medicine out of the Greek tongue, the Hebrew tongue, and many other languages, into their own natural tongue, which was then the Arabian tongue. In like manner the Latinists were no less diligent to collect and gather both out of the Greek and Arabian tongue and wrote it in their own tongue, as you may read in the works of those famous men, Plinius and Cornelius Celsus,[4] with many other more whose works are manifest at this present day. If these worthy men have been moved with good conscience for knowledge sake, and for the better maintenance of their common wealth, in setting forth of this art for the relief, comfort, succour, help, and health of those that be sick and diseased, or other ways wounded or hurt in war or by mischance etc., why should not I then without blame or reproach, for the furtherance of knowledge and other necessary things above rehearsed, set forth in our English tongue some part of this good and necessary art for the

[3] Hippocrates and Galen] Hippocrates was a physician of the late fifth century / early fourth century BC. A Latin text of his aphorisms was published in London in 1567, but no English translation appeared until the seventeenth century. Galen, working in the first century AD, was influenced by Hippocrates's humoral theories and saw himself as a philosopher as well as a physician. His work on oratory was authoritative until Vesalius (1543), who translated much of Galen from Greek into Latin, and on the physiology of circulation until Harvey (1628).

[4] Avicenna [. . .] Celsus] The most significant contributions to medicine in the medieval period came from the Muslim world. Albucasis and Averroes were natives of Cordoba and Mesue and Avicenna were Persian. Many editions of the works of Mesue and Avicenna were published in Italy in Latin translation during the fifteenth and sixteenth centuries. On Pliny see **31**. 15 above and **46**. below. Cornelius Celsus was the Roman author of *De Medicina* (extracts translated into English, 1612).

instruction and further knowledge of those young students which are desirous to learn the same, and to use the same to the profit of the common wealth in the time of necessity. I do not mean that honest artists,° as tailors, shoemakers, weavers, or any other handy occupations, that they should leave their arts wherein they are perfect and fall to this art of medicine, for I do wish with all my heart that politic laws might be made to constrain every man to follow that art in which he hath been well instructed and brought up in. But my meaning is only to instruct those that be brought up in the art of surgery under some experimenters[5] who hath little learning in the tongues and [are] yet desirous to attain knowledge, and forasmuch as these experimenters are permitted by laws to occupy the art of surgery, I thought it my bounden duty both for the furtherance of their knowledge and also for the relief of these that be diseased to set forth this in the English tongue which I have done.

I do not go about to instruct those which be great learned men and understandeth the tongues, neither yet do I go about to satisfy the mind of those that be contentious and captious, that will rather find fault with other men's doings than to further those that be willing to learn with their good doings. My intent is only to further those that be willing to learn, which with humble and gentle heart do accept and take in good part other men's great pain and travails, and forasmuch as prentices and young men which have not been trained up in schools, neither yet can understand the Greek or Latin tongue, and yet can understand and read English very well, and be of ready wit and good memory to carry away that they read and hear, it hath moved me, therefore, the rather to write these books in the English tongue. And forasmuch as the foundation of art doth consist only in reason and experience, neither can there be any third thing added thereunto, as Galen affirmeth in his third book named *Therapeutikon.*[6] It seemeth to me, therefore, that he which understandeth any tongue, whether it be Greek, Latin, or English, it serveth him no more but for the further understanding

[5] experimenters] Predates first citation in the OED; the sense here is more that of 'practitioners'.

[6] Galen's fourth book, not third, is known as the *Therapeutikon*. This had appeared in *The Questyonary of Chirurgyens*, translated from the French of Guy de Chauliac as the 'Terapentyke' and borrowed by Gale for his own translation.

of that thing which he doth read, for it doth not follow that everyone which can speak Greek, Latin, or Hebrew by and by to be a good divine or perfectly to understand the art of medicine, for the common people amongst the Grecians speaketh the Greek tongue, and so in other countries which speaketh their language, and yet [are] neither divines, neither yet physicians. Therefore it doth manifestly appear by Galen that the tongues maketh not an artist, but reasonable knowledge being joined with experience maketh the artist, so that in what tongue soever a man may gather knowledge, whether it be Greek, Hebrew, Latin, English, or what other language soever it be, that same knowledge being joined with reason and experience, maketh a perfect artist.

Yet, my good Lord, I would wish that he that should be a chirurgeon° should understand the tongues, forasmuch as in times past they have been more diligent and careful to further their common wealths in those countries than they be in ours, by means whereof they have brought many noble arts into their own tongues, which we have not so largely set forth in our English tongue. Therefore, if the professors of chirurgery were learned in these tongues, they might more easily understand the principles of their art with their true divisions and definitions, which should the more readier instruct them to follow a true method. And this hath been one cause which hath moved me to take this matter in hand.

35. William Painter, *The Second Tome of the Palace of Pleasure* (1567)

[William Painter (1540?-1595) enjoyed a lucrative career as a civil servant, working as Clerk to Her Majesty's Ordnance at the Tower of London, a position which enabled him to embezzle large sums of money. The work that became *The Palace of Pleasure* (1566) was originally entered in the Stationers' Register as 'The City of Civility', a title that reflects the first stories in the collection, which are translations from Livy and other classical authors. The success of the *Palace* enabled him to bring out a second 'tome' the following year, and the two volumes were republished together in 1575. After completing the first volume of the *Palace*, Painter also published a translation of Ortensio

Landi's *Quattro Libri di Dubbi* as *Delectable Demaundes and Pleasant Questions* (1566).

The Palace of Pleasure owed its success partly to Painter's decision to move away from translations of classical history to the *novelle* of Boccaccio and his followers, Bandello and Marguerite of Navarre. These are almost certainly the Italian tales censured by Roger Ascham in *The Schoolmaster* as morally corrupting. Painter's translations were enormously influential, producing a spate of similar collections of short fictional prose and providing the new London theatres with abundant plot material. Painter's versions of Italian stories were translated from French-language editions: in the case of Boccaccio's *Decameron*, that of Antoine Le Maçon, published in many editions from 1543 onwards; in the case of Bandello, that of François de Belleforest (1559).

See also Lorna Hutson, *The Usurer's Daughter: Male Friendship and Fictions of Women in Sixteenth-Century England* (London: Routledge, 1994); R. W. Maslen, *Elizabethan Fictions: Espionage, Counter-Espionage, and the Duplicity of Fiction in Early Elizabethan Prose Narratives* (Oxford: Clarendon Press, 1997); Hadfield, *Literature, Travel, and Colonial Writing*.]

To the Right Worshipful Sir George Howard,[1] Knight, Master of the Queen's Majesty's Armoury.

Every science[2] having his peculiar commodity° and conducing to the travailer and diligent searcher, a due deserved benefit (besides the exercise and shunning the pestilent monster, idleness) discloseth the miraculous effect of the divinity and the excellency of his creature, who, breathing life into that senseless work framed within the mould of human conception, forceth in him by nature and timely institution such capacity of science, as not only by that knowledge he glorifyeth his creator, but also besides himself helpeth and doth good to other. For prose whereof the science of that surpassing and delightsome pasture of theology is profitable

[1] Howard] (before 1523–1580), brother of Katherine Howard, fifth queen of Henry VIII. Appointed Master of the Armoury by Elizabeth in 1560, he was Painter's employer.

[2] science] Here, 'branch of knowledge, but at l. 7 'knowledge and understanding'.

to teach, argue, reprove, and instruct, that by patience and consolation we may conceive hope of eternity. The knowledge of philosophy cureth the mind, avoideth childish care, expelleth fear, and shunneth fond desires. 'O philosophy, the guide of life', exclaimeth Tully, 'the inquisitor of virtue and expeller of vice'.[3] 'Rhetoric', affirmeth he, 'causeth us to learn that we know not, and that we know to teach to other'. By the same we exhort; with that we persuade; with that we comfort the afflicted; by it we encourage the astoned° and appease the outrageous. Music easeth the troubled mind, lenifieth° sorrow, comforteth the heavy-hearted, and erecteth a contemplation of heavenly things. Astronomy revealeth the nature of the stars and planets, presageth days and times for the help and maintenance of life. Poesy teacheth amendment of manners, directeth what things be meet for imitation and with what detriment wantonness annoyeth the body of man. By means of it, St Augustine sayeth he learned many good lessons to profit himself and do good to other.[4] To be short, every science is so necessary, as the same taken away, reason is deprived, and the life of man, of due order and government defrauded.

Think, sayeth a Greek orator, the knowledge of many things to be more precious and excellent than a chest heaped up with abundance of money: for the one quickly faileth, and the other forever lasteth. For *Scientia*, affirmeth he, is the only immortal storehouse of all possessions. Amongst which troupe of sciences, the knowledge and search of history deserveth a place in the chiefest rank and is for example of human affairs a crystal light to show the paths of our ancestors. The same displayeth the counsels, advices, policies, acts, success and ends of kings, princes, and great men with the order and desciption of time and place, and like a lively image representeth before our eyes the beginning, end, and circumstance of each attempt. The same, like a mistress of our life, by probable[5] examples stirreth up our

[3] Cicero, *Tusculan Disputations* 5.2.

[4] See Augustine, *Confessions* 3.2.2–4. Augustine's belief in the educative powers of poetry was matched by an awareness of how easily this power could be abused.

[5] probable] i.e. credible and persuasive. The case Painter makes for the morally inspiring effects of history is the same that Sidney makes for poetry in the *Apology*, though unlike Sidney Painter makes no clear distinction between history and fiction. Painter's use of the term 'histories' in this preface is

sluggish minds to aspire the eternal glory of praise and fame, and terrifieth the desperate and adventurous from enterprise of things unseemly. The same is a passing picture of verity and an absolute pattern framing the matter greater nor less than it is. And because I am not ignorant what encomia innumerable authors in time past and writers of our time do attribute unto that science, and with what titles the prince of them all decketh the praise of historical knowledge, I only refer the worthiness to the practisers, and the singularity of histories' travail and delight to each willing mind that employs their leisure and time therein. And I for my part do confess that by reading of histories I find the saying which Tully avoucheth of Publius Scipio to be true: that he was never less idle than when he was idle, and never less alone than when he was alone,[6] meaning thereby that when he was at best leisure he was never idle, nor when he was alone, unoccupied. For when labour resteth himself in me and leisure refresheth other affairs, nothing delights more that vacant time than reading of histories in such vulgar speech wherein my small knowledge taketh repast.

And for that my private reading might not delight and pleasure me alone, to avoid the nature of that cankered churl and foe of human company, Timon of Athens,[7] that lived but for himself, I have (after my skill) culled some flowers and fruits from that pleasant store of those my readings to impart for universal gain and benefit, choosing rather hereby to follow the liberality of Cimon, a gentleman of that city, who knowing himself to be born to profit other, and for the enriching of his country, not only achieved marvellous matters for furtherance of common wealth,[8] but left his gardens and orchards open for all men to participate the fruits of his pleasure and travail.[9] Whereby, so well as I can, I follow the tract and practice of other, by whose means so

equivalent to 'stories', and he designates them as 'novelles' in the text. He uses the terms 'novelles' and 'histories' interchangeably in the preface to Tome 1 (STC 19121, sig. ¶¶¶iv, image 14).

6 Cicero, *De Officiis* 3.1, citing Cato.

7 The story of Timon the misanthrope is told in the 28th novel of Tome 1, which may have influenced Shakespeare and Middleton's play.

8 The omission of the definite article implies 'common good' or 'public benefit' rather than 'the state'.

9 See Plutarch's *Lives*, trans. by North (1579), STC 20066, p. 536, image 284, where Cimon is paired with Lucullus. Opening private gardens to the public is a model benefaction to the commonwealth: Shakespeare makes this the climax of Antony's speech in *Julius Caesar* where he reads Caesar's will (3.3.236–41).

manifold sciences in our known tongue and translation of histories be frequent and rife among us. All which be done for our commodity, pleasure, solace, preservation, and comfort, and without the which we cannot long be sustained in this miserable life, but shall become not much unlike the barbarous, ne discrepant from the savage sort. The investigators and bringers to light whereof direct their eyes and meaning to none other end but for the benefit of us and our posterity, and that our faces be not tainted with the blushing colour to see the passing diligence of other countries by curious° embellishing of their states with the troublous travail of their brain and laboursome course of pen, who altogether employ those pains that no science lurk in [a] corner, that no knowledge be shut up in cloisters, that no history remain under the mask and unknown attire of other tongues. Amongst which crew, I say, I crave an inferior place and have undertaken the unfolding of sundry histories from the coverture of foreign language for none other purpose and intent but to universal benefit. Part whereof, two years past (almost), were made common in a former book, now succeedeth a second, furnished with like ornaments that the other was.

36. Thomas Wilson, *The Three Orations of Demosthenes* (1570)

[Sir Thomas Wilson (1523/24–1581) was educated at Eton under Nicholas Udall, who became a life-long friend, and at King's College, Cambridge. At Cambridge he became part of Cheke's Protestant humanist circle, which included Roger Ascham and Sir Thomas Smith. He is best known as the author of the first comprehensive rhetoric in English, *The Arte of Rhetorique* (1553), a companion to his earlier logic manual, *The Rule of Reason* (1551). On the accession of Mary he left the country to study at the University of Padua alongside other exiles, Cheke and Hoby, and it was here that he made his translation of Demosthenes. On moving to Rome he found his books on logic and rhetoric denounced as heretical, and he was imprisoned, but his fortunes improved dramatically with the accession of Elizabeth when he returned to England and enjoyed the patronage of both Sir William Cecil and Robert Dudley, Earl of Leicester. He became active as a diplomat and was eventually appointed Privy Councillor.

Wilson's *The Three Orations of Demosthenes* was originally conceived in tribute to Cheke, whose lectures Wilson had attended at Cambridge and who was trying to keep Greek studies alive among the English exiles at Padua. But when eventually published in 1570, this translation of Demosthenes's *Olynthiacs* and *Philippics*, originally directed against Philip of Macedon, was also meant to be understood as a modern call to arms in support of the Dutch Protestants fighting Philip of Spain. The dedication to Sir William Cecil, a former pupil of Cheke's, underlines both the Cambridge connection and the work's propaganda role. No Greek language texts were printed in England before 1570, so Wilson's source would have been a continental edition, probably used in conjunction with Wolf or one of the other Latin translations which he mentions in the preface.

See Peter E. Medine, *Thomas Wilson* (Boston, MA: Twayne Publishers, 1986); Cathy Shrank, *Writing the Nation*, pp. 182–219; Alastair J. L. Blanshard and Tracey A. Sowerby, 'Thomas Wilson's Demosthenes and the Politics of Tudor Translation', *International Journal of the Classical Tradition*, 12 (2005), 46–80; Robert Cummings in *OHLTE*, pp. 415–16; Susan Doran and Jonathan Woolfson in *ODNB*]

To the right Honourable Sir William Cecil, Knight, Principal Secretary to the Queen's Majesty and of her Privy Council, Master of the Court of Wards and Liveries, and Chancellor of the University of Cambridge, Thomas Wilson, Doctor of the Civil Law, wisheth long and perfect health with increase of God's most holy spirit.

Great is the force of virtue, right honourable counsellor, to win love and good will universally, in whose mind soever it is perfectly known to have once got a dwelling. I speak it for this end, that being solitary of late time from my other studies, and musing on this world in the middest of my books, I did then, as I have oftentimes else done, deeply think of Sir John Cheke, knight, that rare learned man and singular ornament of this land. And as the remembrance of him was dear unto me for his manifold great gifts and wonderful virtues, so did I think of his most gentle nature and godly disposed mind to help all those with his knowledge and understanding that any way made means unto him and sought his favour. And to say for myself amongst others, I found him such a friend to me for communicating the skill and gifts of his mind, as I cannot but during my life speak reverently of so worthy a man and honour in my heart the heavenly remembrance of him. And thinking of my being with him in Italy in that famous university of Padua, I did call to mind his care that he had over all the Englishmen there to go to their books, and how gladly he did read to me and others certain orations of Demosthenes in Greek, the interpretation whereof I and they had then from his mouth.[1]

And so remembering the rather this world by the very argument of those actions, I did then seek out amongst my other writings for the translation of them, and happily finding some, although not all, I was carried straightways (I trust by God's good motion) to make certain of them to be acquainted so nigh as I could with our English tongue, as well for the aptness of the matter and needful knowledge now at this time to be had, as also for the right notable and most excellent handling of the same. And here must I say, confessing mine own weakness and imperfection, that I never found in my life anything so hard for me to do. Yea, the more I look upon this orator to bring his sentences and words known to our common speech and language, the more do I find him hard and unable to be translated according to the excellency of his tongue. And many times I have been ashamed of myself when I compared his Greek and my English together; and no marvel neither, for the Latin translators, being otherwise most excellent men, have not always satisfied themselves, much less answered to their charge and enterprise in the opinion of others that compared their doings and the Greek together.

Hieronymus Wolfius[2] hath translated all Demosthenes (the like thing never yet done by any other) and herein he is very careful to keep himself to the Greek, and doth, as it should seem, better understand Demosthenes than any other, and yet sometimes either he is not well understood or else he faileth of Demosthenes' meaning. And being thus very curious° in his

[1] Cheke seems to have followed his practice as a lecturer at Cambridge described by Wilson at ll. 112–15 below.

[2] Wolfius] He and the other scholars cited by Wilson were German classicists translating Greek into Latin. Wolf's edition was published by Oporinus at Basel in 1549, USTC 632392. On Melanchthon see Norton **8**. n. 8.

translation to follow his author as nigh as may be, his Latin is now and then somewhat harsh and more hard than is the Greek itself. Christopherus Hegendorphius, a notable learned man undoubtedly, makes himself overbold with Demosthenes, enlarging his speech after the manner of a *Paraphrasis*,[3] whereas Demosthenes' praise was chiefly his short knitting up of his matters together. Philip Melanchthon misliketh himself, and yet he hath done very well, but compared to the Greek he is to seek. Ioachimus Camerarius for that which he hath taken in hand deserveth great praise with the best, and yet he doth not fully satisfy all men for his doings. Petrus Clobardus hath very learnedly translated the three first orations made in favour of the Olynthians, and varieth from others in sense, not without their misliking, and perhaps not always expressing the very force and pith of the Greek phrase. Nicholas Carr,[4] our countryman, one notably learned in the Greek tongue when he lived, as it is well known, hath done all these Orations passing well in eloquent Latin that I have done in English, who varieth from all others even in the very sense sometimes and understanding of the author, and seems to have reason with him. Master Cheke, whom I dare match with anyone before-named for his knowledge in the Greek tongue, having travailed in Demosthenes as much as any one of them all, and famous for his learning throughout Europe, yet was he never so passing in his translations that no exception could be made against him.

And then what shall I think of myself, after the naming of so many excellent learned men, but only submit my doings to the favour of others, and desire men to bear with my weakness. For this must I needs confess, that I am altogether unable to do so in English as the excellency of this orator deserveth in Greek. And yet the cunning is no less, and the praise as great in my judgement, to translate anything excellently into English as into any other language. And I think, although there be many doers, yet scant one is to be found worthy amongst us for translating into

[3] On paraphrase see Udall **7b**. n. 1 and Ascham **50**. Wilson contrasts the literal version of Wolf with the expansive and more Ciceronian version of Hegendorph, which misrepresents Demosthenes' tight style.

[4] Carr] Nicholas Carr (1522/23–1568) was a founding Fellow of Trinity College, Cambridge, and officially succeeded Cheke as Regius Professor of Greek in 1551 after deputising for him from 1544. His Latin translation of Demosthenes was not published until 1571 (STC 6578).

our country speech, such a hard thing it is to bring matter out of any one language into another. And perhaps it may be that even those who take themselves to be much better learned than I am (as what is he that is not, having any name for learning at all?) will find it a harder piece of work than they think even to make Greek speak English, if they will make proof thereof as I have done. Whose labour and travail I would as gladly see, as they are like now to see mine, that such an orator as this is might be so framed to speak our tongue as none were able to amend him, and that he might be found to be most like himself.

The which enterprise, if any might have been most bold to have taken upon him, Sir John Cheke was the man, of all that ever I knew or do yet know in England. Such acquaintance had he with this notable orator, so gladly did he read him, and so often, that I think there was never old priest more perfect in his porteous,° nor superstitious monk in Our Lady's Psalter, as they call it, nor yet good preacher in the Bible or Testament than this man was in Demosthenes. And great cause moved him so to be, for that he saw him to be the perfectest orator that ever wrote for these two thousand years almost bypast (for so long it is since he was), and also for that he perceived him to have before his eyes in all his orations the advancement of virtue as a thing chiefly to be sought for, together with the honour and welfare of his country. Besides this, Master Cheke's judgement was great in translating out of one tongue into another, and better skill he had in our English speech to judge of the phrases and properties of words, and to divide sentences, than any else had that I have known. And often he would English his matters out of the Latin or Greek upon the sudden, by looking of the book only, without reading or construing anything at all:[5] an usage right worthy and very profitable for all men, as well for the understanding of the book as also for the aptness of framing the author's meaning, and bettering thereby their judgement and therewithal perfecting their tongue and utterance of speech. Moreover, he was moved

[5] This is the source of the account of Cheke's Cambridge lectures in John Strype, *The Life of the Learned Sir John Cheke* (London, 1705), p. 201. It illustrates how Greek lectures were able to stimulate a translation culture in English, influencing the work of Hoby and Wilson as well as Cecil's patronage of translators such as Golding. Cheke is also the source of the double translation method recommended by Ascham (see **51**. 203–73).

greatly to like Demosthenes above all others, for that he saw him so familiarly applying himself to the sense and understanding of the common people[6] that he sticked not to say that none ever was more fit to make an Englishman tell his tale praiseworthily in any open hearing, either in parliament or in pulpit or otherwise, than this only orator was.

But seeing Master Cheke is gone from us to God, after whom we must all seek to follow, and that this thing is not done by him, the which I would with all my heart had been done, for that he was best able,[7] it cannot be counted now, I trust, any fault in me if I endeavour to do that, the which I never saw done before me. And indeed my labour can be no hurt to anybody, except it be to myself, for the Greek is as it was, and those that were Grecians may read the Greek still, notwithstanding my English. And such as have no Greek may go to the Latin for all my doings, or any other translation else in any other strange tongue or language, for as I do hear say, certain pieces of Demosthenes are translated also into divers other tongues.[8] But such as are grieved with translated books are like to them that eating fine manchet are angry with others that feed on cheat bread, and yet God knoweth men would as gladly eat manchet[9] as they, if they had it. But all cannot wear velvet, or feed with the best, and therefore such are contented for necessity's sake to wear our country cloth and to take themselves to hard fare that can have no better. But what reason have they, I pray you, that will not suffer men to write reason as well as to speak reason? For this I dare say, that even those men, if they have any reason with them at all, will use in their proofs upon weighty matters the arguments of Demosthenes or reasons of like value. And may not I or any

---

[6] Cheke followed Hermogenes in admiring Demosthenes' mastery of each of the three stylistic levels. Ascham cites Hermogenes in *The Schoolmaster*, STC 832, sig. R2[r], image 64; see also Cecil W. Wooten, *Hermogenes' On Types of Style* (Chapel Hill: University of Noth Carolina Press, 1987).

[7] Cheke had made Latin translations of Sophocles and Euripides as well as Demosthenes. None of these were published, but John Bale found a manuscript of the Sophocles translation at the house of the printer, Reginald Wolfe (Paul Strope Needham, 'Sir John Cheke at Cambridge and at Court' (PhD diss., Harvard University, 1971), p. 123.). Cheke had died in 1557.

[8] The Olynthiacs and Philippics had been translated into French by Louis le Roy (1551; 1555) and also into German and Italian.

[9] cheat bread [. . .] manchet] The finest and coarser qualities of wheaten bread.

other set down those reasons by pen in our English language, the which are uttered daily in our common speech by men of understanding? Now wicked is that mind the which doth envy welfare or wisdom to another body, because the same man cannot be so wealthy or as wise as the best.

And therefore in my simple reason there is no harm done, I say, to anybody by this my English translation, except it be to myself. For whereas I might have lived peradventure under the colour° of silence and stillness in some opinion of learning, I may now, perchance, with mine overmuch boldness in seeking to fashion so famous an orator out of Greek into English, happen to bewray mine own unskillful dealing. But howsoever it is, I had rather hazard rebuke, if by this means I could toll° out some other to do this perfectly, the which I have only assayed to do plainly and homely, than to suffer so noble an orator and so necessary a writer for all those that love their country's liberty and welfare to lie hid and unknown, especially in such a dangerous world as this is.

And although your honour hath no need of these my doings, for that the Greek is so familiar unto you, and that you also, as well as I, have heard Sir John Cheke read the same orations at other times, yet I think for divers causes I should in right present unto your honour this my travail, the rather to have it through your good liking and allowance to be made common to many. First, the said Sir John Cheke (whom I do often name, for the honour and reverence due to so worthy a man) was your brother-in-law, your dear friend, your good admonisher and teacher in your younger years to take that way of virtue, the fruit whereof you do feel and taste to your great joy at this day, and shall forever be remembered therefore.[10] Again, by him you have heard these orations read and translated, as I after you (although out of England) have heard the same likewise of him, to my great comfort and profit in learning. Thirdly, the orator himself having been a counsellor in his country as you now are in this realm, he is your glass, I am well assured, whereupon you do often look

[10] Cheke] Cecil was taught by Cheke at St John's College, Cambridge, from 1535 to 1541, when he married Cheke's sister, Mary (d. 1544). He was sufficiently advanced in Greek to have read the Greek lecture at the college at the age of eighteen; see *The 'Anonymous Life' of William Cecil, Lord Burghley*, ed. by Alan G. Smith (Lewiston, NY: Edwin Mellen Press, 1990), p. 44.

and compare his time with this time, country with country, neighbours with neighbours, and king with king. Lastly, your great goodness used to me from time to time, together with that your good conceived opinion to enable me to deal in things much above my power, for it pleased you to like and allow of me.

All these respects, I say, do move me at this time to offer most humbly to Your Honour this mine enterprised travail of so noble an orator of those his seven several famous orations, whereof three are made in favour of the distressed Olynthians, sometimes a warlike people in Thracia, now called Romania, and the other four entitled 'Against King Philip of Macedonia' by name. The arguments whereof and orations also shall hereafter appear translated in order. And after this done, his life and dealings shall be truly set forth, and his faults told as well as his virtues rehearsed, that it may appear he was a man subject to imperfections and lacks as others are. And though he was in some things for his rare virtues and singular gifts most excellent, and passed all others, yet had he his wants, as what is he that hath not? According to that saying in Titus Livius of Maharbal to Hannibal after that great victory got at Cannae in Italy against the Romans: 'God never gave all things to any one man'.[11]

And thus having done my voluntary task, I desire none other thanks for all my labour and travail herein but your favourable defence against certain that will do nothing themselves and yet will find fault with all things, being in nature drones and no bees, lubbers° and no learners, as void of sound judgement and understanding as they are out of reason curious judges over the travail and painstaking of others. But who can stop these open-mouthed talkers? Empty vessels make the greatest sound and ring out a hollow noise to small purpose, and so do these that have the least skill and smallest knowledge make the mightiest brag and are the boldest of all others, without cause or reason, God He knoweth. Of which croaking paddocks° and manifest overweeners of themselves, I do make very little account, or no reckoning at all. Your sound judgement, Sir, and good liking may be of sufficient value with me to hold myself well contented, whatsoever shall be said to the contrary. And thus most heartily I do wish to that heavenly mind of yours a strong and lusty body, that in these perilous days

[11] Titus Livius] See Livy, *History of Rome*, 22.51.

your pain and travail may run in equal course with your knowledge and understanding.

From the Queen's Majesty's Hospital of St Katharine's[12] nigh the Tower of London, the 10th of June, 1570.

37. Margaret Tyler, *The Mirror of Princely Deeds and Knighthood* [Ortúñez de Calahorra] (1578)

[Margaret Tyler (d. 1595) was employed in the household of Thomas Howard, Duke of Norfolk, from about 1558 to 1564, and may have been the wife of Norfolk's factor or land agent, John Tyler. Her employer, who was the father of the dedicatee of the translation, was executed in 1572 for his part in a Catholic plot against Elizabeth. Tyler's own religion has been debated, but it seems unlikely that she was herself a Catholic. The *Mirror* is the first translation of a work of secular literature by a woman to be printed in English and Tyler's preface offers a forceful defence of her right to undertake such an enterprise.

Diego Ortúñez de Calahorra's *Espejo de principes y cavalleros* was printed in 1555 (not 1562 as given in USTC; see Coad (1996)), and like other serial romances it has a complex publishing history both in the original Spanish and in English translation. Tyler's work covers only the first book, but its popularity ensured that the continuations were also translated. They were undertaken by R. P. (probably Robert Parry) and published in 1585 and 1586 by Thomas East, who was also Tyler's publisher.

See Tina Krontiris, 'Breaking Barriers of Genre and Gender: Margaret Tyler's Translation of the Mirrour of Knighthood', *English Literary Renaissance*, 18 (1988), 19–39; Louise Schleiner, 'Margaret Tyler, Translator and Waiting Woman', *English Language Notes*, 29 (1992), 2–5; Lorna Hutson, *The Usurer's Daughter: Male Friendship and Fictions of Women in Sixteenth-Century England* (London: Routledge, 1994), pp. 91–98; *The Early Modern Englishwoman, Vol. 8: Margaret Tyler*, introd. by Kathryn Coad (Aldershot: Scolar Press, 1996); Helen Hackett, *Women and Romance Fiction in the English Renaissance*

[12] St Katharine's] Wilson had been appointed Master of St Katharine's hospital in 1561.

(Cambridge: Cambridge University Press, 2000); Helen Moore in *OHLTE*, pp. 337–38.]

M. T. to the Reader.

Thou hast here, gentle reader, the history of Trebatio, an emperor in Greece: whether a true history of him indeed or a feigned fable, I wot not, neither did I greatly seek after it in the translation, but by me it is done into English for thy profit and delight.[1] The chief matter therein contained is of exploits of wars, and the parties therein named are specially renowned for their magnanimity and courage. The author's purpose appeareth to be this, to animate thereby and to set on fire the lusty courages° of young gentlemen, to the advancement of their line, by ensuing suchlike steps.[2] The first tongue wherein it was penned was the Spanish, in which nation by common report the inheritance of all worldly commendation hath to this day rested – the whole discourse in respect of the end not unnecessary, for the variety and continual shift of fresh matter very delightful, in the speeches short and sweet, wise in sentence° and wary in the provision of contrary accidents.[3] For I take the grace thereof to be rather in the reporter's device° than in the truth of this report, as I would that I could so well impart with thee that delight which myself findeth in reading the Spanish, but seldom is the tale carried clean from another's mouth. Such delivery as I have made I hope thou wilt friendly accept, the rather for that it is a woman's work, though in a story profane and a matter more manlike than becometh my sex. But as for the manliness of the matter, thou knowest that it is not necessary for every trumpeter or drumster° in the war to be a good fighter. They take wage only to incite others, though themselves have privy maims, and are therefore recureless.[4]°

---

[1] **Marg**. The commendation of the story.

[2] Tyler's defence of her subject matter echoes that of Painter **35**. 44–48, though she is working in the genre of chivalric romance rather than the classical histories and Boccaccian *novelle* of *The Palace of Pleasure*; see Hutson, *Usurer's Daughter*, pp. 95–96.

[3] wary [. . .] accidents] careful to provide contrasting events or incidents in the plot.

[4] **Marg**. That a woman may write of war.

So, gentle reader, if my travail in Englishing this author may bring thee to a liking of the virtues herein commended, and by example thereof in thy prince's and country's quarrel to hazard thy person and purchase good name, as for hope of well deserving myself that way, I neither bend myself thereto nor yet fear the speech of people if I be found backward. I trust every man holds not the plough which would the ground were tilled, and it is no sin to talk of Robin Hood though you never shot in his bow;[5] or be it that the attempt were bold to intermeddle in arms (so as the ancient Amazons[6] did, and in this story Claridiana doth, and in other stories not a few), yet to report of arms is not so odious but that it may be borne withal, not only in you men which yourselves are fighters, but in us women, to whom the benefit in equal part appertaineth of your victories, either for that the matter is so commendable that it carrieth no discredit from the homeliness of the speaker, or for that it is so generally known that it fitteth every man to speak thereof, or for that it jumpeth° with this common fear on all parts of war and invasion. The invention, disposition, trimming,[7] and what else in this story is wholly another man's, my part none therein but the translation, as it were only in giving entertainment to a stranger° before this time unacquainted with our country guise.[8] Marry, the worst perhaps is this, that among so many strangers as daily come over – some more ancient and some but new set forth, some penning matters of great weight and sadness° in divinity, or other studies the profession whereof more nearly beseemeth my years, other some discoursing of matters more easy and ordinary in common talk, wherein a gentlewoman may honestly employ her travail[9] – I have notwithstanding made countenance[10] only to this gentleman, whom neither his personage might sufficiently commend

[5] Robin Hood [. . .] bow] there is nothing wrong with talking about things of which you have no experience; proverbial, though commonly used to refer to empty boasting.

[6] Amazons] Painter opens the second tome of *The Palace of Pleasure* with a story of the Amazons.

[7] The first three parts of rhetoric, with the third (*elocutio*: style, expression) presented as dressing up.

[8] our country guise] the customs of our nation. The topos of giving hospitality to a foreign visitor is echoed by Hoby, **30**. 16–31, and Daniel in Florio, **47**. 416–26.

[9] **Marg**. That a woman of your years may write in this argument.

[10] made countenance] addressed myself.

itself unto my sex, nor his behaviour (being light° and soldier-like) might in good order acquaint itself with my years, so that the question now ariseth of my choice, not of my labour, wherefore I preferred this story before matter of more importance.

For answer whereto, gentle reader, the truth is that as the first motion to this kind of labour came not from myself, so was this piece of work put upon me by others, and they which first counselled me to fall to work took upon them also to be my taskmasters and overseers lest I should be idle. And yet because the refusal was in my power, I must stand to answer for my easy yielding and may not be unprovided of excuse wherein, if I should allege° for myself that matters of less worthiness by as aged years have been taken in hand, and that daily new devices are published in songs, sonnets, interludes and other discourses, and yet are borne out without reproach only to please the humour of some men. I think I should make no good plea therein, for besides that I should find thereby so many known enemies, as known men have been authors of such idle conceits, yet would my other adversaries be never the rather quieted. For they would say that as well the one as the other were all naught, and though peradventure I might pass unknown amongst a multitude, and not be the only gaze or odd party in my ill-doing, yet because there is less merit of pardon if the fault be excused as common, I will not make that defence which cannot help me and doth hinder other men.

But my defence is by example of the best, amongst which many have dedicated their labours – some stories, some of war, some physic, some law, some as concerning government, some divine matters – unto diverse ladies and gentlewomen. And if men may and do bestow such of their travails upon gentlewomen, then may we women read such of their works as they dedicate unto us, and if we may read them, why not further wade in them to the search of a truth. And then much more why not deal by translation in such arguments, especially this kind of exercise, being a matter of more heed than of deep invention or exquisite learning. And they must needs leave this as confessed, that in their dedications they mind not only to borrow names of worthy personages, but the testimonies also for their further credit, which neither the one may demand without ambition, nor the other grant without overlightness. If women be excluded from the view of such works as appear in their name, or if glory only be sought in our common inscriptions, it mattereth not whether the parties be men or women, whether alive or dead.

But to return, whatsomever the truth is, whether that women may not at all discourse in learning, for men lay in their claim to be sole possessioners of knowledge, or whether they may in some manner that is by limitation or appointment in some kind of learning, my persuasion hath been thus, that it is all one for a woman to pen a story as for a man to address his story to a woman. But amongst all my ill-willers, some I hope are not so strait° that they would enforce me necessarily either not to write, or to write of divinity,[11] whereas neither durst I trust mine own judgement sufficiently if matter of controversy were handled, nor yet could I find any book in the tongue which would not breed offence to some. But I perceive some may be rather angry to see their Spanish delight turned to an English pastime: they could well allow the story in Spanish, but they may not afford it so cheap, or they would have it proper to themselves.[12] What natures such men be of I list° not greatly dispute, but my meaning hath been to make other partners of my liking, as I doubt not, gentle reader, but if it shall please thee after serious matters to sport thyself with this Spaniard that thou shalt find in him the just reward of malice and cowardice with the good speed of honesty and courage, being able to furnish thee with sufficient store of foreign example to both purposes.[13] And as in such matters which have been rather devised to beguile° time than to breed matter of sad° learning, he hath ever borne away the price[14] which could season such delights with some profitable reading, so shalt thou have this stranger an honest man when need serveth, and at other times either a good companion to drive out a weary night or a merry jest at thy board.°

And thus much concerning this present story, that it is neither unseemly for a woman to deal in, neither greatly requiring a less staid age than mine is. But of these two points, gentle reader, I thought to give thee warning, lest perhaps understanding of my name and years, thou mightest be carried into a wrong suspect of my boldness and rashness, from which I would gladly free

[11] **Marg.** That you may not write of divinity.
[12] **Marg.** That you meant to make a common benefit of your pains.
[13] **Marg.** The use and profit of this Spanish translation.
[14] borne away the price] held in the highest esteem [as a work].

myself by this plain excuse, and if I may deserve thy good favour by like labour, when the choice is mine own I will have a special regard of thy liking.

So I wish thee well.
Thine to use,
M. T.

38. George Pettie, *The Civil Conversation of Master Steven Guazzo* (1581)

[George Pettie (*c.* 1548–1589) was a Scholar of Christ Church, Oxford, where he was friendly with the neo-Latin dramatist William Gager, graduating in 1569. He then travelled on the continent and served as a soldier. His best known work is the collection of stories *A Petite Pallace of Pettie his Pleasure* (1576), which capitalised on the vogue for short prose fiction initiated by Painter. Although the stories are taken from classical sources, they are closer in spirit to the Italian *novella* and are stylistically significant for introducing an early form of Euphuism.

Stefano Guazzo's *La Civil Conversatione* (1574) was the most influential sixteenth-century courtesy book after Castiglione and its title had European currency as a new term for social discourse and relationships. 'Civil conversation' is explained in Pettie's translation as 'an honest and commendable and virtuous kinde of living in the world' (STC 12422, image 28). Pettie translated the first three books, and the fourth, translated by Bartholomew Young, was added in 1586. Pettie's source text was the French translation by Gabriel Chappuys (Lyon: Jean Béraud, 1579), USTC 3599, though he also consulted the Italian.

See John Leon Lievsay, *Stefano Guazzo and the English Renaissance* (Chapel Hill, NC: University of North Carolina Press, 1961); Richards, *Rhetoric and Courtliness*, pp. 20–35; Helen Moore in *ODNB*]

To the Reader.

This, I hope, will satisfy those which mislike that gentlemen should publish the fruits of their study, especially seeing thereby learning is advanced and a great number pleasured and profited, and seeing the only way to win immortality is either to do things worth the writing or to write things worthy the reading. And if they object that that seeking of immortality is a sign of vainglory, to answer them plainly and humanely, I am flat of this mind that they which pass not of praise will never do anything worthy praise. There are some others yet who will set light by my labours because I write in English, and those are some nice travellers who return home with such queasy stomachs that nothing will down with them but French, Italian or Spanish, and though a work be but meanly written in one of those tongues, and finely translated into our language, yet they will not stick far to prefer the original before the translation. The cause is partly for that they cannot so soon espy faults in a foreign tongue as in their own, which maketh them think that to be current which is but coarse, and partly for that strange things do more delight them than that which they are daily used to. But they consider not the profit which cometh by reading things in their own tongue, whereby they shall be able to conceive the matter much sooner, and bear it away far better, than if they read it in a strange tongue; whereby also they shall be enabled to speak, to discourse, to write, to indite,° properly, fitly, finely, and wisely, but the worst is they think that impossible to be done in our tongue, for they count it barren, they count it barbarous, they count it unworthy to be accounted of; and, which is worse, as I myself have heard some of them, they report abroad that our country is barbarous, our manners rude, and our people uncivil. And when I have stood with them in the comparison between other countries and ours, and pointed with my finger to many gross abuses used in the places where we have been, when by no reason they have been able to defend them, they have shrunk in their neck and told me it was the fashion of the country, not considering that the manners and fashions of each country are the only thing that make it counted barbarous or civil, good or bad. But for our country, I am persuaded that those which know it and love it will report it for the civilest country in the world, and if it be thought to be otherwise by strangers, the disorders of those travellers abroad are the chief cause of it. And to speak but of the lightest, their envying one another, their depraving one another, their flouting one another, their falling out one with another, their fighting one with another in the open street (as with blushing I have often beheld in Paris), their contemning of their country fashions, their apish imitation of every outlandish ass in their gestures, behaviour, and apparel, are the only causes that make strangers count our country and our people barbarous. For at home it is well known that we live in laws as orderly, in manners as decently, in apparel as comely, in diet as delicately, in lodging as curiously,° in buildings as sumptuously, in all things as abundantly, and every way as civilly as any nation under heaven.

For the barbarousness of our tongue, I must likewise say that it is much the worse for them, and some such curious fellows as they are, who if one chance to derive any word from the Latin, which is insolent to their ears (as perchance they will take that phrase to be), they forthwith make a jest at it and term it an ink-horn term.[1] And though for my part I use those words as little as any, yet I know no reason why I should not use them, and I find it a fault in myself that I do not use them, for it is indeed the ready way to enrich our tongue and make it copious, and it is the way which all tongues have taken to enrich themselves. For take the Latin words from the Spanish tongue and it shall be as barren as most part of their country; take them from the Italian and you take away in a manner the whole tongue; take them from the French and you mar the grace of it; yea, take from the Latin itself the words derived from the Greek and it shall not be so flowing and flourishing as it is. Wherefore I marvel how our English tongue hath cracked its credit[2] that it may not borrow of the Latin as well as other tongues; and if it have broken, it is but of late, for it is not unknown to all men how many words we have fetched from thence within these few years, which if they should all be counted inkpot terms, I know not how we should speak

---

[1] ink-horn term] English attacks on borrowings from foreign languages run from Cheke (see **30**. 253–58 above) to Richard Verstegan [Rowlands]: 'But doubtlesse yf our selves pleased to use the treasurie of our own tong, wee should as little need to borrow words, from any language, extravagant from ours, as any such borroweth from us: our toung in it self being sufficient and copious enough, without this dayly borrowing from so many as take scorne to borrow any from us', *A Restitution of Decayed Intelligence* (London, 1605), STC 21361, sig. Cc3^{v}, image 116. Yet this is the period when the English language was enormously enriched in the way that Pettie describes.

[2] cracked its credit] Both defenders and opponents of the practice of borrowing from foreign languages in order to enrich ones own use the financial metaphor, with writers such as Cheke and Verstegan implying that loan words have somehow to be repaid.

anything without blacking our mouths with ink. For what word can be more plain than this word 'plain', and yet what can come more near to the Latin? What more manifest than 'manifest', and yet in a manner Latin? What more common than 'rare' or less rare than 'common', and yet both of them coming of the Latin?[3] But, you will say, long use hath made these words current, and why may not use do as much for these words which we shall now derive? Why should not we do as much for the posterity as we have received of the antiquity? And yet if a thing be of itself ill, I see not how the oldness of it can make it good, and if it be of itself good, I see not how the newness of it can make it naught. Whereupon I infer that those words which yourselves confess by use to be made good are good the first time they are uttered, and therefore not to be jested at, nor to be misliked. But how hardly soever you deal with your tongue, how barbarous soever you count it, how little soever you esteem it, I durst myself undertake (if I were furnished with learning otherwise) to write in it as copiously for variety, as compendiously for brevity, as choicely for words, as pithily for sentences, as pleasantly for figures, and every way as eloquently as any writer should do in any vulgar tongue whatsoever.

39. Richard Stanyhurst, *The Aeneid* (1582)

[Richard Stanyhurst (1547–1615) was born in Dublin and studied at University College, Oxford, graduating in 1568. A committed Catholic, he became a protégé of Edmund Campion, who encouraged his work on Porphyry's logic which he published in 1570. He also collaborated with Campion on a history of Ireland and contributed to the Irish section of Holinshed's *Chronicles* (1577). Emigrating to the Low Countries, his translation of *Aeneid* 1–4 was first published at Leiden in 1582 and again the following year in London. Stanyhurst lived abroad for the rest of his life, mainly in the Spanish Netherlands, but with a period of residence at the Spanish court in 1592–5. He was active in promoting the claims of Isabella, daughter of Philip II, to the throne of England and Ireland and was a staunch defender of the Counter-Reformation.

[3] plain [. . .] common] *planus* and *communis* in Latin.

Stanyhurst composed his translation of the *Aeneid* in quantitative metre in deliberate opposition to Thomas Phaer's version in rhymed fourteeners, which had been completed by Thomas Twyne in 1573 and was widely praised. It constitutes part of the debate on whether English can accommodate classical metre that extends to Thomas Campion's *Observations on the Arte of English Poesie* (1602) and Samuel Daniel's *Defence of Ryme* (1603). Stanyhurst oddly combines the supposedly elevated form of quantitative metre with a distinctly rustic and colloquial choice of vocabulary, which was mocked by both Puttenham and Nashe. The vocabulary of the preface is also highly idiosyncratic.

See Derek Attridge, *Well-weighed Syllables: Elizabethan Verse in Classical Metres* (London: Cambridge University Press, 1974); D. E. L. Crane, 'Richard Stanyhurst's Translation of Vergil's Aeneid (1582)' in *Studies in Seventeenth-Century English Literature, History and Bibliography*, ed. by G. A. M. Janssens and F. G. A. M. Aarts (Amsterdam: Rodopi, 1984); Gordon Braden in *OHLTE* (2), pp. 170–71]

To the Right Honourable my very loving brother, the Lord Baron of Dunsany[1]

What deep and rare points of hidden secrets[2] Virgil hath sealed up in his twelve books of Aeneas may easily appear to such reaching wits as bend their endeavours to the unfolding thereof, not only by nibbling upon the outward rind of a supposed history, but also by groping° the pith that is shrined up within the bark and body of so exquisite and singular a discourse. For whereas the chief praise of a writer consisteth in the interlacing of pleasure with profit, our author hath so wisely allayed° the one with the other as the shallow reader may be delighted with a smooth tale and the diving searcher[3] may be advantaged by

[1] Dunsany] Patrick Plunkett, 7th Baron of Dunsany (d. 1601), Stanyhurst's brother-in-law.

[2] secrets] The term frequently appears in book titles in the early modern period, where it usually refers to the secrets of nature uncovered by medicine and science (and revealed to the reader by translators); see Blank, 'Languages of Early Modern Literature', pp. 156–59.

[3] diving searcher] Predates the first citation in the OED for 'diving': 'The industrious search of some diving braine' (Fulbecke, 1602), which glosses the sense here.

sounding° a precious treatise. And certes this pre-eminency of writing is chiefly (if we respect our old Latin poets) to be afforded to Virgil in this work and to Ovid in his *Metamorphoses*. As for Ennius, Horace, Juvenal, Persius, and the rabblement of such cheat[4] poets, their doings are for favour of antiquity rather to be patiently allowed° than highly regarded. Such leavings as we have of Ennius his ragged verses are nothing current, but savour somewhat nappy of the spigot,[5] as one that was never accustomed to strike up the drum and to cry in blazing martial exploits, 'alarm', but when he were half tipsy, as Horace recordeth.[6] The other three, over this that their verses in camfering° wise run harsh and rough, perform nothing in matter but biting quips, taunting darkly certain men of state that lived in their age, besprinkling their invectives with some moral precepts answerable to the capacity of every weak brain. But our Virgil, not content with such meagre stuff, doth labour in telling, as it were, a Canterbury Tale[7] to ferret out the secrets of nature with words so fitly couched, with verses so smoothly slicked, with sentences so featly° ordered, with orations so neatly burnished, with similitudes so aptly applied, with each decorum so duly observed, as in truth he hath in right purchased to himself the name of a surpassing poet, the fame of an odd° orator, and the admiration of a profound philosopher.

Having therefore, my good Lord, taken upon me to execute some part of Master Ascham his will, who in his golden pamphlet, entitled *The Schoolmaster*, doth wish the university students to apply their wits in beautifying our English language with heroical verses,[8] I held no Latinist so fit to give thee onset on as Virgil, who, for his peerless style and matchless stuff, doth

---

[4] cheat] coarse, poor quality; figuratively, from cheat bread.

[5] nappy of the spigot] intoxicated from the beer-barrel.

[6] Horace, *Epistles* 1.19.7–8: 'Father Ennius himself never leaped up to write about war unless he was drunk'. Quintus Ennius (*c.* 239 - *c.*169 BC) was often regarded as the father of Roman poetry.

[7] Canterbury Tale] i.e. a pleasing fiction.

[8] Ascham [. . .] heroical verses] Although Ascham, like Stanyhurst, deplored native English metre ('rhyme') he recognised, unlike Stanyhurst, that hexameters did not work in English. He agreed that iambics did work, but still expected them to be used quantitatively, which was why he failed to understand Surrey's experimental use of blank verse; see *The Schoolmaster*, STC 832, sigs S1^{r}-S1^{v}, images 67–68.

bear the prick and price[9] among all the Roman poets. Howbeit I have here half a guess that two sorts of carpers will seem to spurn at this mine enterprise: the one utterly ignorant, the other meanly lettered. The ignorant will imagine that the passage was nothing craggy,° inasmuch as Master Phaer[10] hath broken the ice before me; the meaner clerks° will suppose my travail in these heroical verses to carry no great difficulty in that it lay in my choice to make what word I would short or long, having no English writer before me in this kind of poetry with whose square I should level my syllables.[11] To shape, therefore, an answer to the first, I say they are altogether in a wrong box, considering that such words as fit Master Phaer may be very unapt for me, which they would confess if their skill were so much as spare in these verses. Furthermore, I stand so nicely on my pantofles° that way as if I could, yet I would not run on the score[12] with Master Phaer or any other by borrowing his terms in so copious and fluent a language as our English tongue is. And in good sooth, although the gentleman hath translated Virgil into English rhyme[13] with such surpassing excellency as a very few (in my conceit) for picked and lofty words can bourd[14] him, none, I am well assured, overgo him. Yet he hath rather doubled than defalked° ought of my pains, by reason that, in conferring his translation with mine, I was forced to weed out from my verses such choice words as were forestalled by him, unless they were so feeling as others could not countervail their signification. In which case, it were no reason to sequester my pen from their acquaintance, considering that, as Master Phaer were not the first founder so he may not be accounted the only owner of such terms. Truly, I am so far from embezzling his travails as that for the honour of the English I durst undertake to run over these books again and to give them

[9] prick and price] highest accolade and honour.
[10] Phaer] See headnote to **22**. above.
[11] square [. . .] syllables] i.e. since no-one has attempted to use quantitative metre for a translation of Virgil into English before, and there is therefore no template to follow, some people will say that my task is easy because I can decide for myself which syllables in English are long and which are short; 'square' = carpenter's square or set-square.
[12] run on the score] run up a debt.
[13] rhyme] i.e. verse in accentual-syllabic metre, which was seen as a defining feature of rhyming verse, reflected in the variant spelling 'rhythme'; see Puttenham, *Art of English Poesy*, 2.6.
[14] bourd] challenge; the closest sense recorded in the OED is 'joust, tilt'.

a new livery in such different wise as they should not jet° with Master Phaer his badges, ne yet be clad with this apparel wherewith at this present they come forth attired, which I speak not of vanity to enhance my cunning,° but of mere verity to advance the riches of our speech. Morever, in some points of greatest price where the matter, as it were, doth bleed,° I was moved to shun Master Phaer his interpretation, and cling more near to the meaning of mine author in slicing the husk and cracking the shell, to bestow the kernel upon the witty and inquisitive reader. [. . .][15]

Now to come to them that guess my travail to be easy, by reason of the liberty I had in English words (for as I cannot divine upon such books that haply ruck° in students' mews,° so I trust I offer no man injury if I assume to myself the maidenhead of all works that hath been before this time in print, to my knowledge, divulged in this kind of verse), I will not greatly wrangle with them therein. Yet this much they are to consider, that as the first applying of a word may ease me in the first place, so perhaps, when I am occasioned to use the selfsame word elsewhere, I may be as much hindered as at the beginning I was furthered. For example: in the first verse of Virgil I make 'season' long; in another case it would stead° me percase° more if I made it short, and yet I am now tied to use it as long, so that the advantage that way is not very great. But as for the general facility, this much I dare warrant young beginners, that when they shall have some firm footing in this kind of poetry, which by a little painful exercise may be purchased, they shall find as easy a vein in the English as in the Latin verses, yea, and much more easy than in the English rhymes. Touching mine own trial, this much I will discover. The three first books I translated by starts,° as my leisure and pleasure would serve me. In the fourth book I did task myself, and perused the matter somewhat hotly. Master Phaer took to the making of that book fifteen days – I huddled up mine in ten, wherein I covet no praise but rather do crave pardon. For like as fore-littering bitches whelp blind puppies, so I may be perhaps entwited° of more haste than good speed, as Sir Thomas More in like case gibeth at one that made vaunt of certain pilled verses clouted up extrumpery:[16]

---

[15] shell [. . .] kernel] cf. the preface to the KJB, **15d**. 123–24.

[16] certain [. . .] extrumpery] certain wretched verses cobbled together on the spur of the moment ('extrumpery' puns on 'trumpery' [trashy finery] and 'extempore').

Hos quid te scripsisse mones ex tempore versus?
Nam liber hoc loquitur, te reticente, tuus.[17]

But to leave that to the verdict of others (wherein I crave the good liking of the courteous and scorn the controlment° of the currish, as those that usually reprehend most and yet can amend least), the odds between verses and rhyme is very great.[18] For in the one, every foot, every word, every syllable, yea, every letter is to be observed; in the other, the last word is only to be heeded [. . .] Good God, what a fry° of such wooden rhymers doth swarm in stationers' shops, who never instructed in any grammar school, not attaining to the parings of the Latin or Greek tongue, yet like blind bayards[19] rush on forward, fostering their vain conceits with such overweening, silly follies as they reck not to be condemned of the learned for ignorant, so they be commended of the ignorant for learned. The readiest way, therefore, to flap° these drones from the sweet-scenting hives of poetry is for the learned to apply themselves wholly (if they be delighted with that vein) to the true making of verses in such wise as the Greeks and Latins, the fathers of knowledge, have done, and to leave to these doltish coistrels° their rude rhyming and balductum° ballads.

To the Learned Reader.

In the observation of quantities of syllables some haply will be so stiffly tied to the ordinances of the Latins as what shall seem to swerve from their maxims they will not stick to score up for errors. In which resolution such curious° Priscianists[20] do attribute greater prerogative to the Latin tongue than reason will afford, and less liberty to our language than nature may permit. For inasmuch as the Latins have not been authors of these verses, but traced in the steps of the Greeks, why should we with the strings of the Latin rules cramp our tongue more than the Latins

[17] More, *Epigrams* (1518), p. 261 ('Why do you announce that you wrote these verses *extempore*? Your book tells us that without your saying a word.')
[18] odds [. . .] great] 'Verse' had a more elevated sense than it does in modern usage and was usually reserved for poetry in classical metre; see Wither, **16a**. 19 above.
[19] blind bayards] see **3**. 310 above.
[20] Priscianists] grammatical pedants. Priscian was the author of the Latin grammar which became a standard text in the Middle Ages.

do fetter their speech, as it were, with the chains of the Greek precepts. Also, that nature will not permit us to fashion our words in all points correspondent to the Latinists may easily appear in such terms as we borrow of them. For example, the first of *breviter* is short, the first of 'briefly' with us must be long. Likewise, *sonans* is short, yet 'sowning' in English must be long, and much more if it were 'sounding', as the ignorant generally, but falsely, do write. Nay, that whereat I wonder more, the learned trip their pens at this stone insomuch as Master Phaer in the very first verse of Virgil mistaketh the word. Yet 'sound' and 'sowne' differ as much in English as *solidus* and *sonus* in Latin [. . .] And, soothly, to my seeming, if the conjuction 'and' were made common in English it were not amiss, although it be long by position, for the Romans are greatly advantaged by their words *et*, *que*, *quoque*, *atque*, which were they disjointed from the Latin poetry, many good verses would be ravelled and dismembered that now carry a good grace among them, having their joints knit with these copulative sinews.[21]

But to rip up° further the peculiar property of our English, let us listen to Tully his judgement, wherein though he seem very peremptory, yet with his favour he misseth the cushion. Thus in his book entitled *Orator* he writeth, *Ipsa natura, quasi modularetur hominum orationem, in omni verbo posuit acutam vocem, nec una plus, nec a postrema syllaba citra tertiam*[22]. In this saying Tully observeth three points: first, that by course of nature every word hath an accent; next, one only; lastly, that the said accent must be on the last syllable, as *propè*, or on the last saving one, as *virtûtis*, or, at the furthest, on the third syllable, as *omnîpotens*. Yet this rule taketh no such infallible effect with us, although Tully maketh it natural, who by the skill of the Greek and Latin did aim at other languages to him unknown, and therefore is to

[21] ravelled [. . .] sinews] Anatomical and corporeal metaphors were used metaphorically in the context of prosody by other contemporary poets; cf. Spenser in the epistle to Harvey prefacing *The Shepheardes Calender*: 'Now for the knitting of sentences, which they call the ioynts and members thereof', *The Shorter Poems*, ed. by Richard A. McCabe (London: Penguin, 1999), p. 28. On joints and sound, see Bruce R. Smith, *The Acoustic World of Early Modern England* (Chicago: University of Chicago Press, 1999), pp. 96–129.

[22] *Ipsa natura* [. . .] *tertiam*] Cicero, *Orator*, 18.58: 'Nature herself, as if to regulate human speech, has placed an accent – no more than one – in every word, and it is never further than the third syllable from the end'.

be born withal. As 'peremptory' is a word of four syllables and yet the accent is on the first, so 'sêcondary', 'ôrdinary', 'mâtrimony', 'pâtrimony', 'plânetary', 'împerative', 'côsmography', 'ôrthography', with many like. For although the ignorant pronounce 'impêrative', 'cosmôgraphy', 'orthôgraphy', giving the accent to the third syllable, yet that is not the true English pronunciation. Now put case° the cantle° of the Latin verse *sapiens dominabitur astris* were thus Englished, 'planetary workings the wiseman's virtue represseth', albeit the middle of *planeta* be long with the Romans, yet I would not make it scrupulous to shorten it in English by reason the natural pronunciation would have it so. For the final end of a verse is to please the ear, which must needs be the umpire of the word, and according to that weight our syllables must be poised.[23] Wherefore, sith the poets themselves avouch *tu nihil invita facies dicesve Minerva*,[24] that nothing may be done or spoken against nature, and that art is also bound to shape itself by all imitation to nature, we must request these grammatical precisians that as every country hath his peculiar law, so they permit every language to use his particular law.

40. N. W., in Samuel Daniel, *The Worthy Tract of Paulus Jovius* (1585)

['N.W.' remains unidentified and may be a pseudonym for Daniel himself. Samuel Daniel (1562/63–1619) was educated at Magdalen Hall, Oxford, where he became friends with John Florio, later marrying his sister. One of the most important poets of the great literary decade of the 1590s, Daniel was widely read by Shakespeare. He made his name with the sonnet sequence

---

[23] weight [. . .] poised] i.e. according to that measure our syllables should be weighed. Stanyhurst's point that aesthetic effect should have priority over the rules of poetry, as nature should over art, and that each language has its own rules, does little to support his case for classical metres in English. A similar argument is advanced in Samuel Daniel's *Defence of Ryme*; see Neil Rhodes, 'Framing and Tuning in Renaissance English Verse', in *Renaissance Transformations: The Making of English Writing and its World* (1480–1650), ed. by Margaret and Thomas Healy (Edinburgh: Edinburgh University Press, 2009), pp. 32–47.

[24] Horace, *Art of Poetry*, l. 385.

Delia (1591) and further established his reputation as a poet with *The Civil Wars* (1594), which left its mark on Shakespeare's Histories. His thinking about literature is reflected in *Musophilus* (1599) and the *Defence of Ryme* (1603), which makes a forceful case for the tradition of native English verse. These works show traces of the influence of Montaigne and he contributed a dedicatory poem to Florio's translation of the *Essayes* (1603) (see below **47**. 369–458).

Paolo Giovio (1483–1532) was an Italian physician employed by the Medici family who in later life amassed an impressive collection of paintings and antiquities. He is best known as a historian of the Italian wars. The *Dialogo dell'imprese militari et amorose* (1555), a series of emblems with mottoes, was Giovio's last published work and the English translation Daniel's first. It gave him an opportunity to put to use the Italian he would have learned from Florio. Italian language editions of Giovio's work were published at Venice and Lyon, the last being Lyon (1574).

See Joan Rees, *Daniel: A Critical and Biographical Study* (Liverpool: Liverpool University Press, 1984); John Pitcher in *ODNB*]

To his good friend Samuel Daniel, N. W. wisheth health.[1]

There is another point in your last letter wherein you seem to mar all that you have made and dash that which so cunningly was devised. Forsooth, you blush to open another man's shop and sell Italian wares as though you were a bankrupt in philosophy and could not afford any pretty conceit without borrowing and embezzling. I pray you, sir, shall Castilio be more reverenced for his courtier than Dr Clerke[2] admired for investing him with so courtly robes? Shall Menander be eternised for his comedies and Terence forgot who gave them credit?[3] Shall Lambin, Cardan, and Scaliger, and the most excellent secretaries of nature, Pliny,

[1] The dedicatory letter is signed 'from Oxenford'.

[2] Clerke] Bartholomew Clerke's Latin translation of Castiglione's *Il Cortegiano* (1571) was more successful than Hoby's English version, going through six editions to 1612.

[3] Roman comedy was indebted to the Greek New Comedy of Menander. On Terence as 'translator' see Cicero, *De Finibus* 1.2.5 and cf. Humphrey **29**. 665.

Matthiolus, and Tolet,[4] shall they be less reverenced for perfecting knowledge than the old philosophers for a shadowed° invention? Shall the wit and capacity of antiquity sit in her throne and disposition and judgement of posterity keep the door? No reason: the one devised, the other disposed.[5] Jovius therefore is bound unto you both for absoluting[6] and blazing° his inventions abroad in this famous island, and we are beholding unto you for revealing them to us, wherein truly both art in translating and knowledge in judging justly may challenge their foes. You cannot forget that which Nolanus (that man of infinite titles among other fantastical toys) truly noted by chance in our schools, that by the help of translations all sciences had their offspring, and in my judgement it is true.[7] The Hebrews hatched knowledge, Greece did nourish it, Italy clothed and beautified it, and the arts which were left as wards in their minority to the people of Rome, by translators as most careful gardeners, are now deduced° to perfect age and ripeness.

Concerning the nakedness of your style, which troubleth you without the colours or flourish of rhetoric, Tully commendeth it, all translators approve it, and no man maketh so much account of the gloss as of the substance, of the gay ivy bush[8] as of the wine. Neither could it prejudice you at all (if it were naked as indeed it is pure) because you have not done it as the Sybaritae,[9]

---

[4] Lambin [. . .] Tolet] With the exception of Pliny (see **45.** and **46.**) these are all modern scholars and scientists: Denis Lambin was a French classical scholar; Girolamo Cardano an Italian mathematician, physician, and scientist; Julius Caesar Scaliger was the author of the *Poetices*, as well as scientific works, and his son Joseph was a classical scholar; Pietro Mattioli was an Italian physician and botanist; Toletus (Francisco de Toledo) published commentaries on Aristotle during the 1570s. ('[S]ecretaries of nature' = those acquainted with the secrets of nature.)

[5] devised [. . .] disposed] The distinction is between invention and disposition, the first two parts of rhetoric.

[6] absoluting] Probably 'giving independence to', but not recorded as a verb in the OED.

[7] Nolanus [. . .] true] Giordano Bruno (1548–1600) was born at Nola in Campania. His remarks on translation are also quoted by Florio (see **47.** 205–7), but there is no trace of them in his extant writings; see Angelo M. Pellegrini, 'Giordano Bruno on Translations', *ELH*, 10 (1943), 193–207.

[8] ivy-bush] Used as a tavern sign to show that wine was sold.

[9] Sybaritae] Inhabitants of the early Greek colony of Sybaris in southern Italy which became a byword for luxury.

that bade their guests a whole year before the feast to make some expectation of a sumptuous banquet. A toy° would require all bravery,° vanity all ornaments, and an ass had need of all his trappings, but your argument is such as can both move and delight, tickle the ear and satisfy the mind. And our time also hath learned to loathe that odd rhyming vein and to persecute the letter[10] is clean out of fashion, which began by a bad portraiture of wit and is ended by a ripe direction of judgement. But why do I rather answer the captious than satisfy the grave and modest, who at the first view (I dare presume upon their wisdom) will subscribe to the supremacy of the wit of your new science. For if courtiers are inwardly ravished in viewing the picture of Fiammetta which Boccace limned°; if ladies entertain Bandello or Ariosto in their closets; if lovers embrace their physician, Ovid, in extremity of their passion;[11] then will gentlemen of all tribes much rather honour your *impresa*° as a most rare jewel and delicate *Enchiridion.*°

41. John Harington, *Orlando Furioso in English Heroical Verse* [Ariosto] (1591)

[Sir John Harington (1560–1612) was the godson of Queen Elizabeth and William Herbert, 2nd Earl of Pembroke. He was educated at Eton and King's College, Cambridge, which he entered in 1576, graduating in 1578. While at Cambridge he was given advice by William Cecil to follow Cheke's method of double translation to develop facility of expression. In addition to his translation of Ariosto Harington wrote epigrams in imitation of Martial, presenting a collection to Lucy, Countess

[10] persecute the letter] use excessive alliteration; cf. Spenser in the preface to *The Shepheardes Calender*: 'I scorne and spue out the rakehellye route of our ragged rymers (for so themselues vse to hunt the letter)', *The Shorter Poems*, ed. by McCabe, p. 28, and Sidney on 'coursing of a letter', *Apology for Poetry*, ed. by Shepherd, rev. by Maslen, p. 113.

[11] Fiammetta [. . .] Ovid] 'Boccace' or 'Bocace' was the usual English spelling of Boccaccio in the sixteenth century. His *Elegia di Madonna Fiammetta*, in which Fiammetta confesses her passion for Panfilo, was not translated into English until 1587. Some of Bandello's *novelle* in the Boccaccio tradition appeared in English versions in Painter's *Palace of Pleasure* (see **35.**) and Ariosto's *Orlando Furioso* was translated by Harington (see **41**.). Ovid acted as the lover's 'physician' in *Remedia amoris*.

of Bedford (dedicatee of Florio's Montaigne), and published a frivolous treatise on sanitary plumbing, *The Metamorphosis of Ajax* (1596). In 1604 he presented a translation of *Aeneid* 6 to King James, whose accession to the English throne he had advocated before Elizabeth's death.

The epic romance *Orlando Furioso*, first published in 1516 and in a third and final version in 1532, was a sixteenth-century best-seller, but it was also given the status of a modern classic, on a par with the *Aeneid.* This view was challenged by neo-Aristotelians, but it gained currency outside Italy in the second half of the century and is echoed by Harington in his preface. Harington's 'apology' is constructed as a general defence of poetry and borrows both from Sidney and from Minturno's *L'arte poetica* (1563). The translation was supposedly undertaken as a penance imposed upon him by Queen Elizabeth for having circulated a risqué version of canto 28 (on Fiammetta) among her ladies-in-waiting. It was expensively published by Richard Field with illustrations and elaborate notes, some personal, which Harington justifies in his preface. This was the first complete translation of Ariosto's poem into English.

See Townsend Rich, *Harington and Ariosto: A Study in Elizabethan Verse Translation* (New Haven: Yale University Press, 1940); *Orlando Furioso, Translated into English Heroical Verse by Sir John Harington (1591)*, ed. by Robert McNulty (Oxford: Clarendon Press, 1972); Daniel Javitch, *Proclaiming a Classic: The Canonisation of Orlando Furioso* (Princeton, NJ: Princeton University Press, 1991); Brian Vickers, ed., *English Renaissance Literary Criticism* (Oxford: Clarendon Press, 1999); Jason Scott-Warren, *Sir John Harington and the Book as Gift* (Oxford: Oxford University Press, 2001); Gavin Alexander, ed., *Sidney's 'The Defence of Poesy' and Selected Renaissance Literary Criticism* (London: Penguin, 2004).]

Now remains the third part of it, in which I promised to speak somewhat for myself, which part, though it have most need of an apology both large and substantial, yet I will run it over both shortly and slightly, because indeed the nature of the thing itself is such that the more one doth say, the less he shall seem to say; and men are willinger to praise that in another man which himself shall debase° than that which he shall seem to maintain.°

Certainly, if I should confess or rather profess that my verse is unartificial,° the style rude, the phrase barbarous, the metre unpleasant, many more would believe it to be so than would imagine that I thought them so. For this same *philautia* or self-pleasing is so common a thing as the more a man protests himself to be free from it, the more we will charge him with it. Wherefore let me take thus much upon me that admit it have many of the forenamed imperfections, and many not named, yet as writing goes nowadays it may pass among the rest. And as I have heard a friend of mine (one very judicious in the beauty of a woman) say of a lady whom he meant to praise that she had a low forehead, a great nose, a wide mouth, a long visage, and yet all these put together she seemed to him a very well-favoured woman, so I hope, and I find already some of my partial friends, that what several imperfections soever they find in this translation, yet taking all together they allow it, or at least wise they read it, which is a great argument of their liking.

Sir Thomas More, a man of great wisdom and learning, but yet a little inclined (as good wits are many times) to scoffing,[1] when one had brought him a book of some shallow discourse and pressed him very hard to have his opinion of it, advised the party to put it into verse. The plain-meaning man, in the best manner he could, he did so, and a twelve-month after at the least came with it to Sir Thomas, who slightly perusing it gave it this *encomium*, that now there was rhyme in it, but afore it had neither rhyme nor reason.[2] If any man had meant to serve me so, yet I have prevented° him, for sure I am he shall find rhyme in mine, and if he be not void of reason, he shall find reason too. Though for the matter I can challenge no praise, having but borrowed it, and for the verse I do challenge none, being a thing that everybody that never scarce baited° their horse at the university take upon them to make. It is possible that if I would have employed that time that I have done upon this, upon some invention of mine own, I could have by this made it have risen to a just volume, and if I would have done as many spare not to do, flown

[1] During the Elizabethan period More's reputation outside Catholic circles was that of jester rather than saint; see for example Nashe, *Works*, III, 317.

[2] rhyme nor reason] An old saying which appears in John Heywood's *Dialogue of Proverbs* (1546). Heywood makes a similar joke about 'ryme without reason, and reason without ryme' in his *Epigrammes* (1550), STC, 13294.5, sig. A1^{v}, image 3.

very high with stolen feathers.[3] But I had rather men should see and know that I borrow all than that I steal any, and I would wish to be called rather one of the not worst translators than one of the meaner makers.[4] Specially sith the Earl of Surrey and Sir Thomas Wyatt, that are yet called the first refiners of the English tongue, were both translators out of Italian.[5]

Now for those that count it such a contemptible and trifling matter to translate, I will but say to them as Master Bartholomew Clerke,[6] an excellent learned man and a right good translator, sayeth in manner of a pretty challenge in his preface (as I remember) upon *The Courtier*, which book he translated out of Italian into Latin: 'You', sayeth he, 'that think it such a toy,° lay aside my book and take my author in your hand and try a leaf or such a matter and compare it with mine'. If I should say so, there would be enow° that would quickly put me down, perhaps, but doubtless he might boldly say it, for I think none could have mended him. But as our English proverb sayeth, 'many talk of Robin Hood that never shot in his bow', and some correct *Magnificat* that know not *quid significat*.[7]

For my part, I will thank them that will amend anything that I have done amiss, nor I have no such great conceit of that I have done but that I think much in it is to be mended; and having dealt

---

[3] Harington mixes the myth of Icarus, who tried to fly with wings attached to his body by wax, with Aesop's fable of the crow, who dressed up in feathers borrowed from a peacock. This combines overreaching with plagiarism.

[4] makers] 'poets', from Greek *poiētēs*, which literally means a 'maker'. On whether translators may be termed 'poets', see Alexander, *Selected Renaissance Literary Criticism*, pp. 262, 418.

[5] Wyatt and Surrey had both translated some of Petrarch's sonnets from the *Canzoniere* and had imitated his translations of the penitential Psalms. Surrey's pioneering use of blank verse in *The Fourth Boke of Virgill* (1554), which the publisher described on the title page (STC 24810a) as a 'strau[n]ge metre', was indebted to Italian *versi sciolti*.

[6] Clerke] see 'N. W', **40**. 8.

[7] *quid significat*] i.e. some will venture to correct the Latin of the Magnificat (the song of Mary at the Visitation) when they don't even know what it means. On Robin Hood cf. **37**. 36 above; on correcting *Magnificat* cf. Gabriel Harvey *in Three Proper and Wittie Familiar Letters* (1580), in *Elizabethan Critical Essays*, ed. by G. Gregory Smith, 2 vols (London: Oxford University Press, 1904), I, 117, 378. On Harvey's use of the expression in his criticism of Spenser's experiments with classical metre, see Richard Helgerson, *Forms of Nationhood: The Elizabethan Writing of England* (Chicago: University of Chicago Press, 1992), pp. 27–28.

plainly with some of my plain-dealing friends to tell me frankly what they heard spoken of it (for indeed I suffered some part of the printed copies to go among my friends, and some more perhaps went against my will), I was told that these in effect were the faults were found with it. Some grave men misliked that I should spend so much good time on such a trifling work as they deemed a poem to be.

Some more nicely° found fault with so many two-syllabled and three-syllabled rhymes. Some (not undeservedly) reproved the fantasticalness° of my notes, in which they say I have strained myself to make mention of some of my kindred and friends that might very well be left out. And one fault more there is which I will tell myself, though many would never find it, and that is, I have cut short some of his cantos in leaving out many staves° of them, and sometimes put the matter of two or three staves into one. To these reproofs I shall pray you, gentle and noble readers, with patience hear my defence, and then I will end.

For the first reproof, either it is already excused or it will never be excused, for I have, I think, sufficiently proved both the art to be allowable and this work to be commendable. Yet I will tell you an accident° that happened unto myself. When I was entered a pretty way into the translation, about the seventh book, coming to write that where Melissa in the person of Rogero's tutor comes and reproves Rogero in the fourth staff:°

> Was it for this that I in youth thee fed
> With marrow? etc.,

and again:

> Is this a means or ready way you trow
> That other worthy men have trod before,
> A Caesar or a Scipio to grow? etc.,[8]

straight I began to think that my tutor,[9] a grave and learned man and one of a very austere life, might say to me in like sort: 'Was it for this that I read Aristotle and Plato to you, and instructed you so carefully both in Greek and Latin, to have you now become a translator of Italian toys?' But while I thought thus, I

[8] See Harington, *Orlando Furioso in English Heroical Verse*, STC 746, sigs I3^{v}–I4^{r}, image 36 [Book 7, stanzas 49, 51].

[9] **Marg.** Samuel Fleming of King's College in Cambridge.

was aware that it was no toy that could put such an honest and serious consideration into my mind.

Now for them that find fault with polysyllable metre,[10] methinks they are like those that blame men for putting sugar in their wine, and chide too bad about it and say they mar all, but yet end with God's blessing on their hearts. For indeed, if I had known their diets I could have saved some of my cost, at least some of my pain, for when a verse ended with 'civility', I could easier, after the ancient manner of rhyme, have made 'see' or 'flee' or 'decree' to answer it, leaving the accent upon the last syllable, than hunt after three-syllabled words to answer it with 'facility', 'gentility', 'tranquility', 'hostility', 'scurrility', 'debility', 'agility', 'fragility', 'nobility', 'mobility', which who mislike may taste lamp oil[11] with their ears. And as for two-syllabled metres, they be so approved in other languages that the French call them the feminine rhyme, as the sweeter, and the one-syllable the masculine.[12] But in a word to answer this, and to make them forever hold their peaces of this point, Sir Philip Sidney not only useth them but affecteth° them: 'signify', 'dignify'; 'shamed is', 'named is', 'blamed is'; 'hide away', 'bide away'. Though if my many blotted papers that I have made in this kind might afford me authority to give a rule of it, I would say that to part them with a one-syllable metre between them would give it best grace. For as men use to sow with the hand and not with the whole sack, so I would have the ear fed but not cloyed with these pleasing and sweet falling metres.

For the third reproof about the notes,[13] sure they were a work (as I may so call it) of supererogation,° and I would wish sometimes they had been left out, and the rather if I be in such fair possibility to be thought a fool or fantastical° for my labour. True it is, I added some notes to the end of every canto, even as if some of my friends and myself reading it together (and so it fell

[10] See Puttenham, *Art of English Poesy*, 2.13.

[11] may taste [. . .] ears] may think these words sound as though they have been laboured over in the small hours.

[12] Chapman asserts the superiority of English monosyllables over French and Italian polysyllabic rhymes in the preface to *The Iliads of Homer*, see **44c**. 82–97.

[13] the notes] Harington describes the notes as being of four kinds: on the moral, the history, the allegory, and the allusions. Many are taken from Simon Fornari's commentary on Ariosto (Florence, 1549–50); see Rich, *Harington and Ariosto*, p. 148.

out indeed many times) had after debated upon them what had been most worthy consideration in them, and so oft-times immediately I set it down. And whereas I make mention here and there of some of mine own friends and kin, I did it the rather because Plutarch in one place, speaking of Homer,[14] partly lamenteth and partly blameth him that, writing so much as he did, yet in none of his works there was any mention made or so much as inkling to be gathered of what stock he was, of what kindred, of what town, nor, save for his language, of what country. Excuse me then if I, in a work that may perhaps last longer than a better thing, and, being not ashamed of my kindred, name them here and there to no man's offence, though I meant not to make everybody so far of my counsel why I did it, till I was told that some person of some reckoning noted° me of a little vanity for it; and thus much for that point.

For my omitting and abbreviating some things, either in matters impertinent° to us or in some too tedious flatteries of persons that we never heard of, if I have done ill I crave pardon, for sure I did it for the best. But if any being studious of the Italian would for his better understanding compare them, the first six books, save a little of the third, will stand him in stead. But yet I would not have any man except° that I should observe his phrase so strictly as an interpreter, nor the matter so carefully as if it had been a story, in which to vary were as great a sin as it were simplicity in this to go word for word.

But now to conclude, I shall pray you all that have troubled yourselves to read this my triple apology to accept my labours and to excuse my errors, if with no other thing, at least with the name of youth (which commonly hath need of excuses); and so, presuming this pardon to be granted, we shall part good friends. Only let me entreat you in reading the book ensuing not to do me that injury that a potter did to Ariosto.[15]

[14] The commentary on Homer is not by Plutarch but it dates from the third to fourth centuries AD and was included in some editions of the *Moralia*.

[15] potter [. . .] Ariosto] In the life of Ariosto that follows the poem Harington recounts the story of Ariosto's hearing a potter sing one of the stanzas from his poem in a mangled way and then breaking some of the potter's wares with his walking stick in a rage; STC 746, sigs Nn^{r}-Nn3^{r}, images 218–222.

42. Thomas Danett, *The History of Philip de Commines* (1596)

[Thomas Danett (1543–1601?) was tutored abroad during Mary's reign by John Aylmer, future Bishop of London, and later studied at Gray's Inn and Jesus College, Cambridge. He was employed on diplomatic missions in France and Spain in the service of Robert Dudley, Earl of Leicester, in the 1560s and 1570s and became an MP for Maidstone in 1572. His first publication was *The Description of the Low Countries* (1593), taken from Guicciardini, and his last a history of France up to 1559 (1600). He was related to William Cecil, Lord Burghley, who was also the dedicatee of the *Description of the Low Countries*.

The original translation of Commines was made in 1565 while Danett was still at Cambridge and dedicated to Dudley. He reported in the preface to the expanded printed version that it had been admired by Sir Christopher Hatton and that he had been urged to publish it after Hatton's death. The translation was popular, with four further editions appearing during the seventeenth century.

See Christina DeCoursey in *ODNB*.]

To the Right Honourable, my very good lord, the Lord Burghley

It is now, Right Honourable, thirty years since I presented to Your Lordship and the late Earl of Leicester,[1] my lord and master, the *History* of Commines rudely translated into our vulgar tongue, the which of later times at the request of the late Lord Chancellor, Sir Christopher Hatton,[2] I perused anew and enlarged with such notes and pedigrees° as seemed necessary, as well for explanation as (in some few places) for correction of the *History*. Since his death certain gentlemen to whose hands the

[1] Earl of Leicester] Robert Dudley (1532/33–1588) was, like Cecil, a patron of translation; see Graham Parry, 'Literary Patronage', in *The Cambridge History of Early Modern English Literature*, ed. by David Loewenstein and Janel Mueller (Cambridge: Cambridge University Press, 2002), pp. 121–23.

[2] Christopher Hatton] (*c.* 1540–1591) enjoyed a close personal relationship with Queen Elizabeth and great political power, becoming Lord Chancellor. He was also a patron of writers and scholars, with at least twelve dedications from authors, and actively supported Thomas Churchyard, John Dee, and Barnaby Rich.

book happened to come took so great pleasure and delight therein that they determined to put it to the press, supposing it a great dishonour to our nation that so worthy a history, being extant in all languages, almost, in Christendom, should be suppressed in ours. Notwithstanding their resolution, they forbore of courtesy to put [it] in execution till their purpose should be made known to me. And albeit that I alleged° many reasons why, in my conceit, books of this nature treating of princes' secrets[3] were unfit to be published to the vulgar sort, the rather because the author in some places seemeth to be of that opinion himself, yet none of my reasons could prevail, but they continued in their former determination, adding thereunto that others besides myself had taken pains in this history, and though I of peevishness would suppress my labours, yet they would not suppress theirs. So that would I, nould I, to the press the book must go, being already warranted by public authority thereunto. I, seeing the matter advanced thus far, thought it no time to draw back any longer, but in the end took the burden upon myself, doubting if I had done otherwise, both the blemishing of the *History*, wherein I may boldly say that I have more travailed than any man that hath intermeddled therewith, and also that the work should be presented to some patron that had no interest therein.

Wherefore, having again examined it and freed it from some faults that methought fit to be reformed, I have presumed to publish it under the protection of your lordship's honourable name, to whom of right it appertaineth in many respects. First, because the author thereof was a noble man – one of your own coat° – the wisest and the best acquainted with all matters of state of any man in his time. Whereunto I add that he continued a counsellor successively to so many French kings that he was reputed one of the ancientest counsellors in Christendom at his death; wherein your lordship's fortune is not only correspondent, but hath also surmounted his. Secondarily, your lordship has the eigne° title to it, and lastly the right of survivor casteth it upon you by course of common law.[4] Wherefore, all these

[3] princes' secrets] as Secretary of State, Burghley was the pre-eminent keeper of state secrets; cf. by analogy, 'secretaries of nature', 'N.W.', **40**. 11, and on the vulgarisation of secrets, Dolman, Gale, and Stanyhurst above.

[4] Cecil (1520/21–1598) survived both Dudley and Hatton. Danett's work had the approval of the three most politically powerful men in England in the 1580s.

circumstances well considered (my particular duties also not forgotten), I thought it a kind of sacrilege to suffer Your Lordship to be robbed of your right. May it therefore please you to receive this *History* into your honourable protection as your own, as well in regard of the author being a man of such condition as above is rehearsed, as also of the work, treating of that subject wherewith Your Lordship at this day is better acquainted than any man living; and lastly, in respect of your own title thereunto.

43. Elizabeth Tudor (Queen Elizabeth I), 'Horace's *De Arte Poetica*' (1598)

[Elizabeth's translation of the first 178 lines of Horace's *Art of Poetry* is preserved in a manuscript which also contains Plutarch's moral essay 'On Curiosity', also made in 1598, and Boethius's *On the Consolation of Philosophy*, made in 1593. It was evidently done quickly and there is considerable obscurity in the syntax. The metre is highly irregular, but the basic pattern is poulter's measure, i.e. alternating fourteen- and twelve-syllable lines. Although this was an old-fashioned metre by the late 1590s, Chapman still thought that the fourteener was appropriate as an English equivalent for Greek hexameters in his first published translation of Homer made at the same time. The passage below deals with matters of composition that are particularly relevant to translation: the value and status of old and new words and the best way to enrich the language of the nation. Pettie (**37.**) offers one point of comparison.

See Caroline Pemberton, ed., *Queen Elizabeth's Englishings of Boethius, 'De Consolatione Philosophiae', Plutarch, 'De Curiositate' and Horace, 'De Arte Poetica'* (London: Early English Text Society, 1899); Leicester Bradner, ed., *The Poems of Queen Elizabeth 1* (Providence, RI: Brown University Press, 1964); Janel Mueller and Joshua Scodel, eds., *Elizabeth 1: Translations 1592–1598* (Chicago: Chicago University Press, 2009.]

Take, you that write, a matter such as equals best your skill;
And long do pause, on what your shoulders do refuse,
Or what they bear may, best.[1]
Who, that he chose,[2] best understands
Nor eloquence shall he want, nor order clear.
Nor grace and virtue shall he place (or far I am beyond[3]),
So as, what now be said, or what hereafter should,
Much he defers and, for the present time, omits;
This, love he doth; this scorn – of promised verse, the scribe.[4]
In placing words, if thou be scant° and wary both,
The speech shall flourish well and be esteemed.
Yea, if new word for old, well-soldered[5] thou do place;[6]
Yea, and need be, with new show the hidden gone[7] expound,
To frame may hap some word girdled[8] Cethegi lacked:
A license thou, with shamefast leave, must take.
The new-made words, and feigned, like credit bears,
If from the Greekish spring they softly be withdrawn.[9]
But, Roman, what to Plautus and Caecilius[10] shall he give,
If, from Varius,[11] leave – or Virgil – it be raught?[12]
Why, if I little get, need envied I to be,
When Cato and Ennius'[13] tongue enriched their country' speech,
And new names to their matters gave?

[1] Or [. . .] best] i.e. 'or what they are best able to bear'.

[2] Who [. . .] chose] i.e. 'whoever makes that choice'.

[3] or [. . .] beyond] i.e. 'if I am not mistaken'.

[4] This [. . .] scribe] i.e. 'The writer of the promised poem will love this point and scorn that'.

[5] well-soldered] Elizabeth's term is more expressive than *callida* [. . .] *iunctura* [skillfully joined] in the original.

[6] Lines 11–12 are transposed in many editions of the Latin text, which may explain the convoluted syntax here.

[7] hidden gone] i.e. 'what has disappeared through being hidden' (expanding *abdita* in the original).

[8] girdled Cethes] *cinctutis*: the *cinctus* was a loin-cloth worn by the Romans before the advent of the *tunica*. The Cethes were the Cethegi.

[9] softly be withdrawn] i.e. the water must be drawn sparingly [*parce*].

[10] Ceacilius] Caecilius Statius, a writer of comedies, died *c.* 168 BC.

[11] Varius] Friend of both Virgil and Horace, who described him as a master of epic (*Odes* 1.6).

[12] But [. . .] raught] i.e. 'why should this licence be given to Plautus and Caecilius and taken away from Varius and Virgil'.

[13] Ennius'] See Stanyhurst **39**. 16 above.

It lawful is, and ever shall, a word assign by mark[14] to know.
As primer° leaves of wood first fall and change to nearest year,
So eldered[15] age of words turns, so, to their decay,
And young-men-like, the born-first flourish and increase.
To death we owe ourselves, and all we have:
Whether Neptune by earth be received,
And reineth in, by Northern wind, the sailing ships,
Which is a work and act for kings;
Or whether accustomed marshes, fit for oars,
Feed the cities near, and makes them feel the plough's weight;
Or stream change the course, the foe to fruits,
By learning better way: all mortal deed shall end,
Nor shall our words know honour ought, nor liveliest grace.
Much shall renew that have been fall'n, and then decay
Such words that have been rev'renced well, if use it grant,[16]
On whose beck,° both force and form of speech depends.

44. George Chapman, *The Iliad*

[George Chapman (1559/60–1634) was born in Hitchin in Hertfordshire, which had a grammar school of some repute, though there is no record of his education either there or at university. He did, however, become one of the most learned playwrights of the English Renaissance, compared by some with Ben Jonson, as well as a considerable poet and translator. Most of his work for the stage was performed in the private theatres by the two principal children's companies, the Children of the Chapel and Paul's Boys. His most famous play is *Bussy d'Ambois* (1603–04), which deals with serious political concerns drawn from French history, but he also pioneered the humours' play, popularised by Jonson, and collaborated with Jonson and Chapman on the satirical comedy *Eastward Ho* (1605), which landed him in jail.

[14] mark] Elizabeth's translation disguises the sense of the original, which is that it is lawful to coin words with the current mint mark. In an English context the 'mark' would be Elizabeth's own head.

[15] eldered] Not in the OED, but the sense is obvious.

[16] Much [. . .] grant] i.e. 'many words that have fallen out of use shall be renewed, and such words as have been held in high repute shall decay, if usage so wills it'.

Chapman's translations from Greek reflect a bardic view of poetry which gave him a sense of mission: he would render in English the very origins of western literature in its pure and primitive phase. He followed his Homer with translations of Musaeus (1616), thought at the time to be one of the earliest Greek poets, and Hesiod (1618). The translation of the *Iliad* was done in stages: books 1–2 and 7–11 appeared in 1598, and book 18 in the same year with the title *Achilles Shield*; books 3–6 and book 12 were added in 1608; the rest of the poem was completed in 1611 along with a revised version of books 1 and 2. A complete translation of the *Odyssey* was added to form *The Whole Works of Homer*, published in 1614.

Chapman's source text was the edition by Spondanus (Jean de Sponde) published in Basel in 1583 (USTC 663916), which contained extensive Latin commentaries and a line by line Latin translation by Andreas Divus in parallel with the Greek. Other Latin resources included the prose paraphase by Eobanus Hessus (Basel, 1540) and Johann Scapula's Greek-Latin lexicon (Basel, 1580).

See Franck L. Schoell, *Études sur l'Humanisme continental en Angleterre à la fin de la Renaissance* (Paris: Champion, 1926); *The Poems of George Chapman*, ed. by Phyllis Brooks Bartlett (London: Oxford University Press, 1941); *Chapman's Homer*, ed. by Allardyce Nicoll, 2 vols (London: Routledge & Kegan Paul, 1957); Robin Sowerby, 'Chapman's Discovery of Homer', *Translation and Literature*, 1 (1992), 26–51; Vickers, ed., *English Renaissance Literary Criticism*.]

a) *Seven Books of the Iliads* (1598)

To the Reader

I suppose you to be no mere° reader since you intend to read Homer, and therefore wish I may walk free from their common objections that can only read. When my disorder is seen, that four books are skipped (as a man would say),[1] and yet the poem continued according to the Greek alphabet, viz. that for gamma which is eta and that for delta which is theta etc., then comes my

[1] i.e, books 3–6.

known condemnation more grievously than charity would wish, especially with those that, having no eyes to peruse and judge of the translation and whatsoever the main matter deserves, will be glad to show they see something in finding fault with that form, and peradventure find their queasy stomachs turned at whatsoever is merited in the much-laboured work.

But to him that is more than a reader I write, and so consequently to him that will disdain those easy objections which every speller may put together.[2] The worth of a skilful and worthy translator is to observe the sentences, figures, and forms of speech proposed in his author, his true sense and height,[3] and to adorn them with figures and forms of oration fitted to the original in the same tongue to which they are translated. And these things I would gladly have made the questions of whatsoever my labours have deserved, not slighted with the slight disorder of some books, which, if I can put in as fit place hereafter without check to your due understanding and course of the poet, then is their easy objection answered that, I expect, will be drowned in the foam of their eager and empty spleens. For likelihood of which ability I have good authority that the books were not set together by Homer himself, Lycurgus[4] first bringing them out of Ionia in Greece as an entire poem, before whose time his verses were sung dissevered into many works: one called 'The Battle Fought at the Fleet', another 'Doloniades', another 'Agamemnon's Fortitude', another 'The Catalogue of Ships', another 'Patroclus' Death', another 'Hector's Redemption', another 'The Funeral Games' etc. – all which are the titles of several *Iliads*, and, if those were ordered by others, why may not I challenge as much authority, reserving the right of my precedent?

But to omit what I can say further for reason to my present alteration, in the next edition, when they come out by the dozen, I will reserve° the ancient and common received form. In the meantime do me the encouragement to confer that which I have

---

[2] From the start Chapman defines his audience exclusively and implies that any perceived inadequacies in his work are the fault of the reader rather than the translator.

[3] height] level of style (i.e. low, middle, or high), in this case the high style.

[4] Lycurgus] (*c.* 800 BC), traditionally regarded as the founder of Sparta's *eunomia* (good order). Chapman's source for the story that he discovered the scattered fragments of Homer in Ionia and then organised them is Plutarch's *Life*.

translated with the same in Homer, and, according to the worth of that, let this first edition pass. So shall you do me but lawful favour and make me take pains to give you this emperor of all wisdom (for so Plato will allow him[5]) in your own language, which will more honour it, if my part be worthily discharged, than anything else [that] can be translated. In the meantime, peruse the pamphlet of errors in the impression and help to point the rest with your judgement; wherein, and in purchase of the whole seven, if you be quick and acceptive,° you shall in the next edition have the life of Homer, a table, a pretty comment, true printing, the due praise of your mother tongue above all others for poesy, and such demonstrative proof of our English wits above beyond-sea muses[6] (if we would use them) that a proficient wit should be the better to hear it.

b) Achilles Shield (1598)

To the most honoured earl, Earl Marshal[7]

And this is it, most honoured, that maketh me thus suddenly translate this Shield of Achilles, for since my publication of the other seven books comparison hath been made between Virgil and Homer,[8] who can be compared in nothing more decisal[9] and cutting of all argument than in these two shields. And whosoever shall read Homer throughly and worthily will know the question comes from a superficial and too unripe a reader. For Homer's poems were writ from a free fury, an absolute and full soul; Virgil's out of a courtly, laborious, and altogether imitatory spirit: not a simile he hath but is Homer's; not an invention,

[5] Plato conceded that Homer was the 'educator of Greece' and the 'most poetic and first of the tragic poets', *Republic* 606e.

[6] beyond-sea muses] Chapman is not consistent in his disparagement of foreign influence and refers to his own 'beyond-sea manner of writing', **44b**. 83.

[7] Earl Marshal] the Earl of Essex, who is identified with Achilles.

[8] Virgil and Homer] The main object of Chapman's wrath is Julius Caesar Scaliger, whose *Poetices libri septem* (Lyons, 1561) had compared Virgil with Homer to the detriment of the latter (see Book 5, chapter 3), but this had not been reprinted after the publication of *Seven Books of the Iliads*.

[9] decisal] Not in the OED. It echoes 'cutting' (incisive) but has the sense of 'decisive'.

person, or disposition but is wholly or originally built upon Homerical foundations, and in many places hath the very words Homer useth. [. . .]

But some will convey their imperfections under his Greek shield and from thence bestow bitter arrows against the traduction,° affirming their want of admiration grows from defect of our language not able to express the copy° and elegancy of the original. But this easy and traditional pretext hides them not enough, for how full of height and roundness° soever Greek be above English, yet is there no depth of conceit triumphing in it, but, as in a mere admirer it may be imagined, so in a sufficient translator it may be expressed. And Homer, that hath his chief holiness of estimation for matter and instruction, would scorn to have his supreme worthiness glozing° in his courtship and privilege of tongue.[10] And if Italian, French, and Spanish[11] have not made it dainty,° nor thought it any presumption to turn him into their languages, but a fit and honourable labour and, in respect of their countries' profit and their poesies' credit, almost necessary, what curious,° proud, and poor shamefastness should let° an English muse to traduce him when the language she works withal is more conformable,° fluent, and expressive, which I would Your Lordship would command me to prove against all our whippers of their own complement in their country's dialect.[12]

O what peevish ingratitude and most unreasonable scorn of ourselves we commit to be so extravagant and foreignly witted to honour and imitate that in a strange tongue which we condemn and contemn in our native! For if the substance of the poets will be expressed and his sentence and sense rendered with truth and elocution, he that takes judicial° pleasure in him in Greek cannot bear so rough a brow to him in English, to entomb his acceptance in austerity. [. . .]

But the chief and unanswerable mean° to his general and just acceptance must be Your Lord's high and of all men expected

[10] scorn [. . .] tongue] i.e. would not devalue his supreme worth by insisting that this depends upon the verbal form rather than the matter.

[11] The first complete translation of the *Iliad* into Italian was by Paolo La Badessa Messinese (Padua, 1564); into French by Jean Saxmon (Paris, 1515); and into Spanish by Juan de Mena (Valladolid, 1519).

[12] all [. . .] dialect] i.e. all those who denigrate the sufficiency of their own country's dialect.

precedent, without which he must, like a poor snail, pull in his English horns that out of all other languages (in regard of the country's affection and royalty of his patrons) hath appeared like an angel from a cloud or the world out of chaos, when no language can make comparison of him with ours if he be worthily converted; wherein before he should have been born so lame and defective as the French midwife hath brought him forth,[13] he had never made question how Your Lordship would accept him, and yet have two of their kings embraced him as a wealthy ornament to their studies and the main battle of their armies.

To the Understander.[14]

You are not everybody. To you, as to one of my very few friends, I may be bold to utter my mind. Nor is it more impair° to an honest and absolute man's sufficiency to have few friends than to an Homerical poem to have few commenders, for neither do common dispositions keep fit or plausible consort with judicial and simple honesty, nor are idle capacities comprehensible of an elaborate poem. My 'Epistle Dedicatory' before my *Seven Books* is accounted dark° and too much laboured, for the darkness there is nothing good or bad, hard or soft, dark or perspicuous, but in respect,[15] and in respect of men's light, sleight° or envious perusals (to whose loose capacities any work worthily composed is knit with a riddle). And that the style is material, flowing and not rank,° it may perhaps seem dark to rank° riders or readers that have no more souls than burbolts,[16] but to your comprehension, and in itself, I know it is not. For the affected° labour bestowed in it, I protest two mornings both ended it and the 'Reader's Epistle', but the truth is, my desire and strange disposition in all things I write is to set down uncommon and most profitable coherents for the time, yet further removed from

[13] The first translation of the *Iliad* into English by Arthur Hall (1581), STC 13630, was based on the French of Hugues Salel (Paris, 1545).

[14] Understander] A reader with knowledge and judgement. Chapman was paired with Jonson as a 'laboured and understanding' writer by Webster in the preface to *The White Devil*.

[15] in respect] by comparison.

[16] burbolts] bird-bolts: a blunt-headed arrow used for shooting birds; cf. Udall, *Ralph Roister Doister*, III.ii: 'as much brain as a burbolt'.

abhorred affectation° than from the most popular and cold digestion.[17]

And I ever imagine that as Italian and French poems to our studious linguists win much of their discountried[18] affection, as well because the understanding of foreign tongues is sweet to their apprehension as that the matter and invention is pleasing, so my far-fetched and, as it were, beyond-sea manner of writing, if they would take as much pains for their poor countrymen as for a proud stranger when once they understand it, should be more gracious to their choice conceits than a discourse that falls naked before them and hath nothing but what mixeth itself with ordinary table talk. For my variety of new words I have none inkpot,[19] I am sure you know, but such as I give passport with such authority, so significant and not ill-sounding, that if my country language were an usurer, or a man of this age speaking it, he would thank me for enriching him.[20] Why, alas, will my young master, the reader, affect nothing common and yet like nothing extraordinary? 'Swaggering' is a new word amongst them and round-headed° custom gives it privilege with much imitation, being created, as it were, by a natural prosopopoeia[21] without etymology or derivation. And why may not an elegancy authentically derived and, as I may say, of the upper house,[22] be entertained as well in their lower consultation with authority of art as their own forgeries licked up by nature? All tongues have enriched themselves from their original (only the Hebrew and Greek, which are not spoken amongst us) with good neighbourly borrowing, and as with infusion of fresh air and nourishment of new blood in their still-growing bodies, and why may not ours? Chaucer, by whom we will needs authorise our true English, had more new words for his time than any man needs to devise now,

---

[17] cold digestion] slow-witted understanding.

[18] discountried] deracinated and loving what is foreign (not in the OED).

[19] inkpot] i.e. ink-horn terms; see Pettie **38**. 57.

[20] Chapman combines the financial metaphor (see Hoby **30**. 253–57 and Pettie **38**. 68–76) with that of naturalisation and immigration (see Florio **47**. 415–26), claiming that the translator can naturalise foreign words on his own authority.

[21] prosopopoeia] The rhetorical figure of impersonation: the swaggerers embody the word that they have invented.

[22] upper house] In parliament, the House of Lords, not the House of Commons. The main drift of Chapman's prefaces is to appeal to an intellectual and discerning audience rather than to the common reader.

and therefore for current wits to cry from standing° brains, like a brood of frogs from a ditch, to have the ceaseless, flowing river of our tongue turned into their frog pool, is a song far from their arrogation° of sweetness and a sin [that] would soon bring the plague of barbarism amongst us; which, in faith, needs not be hastened with defences of his ignorant furtherers° since it comes with meal-mouthed° toleration too savagely upon us.

To be short, since I had the reward of my labours in their consummation, and the chief pleasure of them in mine own profit, no young prejudicate° or castigatory brain hath reason to think I stand trembling under the airy stroke of his fevery° censure or that I did ever expect any flowing applause from his dry fingers. But the satisfaction and delight that might probably redound to every true lover of virtue I set in the seat of my own profit and contentment, and if there be anyone in whom this success is enflowered, a few sprigs of it shall be my garland. Since then this never equalled poet is to be understood, and so full of government and direction to all estates – stern anger and the affrights of war bearing the main face of his subject, soldiers shall never spend their idle hours more profitably than with his studious and industrious perusal, in whose honours his deserts are infinite. Counsellors have never better oracles than his lines; fathers have no morals so profitable for their children as his counsels; nor shall they ever give them more honoured injunctions than to learn Homer without book, that being continually conversant in him, his height may descend to their capacities and his substance prove their worthiest riches. Husbands, wives, lovers, friends, and allies, having in him mirrors for all their duties, all sorts of which concourse and society in other more happy ages, have instead of sonnets and lascivious ballads sung his *Iliad*s. Let the length of the verse never discourage your endeavours, for talk our quidditical° Italianists of what proportion soever[23] their strutting lips affect, unless it be in these couplets into which I have hastily translated this *Shield*, they shall never do Homer so much right in any octaves, canzons, canzonets,[24] or with whatsoever fustian° epigraphs they shall

[23] for talk [. . .] soever] i.e. 'however much quibbling Italophiles may talk pretentiously about the various verse forms they prefer'. On 'proportion' and verse form, see Puttenham, *Art of English Poesy*, Book 2.

[24] octaves, canzons, canzonets] i.e. verse forms more suited to lyric poetry.

entitle their measures. Only the extreme false printing troubles my conscience, for fear of your deserved discouragement in the impair of our poet's sweetness, whose general divinity of spirit, clad in my willing labours (envious of none, nor detracting any), I commit to your good nature and solid capacity.

c) *The Iliads of Homer* (1611)

To the Reader

Volumes of like praise I could heap on this,
  Of men more ancient and more learn'd than these;
But since true virtue enough lovely is
  With her own beauties, all the suffrages
Of others I omit; and would more fain
  That Homer for himself should be belov'd,
Who every sort of love-worth did contain.[25]
  Which how I have in my conversion° prov'd,
I must confess I hardly dare refer
  To reading judgements, since so generally
Custom hath made even th' ablest agents err
  In these translations.[26] All so much apply
Their pains and cunnings, word for word[27] to render
  Their patient authors, when they may as well
Make fish with fowl, camels with whales engender,
  Or their tongues' speech in other mouths compel.
For even as different a production
  Ask Greek and English, since as they in sounds
And letters shun one form and unison,
  So have their sense and elegancy bounds
In their distinguished° natures, and require
  Only a judgement to make both consent
In sense and elocution, and aspire
  As well to reach the spirit that was spent

[25] Volumes [. . .] contain] These lines are based on Spondanus (see Schoell, *Études sur l'Humanisme*, pp. 171–72).
[26] **Marg**. Of translation, and the natural difference of dialects necessarily to be observed in it.
[27] word for word] The most famous attack on word for word translation in Horace, *Art of Poetry*, ll. 133–34, which Chapman cites at l. 212.

In his example, as with art to pierce
  His grammar and etymology of words.[28]
But as great clerks can write no English verse,
  Because (alas! great clerks) English affords,
Say they, no height nor copy[29] – a rude tongue
  (Since 'tis their native) – but in Greek or Latin
Their writs are rare, for thence true poesy sprung,
  Though them (truth knows) they have but skill to chat in
Compar'd with that they might say in their own,
  Since thither th'other's full soul cannot make
The ample transmigration to be shown
  In nature-loving poesy.[30] So the brake°
That those translators stick in, that affect
  Their word-for-word traductions (where they lose
The free grace of their natural dialect[31]
  And shame their authors with a forced gloze°)
I laugh to see;[32] and yet as much abhor
  More licence from the words than may express
Their full compression and make clear the author.
  From whose truth, if you think my feet digress,
Because I use needful periphrases,
  Read Valla, Hessus,[33] that in Latin prose
And verse convert him; read the Messines[34]
  That into Tuscan turns him; and the gloze

[28] **Marg**. Ironicè. [The marginal note indicates Chapman's challenge to received opinion that 'rude' English is inferior to classical Greek; however, he sees more divergence between the two languages than do Tyndale (**1**.) and Elyot (**20**.).]

For even [. . .] etymology of words] 'Only a poet's judgement can hope to render the Greek lines effectively in English, aiming both to enter into the spirit of the original and to understand the individual meaning of its words' (Nicoll).

[29] no height nor copy] i.e. neither stylistic gravity nor abundance of language.

[30] This alludes to Pythagoras's doctrine of the transmigration of souls to illustrate Chapman's contention that nature, not art, enables 'poesy to open poesy' (l. 60) and convey its soul into another language. See also Florio, **47**. 286–87. The point here is that over-literal translations are unable to do this.

[31] natural dialect] This is best glossed by Florio: 'every language hath its genius and inseparable form' (**47**. 287–88).

[32] **Marg**. The necessary nearness of translation to the example.

[33] Valla, Hessus] Lorenzo Valla translated Homer into Latin prose (Brescia, 1474) and Eobanus Hessus into Latin verse (Basel, 1540), which Chapman describes as paraphrases (ll. 194–97 below).

[34] Messines [. . .] Tuscan] The Italian translation by La Badessa Messinese.

Grave Salel[35] makes in French as he translates,
  Which (for th'aforesaid reasons) all must do,
And see that my conversion much abates
  The licence they take, and more shows him too,[36]
Whose right not all those great learn'd men have done
  (In some main parts) that were his commentars;[37]
But, as the illustration of the sun
  Should be attempted by the erring stars,
They fail'd to search his deep and treasurous heart.
  The cause was since they wanted the fit key
Of Nature, in their downright strength of art,[38]
  With poesy to open poesy;
Which in my poem of the mysteries
  Reveal'd in Homer I will clearly prove,[39]
Till whose near birth suspend your calumnies
  And far-wide imputations of self-love.
'Tis further from me than the worst that reads,
  Professing me the worst of all that write;
Yet what, in following one that bravely leads,
  The worst may show, let this proof hold the light.
But grant it clear: yet hath detraction got
  My blind side in the form my verse puts on,
Much like a dung-hill mastiff that dares not
  Assault the man he barks at, but the stone
He throws at him takes in his eager jaws
  And spoils his teeth because they cannot spoil.[40]
The long verse[41] hath by proof receiv'd applause
  Beyond each other number, and the foil°

[35] Salel] Hugues Salel translated the first ten books of the *Iliad*; see also **44b**. 52.
[36] more shows him too] reveals his true nature more effectively.
[37] commentars] commentators; the only known use of the word (invented for the rhyme).
[38] **Marg**. The power of nature above art in poesy.
[39] This poem was never published.
[40] detraction [. . .] spoil] The tone and language of Chapman's preface harks back to the verse satire of the 1590s, which was at its height when his first translations of Homer were published, and makes a fierce assault on 'detraction'; cf. John Marston, 'To Detraction', *The Scourge of Villanie* (1598).
[41] long verse] The fourteen syllable line which Chapman had first used in the *Seven Books of the Iliads*.

That squint-eye'd envy[42] takes is censur'd plain.
For this long poem asks this length of verse,
Which I myself ingenuously maintain
Too long our shorter authors to rehearse.
And for our tongue, that still is so impair'd[43]
By travailing linguists[44], I can prove it clear
That no tongue hath the Muses' utterance heard
For verse, and that sweet music to the ear
Struck out of rhyme, so naturally as this.
Our monosyllables[45] so kindly fall
And meet, opposed in rhyme, as they did kiss;
French and Italian, most immetrical,
Their many syllables in harsh collision,
Fall as they break their necks, their bastard rhymes
Saluting as they jostl'd in transition
And set our teeth on edge, nor tunes nor times
Kept in their falls. And, methinks, their long words
Show in short verse, as ·in a narrow place
Two opposites should meet with two-hand swords
Unwieldily, without or use or grace. [. . .]

The Preface to the Reader

Of all books extant in all kinds, Homer is the first and best. No one before his,[46] Josephus affirms, nor before him, sayeth Velleius Paterculus, was there any whom he imitated, nor after him any that could imitate him.[47] And that poesy may be no

[42] squint-eyed'd envy] Cf. Harington, preface to *Orlando Furioso*, STC 746, sig. ¶ii^{v}, image 3: 'every blind corner hath a squint-eyed Zoilus'. The classical source is Plutarch, 'On Envy and Hatred'.

[43] **Marg**. Our English language above all others for rhythmical poesy.

[44] travailing linguists] Chapman puns on 'travail' and 'travel', but this contradicts his earlier comments on his own 'beyond-sea' terms.

[45] our monosyllables] Chapman's defence of English monosyllables ran counter to much contemporary opinion; see Ascham, *Scholemaster*, STC 832, sig. R4^{v}, image 67, citing Quintilian, though Puttenham's approval gives Chapman a precedent; see *Art of English Poesy*, ed. by Whigham and Rebhorn, p. 166. On polysyllabic rhyme cf. Harington **41**. 102–25.

[46] **Marg**. All books of human wisdom.

[47] The Jewish historian Flavius Josephus in *Against Apion*, 1. 2; Velleius Paterculus wrote a history of Rome beginning with the dispersal of the Greeks after the siege of Troy.

cause of detraction from all the eminence we give him, Spondanus, preferring it to all arts and sciences, unanswerably argues and proves.[48] For to the glory of God and the singing of his glories, no man dares deny, man was chiefly made. And what art performs this chief end of man with so much excitation and expression as poesy – Moses, David, Solomon, Job, Isaiah, Jeremiah, etc. chiefly using that to the end abovesaid? And since the excellence of it cannot be obtained by the labour and art of man, as all easily confess it, it must needs be acknowledged a divine infusion. To prove which, in a word, this distich, in my estimation, serves something nearly:

> Great Poesy, blind Homer, makes all see
> Thee capable of all arts, none of thee.

For out of him, according to our most grave and judicial° Plutarch, are all arts deduced,° confirmed, or illustrated.[49] It is not therefore the world's vilifying of it that can make it vile, for so we might argue and blaspheme the most incomparably sacred. It is not of the world indeed, but (like truth) hides itself from it. Nor is there any such reality of wisdom's truth in all human excellence as in poets' fictions – that most vulgar and foolish receipt of poetical licence [50] being of all knowing men to be exploded (accepting it as if poets had a tale-telling privilege above others), no artist being so strictly and inextricably confined to all the laws of learning, wisdom, and truth as a poet. For were not his fictions composed of the sinews and souls of all those, how could they differ far from and be combined with eternity? To all sciences, therefore, I must still (with our learned and ingenious Spondanus) prefer it, as having a perpetual commerce with the divine majesty, embracing and illustrating all his most holy precepts and enjoying continual discourse with his thrice perfect and most comfortable spirit. And as the contemplative life is most worthily and divinely preferred by Plato to the

[48] See the essay *De Origine et dignitate poeticae* in the prefatory material to Spondanus's edition, which provides the source for much of Chapman's material (Schoell, *Études sur l'Humanisme*, p.172).

[49] The reference is to the pseudo-Plutarchan essay on the life and poetry of Homer, *De Homero*.

[50] poetical licence] This freedom had nonetheless been endorsed by Quintilian; see *Institutio oratoria*, I.viii.14.

active,[51] as much as the head to the foot, the eye to the hand, reason to sense, the soul to the body, the end itself to all things directed to the end, quiet to motion, and eternity to time, so much prefer I divine poesy to all worldly wisdom.

To the only shadow of whose worth yet I entitle not the bold rhymes of every apish and impudent braggart (though he dares assume anything) – such I turn over to the weaving of cobwebs, and shall but chatter on molehills, far under the hill of the Muses, when their fortunatest self-love and ambition hath advanced them highest. Poesy is the flower of the sun and disdains to open to the eye of a candle. So kings hide their treasures and counsels from the vulgar: *ne evilescant*,[52] sayeth our Spondanus. We have example sacred enough that true poesy's humility, poverty and contempt are badges of divinity, not vanity. Bray then and bark against it, ye wolf-faced worldlings. [. . .] I for my part shall ever esteem it much more manly and sacred in this harmless and pious study to sit till I sink into my grave than shine in your vainglorious bubbles and impieties – all your poor policies, wisdoms, and their trappings at no more valuing than a musty nut. And much less I weigh the frontless° detractions of some stupid ignorants, that no more knowing me than their own beastly ends, and I ever, to my knowledge, blest from their sight, whisper behind me vilifyings of my translation: out of the French, affirming them, when both in French and all other languages but his own, our with-all-skill-enriched poet is so poor and unpleasing that no man can discern from whence flowed his so generally given eminence and admiration. And therefore (by any reasonable creature's conference° of my slight comment and conversion°), it will easily appear how I shun them, and whether the original be my rule or not. In which he shall easily see I understand the understandings of all other interpreters and commenters in places of his most depth, importance, and rapture, in whose exposition and illustration, if I abhor° from the sense that others wrest and rack out of him, let my best detractor examine how the Greek word warrants me.[53] For my other fresh fry,° let them fry in their foolish galls,

[51] Vickers points out that the whole point of *The Republic* is to celebrate 'both philosophical activity and involvement in society', *English Renaissance Literary Criticism*, p. 518.

[52] *ne evilescant*] lest they are debased.

[53] warrants me] justifies my translation.

nothing so much weighed as the barkings of puppies or foisting° hounds, too vile to think of our sacred Homer or set their profane feet within their lives' lengths of his thresholds.

If I fail in something, let my full performance in other some restore me, haste spurring me on with other necessities. For as at my conclusion I protest, so here at my entrance, less than fifteen weeks was the time in which all the last twelve books were entirely new translated, no conference had any with anyone living in all the novelties I presume I have found. Only some one or two places I have showed to my worthy and most learned friend, Master Harriot,[54] for his censure how much mine own weighed: whose judgement and knowledge in all kinds I know to be incomparable and bottomless, yea, to be admired as much as his most blameless life and the right sacred expense of his time is to be honoured and reverenced. Which affirmation of his clear unmatchedness in all manner of learning I make in contempt of that nasty objection often thrust upon me, that he that will judge must know more than he of whom he judgeth; for so a man should know neither God nor himself. Another right learned, honest, and entirely loved friend of mine, Master Robert Hughes, I must needs put into my confessed conference touching Homer, though very little more than that I had with Master Harriot's, which two, I protest, are all, and preferred to all. Nor charge I their authorities with any allowance° of my general labour,[55] but only of those one or two places, which for instances of my innovation, and how it showed to them, I imparted. If any tax me for too much periphrasis or circumlocution in some places, let them read Laurentius Valla and Eobanus Hessus, who either use such shortness as cometh nothing home[56] to Homer, or, where they shun that fault, are ten parts more paraphrastical than I.[57] As for example, one place I will trouble you, if you please, to confer with the original, and one interpreter for all.[58] It is in the end of the third book, and is Helen's speech to Venus, fetching her to Paris

[54] Thomas Harriot (*c*. 1560–1621), mathematician and scientist who was part of the circle of the 'wizard' Earl of Northumberland and Sir Walter Ralegh. Chapman addressed verses to him in the preface to *Achilles' Shield*.

[55] Nor charge I [. . .] labour] 'I do not make them responsible for approving the whole of my work' (Nicoll).

[56] cometh nothing home] does not correspond to.

[57] periphrasis [. . .] paraphrastical] See Udall **7b**. 1–8 and Marbury, **14**. 21.

[58] and one interpreter for all] 'and let this one example serve for all' (Nicoll).

from seeing his cowardly combat with Menelaus.[59] [. . .] And this one example I thought necessary to insert here, to show my detractors that they have no reason to vilify my circumlocution sometimes, when their most approved Grecians, Homer's interpreters, generally hold him fit to be so converted. Yet how much I differ, and with what authority, let my impartial and judicial reader judge, always conceiving how pedantical and absurd an affectation it is in the interpretation of any author – much more of Homer – to turn him word for word, when (according to Horace and other best lawgivers to translators) it is the part of every knowing and judicial interpreter not to follow the number and order of words but the material things themselves, and sentences to weigh diligently, and to clothe and adorn them with words and such a style and form of oration as are most apt for the language into which they are converted. If I have not turned him in any place falsely (as all other his interpreters have in many and most of his chief places); if I have not left behind me any of his sentence,° elegancy, height, intention, and invention; if in some few places (especially in my first edition, being done so long since and following the common tract°) I be something paraphrastical and faulty – is it justice in that poor fault (if they will needs have it so) to drown all the rest of my labour?

But there is a certain envious windfucker[60] that hovers up and down, laboriously engrossing all the air with his luxurious ambition and buzzing into every ear my detraction, affirming I turn Homer out of the Latin only etc., that sets all his associates, and the whole rabble of maligners on their wings with him, to bear about my impair and poison my reputation. One that, as he thinks, whatsoever he gives to others, he takes from himself; so whatsoever he takes from others, he adds to himself. [. . .] If any further edition of these my silly° endeavours shall chance, I will mend what is amiss (God assisting me) and amplify my harsh comment to Homer's far more right, and mine own earnest and

[59] Chapman here compares the Greek with the Latin of both Hessus and Spondanus.

[60] windfucker] windhover or kestrel. This may refer to Jonson. (The term had also been used by Nashe of Harvey; *Works*, III. 62). Jonson's marginal annotations (in Latin) in his copy of Chapman's *The Whole Works of Homer, Prince of Poets* (1616) are sharply critical of Chapman's scholarship. Whatever the level of Chapman's understanding of Greek, it is true that some parts of his translation are versifications of the Latin commentary in his source text.

ingenious love of him. Notwithstanding, I know the curious° and envious will never sit down satisfied. A man may go over and over till he come over and over, and his pains be only his recompense. Every man is so loaded with his particular head, and nothing in all respects perfect but what is perceived by few. Homer himself hath met with my fortune in many maligners, and therefore may my poor self put up with motion. And so little I will respect malignity, and so much encourage myself with mine own known strength and what I find within me of comfort and confirmance° (examining myself throughout with a far more jealous° and severe eye than my greatest enemy, imitating this: *iudex ipse sui totum se explorat ad unguem*,[61] etc.), that after these *Iliads* I will (God lending me life and any meanest means), with more labour than I have lost here and all unchecked alacrity, dive through his *Odyssey*.

45. Philemon Holland, *The Roman History* [Livy] (1600)

[Philemon Holland (1552–1637) was the son of a Protestant clergyman who took his family abroad during Mary's reign. He was educated at Chelmsford grammar school and Trinity College, Cambridge, where he was a Fellow from 1573 to 1579. On marriage he became a schoolmaster in Coventry and began his huge output of translation from the classics when he was nearly fifty. In addition to his Livy and Pliny he published translations of Plutarch's *Moralia* (1603), Suetonius's *History of Twelve Caesars* (1606) and, eventually, Xenophon's *Cyropaedia* (1632), which had originally been commissioned by King James as a gift for Prince Henry (d. 1612). Holland also translated the two principal works of British topography: William Camden's *Britannia* (1610) from Latin into English and John Speed's *The Theatre of the Empire of Great Britaine* (1616) from English into Latin. His commitment to popularising the classics and the sheer weight of his published volumes made him something of a celebrity in his own age, and his work continued to be read up to the nineteenth century.

[61] *iudex* [. . .] *unguem*] Pseudo-Virgil, *De institutione viri boni*; Ausonius, *De viro bono* [On the good man]: 'As a judge he examines himself completely, down to his fingernails'.

Livy's history of Rome, *Ab urbe condita*, covered seven-and-a-half centuries in 142 books and had been widely translated into the modern European vernaculars during the sixteenth century, as well as (supposedly) into Arabic, as Holland mentions. Holland's is the first complete English translation of the surviving thirty-five books and includes an ancient summary of the rest of Livy's work. Livy was closely studied in the Renaissance as a source of lessons in political history, most famously by Machiavelli in his *Discorsi*, which is a treatise on republics presented as a commentary on Livy's text. His reception in Elizabethan England was at different levels: he was read in Latin alongside Tacitus as a source of progressive political ideas by scholars such as Gabriel Harvey, but also popularised in English story collections such as Painter's *Palace of Pleasure* (1566). Holland's translation is scholarly and accurate, though he aims for 'a mean and popular style' and prefers 'old words' to ink-horn terms (ll. 89–90). His copy text is the edition published in Paris in 1573 (USTC 138480), but he says that he has compared this with other Latin editions and modern translations (ll. 77–81).

See also F. O. Matthiessen, *Translation: An Elizabethan Art* (Cambridge, MA: Harvard University Press, 1931), pp. 169–227; Lathrop, *Translations from the Classics*; Peter Culhane, 'Philemon Holland's Livy: Peritexts and Contexts', *Translation and Literature*, 13 (2004), 268–86; Gordon Braden in *OHLTE* (2), pp. 95–97; John Considine in *ODNB*.]

To the Most High and Mighty Monarch, Elizabeth

All my labour whatsoever in translating another man's work I present here unto your Highness and consecrate to the happy and immortal memory of your most sacred Majesty – an attempt, I confess, in regard of mine own imperfections, venturous° and overbold as the first enterprise, right, hard, and exposed to peril. Yet, most worthy and powerful empress, who is there so unsufficient that by the favourable aspect of your countenance may not be graced and enabled? What so difficult and dangerous, which under the fortunate auspices of Your Majesty cannot be effected with ease and pass in safety?

Accept, then, most gracious lady, the first fruits of a few years' study for the benefit enjoyed of life and liberty – an offering as well in that respect as of myself, the meanest of many thousands, under all proportion,[1] but considering either the argument or the first author, not much unfitting. He, in penning the history of the greatest state in his time, for exquisite° eloquence had not his equal, no more than Your Highness in glorious government at this day any second. Such are the incomparable perfections resplendent in your royal person, the wonder of the world.

Vouchsafe also of your accustomed clemency showed to aliens,[2] of your fervent zeal to learning and good letters, wherein, among other rare virtues and singular gifts featured in your heroic mind, no prince cometh near unto Your Excellency to reach forth your gracious hand to T. Livius: who, having arrived long since and conversed as a mere stranger in this your famous island, and now for love thereof learned in some sort the language, humbly craveth Your Majesty's favour to be ranged with other free denizens[3] of that kind, so long to live under your princely protection as he shall duly keep his own allegiance and acquaint your liege subjects with religious° devotion after his manner, with wisdom, policy, virtue, valour, loyalty, and not otherwise. [. . .]

To the Reader.

Now in these thirty-five books, so few as they be, preserved as another Palladium[4] out of a general scare-fire,° we may conceive the rare and wonderful eloquence of our writer in the whole; for the further he proceedeth into a world, as it were, of matter, the more copious still he floweth, and with such variety as that he never iterateth one thing twice, but at every change of new affairs returneth always fresh and gay, furnished with new devices,

[1] under all proportion] i.e. the offering is not proportionate to the benefits he has enjoyed.

[2] clemency [. . .] aliens] On policy towards aliens under Elizabeth see Andrew Pettegree, *Foreign Protestant Communities in Sixteenth-Century London* (Oxford: Clarendon Press, 1986), pp. 278–302.

[3] free denizens] naturalized citizens; cf. Hoby **30**. 265; Florio **47**. 422–26.

[4] Palladium] An ancient image on which the safety of the city was thought to depend; especially, the statue of Pallas Athene that Aeneas brought back to the future site of Rome. This is the first citation in the OED for the extended use of the term as a source of protection or safeguard.

inventions, and phrases, much like a second Antaeus,[5] gathering greater strength and more forces still at every turn; or after the manner of a little rill, which issuing from a small source is maintained with fresh springs and new riverets, and hasting toward the vast ocean, carrieth a deeper channel and broader stream. For the form of his style I refer the readers to the sound and staid judgement rather of Quintilian,[6] who compareth him with Herodotus, Thucydides, and the best Greeks, than to the fantastical conceits of some critics of our time, who, seeking *nodum in scirpo*,[7] have dreamed of I wot not Patavinity[8] in him. What should I speak of that pathetical sprit of his in moving affections? But that which most of all commendeth a history, which being *lux veritatis*[9] ought especially to deliver with sincerity the whole truth and nothing but the truth, without respect of face or person, to keep only to the substance and train of the subject argument, the due and orderly regard of the important circumstances thereto belonging, without inserting extravagant and impertinent by-matters, much less than fabulous tales, therein he hath the prick and price[10] above all others. For neither forbeareth he to reprove (as occasion is offered) the Romans, in whose favour he might be thought to have written, nor doubteth to praise the good parts and the valiant exploits of their mortal enemies. The Gauls he may seem to gall more bitterly upon a sinister affection, glancing at them as he doth in many places for their greedy desire of gold and idle sloth, as not able to endure any long travel, and heat least of all; yet so, as the French now living seem not much offended therewith, for above other nations they have given him

[5] Antaeus] A giant, the son of Poseidon and Gaia who wrestled with Hercules and who drew strength from contact with the earth.

[6] Quintilian] See *Institutio oratoria* X. i. 33. What Quintilian actually says is that Livy's style has too much creamy richness (*lactea ubertas*) for forensic use and that Cicero does not regard Thucydides or Xenophon as useful for the orator either.

[7] *nodum in scirpo*] a knot in a bulrush.

[8] Patavinity] Provincial usage. Pollio had criticised Livy's 'Patavinity'; see Quintilian, *Insttutio oratoria* I. v. 56; VIII. i. 3. 'E. K.' refers to a similar criticism by Valla in the preface to Spenser, *The Shepheardes Calender*. *Patavinus* indicates a native of Patavium (modern Padua), Livy's birthplace.

[9] *lux veritatis*] the light of truth.

[10] prick and price] the highest accolade and honour.

most friendly entertainment and twice enfranchised him among them.[11]

I am not unwilling to touch by the way this principal point and virtue of an historiographer, I mean the delivery of a simple truth in his narrations, for that I have observed in him throughout that he hath been most modest in reporting from others by hearsay anything that soundeth to an untruth, so little deserveth he to be noted with the infamous brand of liar. The wary circumspection of his in that behalf which I dare be bold to recommend unto the reader, I proposed unto myself in making him English, endeavouring by conference° especially of the select copies in Latin, yet not rejecting other translations (such as I had some little skill in) to come as near as possibly I could to the true meaning of the author:[12] making this account, that if I could approve my diligence that way to men of reason and understanding, all other my wants and defects might sooner be passed by and pardoned. A desire I had to perform in some sort that which is profitable to the most, namely an English history of that C.W.,[13] which of all others (if I have any judgement) affordeth most plenteous examples of devout zeal in their kind, of wisdom, policy, justice, valour, and all virtues whatsoever. According to this purpose and intent of mine, I framed my pen not to any affected phrase, but to a mean° and popular style, wherein, if I have called again into use some old words, let it be attributed to the love of my country language. If the sentence be not so concise, couched,° and knit together as the original, loath I was to be obscure and dark. Have I not Englished every word aptly? Each nation hath several manners, yea, and terms appropriate, by themselves. Have I varied in some places from the French or Italian?[14] Censured I

[11] most friendly [. . .] among them] cf. l. 27 above; 'enfranchised' means 'given his liberty' as well as 'naturalised' and both are extensions of the hospitality to strangers *topos* (cf. Tyler **37**. 49). The *Roman History* had been translated into French by Antoine de La Faye (Paris, 1582), USTC 94500, and there had been a number of earlier partial translations.

[12] endeavouring [. . .] author] It seems to have been Holland's regular practice to use multiple sources; on this and translators' use of source texts more generally see Braden in *OHLTE* (2), pp. 95–97.

[13] C. W.] commonwealth.

[14] Italian] The *Roman History* had been translated into Italian in the late fifteenth century by Leonardo Bruni Aretino and a new translation by Iacopo Nardi was published in 1540, USTC 838294.

look to be, and haply reproved, but like as Alcibiades said to one, *pataxon oun kai akouson*, 'Strike hardly, Euribiades, so you hear me speak';[15] even so, say I, find fault and spare not, but withal read the original better before ye give sentence. And howsoever I have faulted otherwise by oversight, set against it my affection and desire to do some good whiles I live to my sweet native country, add thereto the long travail that I have taken to testify the same, and if that will not bring down the balance, let the profit and delight both, which you shall find in the argument and discourse of the history, counterpoise and overweigh my wants, more or less.

And thus I recommend unto my countrymen Livy in English habit: Livy, I say, who whether he were more honoured whiles he lived than beloved at this day of foreign nations, I cannot easily determine. For like as then (by the testimony of St Jerome and Pliny in his *Epistles*)[16] there repaired many great and noble personages from the furthest parts of Spain and France only to see his face for the admiration they conceived of him by the fame of his incomparable eloquence; even so, of late time his spirit (which yet liveth in his writings) hath made a voyage by Florence into the same France and Spain and hath passed as far as into Arabia one way and Almaine° another.[17] In which dissite[18] and remote parts he hath found such kind entertainment, not only in courts of emperors and kings, in palaces of princes and great potentates, but also with the people in general, that they seem to strive no less who may endow him with most ample franchises and free burgessy° than those seven cities in old time who every one challenged to themselves the birth of the poet Homer.[19] Since then he hath thus long been desirous to cross the seas into this

[15] *pataxon* [. . .] speak] According to Plutarch in his *Life of Themistocles* these words were spoken by Themistocles, not Alcibiades, to the Spartan general Euribiades at the war council before the Battle of Salamis.

[16] See Pliny the Younger, *Epistles* VI.20; Jerome refers to Livy in his translation of Eusebius's *Chronicon*.

[17] There were complete translations by Pedro de la Vega into Spanish (Strasbourg, 1552), USTC 440156, and into German by Bernhard Schöfferlin and Ivo Wittich (Mainz, 1505), USTC 691424. The Arabic translation was denounced as a forgery in 1800.

[18] dissite] situated apart, remote; first citation in the *OED*.

[19] seven cities] Argos, Athens, Chios, Colophon, Rhodes, Salamis, and Smyrna all claimed to be the birthplace of Homer.

noble island, not as a traveller to sojourn for a time in the court only or the universities, but to remain here still both in city and country, and thereto hath learned our language indifferently; let it now appear that this nation of ours (like to reap as great fruit and benefit by his acquaintance as any other) is ready also to receive and embrace him as friendly as the rest.

46. Philemon Holland, *The History of the World* [Pliny] (1601)

[Pliny the Elder's encyclopaedia of the natural world, *Naturalis Historia*, was completed in thirty-seven volumes in AD 77 and had considerable indirect influence in the Middle Ages and Renaissance. The first printed edition was published at Venice in 1469 by the German brothers Johann and Wendelin of Speyer. There was an abridgement of the work in a French translation by Pierre de Changy (Paris, 1542), USTC 4035, which was used by I. A. (possibly the printer John Apsley) for the first English translation, *A Summarie of the Antiquities and Wonders of the Worlde* (London, 1566), reprinted in 1585 (STC 20031, 20032). Holland's is the first complete English translation and in his preface he is particularly keen to emphasise that it is intended for all classes of people, arguing that Pliny himself wrote 'in that dialect or idiom which was familiar to the basest clown' (ll. 76–7).]

The Preface to the Reader.

Now albeit my intention and only scope° was to do a pleasure unto them that could not read these authors in the original, yet needs I must confess that even myself have not only gained thereby increase of the Latin tongue (wherein these works were written), but also grown to further knowledge of the matter and argument therein contained. For this benefit we reap by studying the books of such ancient authors: that the oftener we read them over, the more still we find and learn in them. [. . .] Well may the newest songs and last devised plays delight our eyes at the first, and for the present ravish our senses, like as horary[1] and early

[1] horary] lasting only for an hour or a short time (here, fruits that will not keep); predates the first citation in the *OED*.

summer fruits content our taste and please the appetite; but surely it is antiquity that hath given grace, vigour, and strength to writings, even as age commendeth the most generous and best wines. In which regard and upon this experience of mine own, I nothing doubt but they also whom I might justly fear as hard censors° of these my labours, will not only pity me for my pains, but also in some measure yield me thanks in the end; when either by the light of the English (if they be young students) they shall be able more readily to go away with the dark phrase and obscure construction of the Latin; or (being great scholars and taking themselves for deep critics), by conferring the one with the other, haply to espy wherein I have tripped, they shall by that means peruse once again and consequently gather new profit out of that author whom peradventure they had laid by for many years as sufficiently understood. When some benefit (I say) shall accrue unto them likewise by this occasion, I less dread their fearful doom to which so wilfully I have exposed myself. Well I wist that among the Athenians order was taken by law that an interlude° newly acted should be heard with silence and applause, which custom, as it was respective and favourable to the first endeavours of the actors, so it implied an inevitable danger of hissing out and utter disgrace if afterwards they chanced to miss and fail in their parts.[2] Having showed myself once before upon the stage,[3] presuming upon this privilege and the courtesy of the theatre, I might have now sitten still and so rested. In mounting up thus soon again I may seem either in the assured confidence of mine own worthiness to proclaim a challenge to all men's censures; or else upon a deep conceit of some general connivency[4] make reckoning of an extraordinary and wonderful favour. [. . .]

Moreover, the title prefixed thereto, so universal as it is, to wit *The History of the World*, or *Reports of Nature*, imported no doubt that he first penned it for the general good of mankind. Over and besides the argument ensuing, full of variety, furnished with discourses of all matters, not appropriate to the learned only, but accommodate to the rude peasant of the country; fitted

[2] Athenians [. . .] parts] There is no evidence that plays at Athens were granted this indulgence on their first performance.

[3] showed [. . .] stage] i.e. in his translation of Livy.

[4] upon [. . .] connivency] confidently presuming upon general approval ('connivency' is Holland's coinage).

for the painful artisan in town and city; pertinent to the bodily health of man, woman, and child; and in one word, suiting with all sorts of people living in a society and commonweal. To say nothing of the precedent given by the author himself who indited° the same, not with any affected phrase, but sorting well with the capacity even of the meanest and most unlettered; who also translated a good part thereof out of the Greek.[5] What should I allege° the example of former times, wherein the like hath evermore been approved and practised? Why should any man therefore take offence hereat, and envy this good to his natural country, which was first meant for the whole world? And yet some there be so gross as to give out that these and such like books ought not to be published in the vulgar tongue. It is a shame (quoth one) that Livy speaketh English as he doth: Latinists only are to be acquainted with him; as who should say, the soldier were to have recourse unto the university for military skill and knowledge; or the scholar to put on arms and pitch a camp. What should Pliny (sayeth another) be read in English, and the mysteries couched in his books divulged?[6] As if the husbandman, the mason, carpenter, goldsmith, painter, lapidary, and engraver with other artificers were bound to seek unto great clerks or linguists for instructions in their several arts. Certes, such *Momi*[7] as these, besides their blind and erroneous opinion, think not so honourably of their native country and mother tongue as they ought: who, if they were so well affected that way as they should be, would wish rather and endeavour by all means to triumph now over the Romans in subduing their literature under the dent of the English pen, in requital of the conquest sometime over this island, achieved by the edge of their sword.[8] As for our speech, was not Latin as common and natural in Italy as English here with us? And if Pliny faulted not but deserved well of the Roman name, in laying abroad the riches and hidden treasures of nature in that dialect or idiom which was familiar to

---

[5] translated [. . .] Greek] More than three-quarters of Pliny's sources were Greek and included Herodotus, Thucydides, Diodorus Siculus, and Theophrastus.

[6] On the divulging of mysteries and 'secrets' cf. Dolman **28**. 50–51; Stanyhurst **39**. 3; Dannet **42**. 18.

[7] *Momi*] carping critics; cf. James **13**. 68.

[8] Cicero himself had represented translation as conquest when he recommended the seizure of cultural capital from the declining Greeks; see *Tusculan Disputations* 2.1.5. Holland anticipates a future stage in the *translatio imperii*.

the basest clown,° why should any man be blamed for enterprising the semblable to the commodity of that country in which, and for which, he was born?[9] Are we the only nation under heaven unworthy to taste of such knowledge? Or is our language so barbarous that it will not admit in proper terms a foreign phrase? I honour them in my heart, who having of late days trodden the way before me in Plutarch, Tacitus and others, have made good proof that as the tongue in an Englishman's head is framed so flexible and obsequent° that it can pronounce naturally any other language, so a pen in his hand is able sufficiently to express Greek, Latin, and Hebrew.

47. John Florio, *The Essays of Montaigne* (1603)

[John Florio (1553–1625) was the son of an Italian immigrant, who was supported in England by William Cecil and other powerful figures, and an Englishwoman. Between 1578 and 1583 he lived in Oxford where he gave Italian lessons, matriculating at the university in 1581. Here he became friendly with Samuel Daniel and married his sister. His first publications were Italian language manuals and he also produced the first comprehensive Italian dictionary, *A Worlde of Wordes*, in 1598. His ornate prose style and elaborate flattery of patrons were parodied by Donne in *The Courtier's Library*, but some of the newfangled words for which he apologises in the preface to his Montaigne have become part of the common vocabulary of English. Florio's assiduous cultivation of the nobility was finally rewarded in 1604 when he became private secretary and Italian tutor to Queen Anne, to whom the revised Italian dictionary was dedicated in 1611.

Florio probably began his work on Montaigne in 1598 when Sir Edward Wotton asked him to do one chapter and Lucy, Countess of Bedford, got him to do the rest. The work circulated in manuscript before publication and is mentioned by Sir William Cornwallis in his *Essayes* (1600). His exaggeration of the Petrarchan language of compliment is one of several aspects of the prefaces which are liable to parody, but the combination of status anxiety, family romance, the itemisation of every conceivable objection to the practice of translation, and Daniel's poem

[9] enterprising [. . .] born] attempting the same for the benefit of his country.

celebrating the 'intertraffic of the mind', together offer a fascinating overview of the conditions of translation at the end of the sixteenth century. There is no single source text for Florio's Montaigne, as Florio himself says that he used multiple editions while working on his translation in London and in the country (ll. 342–49).

See Frances A. Yates, *John Florio: The Life of an Italian in Shakespeare's England* (Cambridge: Cambridge University Press, 1934); Tom Conley, 'Institutionalizing Translation: On Florio's Montaigne', in *Demarcating the Disciplines: Philosophy, Literature, Art*, ed. by Samuel Weber (Minneapolis: University of Minnesota Press, 1986), pp. 45–58; Warren Boutcher, 'A French Dexterity, & an Italian Confidence', *Reformation*, 2 (1997), 39–109; Christopher Johnson, 'Florio's Conversion of Montaigne, Sidney and Six Patronesses', *Cahiers Elisabéthains*, 64 (2003), 9–18; Neil Rhodes, 'Status Anxiety and English Renaissance Translation' in *Renaissance Paratexts*, ed. by Helen Smith and Louise Wilson (Cambridge: Cambridge University Press, 2011), pp. 107–20.]

To the Right Honourable my best-best benefactors and the most-most honoured ladies, Lucy, Countess of Bedford, and her best-most loved-loving mother, Lady Anne Harington.[1]

Strange it may seem to some, whose seeming is mis-seeming, in one worthless patronage to join two so severally all-worthy ladies. But to any in the right, it would be judged wrong to disjoin them in ought, who never were nearer in kind than ever in kindness. None dearer (dearest ladies) I have seen, and all may say, to your honourable husbands than you; to you than your

[1] Florio dedicated his Montaigne to six noble women. Lucy Russell, Countess of Bedford (1581–1627) was a notable patron of literature, a good linguist, and a poet herself, although none of her work has survived. She was associated with Drayton, Daniel, Jonson, and Donne, and was the dedicatee of many works; Donne addressed several poems to her and also named his daughter after her. Her mother was the wife of John Harington, first Baron Harington of Exton, Rutland (not the translator of Ariosto). The other dedicatees were Elizabeth, Countess of Rutland, Lady Penelope Rich (the 'Stella' of Sidney's *Astrophil and Stella*), Lady Elizabeth Grey and Lady Mary Neville (daughter of Sir Thomas Sackville, author of *Gorboduc*).

honourable husbands; and than to other than either is to the other. So as were I to name but the one, I should surely intend the other, but intending this dedication to two I could not but name both. To my last birth,[2] which I held masculine (as are all men's conceits that are their own, though but by their collecting; and this was to Montaigne like Bacchus, closed in, or loosed from his great Jupiter's thigh[3]), I the indulgent father invited two right honourable godfathers with the one of your noble ladyships to witnesss. So to this defective edition (since all translations are reputed females, delivered at second hand, and I in this serve but as Vulcan to hatchet this Minerva from that Jupiter's big brain), I yet at least a fondling foster-father, having transported it from France to England, put it in English clothes, taught it to talk our tongue (though many times with a jerk[4] of the French jargon) would set it forth to the best service I might, and to better I might not than you that deserve the best.

Yet hath it this above your other servants: it may not only serve you two to repeat in true English what you read in fine French, but many thousands more to tell them in their own what they would be taught in another language. How nobly it is descended let the father in the ninth chapter of his third book[5] by letters testimonial of the Roman senate and city bear record; how rightly it is his and his beloved let him by his discourse in the eighth of his second, written to the Lady of Estissac (as if it were to you concerning your sweet heir, most motherly affected Lady Harington);[6] and by his acknowledgement in this first to all

---

[2] my last birth] His Italian-English dictionary, *A Worlde of Wordes* (1598), which was dedicated to the Earl of Southampton, the Earl of Rutland and Lucy, Countess of Bedford, all his pupils in Italian.

[3] In Greek myth Dionysus (Bacchus) was the child of Zeus (Jupiter) and Semele, who was consumed by lightning before she could give birth. Zeus sewed him up in his thigh from where he was born after full gestation. In the second legend Zeus swallowed Metis after she refused him; later, complaining of a headache, he had Hephaistus (Vulcan) split open his head with an axe, from where Athena (Minerva) emerged.

[4] jerk] a short, sharp witty speech; cf. Shakespeare, *Love's Labour's Lost* 4.2.125: 'the jerks of invention'.

[5] *Essays* 3.9, 'Of Vanity'.

[6] *Essays* 2.8, 'Of the Affection of Fathers to their Children'. This very personal essay moves from children to brain-children and is the likely origin of Florio's coinage 'brain-babe' in the dedication to Queen Anne in the revised *Worlde of Wordes* (1611), STC 11099, sig. ¶2^v, image 3, as well as of the mythologising of

readers, give evidence first that it is *de bonne foi*, then more than that, *c'est moi.*[7] How worthily qualified, embellished, furnished it is, let his fair-spoken and fine-witted daughter by alliance pass her verdict, which she need not recant. Here-hence to offer it into your service, let me for him but do and say as he did for his other self, his peerless pair, Steven de Boetie in the 28th of this first,[8] and think he speaks to you, my praise-surmounting Countess of Bedford, what he there speaks to the Lady of Gramont, Countess of Guissen. Since as his master poet said,

mutato nomine, de te
fabula narratur[9]
(Do you but change the name,
Of you is said the same),

so do her attributes accord to your demerits. Whereof, to run a long-breathed career,[10] both so fair and large a field might invite me, and my inburning spirits would incite me, if I were not held in by your sweet-reining hand (who have ever held this desire, sooner to exceed what you are thought than be thought what you are not); or should I not prejudice by premonstration° your assured advantage when your value shall come to the weighing.

And yet what are you not that may excel? What weight would you not elevate in truest balance of best judgements? More to be followed by glory since you fly it, which yet many good follow; most to be praised for refusing all praises, which yet will press on virtue; will she, nill she. In which matter of fame (and that exceeding good) well may you, I doubt not, use the word which my author here, I fear, usurpeth:

viresque acquirit eundo[11]
(The further that she goeth,
The more in strength she groweth),

---

birth and parentage in the Montaigne preface. (The first citation in the OED for 'brainchild' is 1921.)

[7] *de bonne foi* [. . .] *c'est moi*] in good faith [. . .] it is myself.

[8] *Essays* 1.28, 'Nine and Twenty Sonnets of Steven de Boetie'. Etienne de la Boëtie was Montaigne's intimate friend and this follows the essay 'Of Friendship'.

[9] **Marg**. Horace, *Satires* 1.69.

[10] to run [. . .] career] to make a long-winded discourse.

[11] **Marg**. Virgil, *Aeneid*, I.iv.175.

since (as in the original) if of his virtue or glory, more of yours, his arch-poet might verify:

ingrediturque solo, et caput inter nubila condit[12]
(She, great and good, on earth doth move,
Yet veils her head in heaven above).

But being by your limitless moderation locked in limits (who more desire, nothing may be said than too much – though I can never say too much); as he of Carthage, so I of your praiseworthiness, were better to say nothing than too little.[13] For this in hand, if it may be so honoured to kiss your honour's gracious hand, if any grace or good be either afforded to it or deserved by it, all that by the father, foster-father, and all that are of kin or kind unto it, must be to your honour, grace, and goodness imputed and ascribed. For (that I may discharge me of all this and charge you with your own, pardon, Madam, my plainness) when I with one chapter found myself overcharged, whereto the charge or choice of an honourable person and by me not-to-be-denied benefactor (noble and virtuous Sir Edward Wotton[14]) had engaged me, which I finished in your house, Your Honour having deigned to read it, without pity of my failing, my fainting, my labouring, my languishing, my gasping for some breath (O could so honourable be so pitiless? Madam, now do I flatter you?), yet commanded me on (and let me die outright ere I do not that command). I say not you took pleasure at shore, as those in this author, to see me sea-tossed, weather-beaten, shipwrecked, almost drowned.[15] Nor say I, like this man's Indian king, you checked with a sour-stern countenance the yearnful complaint of your drooping, near-dying subject.[16] Nor say I, as he allegeth out of others, like an ironically modest virgin you induced, yea

[12] **Marg**. Virgil, *Aeneid*, I.iv.177.
[13] he of Carthage [. . .] too little] On parting from Dido at Carthage Aeneas remained silent, despite her pleas for him to stay.
[14] Sir Edward Wotton (1548–1620) was a diplomat who had lived for several years in Naples and could speak Italian, French, and Spanish; he was one of Florio's benefactors.
[15] **Marg**. Essays I.1, 'Of Profit and Honesty'. [The reference is to the famous passage in Lucretius on the pleasure of standing safely on the shore and watching others being shipwrecked, *De Rerum natura* 2.1, 'O soave mari magno [. . .]'.]
[16] **Marg**. *Essays* III. 6, 'Of Coaches'.

commanded, yea delighted to see me strive for life, yea fall out of breath.[17] Unmerciful you were, but not so cruel (Madam, now do I flatter you?). Yet this I may and must say, like in this Frenchman's report, our third in name but first and chief in fame, King Edward, you would not succour your black, not son, but servant, but bade him fight and conquer, or die.[18] Like the Spartan imperious mother, a shield indeed you gave me, but with this word: *aut cum hoc, aut in hoc.*[19] I must needs say while this was in doing, to put and keep me in heart like a captived cannibal fattened against my death, you often cried *coraggio*, and called *ça ça*, and applauded as I passed, and if not set me in, yet set me on, even with a siren's *O tres-loüable Ulisse.*[20] O, Madam, who then spake fair? As for me, I only say, as this man's embossed hart out of heart,[21] I sweat, I wept, and I went on, till now I stand at bay. Howsoever, I hope that may yet save me, which from others strangles others: I mean the collar you have put about my neck with your inscription,

Noli me caedere, nam sum Dianae.[22]

Yet nor can you deny, nor I dissemble, how at first I pleaded this author's tedious difficulty, my self-known insufficiency and others' more leisureful ability. But no excuse would serve him that must serve without excuse. Little power had I to perform, but less to refuse what you imposed. For his length you gave time; for his hardness you advised help; my weakness you might bid do its best; others' strength you would not seek for further. Yet did your honoured name rally to my succour the forces of two dear friends, both devoted to your service, both obliged to your

---

[17] **Marg.** *Essays* II. 23, 'Of Bad Means Employed to a Good End'.

[18] **Marg.** *Essays* I.41, 'That a Man should not communicate his Glory'. [The son of King Edward III was known as the Black Prince. Both fought at the battle of Crécy in 1346, an English victory which Montaigne writes about in this essay.]

[19] *aut* [. . .] *hoc*] Spartan mothers were said to have sent their sons off to battle with the words '[come back] either with this or on it.'

[20] **Marg.** *Essays* II. 6, 'Of Glory'. ['O thrice-renowned Ulysses'. The sirens' song is from *Odyssey* XII, but the phrase does not correspond to the Greek.]

[21] **Marg.** *Essays* II.11, 'Of Cruelty'.

[22] *Noli* [. . .] *Dianae*] 'Do not kill me, for I am Diana's'. The reference is to Petrarch's 'Una candida cerva' [a white doe] (*Rime sparse* 190) imitated by Sir Thomas Wyatt in 'Whoso list to hunt'.

virtues: the one, master Theodoro Diodati,[23] as in name, so indeed God's gift to me, my *bonus genius*, and sent me as the good angel to Raimond in Tasso for my assistant to combat this great Argantes.[24] Who as he is happy in you, and you in him, that like Aristotle to Alexander he may in all good learning, and doth with all industrious attention instruct, direct, adorn that noble, hopeful, and much-promising spirit of your beloved brother and house-heir, Master John Harington. So was he to me in this inextricable labyrinth like Ariadne's thread; in this rocky-rough ocean, a guide-fish to the whale; in these dark-uncouth ways, a clear, relucent light. Had not he been, I had not been able to wade through, and had not he dissolved these knots, none had, few could. The other, my only dearest and in-love-sympathising friend, Master Doctor Gwinne,[25] of whom I may justly say what my author sayeth of his second self, Steven de la Boétie, for he could not better portray him for himself than he hath lively delineated him for me, willing to do me ease, and as willing to do Your Honour service. As you know him a scholar, and pity is it the world knows not his worth better, for as the Prince of Italian poets said of Valerius Corvinus, *Non so se meglio, duce o cavalliero*,[26] so I may truly say of him, *Non so se meglio, oratore e poeta o philosopho e medico*, so scholarlike did he undertake what Latin prose, Greek, Latin, Italian, or French poesy should cross my way, which as bugbears affrighted my unacquaintance with them, to rid them all afore me and for the most part drawn them from their dens. Wherein what indefatigable pains he hath undergone, and how successfully overgone (I refer to Your Honour), I remit to the learned, for who but he could have quoted so diverse authors and noted so several places? So was he to me in this

[23] Diodati] Theodore Diodati was another Italian Protestant who helped Florio with difficult passages (both his names mean 'a gift from God'). He was the father of Milton's friend, Charles.

[24] In canto 7 of Tasso's *Gerusalemme Liberata* the elderly crusader Raimond, standing in for Tancred, almost defeats Argantes with the help of an angel sent from God.

[25] Gwinne] Matthew Gwinne was a friend of Florio's from Oxford who was appointed the first Professor of Physic [medicine] at Gresham College in 1597. He identified the sources of all Montaigne's quotations and may also have translated them.

[26] *Non so* [. . .] *cavalliero*] 'I do not know in which role he was better, general or horseman'. Florio is citing Petrarch's life of the Roman general Valerius Corvinus in *De viris illustribus*.

bundle of riddles an understanding Oedipus, in this perilous-crooked passage a monster-quelling Theseus or Hercules. With these two supporters of knowledge and friendship, if I upheld and armed have passed the pikes, the honour be all yours, since all by yours was done for Your Honour.

That all this is thus, the reply of that friend upon my answer to Your Ho[nour's] invitation in a sonnet of the like (but not same) terminations may signify and testify to all the world. Then let none say I flatter when I forbear not to tell all. Yet more I must needs say, if poets be inspired by their muse, if soldiers take courage by the eye or memory of their mistresses (as both have made some long believe), having already said, as Petrarch to his mistress:

In questo stato son Donna per vuoi[27]
(By you or for you, Madam thus am I.)

I now rather aver as the lyric to his Melpomene:

Quod spiro et placeo, si placeo tuum est.[28]
(That I do breathe and please, if please I do,
It is your grace, such grace proceeds from you.)

For besides your own inexplicable bounty, first-mover of my good, *la quale ritogli me peregrino errante, e fra gli scoglii e l'onde agitato, al furor di Fortuna, e benignamente guidi in porto di salute e pace*,[29] your noblest Earl's beneficence, forerunning all as far in courtesy as pedigree, and bearing not only in his heart or hand, but even in aspect and due respect the native magnanimity of Bedford and magnificent frank nature of the Russells, hath so kindly bedewed my earth when it was sunburnt, so gently thawed it when it was frost-bound, as (were there any good in me) I were more senseless than earth if I returned not some fruit in good measure. This may be thought too much for no better a deserver than I am, yet more must I acknowledge joined to this: for as to

[27] **Marg**. Petrarch, Sonnet 107 [Given as 134 in modern editions of the *Canzoniere*].

[28] **Marg**. Horace, *Odes* IV.3. [Melpomene is the muse of tragedy.]

[29] *la quale* [. . .] *pace*] **Marg**. Tasso, *Gerusalemme Liberata*, Canto 1, stanza 4. ['who set me free, the wandering traveller, and guided me with kindness through the rocks and troubled seas of Fortune's storm into the peace and safety of the harbour' (Tasso is addressing Alfonso d'Este, Duke of Ferrara). Florio's quotation is not entirely faithful to the text].

all that profess any learning, and do you but small stead therein, you and your husband's hand, most bounteous Lady Harington, have been still open, and your hospitable house my retreat in storms, my relief in need, yea, your hearts ever enlarged. So for an instance in doing well by me, the meanest, as if honourable father and mother with their noblest son and daughter should contend in that only praiseworthy emulation of well-doing, you seemed even to strive who should excel each other, who should best entertain, cherish, and foster me. And as if this river of benignity did run in a blood, your worthy son-in-law and virtuous daughter Chichester with like sweet liquor have supplied my dry cisterns. So as to the name and house of Bedford and Harington, without profaneness let me vow but one word of the pastoral, *illius aram*,[30]
and with that word myself

Your Honourable Ladyship's in humble, hearty service
John Florio.

To the Courteous Reader

Shall I apologise translation? Why, but some hold (as for their freehold)[31] that such conversion is the subversion of universities.[32] God hold with them, and withhold them from impeach or impair. It were an ill turn, the turning of books should be the overturning of libraries. Yea, but my old fellow Nolano[33] told me, and taught publicly, that from translation all science had its offspring. Likely, since even philosophy, grammar, rhetoric, logic, arithmetic, geometry, astronomy, music, and all the

---

[30] *illius aram*] 'the altar of that man' (Virgil, *Eclogues*, I.7). Here, 'of that woman' since it refers to the altars in the frontispiece to the volume on which the names of Florio's female benefactors are inscribed.

[31] as for their freehold] as if it were their right.

[32] subversion of universities] Cf. John Dee, 'Mathematical Preface' to Euclid, *The Elements of Geometrie* (London, 1570), STC 10560, sig. A3^{v}, image 28: 'the Honour, and Estimation of the Universities, and Graduates, is, hereby, nothing diminished. Seing, from, and by their Nurse Children, you receave all this Benefit: how great soever it be'. Dee then cites the example of universities in Italy where translation has flourished; cf. also Hoby **30**. 111–19.

[33] Nolano] Giordano Bruno, whom Florio met at the French embassy in 1583; 'Nolano' is a character in the first dialogue of Florio's *Second Frutes* (1591). See also 'N. W.', **40**. 22–23.

mathematics yet hold their name of the Greeks, and the Greeks drew their baptising water from the conduit-pipes of the Egyptians, and they from the well-springs of the Hebrews or Chaldees. And can the well-springs be so sweet and deep, and will the well-drawn water be so sour and smell? And were their countries so ennobled, advantaged, and embellished by such deriving, and doth it drive our noblest colonies upon the rocks of ruin? And did they well? And proved they well? And must we prove ill that do so? Why, but learning would not be made common. Yea, but learning cannot be too common, and the commoner the better.[34] Why, but who is not jealous, his mistress should be so prostitute? Yea, but this mistress is like air, fire, water: the more breathed, the clearer; the more extended, the warmer; the more drawn, the sweeter. It were inhumanity to coop her up and worthy forfeiture close to conceal her. Why, but scholars should have some privilege of pre-eminence. So have they: they only are worthy translators. Why, but the vulgar should not know all. No, they cannot, for all this; nor even scholars for much more. I would both could, and knew much more than either doth or can. Why, but all would not be known of all. No, nor can: much more we know not than we know; all know something, none know all. Would all know all? They must break ere they be so big: God only, men far from God. Why, but pearls should not be cast to swine.[35] Yet are rings put in their noses, and a swine should know his sty, and will know his meat and his medicine, and as much beside, as any swine doth suppose it to be marjoram.[36] Why, but it is not well Divinity should be a child's or old wives', a cobbler's or clothier's tale, or table talk.[37] There is use and abuse: use none, too much; abuse none, too little. Why, but let learning be wrapped in a learned mantle. Yea, but to be unwrapped by a learned nurse; yea, to be lapped° up again; yea, and unlapped again. Else hold we ignorance the mother of devotion, praying and preaching in an unknown tongue,[38] as

[34] commoner the better] Echoing the maxim '*bonum quo communius eo melius*'; see James, **13**. 91–92.

[35] See Matthew 7.6.

[36] swine [. . .] marjoram] proverbial; see Erasmus *Adages*, 1.4.38.

[37] table-talk] A point of contention between Martin and Fulke; see **11**. 135–40 and **12**. 331–38

[38] ignorance [. . .] tongue] proverbial, but another contentious issue for Protestants; see Tyndale, **1**. 70–78.

sorry as a mother, as a seely daughter; a good mind perhaps, but surely an ill manner. If the best be meet for us, why should the best be barred? Why, but the best wrote best in a tongue more unknown; nay, in a tongue more known to them that wrote and not unknown of them to whom they wrote. Why, but more honour to him that speaks more learned. Yea, such, perhaps as Quintilian's orator, a learned man, I warrant him, for I understand him never a word. Why, but let men write for the most honour of the writer – nay, for the most profit of the reader – and so haply most honour. If to write obscurely be perplexedly offensive, as Augustus well judged, for our own not to write in our own, but unintelligibl[y], is haply to fewer and more critical,[39] but surely without honour, without profit, if he go not or send not an interpreter; who else what is he but a translator? Obscure be he that loves obscurity, and therefore willingly I take his word, though wittingly I do mistake it, *translata proficit*.[40] Why, but whoever did well in it? Nay, who did ever well without it? If nothing can be now said but hath been said before, as he said well, if there be no new thing under the sun.[41] What is that that hath been? That that shall be, as he said that was wisest. What do the best then but glean after others harvest? Borrow their colours, inherit their possessions? What do they but translate; perhaps usurp; at least collect?[42] If with acknowledgement, it is well; if by stealth, it is too bad. In this, our conscience is our accuser, posterity our judge; in that, our study is our advocate and you readers our jury. Why, but whom can I name that bore a great name for it? Nay, who great else but either in part, as Plato and Aristotle out of many; Tully, Plutarch, Pliny out of Plato, Aristotle and many; or of purpose, as all that since have made most know the Greek, and almost the Latin, even translated their whole treatises? Why, Cardan maintaineth neither Homer's verse can be well expressed in Latin, nor Virgil's in Greek, nor Petrarch's in either.[43] Suppose

[39] haply [. . .] critical] i.e. 'is perhaps to write for a smaller and more critical audience'.

[40] *translata proficit*] Used in the phrase *translata proficit arbos* [a transplanted tree flourishes], but *translata* also means 'metaphors', in which the sense is transferred from one word to another.

[41] See Ecclesiastes 1.9.

[42] collect] As did Montaigne himself; see l. 15 above.

[43] Cardan [. . .] either] Girolamo Cardano (1501–76), physician and mathematician (not an obvious authority on literary translation).

Homer took nothing out of any, for we hear of none good before him, and there must be a first. Yet Homer by Virgil is often so translated as Scaliger[44] conceives there is the armour of Hercules most puissant put on the back of Bacchus most delicate; and Petrarch, if well tracked, would be found in their footsteps, whose very garbage less poets are noted to have gathered. Why, but that Scaliger thinks that Ficinus[45] by his rustical simplicity translated Plato, as if an owl should represent an eagle, or some tara-rag player should act the princely Telephus[46] with a voice as ragged as his clothes, a grace as bad as his voice. If the famous Ficinus were so faulty, who may hope to scape scot-free? But for him and us all let me confess, as he here censureth, and let confession make half amends, that every language hath its genius and inseparable form. Without Pythagoras his metempsychosis it cannot rightly be translated.[47] The Tuscan altiloquence,[48] the Venus° of the French, the sharp state of the Spanish, the strong significancy of the Dutch cannot from here be drawn to life. The sense may keep form, [though] the sentence is disfigured, the fineness, fitness, featness° diminished: as much as art's nature is short of nature's art, a picture of a body, a shadow of a substance. Why then, belike I have done by Montaigne as Terence by Menander, made of good French no good English. If I have done no worse, and it be no worse taken, it is well. As he, if no poet yet am I no thief, since I say of whom I had it rather to imitate his and his author's negligence than any backbiter's obscure diligence. His horse I set before you, perhaps without his trappings, and his meat without sauce. Indeed, in this specially find I fault with my master, that as Crassus and Antonius in

---

[44] See Julius Caesar Scaliger (1484–1558), *Poetices*, Book V ('Criticus') for the comparison of Homer and Virgil. His preference for Virgil was vigorously attacked by Chapman in the preface to *Achilles Shield* (1598).

[45] Ficinus] Marsilio Ficino (1433–1499) was the leading Florentine Neoplatonist; his Latin translation of Plato's works was published in 1584–5, USTC 991952.

[46] tara-rag [. . .] Telephus] 'tara-rag' is not in the OED but evidently means 'beggarly'; Telephus was the son of Hercules. See also Horace, *Art of Poetry*, ll. 95–6.

[47] On translation and Pythagoras's doctrine of the transmigration of souls (metempsychosis) cf. Chapman **44c**. 36. Donne had written a poem on 'the progress of the soul' entitled *Metempsychosis* in 1601.

[48] altiloquence] high speech, height of eloquence (not recorded in the OED before 1731).

Tully,[49] the one seemed to contemn,° the other not to know the Greeks; whereas the one so spake Greek as he seemed to know no other tongue, the other in his travels to Athens and Rhodes had long conversed with the learnedest Grecians. So he, most writing of himself, and the worst rather than the best, disclaimeth all memory, authorities, or borrowing of the ancient or modern, whereas in course of his discourse he seems acquainted not only with all, but no other but authors, and could out of question like Cyrus or Caesar call any of his army by his name and condition. And I would for us all he had in this whole body done as much as in most of that of other languages my peerless, dear-dearest and never sufficiently commended friend hath done for mine and your ease and intelligence. Why then again, as Terence, I have had help? Yea, and thank them for it, and think you need not be displeased by them that may please you in a better matter. Why, but essays are but men's school themes pieced together:[50] you might as well say, several texts; all is in the choice and handling? Yea, marry, but Montaigne, had he wit, it was but a French wit *fertillant*, *léger*[51] and extravagant.

Now, say you, English wits by the staidest censure of as learned a wit as is among you. The counsel of that judicious, worthy counsellor, honourable Sir Edward Wotton, would not have embarked me to this discovery, had not his wisdom known it worth my pains and your perusing. And should or would any dog-toothed critic or adder-tongued satirist scoff or find fault that in the course of his discourses, or web of his essays, or entitling of his chapters, he holdeth a disjointed, broken, and gadding° style, and that many times they answer not his titles and have no coherence together, to such I will say little, for they deserve but little. But if they list,° else let them choose, I send them to the ninth chapter of the third book,[52] folio 596, where himself preventeth their carping, and foreseeing their criticism answereth them for me at full. Yet are there herein errors: if of matter, the author's; if of omission, the printer's. Him I would

[49] Crassus [. . .] Tully] Speakers in Cicero's *De Oratore*, which is set at Crassus's villa at Tusculum but which has an Athenian model.

[50] essays [. . .] pieced together] On Montaigne's use of quotation and his avoidance of 'school themes' see Hugo Friedrich, *Montaigne*, trans. by Philippe Desan (Berkeley: University of California Press, 1991), pp. 378–79.

[51] *fertillant, léger*] fertile; with a light touch.

[52] **Marg**. *Essays* I. 3, 'Of Vanity'.

not amend, but send him to you as I found him; this I could not attend, but where I now find faults, let me pray and entreat you for your own sake to correct as you read, to amend as you list. But some errors are mine, and mine by more than translation. Are they in grammar or orthography? – as easy for you to right as me to be wrong. Or in construction, as misattributing him, her or it to things alive, or dead, or neuter? – you may soon know my meaning and eftsoons use your mending. Or are they in some uncouth° terms as entrain, conscientious, endear, tarnish, comport, efface, facilitate, amusing, debauching, regret, effort, emotion, and suchlike?[53] If you like them not, take others most commonly set by them to expound them, since there they were set to make such likely French words familiar with our English, which well may bear them. If any be capital in sense mistaking,[54] be I admonished and they shall be recanted. Howsoever, the falseness of the French prints, the diversities of copies, editions, and volumes (some whereof have more or less than others), and I in London having followed some, and in the country others; now those in folio, now those in octavo, yet in this last survey reconciled all; therefore, or blame not rashly or condemn not fondly the multitude of them set for your further ease in a table (at the end of the book), which ere you begin to read I entreat you to peruse. This printer's wanting a diligent corrector, my many employments and the distance between me and my friends I should confer with may extenuate, if not excuse, even more errors. In sum, if any think he could do better, let him try; then will he better think of what is done. Seven or eight of great wit and worth have assayed, but found these essays no attempt for French apprentices or Littletonians.[55] If thus done it may please you, as I wish it may and I hope it shall, I with you shall be pleased; though not, yet still I am
the same resolute
John Florio

---

[53] entrain [. . .] suchlike] Of these the *OED* gives Florio as the first citation for particular senses of the following: conscientious; endear; tarnish (in the *Worlde of Wordes*, 1598); debauch; emotion. Florio's use of 'efface' predates the first citation in the *OED* other than in a figurative sense.

[54] capital [. . .] mistaking] guilty of a fatal error in understanding.

[55] Littletonians] Those who have to rely upon Claudius Holyband's French language primer, *The French Littleton* (London, 1578).

To my dear friend Master John Florio, concerning his translation of Montaigne.

Books, the amass° of humours, swoll'n with ease,
The grief of peace, the malady of rest,
So stuff the world, fall'n into this disease,
As it receives more than it can digest;
And do so overcharge, as they confound
The appetite of skill with idle store:
There being no end of words, nor any bound°
Set to conceit, the ocean without shore.
   As if man laboured with himself to be
As infinite in words as in intents,
And draw his manifold uncertainty
In ev'ry figure passion represents
That these innumerable visages
And strange shapes of opinions and discourse,
Shadowed in leaves, may be the witnesses
Rather of our defects than of our force.
And this proud frame of our presumption,
This Babel of our skill, this tower of wit,
Seems only checked with the confusion
Of our mistakings that dissolveth it.
And well may make us of our knowledge doubt,
Seeing what uncertainties we build upon,
To be as weak within book as without,
Or else that truth hath other shapes than one.
   But yet although we labour with this store,°
And with the press of writings seem oppress'd,
And have too many books, yet want we more,
Feeling great dearth and scarceness of the best,
Which cast in choicer shapes have been produced
To give the best proportions to the mind
Of our confusion, and have introduced
The likeliest images frailty can find.[56]
And wherein most the skill-desiring soul
Takes her delight, the best of all delight,

[56] The likeliest [. . .] find] the most convincing appearances of truth that our weak minds can discover.

And where her motions evenest come to roll
About this doubtful centre of the right.
  Which to discover this great potentate,
This prince Montaigne (if he be not more)
Hath more adventur'd of his own estate[57]
Than ever man did of himself before,
And hath made such bold sallies out upon
Custom, the mighty tyrant of the earth,
In whose seraglio° of subjection
We all seem bred up from our tender birth.
As I admire his powers, and out of love
Here at his gate do stand, and glad I stand
So near to him whom I do so much love,
To applaud his happy settling in our land
And safe transpassage[58] by his studious care
Who both of him and us doth merit much,
Having as sumptuously, as he is rare,
Placed him in the best lodging of our speech
And made him now as free as if born here;
And as well ours as theirs, who may be proud
That he is theirs, though he be everywhere
To have the franchise of his worth allowed:[59]
  It being the portion of a happy pen
Not to be envassalled[60] to one monarchy,
But dwell with all the better world of men
Whose spirits are all of one community,
Whom neither ocean, deserts, rocks, nor sands
Can keep from th'intertraffic of the mind,[61]
But that it vents° her treasure in all lands
And doth a most secure commercement° find.

---

[57] more [. . .] estate] i.e. invested and risked so much of himself in his own writing. Florio has already commented on Montaigne's making himself the subject of his essays at l. 298.

[58] transpassage] The only citation in the OED.

[59] As I admire [. . .] allowed] On the naturalisation and enfranchisement of the 'stranger' text, cf. Holland **45**. 27, 71–73, 126–28.

[60] envassalled] reduced to servitude; predates first citation in OED (also from Daniel).

[61] intertraffic of the mind] The phrase has become a well-known conceptualisation of translation through George Steiner's discussion in *After Babel: Aspects of Language and Translation*, 3rd edn (Oxford: Oxford University Press, 1998), p. 261.

Wrap excellency up never so much
In hieroglyphics, ciphers, characters,
And let her speak never so strange a speech,
Her genius yet finds apt decipherers;
And never was she born to die obscure,
But guided by the stars of her own grace
Makes her own fortune, and is ever sure
In man's best hold, to hold the strongest place.
And let the critic say the worst he can,
He cannot say but that Montaigne yet
Yields most rich pieces and extracts of man,
Though in a troubled frame confus'dly set,[62]
Which yet he is blest that he hath ever seen,
And therefore, as a guest in gratefulness,
For the great good the house yields him within,
Might spare to tax th'unapt conveyances.[63]
But this breath hurts not, for both work and frame,
Whilst England English speaks, is of that store
And that choice stuff, as that without the same
The richest library can be but poor;
And they unblest who letters do profess
And have him not, whose own fate beats their want
With more sound blows than Alcibiades
Did his pedant that did Homer want.[64]

Sam[uel] Daniel

48. Richard Carew, *A World of Wonders* [Henri Estienne] (1607)

[Richard Carew (1555–1620), a native of Cornwall, entered Christ Church, Oxford, where he met Sir Philip Sidney and William Camden. He was one of the founding members, with Camden, of the Society for Antiquaries and published an essay

[62] Though [. . .] set] Daniel refers both to Montaigne's rhapsodic method of composition, stitching together quotations and allusions from different sources, and to the exploratory nature of the essay form.

[63] unapt conveyances] inadequate amenities.

[64] sound [. . .] want] see Plutarch, *Life of Alcibiades* VII.1. Plutarch recounts that Alcibiades hit his tutor after being told that he did not have a copy of Homer.

on 'The Excellencie of the English Tongue' in the second edition of Camden's *Remaines* (1614). He published a translation of the first five cantos of Tasso's *Gerusalemme Liberata* in 1594, which was superseded by Edward Fairfax's complete version (1600), but he is best known for his *Survey of Cornwall* (1602), dedicated to Sir Walter Raleigh.

Henri Estienne and his father, Robert, were both enormously productive lexicographers and printers, though the text that Carew translated is the satirical *L'Introduction au traité de la conformité des merveilles anciennes avec les modernes* (Antwerp, 1567), USTC 18579. Carew dedicated his translation to the brothers William and Philip Herbert who were the dedicatees of the Shakespeare First Folio and the 1620 *Decameron.*

See D. N. C. Wood, 'Elizabethan English and Richard Carew', *Neophilologus*, 61 (1977), 304–15; Morini, *Tudor Translation*, pp. 118–28; John Considine, *Dictionaries in Early Modern Europe: Lexicography and the Making of Heritage* (Cambridge: Cambridge University Press, 2008), pp. 56–100 ('Henri Estienne and his World'); Considine in *ODNB*.]

The Translator to the Reader.

Touching the translation I have not much to say, for I do not profess myself a translator, neither do I arrogate° any extraordinary skill in the French tongue. I leave both to the skilful linguists of our modern languages, as stately Savile,[1] flourishing Florio, grave Grimeston,[2] facile° and painful° Holland etc.. Yet this I hope I may truly say, that I have expressed the meaning of my author both truly and fully, and that I have not lost either the life or the grace of any conceit where it was possible to be kept. Which I speak not as doting upon mine own doings, for I am not so in love either with the work or workmanship, with the matter of the book or the manner of handling, nor the gay coat that I have put upon it, as Heliodorus was of his amorous discourse of

[1] Savile] Sir Henry Savile (1549–1622), Warden of Merton College, Oxford, and Provost of Eton; an exceptionally learned scholar who had published a translation of Tacitus (1591).

[2] Grimeston] Edward Grimeston (before 1570 - after 1640) specialised in translating large works of national European history, mainly from the French. His last major work was a translation of the Greek historian Polybius (1633).

Chariclea (called *The Ethiopian History*),[3] who chose rather to leave his bishopric than to call in his book. I am rather of Marsilius Ficinus his mind, who having translated Plato into Latin, came to his learned friend Musurus Candiot[4] to know his opinion of it; where Candiot, after he had perused some few leaves, perceiving that it would not satisfy the expectation of the learned, considering it was but slubbered° over and that it resembled the original (as Cicero the younger did his father) in nothing but in name, takes a sponge, and having dipped it in an inkpot, blots out the first page. Then, turning him to Ficinus: 'Thou seest', quoth he, 'how I have corrected the first page. If thou wilt, I will correct the rest in like sort'. To whom Ficinus very mildly answered: 'No reason that Plato should be disgraced through my default', and so refined it again. Who, notwithstanding having done the best he could, by his rustical simplicity resembles the majesty of Plato's style (if we may believe Scaliger[5]) no otherwise than if an owl should represent an eagle. If, therefore, any candid Candiot (for I appeal only to such as have skill in the French tongue) shall show me that I have done the like in translating this Apology, and that I have not attained to the Venus° of the French, the fineness, fitness, and featness° of the phrase, I refuse not the sponge so that he will correct me and not control° me. As for the rest, I shall desire them to spare their censure till they have learned their Littleton.[6]

But lest any carping companion should brag that he had found a hole in my coat, and that he could show where I have missed the cushion,° I do here correct myself and confess a fault in the translation, chapter 15, § 1, which as (in my necessary absence) it passed the press before I was aware, so if it come to a second review shall have his due correction. As for other scapes (saving

[3] *Ethiopian History*] Heliodorus's work was popularised by Thomas Underdowne's translation, *An Aethiopian Historie* (1569), which went through four subsequent editions to 1617.

[4] Ficinus [. . .] Candiot] The source of the anecdote is Simon Goulart, *Histoires admirables et memorables de nostre temps* (Paris, 1600); see the translation by Grimeston (London, 1607), STC 12135, pp. 444–45, image 228. Marcus Musurus was a Greek scholar born on Crete when it was a colony of the republic of Venice, i.e. the kingdom of Candia; hence 'Candiot'.

[5] Scaliger] Carew is echoing Florio **47**. 280–89 both on Scaliger and 'the Venus of the French'.

[6] Littleton] See Florio **47**. 364.

such as have escaped the corrector's care) I know none except some *sciolus*[7] shall judge it a fault to translate *à pain et à pot*, at bed and board; *à pain et à cueillier*, at rack and manger; *entre Paris et Lyon*, betwixt York and London; *chien de St Roche*, Toby's dog, etc., as though it were never lawful to translate *sexcenta*, five hundred. And albeit it be bootless to complain of those infinite rubs° that lay in my way, and those many difficulties which encountered me in my course, yet he that shall duly consider the author's intricate notions, his obscure allusions, his manifold (though not impertinent) excursions, his continual repetitions of the same phrase in divers senses (for Homer's *ton d'apameibomenos* noted by Martial, and Tully's *esse videatur* by Montaigne,[8] are not so frequent as Stephen's[9] *à ce propos*) and last of all his infinite parentheses, which were enough to exercise the patience of a saint, will no doubt, if he have but a grain of candour, as well with connivency° pass over such faults as are trivial as tax those with some easy censure which he shall find to be material. As for the rigid censurer who is *crudelis in animadvertendo*,[10] I shall desire him but to make trial himself in translating of two or three paragraphs, and then I doubt not, *quin fuerit studiis aequior ille meis*.[11] Touching the phrase,[12] I desire the less favour, for albeit I am not ignorant that tailors and writers are now in like esteem – that if they have not new fashions, they are not fancied, and if the style be not of the new stamp, the author is but a simple fellow and may put up his pipes[13] – yet I have of purpose so tempered my style as that it might content the judicious, nothing respecting the judgement or censure of our finical affecters[14] who are so humorous, leaving inkhorn phrases and tapster-like terms for the tavern and

---

[7] *sciolus*] someone with little knowledge (late Latin).

[8] **Marg.** Martial, *Epigrams* [1.45]; Montaigne, *Essays* 2.10, 'Of Books'. [Carew is conflating Estienne's repetition of the phrase with Cicero's use of the *cursus* and Homer's use of oral formulae, which have rhythmic and metrical functions.]

[9] Stephen's] i.e. Etienne's (also known as Stephanus).

[10] *crudelis in animadvertendo*] cruel in noticing faults.

[11] *quin* [. . .] *meis*] he will look on my work more favourably.

[12] phrase] expression (Greek *phrasis*; Latin *elocutio*); see Quintilian, *Institutio oratoria*, VIII.i.1.

[13] put up his pipes] stop speaking, shut up.

[14] finical affecters] those who artificially affect a style; first citation in the OED.

affected strains of oratory for the stage, and avoiding especially the French frippery because I would not have it seem to be a translation.

49. John Healey, *Theophrastus' Characters* (1616)

[John Healey (*c.* 1585–*c.* 1616) attended St John's College, Cambridge, and then travelled in Europe from 1603–04. A Catholic, he was interrogated at York Castle in the aftermath of the Gunpowder Plot. His major work is the translation of Augustine's *City of God* with the commentary by Vives (1610), but he was also capable of writing in an entirely different style of exuberant comic prose, illustrated by *The Discoverie of a New World* (1609), his translation of Joseph Hall's Latin satire *Mundus alter idem*. In 1610 he published translations of two Greek philosophical texts by Epictetus and Cebes with the aid of the Latin translation by Hieronymus Wolf. Thomas Thorpe, publisher of the Augustine translation also claimed that Healey had visited Virginia.

The *Characters* was published in a reissue of the Epictetus and Cebes translation after Healey's death (reprinted in 1636) and is in a similar stylistic vein to the translation from Hall. The fashion for the prose 'Character' derives from the magisterial edition of Theophrastus by the great French classical scholar Isaac Casaubon (Geneva and Lyon, 1592), USTC 158345 and 451345, expanded in 1599. Healey's translation is a free version of the Latin text of the 1592 edition.

See Lathrop, *Translations from the Classics*, pp. 261–64; Benjamin Boyce, *The Theophrastan Character in England to 1642* (Cambridge, MA: Harvard University Press, 1947); John Considine in *ODNB*.]

To the Reader

Gentle reader, to be too servile or too licentious° are alike amiss in a translator, for the one oftentimes darkeneth the beauty of the work, there being certain properties almost in every language, which cannot, word for word, in terms terminant,° be expressed in another. And likewise, to swerve too much from the author implieth a secret disabling, as if the original might be bettered, which cannot but savour of much self-opinion° and singularity. Yet if there were a necessity to err in either, I had rather be over-strict than any whit too bold, having to precedent (it were contumely to say less) that great magazine or storehouse of all learning, Master Casaubon, who in the translation of this piece hath tied himself very precisely to his text. From so learned a hand the author can lose little lustre, less vigour. However, by poring° it out of the Latin into the vulgar, the great disproportion of languages and abilities considered, it cannot but (by my unskilfulness) it hath taken some wind.[1]

In this mention it cometh oftentimes into my mind to marvel whence it should be that Homer, Theocritus, Plutarch, Heliodorus, with divers others, are so lamely done in the Latin (be it spoken with the supportation of better judgements) and so happily in the French. We may not challenge the poverty of the Latin, the negligence of the translators (having been all very learned), much less the Latin idiom, as disobedient or refractory° to the Greek. We should be almost as vain as Picardus to advance the French before the Latin, who maintaineth after his mountebank, impudent fashion that the French is more ancient and copious than the Greek, and that they spake Greek in Marseilles before they spake it in Athens.[2] The French is elegant enough, passably copious, happy in composition, and hath many Graecisms, which couch very aptly when they are called for, yet in no degree comparable with the learned languages.

---

[1] taken some wind] received some publicity.

[2] Picardus [. . .] Athens] See Jean Picard, *De Prisca Celtopaedia* (Paris, 1556), USTC 78184. This is a variation on the theme of the conformity between Greek and French, which echoes Tyndale's assertion of the affinity between Greek and English at the start of this volume. See J. B. Trapp, 'The Conformity of Greek and the Vernacular: The History of a Renaissance Theory of Language' in *Classical Influences on European Culture, AD 500–1500* (Cambridge: Cambridge University Press. 1971), pp. 239–44; Considine, *Dictionaries in Early Modern Europe*, pp. 61–63; but neither cites this anecdote.

PART THREE
TRANSLATION IN THE ACADEMY

50. John Palsgrave, *Acolastus* (1540)

[John Palsgrave (d. 1554) graduated from Cambridge in 1504 and then studied in Paris. From 1513 he was a tutor in the most powerful families in England, teaching Henry VIII's younger sister, Mary, and his illegitimate son, Henry Fitzroy, and later the sons of the Duke of Norfolk and Thomas Cromwell. He was also highly regarded in humanist circles and was recommended to Erasmus by Thomas More. Ordained priest in 1533, he was presented with a living in Northamptonshire by one of his former pupils, Charles Blount, 5th Baron Mountjoy, a patron of humanist learning whose father had been tutored by Erasmus. His most distinctive achievement, unusually for a humanist, was his work on the two vernaculars, French and English, represented by his *magnum opus*, *L'Eclaircissement de la Langue Françoyse* (1530), which included a French-English dictionary. His respect for the vernacular is also reflected in his parallel Latin-English edition of the school comedy, *Acolastus*.

Acolastus (Antwerp, 1529) is a prodigal son play in the style of Terence, written by the Dutch scholar Gnapheus or Fullonius (the Greek and Latin pseudonyms of Willem de Volder), which enjoyed European popularity as a teaching text both for Latin and the vernaculars throughout the sixteenth century. Printed in multiple Latin editions at Antwerp, Cologne, and Paris, it was also translated into German and French as well as English. The USTC records 42 editions to 1585. Palsgrave's own comparative work on French and English led him to recognise that inadequate expression in the vernaculars was a problem throughout Europe. In his preface he cites the examples of scholars in other countries who have tried to rectify this.

See also John Palsgrave, *The Comedye of Acolastus*, ed. by P. L. Carver (London: EETS, 1937); Guglielmus Gnaphaeus, *Acolastus*, ed. and trans. by W. E. D. Atkinson (London, Ontario: University of Western Ontario Studies in the Humanities, 1964); Marvin T. Herrick, *Tragicomedy: Its Origins and Development in Italy and France* (Urbana: University of Illinois Press, 1962), pp. 17–46; Gabriele Stein, *John Palsgrave as Renaissance Linguist: a Pioneer in Vernacular Language Description* (Oxford: Clarendon, 1997); José María Pérez Fernández, 'Andres Laguna: Translation and the Early Modern Idea of Europe', *Translation and Literature*, 21 (2012), 299–318.]

Ioannis Palsgravi Londoniensis, ecphrasis Anglica in comoediam Acolasti[1]

The comedy of *Acolastus* translated into our English tongue after such manner as children are taught in the grammar school, first word for word as the Latin lieth, and afterward according to the sense and meaning of the Latin sentences, by showing what they do value° and countervail° in our tongue; with admonitions set forth in the margin so often as any such phrase° (that is to say, kind of speaking used of the Latins), which we use not in our tongue, but by other words express the said Latin manners of speaking; and also adages, metaphors, sentences, or other figures poetical or rhetorical do require for the more perfect instructing of the learners, and to lead them more easily to see how the exposition goeth. And afore the second scene of the first act is a brief introductory to have some general knowledge of the divers sorts of metres used of our author in this comedy; and afore Acolastus' ballad is showed of what kinds of metres his ballad is made of; and afore the sixth scene of the fourth act is a monition° of the rhetorical composition used in that scene and certain other after it ensuing.[2]

Interpreted° by John Palsgrave, Anno MDXL.

To the most excellent prince and our most redoubted sovereign lord, Henry VIII

Some instructors of Your Highness's youth, for want of a perfect judgement in this behalf, so much desire to seem affectately° curious, that having no due consideration to the tender wits which they take under their charge to teach, in the stead of pure English words and phrases, they declare to their children one Latin word by another and confound the phrases of the tongues, and thus not a little do hinder their young scholars, while they

[1] *Ioannis* [. . .] *Acolasti*] John Palsgrave of London, an English *ekphrasis* on the comedy of *Acolastus*. '*Ekphrasis*' (or '*ekphrastes*', as Palsgrave also calls it) is a speaking picture which depends for its effects upon *enargeia* or 'liveliness'.

[2] rhetorical [. . .] composition] Palsgrave's 'monition' lists the rhetorical figures which Fullonius uses at this point, but also explains that the scene is 'made of interrogations [. . .] to move the audience to compassion', STC 11470, sig. U3^{r}, image 83.

would seem for their own parts to have a knowledge and erudition above the common sort. And some other again there be, which having undoubtedly learning enough, vailable° and sufficient, yet while they by sundry ways and manners of speaking used in our tongue labour to express such Latin authors' minds as they do take upon them for the time to interpret, and for to seem therein more diligent than the common sort, dispend° in manner whole forenoons and afternoons in the declaring of a few lines of such Latin authors as they for the season have in hand (as to confess the very truth, the schoolmaster's whole diligence tendeth in manner[3] chiefly to that effect and purpose). They do by that means not only right little for the time further their young audience, but also by that ways do oppress and overlay° the tender wits, the which they would so feign° further with their multitude of sundry interpretations confusedly by them uttered; so that finally, their young scholars, to help their memory with, be forced to fall a-glozing – or rather a-blotting[4] – of their Latin books, and as their childish judgement doth for the time serve them, of divers English words in our tongue being synonyms, or of divers manners of interpretations used by their master, they choose most commonly the very worst, and therewith scribble the books of their Latin authors.

And some other furthermore there be, which though they have by their great study at Your Grace's universities so much profited in the Latin tongue that to show an evident trial of their learning they can write an epistle right Latin-like, and thereto speak Latin as the time shall minister occasion, very well, yea, and have also by their diligence attained to a comely vein in making of verses, yet for all this, partly because of the rude language used in their native countries where they were born and first learned, as it happened, their grammar rules, and partly because that coming straight from thence unto some of Your Grace's universities, they have not had occasions to be conversant in° such places of your realm as the purest English is spoken, they be not able to express their conceit° in their vulgar tongue, ne be not sufficient perfectly to open the diversities of phrases between our tongue and the Latin, which in my poor judgement is the very chief thing that the schoolmaster should travail in. Insomuch that for want of

[3] in manner] in such a manner.

[4] a-glozing [. . .] a-blotting] making annotations and then crossing them out.

this sufficient perfection in our own tongue I have known diverse of them, which have still continued their study in Your Grace's universities, that after a substantial increase of good learning by their great and industrious study obtained, yet when they have been called to do any service in Your Grace's commonwealth, either to preach in open audience or to have other administration° requiring their assiduous conversance[5] with your subjects, they have then been forced to read over our English authors by that means to provide a remedy unto their evident imperfection in that behalf. And when it hath fortuned any such for their good name and estimation to be called from your universities to instruct any of Your Grace's noblemen's children, then evidently hath appeared their imperfection in that case to be notable, and that to no small detriment and hindrance of such as they have taken charge to instruct and bring forward.

Being therefore for my part desirous that these inconveniences might also be provided for,° and thereupon taking occasion more attentively to bethink me upon this matter, then began the great difficulty of the well-achieving thereof the more plainly to appear unto me, not only because the like thing hath not yet hitherto (that ever I could know of) been throughly attempted of any clerk° within this Your Grace's noble realm, but also for so much as that to be *ekphrastes* in their mother tongue upon any Latin authors hath never hitherto (so far as I can yet perceive) been assayed° in any other region of Europe; except perchance that some such as be lettered have for their own ease and the more brief and speedy furtherance of their scholars used such kind of interpretation° in their own tongue upon some excellent Latin author, which they would never suffer to pass the bounds of their private houses.[6] The not attempting of which kind of interpretation in other regions hath not proceeded of any notable perfection or furtherance which the other regions have in their languages, over and beyond Your noble Grace's subjects. For how much the phrase of the French tongue is different from the pure Latinity may appear by a book of late years made by Robert Stephanus, which he entitleth *De corrupti sermonis*

[5] conversance] intercourse or communication (predates first citation in the *OED*).

[6] Palsgrave is thought to have guarded his own work on French in this way in order to protect his income as a teacher (see Carver, ed., *Acolastus*, p. 184).

emendatione.[7] And how much the Spanish be with this self-imperfection intact may appear by the testimony of Nebrisensis,[8] which with many words doth lament the notable corruption of the Latin tongue amongst his countrymen, rising upon this occasion, and earnestly doth exhort them to be more diligent in the observing of the perfect and approved Latin authors. And as for the Germans, notwithstanding the great excellency that they now at these days be come unto, yet is there no doubt but that there is no vulgar phrase used within the bounds of Europe that more swerveth from the exact Latinity than this doth. So that when I consider by how earnest manner Bebelius[9] called upon the Germans to leave their own phrase and to take them to the assiduous reading and observing of the good Latin authors, the which was but a little before Reuchlin's days,[10] and how prosperously the thing hath since that time amongst them succeeded, I take that Bebelius was in manner to the Germans as was Laurence Valla[11] unto the Italians, by whose first exhortation and setting on so many excellent writers have risen amongst the Italians within the time of memory.

51. Roger Ascham, *The Schoolmaster* (1570)

[Roger Ascham (1514/15–1568) studied at St John's College, Cambridge, where he excelled in Greek, encouraged by the young John Cheke. Elected Fellow in 1534, he tried unsuccessfully to succeed Cheke in the Regius Chair of Greek when Cheke was appointed tutor to Prince Edward in 1544, but he did become

[7] *De corrupti sermonis emendatione*] Written by Mathurin Cordier and published by Robert Estienne (Stephanus), father of Henri, at Paris in 1530 and many times reprinted.

[8] Nebriensis] Antonio de Nebrija (1441–1522), leading Spanish humanist who published a Castilian grammar and a Latin-Spanish dictionary in 1492. His *De Corruptis Hispanorum* was printed in *Repetitio secunda* (Salamanca, 1486), USTC 333153.

[9] Bebelius] Heinrich Bebel (1472–1518), *Commentaria de abusione lingua Latinae apud Germanos* (Pforzheim, 1509), USTC 623474.

[10] Reuchlin's days] Johann Reuchlin (1455–1522), German humanist, known principally for his *Epistolae obscurorum virorum* (1515) rather than as a grammarian.

[11] Valla's guide to Latin eloquence, *Elegantiae linguae Latinae*, first printed in 1471, was a model for later authors including Erasmus.

Reader in Greek at St John's and public orator of the university in place of Cheke in 1546. When Princess Elizabeth's first tutor, William Grindal (a former pupil of Ascham), died of the plague in 1548, Elizabeth insisted on having Ascham as his replacement. Under his regime Elizabeth studied Greek authors, including Sophocles, Demosthenes, Isocrates, and the New Testament, in the morning, and Latin authors, including Cicero, Livy, and the early church fathers, in the afternoon. With Ascham Elizabeth practised the double translation method he had learned from Cheke at Cambridge and which inspired her to continue practising translation at various times during the rest of her life.

A manuscript of the first book of *The Schoolmaster* (*c*. 1564), now in the British Library (Royal MS. 18.B.xxiv), may have circulated before the posthumous publication of the completed work and supplies evidence that Ascham was writing with an elite private tutor in mind rather than a teacher in the grammar schools. The work has two parts – 'The Bringing-Up of Youth' and 'The Ready Way to the Latin Tongue' – and translation is dealt with in the second of these as a means of achieving expressive fluency in Latin. Ascham claimed that *The Schoolmaster* was conceived after reading Demosthenes with Elizabeth one evening early in her reign, and in a letter to Johann Sturm of late 1568 Ascham says that he has nearly completed it. His widow, Margaret, arranged for the publication of this and other of Ascham's works.

See also William E. Miller, 'Double Translation in English Humanistic Education', *Studies in the Renaissance*, 10 (1963), 163–74; Lawrence V. Ryan, *Roger Ascham* (Stanford, CA: Stanford University Press, 1963); *The Schoolmaster (1570)*, ed. by Lawrence V. Ryan (Charlottesville: University of Virginia Press, 1967); Rebecca W. Bushnell, *A Culture of Teaching: Early Modern Humanism in Theory and Practice* (Ithaca, NY: Cornell University Press, 1996); Mike Pincombe, *Elizabethan Humanism: Literature and Learning in the Later Sixteenth Century* (Harlow: Longman, 2001), pp. 72–83; Fred Schurink, 'The Intimacy of Manuscript and the Pleasure of Print: Literary Culture from *The Schoolmaster* to *Euphues*' in *The Oxford Handbook of Tudor Literature*, ed. by Mike Pincombe and Cathy Shrank (Oxford: Oxford University Press, 2009), pp. 671–86; Rosemary O' Day in *ODNB*.]

The Second Book

After that your scholar, as I said before, shall come indeed, first, to a ready perfectness in translating, then, to a ripe and skilful choice in marking out his six points, as:

1. *Proprium*
2. *Translatum*
3. *Synonymum*
4. *Contrarium*[1]
5. *Diversum*
6. *Phrases*

Then take this order with him: read daily unto him some book of Tully,[2] as the third book of *Epistles* chosen out by Sturmius, *De amicitia, De senectute*, or that excellent epistle containing almost the whole first book, *Ad Quintum fratrem*, some comedy of Terence or Plautus (but in Plautus skilful choice must be used by the master to train his scholar to a judgement in cutting out perfectly over-old and unproper words); Caesar's *Commentaries*[3] are to be read with all curiosity, [where]in specially, without all exception to be made either by friend or foe, is seen the unspotted propriety of the Latin tongue, even when it was, as the Grecians say, in *akmē*, that is, at the highest pitch of all perfectness, or some orations of Titus Livius, such as be both longest and plainest.

These books I would have him read now a good deal at every lecture, for he shall not now use daily translation but only construe again and parse[4] where ye suspect is any need; yet let him not omit in these books his former exercise in marking diligently and writing orderly° out his six points. And for

[1] *Proprium* [. . .] *Contrarium*] The first four points form two contrasting pairs: literal meaning (*proprium*) and metaphorical meaning (*translatum*), cf. Quintilian, *Institutio oratoria* I.v.71; identity of meaning (*synonymum*) and antithesis (*contrarium*), cf. *Instiutio oratoria*, IX.iii.90.

[2] Tully] The recommendations from Cicero are Sturm's selection from the letters (Strasbourg, 1539), USTC 674017, *On Friendship*, *On Old Age*, and the first of the *Letters to his Brother Quintus*.

[3] Caesar's *Commentaries*] i.e. on the Gallic and civil wars.

[4] construe [. . .] parse] The distinction is between explaining the grammatical construction of a whole sentence in order to show its meaning and explaining the grammatical function of individual words.

translating, use you yourself, every second or third day, to choose out some epistle *Ad Atticum*,[5] some notable commonplace[6] out of his orations, or some other part of Tully, by your discretion, which your scholar may not know where to find, and translate it you yourself into plain, natural English, and then give it him to translate into Latin again, allowing him good space and time to do it both with diligent heed° and good advisement.° Here his wit shall be new set on work, his judgement for right choice truly tried, his memory for sure retaining better exercised than by learning anything without the book, and here how much he hath profited shall plainly appear. When he bringeth it translated unto you, bring you forth the place of Tully: lay them together; compare the one with the other; commend his good choice and right placing of words; show his faults gently, but blame them not oversharply, for of such missings, gently admonished of, proceedeth glad and good heed-taking. Of good heed-taking springeth chiefly knowledge, which after groweth to perfectness if this order be diligently used by the scholar and gently handled by the master. For here shall all the hard points of grammar both easily and surely be learned up, which scholars in common schools, by making of Latins, be groping at with care and fear, and yet in many years they scarce can reach unto them.

I remember when I was young, in the north, they went to the grammar school little children; they came from thence great lubbers,° always learning and little profiting: learning without book everything, understanding within the book little or nothing. Their whole knowledge, by learning without the book, was tied only to their tongue and lips, and never ascended up to the brain and head, and therefore was soon spit out of the mouth again. They were as men always going, but ever out of the way. And why? For their whole labour, or rather great toil without order, was even vain idleness without profit. Indeed, they took great pains about learning, but employed small labour in learning, when by this way prescribed in this book, being straight, plain, and easy, the scholar is always labouring with pleasure and ever going right on forward with profit. Always labouring, I say, for or° he have construed, parsed, twice translated over by good advisement, marked out his six points by skilful judgement, he

[5] *Ad Atticum*] Letters to Titus Pomponius Atticus, Roman philosopher.
[6] commonplace] Here, a theme or topic rather than a quotable saying.

shall have necessary occasion to read over every lecture a dozen times, at the least. Which, because he shall do always in order, he shall do it always with pleasure. And pleasure allureth love; love hath lust to labour; labour always obtaineth his purpose, as most truly both Aristotle in his *Rhetoric* and *Oedipus* in Sophocles do teach saying: *pan gar ekponoumenon haliske* etc.[7] And this oft reading is the very right following of that good counsel which Pliny doth give to his friend Fuscus, saying, *multum non multa*.[8] But to my purpose again.

When, by this diligent and speedy reading over those fore-named good books of Tully, Terence, Caesar, and Livy, and by this second kind of translating out of your English, time shall breed skill and use shall bring perfection, then ye may try, if you will, your scholar with the third kind of translation, although the two first ways, by mine opinion, be not only sufficient of themselves but also surer, both for the master's teaching and scholar's learning, than this third way is. Which is thus: write you in English some letter, as it were from him to his father or to some other friend, naturally, according to the disposition of the child, or some tale, or fable, or plain narration, according as Aphthonius beginneth his exercises of learning,[9] and let him translate it into Latin again, abiding in such place where no other scholar may prompt him. But yet use you yourself such discretion for choice therein as the matter may be within the compass, both for words and sentences, of his former learning and reading. And now take heed lest your scholar do not better in some point than

[7] **Marg**. Aristotle, *Rhetoric*, Book 2; Sophocles, *Oedipus the King*. Plato, Letter 7. [The saying quoted by Ascham does not appear anywhere in classical Greek and *haliske* is a non-existent Greek form. If taken to be *halisketai* then the Greek means 'everything that is worked hard at can be achieved'. I am grateful to Stephen Halliwell for this explanation.]

[8] *multum non multa*] Pliny, *Letters* VII.x.6., meaning that it is better to read deeply than to read widely.

[9] Aphthonius [. . .] learning] The *Progymnasmata* of Aphthonius, a Greek rhetorician of the fourth century, were a series of fourteen composition exercises graded in terms of difficulty and widely used in sixteenth-century schools. There were Latin translations by Giovanni Cataneo (1507) and Rudolph Agricola, and a loose version in English by Richard Rainolde (1564). The most popular classroom editions were those with the commentary by Reinhard Lorich. See George A. Kennedy, ed., *Progymnasmata: Greek Textbooks of Prose Composition and Rhetoric* (Leiden: Brill, 2003).

you yourself, except ye have been diligently exercised in these kinds of translating before.

I had once a proof hereof, tried by good experience by a dear friend of mine when I came first from Cambridge to serve the Queen's Majesty, then Lady Elizabeth, lying at worthy Sir Anthony Denny's[10] in Cheshunt. John Whitney, a young gentleman, was my bedfellow, who, willing by good nature and provoked by mine advice, began to learn the Latin tongue after the order declared in this book. We began after Christmas: I read unto him Tully, *De amicitia*, which he did every day twice translate, out of Latin into English and out of English into Latin again.[11] About St Laurence's tide[12] after, to prove how he profited, I did choose out Torquatus's talk, *De Amicitia*, in the latter end of the first book, *De Finibus*,[13] because that place was the same in matter, like in words and phrases, nigh to the form and fashion of sentences as he had learned before in *De Amicitia*. I did translate it myself into plain English and gave it him to turn into Latin, which he did so choicely, so orderly, so without any great miss in the hardest points of grammar, that some in seven year in grammar schools, yea, and some in the universities too, cannot do half so well. This worthy young gentleman, to my greatest grief, to the great lamentation of that whole house, and specially to that most noble lady, now Queen Elizabeth herself, departed within few days out of this world.

And if in any cause a man may without offence of God speak somewhat ungodly, surely it was some grief unto me to see him hie so hastily to God as he did. A court full of such young gentlemen were rather a paradise than a court upon earth. And though I had never poetical head to make any verse in any tongue, yet either love, or sorrow, or both, did wring out of me then certain careful thoughts of my good will toward him, which, in my

[10] Sir Anthony Denny's] Denny (1501–49) was a patron of humanist learning who had studied at St Paul's under Colet and then at St John's College, Cambridge, in Ascham's time. He was close to Henry VIII and was named as an executor of Henry's will.

[11] i.e. the double translation method, which Ascham learned from Cheke at Cambridge.

[12] St Laurence's tide] 10 August.

[13] Torquatus's talk [. . .] *De Finibus*] Torquatus is a speaker in *De Amicitia*; Ascham's exercise for Whitney was taken from Cicero, *De Finibus bonorum et malorum* [On the ends of good and evil], I.20.65–66.

mourning for him, fell forth more by chance than either by skill or use into this kind of misorderly° metre:

> Mine own John Whitney, now farewell, now death doth part us twain,
> No death, but parting for a while, whom life shall join again.
> [. . .][14]

In this place, or I proceed further, I will now declare by whose authority I am led and by what reason I am moved to think that this way of double translation out of one tongue into another is either only, or at least chiefly, to be exercised, specially of youth, for the ready and sure obtaining of any tongue.

There be six ways appointed by the best learned men for the learning of tongues and increase of eloquence, as:

1. *Translatio linguarum*
2. *Paraphrasis*
3. *Metaphrasis*
4. *Epitome*[15]
5. *Imitatio*[16]
6. *Declamatio*.[17]

All these be used and commended, but in order and for respects, as person, ability, place, and time shall require, the five last be fitter for the master than the scholar, for men than for children, for the universities rather than for grammar schools. Yet nevertheless, which is fittest in mine opinion for our school, and which is either wholly to be refused or partly to be used for our purpose, I will by good authority and some reason, I trust, particularly of everyone and largely° enough of them all, declare orderly unto you.

---

[14] There are a further twenty lines of platitudes (though there is no reason to doubt the sincerity of Ascham's grief).

[15] *Epitome*] Ascham is critical of *epitomes* or digests, which he regards as the enemies of learning, especially in the universities; see *Scholemaster*, sig. N2^{v}, image 50.

[16] *Imitatio*] 'a facultie to expresse livelie and perfitelie that example: which ye go about to folow', *Scholemaster*, STC 832, sig. O1^{v}, image 53; see also Thomas M. Greene, *The Light in Troy*, pp. 268–70.

[17] *Declamatio*] A rhetorical exercise which involved making a speech for or against a given proposition; see Neil Rhodes, *Shakespeare and the Origins of English* (Oxford: Oxford University Press, 2004), pp. 92–117. (Ascham does not, in fact, discuss *declamatio* any further.)

Translatio linguarum

Translation is easy in the beginning for the scholar and bringeth all much learning and great judgement to the master. It is most common and most commendable of all other exercises for youth: most common, for all your constructions[18] in grammar schools be nothing else but translations; but because they be not double translations, as I do require, they bring forth but simple and single commodity;° and because also they lack the daily use of writing, which is the only thing that breedeth deep root, both in the wit for good understanding and in the memory for sure keeping of all that is learned, most commendable also, and that by the judgement of all authors which entreat° of these exercises. Tully in the person of Lucius Crassus,[19] whom he maketh his example of eloquence and true judgement in learning, doth not only praise specially and choose this way of translation for a young man, but doth also discommend and refuse his own former wont in exercising *paraphrasin* and *metaphrasin*. *Paraphrasis* is to take some eloquent oration or some notable commonplace in Latin and express it with other words. *Metaphrasis* is to take some notable place out of a good poet and turn the same sense into metre or into other words in prose. Crassus, or rather Tully, doth mislike both these ways because the author, either orator or poet, had chosen out before the fittest words and aptest composition for that matter, and so he, in seeking other, was driven to use the worse.

Quintilian also preferreth translation before all other exercises,[20] yet having a lust to dissent from Tully (as he doth in very many places, if a man read his rhetoric over advisedly) and that rather of an envious mind than of any just cause, doth greatly commend *paraphrasis*, crossing spitefully Tully's judgement in refusing the same, and so do Ramus and Talaeus[21] even

[18] constructions] Exercises in construing in which the sentence structure is analysed and then translated word for word.

[19] **Marg**. *De Oratore* I.[xxxiv.154–5.]

[20] **Marg**. *Institutio oratoria* 1.X. [v.2–11; a discussion of paraphrase follows the discussion of translation].

[21] Ramus and Talaeus] Pierre de La Ramée (1515–72) and Omer Talon (*c.* 1510–62) introduced a radical new approach to the teaching of logic and rhetoric. The name of 'Ramus' was associated with rhetoric textbooks that concentrated exclusively on stylistic figures and with 'method', which used

at this day in France, too. But such singularity in dissenting from the best men's judgements, in liking only their own opinions, is much misliked of all them that join with learning discretion and wisdom. For he that can neither like Aristotle in logic and philosophy, nor Tully in rhetoric and eloquence, will from these steps likely enough presume by like pride to mount higher to the misliking of greater matters: that is, either in religion to have a dissentious head or in the commonwealth to have a factious° heart, as I knew one, a student in Cambridge, who, for a singularity, began first to dissent in the schools from Aristotle and soon after became a perverse Arian,[22] against Christ and all true religion, and studied diligently Origen, Basil, and St Jerome, only to glean out of their works the pernicious heresies of Celsus, Eunomius, and Helvidius, whereby the church of Christ was so poisoned withal.

But to leave these high points of divinity, surely, in this quiet and harmless controversy for the liking or misliking of *paraphrasis* for a young scholar, even as far as Tully goeth beyond Quintilian, Ramus, and Talaeus in perfect eloquence, even so much, by mine opinion, come they behind Tully for true judgement in teaching the same.

Plinius Secundus,[23] a wise senator, of great experience, excellently learned himself, a liberal patron of learned men, and the purest writer, in mine opinion, of all his age (I except not Suetonius, his two schoolmasters, Quintilian and Tacitus, nor yet his most excellent learned uncle, the elder Plinius), doth express in an epistle to his friend Fuscus many good ways for order in study, but he beginneth with translation and preferreth it to all the rest. And because his words be notable, I will recite them:

---

binary trees to organise knowledge. Ramus's simplification of arts teaching was opposed by conservatives but was influential into the eighteenth century. He was killed in the St Bartholomew's Day Massacre of 1572.

[22] perverse Arian] The Arian heresy, first advanced in the fourth century AD, was to deny the divinity of Christ. John Proctor's *The Fal of the Late Arian* (1549), which listed and refuted the main points of the heresy was linked to a later Cambridge student, Christopher Marlowe. Ascham suggests that questioning secular authorities such as Aristotle, as Ramus did, leads on to more serious forms of religious dissent and heresy.

[23] **Marg.** *Plinius dedit Quintiliano praeceptori suo, in matrimonium filiae, 60,000 nummos* [Pliny gave 60,000 sersteces to his tutor Quintilian on the marriage of his daughter], *Epistles* 67.

> *Utile in primis, ut multi praecipiunt, ex Graeco in Latinum et ex Latino vertere in Graecum: quo genere exercitationis proprietas splendorque verborum, apta structura sententiarum, figurarum copia et explicandi vis colligitur. Praeterea, imitatione optimorum, facultas similia inveniendi paratur: et quae legentem fefellissent, transferentem fugere non possunt. Intelligentia ex hoc et judicium acquiritur.*[24]

Ye perceive how Pliny teacheth that by this exercise of double translating is learned easily, sensibly, by little and little, not only all the hard congruities of grammar, the choice of aptest words, the right framing of words and sentences, comeliness of figures and forms, fit for every matter and proper for every tongue, but that which is greater also, in marking daily and following diligently thus the steps of the best authors: like invention of arguments, like order in disposition, like utterance in elocution[25] is easily gathered up, whereby your scholar shall be brought not only to like eloquence but also to all true understanding and right judgement, both for writing and speaking. And where Dionysius of Halicarnassus[26] hath written two excellent books, the one *De delectu optimorum verborum*, the which I fear is lost, the other, of the right framing of words and sentences, which doth remain yet in Greek, to the great profit of all them that truly study for eloquence, yet this way of double translating shall bring the whole

[24] Pliny the Younger (61/62–113 AD), letter to Fuscus Salinator, *Letters* VII.ix.1: 'The most useful thing, which is always being suggested, is to translate Greek into Latin and Latin into Greek. This kind of exercise develops in one a precision and richness of vocabulary, a wide range of metaphor and power of exposition, and moreover, imitation of the best models leads to a like aptitude for original composition. At the same time, any point which might have been overlooked by a reader cannot escape the eye of a translator. All this cultivates perception and critical sense', *The Letters of Pliny the Younger*, trans. by Betty Radice (Harmondsworth: Penguin, 1963; repr. 1981), pp. 190–92.

[25] invention [. . .] elocution] Ascham refers to the first three parts of rhetoric.

[26] Dionysius of Halicarnassus] (*c.* 60 BC–after 7 BC), Greek teacher of rhetoric whom Ascham placed next after Aristotle, Plato and Cicero as an authority on eloquence in his discussion of *imitatio* (*Scholemaster*, sigs R1^{v}–R2^{r}, image 57). The two works referred to here are *Peri mimēseos* ('On imitation') and *Peri synthēseōs onomaton* ('On the arrangement of words'). The first of these only survives in fragments and was Quintilian's source for *Institutio oratoria* X.i–ii; see D. A. Russell, '*De Imitatione*', in *Creative Imitation and Latin Literature*, ed. by David West and Tony Woodman (Cambridge: Cambridge University Press, 1979), pp. 1–16.

profit of both these books to a diligent scholar, and that easily and pleasantly both for fit choice of words and apt composition of sentences. And by these authorities and reasons am I moved to think this way of double translating, either only or chiefly, to be fittest for the speedy and perfect attaining of any tongue.

And for speedy attaining, I durst venture a good wager, if a scholar in whom is aptness, love, diligence, and constancy would but translate after this sort one little book in Tully, as *De senectute*, with two epistles, the first *Ad Quintum fratrem*, the other *Ad Lentulum* (the last, save one, in the first book), that scholar, I say, should come to a better knowledge in the Latin tongue than the most part do that spend four or five years in tossing all the rules of grammar in common schools. Indeed, this one book with these two epistles is not sufficient to afford all Latin words (which is not necessary for a young scholar to know), but it is able to furnish him fully for all points of grammar, with the right placing, ordering, and use of words in all kind of matter. And why not? For it is read that Dionysius Prusaeus, that wise philosopher and excellent orator of all his time, did come to the great learning and utterance that was in him by reading and following only two books, *Phaedon Platonis* and Demosthenes' most notable oration, *Peri Parapresbeias*.[27]And a better and nearer example herein may be our most noble Queen Elizabeth,[28] who never took yet Greek nor Latin grammar in her hand after the first declining of a noun and a verb, but only by this double translating of Demosthenes and Isocrates daily without missing every forenoon, and likewise some part of Tully every afternoon, for the space of a year or two, hath attained to such a perfect understanding in both the tongues and to such a ready utterance of the Latin, and that with such a judgement as they be few in number in both the universities, or elsewhere in England, that be in both tongues comparable with Her Majesty. And to conclude in a short room the commodities of double translation: surely the mind by daily marking, first, the cause and matter; then, the

[27] Dionysius [. . .] *Peri Parapresbeias*] Dion Prusaeus (d. *c.* 117 AD), also known as Dion Chrysostom, Greek rhetorician and spokesman for republican values, cited by Milton in *Areopagitica*. His recommendations are Plato, *Phaedo*, and Demosthenes, 'On the False Embassy'.

[28] Queen Elizabeth] For a more critical view of Ascham's pedagogy see *Queen Elizabeth 1: Selected Works*, ed. by Steven F. May (New York: Washington Square Press, 2004), pp. xxv–xxvi.

words and phrases; next, the order and composition; after, the reason and arguments; then, the forms and figures of both the tongues; lastly, the measure and compass[29] of every sentence, must needs by little and little draw unto it the like shape of eloquence as the author doth use which is read.

And thus much for double translation.

Paraphrasis

Paraphrasis, the second point, is not only to express at large with more words, but to strive and contend (as Quintilian sayeth)[30] to translate the best Latin authors into other Latin words, as many or thereabouts.

This way of exercise was used first by Gaius Carbo and taken up for a while by Lucius Crassus,[31] but soon after, upon due proof thereof, rejected justly by Crassus and Cicero, yet allowed and made sterling° again by Marcus Quintilian; nevertheless shortly after, by better assay, disallowed of his own scholar, Plinius Secundus, who termeth it rightly thus: *audax contentio*.[32] It is a bold comparison indeed to think to say better than that is best. Such turning of the best into worse is much like the turning of good wine out of a fair, sweet flagon of silver into a foul, musty bottle of leather, or to turn pure gold and silver into foul brass and copper.

Such kind of *paraphrasis*, in turning, chopping, and changing the best to worse, either in the Mint[33] or schools (though Master Broke[34] and Quintilian both say the contrary), is much misliked of the best and wisest men. I can better allow another kind of *paraphrasis*, to turn rude and barbarous into proper and eloquent, which nevertheless is an exercise not fit for a scholar but for a

---

[29] measure and compass] rhythm and proportion.

[30] **Marg**. *Instiutio oratoria* 10 [5.4–8].

[31] Carbo [. . .] Crassus] Gaius Papirius Carbo, Roman tribune and orator, who was impeached for complicity in the murder of Gaius Gracchus by Lucius Crassus. Crassus was regarded as an outstanding orator by his pupil, Cicero.

[32] Pliny the Younger, *Letters* VII.ix.4.

[33] Mint] Ascham develops the image of coinage from 'sterling' above.

[34] Broke] Thomas Broke (*c.* 1513 - *c.* 1555), an active Protestant who enjoyed Cromwell's patronage. He added paraphrases of the Ten Commandments and the Lord's Prayer to William Huyecke's translation of Calvin's *Geneva* (London, 1550).

perfect master, who in plenty hath good choice, in copy° hath right judgement and grounded skill, as did appear to be in Sebastian Castalio[35] in translating Kempis's book *De imitando Christi.*

But to follow Quintilian's advice for *paraphrasis* were even to take pain to seek the worse and fouler way when the plain and fairer is occupied before your eyes.

The old and best authors that ever wrote were content, if occasion required to speak twice of one matter, not to change the words, but *rhētōs*, that is, word for word to express it again. For they thought that a matter well expressed with fit words and apt composition was not to be altered, but liking it well themselves, they thought it also would be well allowed of others.

A schoolmaster (such one as I require) knoweth that I say true.

He readeth in Homer, almost in every book, and specially in *secundo et nono Iliados*,[36] not only some verses, but whole leaves, not to be altered with new, but to be uttered with the old selfsame words.

He knoweth that Xenophon,[37] writing twice of Agesilaus, once in his *Life*, again in the *History of the Greeks*, in one matter keepeth always the selfsame words. He doth the like, speaking of Socrates, both in the beginning of his *Apology* and in the last end of *Apomnemoneumatoǹ*.

Demosthenes also in *Philippica* 4[38] doth borrow his own words uttered before in his oration *De Chersoneso*. He doth the like, and that more at large, in his orations against Androtion and Timocrates.

In Latin also, Cicero in some places, and Virgil in more, do repeat one matter with the selfsame words. These excellent authors did thus, not for lack of words, but by judgement and skill, whatsoever other more curious and less skillful do think, write, and do.

Paraphrasis nevertheless hath good place in learning, but not, by mine opinion, for any scholar, but is only to be left to a perfect

---

[35] Castalio] Sébastian Châteillon, who published a version of Thomas à Kempis's *Imitation of Christ* in more elegant Latin (Basel, 1563).

[36] *Iliad*, books 2 and 9.

[37] Xenophon] See Xenophon's accounts of Agesilaus's campaign against the Persians in *Agesilaus* I.6–35 and *Hellenica* III.iv.2–25; also the debate between Hermogenes and Socrates in *Apology of Socrates to the Jury* 2–6 and *Memorabilia* IV.viii.4–7.

[38] *Philippica* 4] The authenticity of this is disputed.

master either to expound openly a good author withal or to compare privately, for his own exercise, how some notable place of an excellent author may be uttered with other fit words. But if ye alter also the composition, form, and order, then that is not *paraphrasis* but *imitatio*, as I will fully declare in fitter place.[39] [. . .]

If a master would have a perfect example to follow, how in *genere sublimi* to avoid *nimium*, or in *mediocri* to attain *satis*, or in *humili* to eschew *parum*,[40] let him read diligently for the first *Secundam Philippicam*, for the mean *De natura deorum*, and for the lowest *Partitiones*.[41] Or if in another tongue ye look for like example, in like perfection for all those three degrees, read *Pro Ctesiphonte*, *Ad Leptinem*, and *Contra Olympiodorum*, and what wit, art, and diligence is able to afford ye shall plainly see.

For our time, the odd° man to perform all three perfectly, whatsoever he doth, and to know the way to do them skillfully, whensoever he list, is, in my poor opinion, Ioannes Sturmius.[42]

He also counselleth all scholars to beware of *paraphrasis*,[43] except it be from worse to better, from rude and barbarous to proper and pure Latin, and yet no man to exercise that neither, except such one as is already furnished with plenty of learning and grounded with steadfast judgement before.

All these faults that thus many wise men do find with the exercise of *paraphrasis* in turning the best Latin into other as good as they can, that is, ye may be sure, into a great deal worse than it was, both in right choice for propriety and true placing for good order, is committed also commonly in all common schools by the schoolmasters in tossing and troubling young wits (as I said in the beginning) with that butcherly° fear in making of Latins.[44]

---

[39] in a fitter place] Ascham proposed to write a separate treatise on *imitatio*; see STC 832, image 64.

[40] *genere sublimi* [. . .] *parum*] 'in the high style to avoid bombast; in the middle style to attain sufficiency; in the low style to avoid poverty.'

[41] for the first [. . .] *Contra Olympiodorum*] The first are orations by Cicero, the second by Demosthenes.

[42] Sturm] Johann Sturm (1507–89) was rector of the gymnasium at Strasbourg and author of works on rhetoric and education. Ascham maintained a friendly correspondence with him over eighteen years, which was published with his other letters in 1576. See also Lewis W. Spitz and Barbara Sher Tinsley, eds., *Johann Sturm on Education: the Reformation and Humanist Learning* (St Louis: Concordia, 1995), which includes a translation of *De Litterarum ludis* (1539).

[43] See Sturm, *De Imitatione oratoria* (Strasbourg, 1574), sig. C8^{v}.

Therefore, in place of Latins for young scholars and of *paraphrasis* for the masters, I would have double translation specially used. For in double translating a perfect piece of Tully or Caesar, neither the scholar in learning nor the master in teaching can err. A true touchstone, a sure metewand° lieth before both their eyes. For all right congruity, propriety of words, order in sentences, the right imitation – to invent good matter, to dispose it in good order, to confirm it with good reason, to express any purpose fitly and orderly – is learned thus both easily and perfectly. Yea, to miss sometime in this kind of translation bringeth more profit than to hit right either in *paraphrasis* or making of Latins. For though ye say well in a Latin making or in a *paraphrasis*, yet you being but in doubt and uncertain whether ye say well or no, ye gather and lay up in memory no sure fruit of learning thereby; but if ye fault in translation, ye are easily taught how perfectly to amend it, and so well warned how after to eschew all such faults again.

Paraphrasis therefore, by mine opinion, is not meet for grammar schools, nor yet very fit for young men in the university, until study and time have bred in them perfect learning and steadfast judgement.

Metaphrasis

This kind of exercise is all one with *paraphrasis*, save it is out of verse either into prose or into some other kind of metre, or else out of prose into verse, which was Socrates' exercise and pastime (as Plato reporteth)[45] when he was in prison, to translate Aesop's *Fables* into verse. Quintilian doth greatly praise also this exercise, but because Tully[46] doth disallow it in young men, by mine

[44] making of Latins] Pupils proceeded to Latin composition after instruction in grammar.

[45] **Marg**. Plato, *Phaedo* [60 D].

[46] Quintilian [. . .] Tully] *Institutio oratoria* X.v.4: 'I do not want Paraphrase to be a mere passive reproduction, but to rival and vie with the original in expressing the same thoughts. I therefore disagree with those who forbid paraphrases of Latin speeches', trans. by D. A. Russell, *The Orator's Education*, 5 vols (Cambridge, MA: Harvard University Press, 2001), IV, 357, disagreeing with Cicero at *De Oratore* I.xxxiv.154: 'I saw that to employ the same expressions profited me nothing, while to employ others was a positive hindrance, in that I was forming the habit of using the less appropriate', trans. by E. W. Sutton and H. Rackham (London: William Heinemann, 1948), I, 107.

opinion it were not well to use it [in] grammar schools, even for the selfsame causes that be recited against *paraphrasis*. And therefore, for the use, or misuse, of it the same is to be thought that is spoken of *paraphrasis* before.

52. Abraham Fleming, *The Bucolics of Virgil* (1575)

[Abraham Fleming (*c.* 1552–1607) was a sizar (a poor scholar) at Peterhouse, Cambridge, from 1570, and published his translation of Virgil's *Eclogues* (also known as the *Bucolics*) as a student. Before graduating in 1582 he had already worked for a number of London publishing houses as a translator, editor, and indexer, and he eventually contributed in various ways to more than 50 books. These included a translation of Aelian as *The Registre of Hystories* and the index for Barnabe Googe's popular translation of Palingenius, *The Zodiake of Life*, both of which appeared the year after his *Bucolics*. His most important work was the revision of Holinshed's *Chronicles* (1587) and he also revised his *Bucolics* for publication with a new translation of the *Georgics* in 1579.

Virgil's position as the premier Roman poet is based on the *Aeneid*, but the pastoral *Eclogues* were also an established part of the school curriculum. Latin editions were printed in England as early as 1512, but Fleming's is the first English translation to appear in print and is done in rhyming fourteeners. There is evidence that he used the edition with commentary by Badius (Paris, 1501). Fleming abandoned rhyme for his 1579 revision and a prose translation of the *Eclogues* was published by John Brinsley in 1620.

See also Margaret Tudeau-Clayton, *Jonson, Shakespeare and Early Modern Virgil* (Cambridge: Cambridge University Press, 1998); Andrew Wallace, *Virgil's Schoolboys: the Poetics of Pedagogy in Renaissance England* (Oxford: Oxford University Press, 2010); George W. Pigman III in *OHLTE* (2), pp. 248–57; Cyndia Susan Clegg in *ODNB*.]

To the Right Worshipful Master Peter Osborne,[1] Esquire, a favourer and furtherer of learning.

Taking a view, right worshipful, of Virgil's *Bucolics*, and finding therein many difficulties and obscurities, as well for the interpretation as for the construction,° I addressed my pen to wade° through that work that by mine endeavour and travail in the translation thereof employed, some commodity might redound to weaker wits which cannot comprehend (for want of understanding and perseverance) the poet's phrase,° nor the stateliness of his style. Which labour I attempted partly for my private practice (using it as a preservative against idleness rather than a preparative to gain and profit) and partly for the benefit of young learners of the Latin tongue. I account the work worthy of my travail, and I persuade myself of a sufficient recompense by the measure of that knowledge which I have reaped in this English conversion,° for after I had traced° through thick and thin, through deep and shallow, through hard and soft, through rough and smooth, and what not, I obtained in the end such familiarity and acquaintance with Virgil's verse that such things as appeared at a sudden blush[2] to surmount my capacity many degrees, by earnest perusing and serious searching out of the sense, which sometime lay secret and hidden, offered themselves plain, open, and (as I may say) naked to my understanding. And now at the length I have broken the bone that other may taste the marrow; I have cut the ice that other may wade in the water; I have cracked the shell that other may eat the kernel; I have pressed the grapes that other may suck the juice; I have reaped the wheat that other may enjoy the harvest.[3]

It was not my meaning that this translation should be published after it was fully finished and throughly performed, but a true and an approved friend of mine to his ability,° regarding my study and pains bestowed in the same and the benefit which might spring and issue therefrom, counselled me to put it in print, persuading me that the edition thereof would be very

---

[1] Peter Osborne] (1521–92), a Member of Parliament who held an administrative position at the Exchequer. He enjoyed the patronage of Sir William Cecil and was related by marriage to Sir John Cheke.

[2] at a sudden blush] at first sight.

[3] The construction and some of the metaphors are echoed in the preface to the KJB; see **15d**. 122–28].

commodious° and necessary, whose words (uttered of special good will and favour to the furtherance of young beginners in grammatical exercises) I thought it wisdom and modesty to obey, foolishness and insolency to withstand. It is well known that there be in this English land many ignorant and unskillful instructors of youth in the Latin language, who sometime read that to their hearers which they themselves understand not and teach their scholars that which they themselves had need to learn. Some stumble at straws and leap over logs, and that is mere blindness. Some are drowned in doubts where every line is as lightsome as a lamp, and that is gross foolishness. Some pervert and wrest awry many things with oblique and crooked interpretations, and that is weakness of wit. Some expound after their own opinion and reason without further ground of authority, and that is impudency or boldness void of shame. Some follow their own fantasies and forsake the judgements of other writers, and that is self-love and contempt. Some fill their hearers' ears with variety of discourses upon a letter, a word, a line, or a sentence, and that is curiosity° without necessity. These are not pathways to tread to Virgil's poetry, but rather stops and impediments. These are not keys to open hard and obscure clauses, but bars and bolts to shut them up closer. These are not stiles and bridges to pass over into the plain fields of the poet's meaning, but hedges and ditches to compass them in. Finally, these are not glittering stars to shine in dark corners, but misty clouds to procure greater blindness.

A plain interpretation° and a literal explication maketh a ready and a speedy passage to understanding and knowledge, whereof I have had a principal care in this translation, leaving nothing unsifted° which might appertain to the uttermost exposition of these *Bucolics*, that weaklings in poetry might rather be supported than suppressed, quickened than dulled, emboldened than discouraged, furthered than hindered. In this conversion, for the avoiding of confusion and disorder in proper names of men, women, rivers, springs, hills, cities etc., whereof the ignorant oftentimes make a hotchpotch and mingle-mangle, whilst they know not how to distinguish the one from the other, applying erewhile the name of a mountain to a man, the name of a fountain to a town, the name of a village to a flood, the name of a city to a river etc., – which false applications the unskilful commonly use, supposing they hit the mark when indeed they wander wide – I have after the order of the alphabet or ABC collected such annotations as seemed convenient and necessary for the understanding of such proper names as the poet enfarceth° in this his bucolical discourse, so that whosoever readeth the verse and findeth therein any proper name, by casting an eye to the margin of the page they shall be disburdened of all doubt in that case, which in mine opinion is a benefit not to be neglected. Other annotations besides these I couched together, as it were in a heap, wherein obscure and dark phrases of speech, natures of heaths and plants, qualities and dispositions of beasts and birds, properties of trees and fruits, and whatsoever else was expedient, very briefly and yet plainly were expressed. But the printer hereof sparing cost, and coveting to compass much with little charge, besides that making haste to have it dispatched, lightly regarded these annotations which I, by tossing, tumbling, and ruffling° divers authors to and fro, collected and gathered.

Therefore they remain in mine own hands, and I intend to preserve them until such time as I have translated Virgil's *Georgics* into English[4] (which I mean to do, by God's assistance, at my convenient leisure when I have cleared my hands of other exercises and as I feel my mind discharged of clogging° cares) than to broach them, that the liquor of the same may run abroad for every young scholar to taste and sup. Wherefore it remaineth that such whose chance it is to see and read this translation and to confer it with the Latin, to increase their knowledge in that whereof they are ignorant, that such, I say, content themselves with this handgrip[5] of notes, yet my will, my wit, and my work wrestled to have them fully satisfied.

To the Indifferent Reader.

The *Bucolics* of Virgil, which Cicero (the flowing fountain of eloquence) desired to hear with greediness,[6] and never heard to

---

[4] Virgil's *Georgics*] Fleming's was the first printed English translation of both the *Eclogues* and the *Georgics*, which he published together in 1589, STC 24817.

[5] handgrip] Fleming may be imagining the marginal notes as a handrail or banister to help in climbing the stairs.

[6] Cicero [. . .] greediness] Fleming is citing an anecdote from Servius: 'as for Cicero, when he had heard some of the verses, his piercing judgement immediately perceived that these were productions of uncommon genius, and ordered the whole eclogue to be recited from the beginning'. Since the *Eclogues* did not become available until after Cicero's death, this must be apocryphal. See David

the accomplishment and contentation of his mind, I have translated into the English tongue, wedding myself as it were to the vulgar and common phrase of speech, and yet observing (as near as I could) the natural significations of such words as the poet hath used to garnish and deck this his worthy work, as clusters of purple grapes a green vine; as crimson roses a beautiful garland; as velvet violets an odoriferous nosegay; as precious pearls a gorgeous garment; as golden letters polished alabaster; as a rich diamond a glorious diadem etc. So that in all Virgil's verses pleasure and profit draw (as it were) in one yoke, and where these twain are linked in a chain, what can be tedious, what can be wearisome, what can be laborious, what can be undelightsome?

This translation affordeth a double advantage: the first a mitigation of expense, or (that I may speak more familiarly) a saving of money, for it containeth an abridgement of a commentary or dictionary, which being bought alone (I mean the whole volume or book as it is set forth by learned men both of this our native country and also of foreign lands) doth exceed the price of this libel° by pence, groats,° and shillings. The second, a ready introduction or an easy entrance to the knowledge of proper names (placed after the manner of marginal notes) that such as have not seen the substance, or scarcely the shadow or glimmering of the Latin tongue, might perceive without curious inquisition or further search in any other author the meaning of that which they read, understand circumstances, discern doubts, interpret with judgement, follow order, and avoid confusion. I am determined (God prosper my purpose) to bestow semblable° labour in the translation of Virgil's *Georgics*, if I be not prevented nor intercepted by infortunate casualties (from them the Lord God protect me and mine), which commonly are allotted to our unlucky life. In the mean season, take and use the benefit and commodity of this my travail with courtesy and soberness, not barking nor biting at me after a currish kind in mine absence, nor stinging me with unreverent terms for my good will herein employed. To be brief, as you judge and talk of me and my labour, *sic venite et valete*.[7]

Abraham Fleming, Student.

Scott Wilson-Okamura, *Virgil in the Renaissance* (Cambridge: Cambridge University Press, 2010), p. 54.

[7] *sic venite et valete*] 'So hail and farewell.'

53. Maurice Kyffin, *Andria: The First Comedy of Terence, in English* (1588)

[Maurice Kyffin (*c.* 1555–1598) came from the Welsh-speaking town of Oswestry on the English-Welsh border and his *magnum opus* was a translation into Welsh of Bishop John Jewel's defence of the Church of England, *Apologia Ecclesiae Anglicanae* (1562), which he published in 1595. After moving to London in 1578 he became tutor to the sons of Thomas Sackville, Lord Buckhurst, the co-author of *Gorboduc*, and was acquainted with the most distinguished writers and scholars of the day, including John Dee, William Camden, Edmund Spenser, and Sir John Harington. He was the author of a celebrated patriotic poem, *The Blessedness of Britain* (1587), reissued in the Armada year of 1588, which also saw the publication of his translation of Terence's *Andria.*

Terence is, with Plautus, the most important writer of Roman comedy, basing his plays on the Greek New Comedy of Menander, which allowed some sixteenth-century English translators to describe his work as 'translation' like their own (see 'N. W.', **40**. 9–10). He was popularised in the Middle Ages by the commentary of Donatus, teacher of Jerome, who also described Terence as a 'translator' in his letter to Pammachius. Widely regarded as the best example of pure, simple, and colloquial Latin, he was used as a model for Latin speaking in sixteenth-century school textbooks. Nicholas Udall, Eton headmaster and translator of Erasmus's *Paraphrases*, gathered his *Floures for Latine Spekynge* (1534) from Terence. Printed teaching texts called *Vulgaria*, which presented conversational phrases from Terence in Latin and English, date back to 1483, and the first English translation of *Andria* appeared *c.* 1520 with the title *Terens in Englysh* (STC 23894).

See also T. W. Baldwin, *William Shakspere's Small Latine and Lesse Greeke*, 2 vols (Urbana: University of Illinois Press, 1944); Marvin T. Herrick, *Comic Theory in the Sixteenth Century* (Urbana: University of Illinois Press, 1964); Joel B. Altman, *The Tudor Play of Mind* (Berkeley: University of California Press, 1978), pp. 130–47; Hutson, *The Usurer's Daughter*, pp. 163–91; Gordon Braden in *OHLTE* (2), pp. 280–92; Glanmor Williams in *ODNB*.]

A furtherance for the attainment unto the right knowledge and true propriety of the Latin tongue. And also a commodious° mean of help to such as have forgotten Latin for their speedy recovering of ability to understand, write, and speak the same.

R. Cook[1] to the Readers of Master Kyffin's Translation.

The perfect pattern of pure Latin speech,
In English phrase most fitly here expressed,
Yields pleasure, profit, ease, and aid to each,
That would of Latin language be possessed.
Thank Kyffin then, whose pen hath purchased praise:
His pain (your gain) deserves the same always.

To the Right Worshipful gentlemen, Master Henry and Master Thomas Sackville, sons to the Right Honourable, the Lord Buckhurst.

It is now full seven years (as you can well remember) since I first attempted the translation of *Andria* into English verse, being thereto partly incited by your means. But afterward perceiving what difficulty it was to enforce the pithy and proverbial sayings of Terence into rhyme, and withal what inconvenience grew by reason of divers several speakers, sometime severally happening within the length of one line or less, I plainly saw that such manner of forced translation must needs be both harsh and unpleasant to the reader, and also not half seemly befitting the sweet style and eloquence of the author. So as having thus translated the whole comedy in verse (saving the two last leaves) my pains bestowed therein did so much mislike me, as that ever sithence° it lay by me utterly neglected and never fully finished. Till that now of late, being by some much requested to make common the same for the benefit of such as study the Latin, I have thereupon somewhat altered my course and endeavoured to turn it into prose as a thing of less labour in show and more liberty in substance, seeming withal most accordant with this comical kind of writing. And because I am not ignorant with what ardent love and liking you have always most studiously

[1] Cook] Probably Roger Cook, one of John Dee's apprentices.

embraced all good authors (being of yourselves even naturally inclined to all learning and knowledge), I cannot therefore but recommend to your favour this piece of Terence, bearing the frame of my poor workmanship, which I desire you at idle and vacant times to vouchsafe to peruse, both for Terence's sake, whom I am sure you love, and also at my request, whom I know you do not hate. And so I commit you to the most gracious protection of the Highest.

A Preface to the courteous reader.

Among all the Roman writers, there is none (by the judgement of the learned) so much available to be read and studied for the true knowledge and purity of the Latin tongue as Publius Terentius.[2] For sith° the chiefest matter in speech is to speak properly and aptly,[3] and that we have not a more cunning craftsmaster of apt and proper speech than Terence, well worthy is he then, even with all care and diligence, to be both taught and learned before any other. And surely, great is the pity, that Terence were not more used of masters in teaching and made more familiar to scholars in learning than commonly it is,[4] being (as I have known myself) by divers men in divers sentences diversely misunderstood. For the author in many places using abbreviations and figurative speeches, as well in regard of his verse as also that such manner of writing, was very eloquent and familiar in his time, doth thereby cause the sense [to] seem very doubtful to such readers as are not fully acquainted with him. Which comes to pass by means that this book is not so frequented in schools, nor laboured in study, according to the worthiness of it, but other base and inferior books commonly preferred before

[2] Purity [. . .] Terentius] Terence himself advertised this in the prologue to *Heautontimoroumenos* ('The Self-Tormentor'): 'In this play there is pure language'.

[3] speak [. . .] aptly] Kyffin follows earlier school texts such as Udall's *Floures for Latine spekynge* (1534) in presenting Terence as a model for speaking rather than writing Latin. Palsgrave's bilingual version of the Terentian *Acolastus* is similarly concerned with speech.

[4] pity [. . .] commonly it is] This is a strange observation, since Terence had long been used for Latin language teaching in schools. As well as the bilingual dialogues of the *Vulgaria*, a Latin edition of the six comedies by Badius Ascensius had been published in 1497 and many times reprinted.

it, to the utter marring and maiming of scholars both in style and judgement.

Though this comedy, now Englished, perhaps seem not altogether so pleasant as could be wished, neither in matter nor manner of handling, yet is it to be considered (besides that it leeseth° his natural grace, being turned into another language) that the time when and the place where it was first published in Latin, afforded no other sort of comedies than this is. And therefore it was no part of my meaning to translate the same as a thing either pleasant to be played or very delightful to be read (notwithstanding that this author was most excellent and most learned of any that wrote in this kind), but especially for that the Latin is pure and eloquent, much commended by Tully himself,[5] and right requisite to be studied of all such as would attain to the knowledge of right speaking and readiness of well writing in the Latin tongue; for whose sakes (and also at the earnest request of some whom I was desirous to satisfy) I have adventured the Englishing hereof, wishing that as I have thus boldly begun with the first, so some other, having more leisure and learning, would go thorough with the rest of the comedies. I have used, as near as I could, the most known, usual, and familiar phrases in common speech to express the author's meaning, as (to my thinking) best agreeing therewithal.

To all young students of the Latin tongue (for whose only help and benefit this comedy is published) Maurice Kyffin wisheth increase of knowledge and final perfection.

How necessary the use and familiarity of Terence is for all such as would attain unto ripeness° in understanding, readiness in speaking, and right judgement in writing Latin, is a thing so commonly known and confessed of all men as I shall not need any reasons to prove the same. Therefore, for the better furthering of those that as yet are unacquainted with him, I was the rather persuaded to publish this my translation of *Andria*, wherein, whither my labour meriteth ought or nought, *aliorum sit iudicium*.[6] My chiefest care hath been to lay open the meaning

[5] Cicero's teacher, the grammarian Antonius, had encouraged him to write verses in praise of Terence's purity of language. See *The Fragmentary Latin Poets*, ed. by Edward Courtney (Oxford: Oxford University Press, 2003), p. 155.
[6] *aliorum sit iudicium*] 'let others be the judge'.

of the author, especially in all hard and difficult places of this comedy, and to utter the same in such apt, plain, and familiar words as are most meet for this low style and argument, for to handle a mean matter with high and lofty phrase were as great oversight and lack of judgement as could be. Touching the interpretation° of some places in *Andria*, I was forced to dissent from some of no small authority,[7] and specially from one very learned man who, occasioned° (in a work that he wrote) to English certain dispersed° phrases of Terence, hath (without offence be it spoken) so Englished some, and namely in *Andria*, as I am fain to forsake the same and give other quite contrary English unto them. One of those places in *Andria* hath these words: *aliquid monstri alunt*;[8] by him thus Englished: 'they bring some monstrous creature', and by me in this sort: 'they cloak some secret fault in her', which may be seen, interpreted to that effect, by Erasmus of Rotterdam handling that place in his *Chiliades*.[9] [. . .]

Moreover, for that the not well understanding of the argument of this comedy hath in divers bred errors and mistakings, I have therefore been careful herein to explain the argument° at large unto you and withal to set down each particular argument before every scene. Likewise, by my notes in the margin you shall be instructed, as occasion is offered, touching any doubtful speeches of the speakers, as whether they speak unto him that spake last before, or else to the audience, or to themselves.

54. John Brinsley, *Ludus Literarius* (1612)

[John Brinsley (1566–1624) was a sizar at Christ's College, Cambridge, and became a schoolmaster at Ashby-de-la-Zouch in Leicestershire. A strict puritan, his approach to education was

---

[7] no small authority] Thomas Cooper in his Anglo-Latin *Thesuarus* (1565); see STC 5688 (1578 edition), sig. G2^{v}, image 44.

[8] *aliquid monnstri alunt*] Terence, *Andria*, 250 and Erasmus *Adagia* 2.4.98: '*Monstrum alere* / To breed a monster. We speak of breeding a monster when we wish to convey that some frightful thing is being concealed and kept dark', *CWE* 33, trans. by R. A. B. Mynors (Toronto: Toronto University Press, 1991), p. 236.

[9] *Chiliades*] A title used by Erasmus for some editions of his proverb collection, *Adagia* (*Adagiorum chiliades:* 'thousands of proverbs').

pragmatic and his published work was designed for a very broadly based audience within education. His *Consolation for our Grammar Schooles* (1624), a shorter and more general version of *Ludus Literarius*, advertised itself as being 'for all those of the inferiour sort, namely, for Ireland, Wales, Virginia, with the Sommer Ilands [Bermuda] that all may speake one and the same language' (tp.). He also wrote a highly successful grammar, *The Posing of Parts* (1612), which went through ten editions to 1639, and a number of 'grammatical translations' which illustrate the method set out in *Ludus Literarius*.

Ludus Literarius was aimed at the 'common' or country schools rather than the elite audience that Ascham was assuming. It was based on consultation with other schoolmasters and also reflects contemporary ideas about pedagogy. Brinsley invited feedback from readers in order to establish a consensus on the most effective methods of teaching Latin, and despite its date it is likely to reflect common grammar school practice in the Elizabethan period. The treatise is constructed as a dialogue between two schoolmasters: Spoudaeus is a traditionalist, whose name means 'hasty' (and, it is implied, 'superficial'), while Philoponus ('lover of hard work') is a reformer.

See Vivian Salmon, 'John Brinsley: 17th-Century Pioneer in Applied Linguistics', in *The Study of Language in Seventeenth-Century England*, 2nd edn (Amsterdam: Benjamins, 1988), pp. 33–46; Peter Mack, *Elizabethan Rhetoric: Theory and Practice* (Cambridge: Cambridge University Press, 2002); Rhodes, *Shakespeare and the Origins of English*; John Morgan in *ODNB*.]

Of Grammatical Translations.

There is a way, sayeth Master Ascham,[1] touched in the first book of Cicero, *De Oratore*, which wisely brought into schools, truly taught and constantly used, would not only take wholly away that butcherly fear in making Latins,[2] but would also with ease

[1] **Marg**. Master Ascham, book 1, page 1. [Subsequent marginalia merely abbreviate the points made in the main text and have been omitted.]

[2] butcherly [. . .] Latins] echoing Ascham **51**. 357. Brinsley then recapitulates the six points made by Ascham at ll. 4–10; for Ascham on double translation see ll. 203–73 and on Whitney ll. 95–134.

and pleasure and in short time, as I know by good experience, work a true choice and placing of words, a right ordering of sentences, an easy understanding of the tongues, a readiness to speak, a facility to write, a true judgement both of his own and other men's doings, what tongue soever he doth use.

This way, as he showeth, is by causing the scholar first to understand the matter which he learneth; secondly, to construe truly; thirdly, to parse exactly; fourthly, to translate into English plainly; fifthly, to translate out of the English into the Latin of the author again, and so after to compare with the author how near he came unto it. Finally, by much translating both ways, chiefly out of the English into Latin, as he setteth down in the beginning of his second book; and hereby he saw those strange experiments of the increase of learning which he reporteth of Master John Whitney and others. Now whereas these things are very hard to be performed in the common schools, especially for lack of time to try and compare every scholar's translation, and ever giving them new pieces to translate and those such as are meet for every form, by the means of these translations of our first school authors all these things may be performed in every author and form most certainly and constantly, and with much ease and delight both to master and scholars, as I trust will be found. The manner hereof I have set down in the 8th chapter and others following.

Therefore, since the time that God made these known unto me (which was about some four years ago, or not much above, upon the occasion of a late worthy experiment related unto me confirming the testimony of Master Ascham) I have laboured in these translations above all other things: first, to find out the grammar rule of construing truly and perfectly whereby to guide these translations, and whereupon they chiefly depend; secondly, to find out the particular uses and benefits of them; thirdly, to find out and set down such directions as whereby to frame the translations to serve for all the uses most plainly; fourthly, to translate so many of our first authors after the same manner as since that time I have had occasion for my scholars in each form to read;[3] fifthly, to have certain trial and experience of

[3] translate [. . .] read] Brinsley made grammatical translations of Cato (1612) and Aesop (1617), the most elementary authors on the school curriculum, and also of Corderius's *Dialogues* (1614), Cicero's *De Officiis* (1616), Ovid's *Metamorphoses* (1618), and Virgil's *Eclogues* (1620); see also n. 25 below.

everything,[4] so much as in this time I could, and upon trial to commend them to schools to help hereby to bring into schools that excellent way of learning which he so highly commendeth, and whereof I have very great hope, and so by them a perpetual benefit to all schools and good learning, which I unfeignedly wish and pray for.

Particular Benefits of the Use of Grammatical Translations and of the Rule.

SPOUDEUS: It is apparent by that which you have said that you take the benefit to be very great which may come by such translations, rightly used.

PHILOPONUS: I do indeed, and that for all these things following, which seem most strange and hard to be done by children:

1. Teaching to resolve Latin grammatically, which is the foundation of the rest.

2. In construing,[5] to direct to do it artificially by rule, and also in propriety of words and in true sense.

3. For parsing, to do it of themselves: as reading a lecture[6] without any questions asked, unless some which they omit; which manner of parsing gaineth half the time which is spent therein commonly, when otherwise each question is asked and stood upon.

4. For making Latin, to be able to make the very same Latin of their authors upon sure grounds, and thereby to be encouraged to go on boldly and certainly with cheerfulness and confidence, when little children shall see that they are able to make the same Latin which their authors do, as was said, and have also the author to justify that which they have done.

---

[4] Brinsley says that he held 'yearely trials' in *A Consolation for our Grammar Schooles* (1622), STC 3767, p. 22, image 19.

[5] construing] On the difference between construing and parsing see Ascham **51**. 26.

[6] lecture] lesson, and by extension the text set for that lesson.

5. For proving° Latin, specially for the syntax, when each principal word going before directs those which follow, except in some few.

6. For composing artificially° by continual comparing this grammatical order to the order of the author, and marking why the author placed otherwise, and by being helped by a few rules which I will show after.

7. To help the younger scholars to understand their lectures, so far as need is; of the benefit of which understanding we have spoken before.

8. Also, to take their lectures for most part of themselves, as was said; to get and bring their lectures more surely and sooner than by the master's teaching alone, as a little experience will show.

9. To construe and parse their lectures out of the English as out of the Latin (which is a continual making Latin, as we heard), and so to read their lectures first in the natural[7] order, then as they are in their authors.

10. To be able to correct their authors of themselves if they be false printed.

11. To keep all which they have learned in their authors so perfectly as to be able in good sort to construe or parse at any time, in any place, out of the bare[8] translation, only by reading them oft over out of the translation.

12. To save all the labour of learning most authors without book, as all authors in prose, which labour in many schools is one of the greatest tortures to the poor scholars, and cause of impatience and too much severity to the masters, though with very little good for most part; to be able, as it were, by playing, only reading their authors out of the English over and over at meet times, to have them much better for all true use and each good purpose than by all saying without book; to trouble the memory only with getting rules of grammars and the like, and

[7] natural] i.e. grammatical (cf. l. 186 below); this is exactly the opposite of the way in which Webbe understands 'nature' in a linguistic context in **55.** below.
[8] bare] i.e. without further glosses or other commentary.

such other of most necessary use as the poets, which also are exceedingly furthered hereby.

13. To help to proceed as well in our English tongue as in the Latin for reading and writing true orthography;[9] to attain variety and copy° of English words to express their minds easily and utter any matter belonging to their authors; and so in time to come to propriety, choice and purity, as well in our English as in the Latin.[10]

14. To learn the propriety of the Latin tongue as they go forward; to be able to justify each phrase, and in time to remember words and phrases for almost whatsoever they have learned, and where. Also, by reading Tully and other purer authors constantly out of such translations – first grammatically, then rhetorically – to attain to make a more easy entrance to that purity of the Latin tongue, whereof sundry great learned men have given precepts, than by precepts alone, and much more by joining precepts and this practice together.

15. By the translations of the poets, as of Ovid and Virgil, to have a most plain way into the first entrance into versifying, to turn the prose of the poets into the poets' own verse with delight, certainty, and speed without any bodging;° and so by continual practice to grow in this facility for getting the phrase and vein of the poet.[11]

16. To be (as was noted) not only instead of masters or ushers,° to give each lower lecture perfectly for all the substance, but also to be after instead of their own presence, or of dictionaries, in every one of those forms continually to direct them until every one of the form can construe, parse,

---

[9] true orthography] correct spelling; though even in the sixteenth century attempts were made to simplify English spelling. Would-be reformers included the influential headmaster of Merchant Taylors', Richard Mulcaster, in *The First Part of the Elementarie* (1582).

[10] propriety [. . .] Latin] Brinsley's Aesop was advertised as being translated 'both grammatically, and also in propriety of our English phrase', STC 187.5, tp, image 1.

[11] continual [. . .] poet] On the imitation of Ovid as a spur to creativity see Jonathan Bate, *Shakespeare and Ovid* (Oxford: Clarendon Press, 1993), pp. 21–22, quoting this passage.

make the same Latin, and prove it. Hereby both to free the children from that fear which they will have ordinarily to go to their masters for every word, and also to free the masters from that trouble and hindrance to tell them every word, so oft as they forget, and the vexation and fretting to see the children's dullness and forgetfulness. For the help of the master or usher in the meantime, what it ought to be we shall see after in the use of these.

17. Hereby scholars having been well entered and exercised in their lower authors shall be able to proceed to their higher authors *ex tempore*,[12] and go on with ease by the assistance of the master where they need, and by the help of the commentaries, that they may be thus enabled to construe any author and be fitted for the studies of the university at their first entrance thither.

18. These will be also a help to many weaker schoolmasters for right and certain construction without so oft seeking dictionaries for English and propriety of words, and so for parsing and all sorts of the former directions.

19. Also, weaker scholars in the universities, who have not been so well grounded in the grammar schools, may proceed in their private studies by the use of some of these translations, either one alone or two or three together, and increase both for construing, understanding, and writing Latin. Also, they may have continual use of translating both into English and Latin, whether reading out of the author into the translation, or out of the translation into the author, or doing it by pen; and ever a direction to try all by, and as a private help, which continually translating both ways is a most speedy way to learning, as Master Ascham proveth at large.

20. Likewise, any who have lost the knowledge of the Latin tongue may recover it hereby within a short time, and they who have had but a smattering, or some little beginning, may soon come to understand any ordinary author and proceed with pleasure and certainty.

[12] *ex tempore*] without preparation or study aids.

21. Finally, hereby scholars may have daily much sure practice both of analysis and genesis,[13] that is, resolving and making Latin, which (as was noted) all the learned do acknowledge to be almost all in all in getting all learning. For all this practice by them is nothing else but analysis and genesis.

Things more specially observed in the translating of the school authors.

SPOUDEUS: These benefits are indeed very great and worthy the labour of every child, or other who would attain them, if it be as you say. Yet, by your favour, many of them cannot be obtained by bare grammatical translations alone as to get the propriety of both the tongues, both of Latin and English together, with variety of phrase, the sense, and the like. Therefore what course have you observed in your translations to make them to serve to all these purposes?

PHILOPONUS: I have observed these things following, so near as I have been able for the present. I shall amend them after, God willing.

1. This natural or grammatical order throughout.

2. That the English translation is set down alone without the Latin adjoining, to avoid the inconveniences of having the Latin and English together, as of making truant[14] or the like, whereof I shall speak after.

3. The propriety of the English words answering to the Latin in the first and natural signification, and expressing the force of the Latin words so near as I could, is set down in the first place. And where the Latin phrase is somewhat hard or obscure to be expressed in our English tongue word for word, there I have also expressed that by a more plain phrase, sometimes included within two marks, almost like a parenthesis, with [or] thus. Or else I have set it ever in the margent, where

[13] analysis and genesis] The breaking down of a sentence into its grammatical components (the first citation in the *OED* in this sense) and composition. The process of deconstruction, which enables the pupil to understand how the language works, is the foundation for reconstruction or composition.
[14] making truant] encouraging idleness.

also I have oft placed the meaning, with variety of other phrases over against the word, and noted them with a character or letter answering to the word in the text.

Moreover, where any phrase is over-harsh° in our English tongue to express the Latin *verbatim*, viz. word for word, or in good propriety, that harsh phrase is also placed in the margent over against the Latin phrase with this mark (*Verb*) or (*ver*. (or *v*.)), signifying verbatim, word by word, or word for word, and the more easy phrase set in the text.

Likewise, where there may be two senses or constructions I have commonly expressed both: the more likely and natural in the text, the other in the margent. This I have done to the end that the scholar may see both construction and meaning, together with the propriety of the tongue, whereunto I have chiefly laboured.

Objections against the use of translations in schools answered.

[SPOUDEUS] Objection 1. Translations in schools have not been found to bring any such benefit, but rather much hurt, and therefore the best and wisest schoolmasters have not been wont to suffer any of them amongst their scholars.

PHILOPONUS: I will first answer you for the benefits. That it is true indeed that these uses and benefits cannot be made of any other translation of any one of our school authors, the reasons are evident: first, because none of the translators have followed, nor so much as propounded to themselves to follow this grammatical rule in translating,[15] which you see is the mean° foundation of all true construing, parsing, making, and trying Latin, and of all these benefits to keep scholars to go surely. Secondly, none of them which I know have laboured to express the propriety and force of the Latin in the first and native signification, which this intendeth continually, and how much lieth upon the knowledge of the propriety of the words for the certain getting of any tongue, every scholar knoweth. Thirdly, none of them have endeavoured by a double translation to make all things plain, as these do everywhere: labouring to express with the words and grammar the sense and meaning also, in all

[15] None [. . .] translating] Fleming claims to have translated Virgil's *Eclogues* grammatically; see **52**. 36–37; 60–62.

obscure places, with variety of English words or phrase, to the end to teach children thereby grammar, propriety, sense, with variety of phrase to express their minds in English as well as in Latin; and all under one, that nothing be wanting.

The translators have seemed to aim either only or principally at the meaning and drift of the author, which benefit alone they do in some sort perform; but for the rest of the benefits and uses, or for the most of them (as for true construing, parsing, making, and trying Latin, which are the chief things here mentioned), they either set the learner at a *non plus*,[16] or carry him ordinarily clean amiss. And therefore there is no marvel if in that respect they be utterly disliked. Trial in any of them compared to the rule and the other limits, and especially how in construing, parsing, and the like they carry the learner utterly out of the way, will presently show the truth hereof, and commonly in the very first sentence of them. [. . .]

SPOUDEUS: Objection 2. Besides that they lead scholars amiss very ordinarily in construing, almost in every sentence, they are found also to make scholars truants, or to go by rote[17] (as we commonly call it), which is worse.

PHILOPONUS: Answer. For the first part, that they lead scholars amiss, I have answered that that is only in such translations which respect the sense alone, but do not respect the grammar.

Secondly, for making truants I answer that these grammatical translations, being thus merely English and separate from the Latin altogether, can never endanger any way to make truants if they be used according to the directions prescribed. For first, for construing Latin there can be no likelihood hereof if the translation be only used: first, to give some light and understanding of the lecture amongst the younger; after, to be only in place of the master where he cannot be himself. [. . .]

Indeed, where the translation is joined with the author, and so they are set together answerably[18] word for word, either as the

[16] *non plus*] a point at which the pupil is baffled and cannot proceed any further.

[17] by rote] Spoudaeus is objecting that pupils will simply memorise the translation without understanding it. Ascham comments on rote learning at **51**. 55–57 ('tied only to [the pupils'] tongue and lips, and never ascended up to the brain and head').

[18] answerably] i.e. the Latin word is keyed directly to its English equivalent placed either above the line or side by side.

interlineal set over the head, or the English word or phrase set after the Latin, there the eye of the child is no sooner upon the one but it will be upon the other, and so the memory is not exercised, neither can this mischief be avoided. Yea, where the author is of the one page, [and] the translation is on the other over against it (like as it is in Theognis[19] and some other Greek poets), there must be much discretion for the right using of them, otherwise many inconveniences must needs follow amongst children. But in these bare translations so by themselves these surmised dangers are prevented, if they be used as hath been showed. Although for them who are of full discretion to use them (as those who would study privately for the recovering their Latin, or increasing therein), it may be the most profitable of all to have the translation over against the Latin, directly on the other page, after the manner that Theognis is printed: that, folding the book, they may look upon the one when they would find out the other, and yet have the other ever at hand, as a master, to help in an instant where they need.

Translating into Latin and English

[PHILOPONUS:] For going on faster and dispatching more in translating, beside their writing so, you may only ask them the words or phrases in English, how they can utter them in Latin, and then let them give them in Latin, every one his piece: first naturally, after placing each sentence. Thus to go through daily a side or a leaf at a time, or as leisure will serve.

Besides these, this may be a most profitable course[20] as they proceed to cause them to translate of themselves Aesop's *Fables* or Tully's *Sentences*[21] or the like into plain, natural English so as was showed, and to cause them the next day for their exercise to bring the same thus in English, and to be able without book first to make a report of it (striving in the *Fables* who shall tell his tale

[19] Theognis] Parallel Greek-Latin editions of the *sententiae elegiacae* of Theognis had been published since 1537, though not in England. Melanchthon was a major contributor to several of these.

[20] **Marg**. Translating into English after Master Ascham's manner. Use hereof.

[21] Tully's *Sentences*] Thomas Vautrollier and then Richard Field, who had published popular Latin editions of Ovid, also brought out Cicero's *Sententiae* (along with extracts from Demosthenes and Terence) as a school text in 1584 and 1603.

in best words and manner) and then to read it into the Latin of the author out of the English and be able to prove it, and where they have read the hard words.[22] And after all these to try (if your leisure will serve) how they can report the same in Latin, either in the words of the author, or otherwise, as they can of themselves, which all who are pregnant° and will take pains will be able to do very readily. By this you shall find a great increase.°

Lastly, this is yet the most speedy and profitable way of all, as my experience doth assure me, to cause them to read *ex tempore* some easy author daily out of the translation into the Latin of the author, or out of the author into English: first plainly, then artificially.[23] And to this purpose I have translated, as I showed, Corderius's *Dialogues*,[24] whose Latin you know to be most easy, familiar, and pure, and also Terentius Christianus,[25] with Tully's *Sentences* to help hereunto.

For further translating or turning any author, or piece of author, or other matter into Latin, if it be difficult direct your scholars to resolve the speech into the natural order of the words, so near as they can. Secondly, if there be any phrase which they cannot express, to resolve and express it by some other easier words and phrase of speech with which they are better acquainted, and to do it by periphrasis (that is, more words) if need be. Besides, for such English words which they know not to give Latin unto, let them use the help of some dictionary, as Holyoake or Baret:[26] Holyoake is best, wherein the proper words, and more pure, are first placed.

---

[22] **Marg**. Here you must be sure they have no translation to help them secretly.

[23] first plainly, then artificially] first literally or grammatically, then expressively or rhetorically.

[24] Corderius's *Dialogues*] For Corderius (Mathurin Cordier, 1479–1564) see STC 5762, which is Brinsley's translation of the *Colloquia scholastica*.

[25] Terentius Christianus] Editions of *Juditha* and *Tobaeus*, Christianised comedies in the style of Terence by Cornelis Schonaeus, had been published in 1609 and 1610, but Brinsley's published translations are from Terence's own comedies. Philoponus goes on to list 'Schoole Authors translated or in hand'; in addition to those mentioned above they include '*Sententiae pueriles* [. . .] *Tullies* Epistles gathered by *Sturmius* [. . .] *de Amicitia, Senectute, Paradoxes*; *Ovid de Tristibus*', STC 3768, sig. R1r, image 75.

[26] Holyoake or Baret] Francis Holyoake's revision of John Rider's *Bibliotheca scholastica* was first published in 1606 as *Rider's Dictionarie corrected and augmented*, STC 21032. John Baret's *Alvearie* (1580) was a 'quadruple dictionarie' covering Latin, Greek, English, and French, STC 1411.

In all such translating, either English or Latin, this is carefully to be observed: ever to consider well the scope and drift of the author and the circumstances of the place,[27] and to labour to express lively not only the matter, but also the force[28] of each phrase, so near as the propriety of the tongue will permit.

But for all this matter of translating, that practice of reading the English out of the authors, and the authors back again out of the translations, shall fully teach it, so far as it concerneth the scholar for propriety and getting of the tongues. For translating any Latin author into English only to express the sense and meaning of it, the sense and drift of the Latin author is principally to be observed, and not the phrase nor propriety of the tongue to be so much sought or stuck unto. The like may be said for the Latin. But this kind of translating into Latin is only for such scholars as are well grounded thorough long exercise and practice in the former kind of grammatical translation and in Tully's or their author's phrase.

SPOUDEUS: I hope I understand you right, and do like very well of all, so far as I conceive. Only let me entreat you as in the former to rehearse the principal heads briefly concerning this matter.

PHILOPONUS: This is the sum of all for this entrance in making and writing Latin:

1. Readiness in their rules, chiefly in examples of nouns and verbs;

2. Making their own lectures into Latin daily;

3. Continual reading or repeating lectures, and all their authors which they have learned out of the grammatical translations, into the Latin of the authors;

4. Translating into Tully's Latin out of a perfect grammatical translation, or as the English is so dictated unto them, and reading or repeating the same out of the English into Latin; and lastly, out of the natural order into the order of Tully;

5. Translating into English grammatically of themselves, and reading forth of the English into the Latin of the author, or writing it down.

---

27 circumstances of the place] i.e. context.

28 lively [. . .] force] Brinsley is referring to the rhetorical figures of *enargeia* and *energia*.

55. Joseph Webbe, *The Familiar Epistles of Cicero* (1620)

[Joseph Webbe (*c.* 1560–*c.* 1630) was a teacher of Latin and a medic and is known chiefly for his published work on language pedagogy. A Catholic, he grew up speaking Latin (a distinction he shares with Montaigne) and this formative experience determined his approach to the teaching of the language. He visited the English College at Rome in 1600 and 1603 and also obtained a doctorate from the University of Padua. He had difficulty obtaining a licence to practise medicine without having studied at either Oxford or Cambridge, and he made a living from teaching Latin by the method set out in *An Appeal to Truth*. His system found support both from the schoolmaster and author Thomas Hayne, who taught at Merchant Taylors' and Christ's Hospital, and the educational reformer Samuel Hartlib, and it was officially recognised by parliament following his *Petition in the behalfe of Auncient and Authentique Authors* (1623), when he was granted a monopoly on his teaching method for twenty-one years. He claims in this work that his method had the approval of King James.

Webbe's translation of all sixteen books of Cicero's *Epistulae ad Familiares* [Letters to his Friends] was 'conferrred with the French, Italian and other translations'. The text is in parallel Latin and English columns with an elaborate system of cross-referencing to show the exact correspondence between the words and phrases. He then embarked on an ambitious programme of translation to extend the system throughout the canonical school texts. This included *Lessons and Exercises out of Cicero ad Atticum* (1627) and Terence's comedies *Andria* and *Eunuchus*, 'claused after the method of Dr. Webbe' (both 1629).

See also Vivian Salmon, 'Joseph Webbe: Some Seventeenth-Century Views on Language Teaching and the Nature of Meaning' in *The Study of Language in Seventeenth-Century England*, 2nd edn (Amsterdam: Benjamins, 1988), pp. 15–31; A. P. R. Howatt with H. G. Widdowson, *A History of English Language Teaching* 2nd edn (Oxford: Oxford University Press, 2004); Salmon in *ODNB*.]

Joseph Webbe, Doctor of Physic,° to his much esteemed friend, Francis L[. . .] Esquire.[1]

Your inbred love of knowledge equalised with able industry, and your applause and furtherance of a public benefit, brought us acquainted. In that, an office freely done to any peculiar person is very laudable, but extending itself to an universality obligeth and uniteth all men. For as the mutual participation of particulars, and their use and faculties in a body natural, so breedeth it a loving harmony and perpetuity in that which is political: harmony of minds through uniting courtesies, perpetuity of being so by an affectionate acceptance and grateful acknowledgement. Whereupon there is not only an exchange of favours out of the endowments of fortune, but from the elaborated experience also of such as are not envious proceedeth a willing demonstration of all either infused° or acquired sciences, ever binding, by reiterated offices, the receiver to a new addition of thankfulness and the giver to participate through a former deserving gratitude. And this was the main occasion that I, true friend, breaking the ice of my long concealed blessings and inventions, laid open to your view those crystal and abounding fountains, which whoso tasteth instantly bedeweth his understanding with so recreating a balsamum° that it springeth in the coldest winter and is ever fruitful. This powerful and celestial water is, as you beheld, environed with a guard of ancient authors of the most admired perfection in all professions, and such as from the riches of their wisdoms have left rules, precepts, and authorities as legacies, regalities, and prerogatives, by which all after ages, conditions of men and dominions have been and must be instituted, maintained, and governed.

All these, though they bewrayed° a willingness to embrace you and grant you access unto that fountain, yet through an ancient familiarity begun in childhood between yourself and Cicero, which was one of them, you sought this courtesy rather from him, and he gave rather way thereto, than any other. And as he was ever of an affable disposition and had been well-read in the conditions of all men, and delighted to be frequented by the most illuminated understandings, he so tasted your inclination that, calling me from cleansing (as my custom is) and purifying that fountain, he requested me in token of his affection, to present you with one

[1] Francis L.] Not identified.

volume of his *Epistles*. I asked him 'Which?' He answered, 'The *Familiar*'. 'In what language?' 'English'. Whereat I blushed, and smiled. He, gathering mine inward thoughts by mine outward carriage, said, 'Blush not to be made a translator of so ordinary books as mine *Epistles*. In that, things the more ordinary they are argue the more universal acceptance, and besides, men of greater show have held their translations of lesser moment for their greatest ornaments. But blush to think that Cicero, whose letters bewray his conversation, and whose conversation was with consuls, kings, imperators, praetors, quaestors, tribunes, generals, and friends of his own rank, Caesar, Pompeius, Lepidus, Antonius, Brutus, Cassius, Cato, Plancus, Lentulus, Deiotarus, Octavianus, and such great potentates – and at that time when all the world was subject unto one dominion, and himself in it a chief commander – I say, blush to conceit° that he should reduce such epistles into volumes only for little ones, and wrong not thine own judgement so far as to imagine that every man of thy nation and country which is desirous and worthy to read mine *Epistles* is able to understand them in their original. Go on, then, for those that ruled all men have been ruled by me. Be thou then ruled, and go on'.

When I heard this, my shameful blush was turned to a daring boldness, which made me reply, 'Command – but thou art the world's greatest orator, and I, when these are ended, shall be but a young translator. Let me bring thee a Sidney, a great Lord Chancellor, or a Sandys,[2] that can parallel thy Latin with our English language.' 'No', said mine author, 'they have done; do thou!' With that, I asked him, 'How?' 'Hast thou forgotten', said he, 'that *epistolas quotidianis verbis texere solemus*?'[3] Here I grew silent, but not so silent as presumptuous, for hence came these *Epistles*. Neither did I forget a French Doletus[4] and Italy's Manutius,[5] who had dared as much and were applauded.

---

[2] Sandys] Sir Edwin Sandys (1561–1629), parliamentarian and noted orator, educated by Richard Mulcaster, who spoke on behalf of the gentry and free trade.

[3] *epistolas* [. . .] *solemus*] Cicero, *Letters to Friends* [*Epistolae ad Familiares*] 9.21: 'it is our practice to weave letters out of everyday words'.

[4] Doletus] Etienne Dolet (1509–1546), French humanist scholar, printer, and translator who was executed for supposedly mistranslating the *Axiochus* (attributed to Plato) to suggest that there is no life after death. He is the author of the most important French work of translation theory in the sixteenth century, *La Maniere de bien traduire d'une langue en aultre* (Lyon, 1540).

[5] Manutius] Aldus Manutius (1449–1515), famed Italian publisher and Greek scholar who founded the Aldine press at Venice.

But when I was almost at an end, and met with *aliter scribimus, quod eos solos, quibus mittimus, aliter quod multos lecturos putamus*,[6] I was absolutely determined to commend my former labours to the secretest of all friends, a fire. But you, at that very instant sent by destiny, reprieved them and requested my patience once more to read them and return you them.'Tis done and by these you shall receive them. Send back your censure, and farewell.

56. Joseph Webbe, *An Appeal to Truth in the Controversy between Art and Use* (1622)

[*An Appeal to Truth* argues for a colloquial rather than a grammar-based method of teaching Latin, where 'art' (grammar) is contrasted with 'use'. The distinction is repeated in his later work *Usus et authoritas* (1626) and is also reflected in the colloquial examples set out in *Pueriles confabulatiunculae*, or *Childrens Talke* (1627). He frequently cites the work of the Flemish scholar Georgius Haloinus Cominius, which should not be confused with the much more influential educational theories of the Moravian John Amos Comenius (1592–1670). It was the work of Comenius that superseded Webbe's attempts to recreate Latin as a living language.]

No man can run speedily to the mark of languages that is shackled and engined[1] with grammar precepts. And hence it proceeds that such as only depend on the rules of grammar wrote barbarously, as appeareth *ex libris Tenebriorum seu Dunsarum et ex epistolis obscurorum virorum*.[2] And such as attribute much to precepts and something to authority must needs be fearful and irresolute. For, following authority, they many times run against

---

[6] *aliter* [. . .] *putamus*] Cicero, *Familiar Epistles* 15.21: 'We write in one way when we think that only those to whom we send them will read them, and in another way when we think that many will'.

[1] engined] ensnared; but can also mean 'to be put on the rack'.

[2] *ex libris* [. . .] *virorum*] 'From the books of darkness and stupidity and the letters of obscure men.' *Epistolae obscurorum virorum* (1518) was a satire by the German humanist Ulrich von Hutten.

rules, and obeying rules, they disturb authority, without whose hand and seal the best of rules is but irregular.

And Cominius concludes[3] that they teach and command children, and such as would learn the tongue, to follow things of a contrary nature. For first they would have them learn by grammar, and then they send them to read authors, which things are contrary. And Despauterius runs with him against himself, for he is constrained to say:

Construit orator propriè, qua destruit ipse
Grammaticus; quibus est fermè contrarius ordo.[4]
(What the orator builds decently's destroyed
By the grammarian, other ways employed.)

And in another place:

Si bene discutias doctorum scripta virorum,
Multa secus cernes quam lex vult Grammaticorum.
(If thou with care discuss what wise men wrote,
Thou'lt oft find other things than grammars note.)

Whereunto Cicero alluding sayeth, 'I omit to speak of mathematicians, grammarians, and musicians, with whose arts this of oratory hath not so much as the least coherence.'[5]

Howbeit we are not ignorant, sayeth Cominius,[6] that grammarians endeavouring to uphold their errors (either to please the people or, rather, because they had no better way to get or teach by) have wrested all the sentences and authorities of the ancients to the approbation of their art of grammar. For whereas Varro,[7] Quintilian, and others disputing about grammar are enforced to allege the arguments that may be brought on both sides, the grammarians catch those that make for themselves and produce

---

[3] **Marg**. [Georgius Haloinus Cominius,] *De Resturatione* [*linguae Latinae* (Antwerp, 1533),]1.1. [George Halewyn, of Comines in modern Belgium, was a friend and correspondent of Erasmus and patron of the grammarian Despauterius. Salmon states that this work is not extant (*Study of Language*, p. 16), and it does not appear in the USTC, but there is a modern edition edited by Constantinus Mattheeusen (Leipzig: Teubner, 1978)].

[4] **Marg**. [Pantaléon Bartelon, with Johannes Despauterius,] *Syntaxis Latina* [(Lyon, 1548), the standard grammar in France and the Netherlands in the sixteenth century.]

[5] **Marg**. *De Oratore* 1. 1.

[6] **Marg**. *De Restauratione*, 1. 1. 5

them as the judgement and established opinions of the same authors on their behalf. But such arguments as made against them, as also the conclusions and absolute determinations of those authors in the shutting up of their disputations they overslip without remembrance. And therefore, sayeth he (though somewhat roughly), they have hitherto deceived us and are themselves full oft deceived. Neither doth he exclude our new writers from this censure, for he holds that they have nothing but what they have taken from others.[8] And he wrote since Lily's *Grammar* was composed.[9]

But, sayeth he, let these and many other authors speak their pleasures, grammarians will not be reformed.[10] True it is that, finding their collections taxed of being vain, tedious, disordered, and superfluous, they affect brevity and better method; but as they grow shorter, so are they more insufficient and less intelligible, ever intricated in the selfsame labyrinth, commending their reproved precepts and persuading all the world to follow them.

Thus far our authors have declared themselves concerning grammarians; now let us patiently hear them about their art.

It is very likely, sayeth our alleged° author, that those which in speech proceed by art, rules, and reason ought to speak better than those that follow the people and such as are unlearned.[11] So is there a likelihood in music that the distances° of a third, a fifth, a sixth, and an eighth should by reason of these numbers make a concord or consonant harmony; but, sayeth he, this dependeth merely upon the judgement of the ear, because God and nature would have it so. And they were not found out by numbers but by experience, for this observation of numbers therein came afterwards. We may also by likelihood say the sun's rising is a cause of the cock's crowing and the setting

[7] Varro] Marcus Terentius Varro (116 BC–27 BC), prolific Roman scholar; author of a treatise on the Latin language in twenty-five books and many other works now lost.

[8] **Marg.** Epistle to *De Restauratione.*

[9] Lily's *Grammar*] A composite work atributed to William Lily which was the authorised grammar school text in England from 1540 onwards. The first part is in English and the second in Latin. See T. W. Baldwin, *William Shakspere's Small Latine*, I, 94–99; II, 690–701.

[10] **Marg.** *De Restauratione.* 1. 1. 15

[11] **Marg.** *De Restauratione*, 1. 1. 10.

thereof of the owl's better seeing. But presumption upon likelihood is often a wronger of blameless truth and an overthrow of greatest knowledges, and in many things there are seeming reasons at the first encounter thought to be irrefragable,° which experience at length assureth us to be vain and frivolous. And this appears in grammar in that there is a likelihood that all nouns and verbs should follow by analogy the grammatical declensions and conjugations;[12] yet looking into custom and authority we find daily some irregularities which we cannot excuse, or make good, but by new-found exceptions and enlarging the doctrine of the Heteroclites.[13] And all our actions that proceed from nature are sooner and better learned by use and exercise than by art or precept. For Quintilian sayeth there are many things that cannot be delivered by art, as sucking, eating, drinking, standing, running; to which we may add the actions of our outward senses and the like, which are not only given to men, but children and unreasonable creatures.[14] And as in these, so in speech (which is the first external sense according to Raimundus),[15] we begin not by art but by nature and proceed by use, custom, authority, and exercise, governed by the ear,[16] which is in this kind pleased or displeased by an inbred, secret, and unpenetrable harmony in nature. And let us be content to know thus much *de facto*, for of the first causes we never yet had solider doctrine than those likelihoods. Neither will nature be compelled to dance within our circle, or have a coat or coxcomb put upon her by her own apes, though I must confess that all these may be helped by art and also adorned. But this is not to be understood in childhood, but in men of judgement and of good discretion that are capable of art and the reasons thereof. And that made Quintilian say they would do it better

[12] **Marg**. Priscian, Book 7: chapter on datives and ablatives.

[13] Heteroclites] Those who believed in the doctrine of universal reconciliation, though the term was often applied in the seventeenth century to anyone of unusual or irregular opinions.

[14] Quintilian [. . .] creatures] See *Insitutio oratoria* XI.iii, on delivery.

[15] **Marg**. Raimondus [Ramon Llull] *Ars Magna* [The ultimate general art (1305)]; Plato, *Cratylus*.

[16] governed by the ear] For a contrasting view of use, custom, and the role of sound in a linguistic context see Richard Mulcaster, *The First Part of the Elementarie* (1582) and John Wesley, 'Mulcaster's Tyrant Sound', in *Sound Effects: the Oral/Aural Dimensions of Literature in English*, ed. by Neil Rhodes and Chris Jones, *Oral Tradition* 24.2 (2009), 337–58.

conducted by nature than by art; yet nature, sayeth he, hath in it art.[17]

But though there be an art of helping and adorning speech, yet is it not grammar, except we take it in the first simplicity.[18] For our fore-alleged author Cominius would have us know that grammar hindreth the elegancy of speech, because grammatical construction and precepts command that words be otherwise placed than ancient authors placed them. And this, sayeth he, is a great error amongst us that we are now afraid to produce the same sentences and periods which were used by them, in the same words that they did, and in their manner of position; but by art of grammar we invent new words and put them in another order than the best writers placed them. Though Quintilian say that if any man dissolve a clause, sentence, or period that is in itself sweet, full, and well-spoken, he will drive away all the force, pleasure, and ornament thereof and altogether foil the composition.[19] And he takes his authority from Cicero, who, dissolving periods of his own, makes them harsh and ill-sounding, and by correcting the hard and crabbed compositions of Gracchus[20] makes them sweet and pleasing, the better to demonstrate that which otherwise might have been thought but mere imaginary.

Wherefore it appeareth that in following grammar we abandon elegancy and the pleasure of the ear and speak and write grammar-Latin, English-Latin, Dutch-Latin, French-Latin; and, in a word, every nation by this art writes its own peculiar Latin and not the Latin of the Latins, nor any foreign language as it should be. For in every tongue there are many things which, if we should utter by any other order than as they are vulgarly spoken, they would not run well and we should be thought to speak improperly; as every man may judge by the clauses, sentences, and especially proverbs of his own language, which, transposed or made up with other words than common, would for the most part lose their pleasing grace, delightful sound, and (many times) their sense and meaning. Whereupon Cicero concludes that these men separate words from sentences

[17] **Marg.** *De Restauratione*, 9. 4.

[18] **Marg.** *De Restauratione*, 1. 10.

[19] **Marg.** *De Restauratione*, 9. 4.

[20] Gracchus] Gaius Gracchus, Roman senator of the second century BC. Webbe may be referring to Cicero, *In Verrem* II.v.160–02.

in the same manner that the soul is separated from the body, which is not to be done, sayeth he, without their manifest destructions.[21] [. . .]

I cannot think these ancient authors would in this manner[22] slight either grammar or grammarians, had they thought the tongues of nations might have been sufficiently learned by their grammatical rules or precepts, for none made more account of speech than they did, or were more diligent in adorning it, or more desired to make themselves and posterity orators and eloquent. But they knew full well that there were other courses to come sooner, and with greater ease, in all perfection unto languages; whereof though something have been said already, yet because we have had the judgements of grave men to dissuade from art and precepts, let us also use them to direct us to that way of greater benefit.

If we ask Quintilian what this way is,[23] he will tell us plainly that custom is the best approved schoolmistress for languages, and that all the Latins were taught by use and custom from the mouths of nurses and other women which had the keeping of them from their cradle, and not by grammar or grammarians, as was erroneously thought by Leonardus Aretinus[24] and his followers. And he boldly affirmeth that speech depends not on reason but example, neither will he hear of any other law therein but observation, or that the art itself had any ground or foundation but in custom.

Experience also confirms that if we speak not according to custom, few or none will give us hearing, and amongst those that will, the most part of them will deride us because they cannot understand our meaning. Whereupon the Apostle sayeth, 'If I know not the meaning of the voice, I shall be unto him that speaketh a barbarian, and he that speaketh shall be a barbarian unto me' (1 Corinthians 14).

---

[21] **Marg**. *De Oratore*, I. 3.

[22] **Marg**. Use approved.

[23] **Marg**. *Institutio oratoria*, 1. 11.

[24] Leonardus Aretinus] Leonardo Bruni (*c*. 1370–1444), Italian literary scholar and historian; see *De Studiis et litteris* (1470). Bruni translated Plato, Aristotle, and Xenophon into Latin and was the author of *De Interpretatione recta* [On the correct way to translate] (*c*. 1425). He is the originator of the term *studia humanitatis*, on which the concept and principles of humanism are founded.

Yet was this custom limited by the judgement of hearing, and therefore Cominius sayeth,[25] custom, concurring with the pleasure of hearing, is the surest rule and foundation of the Latin language.

By custom, ancient authors understand the common form of speaking used by the people, and especially, as Quintilian sayeth, by consent of that part of them that are learned. But sayeth Cominius,[26] these learned must be such as are least tainted with grammatical instructions or corrupted with extern° custom; for, sayeth he, Quintilian understood not the consent of grammarians, but of men that by much knowledge and experience came by learning and understanding, as being exercised by frequent custom of speaking both in private and in public places, and of such as resorted daily to princes' palaces, as Cicero, Caesar, Livius, Sallustius, and the like, who as well in war as peace were courtiers, and joined to their own learning much other study and diligence in reading, and experience of all other matters that might enrich their tongue in speaking. [. . .]

And for mine own part, I have as long sucked the milk of universities and acknowledge as much respect and obedience unto them as many others, and therefore have some reason to know their motherly love to be such that what we receive they had rather should turn to wholesome and effectual nourishment than a seeming and diseasing fullness. But let deeds dispute the rest and let us return to custom, in which I had rather satisfy the world with other men's authority than mine own opinion.

And to this purpose Cominius sayeth,[27] if we would follow the example of ancient authors, orators, historians, and poets, either in Latin or in Greek, and should be exercised in their custom of speaking, which we find within their writings, there is no doubt but we may arrive unto their very height of elegancy.

But there are four especial reasons alleged by mine author why few or none perceive the custom of the ancients.

First, they put whatsoever they would speak word for word into another language, in the same order wherein they speak it in their own. Now though this may in some fall out well, yet there are many speeches, sentences, proverbs, sayings, and authorities,

[25] **Marg.** *De Restauratione*, 1. 11.

[26] **Marg.** *De Restauratione*, 1. 11.

[27] **Marg.** *De Restauratione*, 1. 3.

of two words only or of more, which, translated into three or four languages, are to be set down in every one after a diverse order, and other words are to be received. For every tongue hath proper and peculiar words, which are neither agreeable to other tongues or liable to translation, by which the eleganter sayings, the graver sentences, and the more usual proverbs are especially composed. Wherefore they are deceived which speak according to the order of other languages, which is known to be much used, and most amongst the more unlearned.

Secondly, though such as follow grammar, and are a middle sort of scholars, do not always translate verbally, yet they speak not by the order and custom of the ancients, but place their words after a grammatical order and construction, rather obeying the rules and precepts of grammarians than the custom of the ancients and the judgement of hearing, which is contrary to the precepts of Cicero.

Thirdly, though the learned sort, and such as would be called poets and orators, translate not always word for word, nor do everywhere observe a grammatical construction, yet they come not near the Latin elegancy, as having been brought up from their childhood by the art of grammar and analogy. They take a pride to frame new words without regard unto the judgement of the ear, which though they be sometimes placed according to the order of the ancients, yet are they harsh and without elegancy, because they are not moderated and measured by the ear as their ancestors would have them.

Fourthly, the greater part of men, and especially of the learneder sort, are ashamed forsooth to speak in the same words, and in the same order placed, that the ancients spake them, lest it might be cast in their teeth that they knew not how to speak of themselves without using the ways and words of others.

From these fore-alleged reasons there arise, sayeth he, innumerable solecisms and barbarisms, not only in the Latin, but all other languages, of which, sayeth he, grammarians dream many things; but I dare say that few of them know what either a solecism or a barbarism meaneth because they make all to have relation to their grammar.

TEXTUAL NOTES[1]

Louise Wilson

The textual notes do not aim to be exhaustive but list the substantive differences in spelling and punctuation between the edited text and copy-text as well as substantive differences between the copy-text and other early modern editions. Where the editor has consulted a modern edition, this is also indicated. Publication information is taken from STC unless otherwise stated. In keeping with the edition's aim to be used in conjunction with electronic resources, the collation comprises those editions available on EEBO.

PART ONE: TRANSLATING THE WORD OF GOD

1. William Tyndale, *The Obedience of a Christian Man* (1528)

Copy-text

William Tyndale, *The obedie[n]ce of a Christen man and how Christe[n] rulers ought to governe* (Marlborow in the la[n]de of Hesse: H. luft [Antwerp: Martin de Keyser],[2] 1528) STC 24446

Other early editions

STC 24447 (Marlborow in the lande of Hesse, H. luft [Antwerp: Heyndrik Peetersen von Middelburch?], 1535)
STC 24447.3 (Marlborow in the lande of Hesse, H. luft [Antwerp: Heyndrik Peetersen von Middelburch?], 1537) [not on EEBO]
STC 24447.7 [formerly 24452] (s.n., [1537?])
STC 24448 ([William Hill, 1548])
STC 24450 (Thomas Ranalde and Wylliam Hyll, solde by Richard Jugge, [1548?])
STC 24451 (Wyllyam Coplande, [1548?])
STC 24453 (Wyllyam Coplande, 1561)

[1] The place of publication is London unless otherwise stated.
[2] STC lists the printer as Johannes van Hoochstraten. Recent scholarship has shown that it was in fact de Keyser working under a pseudonym. See David Teems, *Tyndale: The Man Who Gave God an English Voice* (Nashville, Tennessee: Thomas Nelson, 2012), p. 106.

STC 24436 *The whole workes of W. Tyndall, Iohn Frith and Doct. Barnes*, 2 vols (John Daye, 1572–73) [STC: Several copies have the general title-page dated 1572 and altered in ink to 1573.]

Modern edition consulted

Tyndale, William, *The obedience of a Christian man*, ed. by David Daniell (Penguin, 2000) [Abbreviated to D. below]

4 spirits] sprites 24446, 24447, 24450, 24451, 24453, 24436; spirytes 24447.7, 24448; spirits D.

11–12 tongue, and all the prophets wrote in their mother tongue, and all the Psalms were in the mother tongue. And] tongue. And all the prophets wrote in their mother tongue. And all the Psalms were in the mother tongue. And 24446, 24447, 24447.7, 24448, 24450, 24451, 24453, 24436, D.

33 Moseses] Moyseses 24446, 24447, 24447.7; Moyses 24448, 24450, 24451, 24453; Moysesses 24436; Moseses D.

34 threat] threat 24446, 24447, 24450, 24451, 24453, D.; threate 24447.7, 24448; threaten 24436

41 observances] observances 24446; obseruaunces 24447, 24447.7, 24448, 24450, 24451, 24453, 24436; observations D.

48 worldly] wordly 24446, 24450; worldly 24447, 24447.7, 24448, 24436, D.; wordlye 24451, 24453

51 worldly] wordly 24446; worldly 24447, 24447.7, 24448, 24450, 24453, 24436, D.; worldely 24451

71–72 which yet they] which yet they 24446, 24447, 24447.7, 24448, 24453, 24436; whyche yet they 24450, 24451; which they D.

84 alleged] alleged 24446, 24447, 24447.7, 24448, 24450, 24451, 24453, D.; alleaged 24436

84 likewise see whether] lyke wise se / whether 24446; lykwyse se / whether 24447; lykewyse se / whether 24447.7; lykewyse se, whether 24448; lykewyse se whether 24450, 24451; lyke wise se whether 24453; likewise see, whether 24436; likewise, whether D.

121 that King Æthelstan] that kynge Adelstone 24446, 24447; that kyng Adelstone 24447.7, 24448, 24436; that kynge.Adelstone 24448, 24451, 24453; the king Athelstan D.

153 other] other 24446, 24447, 24447.7, 24450, 24451, 24453; either 24448, 24436; or D.

157 seeing] seinge 24446; seing 24447, 24451; seynge 24447.7, 24448; seyng 24450, 24436; seng 24453; saying D.

160 forbidden] forbyddige 24446; forbydding 24447; forbyddynge 24447.7, 24448, 24453; forbyddinge 24450, 24451; forbidding 24436, D.

2. William Tyndale, *The First Book of Moses called Genesis* (1530)

Copy-text

William Tyndale, [*The Pentateuch*] (Malborow in the lande of Hesse: H. Luft [Antwerp: Martin de Keyser],[3] 1530) STC 2350

The text of 'W. T. To the Reader' is not found in subsequent editions where 'Vnto the Reader W. T.' is used as a title for what appears in STC 2350 as 'A Prologe shewinge the use of the scripture'. These editions are:

STC 2351 *The firste boke of Moses called Genesis* ([Antwerp: M. de Keyser], 1534) [Part 1 reprinted and parts 2–5 reissued from STC 2350]

STC 2087 *The fyrste parte of the Bible called the .v. books of Moses* [. . .] *Genesis. Exodus. Leuiticus. Numeri. Deuteronomium* (John Day, 1551)

The text is reprinted as 'The Preface of master William Tyndall, that he made before the fiue bookes of Moses, called Genesis. An. 1530. Ianua. 17.'

STC 24436 *The whole workes of W. Tyndall, Iohn Frith and Doct. Barnes*, 2 vols (John Daye, 1572–73) [STC: Several copies have the general title-page dated 1572 and altered in ink to 1573.]

17 obeyed, and] obeyed. And 2350, 24436
22 corrected] correcte 2350; correct 24436
36 sit] sirt 2350; sit 24436
41 liefer] lever 2350; leuer 24436
46 worldly] wordly 2350; worldly 24436
56–57 Testament, because] Testament. Because 2350, 24436
60 text. For] texte: for 2350; text: for 24436
77 sorely] soryly 2350; sorily 24436
82–83 withal. For] with all: for 2350, 24436
87 two] to 2350, 24436
101 got] gate 2350; gatte 24436

[3] See n. 2 above.

102 acquaintance] accoyntaunce 2350; acquaintance 24436
109 acquaintance] accoyntaunce 2350; acquaintaunce 24436
111 purpose, and] purpose. And 2350, 24436
112 got] gate 2350; gatte 24436
115 service. And] service, And 2350; seruice, And 24436
120 unity] unite 2350; vnite 24436
145 burn] borne 2350; burne 24436
146 slay] sle 2350; slea 24436
148 either] other 2350; either 24436

3. Thomas More, *A Dialogue of Heresies* (1529)

Copy-text

Thomas More, *A dyaloge of syr Thomas More [. . .] wherin be treatyd dyuers maters, as of the veneration & worship of ymagys* ([J. Rastell,] 1529) STC 18085

Other early editions

STC 18084 ([W. Rastell,] 1530) [STC – Privilege dated May 1531 at end; in O, HD copies it is altered to 1530 by erasure of the 'i'.] [N. B. Although this is an earlier edition than the copy-text, parts are illegible.]
STC 18076 *The workes of Sir Thomas More Knyght, sometime Lorde Chauncellour of England, wrytten by him in the Englysh tonge* (at the costes and charges of Iohn Cawod, Iohn Waly, and Richarde Tottell, 1557)

37 be, but] be. But 18085, 18084, 18076
49 seniors] senyours 18085, 18084; Seniours 18076
66 office, and] office. And 18085, 18076; offyce. And 18084
78 common] comen 18085; comē 18084; cōmen 18076
91 forbidden] forboden 18085, 18084, 18076
113 mastery] maystrye 18085, 18084; maistry 18076
114–15 realm, and] realme. And 18085, 18076; reame. And 18084
122 him, saving] hym. Sauynge 18085, 18084; him. Sauĩg 18076
134 then] than 18085, 18076; thā 18084
165 weened] went 18085, 18076; wente 18084
172 he, but] he. But 18085, 18084, 18076
183 wholly] hole 18085, 18084, 18076
199 better, which] better. Whiche 18085; better. Whych 18084; better. Which 18076

201 peril] 18076; parell 18085, 18084
216 wholly] hole 18085, 18084, 18076
240 enough, if] ynough and yf 18085, 18084; ynough, and if 18076
257 Nazianzanus] Nazianzen 18085; Naziazenus 18084, 18076
267 therewith: not] therwith. Not 18085; therwyth. Not 18084; ther-with: not 18076
304 fantasy, for] fantasye. For 18085, 18076; fantesye. For 18084
327 them, nor] them. Nor 18085, 18076; theym. Nor 18084
353 after –] after / 18085; after 18084; after, 18076
354 newfangledness –] newe fanglenes / 18085; newfāglenes / 18084; new fanglenesse 18076
378 well-learned] well lerued 18085; well lerned 18084; well learned 18076

4. William Tyndale, An Answer to More's Dialogue (1531)

Copy-text

William Tyndale, *An answere vnto Sir Thomas Mores dialoge made by VVillyam Tindale* ([Antwerp: Martin de Keyser,[4] 1531]) STC 24437

Other early editions

STC 24436 *The whole workes of W. Tyndall, Iohn Frith and Doct. Barnes*, 2 vols (John Daye, 1572–73) [STC: Several copies have the general title-page dated 1572 and altered in ink to 1573.]

64 him; as] him. As 24437, 24436
66 murdering] murtherynge 24437; murtheryng 24436
84 before; for] before. For 24437; before, for 24436
100 years,] yeres. 24437; yeares: 24436
112 behind] 24436; behide 24437
126 murder] murther 24437, 24436
129 epistles] pistles 24437; Epistles 24436
130 aught] ought 24437, 24436
133 it; of] it. Of 24437, 24436

[4] STC conjectures the printer to be S. Cock. This is a pseudonym for Tyndale's usual printer, de Keyser. See n. 2 above.

5. Thomas More, *The Confutation of Tyndale's Answer* (1532)

Copy-text

Thomas More, *The cõfutation of Tyndales answere made by syr Thomas More knight lorde chaũcellour of Englonde* (Wyllyam Rastell, 1532) STC 18079

Other early editions

STC 18076 *The workes of Sir Thomas More Knyght, sometime Lorde Chauncellour of England, wrytten by him in the Englysh tonge* (at the costes and charges of Iohn Cawod, Iohn Waly, and Richarde Tottell, 1557)

5 senior] senyour 18079; seniour 18076
18 object,] obiecte: 18079, 18076
24 words,] wordes: 18079; woordes: 18076
31 grace,] grace: 18079, 18076
48 thereof,] therof: 18079, 18076
64 Church,] chyrche: 18079; church: 18076
79 "Church",] chirche: 18079; church: 18076
97 priesthood] presthed 18079; Priesthoode 18076
131 tongue,] tongue: 18079; tounge: 18076
136 assembly] assemble 18079; as-semble 18076
143 them.] thẽ: 18079; them: 18076
154 eyes] eyen 18079, 18076
218 write. If] wryte: yf 18079, 18076

6. Miles Coverdale, *Biblia: The Bible Faithfully Translated into English* (1535)

Copy-text

Miles Coverdale, *Biblia the Byble, that is, the holy Scrypture of the Olde and New Testament, faithfully translated in to Englyshe* ([Preliminaries printed: Southwark: J. Nicholson, 1535]) STC 2063.3 [This is another issue of STC 2063 with 8 leaves of preliminaries printed in English black letter type – STC]

Other early editions

STC 2063 ([Cologne?: E. Cervicornus and J. Soter?], 1535)
STC 2063.5 [A variant with tp dated '1536'] [not on EEBO]
STC 2064 (Sowthwarke: Iames Nycolson, [1537])

STC 2065 ([Southwark: J. Nycolson, 1537]) [Preliminaries missing in EEBO copy]
STC 2079.8 (Zürych: C. Froschower, 1550) [Not on EEBO]
STC 2080 ([Zürich: Christoph Froschauer and S. Mierdman?] for Andrewe Hester, [1550]) [Another issue with cancel preliminaries printed by S. Mierdman? – STC]
STC 2090 (Richard Jugge, [1553]) [A reissue of the Zürich sheets of 2079.8 and retaining its colophon, with cancel preliminaries probably printed by S. Mierdman for Jugge – STC] [Not on EEBO]

10 impediment –] impediment: 2063.3, 2063, 2064; impedimentes: 2080
12–13 it –] it: 2063.3, 2063, 2064, 2080
20 hand. Nevertheless] hande: neuertheles 2063.3, 2063; hande: neuerthelesse 2064, 2080
26 so. For] so: for 2063.3, 2063, 2064, 2080
44 spirit] 2080; sprete 2063.3, 2063, 2064
44 stirreth] stereth 2063.3, 2063; steareth 2064; stereth 2080
50 eyes,] 2080; eyes: 2063.3, 2063, 2064, 2080
60 love,] loue: 2063.3, 2063, 2064, 2080
71 another –] another, 2063.3, 2063, 2064, 2080
85 construe] constyrre 2063, 2063.3; cõstyrre 2064; consterre 2080

7. Nicholas Udall, *The Paraphrase of Erasmus upon the New Testament* (1548)

Copy-text

Nicholas Udall, *The first tome or volume of the Paraphrase of Erasmus vpon the Newe Testamente* (London: Edwarde Whitchurche,1548) STC 2854.5

Other early editions

STC 2854 (Edwarde Whitchurche, 1548) [Not on EEBO]
STC 2854.2 (Edwarde Whitchurche, 1548)
STC 2854.3 (Edwarde Whitchurche, 1548)
STC 2854.4 (Edwarde Whitchurche, 1548)
STC 2866 ([Edward Whitchurch], 1552)

a) [Epistle to King Edward VI]

4 able] hable 2854.5, 2854.2, 2854.3, 2854.4, 2866
4 done,] doen: 2854.5; dooen: 2854.2, 2854.3, 2854.4, 2866
13 able] hable 2854.5, 2854.2, 2854.3, 2854.4, 2866
16 realm] Royalme 2854.5, 2854.2, 2854.3, 2854.4, 2866
30 realms] Royalmes 2854.5, 2854.2, 2854.3, 2854.4, 2866
37 oppress] oppresse: 2854.5, 2854.2, 2854.3, 2854.4, 2866
44 shot –] shot, 2854.5, 2854.2, 2854.3, 2854.4, 2866
45 burning –] burning: 2854.5; burnyng: 2854.2, 2854.3, 2854.4, 2866
52 bushel,] bushell: 2854.5, 2854.2, 2854.3, 2854.4, 2866
57 doctrine,] doctrine: 2854.5, 2854.2, 2854.3, 2854.4, 2866
67 silly] sely 2854.5; selie 2854.2, 2854.3, 2854.4; selye 2866
84 realm] Royalme 2854.5, 2854.3, 2854.4, 2866; royalme 2854.2
85 universally,] uniuersally: 2854.5, 2854.2, 2854.3, 2854.4, 2866
85 able] hable 2854.5, 2854.2, 2854.3, 2854.4, 2866
102 requireth,] requireth: 2854.5, 2854.2, 2854.3, 2854.4, 2866
105 able] hable 2854.5, 2854.2, 2854.3, 2854.4, 2866
112 service,] seruice: 2854.5, 2854.2, 2854.3, 2854.4, 2866
117 writers,] writers: 2854.5, 2866; wryters: 2854.2, 2854.3, 2854.4

b) To the gentle Christian reader.

12 volumes,] volumes: 2854.5, 2854.2, 2854.3, 2854.4, 2866
35 able] hable 2854.5, 2854.2, 2854.3, 2854.4, 2866
53 corrected,] corrected: 2854.5, 2854.2, 2854.3, 2854.4, 2866
61 window] windoore 2854.5, 2854.3, 2854.4; wyndoore 2854.2, 2866
62 frame,] 2866; frame: 2854.5, 2854.2, 2854.3, 2854.4
64 other,] other: 2854.5, 2854.2, 2854.3, 2854.4, 2866
72 altered,] altered: 2854.5, 2854.2, 2854.3, 2854.4, 2866

8. Thomas Norton, *The Institution of Religion by Calvin* (1562)

Copy-text

Jean Calvin, *The institution of Christian religion, written in Latine by maister Iohn Caluine, and translated into Englishe according to the authors last edition, by T. N.*(Richarde Harrison, 1562) STC 4416

Other early editions

STC 4417 [T. Vautrollier for] the widowe of R. Wolffe, 1574
STC 4418 T. Vautrollier for W. Norton, 1578
STC 4419 [A variant, with imprint:] T. Vautrollier for H. Toy, 1578
STC 4421 H. Middleton for W. Norton, 1582
STC 4422 H. Middleton for W. Norton, 1587
STC 4423 A. Hatfield for B. Norton, 1599
STC 4424 [Eliot's Court Press] for J. Norton, 1611
STC 4425 A. Griffin for Joyce Norton and R. Whitaker, 1634

10 nighly] nyely 4416; niely 4417, 4418, 4419, 4421, 4422, 4423; nicely 4424, 4425
111 oftener] 4424; ofter 4416, 4417, 4418, 4419, 4421, 4422, 4423; oftner 4425

9. Gregory Martin, *A Discovery of the Manifold Corruptions of the Scriptures* (1582)

Copy-text

Gregory Martin, *A Discoverie of the Manifold Corruptions of the Holy Scriptures* (Rhemes: John Fogny, 1582) STC 17503

There are no further early modern editions.

Modern edition consulted

Sections from the beginning of the text to the end of 5, and from 20 to the end of 24, are available in Douglas Robinson (ed.), *Western Translation Theory from Herodotus to Nietzsche*, 2nd edn (Manchester: St Jerome Publishing, 2002) [Abbreviated to R. in textual notes below]

22 refuted] refused 17503, R.
66 possible] possibly 17503
128 Hebrew, which] Hebrew. Which 17503, R.

10. William Fulke, *A Defence of the Translations of the Holy Scriptures* (1583)

Copy-text

William Fulke, *A defense of the sincere and true translations of the holie Scriptures into the English tong* (London: Henry Bynneman, 1583) STC 11430.5

Other early editions

STC 11431 (Eliot's Court Press for Thomas Adams, 1617)
STC 11431a (John Bill, 1617)

Modern edition consulted

Various sections to the end of 24 are in Douglas Robinson (ed.), *Western Translation Theory from Herodotus to Nietzsche*, 2nd edn (Manchester: St Jerome Publishing, 2002) [Abbreviated to R. in textual notes below]

6 cause,] cause: 11430.5, 11431, 11431a
32 them?] them. 11430.5, 11431, 11431a; them? R
52 a] a the 11430.5; a 11431, 11431a, R.
60 not', whereas] not. Whereas 11430.5, 11431, 11431a; not"; whereas R.
70 heresy,] heresie: 11430.5, 11431, 11431a; heresy; R.
83 perverted. But] peruerted: but 11430.5, 11431, 11431a; perverted; but R.
84 howsoever] howsoeuer 11430.5, 11431, 11431a; however R.
87 errors,] errours: 11430.5; errors; 11431, 11431a, R.
87 lest] 11431, 11431a, R.; least 11430.5
89 iota] R.; iote 11430; iot 11431, 11431a
109 uncorrupted,] vncorrupted: 11430.5, 11431, 11431a
114 (God be praised!)] R.; God be praised 11430.5; God bee praised 11431, 11431a
118 New, not] new. Not 11430.5, 11431, 11431a; New; not R.
120–22 them; and] them. And 11430.5, 11431, 11431a, R.
125 tongue? Neither] R.; tongue, neither 11430.5; tongue neither 11431, 11431a
128 tongues] 11430.5, 11431, 11431a; tongue R.
152 negligent,] negligēt: 11430.5; negligent: 11431, 11431a; negligent; R.
167 complaineth,] complayneth: 11430.5; complaineth 11431, 11431a; complains R.
177 Septuagint] R.; Septuagintaes 11430.5, 11431, 11431a
204 Hebrew,] R.; Hebrew: 11430.5; Hebrue: 11431, 11431a
205 'out] Out 11430.5, 11431, 11431a; "Out R.
205–06 son', and] sonne. And 11430.5; son. And 11431, 11431a; son" [. . .], and R.
206 'he] he 11430.5, 11431, 11431a; "he R.
206 Nazarite'] Nazarite 11430.5, 11431, 11431a; "Nazarite R.

210–11 *Cainan*, because] R.; *Cainan*. Because 11430.5, 11431, 11431a
211 Moses;] R.; Moises, 11430.5; Moses 11431, 11431a
223 done;] R.; done, 11430.5, 11431, 11431a
227 Arphachshad] Arphaxad 11430.5, 11431, 11431a, R.
227 Shelah] Sala 11430.5, 11431, 11431a, R.
229 number, and] number. And 11430.5, 11431, 11431a, R.
237 Testament, seeing] Testament. Seing 11430.5; Testament. Seeing 11431, 11431a; Testament; seeing R.
241 ours,] ours (11430.5, 11431, 11431a, R.
273 Zwingli] Zwinglius 11430.5; Zuinglius 11431, 11431a, R.
277 loseth] leeseth 11430.5, 11431, 11431a; loses R.
284 slander] 11431, 11431a, R.; sclaunder 11430.5
343 have] hane 11430.5; haue 11431, 11431a

11. Gregory Martin, *The New Testament Faithfully Translated into English* (1582)

Copy-text

Gregory Martin, *The New Testament of Iesus Christ, translated faithfully into English, out of the authentical Latin* (Antwerp: Daniel Vervliet, 1600) STC 2898

Other early editions

STC 2884 (Rhemes: John Fogny, 1582)
STC 2923 (Antwerp: Iames Seldenslach, 1621) [Not on EEBO]
STC 2937.5 (Antwerp: Iames Seldenslach, 1630) [A reissue of STC 22923 with cancel title-page – not on EEBO]

Modern edition consulted

A section of the text is in Douglas Robinson (ed.), *Western Translation Theory from Herodotus to Nietzsche*, 2nd edn (Manchester: St Jerome Publishing, 2002) [Abbreviated to R. in textual notes below]

14 proper] R.; propre 2884, 2898
33 indiscreet] R.; indiscrete 2884, 2898
50 Slavonians] Slauonians 2884, 2898; Sclavonians R.
51 Jerome] Hierom 2884, 2898, R.
59 hands] hãdes 2884; handes 2898; heads R.
70 held] R.; holden 2884, 2898

112 discreet] R.; discrete 2884, 2898
120 counsels] Councels 2884, 2898; Councils R.
137 alleged] alleaged 2884, 2898
138 rhymer] rimer 2884, 2898
171 since] sithence 2884, 2898
194 use.] vse: 2884, 2898

12. William Fulke, *The New Testament with a Confutation of Manifest Impiety* (1589)

Copy-text

[William Fulke], *The Text of the New Testament of Iesus Christ [. . .] with A Confutation of all such arguments, glosses, and annotations, as conteine manifest impietie* (London: deputies of Christopher Barker,1589) STC 2888

Other early editions

STC 2900 (Robert Barker, 1601)
STC 2900.3 (G. B[ishop]., 1601) [A variant of STC 2900]
STC 2917 ([Adam Islip] for Thomas Adams, 1617)
STC 2918 ([Adam Islip] for John Bill, 1617) [A variant of 2917]

Modern edition consulted

Douglas Robinson (ed.), *Western Translation Theory from Herodotus to Nietzsche*, 2nd edn (Manchester: St Jerome Publishing, 2002) [Abbreviated to R. in textual notes below]

4 lain] lyen 2888, 2917, 2918; lien 2900, 2900.3
91 account] 2900, 2900.3, 2917, 2918; accompt 2888
96 counted] 2900, 2900.3, 2917, 2918; compted 2888
97 hundred] 2900, 2900.3, 2917, 2918; hundreth 2888
131 lose] leese 2888, 2900, 2900.3, 2917, 2918
171 implieth] emplieth 2888, 2900, 2900.3, 2917, 2918
272 straiter] straighter 2888, 2900, 2900.3, 2917, 2918
302 alleged] alleadged 2888; alleaged 2900, 2900.3; alledged 2917 2918
333 rhymers] Rymers 2888; Rimers 2900, 2900.3, 2917, 2918
334 entertainment] 2917, 2918; interteynement 2888; intertainement 2900, 2900.3
342 account] 2900, 2900.3, 2917, 2918; accompt 2888

13. Thomas James, *A Commentary upon the Canticle of Canticles by Brucioli* (1598)

Copy-text

Thomas James, *A commentary vpon the canticle of canticles, written first in Italian by Antonio Brucioli* (R. F[ield] for Tho[mas] Man, 1598) STC 3928

There are no further early modern editions.

4 deserve.] deserue 3928
17 supererogating] superogating 3928
18 much. There] much: there 3928
33 affords. He] affords, he 3928
36 fine. The] fine: the 3928
52 are. But] are: but 3928
53 frogs. There] frogs: there 3928
56 found. A] found: a 3928
68 'But what!', sayeth] But what saith 3928
69–70 translations. It] translations, it 3928
71 English. Their] english, their 3928
90 common. The] common: the 3928
92 is'. If] is: if 3928
97 own. For] own; for 3928

14. Francis Marbury, in *A Treatise of God's Effectual Calling by Robert Rollock* (1603)

Copy-text

Robert Rollock, *A treatise of Gods effectval calling: written first in the Latin tongue, by the reuerend and faithfull seruant of Christ, Maister Robert Rollock, Preacher of Gods word in Edenburgh. And now faithfvlly translated for the benefite of the vnlearned, into the English tongue, by Henry Holland, Preacher in London* (Felix Kingston, 1603) STC 21286

There are no further early modern editions.

3 outweigh] out-way 21286
12 through] thorough 21286
21 translator. For] translator: for 21286

15. The King James Bible

a) William Barlow, *The Sum of the Conference at Hampton Court* (1604)

Copy-text

William Barlow, *The summe and substance of the conference, which, it pleased his majestie to have with the lords, bishops, and other clergie, at Hampton Court* (J. Windet [and Thomas Creede] for M. Law, 1604) STC 1456

Other early editions

STC 1456.5 J. Windet [and T. Creede] for M. Law, 1604
STC 1457 V. S[immes] for M. Law, 1605
STC 1458 [Eliot's Court Press for] J. Bill, 1625
STC 1459 J. Norton, sold by J. Kirton and T. Warren, 1638

13 answered. Only] aunswered; onely 1456, 1456.5, 1457; answered; onely 1458, 1459
22 authority. And] authoritie; and 1456, 1456.5, 1457; authority; and 1458, 1459
23 other.] other: 1456, 1456.5, 1457, 1458, 1459
29 conceits.] 1458 1459; conceites: 1456, 1456.5; conceites. 1457
32 her.] her: 1456, 1456.5, 1457, 1458, 1459
33 advice.] 1458, 1459; aduise. 1456, 1456.5; advise. 1457
41 me. Some] me; some 1456, 1456.5, 1457, 1459; mee; some 1458

b) King James, Letter to Richard Bancroft (1604)

Copy-text

Cambridge University Library MS. Mm.1.43

1 Lordship] lordship:
13 straitly] straightlie
41 thoroughly viewed] throughly vewed
69 31st] 30 [crossed out] 29:31

c) Richard Bancroft, *Rules to be Observed in the Translation of the Bible* (1604)

Copy-text

BL MS Egerton 2884 collated with MS Harley 750 and Add 28721.

title] An order agreed upon for translation of the Bible. The Rules to be observed in Translation (Harl.); The Rules to be observed in Translating the Byble (Ege.)
4 and the holy writers] (Ege; Add.); and holy writers (Harl.)
5–6 as near [. . .] used.] neere as may be accordinly as the vulgarly used (Harl.); as neer as may be accordingly as they ar vulgarly used (Ege; Add.)
7–12 Rules 3 and 4 are run together in Ege.
13 not at all] notes not at all (Ege.); notes at all (Harl; Add.)
14 so require] (Ege; Add.); doth require (Harl.)
17 expressed in the text] (Ege; Add.); explaned in the Text (Harl.)
21 translated or amended] (Ege; Add.); amended & translated (Harl.);
23 for their parts] for their parte (Harl., Add.); for their partes (Ege.)
25 any one company] (Ege.); one company (Harl., Add.)
25 any one book] any one booke (Harl., Add.); one booke (Ege.)
29–30 to send [. . .] place] to send them worde thereof, note the place (Ege; Add; omitted in Harl.)
35–41 Rules 11 and 12 are run together in Ege.
36 on such a place] (Harl.); in such a place (Ege; Add.)
39 in the tongues] in the Tongues (Harl; Add.); in the tongue (Ege.)
48–53 Rule 15 omitted in Harl. and Add.

d) *The Translators to the Reader* [Preface to the King James Bible] (1611)

Copy-text

The Holy Bible conteyning the Old Testament, and the New (Robert Barker, 1611) STC 2216

There are numerous other early editions of the King James Bible; it is not possible, within the scope of this section, to collate them here. For detailed bibliographic information on the text, see David Norton, *A Textual History of the King James Bible* (Cambridge: Cambridge University Press, 2005).

19 sensuality; by] sensualitie: By 2216
21 violence; by] violence: By 2216
23 ourselves; briefly] our selues: Briefly 2216
25 endless; and] endlesse: And 2216
82 finewed] fenowed 2216
86 finally] Finally
91 matter –] matter, 2216
92 form –] forme, 2216
94 effects –] effects, 2216
99 happy] Happie 2216
104 As] as 2216
226 Ulfilas] Vlpilas 2216
229 Seville] Siuil 2216
233 Alfred] Alured 2216
236 Slavonian] Sclauonian 2216
238 rhyme] rithme 2216
272 men –] men, 2216
300–01 understand, since] understand? Since 2216
302 profit?] profit, 2216
336 answer] answere; 2216
356 cause. Then] cause: then 2216
365 us.] vs: 2216
431 commentators –] Commentators, 2216
432 Latin –] Latine, 2216
486 'travelling'] Traueiling 2216

e) Samuel Ward, *Report to the Synod of Dordt* (1618)

Copy-text

The translation by A. W. Pollard in Alfred W. Pollard, *Records of the English Bible: the documents relating to the translation and publication of the Bible in English, 1525–1611* (London: Oxford University Press, 1911)

16. George Wither, *The Psalms*

Copy-text

a) George Wither, *A Preparation to the Psalter* (Nicholas Okes, 1619) STC 25914

There are no further early modern editions.

35 words.] words: 25914
46 is, there] is; There 25914
76 Apostles, and] Apostles. And 25914
115 imagination, for] imagination. For 25914
130 judgement.] iudgement: 25914
134 Church – yea] Church; Yea 25914
142 done. For] done: for 25914
180 gives, whose] giues. Whose 25914
193–94 nonsense, therefore] Non-sense; Therefore 25914
205 unseemly,] vnseemely: 25914
212 another.] another: 25914
213 them, so] them; So 25914
231 synonyms] Synonomaes 25914

b) George Wither, *The Psalmes of David translated into lyrick-verse, according to the scope, of the original. And illustrated with a short argument, and a briefe prayer, or meditation; before, & after, every psalme* ([Amsterdam?] Netherlands: Cornelis Gerrits van Breughel, 1632) STC 2735

There are no further early modern editions.

4 obtain, be] obtaine; Be 2735
6 performance, but] performance: But 2735
27 obscurer, but] obscurer; But 2735
34 expectation, for] expectation: For 2735
36 text. And] Text: And 2735
42 another, yet] another: Yet 2735
49 strain, it] straine; It 2735

PART TWO: LITERARY TRANSLATION

17. William Caxton, *The Recuyell of the Histories of Troy* (1473–74)

Copy-text

Raoul Le Fèvre, *hEre* [sic] *begynneth the volume intituled and named the recuyell of the historyes of Troye*, trans. by William Caxton ([Bruges: William Caxton and C. Mansion, 1475?]) STC 15375

Other early editions

STC 15376 (Wynkyn de Worde, 1502) [does not have sections]
STC 15377 (Wynkyn de Worde, 1503) [A variant of STC 15376]
STC 15378 (William Copland, 1553)
STC 15379 (Thomas Creede and Valentines Simmes, 1596 (1597))
STC 15380 (Thomas Creede, 1607)
STC 15381 (Bernard Alsop, 1617)
STC 15382 (Bernard Alsop and Thomas Fawcett, 1636)

[Caxton's parts do not appear in any text after 15378; title is changed in 15378 so first few lemmata in Textual Notes do not appear in the edition]

4 man,] man. 15375
4 Fèvre,] ffeure. 15375
7 four, and] foure, And 15375
11 God] god. 15375
15 eight, and] eyghte, And 15375
46 written five] wretyn a fyue 15375; wryten a fyue 15378
48 those] tho 15375, 15378
49 work, and] werke And 15375; werke, and 15378
57 grace. And] grace and 15375; grace, and 15378
62 receive] resseyne 15375; receyue 15378
68 following. And] folowyng.and 15375; folowynge, and 15378
78 said, and] said/ And 15375; sayd, and 15378
80 Bourgogne.] Bourgone: 15375; Burgoine. 15378
83 Ghent and] gaunt And 15375; Gaunte, and 15378
95 rhyme, and] ryme/ And 15375; rime, and 15378
96 tongue, and] tonge/ And 15375; tonge, and 15378
97 is, and] is/ And 15375; is. And 15378
98 desires, some] desyres. Some 15375, 15378
110 praising.] preysyng/ 15375; praysynge. 15378
120 at once. For] attones/ ffor 15375; attones. For 15378
122 imprinted] enpryntid 15375; enprinted 15378
124 said, and] sayd. And 15375; sayde, and 15378
126 life, praying] lyf. Prayng 15375; lyfe, prayinge 15378
134 do,] doo/ 15375; doo, 15378
141 re-edified, which] reedefyed whyche 15375; re edefyed which 15378
148 rood-tree.] rood tree/ 15375; Rood tree, 15378

18. Willam Caxton, *Eneydos* [The Aeneid] (1490)

Copy-text

Virgil, (*Here fynysseth the boke yf Eneydos, compiled by Vyrgyle, which hathe be translated oute of latyne in to frenshe, and out of frenshe reduced in to Englysshe by me w. Caxton*), trans. by William Caxton ([Westminster: William Caxton, 1490]) STC 24796

There are no further early editions.

2 pamphlets] paunflettis 24796
6 Virgil.] Vyrgyle/ 24796
11 the history] thystorye 24796
18 past] passed 24796
20 places,] places/ 24796
20 metre.] metre/ 24796
24 it.] it/ 24796
27 understood] understande 24796
32 did show] ded do shewe 24796
34 used.] used/ 24796
35 English.] englysshe 24796
36 understood.] understonden/ 24796
37 born,] borne/ 24796
49 not.] not/ 24796
51 well.] well/ 24796
52 eyren?] eyren/ 24796
57 them.] theym/ 24796
62 English.] englysshe/ 24796
71 epistles] pystles 24796
73 and] dna 24796
78 emprise] enpryse 24796
78 work.] werke/ 24796
83 therein.] therein/ 24796
88 unknown.] unknowen: 24796
89 understood] understande 24796
95 correction.] correction/ 24796
102 servant.] seruaũt/ 24796
107 heaven.] heuen/ 24796

19. Gavin Douglas, *Eneados* [The Aeneid] (1513)

Copy-text

Virgil, *The .xiii.bukes of Eneados [. . .]*, trans. by Gavin Douglas [the 13th Book by M. Vegius] ([William Copeland,] 1553) STC 24797

There are no further early editions.

For textual notes, see Gavin Douglas, *The Aeneid (1513)*, ed. by Gordon Kendal, MHRA Tudor and Stuart Translations (London: MHRA, 2011), pp. 1–15.

20. Thomas Elyot, *The Doctrinal of Princes by Isocrates* (1533)

Copy-text

Isocrates, *The doctrinal of princes*, trans. by Thomas Elyot (in the house of Thomas Berthelet, [*c.*1550]) STC 14279

Other early editions

STC 14278 (in the house of Thomas Berthelet, [1533?]) [Not on EEBO]

6 might] mought 14279
11 use] use: 14279
15 these words] this wordꝫ 14279
18 was] was: 14279

21. Thomas Elyot, *The Knowledge which Maketh a Wise Man* (1533)

Copy-text

Thomas Elyot, *Of that knowlage, whiche maketh a wise man. A disputacion Platonike* (in the house of Thomas Berthelet, [after 1548?]) STC 7670

Other early editions

STC 7668 (in aedibus Thomae Bertheleti, 1533)

5–6 country, whereunto] countrey: Whervnto 7670, 7668
16 it, like] it. Like 7670; it. Lyke 7668
22 this, some] this: Some 7670, 7668
31 lord,] lorde? 7670, 7668

38 purpose,] purpose: 7670; pourpose: 7668
44 understood] vnderstande 7670, 7668
48 Highness.] highnes: 7670; hyghnes: 7668

22. Thomas Phaer, *The Regiment of Life* [Jehan Goeurot] (*c.* 1543) N.B. Phaer is author of Book of Children

Copy-text

Jehan Goeurot, *The regiment of life, whereunto is added a treatise of the pestilence, with the boke of children*, trans. by Thomas Phaer (E. Whitchurch, 1550) STC 11970

Other early editions

STC 11966.5 (E. Whitchurch, to sell by W. Tilletson,) [1543?] [No *Book of Children* – not on EEBO]
STC 11967 (E. Whitchurch, 1544) [Preceded by Phaer's *Book of Children*]
STC 11969 (E. Whitchurch, 1546)
STC 11971 (J. Kingston and H. Sutton, 1553)
STC 11972 [R. Wolfe? for] (E. Whitchurch, 1560)
STC 11974 (Thomas East and H. Middleton,) 1567
STC 11975 (W. How for A. Veale [1578])
STC 11976 (E. Allde, 1596)

16 languages;] lāguages, 11969, 11970, 11972; languages, 11967, 11971, 11974, 11975, 11976
29 themselves – merchants] thēselues? Marchauntes 11969, 11970; them selues? Marchauntes 11967, 11975, 11976; them selues? Marchantes 11971, 11972; them selues? Marchātes 11974
30 deaths? –] deathes, 11967, 11970, 11971, 11972, 11974, 11975, 11976; deathes 11969
39 hugger-mugger] huther muther 11967, 11969, 11970, 11971, 11972, 11974, 11975, 11976
50 sicknesses] 11972, 11974, 11975, 11976; sickuesses 11970; sycknesses 11967, 11969, 11971
51 benefits] beuefites 11970; benefites 11967, 11969, 11971, 11972, 11974. 11975, 11976
53 constraineth] 11969, 11976; onstraineth 11970; constrayneth 11967, 11971, 11975; cōstraineth 11972, 11974
55 death –] death, 11970, 11972, 11975, 11976; deathe, 11967, 11969, 11971; death 11974

60 commandments. In] commaundementes: in 11969, 11970, 11975; cōmaundementes, in 11967; commandementes: in 11971; cōmandementes: in 11972; commaundements: in 11974, 11976

62 rewarded; otherwise] rewarded. Otherwyse 11970, 11971, 11975; rewarded: Otherwyse 11967; rewarded, Otherwyse 11969; rewarded. Otherwise 11972, 11974, 11976

68 glosses. The] gloses, the 11969, 11970, 11971, 11974, 11975, 11976; gloses, ye 11967, 11972

23. Elizabeth Tudor (Princess Elizabeth), 'The Glass of the Sinful Soul' [Marguerite of Navarre] (1544)

Copy-text

Bodleian MS Cherry 36 in the facsimile edition by Percy W. Ames, ed. *The Mirror of the Sinful Soul* (London: Asher, 1897) which has been compared with the transcript in Mueller and Scodel (2009).

12 study. Which things] study Which thinges
14 as for assay] as for a seye
31 howbeit] hubei
39 lest] lesse
43 grant] garaunte

24. Mildred Cecil, 'An Homily or Sermon of St Basil' (c. 1548)

Copy-text

MS BL Royal 17 B. XXI

4 Somerset] Summarsid
10 debt, so] debt. So
17 worthy] wordy
19 claim] cleame
32 performation] performacton
34 Cecil] Cicill

25. William Thomas, 'The Book of the Sphere' (*c.*1551)

Copy-text

BL MS Egerton 837, fols. 2^{r}–3^{v}

4 – appear] (Appear
6 to the intent] to thentent
12 triumphing] triumphnig
16 common, therefore] common. Therefore
20 government – a thing] governe. A thing
48 tongues, because] tongues. Because
50 matter] matier
51 attain] atteigne

26. Henry Parker (Lord Morley), *The Triumphs of Petrarch* (1555)

Copy-text

Francesco Petrarca, *The tryumphes of Fraunces Petrarcke [. . .] (Vyrgyll in his epigrames of Cupide and Dronkenesse)*, trans. by Henry Parker (J. Cawood, [1555?]) STC 19811

There are no further early editions.

12 thee? Thou] the, thou 19811
22 six] syxte 19811
30–31 works? Surely] workes, suerlye 19811
36 countries.] countreys: 19811
45–46 had. Which] hadde: whiche 19811
55 I. But] I: but 19811

27. Nicholas Grimald, *Cicero's Three Books of Duties* (1556)

Copy-text

Marcus Tullius Cicero, *Marcus Tullius Ciceroes thre bokes of duties*, trans. by Nicholas Grimald (R. Tottel,) 1556 STC 5281

Other early editions

STC 5281.8 (R. Tottel, 1558)
STC 5282 (R. Tottel, 1558 [1563?])
STC 5283 (R. Tottel, 1568)
STC 5284 (R. Tottel, 1574 (1575))

STC 5285 (R. Tottel, 1583) [One page of epistle to reader missing]
STC 5286 (Thomas East, 1596)
STC 5287 (Thomas East, [1600?]) [Epistle to Bishop of Ely missing]

7 furthered] furdered 5281, 5281.8, 5282, 5283, 5284, 5285, 5286
8 learning] lerning: 5281; lerning, 5281.8; learning, 5282, 5285, 5286; lernig, 5283, 5284
13 travelling] trauailīg 5281, 5281.8, 5282; trauayling 5283; trauailing 5284, 5285, 5286
14 commodities] commodities: 5281, 5283, 5284, 5285, 5286; cōmodities: 5281.8, 5282
25 Homer.] Homer: 5281, 5281.8, 5282, 5283, 5284, 5285, 5286
27 before] before: 5281, 5281.8, 5282, 5283, 5284; before, 5285, 5286
28 easy,] easie: 5281, 5281.8, 5282, 5283, 5284; easie, 5285, 5286
30 espying] espyeng: 5281, 5281.8, 5282; espying: 5283, 5284, 5285, 5286
37–38 myself. And] myself: & 5281; my selfe: & 5281.8, 5282, my self: & 5283, 5284; my selfe, and 5285, 5286
40 countrymen] contriemēne: 5281; contrimen: 5281.8; contrymen: 5282; countreymen: 5283, 5284; countrimen, 5285, 5286
46 many. So] meany: so 5281, 5281.8; many, so 5283, 5284, 5285, 5286
48 humanity] humanitie: 5281, 5281.8; humanite: 5282; humanitie, 5283, 5284, 5285, 5286
54 also] also: 5281, 5281.8, 5282; also, 5283, 5284, 5285, 5286
63 honourable] honorable: 5281, 5281.8, 5282; honorable, 5283, 5284; honourable, 5285, 5286
66 entreated] 5281.8, 5282, 5284; entreated: 5281, 5283; intreted 5285, 5286
69 thing] thing: 5281, 5281.8, 5282; thing, 5283, 5284, 5285, 5286
71 state. To] 5285, 5286; state: to 5281, 5281.8, 5282, 5283; state, to 5284
89 excellence] excellence: 5281, 5281.8, 5282; excellence, 5283, 5284, 5286
97 Athenians] Athenians: 5281; Atheniās: 5281.8, 5282; Athenians, 5283, 5284, 5286
134 man'. Eloquent] man, eloquent 5281, 5281.8, 5282, 5283 5284, 5285, 5286, 5287
144 words:] wordes. 5281, 5281.8, 5282, 5284; woordes. 5283; words, 5285, 5287; words. 5286

153 vanities] vanities: 5281, 5281.8, 5282, 5283; vanyties: 5284; vanities, 5285, 5286, 5287

167 liked] liked: 5281, 5281.8, 5282; lyked, 5283, 5284; liked, 5285, 5286, 5287

167–68 none. Yet] none: yet 5281, 5281.8, 5282; none, yet 5283, 5284, 5285, 5286, 5287

168 nothing,] 5283, 5284, 5285, 5286, 5287; nothing: 5281, 5281.8, 5282

171 tale –] tale: 5281, 5281.8, 5282; tale, 5283, 5284, 5285, 5286, 5287

173 truth –] trouth: 5281; trouthe 5281.8, 5282; trouth, 5283, 5284, 5285, 5286, 5287

179 wrested] 5285, 5286, 5287; wrasted 5281, 5281.8, 5282, 5283, 5284

184 interpretation] interpretation: 5281; interpretacion: 5281.8; enterpretacion: 5282; enterpretation, 5283, 5284; interpretation, 5285, 5286, 5287

185 perform] 5285; pfourme 5281; parfourme 5281.8, 5282; perfourme 5283, 5284; performe 5286, 5287

191 already] allredy: 5281; already: 5281.8, 5282; alredy, 5283, 5284; already, 5285, 5286, 5287

194 better] better: 5281, 5281.8, 5282; better, 5283, 5284, 5285, 5286, 5287

201 tongue.] 5285; 5287; toung: 5281, 5281.8, 5282; tongue, 5283, 5286; tong. 5284

208 man] man: 5281, 5281.8, 5282; manne: 5283, 5284; man, 5285, 5286, 5287

214 again. First] againe: first 5281, 5281.8, 5287; agayne: first 5282, 5286; again: first 5283, 5284, 5285

227 travail] tranail 5281; trauail 5281.8; trauaill 5282; trauaile 5283; trauayle 5284; trauel 5285; trauell 5286, 5287

227 worth] worthe: 5281, 5281.8, worthe, 5282; worth, 5283, 5284, 5285, 5286, 5287

28. John Dolman, *Tusculan Questions* [Cicero] (1561)

Copy-text

Marcus Tullius Cicero, *Those fyue questions, which Marke Tullye Cicero, disputed in his manor of Tusculanum*, trans. by John Dolman (T. Marsh, [1561]) STC 5317

There are no further early editions.

14 this, which] this. Which 5317
33–34 travail, thinking] trauayle. Thinking 5317
35 Tully, whom] Tullie. Whom 5317
48 these: first] these. Firste 5317
50 day; then] daye. Then 5317
52 multitude, and] multitude. And 5317
65 eloquence, first] eloquēce. First 5317
66 grant: that] graūt. That 5317
67 eloquently] eloquently: 5317
88 dark, especially] darke. Especially 5317
90–91 philosophy, inasmuch] philosophye. Inasmuche 5317
93 learned, but] learned. But 5317
101 himself] him selfe: 5317
102 own; which] owne. Which 5317
104 gentleness, knowing] gentlenes. Knowynge 5317
113 afford] forde 5317
134 then] the 5317
138 perform; who] performe. Who 5317
143 part] part: 5317
144 fault; but] fault. But 5317
146 day and] daye. And 5317
148 said, ‘No] sayde. No 5317
148–49 souter’, showing] sowter. Shewynge 5317
151 nothing, but] nothinge. But 5317
154–55 Tully, do] Tullye. Do 5317
156 faults, but] faultes. But 5317

29. Laurence Humphrey, *Interpretatio linguarum* [Interpreting Language] (1559)

Copy-text

Laurence Humphrey, *Interpretatio linguarum, seu de ratione convertendi et explicandi autores tam sacros quam prophanos, libri tres* [The translation of languages, or How to re-express and make clear sacred as well as secular writers. Three books] (Basle, 1559)

30. Thomas Hoby, *The Courtier of Count Baldessar Castilio* (1561)

Copy-text

Baldassare Castiglione, *The courtyer of count Baldessar Castilio*, trans. by Thomas Hoby (William Seres, 1561) STC 4778

Other early editions

STC 4779 H. Denham, 1577 [Cheke's letter missing from EEBO]
STC 4780 Thomas Creede, 1603 [Prelims missing from EEBO]
STC 4781 John Wolfe, 1588 [Italian, French, and English in parallel columns – Cheke's letter not included]

8 cause.] cause: 4778, 4779, 4781
40 fashions] 4781; facions 4778, 4779
41 you, and] you: And 4778, 4779, 4781
45 company, and] company: And 4778, 4779; companie: And 4781
55 men, for] men: For 4778, 4779, 4781
59 kings; to] kinges: To 4778, 4779; Kings. To 4781
61 age; to] age: To 4778, 4779, 4781
64 end; to] ende: To 4778, 4779; end. To 4781
66 men; and] men: And 4778, 4779, 4781
76 him, but] him: But 4778, 4779, 4781
103 nations.] Nations: 4778, 4779, 4781
149 question how] question. How 4778, 4781; question. Howe 4779
150 unlearned.] unlearned, 4778, 4779; vnlearned, 4781
166 are, and] are. And 4778, 4779; are: And 4781
175 forbore] forbare 4778, 4779, 4781
178–79 benefit. And] benefite: and 4778; benefit: and 4779, 4781
181 informed] enfourmed 4778; enformed 4779, 4781
188 leisure] 4781; leyser 4778; leysure 4779
196 betters.] betters: 4778, 4779, 4781
206 readers.] readers: 4778, 4779, 4781
207 good; if] good: Yf 4778; good: If 4779, 4781
207 practised; if] practised: Yf 4778; practised: If 4779, 4781

225 parcel] percell 4778; parcell 4779; 4781
227 themselves] themselnes 4778; thēselues 4779; themselues 4781
230 hands. And] handes: and 4778; hands: & 4779; hāds: 4781
252 fancy] phansie 4778
262 unperfect] unperfight 4778
264 fashion] fascion 4778
265 denizened] denisoned 4778
266 words.] wordes 4778
270 over-strait] ouerstraight 4778
271 account] accompt 4778
273 away –] awai, 4778
275 leisure] leisor 4778

31. Richard Eden, Letter to Sir William Cecil (1562)

Copy-text

MS BL Lands. 101, art. 5

2 device] divise
4 allotted] lotted
13 could be translated] could not be translated
14 your] you
17 accounted] accompted
27 *atra*] *atrium*
27 *scite*] *seite*
28 *designateque*] *designataeque*

32. Arthur Golding, *The Histories of Trogus Pompeius* (1564)

Copy-text

Trogus Pompeius, *Thabridgment of the histories of Trogus Pompeius, collected by Justine*, trans. by Arthur Golding (T. Marshe, 1564) STC 24290

Other early editions

STC 24291 T. Marshe, 1570
STC 24292 T. Marsh, 1578

2 wrote] wrate 24290, 24291, 24292
2 world] worlde: 24290; Worlde: 24291, 24292

4 Augustus, the abridgement] Augustus. Thabridgement 24290; Augustus. Thabridgemente 24291, 24292
9–10 the author. Wherein] Thaucthour: wherin 24290; Thauthor. Wherin 24291; Thauthor Wherin 24292
24 oftentimes] 24291, 24292; oftentymeg 24290
27 garments, even] garmentes: Euen 24290, 24291, 24292
34 closure] 24292; closur 24290, 24291

33. Thomas Drant, *A Medicinable Moral* [Horace's Satires] (1566)

Copy-text

Quintus Horatius Flaccus, *A medicinable morall, that is, the two bookes of Horace his satyres, Englyshed according to the prescription of saint Hierome. Quod malum est, muta. The wailyngs of Hieremiagh. Also epigrammes*, trans. by Thomas Drant (T. Marshe, 1566) STC 13805

There are no further early editions.

3 quips] quippies 13805
12 sin] synne: 13805
12 sin. Not] synne Not 13805
20 Democriti] Democrati 13805
27 fledge] flydge 13805
47 off] of 13805
47 off] of 13805
55 curtal] cortall 13805
58 interpreters. And] interpreters: and 13805
66 matter, so] matter. So 13805
68 thee. Thou] thee Thou 13805

34. Thomas Gale, *Certain Works of Galen's* (1566)

Copy-text

Galen, *Certaine workes of Galens, called Methodus medendi*, trans. by Thomas Gale (Thomas East, 1586) STC 11531

Other early editions

STC 11530.5 *The [second part of the] institucion of chyrurgerie: newly published by T. Gaille* ([J. Kingston and H. Denham,] 1567)

11 gain. For] gaine, for 11531; gaynes, for 11530.5
18 tongue. But] tongue, but 11531; tounge, but 11530.5
35 understood] vnderstanded 11531, 11530.5
39 Hebrew] Ebrue 11531; Ebru 11530.5
45 day. If] daie: If 11531; daye: If 11530.5
50 etc., why] &c. Why 11531, 11530.5
56 necessity.] necessitie, 11531, 11530.5
69 done.] done, 11531, 11530.5
92 speaketh] 11530.5; spake 11531
94–95 physicians. Therefore] Phisitions, therefore 11531; Phisitions, therfore 11530.5
101–02 artist. Yet] Artist: yet 11531; artist, yet 11530.5
111 method. And] methode, and 11531, 11530.5

35. William Painter, *The Second Tome of the Palace of Pleasure* (1567)

Copy-text

William Painter, *The second tome of the palace of pleasure* (Henry Bynneman for N. England, 1567) STC 19124

Other early editions

STC 19125 T. Marshe [1580?]

7 creature, who] Creature: Who 19124, 19125
19 other'.] other: 19124, 19125
21 astoned] astonned 19124; astōned 19125
37 possessions.] 19125; possessions: 19124
43 place, and] place, And 19124; place. And 19125
55 employs] imploy 19124; imploye 19125
57 that] That 19124, 19125
59 alone, meaning] alone: Meaning 19124; alone, Meaning 19125
72 marvellous] marueious 19124; maruailous 19125
85 embellishing] imbellishing 19124; imbelishinge 19125
87 pen, who] penne, Who 19124, 19125
87 employ] imploye 19124; imploi 19125

36. Thomas Wilson, *The Three Orations of Demosthenes* (1570)

Copy-text

Demosthenes, *The three orations of Demosthenes [. . .] in fauoour of the Olynthians, with fower orations against king Philip most nedefull to be redde in these daungerous dayes*, trans. by Thomas Wilson (Henry Denham, 1570) STC 6578

There are no further early editions.

42–43 together; and] togither. And 6578
87 speech, such] speach. Such 6578
105 wrote] wrate
116 an] An 6578
136–37 language, for] language. For 6578
140 bread, and] breade. And 6578
162 toll] towle 6578
188 enable] enhable 6578
189 power, for] power: (for 6578
189–90 me. All] me) all 6578
199 rehearsed, that] rehearsed. That 6578
200 are. And] are: and 6578

37. Margaret Tyler, *The Mirror of Princely Deeds and Knighthood* [Ortúñez de Calahorra] (1578)

Copy-text

Diego Ortúñez de Calahorra, *The first part of the mirrour of princely deedes and knighthood*, trans. by Margaret Tyler (Thomas East, [1580?]) STC 18860

Other early editions

STC 18859 Thomas East [1578?] [Missing two pages on EEBO]
STC 18861 Thomas East [1599?]

13 rested – the] rested. The 18860, 18859, 18861
25 drumster] drumstare 18860, 18859, 18861
34 backward.] 18859; backward, 18860, 18861
51 over –] ouer, 18860, 18861
56 travail –] trauaile. 18860, 18861
60 years, so] yeares. So 18860; yæres. So 18861
67 idle. And] idle, and 18860, 18861

74 men.] men: 18860, 18861
87 gentlewomen] Gentlewoman 18860; Gentlewomen 18861
98 overlightness. If] ouerlightnesse: if 18860, 18861
102 return,] returne 18860, 18861
109 strait] straight 18860, 18859 ; strayght 18861

38. George Pettie, *The Civil Converation of Master Steven Guazzo* (1581)

Copy-text

Stefano Guazzo, *The ciuile conuersation of M. Steeuen Guazzo written first in Italian, and nowe translated out of the French* [. . .], trans. by George Pettie ([T. Dawson for] R. Watkins, 1581) STC 12422

Other early editions

STC 12423 Thomas East, 1586

6 reading.] readyng? 12422; reading? 12423
16 translation. The] Translation: the 12422, 12423
20 to. But] to: but 12422, 12423
30 uncivil. And] vnciuile: and 12422, 12423
48 barbarous. For] barbarous: for 12422, 12423
62 themselves. For] them selues: 12422; themselues: 12423
69 cracked its] cracke it 12422; crackt it 12423
74 ink. For] inke: for 12422; 12423
76 'manifest',] manifest? 12422; (manifest)? 12423
77 Latin?] Latine: 12422, 12423
82 And] and 12422, 12423
84 naught.] naught: 12422, 12423

39. Richard Stanyhurst, *The Aeneid* (1582)

Copy-text

Publius Virgilius Maro, *The first foure bookes of Virgil his Aeneis translated intoo English heroical verse [. . .] wyth oother poëtical diuises theretoo annexed*, trans. by Richard Stanyhurst (Leiden: J. Pates, 1582) STC 24806

Other early editions

STC 24807 Henry Bynneman, 1583

6 rind] ryne 24806; rine 24807
13 sounding] sowning 24806, 24807
43 guess] guesh 24806; gesse 24807
44 enterprise: the] entreprise. Thee 24806; enterprise. The 24807
59 rhyme] rythme 24806, 24807
61 picked] pyekt 24806, pickte 24807
62 him. Yet] hym: yeet 24806; him: yet 24807
66 signification.] signification: 24806, 24807
73 attired, which] atyred. Which 24806; attyred. Whiche 24807
80 guess] guesh 24806; gesse 24807
86 therein. Yet] therein: yeet 24806; therein: yet 24807
87 applying] 24807; applinyg 24806
90 example: in] example. In 24806; example: In 24807
92 long, so] long. So 24806; lōg. So 24807
98 rhymes] rythmes 24806; rithmes 24807
101 hotly] hoatlie 24806; hotely 24807
102 days –] dayes. 24806; dayes: 24807
103 ten, wherein] ten. Wherein 24806, 24807
113 rhyme] rythme 24806, 24807
116 rhymers] rythmours 24806, 24807
139 example, the] exemple: The 24806; example: The 24807
143 write. Nay] wryte; nay 24806; write, nay 24807
145 word.] woorde, 24806; worde. 24807
149 position, for] position: For 24806, 24807
154 property] propretye 24806; proprietie 24807
160 points: first] poinctes. First 24806; points. Firste 24807
161 accent; next] accēt. Next 24806; accent. Next 24807
162 saving] saluing 24806; sauing 24807
168 first, so] first. So 24806; firste. So 24807
181–82 *Minerva*, that] Minerua. That 24806, 24807

40. N. W., in Samuel Daniel, *The Worthy Tract of Paulus Jovius* (1585)

Copy-text

Paolo Giovio, *The worthy tract of Paulus Jouius, contayning a discourse of rare inuentions, called imprese [. . .]*, trans. by Samuel Daniel ([G. Robinson] for S. Waterson, 1585) STC 11900

Other early editions

STC 11900.5 A variant with imprint: [G. Robinson] for S. Waterson [1585]

9 Shall] shall 11900, 11900.5
14 Shall] shal 11900, 11900.5
15 door? No] dore: no 11900, 11900.5
22 truly] rruely 11900, 11900.5
33 wine.] wine: 11900, 11900.5
37 bravery, vanity] brauerie: Vanitie 11900, 11900.5
38 trappings, but] trappings. But 11900, 11900.5
47 limned; if] limned. If 11900, 11900.5
48 closets; if] Closets. If 11900, 11900.5

41. John Harington, *Orlando Furioso in English Heroical Verse* [Ariosto] (1591)

Copy-text

Ludovico Ariosto, *Orlando Furioso in English heroical verse*, trans. by John Harington (Richard Field, 1591) STC 746

Other early editions

STC 747 Richard Field for J. Norton and Simon Waterson, 1607
STC 748 G. Miller for J. Parker, 1634 (1633)

11 so. For] so: for 746, 747, 748
16 rest. And] rest: and 746, 747, 748
28 pressed] preassed 746, 747, 748
29 verse. The] verse; the 746, 747, 748
54 Latin:] Latin. 746, 747, 748
84 commendable. Yet] commendable: yet 746, 747, 748
91 and] And 746, 747, 748
95 straight] Straight 746, 747, 748
96 sort: 'Was] sort, Was 746, 747, 748
98 Latin,] Latin? 746, 747, 748
160 excuses);] excuses) 746, 747, 748

42. Thomas Dannett, *The History of Philip de Commines* (1596)

Copy-text

Philippe de Comines, *The historie of Philip de Commines*, trans. by Thomas Dannett (A. Hatfield for J. Norton, 1596) STC 5602

Other early editions

STC 5603 A. Hatfield for J. Norton, 1601
STC 5604 [Eliot's Court Press] for J. Bill, 1614

2 Right] 5604; R. 5602, 5603
3 Lordship] L. 5602, 5603; L 5604
4 *History*] historie 5602, 5603, 5604
9 *History*] historie 5602, 5603; history 5604
15 forbore] forbare 5602, 5603, 5604
16 alleged] alleaged 5602, 5603, 5604
29 *History*] historie 5602, 5603; history 5604
29 travailed] trauelled 5602, 5603, 5604
36 man –] man, 5602, 5603, 5604
37 coat –] cote, 5602, 5603, 5604
43 eigne] aisne 5602, 5603, 5604
48 *History*] historie 5602, 5603, 5604

43. Elizabeth Tudor (Queen Elizabeth I), 'Horace's *De Arte Poetica*' (1598)

Copy-text

National Archives SP 12/289, fols. 84r-88v, online facsimile, which has been compared with the transcript in Mueller and Scodel (2009). The ms is unpunctuated and in most cases the careful pointing of Mueller and Scodel has been followed.

3 they bear] the beare
4 chose] chase
6 far] fur
12 well-soldered] WeL soldered
13 need] nide
16 feigned] faned
17 they softly] the softly
18 Plautus] Plauto
20 need] nide
21 Cato] Caton
24 nearest] nirest

44. George Chapman, *The Iliad*

a) *Seven Books of the Iliads* (1598)

Copy-text

Homer, *Seaven bookes of the Iliades*, trans. by George Chapman (John Windet, 1598) STC 13632

Other early editions

STC 13633 *Homer prince of poets: translated according to the Greeke, in twelue bookes of his Iliads* [Anr ed. with additions and different title] [H. Lownes] for S. Macham [1609?] [Does not contain same epistle to the reader]
STC 13634 [See part c below] [Does not contain the same epistle to the reader]

20 translated. And] translated: and 13632
27 ability] habilitie 13632
29 time] time: 13632
34 – all] All 13632
36 precedent] president 13632
39 form. In] forme: in 13632
42 pass. So] passe: so 13632

b) *Achilles Shield* (1598)

Copy-text

Homer, *Achilles shield*, trans. by George Chapman (John Windet, 1598) STC 13635

There are no further early editions.

5 decisal] decysall 13635
6 shields. And] Shieldes; and 13635
8 reader. For] reader: for 13635
19 original. But] originall: but 13635
39 native!] natiue? 13635
49 chaos, when] Chaos. When 13635
58 everybody. To] euery bodie, to 13635
59 mind. Nor] minde, nor 13635
59 impair] empaire 13635
69 riddle). And] riddle) & 13635
78 digestion] disgestion 13635

97 derivation. And] deriuation; and 13635
106–07 now, and] now. And 13635
119 fingers. But] fingers; but 13635
124 estates –] estates; 13635
128 infinite.] infinite: 13635
139 strutting] strooting 13635
145 impair] empaire 13635

c) *The Iliads of Homer* (1611)

Copy-text

Homer, *The Iliads of Homer prince of poets Neuer before in any languag truely translated* [. . .], trans. by George Chapman ([Richard Field] for Nathaniel Butter, [1611?]) STC 13634 [Listed as anr ed. of a) *Seven Books* . . . in STC]

Other early editions

The verse epistle to the reader is also in Homer, *Homer prince of poets: translated according to the Greeke, in twelue bookes of his Iliads*, trans. by George Chapman ([Humphrey Lownes] for Samuel Macham, [1609?]) STC 13633

13 translations. All] translations, all 13634, 13633
19 Ask] Aske 13634; Asks 13633
26 example] 13633; exanple 13634
30 copy –] copie; 13634, 13633
31 native) –] Natiue): 13634, 13633
37 poesy. So] Poesie: So 13634, 13633
61 poesy;] Poesie. 13634, 13633
63 prove,] proue. 13634, 13633
67 write] wright 13634, 13633
82 impair'd] empayr'd 13634; empayrde 13633
84 heard] heyr'd 13634; heyrde 13633
92 jostl'd] iustl'd 13634, 13633
93 our] 13633; out 13634,
108 poesy –] Poesie? 13634
109 abovesaid?] abouesaid. 13634
122 fictions – that] fictions. That 13634
141 anything) –] any thing) 13634
146 Spondanus. We] Spond.) we 13634
162 slight] sleight 13634
166 rapture, in] rapture. In 13634

169 galls] gals 13634
177 translated, no] translated. No 13634
185 learning] learning; 13634
209 judge, always] iudge. Alwaies 13634
223 faulty –] faulty; 13634
227 ambition] ambition; 13634
238–39 recompense. Every] recompence: euery 13634
247 etc.), that] &c.) That 13634

45. Philemon Holland, *The Roman History* [Livy] (1600)

Copy-text

Titus Livius, *The Romane historie* [. . .], trans. by Philemon Holland (Adam Islip, 1600) STC 16613

There are no further early modern editions.

4 Majesty – an] Majestie. An 16613
7 empress, who] Empresse; Who 16613
13 liberty – an] libertie. An 16613
19 second.] second: 16613
94 style, wherein] stile. Wherein 16613
96 language. If] language: if 16613
97 dark. Have] darke: have 16613
99 themselves. Have] themselves: have 16613

46. Philemon Holland, *The History of the World* [Pliny] (1601)

Copy-text

Caius Plinius Secundus, *The historie of the world*, trans. by Philemon Holland (Adam Islip, 1601) STC 20029

Other early editions

STC 20029.5 [Anr issue, with cancel tp, w. imprint:] imp. G. B[ishop,] 1601
STC 20030 Adam Islip, 1634
STC 20030a [Anr issue, with imprint:] A. Islip, sold by J. Grismond, 1635

8 authors: that] authours, That 20029, 20029.5 20030, 20030a
29 law that] lavv, That 20029, 20029.5; law, That 20030, 20030a
36 rested.] rested: 20029, 20029.5, 20030, 20030a

41 Moreover] more-ver 20029, 20029.5; moreo-over 20030, 20030a
61 him; as] him: As 20029, 20029.5; him: as 20030, 20030a
65 divulged? As] divulged: as 20029, 20029.5, 20030, 20030a
77 us?] us. 20029, 20029.5; vs. 20030, 20030a
82 born?] borne. 20029, 20029.5, 20030, 20030a
83 Or] or 20029, 20029.5, 20030, 20030a

47. John Florio, *The Essays of Montaigne* (1603)

Copy-text

Michel de Montaigne, *The essayes or morall, politike and militarie discourses* (Valentine Simmes for E. Blount, 1603) STC 18041

Other early editions

STC 18042 M. Bradwood for E. Blount and W. Barret, 1613 [Contains Daniel's poem only, with first six lines altered from 18041]
STC 18043 M. Flesher for R. Royston, 1632 (1631) [Contains Daniel's poem only, with first six lines altered from 18041]

31 record; how] record: How 18041
37 *moi.*] moy: 18041
44 Guissen.] Guissen: 18041
49 so] So 18041
58–59 follow; most] fellow: Most 18041
66 since] Since 18041
72 much –] much) 18041
86 deigned] dayned 18041
87 you?), yet] you?) Yet 18041
102 word: *aut*] Word. Aut 18041
109 bay. Howsoever] bay: howsoever 18041
118 imposed. For] impos'de: for 18041
123 the] The 18041
126 Argantes.] Argante: 18041
130 Harington.] Harrington: 18041
140 service. As] service, as 18041
144 *medico*, so] Medico) So 18041
148 dens.] dennes: 18041
153 Hercules.] Hercules: 18041
182 am, yet] am: Yet 18041

186 enlarged. So] enlarged: so 18041
191 me.] mee: 18041
204 impair] empaire 18041
245 unknown; nay] unknowne: Nay 18041
250 writer – nay] Writer. Nay 18041
250 reader –] Reader: 18041
256 obscurity, and] obscuritie. And 18041
263 translate;] translate? 18041
263 usurp;] vsurpe? 18041
265 bad. In] bad: in 18041
267 bore] bare 18041
275 first. Yet] first; yet 18041
287 form. Without] forme; without 18041
305 Grecians.] Græcians: 18041
307 modern] moderne; 18041
315 help?] helpe. 18041
318 texts; all] texts. Al 18041
318 handling?] handling. 18041
331 little. But] little; but 18041
333 criticism] critikisme 18041
334 errors: if] errors. If 18041
335 printer's. Him] printers: him 18041
340 orthography? – as] Ortographie? as 18041
341 wrong. Or] wrong; or 18041
342 neuter? – you] newter; you 18041
343 mending. Or] mending: or 18041
346 suchlike? If] like; if 18041
350 recanted.] recanted: 18041
358 peruse. This] pervse: this 18041
381 uncertainty] incertaintie 18041; vncertaintie 18042; uncertaintie 18043
414 birth.] birth; 18041, 18042, 18043
418 To applaud] T'applaude 18041, 18042; T'applaud 18042
422 speech] speach. 18041, 18042; speech, 18043
428 be envassalled] b'invassal'd 18041, 18042, 18043
430 community,] communitie. 18041; communitie, 18042, 18043
447 he is] h'is 18041, 18042, 18043
454 poor;] poore. 18041, 18042, 18043

48. Richard Carew, *A World of Wonders* [Henri Estienne] (1607)

Copy-text

Henri Estienne, *A world of wonders: [. . .] or a preparative treatise to the Apologie for Herodotus*, trans by Richard Carew ([Richard Field] for J. Norton, 1607) STC 10553

Other early editions

STC 10554 [Anr issue] Edinburgh: A. Hart and R. Lawson, 1608

23 page. Then] page: then 10553, 10554
24 page. If] page: if 10553, 10554
35 sponge] sponge: 10553, 10554
48 etc., as] &c. As 10553, 10554
66 esteem –] esteeme; 10553, 10554
69 pipes –] pipes: 10553, 10554

49. John Healey, *Theophrastus' Characters* (1616)

Copy-text

Epictetus, *Epictetus manuall. Cebes table. Theophrastus Characters*, trans. by John Healey (G. Purslowe for E. Blount, 1616) STC 10426

Other early editions

STC 10427 [Anr issue with imprint:] R. B[adger?] sold by J. Stafford, 1636

6 another.] another: 10426, 10427
8–9 singularity. Yet] singularity, yet 10426, 10427
15 poring] powring 10426, 10427
24 refractory] refractiory 10426, 10427

PART THREE: TRANSLATION IN THE ACADEMY

50. John Palsgrave, *Acolastus* (1540)

Copy-text

Gulielmus Fullonius, *Joannis Palsgraui Londoniensis, ecphrasis Anglica in comoediam Acolasti. The comedye of Acolastus translated into englysshe after such maner as chylderne are taught in the grammer schole*, trans. by John Palsgrave (in aedibus T. Berthel[eti], 1540) STC 11470

There are no further early editions.

4 children] chylderne 11470
14 goeth. And] gothe, and 11470
16 comedy; and] comedy. And 11470
17–18 of; and] of. And 11470
24 Some] some 11470
28 children] chylderne 11470
29 another] an nother 11470
29–30 tongues, and] tongues: And 11470
38 whole] hole 11470
40 whole] hole 11470
41 purpose). They] purpose) they 11470
45–46 uttered; so] uttered. So 11470
47 a-glozing] a glosynge 11470
47 a-blotting] a blottyng 11470
51 scribble] scryble 11470
54 profited] prouffyted 11470
68 in.] in) 11470
71 increase] encrease 11470
75 conversance] conuersantynge 11470
93 Europe] Europa 11470
100 furtherance] furderaunce 11470
105 Spanish] Spaynes 11470
106 intact] intached 11470
108 countrymen] countrey meu 11470
113 Europe] Europa 11470

51. Roger Ascham, *The Schoolmaster* (1570)

Copy-text

Roger Ascham, *The scholemaster or plaine and perfite way of teachynge children the Latin tong* (John Day, [1570?]) STC 832

Other early editions

STC 833 [A ghost]
STC 834 John Day, 1571
STC 835 John Day, 1573
STC 835.5 John Day, 1579
STC 836 Abel Jeffes, 1589

14 *Ad Quintum fratrem,*] *ad Q. fra:* 832, 834, 835, 835.5, 836

17 over-old] ouer old 832; ouer olde 834, 835, 835.5, 836
42 words; show] wordes: Shew 832, 834, 835, 835.5; words: Shewe 836
44 heed-taking. Of] heed taking: of 832, 834, 835, 835.5, 836
47 master. For] master: for 832; Master: for 834, 835, 836; Maister: for 835.5
54 nothing.] nothing: 832, 834, 835, 835.5, 836
57 again.] againe: 832, 834, 835, 836; agayne. 835.5
58 way. And] way: and 832, 834, 835, 835.5, 836
61–62 learning, when] lear-ning: Whan] 832, 834; lear-ning: When 835; lear-ning. When 835.5; learning: When 836
64 profit. Always] proffit: Al-wayes 832, 834; profit: Al-wayes 835, 835.5; profit: Always 836
69 pleasure. And] pleasure: And 832, 834, 835, 835.5, 836
75 again.] againe: 832, 834, 835; agayne. 835.5; againe. 836
83 thus:] 836; thus. 832, 834, 835, 835.5
94 before.] 836; before: 832, 834, 835, 835.5
98 Cheshunt] Cheston 832, 834, 835, 835.5, 836
104 Laurence's] Laurence 832, 834, 835, 835.5, 836
106 *De Finibus*] *de finib*. 832, 834, 835, 835.5, 836
110 Latin, which] Latin: Which 832, 834, 835.5; Latine: Which 835, 836
125 metre:] meter. 832; metre. 834; meeter. 835, 836; meeter 835.5
130 further] farder 832, 834; farther 835, 835.5, 836
132 is] 835.5; in 832, 834, 835, 836
144 require, the] require. The 832, 834, 835, 835.5, 836
146 schools. Yet] scholes: yet 832, 834, 835.5; schooles: yet 835, 836
161 learned, most] learned. Most 832, 834, 835.5; learned: Most 835, 836
165 choose] chose 832; chuse 834, 835, 835.5, 836
169 words.] 835.5, 836; wordes: 832; wordes. 834, 835
210 rest. And] rest: and 832, 836; rest: & 834, 835, 835.5
210 them:] them. 832, 834, 835, 835.5, 836
242 *Ad Quintum fratrem*] *ad Q. fra* 832; *ad Q. Fra.* 834, 835, 835.5, 836
251 For] for 832, 834, 835, 835.5, 836
266 room] rowme 832, 834, 835, 835.5, 836
279 Gaius] C. 832, 834, 835, 835.5, 836
288 leather] 834, 835, 835.5, 836; ledder 832
299 Quintilian's] Quintilianus 832, 834, 835, 835.5, 836

306 themselves] their selues 832, 835, 835.5, 836; theyr selues 834
320 Androtion] Andration 832, 834, 835, 835.5, 836
322 more] mo 832, 834, 835, 835.5, 836
331 words.] wordes: 832, 834, 835, 835.5, 836
336 eschew] 835, 835.5, 836; exchew 832, 834
341 able] 835.5, 836; hable 832, 834, 835
356 butcherly] 836; boocherlie 832; boocherly 834, 835 835.5
364 imitation –] imitation, 832, 834, 835, 835.5, 836
366 orderly –] orderlie, 832; orderly, 834, 835, 835.5, 836
366 perfectly.] perfitlie: 832; perfitly: 834, 835, 836; perfytly: 835.5
371–72 thereby; but] thereby: But 832, 834, 835, 835.5, 836
373 eschew] 835, 835.5, 836; exchew 832; eschow 834

52. Abraham Fleming, *The Bucolics of Virgil* (1575)

Copy-text

Publius Virgilius Maro, *The Bucolikes of Publius Virgilius Maro, with alphabeticall annotations*, trans. by Abraham Fleming (John Charlewood for T. Woodcock, 1575) STC 24816

Other early editions

STC 24817 T. O[rwin] for T. Woodcock, 1589 [Does not contain the epistle]

10 style. Which] stile: which 24816
18 not,] not? 24816
25 ice] yse 24816
30 but] But 24816
31 ability] habyllitie 24816
42 learn.] learne: 24816
43 blindness.] blindnes: 24816
45 foolishness.] foolishnes: 24816
47 wit.] wit: 24816
49 shame.] shame: 24816
49 fantasies] phantasies 24816
51 contempt.] contempt: 24816
56 closer.] closer, 24816
66 conversion] couersion 24816
68 whereof] VVhereof 24816
73 etc., –] &c 24816
75 wide –] wyde, 24816

80 margin] margen 24816
82 neglected.] neglected 24816
86 expressed.] expressed: 24816
105 heard] hard 24816
113 alabaster] alablaster 24816
136 life.] life: 24816
141 *venite*] *vinite* 24816

53. Maurice Kiffin, *Andria: The First Comedy of Terence, in English* (1588)

Copy-text

Publius Terentius, *Andria the first comoedie of Terence, in English*, trans. by Maurice Kiffin (Thomas E[ast] for T. Woodcock, 1588) STC 23895

There are no further early editions.

18 means.] meanes: 23895
27 so much] somuch 23895
28 sithence] sithens 23895
28 finished.] finished: 23895
40 Terence's] Terence 23895
41 love, and] loue: And 23895
48 Terentius. For] Terentius: for 23895
49 cunning] conning 23895
56 misunderstood. For] misvnderstood: for 23895
60–61 him. Which] him: which 23895
68 yet] Yet 23895
73–74 notwithstanding] Notwithstanding 23895

54. John Brinsley, *Ludus Literarius* (1612)

Copy-text

John Brinsley, *Ludus literarius: or, the grammar schoole. Intended for the helping of the younger sort of teachers, and of all schollars* ([H. Lownes] for T. Man, 1612) STC 3768

Other early editions

STC 3769 Felix Kingston for William Leake, 1637
STC 3770 [A variant with imprint:] Felix Kingston for A. Hebb, 1627

STC 3770a [A variant with imprint:] Felix Kingston for R. Meighen, 1627

STC 3770b [A variant with imprint:] Felix Kingston for J. Bill, 1627

STC 3770b.2 [A variant with imprint:] Felix Kingston for J. Bellamie, 1627

2 Ascham] Askame 3768, 3769, 3770, 3770a, 3770b, 3770b.2

32 Ascham] Askam 3768, 3769, 3770, 3770a, 3770b, 3770b.2

36 particular] 3769, 3770, 3770a, 3770b, 3770b.2; parricular 3768

46 unfeignedly] vnfainedly 3768, 3769, 3770, 3770a, 3770b, 3770b.2

55 children:] children. 3768, 3769, 3770, 3770a, 3770b, 3770b.2

109 copy] 3769, 3770, 3770a, 3770b, 3770b.2; copie 3768

110 authors; and] Authors. And 3768, 3769, 3770, 3770a, 3770b, 3770b.2

117 translations –] translations, 3768, 3769, 3770, 3770a, 3770b, 3770b.2

118 rhetorically –] Rhetorically, 3768, 3769, 3770, 3770a, 3770b, 3770b.2

163 Ascham] Askam 3768, 3769, 3770, 3770a, 3770b, 3770b.2

172 learning. For] learning: for 3768; learning, for 3769, 3770, 3770a, 3770b, 3770b.2

179 say. Yet] say: yet 3768, 3769, 3770, 3770a, 3770b, 3770b.2

186 present.] present: 3768, 3769, 3770, 3770a, 3770b, 3770b.2

210 constructions] 3769, 3770, 3770a, 3770b, 3770b.2; constrctions 3768

221 benefits.] benefites: 3768; benefits: 3769, 3770, 3770a, 3770b, 3770b.2

223 authors, the] Authours. The 3768; Authors. The 3769, 3770, 3770a, 3770b, 3770b.2

282 recovering] reoouering 3768; recouering 3769, 3770, 3770a, 3770b, 3770b.2

284 over against] ouer-against 3768; oueragainst 3769, 3770, 3770a, 3770b, 3770b.2

308 readily. By] readily: by 3768, 3769, 3770, 3770a, 3770b, 3770b.2

340 stuck] stucken 3768, 3769, 3770, 3770a, 3770b, 3770b.2

55. Joseph Webbe, *The Familiar Epistles of Cicero* (1620)

Copy-text

Marcus Tullius Cicero, *The familar epistles of M. T. Cicero Englished and conferred with the French Italian and other translations*, trans. by Joseph Webbe (E. Griffin, [1620]) STC 5305

There are no further early editions.

1 Physic] PHYS: 5305
2 Francis] FRA: 5305
6 obligeth] obliegeth 5305
20 whoso] who so 5305
27 after ages] after-ages 5305
43 *Epistles*.] Epistles; 5305
46 ornaments.] ornaments: 5305
48 imperators] Imperator's 5305
51 potentates –] Potentates; 5305
52 commander –] Commander; 5305
57 original. Go] originall: goe 5305
58 me. Be] me; be 5305
60 Command –] Commaund: 5305
62 translator.] Translator; 5305
67 presumptuous, for] presumptuous; For 5305
72 *putamus*,] putamus. 5305

56. Joseph Webbe, *An Appeal to Truth in the Controversy between Art and Use* (1622)

Copy-text

Josephe Webbe, *An appeale to truth, in the controversie betweene art, & use; about the best and most expedient course in languages* (H. L[ownes] for G. Latham, 1622) STC 25169

There are no further early editions.

2 engined] ingiu'd 25169
37 behalf. But] behalf: but 25169
60 eighth] eight 25169
63 so.] so: 25169
67 seeing.] seeing: 25169
92 apes, though] Apes; Though 25169

93 adorned.] adorned: 25169
109 them.] them; 25169
121 its] it 25169
141 eloquent. But] eloquent: but 25169
224 without] withont 25169

GLOSSARY

A

abashed	disconcerted
abhor	diverge
ability	aptness, suitability
acceptive	receptive
accident	event
accommodate	suited, adapted
administration	duty, office
admonish	notify, inform
advisement	consideration, reflection
affect	strive for
affectation	artificiality
affected	presumed
affectuous	earnest, ardent
algorism	the Arabic numeral system
allay	intermix
allege	1. cite or quote as an authority; 2. plead as an excuse
allegation	citation
allow	1. praise; 2. grudgingly accept
allowance	praise
Almaine	Germany
amass	accumulation
analogy	agreement
and	if
antitheton	the rhetorical figure of antithesis (opposition)
apaid	rewarded
apply	attribute
appropred	assigned
aret	attribute
argument	plot
arride	please
arrogate	claim
artificial	skillfully made
artificially	1. skillfully; 2. rhetorically
artists	artisans, craftsmen
assay	attempt

assoil	grant absolution
astoned	overwhelmed with amazement or dismay
attent	intent, focused

B

bait	provide fodder for
balductum	trashy
balsamum	balm
beck	control, command
beguile	pass, spend
bewray	reveal
blaze	publicise
blur	blot with ink
board	table
bodging	bungling
bound	limit
brake	thicket
bravery	finery
brittle	unreliable, not tenacious
burgessy	citizenship
butcherly	torturing

C

calendar	register, record
calling	name
camfering	mettlesome, high-spirited
can	know
cantle	separate part, portion
censor	critic
cham	chew
checker	fault-finder
chirurgeon	surgeon
clerk	scholar
cloak	reason of a specious kind, pretext
clogging	encumbering, burdensome
clown	peasant
coat	class
coistrel	base person (general term of abuse)
colour	[see cloak]
colourably	plausibly

commercement	dealings, intercourse
commodious	1. beneficial, profitable; 2. convenient
commodity	1. private benefit; 2. useful resource for the general good
composure	composition
con	acknowledge, express gratitude
conceit [noun]	personal opinion, idea
conceit [verb]	conceive, imagine
confer	compare
conference	comparison, collation
confirmance	confirmation, reassurance
conformable	fitting, harmonious
connivency	tacit approval or permission
construction	grammatical structure
contemn	despise
contemple	contemplate
contentation	contentment
control	challenge, censure
controlment	calling into question
conversant in	familiar with
conversion	translation
conveyance	form of expression
copy	copiousness, linguistic abundance
couched	compressed, covert
countervail	be the equivalent of
courage	spirit, heart
craggy	hard to get through
crooked	tortuous, strained
cruse	jar
cunning	learning, skill
curious	1. fastidious; 2. ingenious, elaborate; 3. painstaking
curiosity	unnecessary scrupulosity
curtal	abbreviated
cushion	mark, target

D

dainty	over-particular
dark	obscure
debase	depreciate

deduce	bring forth, derive
defalk	reduce
deliber	resolve
delicate	charming, pleasurable
denizened	naturalised
deprave	disparage
descant	comment, explicate
device	invention, design
digestion	reduction
diocesan	Bishop
disour	storyteller, jester
dispend	waste
dispense	expense
dispersed	scattered
dispician	discussion
dissimule	conceal
distance	interval (in music)
distinguished	distinct

E

eftsoons	from time to time
eigne	prior, superior
eke	expand
emprise	undertake
enchiridion	handbook, reference guide
enfarce	stuff
enow	enough
ensearch	examine closely
enter	to give initial instruction
entermete	occupy oneself
entreat	treat
entwited	reproached
estrange	foreign
ethnic	pagan, i.e. neither Christian nor Jew
except	object
exhibition	act of provision or support
exigent	writ summoning a defendant
expone	explain
exquisite	accomplished, perfected
extern	foreign

F

facile	fluent, easy to understand
factious	seditious
fantastical	eccentric
fantasticalness	whimsicality
fantasy	groundless supposition
feat	fitting
feign	fashion
fevery	feverish
fine	1. purify; 2. beautify
finewed	mouldy
flap	drive away
fledge	fit to fly
flush	sudden rush of water
foil	defeat
foisting	farting
forehead	sense of shame or decency
forwardness	zeal
frontless	shameless
froward	perverse, evilly-disposed
fry	litter of children
furtherer	supporter
fustian	inflated, bombastic

G

gadding	wandering, digressive
garnish	equip, furnish
gentle	courteous
glout	frown, scowl
gloze [noun]	gloss, explanatory marginal comment
gloze [verb]	1. make excuses for; 2. use ingratiating or fawning language
gnap	bite in a snapping fashion
groat	coin worth four old pence
gree	favour
grutch [noun]	complaint
grutch [verb]	begrudge

H

head point, topic
heed care

I

impair impairment, detriment
imperfect irrelevant
impresa emblem (or book of emblems)
imputation 1. the attributing to believers of the righteousness of Christ; 2. accusation
increase progress
indifferent 1. impartial; 2. non-essential
indign undeserving
indite to put into words, compose
infused imparted by nature
interfarce stuff in between
interlude play
intermeddle intermingle
interpret translate
irrefragable incontrovertible

J

jealous protective, mistrustful
jet swagger, parade
judicial judicious
juggle to play tricks in order to deceive
jump coincide

L

lapped folded
largely generally
leese lose
lewd lay, unlearned
libel booklet
light easy
lief(er) 1. (more) gladly; 2. like
lenify soothe
let [verb] 1. refrain; 2. prevent
let [noun] hindrance

licentious	free
light	frivolous
like	please
linger	draw out, prolong
list	wish to do something
lubber	idle or stupid person

M

maintain	take pride in
manqueller	murderer
massy	huge, widespread
maugre	in spite of
meal-mouthed	unwilling to speak out
mean [noun]	1. method; 2. mediator, ambassador
mean [adj.]	1. middling; 2. common, mutual
meetly	moderately
mere	ordinary
metewand	yardstick, criterion
meteyard	measuring rod, yardstick
mews	lodgings
minish	diminish, reduce
misorderly	irregular
monition	instruction, direction
mortuary	money claimed by the Church from the estate of a deceased parishioner
motioner	instigator

N

nicely	fussily, pedantically
nighly	closely
note	accuse
nought	worthless, a 'nothing'
number	stress pattern, measure; (in plural), metre

O

obsequent	compliant
occasion	have the opportunity (to do something)
odd	1. famous, distinguished; 2. only
or	before

ordain set up
orderly in the correct order, according to the established rule
ordinary [noun] 1.ecclesiastical authority (eg. the Bishop or his deputy); 2. rule-book
ordinary [adj.] authorised
overlay overburden
over-harsh too strained, clumsy
over-strait excessively strict

P

paddock frog or toad
painful painstaking
panary storehouse for bread
pandect complete body of the laws of a country
pantofles slippers
pap baby food
parcel small part
patter to gabble or mumble through a prayer (especially the paternoster)
pedigree source of an idea, origin of a word
penner pen
pensive sorrowful
percase perhaps
performation fulfilment
period pause
phrase expression, idiom
physic medicine
pie magpie
plaster soothing substance
plausible pleasing
plight condition
pore out earnestly examine
porteous portable breviary
prebend land from which income is derived to support cathedral clergy
pregnant 1. full of meaning, highly significant; 2. quick-witted
prejudicate prejudiced
premonstration making something known beforehand

prepensed	premeditated, planned
pretend	to use in support (with intent to deceive)
prevent	anticipate, pre-empt
primer	early
probable	credible, convincing
prove	test
provide for	take measures to prevent
put case	suppose

Q

quidditical	quibbling

R

race	course of action
rank	1. crowded, dense; 2. hasty
rare	excellent
recureless	incurable
recuyell	literary compilation or collection
reduce	translate
refell	disprove
refractory	not responsive to or compliant with
religious	scrupulous, strict
remanant	remainder
remit	refer
reserve	1. except; 2. preserve unaltered
respective	attentive
rhymer	popular poet (more specifically, ballad-maker)
rip up	anatomise
ripeness	maturity
round	1. open, direct; 2. categorical; 3. perfectly constructed
round-headed	common, vulgar
rub	obstacle
ruck	huddle together
ruffle	rifle, ransack

S

sad	serious, sober
sapience	wisdom
saucy	insolent, dismissive
scant	sparing
scare-fire	sudden conflagration
scope	goal, object
self-opinion	self-conceit, high opinion of oneself
semblable	similar, in the same way
sentence	1. sense of a passage, meaning; 2. maxim, pithy saying
sequel	logical consequence, ensuing course of affairs
seraglio	place of confinement
shadowed	kept in the dark, concealed
shift	means, device
shore	sheared
sinisterly	disparagingly
silly	1. weak; 2. simple, ignorant
sith(ence)	since
sleight	wily, deceptive
slubbered	hurriedly done
smatterer	dabbler
soil	1. resolve; 2 refute
sound	get to the bottom of something
souter	shoemaker
staff	stanza
standing	stagnant
[by] starts	intermittently
stave	stanza
stead	be of benefit to
sterling	current
store	abundance, stock of vocabulary
storial	historical
story	history
strait	strict
strange, stranger	foreign, foreigner
supererogation	going beyond what is strictly necessary
superstitiously	punctiliously
supply	supplicate
sustentation	sustenance, support

T

table	index of topics
(by) tale	(by) number
terminant	determining, defining
though	if
to-coming	future
tofore	before
toll	entice
toward	promising
toy	piece of trivia
trace	travel, tread
tract	literary treatment
trade	1. manner of life; 2. method
traduction	translation
treaty	literary treatment

U

unartificial	unskilled
uncouth	strange, unusual
unmingled	unadulterated
unshamefastness	lack of modesty or decency
unsifted	unexamined
uplandish	rustic, uncultivated
usher	schoolmaster's assistant

V

vacant	unoccupied, free from work
vailable	profitable
value	equal
vantage	pecuniary profit
Venus	grace, charm
vent	sell
venturous	bold, risky

W

wade	advance, proceed
ween	suppose
weet	know
wot	know
wrested	strained, perverted
wroth	moved by anger

BIBLIOGRAPHY

Alexander, Gavin, ed., *Sidney's 'The Defence of Poesy' and Selected Renaissance Literary Criticism* (London: Penguin, 2004)

Allen, Ward, ed., *Translating for King James: Notes Made by a Translator of King James's Bible* (London: Allen Lane, 1970)

Altman, Joel B., *The Tudor Play of Mind* (Berkeley: University of California Press, 1978)

Amos, Flora Ross, *Early Theories of Translation* (New York: Columbia University Studies in English and Comparative Literature, 1920)

Arber, Edward, ed., *The First Three English Books on America* (Birmingham: [s. n.], 1885)

Ariosto, Lodovico, *Orlando Furioso, Translated into English Heroical Verse by Sir John Harington* (1591), ed. by Robert McNulty (Oxford: Clarendon Press, 1972)

Ascham, Roger, *The Schoolmaster (1570)*, ed. by Lawrence V. Ryan (Charlottesville: University of Virginia Press, 1967)

Athanasius, *The Life of Antony and the Letter to Marcellinus*, trans. by Robert C. Gregg (New York: Paulist Press, 1980)

Attridge, Derek, *Well-weighed Syllables: Elizabethan Verse in Classical Metres* (London: Cambridge University Press, 1974)

Augustine, *De Doctrina Christiana*, ed. and trans. by R. P. H. Green (Oxford: Clarendon Press, 1995)

—, *The Confessions and Letters of St Augustine*, in *Nicene & Post-Nicene Fathers*, vol. 1, ed. by Philip Schaff (Edinburgh: T. and T. Clark, 1996)

Axton, Marie, and James P. Carley, eds, *Triumphs of English: Henry Parker, Lord Morley: Translator to the Tudor Court* (London: British Library, 2000)

Bacon, Francis, *The Advancement of Learning*, ed. by Michael Kiernan (Oxford: Oxford University Press, 2000)

Baldwin, T. W., *William Shakspere's Small Latine and Lesse Greeke*, 2 vols (Urbana: University of Illinois Press, 1944)

Bale, John, *John Bale's Catalogue of Tudor Authors: An Annotated Translation of Records from the Scriptorum illustrium maioris Brytanniae catalogus (1557–1559)*, ed. by J. Christopher Warner (Tempe, AZ: MRTS, 2010)

Bassnett-McGuire, Susan, *Translation Studies*, 4th edn (London: Routledge, 2013)

Bate, Jonathan, *Shakespeare and Ovid* (Oxford: Clarendon Press, 1993)

Belle, Marie-Alice, ed., *Women and Translation in Early Modern England and France*, special issue, *Renaissance and Reformation / Renaissance et Réforme*, 36 (2013)

Bennett, H. S., *English Books and Readers*, 2nd edn, 3 vols (Cambridge: Cambridge University Press, 1969–70)

[Bible] *Tyndale's Old Testament*, ed. by David Daniell (New Haven: Yale University Press, 1992)

—, *The New Testament translated by William Tyndale*, ed. by W. R. Cooper (London: British Library, 2000)

—, *The Coverdale Bible, 1535*, introd. by S. L. Greenslade (Folkstone: Dawsons, 1975)

—, *The Bible: Douay-Rheims Version*, ed. by Richard Challoner (London: Baronius Press, 2008)

—, Rhodes, Erroll F. and Líana Lupas, eds, *The Translators to the Reader: the Original Preface of the King James Version of 1611 Revisited* (New York: American Bible Society, 1997)

—, *The Bible: Authorized King James Version*, ed. by Robert Carroll and Stephen Prickett (Oxford: Oxford University Press, 2008)

Binns, J. W., *Intellectual Culture in Elizabethan and Jacobean England: The Latin Writings of the Age* (Leeds: Francis Cairns, 1990)

Blake, N. F., *Caxton and his World* (London: André Deutsch, 1969)

Blank, Paula, *Broken English: Dialects of English and the Politics of Language in Renaissance Writings* (London: Routledge, 1996)

—, 'Languages of Early Modern Literature in Britain', in *The Cambridge History of Early Modern English Literature*, ed. by David Loewenstein and Janel Mueller (Cambridge: Cambridge University Press, 2002), pp. 141–69

Blanshard, Alastair J. L. and Tracey A. Sowerby, 'Thomas Wilson's Demosthenes and the Politics of Tudor Translation', *International Journal of the Classical Tradition*, 12 (2005), 46–80

Bolgar, R. R., *The Classical Heritage and Its Beneficiaries* (Cambridge: Cambridge University Press, 1954)

Botley, Paul, *Latin Translation in the Renaissance: The Theory and Practice of Leonardo Bruni, Giannozzo Manetti and*

Desiderius Erasmus (Cambridge: Cambridge University Press, 2004)

—, *Learning Greek in Western Europe, 1396–1529: Grammars, Lexica, and Classroom Texts* (Philadelphia: American Philosophical Society, 2010)

Boutcher, Warren, 'A French Dexterity, & an Italian Confidence', *Reformation*, 2 (1997), 39–109

—, 'The Renaissance', in *The Oxford Guide to Literature in English Translation*, ed. by Peter France (Oxford: Oxford University Press, 2000)

Boyce, Benjamin, *The Theophrastan Character in England to 1642* (Cambridge, MA: Harvard University Press, 1947)

Braden, Gordon, 'Translation Procedures in Theory and Practice', in *OHLTE* (2), pp. 89–100

Braden, Gordon, Robert Cummings, and Stuart Gillespie, eds, *The Oxford History of Literary Translation in English: Volume 2, 1550–1660* (Oxford: Oxford University Press, 2011)

Bruce, F. F., *The English Bible: A History of Translations from the Earliest English Versions to the New English Bible*, rev. edn (London: Lutterworth Press, 1970)

Bruni, Leonardo, 'On the Correct Way to Translate', in *The Humanism of Leonardo Bruni: Selected Texts*, ed. by Gordon Griffiths, James Hankins, and David Thompson (Binghamton, NY: MRTS, 1987), pp. 216–29

Burke, Peter, *The Fortunes of The Courtier* (Cambridge: Polity Press, 1995)

Burke, Peter and R. Po-chia Hsia, eds, *Cultural Translation in Early Modern Europe* (Cambridge: Cambridge University Press, 2007)

Burrow, Colin, 'Horace at Home and Abroad: Wyatt and Sixteenth-Century Horatianism', in *Horace Made New: Horatian Influences on British Writing from the Renaissance to the Twentieth Century* (Cambridge: Cambridge University Press, 1993)

—, 'Shakespeare and Humanistic Culture', in *Shakespeare and the Classics*, ed. by Charles Martindale and A. B. Taylor (Cambridge: Cambridge University Press, 2004), pp. 9–27

Bushnell, Rebecca W., *A Culture of Teaching: Early Modern Humanism in Theory and Practice* (Ithaca, NY: Cornell University Press, 1996)

Butterfield, Ardis, *The Familiar Enemy: Chaucer, Language, and*

Nation in the Hundred Years War (Oxford: Oxford University Press, 2009)
Campbell, Gordon, *Bible: The Story of the King James Version* (Oxford: Oxford University Press, 2010)
Campbell, Lily B., 'John Dolman', *ELH*, 4 (1937), 192–200
Castiglione, Baldassare, *The Book of the Courtier* [trans. by Thomas Hoby], ed. by Virginia Cox (London: Dent, 1994)
Caxton, William, *Caxton's Eneydos*, ed. by W. T. Culley and F. J. Furnivall (London: EETS, 1890)
—, *Caxton's Own Prose*, ed. by N. F. Blake (London: André Deutsch, 1973)
Chapman, George, *The Poems of George Chapman*, ed. by Phyllis Brooks Bartlett (London: Oxford University Press, 1941)
—, *Chapman's Homer*, ed. by Allardyce Nicoll, 2 vols (London: Routledge & Kegan Paul, 1957)
Cheke, John, *The Gospel according to Saint Matthew*, ed. by James Goodwin (Cambridge: J. and J. J. Deighton, 1843)
Cicero, *De Finibus bonorum et malorum*, trans. by H. Rackham (London: William Heinemann, 1914)
—, *De Inventione, De Optimo genere oratorum, Topica*, trans. by H. M. Hubbell (London: William Heinemann, 1949)
—, *De Oratore*, trans. by E. W. Sutton and H. Rackham (London: William Heinemann, 1942)
—, *Marcus Tullius Ciceroes Thre Bokes of Duties*, ed. by Gerald O'Gorman (Washington: Folger Shakespeare Library, 1990)
Clarke, Danielle, 'Translations', in *The Cambridge Companion to Early Modern Women's Writing*, ed. by Laura Lunger Knoppers (Cambridge: Cambridge University Press, 2009), pp. 167–80
Coldiron, A. E. B., 'William Caxton', in *OHLTE* (1), pp. 160–69
—, 'Commonplaces and Metaphors', in *OHLTE* (2), pp. 109–17
Conley, Tom, 'Institutionalizing Translation: On Florio's Montaigne', in *Demarcating the Disciplines: Philosophy, Literature, Art*, ed. by Samuel Weber (Minneapolis: University of Minnesota Press, 1986), pp. 45–58
Considine, John, *Dictionaries in Early Modern Europe: Lexicography and the Making of Heritage* (Cambridge: Cambridge University Press, 2008)
Courtney, Edward, ed., *The Fragmentary Latin Poets* (Oxford: Oxford University Press, 2003)
Craig, John, 'Forming a Protestant Consciousness? Erasmus's

Paraphrases in English Parishes, 1547–1666', in *Holy Scripture Speaks: The Production and Reception of Erasmus's Paraphrases on the New Testament*, ed. by Hilmor M. Pabel and Mark Vessey (Toronto: University of Toronto Press, 2002), pp. 313–58

Crane, D. E. L., 'Richard Stanyhurst's Translation of Vergil's *Aeneid* (1582)', in *Studies in Seventeenth-Century English Literature, History and Bibliography*, ed. by G. A. M. Janssens and F. G. A. M. Aarts (Amsterdam: Rodopi, 1984)

Culhane, Peter, 'Philemon Holland's Livy: Peritexts and Contexts', *Translation and Literature*, 13 (2004), 268–86

Cummings, Brian, *The Literary Culture of the Reformation: Grammar and Grace* (Oxford: Oxford University Press, 2002)

Cummings, Robert, 'Classical Moralists and Philosophers', in *OHLTE* (2), pp. 371–89

Daniell, David, *William Tyndale: A Biography* (New Haven: Yale University Press, 1994)

—, *The Bible in English: Its History and Influence* (New Haven: Yale University Press, 2003)

Demers, Patricia *Women's Writing in English: Early Modern England* (Toronto: University of Toronto Press, 2005)

—, '"Nether bitterly nor brablingly": Lady Anne Cooke Bacon's Translation of Bishop Jewel's *Apologia Ecclesiae Anglicanae*', in *English Women, Religion, and Textual Production, 1500–1625*, ed. by Micheline White (Farnham: Ashgate, 2011), pp. 205–17.

Devereux, E. J., 'The Publication of the English Paraphrases of Erasmus', *Bulletin of the John Rylands University Library of Manchester*, 51 (1969), 348–67

Donne, John, *Devotions upon Emergent Occasions*, ed. by Anthony Raspa (New York: Oxford University Press, 1987)

—, *The Poems of John Donne*, ed. by Robin Robbins, 2 vols (Harlow: Pearson, 2008)

Douglas, Gavin, *The Aeneid (1513)*, ed. by Gordon Kendal, 2 vols (London: MHRA, 2011)

Eden, Kathy, *Friends Hold All Things in Common* (New Haven, CT: Yale University Press, 2001)

Edgar, David, *Written on the Heart* (London: Nick Hearn Books, 2001)

Elizabeth 1, *The Mirror of the Sinful Soul*, ed. by Percy W. Ames (London: Asher, 1897)

—, *Queen Elizabeth's Englishings of Boethius, 'De Consolatione Philosophiae', Plutarch, 'De Curiositate' and Horace, 'De Arte Poetica'*, ed. by Caroline Pemberton (London: Early English Text Society, 1899)

—, *The Poems of Queen Elizabeth 1*, ed. by Leicester Bradner (Providence, RI: Brown University Press, 1964)

—, *Queen Elizabeth 1: Selected Works*, ed. by Steven F. May (New York: Washington Square Press, 2004)

—, *Translations, 1544–1589*, ed. by Janel Mueller and Joshua Scodel (Chicago: University of Chicago Press, 2009)

—, *Translations, 1592–1598*, ed. by Janel Mueller and Joshua Scodel (Chicago: University of Chicago Press, 2009)

Ellis, Roger, ed., *The Oxford History of Literary Translation in English: Volume 1, To 1550* (Oxford: Oxford University Press, 2008)

Erler, Mary C., 'The First English Printing of Galen: The Formation of the Company of Barber-Surgeons', *HLQ*, 48 (1985), 159–71

Erasmus, Desiderius, *Adages*, ed. and trans. by R. A. B. Mynors and Margaret Mann Philips, *CWE* 31–36 (Toronto: University of Toronto Press, 1962-)

—, *Correspondence*, ed. and trans. by R. A. B. Mynors and D. F. S. Thomson, *CWE* 1–10 (Toronto: University of Toronto Press, 1974-)

—, *Paraphrase on Matthew*, ed. by Robert D. Sider and Dean Simpson, *CWE* 45 (Toronto: University of Toronto Press, 2008)

—, 'Two Forewords to the Latin Translation of the New Testament', in *The Praise of Folly and Other Writings*, ed. and trans. by Robert M. Adams (New York: W. W. Norton, 1989)

Ferguson, Margaret W., *Trials of Desire: Renaissance Defenses of Poetry* (New Haven, CT: Yale University Press, 1983)

Firth, Katharine R., *The Apocalyptic Tradition in Reformation Britain* (Oxford: Oxford University Press, 1979)

Folena, Gianfranco, *Volgarizzare e tradurre* (Torino: Einaudi, 1993)

Friedrich, Hugo, *Montaigne*, trans. by Philippe Desan (Berkeley: University of California Press, 1991)

Fulke, William, *A Defence of the Sincere and True Translations of the Holy Scriptures into the English Tongue*, ed. by C. H. Hartshorne (Cambridge: Cambridge University Press, 1843)

Fuller, Thomas, *The History of the Worthies of England*, ed. by P. A. Nuttall, 3 vols (London: Thomas Tegg, 1840)

Gillespie, Stuart, *English Translation and Classical Reception: Towards a New Literary History* (Oxford: Wiley-Blackwell, 2011)

Gnaphaeus, Guglielmus [Fullonius], *Acolastus*, ed. and trans. by W. E. D. Atkinson (London, Ontario: University of Western Ontario Studies in the Humanities, 1964)

Gray, Douglas, 'A Note on Sixteenth-Century Purism', in *Words: for Robert Burchfield's Sixty-Fifth Birthday*, ed. by E. G. Stanley and T. F. Hoad (Woodbridge: D. S. Brewer, 1988)

Green, Ian, *Print and Protestantism in Early Modern England* (Oxford: Oxford University Press, 2000)

Greenblatt, Stephen, *Renaissance Self-Fashioning: From More to Shakespeare* (Chicago: University of Chicago Press, 1980)

Greene, Thomas M., *The Light in Troy: Imitation and Discovery in Renaissance Poetry* (New Haven, CT: Yale University Press, 1982)

Greenslade, S. L., ed., *The Cambridge History of the Bible, Vol. 3: The West, from the Reformation to the Present Day* (Cambridge: Cambridge University Press, 1963)

Grossman, Edith, *Why Translation Matters* (New Haven: Yale University Press, 2010)

Hackel, Heidi Brayman, *Reading Material in Early Modern England: Print, Gender and Literacy* (Cambridge: Cambridge University Press, 2005)

Hackett, Helen, *Women and Romance Fiction in the English Renaissance* (Cambridge: Cambridge University Press, 2000)

Hadfield, Andrew, *Literature, Travel, and Colonial Writing in the English Renaissance, 1545–1625* (Oxford: Oxford University Press, 1998)

Hamlin, Hannibal, *Psalm Culture and Early Modern English Literature* (Cambridge: Cambridge University Press, 2004)

Hammond, Gerald, *The Making of the English Bible* (Manchester: Carcanet, 1982)

—, 'The Authority of the Translated Word of God', *Translation and Literature*, 2 (1993), 17–36

—, 'The Sore and Strong Prose of the English Bible', in *English Renaissance Prose: History, Language, and Politics*, ed. by Neil Rhodes (Tempe, AZ: MRTS, 1997), pp. 19–34

Hannay, Margaret Patterson, ed., *Silent But for the Word: Tudor Women as Patrons, Translators, and Writers of Religious Works* (Kent, OH: The Kent State University Press, 1985)

Harington, John, *Nugae Antiquae* (London: Vernor and Hood, 1804)

Helgerson, Richard, *Forms of Nationhood: The Elizabethan Writing of England* (Chicago: Chicago University Press, 1992)

Hellinga, Lotte, *Caxton and Early Printing in England* (London: British Library, 2010)

Hermans, Theo, 'Images of Translation: Metaphor and Imagery in the Renaissance Discourse on Translation', in *The Manipulation of Literature*, ed. by Hermans (London: Croom Helm, 1985), pp. 103–35

Herrick, Marvin T., *Tragicomedy: Its Origins and Development in Italy and France* (Urbana: University of Illinois Press, 1962)

—, *Comic Theory in the Sixteenth Century* (Urbana: University of Illinois Press, 1964)

Higman, Francis, 'Calvin's Works in Translation', in *Calvinism in Europe, 1540–1620*, ed. by Andrew Pettegree, Alistair Duke, and Gillian Lewis (Cambridge: Cambridge University Press, 1994), pp. 82–99

Höfele, Andreas and Werner von Koppenfels, eds, *Renaissance Go-Betweens: Cultural Exchange in Early Modern Europe* (New York: Walter de Gruyter, 2005)

Horace, *Epistles, Satires and Ars Poetica*, trans. by H. Rushton Fairclough (London: William Heinemann, 1926)

Hosington, Brenda M., 'Tudor Englishwomen's Translations of Continental Protestant Texts: The Interplay of Ideology and Historical Context', in *Tudor Translation*, ed. by Fred Schurink (Basingstoke: Palgrave Macmillan, 2011), pp. 121–42

Howatt, A. P. R. with H. G. Widdowson, *A History of English Language Teaching*, 2nd edn (Oxford: Oxford University Press, 2004)

Hutson, Lorna, *The Usurer's Daughter: Male Friendship and Fictions of Women in Sixteenth-Century England* (London: Routledge, 1994)

James VI and I, *Selected Writings*, ed. by Neil Rhodes, Jennifer Richards, and Joseph Marshall (Aldershot: Ashgate, 2003)

Javitch, Daniel, *Proclaiming a Classic: The Canonisation of Orlando Furioso* (Princeton, NJ: Princeton University Press, 1991)

Jerome, *The Principal Works of St Jerome*, trans. by W. H. Fremantle, in *Nicene & Post-Nicene Fathers*, vol. 6, ed. by Philip Schaff and Henry Wace (Edinburgh: T. and T. Clark, 1996)

Johnson, Christopher, 'Florio's Conversion of Montaigne, Sidney and Six Patronesses', *Cahiers Elisabéthains*, 64 (2003), 9–18

Jones, Howard, *Master Tully: Cicero in Tudor England* (Nieuwkoop: de Graaf, 1998)

Jones, R. F., *The Triumph of the English Language* (Stanford, CA: Stanford University Press, 1953)

Kelly, L. G., *The True Interpreter: A History of Translation Theory and Practice in the West* (Oxford: Basil Blackwell, 1979)

Kendal, Gordon, *Translation as Creative Retelling: Constituents, Patterning and Shift in Gavin Douglas' Eneados* (Saarbrücken: Lambert, 2010)

Kennedy, George A., ed., *Progymnasmata: Greek Textbooks of Prose Composition and Rhetoric* (Leiden: Brill, 2003)

Kristeller, Paul Oskar, *Renaissance Concepts of Man* (New York: Harper & Row, 1972)

Krontiris, Tina, 'Breaking Barriers of Genre and Gender: Margaret Tyler's Translation of the *Mirrour of Knighthood*', *English Literary Renaissance*, 18 (1988), 19–39

Lamb, Mary Ellen, 'The Cooke Sisters: Attitudes Towards Learned Women in the Renaissance', in *Silent But for the Word*, ed. by Hannay, pp. 107–25

Lathrop, Henry Burrowes, *Translations from the Classics into English from Caxton to Chapman* (Madison: University of Wisconsin Press, 1933)

Laoutaris, Chris, 'Translation/Historical Writing', in *The History of British Women's Writing, 1500–1610*, ed. by Caroline Bicks and Jennifer Summit (Basingstoke: Palgrave Macmillan, 2010), pp. 296–327

Lees-Jefferies, Hester, *England's Helicon: Fountains in Early Modern Literature and Culture* (Oxford: Oxford University Press, 2007)

Lehmberg, Stanford E., *Sir Thomas Elyot, Tudor Humanist* (Austin: University of Texas Press, 1960)

—, *The Reformation Parliament: 1529–1536* (Cambridge: Cambridge University Press, 1970)

Lievsay, John Leon, *Stefano Guazzo and the English Renaissance* (Chapel Hill: University of North Carolina Press, 1961)

Lindeman, Yehudi, 'Translation and the Renaissance: A Context and a Map', *Canadian Review of Comparative Literature*, 8 (1981), 204–16

Lyne, Raphael, *Ovid's Changing Worlds: English 'Metamorphoses' 1567–1632* (Oxford: Oxford University Press, 2001)

Mack, Peter, *Elizabethan Rhetoric: Theory and Practice* (Cambridge: Cambridge University Press, 2002)

Mantel, Hilary, *Wolf Hall* (London: Fourth Estate, 2009)

Márquez, Miguel, 'Aspects of Vocabulary Building in Caxton's *Recuyell of the Historyes of Troy*', *English Studies*, 72 (1991), 328–49

Maslen, R. W., *Elizabethan Fictions: Espionage, Counter-Espionage, and the Duplicity of Fiction in Early Elizabethan Prose Narratives* (Oxford: Clarendon Press, 1997)

Matthiessen, F. O., *Translation: An Elizabethan Art* (Cambridge, MA: Harvard University Press, 1931)

Mazzio, Carla, *The Inarticulate Renaissance: Language Trouble in an Age of Eloquence* (Philadelphia: University of Pennsylvania Press, 2008)

McIntosh, Marjorie K., 'Sir Anthony Cooke: Tudor Humanist, Educator and Religious Reformer', *Proceedings of the American Philosophical Society*, 119:3 (1975), 233–50

Medine, Peter E., *Thomas Wilson* (Boston, MA: Twayne Publishers, 1986)

Miller, William E. 'Double Translation in English Humanistic Education', *Studies in the Renaissance*, 10 (1963), 163–74

Milton, Anthony, ed., *The British Delegation and the Synod of Dort (1618–1619)* (Woodbridge: The Boydell Press, 2005)

More, Thomas, *Selected Letters*, ed. by Elizabeth Frances Rogers (New Haven, CT: Yale University Press, 1961)

—, *A Dialogue Concerning Heresies*, ed. by Thomas M. C. Lawler, Germain Marc'hadour, and Richard C. Marius, *CWM* 6, 2 vols (New Haven: Yale University Press, 1981)

—, *The Confutation of Tyndale's Answer* ed. by L. A. Schuster et al., *CWM* 8, 3 vols (New Haven: Yale University Press, 1973)

Morini, Massimiliano, *Tudor Translation in Theory and Practice* (Aldershot: Ashgate, 2006)

Morley, Henry Parker, Lord, *Lord Morley's Tryumphes of*

Fraunces Petrarcke, ed. by D. D. Carnicelli (Cambridge, MA: Harvard University Press, 1971)

Mukherjee, Neel, 'Thomas Drant's Rewriting of Horace', *Studies in English Literature 1500–1900*, 40 (2000), 1–20

Nashe, Thomas, *The Works of Thomas Nashe*, ed. by R. B. McKerrow, rev. by F. P. Wilson (Oxford: Blackwell, 1958)

Needham, Paul Strope, 'Sir John Cheke at Cambridge and at Court', Unpublished PhD diss., Harvard University, 1971

Norton, David, *A History of the Bible as Literature: Volume 1, From Antiquity to 1700* (Cambridge: Cambridge University Press, 1993)

—, *The King James Bible: A Short History from Tyndale to Today* (Cambridge: Cambridge University Press, 2011)

Norton, Glyn P., *The Ideology and Language of Translation in Renaissance France and their Humanist Antecedents* (Geneva: Droz, 1984)

Ong, Walter J., *Ramus, Method, and the Decay of Dialogue* (Cambridge, MA: Harvard University Press, 1958)

Palsgrave, John, *The Comedye of Acolastus*, ed. by P. L. Carver (London: EETS, 1937)

Parr, Katherine, *Complete Works and Correspondence*, ed. by Janel Mueller (Chicago: Chicago University Press, 2011)

Parry, Graham, 'Literary Patronage', in *The Cambridge History of Early Modern English Literature*, ed. by David Loewenstein and Janel Mueller (Cambridge: Cambridge University Press, 2002)

Partridge, A. C., *English Biblical Translation* (London: André Deutsch, 1973)

Partridge, Mary, 'Thomas Hoby's English Translation of Castiglione's *Book of the Courtier*', *The Historical Journal*, 50.4 (2007), 769–86

Pellegrini, Angelo M.,'Giordano Bruno on Translations', *ELH*, 10 (1943), 193–207

Pérez Fernández, José María, 'Andres Laguna: Translation and the Early Modern Idea of Europe', *Translation and Literature*, 21 (2012), 299–318

Pettegree, Andrew, *Foreign Protestant Communities in Sixteenth-Century London* (Oxford: Clarendon Press, 1986)

—, 'Translation and the Migration of Texts', in *Borders and Travellers in Early Modern Europe*, ed. by Thomas Betteridge (Ashgate: Aldershot, 2007), pp. 113–25

Philo of Alexandria, *On the Life of Moses* in *Philo*, trans. by F. H. Colson and G. H. Whitaker, 10 vols (London: Heinemann, 1950), VI, 273–95

Pigman III, George W., 'Versions of Imitation in the Renaissance', *Renaissance Quarterly*, 33 (1980), 1–32

Pincombe, Mike, *Elizabethan Humanism: Literature and Learning in the Later Sixteenth Century* (Harlow: Longman, 2001)

Pineas, Rainer, *Thomas More and Tudor Polemics* (Bloomington: Indiana University Press, 1968)

Pliny, *The Letters of Pliny the Younger*, trans. by Betty Radice (Harmondsworth: Penguin, 1963; repr. 1981)

Pollard, Alfred W., *Records of the English Bible: the documents relating to the translation and publication of the Bible in English, 1525–1611* (London: Oxford University Press, 1911)

Prescott, Anne Lake, 'The Pearl of the Valois and Elizabeth I: Marguerite de Navarre's *Miroir* and Tudor England', in *Silent But for the Word*, ed. by Hannay, pp. 61–76

Purkiss, Diane, ed., *Three Tragedies by Renaissance Women Writers* (London: Penguin, 1998)

Puttenham, George, *The Art of English Poesy*, ed. by Frank Whigham and Wayne A. Rebhorn (Ithaca: Cornell University Press, 2007)

Quintilian, *The Orator's Education*, ed. and trans. by D. A. Russell, 5 vols (Cambridge, MA: Harvard University Press, 2001)

Rabil, Albert, 'Erasmus' Paraphrases of the New Testament', in *Essays on the Works of Erasmus*, ed. by Richard L. De Molen (New Haven: Yale University Press, 1978), pp. 145–61

Read, Conyers, *Mr. Secretary Cecil and Queen Elizabeth* (London: Jonathan Cape, 1955)

Rees, Joan, *Daniel: A Critical and Biographical Study* (Liverpool: Liverpool University Press, 1984)

Rener, Frederick M., *Interpretatio: Language and Translation from Cicero to Tytler* (Amsterdam: Rodopi, 1989)

Rich, Townsend, *Harington and Ariosto: A Study in Elizabethan Verse Translation* (New Haven: Yale University Press, 1940)

Rhodes, Neil, *Shakespeare and the Origins of English* (Oxford: Oxford University Press, 2004)

—, 'Framing and Tuning in Renaissance English Verse', in *Renaissance Transformations: The Making of English Writing and its World (1480–1650)*, ed. by Margaret and Thomas Healy (Edinburgh: Edinburgh University Press, 2009), pp. 32–47

—, 'Status Anxiety and English Renaissance Translation', in *Renaissance Paratexts*, ed. by Helen Smith and Louise Wilson (Cambridge: Cambridge University Press, 2011), pp. 107–20

Richards, Jennifer, *Rhetoric and Courtliness in Early Modern Literature* (Cambridge: Cambridge University Press, 2003)

Ricoeur, Paul, 'Being a Stranger', trans. by Alison Scott-Baumann, in *Theory, Culture & Society*, 27 (2010), 37–48

Robinson, Douglas, ed., *Western Translation Theory from Herodotus to Nietzsche*, 2nd edn (Manchester: St Jerome, 2002)

Robinson, Ian, *The Establishment of Modern English Prose in the Reformation and Enlightenment* (Cambridge: Cambridge University Press, 1998)

Rollison, David, *A Commonwealth of the People: Popular Politics and England's Long Social Revolution, 1066–1649* (Cambridge: Cambridge University Press, 2010)

Russell, D. A., '*De Imitatione*', in D. West and T. Woodman, eds, *Creative Imitation and Latin Literature* (Cambridge: Cambridge University Press, 1979), pp. 1–16.

Ryan, Lawrence V., *Roger Ascham* (Stanford, CA: Stanford University Press, 1963)

Salmon, Vivian, 'John Brinsley: 17th-Century Pioneer in Applied Linguistics', in *The Study of Language in Seventeenth-Century England*, 2nd edn (Amsterdam: Benjamins, 1988), pp. 33–46

—, 'Joseph Webbe: Some Seventeenth-Century Views on Language Teaching and the Nature of Meaning', in *The Study of Language*, ed. by Salmon, pp. 15–31

Schleiner, Louise, 'Margaret Tyler, Translator and Waiting Woman', *English Language Notes*, 29 (1992), 2–5

Schoell, Franck L., *Études sur l'Humanisme continental en Angleterre à la fin de la Renaissance* (Paris: Champion, 1926)

Schurink, Fred, 'Print, Patronage, and Occasion: Translations of Plutarch's *Moralia* in Tudor England', *Yearbook of English Studies*, 38 (2008), 86–101

—, 'The Intimacy of Manuscript and the Pleasure of Print: Literary Culture from *The Schoolmaster* to *Euphues*', in *The Oxford Handbook of Tudor Literature*, ed. by Mike Pincombe and Cathy Shrank (Oxford: Oxford University Press, 2009), pp. 671–86

—, ed., *Tudor Translation* (Basingstoke: Palgrave Macmillan, 2011)

Schwarz, W., *Principles and Problems of Biblical Translation: Some Reformation Controversies and their Background* (Cambridge: Cambridge University Press, 1955)

Scott-Warren, Jason, *Sir John Harington and the Book as Gift* (Oxford: Oxford University Press, 2001)

Shakespeare, William, *The Norton Shakespeare based on the Oxford Edition*, ed. by Stephen Greenblatt et al. (New York: W. W. Norton, 1997)

Shrank, Cathy, *Writing the Nation in Reformation England, 1530–1580* (Oxford: Oxford University Press, 2004)

—, 'Sir Thomas Elyot and the Bonds of Community', in *The Oxford Handbook of Tudor Literature, 1485–1603*, ed. by Pincombe and Shrank (2009), pp. 154–69

Simpson, James, *Burning to Read: English Fundamentalism and its Reformation Opponents* (Cambridge, MA: Harvard University Press, 2007)

Skinner, Quentin, *Reason and Rhetoric in the Philosophy of Hobbes* (Cambridge: Cambridge University Press, 1996)

Skretkowicz, Victor, *European Erotic Romance: Philhellene Protestantism, Renaissance Translation and English Literary Politics* (Manchester: Manchester University Press, 2010)

Smith, Alan G. ed., *The 'Anonymous Life' of William Cecil, Lord Burghley* (Lewiston, NY: Edwin Mellen Press, 1990)

Smith, Bruce R., *The Acoustic World of Early Modern England* (Chicago: University of Chicago Press, 1999)

Smith, G. Gregory, ed., *Elizabethan Critical Essays*, 2 vols (London: Oxford University Press, 1904)

Smith, Sir Thomas, *De recta et emendata linguae Anglicae scriptione, Dialogus* in *Literary and Linguistic Works*, vol. 3, ed. by Bror Danielsson (Stockholm: Almquist and Wiskell, 1983)

Sowerby, Robin, 'Chapman's Discovery of Homer', *Translation and Literature*, 1 (1992), 26–51

Spenser, Edmund, *The Shorter Poems*, ed. by Richard A. McCabe (London: Penguin, 1999)

Spitz, Lewis W. and Barbara Sher Tinsley, eds, *Johann Sturm on Education: the Reformation and Humanist Learning* (St Louis, MI: Concordia, 1995)

Steiner, George, *After Babel: Aspects of Language and Translation*, 3rd edn (Oxford: Oxford University Press, 1998)

Stein, Gabriele, *John Palsgrave as Renaissance Linguist: a Pioneer in Vernacular Language Description* (Oxford: Clarendon, 1997)

Stevenson, Jane, *Women Latin Poets: Language, Gender, and Authority, from Antiquity to the Eighteenth Century* (Oxford: Oxford University Press, 2005)

Struever, Nancy S., *Theory as Practice: Ethical Enquiry in the Renaissance* (Chicago: Chicago University Press, 1992)

Strype, John, *The Life of the Learned Sir John Cheke* (London, 1705)

Tadmor, Naomi, *The Social Universe of the English Bible* (Cambridge: Cambridge University Press, 2010)

Tanner, Norman P., ed., *Decrees of the Ecumenical Councils*, 2 vols (London: Sheen & Ward, 1990)

Taylor, Andrew, 'The Bible' in *OHLTE* 2, pp. 121–40

Teems, David, *Tyndale: The Man Who Gave God An English Voice* (Nashville, Tennessee: Thomas Nelson, 2012)

Tilley, M. P., *A Dictionary of the Proverbs in England in the Sixteenth and Seventeenth Centuries* (Ann Arbor: University of Michigan Press, 1950)

Trapp, J. B., 'The Conformity of Greek and the Vernacular: The History of a Renaissance Theory of Language', in *Classical Influences on European Culture, AD 500–1500*, ed. by R. R. Bolgar (Cambridge: Cambridge University Press. 1971), pp. 239–44

Treharne, Elaine, '*Tristis Amor*: An Unpublished Verse Love Letter from Elizabeth Dacre Howard to Sir Anthony Cooke', *Renaissance Studies*, forthcoming

Tudeau-Clayton, Margaret, *Jonson, Shakespeare and Early Modern Virgil* (Cambridge: Cambridge University Press, 1998)

[Tyler] *The Early Modern Englishwoman, Vol. 8: Margaret Tyler*, introd. by Kathryn Coad (Aldershot: Scolar Press, 1996)

Tyndale, William, *The Obedience of a Christian Man*, ed. by David Daniell (London: Penguin, 2000)

—, *An Answer unto Sir Thomas Mores Dialogue*, ed. by Anne M. O'Donnell and Jared Wicks (Washington, DC: Catholic University Press of America, 2000)

Venuti, Lawrence, *The Translator's Invisibility* (London: Routledge, 1995)

Vickers, Brian, ed., *English Renaissance Literary Criticism* (Oxford: Clarendon Press, 1999)

Walker, Greg, *Writing Under Tyranny: English Literature and the Henrician Reformation* (Oxford: Oxford University Press, 2005)

Wallace, Andrew, *Virgil's Schoolboys: the Poetics of Pedagogy in Renaissance England* (Oxford: Oxford University Press, 2010)

Walsham, Alexandra, 'The Spider and the Bee: the Perils of Printing for Refutation in Tudor England', in *Tudor Books and Readers: Materiality and the Construction of Meaning*, ed. by John N. King (Cambridge: Cambridge University Press, 2010)

—, 'Unclasping the Book? Post-Reformation English Catholicism and the Vernacular Bible', *Journal of British Studies*, 42 (2003), 141–66

Waswo, Richard, *Language and Meaning in the Renaissance* (Princeton, NJ: Princeton University Press, 1987)

Watson, Nicholas, 'Theories of Translation', *OHLTE* (1), pp. 73–91

Watt, Tessa, *Cheap Print and Popular Piety, 1550–1640* (Cambridge: Cambridge University Press, 1991)

Weissbort, Daniel and Astradur Eysteinsson, eds, *Translation – Theory and Practice: A Historical Reader* (Oxford: Oxford University Press, 2006)

Wesley, John, 'Mulcaster's Tyrant Sound', in *Sound Effects: the Oral/Aural Dimensions of Literature in English*, ed. by Neil Rhodes and Chris Jones, *Oral Tradition* 24.2 (2009), 337–58

Westcott, Brooke Foss, *A General View of the History of the English Bible*, rev. by W. A. Wright (London: Macmillan, 1905)

Whiting, Bartlett, *Proverbs, Sentences, and Proverbial Phrases from English Writings mainly before 1500* (Cambridge, MA: Harvard University Press, 1968)

Wilson-Okamura, David Scott, *Virgil in the Renaissance* (Cambridge: Cambridge University Press, 2010)

Woolfson, Jonathan, 'Thomas Hoby, William Thomas, and Mid-Tudor Travel to Italy', in *The Oxford Handbook of Tudor Literature, 1485–1603*, ed. by Pincombe and Shrank, pp. 404–17

Wood, D. N. C., 'Elizabethan English and Richard Carew', *Neophilologus*, 61 (1977), 304–15

Wooten, Cecil W., *Hermogenes' On Types of Style* (Chapel Hill: University of North Carolina Press, 1987)

Worth-Stylianou, Valerie, '*Translatio* and Translation in the Renaissance: from Italy to France', in *The Cambridge History of Literary Criticism, Vol. 3: The Renaissance*, ed. by Glyn P. Norton (Cambridge: Cambridge University Press, 1999), pp. 127–35

Wright, Louis B., 'Translations for the Elizabethan Middle Class', *The Library*, 13 (1932), 312–31

Wrightson, Keith, 'Estates, Degrees, and Sorts: Changing Perceptions of Society in Tudor and Stuart England', in *Language, History and Class*, ed. by Penelope J. Corfield (Oxford: Blackwell, 1991), pp. 30–52

Yates, Frances A., *John Florio: The Life of an Italian in Shakespeare's England* (Cambridge: Cambridge University Press, 1934)

Zim, Rivkah, *English Metrical Psalms: Poetry as Praise and Prayer* (Cambridge: Cambridge University Press, 1987)

INDEX

www.ingramcontent.com/pod-product-compliance
Lightning Source LLC
Chambersburg PA
CBHW060258100726
47907CB00002B/201

* 9 7 8 1 7 8 1 8 8 0 4 1 8 *